SHILOH: BLOODY APRIL

SHILOH: BLOODY APRIL

by Wiley Sword

WILLIAM MORROW & COMPANY, INC., NEW YORK, 1974

Design by Helen Roberts

Library of Congress Cataloging in Publication Data

Sword, Wiley.
   Shiloh: bloody April.
   Bibliography: p.

   1. Shiloh, Battle of, 1862. I. Title.
E473.54.S96   973.7'33   74-7455
ISBN 0-688-00271-4

To Marianne, Gregory and Andrew

*—that they may never know the
agony of another Shiloh*

Foreword

When my good friend and near neighbor, the author of *Shiloh: Bloody April,* asked me to write an introduction to his first book, he had just finished correcting the galley proofs, an abominable chore even for those of us who write that we may stay out of the breadline.

For the first and only time on being thus favored, it was unnecessary for me to follow the lead of the author and work through galley proofs toward distilling the values of someone else's work and writing an appreciation. On and off, I have been pretty much living with this manuscript since well before my last tour in South Vietnam, which was in 1968.

That long ago we met by chance over lunch at the Plum Hollow Golf Club, which is not far from his home and mine. There, the author enjoys a delightfully low handicap, and there also a mutual friend introduced us. I got the name at first hearing, this after being told that my new acquaintance was starting to write a book about the Battle of Shiloh. Nothing seemed less likely to me than that the person christened Wiley Sword should ever mature as a first-rank military writer unless it was that a young man, wholly lacking in combat experience, could write a publishable book, let alone a classic, about the most confused battle of the Civil War.

On being asked, I agreed to read through the first three chapters, all that had been written until then. Thus began the connection that lasted until now. As through the years more copy came from his mill, I went over it with him, until came completion. Frankly, I never expected him to finish it. Wiley Sword is a highly successful businessman, and a devoted husband and father. His time seemed fully occupied. But the book was to him a labor of love, and it became so to me, there being no other incentive.

His part was the research and writing, mine the tactical criticism, pointing up where descriptions of ground were inadequate, the adding of observations about command failures and foibles, and early in the exchange, some suggestions about the sharpening of writing style. In this association, there was none of the customary sweat between the new writer and the jaundiced professional critic. Like U. S. Grant, Wiley Sword never made the same mistake twice. But then there was another attraction: For the first time, I was reading that about Civil War fighters and fighting which ran directly parallel to my own personal experience with battle forces in later wars.

Though the Civil War has never been my dish of tea, about Shiloh, that terrible field the name of which ironically is supposed to mean tranquillity, I had read many times. What I remembered chiefly was that it was a meeting engagement on the largest scale, a monstrous surprise to begin, of which came numerous subsequent surprises, which is ever the case in battle. Among other vague flashbacks, there was the familiar picture of Grant, his leg crippled, heroically striving to turn routed forces at the landing, Johnston dying untimely with irreparable loss to the Confederates, Lew Wallace dragging his feet, Garfield coming up too late, Sherman riding through as if death didn't want him, and Halleck frittering away the fruits of the field out of timidity or stupidity.

It was through reviewing Civil War histories, however, in between the two World Wars, that I first became convinced that much of the writing was sheer romance, and that there must be some better system of reconstructing the events, ordered or happenstantial, of the battlefield. Generals were forever "hurling" forward a right or left flank, which generals never do, tired and fear-ridden troops not being that responsive. Weather, visibility and footing were ignored. Troops were described as advancing in perfect order under fire, though how they went, whether crawling, or bounding or with a few brave souls charging straight on while the rest hugged dirt, was left unsaid. The story of maneuver and counter-maneuver was related as if the fire field is as subject to tight control as a checkerboard though, then as now, lateral communications practically cease to exist once the guns begin to speak.

It was the rifle bullet that, beginning with Shiloh, made all such terms unrealistic forever after. That bullet begot entrenched works, sheathed the bayonet, drove back the cannon, obsoleted the sword and spelled doom to cavalry. One good man in an earthwork became worth three who were charging him in the open, though the muzzle-loading rifle was still the common weapon. But at Shiloh neither side understood that. The war was itself too new, the troops too green and the commanders too limited in mental horizon to be aware. Many years would pass, more wars would be fought, and the lesson would still be missed. On the field of Shiloh, at least, there was some excuse for the command mismanagement of which came troop wastage and bloodshed otherwise unpardonable.

Battle is more like a schoolyard in a rough neighborhood at recess time than a clash between football giants at the Rose Bowl. The extreme in chaos and disorder, it is messy, inorganic and little coordinated. It is only much later, after the clerks have tidied up their reports and the commanders, in retrospect, have made their estimates of situation *ex post facto,* that the historian, with his orderly mind, professes to discern a moving hand and sensible pattern in what was at the time a frenzied and fear-filled scrambling, a desperate groping in the dark.

Though the clash may be widespread and immediate, what happens in any one sector is little, if any, related to the action in any other. With the firing of the first shell or bullet, units start to become fractionalized and to fight mainly for themselves, not only to survive, but to vindicate that which is never clearly understood. They are as likely to battle to the death for worthless ground as to recognize the advantage of a superior position. The horizon is always only a few yards away. Armies have no feel of fighting other armies; the enemy is the small group holding the next rise. Within one company, each platoon may have its own fight virtually in isolation. Within any battalion, each company may get the feeling that it is standing at Armageddon and battling almost alone for the Lord. The prevailing emotion of the rifleman when first committed to close combat is a nigh paralyzing lonesomeness. He has almost no sense of the people to his flanks or rear who are helping him: out of his need for cover, his perspective shrinks to that of a burrowing creature. He goes mute, as do the others near him, and from that the grip of fear tightens.

Soldiers may win a battle or a skirmish and still not know it until someone tells them. The tiding rarely lifts their hearts or evokes cheers. Fear dulls the mind even as it exhausts the body and with it the emotions. Blessed sleep is the only restorative and tired fighters prize it more than victory.

The proper command spot for a field general during the fight is up front, sharing the risks with his soldiers. His presence and his courage will brace and benefit them more than his broodings and calculations at a command post far in rear. If he cannot depend on his headquarters staff to run their part of the show, then he is a poor organizer. General W. T. Sherman was the most lustrous figure on the field of Shiloh. Inspiring personal action, rather than inspired thought, so made him. He was as undaunted as was General Matthew B. Ridgway when in 1950 he took over the beaten Eighth Army in Korea and within one month restored its confidence and energy, all the time staying up front with his soldiers.

In battle, moments of high crisis as often as not slip past unnoticed. The effects of a success or reverse at some corner of the field as related to the whole are seldom grasped. Messages almost invariably get garbled. The information flow to higher commands is usually late and generally exaggerated. Hence the issue of battle is as apt to turn on a fluke or a folly as on the logic of an order or the perception of tactical opportunity. As was said by Edmund Burke, "A common soldier, a child, a girl at the door of an inn, have changed the face of fortune and almost of Nature."

These are among the lessons I have learned slowly over many years in the school of war by being with the United States Army, early as a junior leader of riflemen, and later as a combat historian and operations analyst. My friend, Wiley Sword, has learned them over a gratifyingly shorter course in his researching of Shiloh. It is his perception of the chanciness of fighting operations and his revelation of raw human nature in the worst of circumstances that make an old story as freshly new as the next second. His battlefield episodes convey much of the apparent inconsequence of real life. His literary style is distinctly his own, its movement and color are satisfying, and it is rich, and indeed fascinating, in historical allusion as in its character sketching.

Though it is said that the pen is mightier than the sword, that is not a whole truth. All depends on who is wielding either. In this novel instance, however, in which the Sword wields the pen, much comes forth that military professionals and scholars, and probably the critics, should delight to ponder.

S. L. A. MARSHALL
Brig. Gen.-Ret.

Dherran Dhoun
Birmingham, Michigan

About This Book

In researching a subject as complex and fraught with emotion as was Shiloh, it is inevitable that conflicting or contradictory accounts are uncovered. For this reason, where possible, accounts contemporary to the battle have been used as primary sources. Particularly revealing among these are the personal letters, diaries, and journals of the participants, providing a vivid insight into events, opinions, and emotions long before they were distorted by failing memory or the pressure of public scrutiny.

Generally only eyewitness descriptions of those actually present at a particular phase or incident of the battle have been utilized. Beyond this all accounts have been carefully examined and compared for verisimilitude, in order to delete inaccurate or misleading material. Some descriptions, such as William G. Stevenson's *Thirteen Months in the Rebel Army,* have been found so wanting in credibility that they have been disregarded altogether. Quotations by individuals have been given as found, except for corrections, largely in grammar and sentence structure, to provide a more readable text.

What has been strived for, is to present the story of Shiloh as accurately and objectively as possible without regard to personalities or partisanship. In this sense, no especial disparagement of such prominent Americans as Ulysses S. Grant and William T. Sherman is intended. Both were great men—if for no better reason than that they accomplished great tasks. Yet it is also important to recognize that as human beings, no matter how gifted, they were subject to the same frailties and failings as others. Both made grave mistakes at Shiloh, as in later life, yet they learned the hard lessons of war well. That they went on to achieve great success was, to a large extent, due to their ability to profit from former mistakes.

Indeed, if the more meaningful aspect of this book is to be defined, it must lie in the vignette of life itself—the inevitable mixture of good and bad that is inherent in all human endeavor.

xi

For the generous assistance of the following persons I am particularly indebted: Brigadier General S. L. A. Marshall, U. S. A., retired, whose advice and critique of the manuscript have been invaluable; David Green, Windsor, Ontario, Canada; Herb Peck, Jr., Nashville, Tennessee; Charles P. Roland, Lexington, Kentucky; Robert Guinn, Savannah, Tennessee; J. P. Barnett, Omega East, Herbert Olsen, Alvoid L. Rector, and Edward Tinney, all formerly or presently with the Shiloh National Military Park, Shiloh, Tennessee; Dr. D. Emerick Szilagyi, Henry Ford Hospital, Detroit, Michigan; and Dr. Charles G. Child, 3d, University of Michigan, Ann Arbor, whose expert medical knowledge was of great help to me in investigating Sidney Johnston's fatal wound; Edward F. Williams, Memphis, Tennessee; Truman R. Strobridge, Kaneoke, Hawaii; Edwin C. Bearss, Arlington, Virginia; Ezra J. Warner, Solana Beach, California.

I also wish to express my appreciation for the cooperation of the following libraries, societies, associations, and branches of government:

Blue Grass Trust, Lexington, Kentucky
Chicago Historical Society
Corinth, Mississippi, Chamber of Commerce
Detroit Public Library, Burton Historical Collection
Duke University Library, Durham, North Carolina
General Services Administration, National Archives & Records
    Service
Henry E. Huntington Library, San Marino, California
Illinois State Historical Library, Springfield
Indiana Historical Society, Indianapolis
Indiana State Library, Indianapolis
Iowa State Department of History & Archives, Des Moines
Library of Congress, Washington, D. C.
Louisiana State University, Department of Archives, Baton Rouge
Marietta College Library, Marietta, Ohio
Mississippi Department of Archives & History, Jackson
Missouri Historical Society, St. Louis
Ohio Historical Society, Columbus
Shiloh Military Trail, Inc., Memphis, Tennessee
State Historical Society of Wisconsin, Madison
State of Illinois, Office of the Secretary of State
State of Louisiana, Adjutant General's Office, New Orleans
Tennessee State Library, Nashville
Toledo Public Library, Toledo, Ohio
Tulane University, Howard Tilton Memorial Library, New Orleans
University of Michigan, Michigan Historical Collection, Ann
    Arbor

University of Michigan, William L. Clements Library, Ann Arbor
University of North Carolina Library, Chapel Hill
U. S. Department of the Interior, National Park Service
Western Reserve Historical Society, Cleveland, Ohio
Yale University Library, New Haven, Connecticut

Last but not least, the following persons helped prepare the manuscript: Pat Perez, Sue Comito, Pamela Hood, and especially Linda Lindquist. For their help and patience I am particularly grateful.

WILEY SWORD

West Bloomfield
Michigan
1973

Contents

List of Maps

List of Illustrations

On paper, Shiloh was a draw; actually it was one of the decisive battles of the war. It was a battle the Confederacy simply had to win. For it had been a blow struck to restore a disastrously lost balance, a desperate attempt to re-establish the Confederate frontier in the Kentucky-Ohio Valley. It had failed, and the fact that it had come close to being a dazzling victory did not offset the failure. . . .

—BRUCE CATTON, *This Hallowed Ground*

What a pity it is that men do not use reason instead of rifles, and common sense instead of cannon.

—A Shiloh veteran

SHILOH: BLOODY APRIL

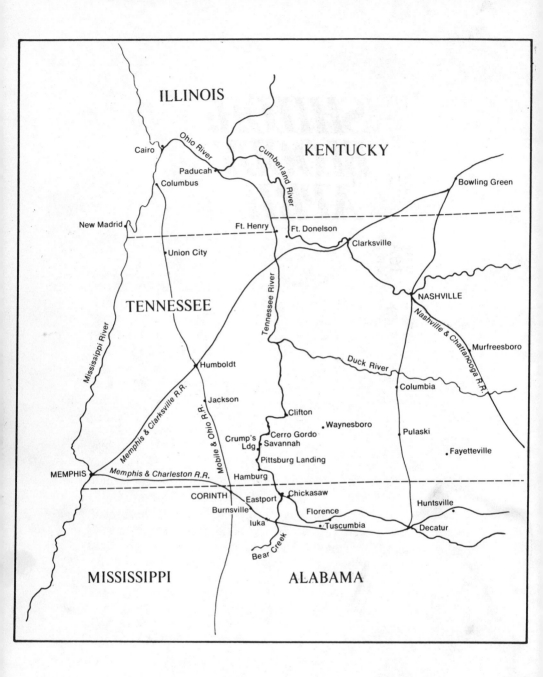

MAP 1
Field of Operations, Western Theater
February–April, 1862 (Chapters 1–2, 5)

CHAPTER I

The River Has Risen

Each spring in the Middle South the muddy, rain-swollen Tennessee River becomes a vast water highway. Racing through a picturesque land once the wilderness domain of the Cherokee, Creek, and Chickasaw nations, the Tennessee flows in a relentless torrent from the mountains of the Cumberland to a confluence with the Ohio River, 652 miles distant.

At the mouth of the Tennessee, amid the rolling farmland of southwestern Kentucky, the river is broad and unpretentious. Here glistening white farmhouses dot the countryside and country lanes crisscross the meadows.

In its distant upper reaches, however, the Tennessee is ruggedly spectacular. Fed by a system of boulder-strewn mountain streams, a wild and unsubdued Tennessee rushes through deep gorges and almost primeval forests of spruce and balsam.

Between these turbulent headwaters and the river's placid junction with the Ohio lies a rich land of towering trees and fertile soil. It is also one of America's most historic dark and bloody grounds.

Through a hundred years of Colonial history the whir of the Indian arrow and the roar of the long rifle were familiar sounds in the Tennessee Valley. Sweeping from the mountains like a giant serpent, the mighty river with its vast opportunities for land development seemed to be one of pioneer America's important assets. Yet the early immigrants, hurrying to cash in on the post-Revolution land schemes, soon learned that the mid-Tennessee was an aberrant and forbidding river.

Doubling back on its course after flowing southwest for three hundred fifty miles, the Tennessee turns in a great bend and rushes north for two hundred miles. Headed by a thirty-mile stretch known as the Narrows, where the waters of the upper Tennessee are constricted by an abrupt narrowing of the channel, the obstructions continue downriver, terminating with Muscle Shoals in north-

1

ern Alabama. A labyrinth of jagged rocks, sunken reefs, and hidden sandbars, the shoals extend for forty miles, creating an extensive rapids and an average drop in the river of three and a half feet to the mile.

These great obstacles of the Tennessee not only impeded navigation in an era known for skillful rivermen, they remained an unyielding deterrent to rapid civilization by nineteenth-century America. Although territory adjacent to the Mississippi, Ohio, and other rivers soon was settled and exploited, the land bordering the mid-Tennessee lagged behind in development. Through the first quarter-century much of the Tennessee Valley was still Indian country, particularly in the Great Bend region. Chattanooga at the time was merely an obscure stopping spot on the river known as Ross's Landing.

The first engineering survey, delayed until 1830, did little to change the habitation of the region. Later, when the extensive canal and construction projects recommended were not completed for lack of appropriations, the newly developed railroads provided the region with a viable means of progress. River sites such as Chattanooga, Decatur, and Tuscumbia soon became bustling railroad towns, bringing more settlers to exploit the Tennessee Valley's vast natural resources. In the decade before the Civil War a network of narrow-gauge railroads busily hauled freight and passengers across hundreds of miles of the once trackless wilderness. The treacherous Tennessee, wild and unfriendly, had been largely bypassed as a major means of transportation.

During the golden era of steamboating, only the lower Tennessee enjoyed much of the river commerce familiar to the Ohio and Mississippi. Plying between Paducah, Kentucky, and Florence, Alabama, some of the regular packets hauled up to five thousand bales of cotton in a single shipment, providing the planters and farmers of the lower Tennessee with a profitable means for marketing their produce.

Although this prosperity resulted in the development of several vast plantations in the district, many of the counties bordering on the Tennessee were among the wildest backwoods regions in the state. Forests of tall, gray-barked oaks stood on the high bluffs in leaning groves, as they had for centuries. Fern and wildflowers graced the riverbank. Houses were few, and often only the winging heron disturbed the tranquil repose of the river.

In the days before the Civil War it was a serenely quiet and majestic land with an aura of unspoiled natural beauty. Here the simple country people of the lower valley enjoyed the homespun life of the outdoors, oblivious of the supreme crisis about to divide the nation. Strong in folk culture and frontier tradition, they pursued happiness with a carefree, backwoods informality.

The advent of the Civil War, however, brought storm clouds of ominous portent. Life in the Tennessee Valley—robust, simple, and unassuming—somehow was never to be quite the same again. By a cruel twist of fate an obscure river landing in a backwoods county of Tennessee was destined to become one of the bloodiest places on earth. Where there had been only unspoiled natural wilderness, there would be brutal, almost indescribable suffering and a horrid pall of death. Beyond the anguish of a nation divided by civil war, there occurred in this placid, backwoods setting one of the most decisive battles of the great American crisis.

Ironically, the Tennessee River was the source of ruin for the Confederacy. Because it ran in the wrong direction it was an open route of invasion, a broad, two-hundred-mile river highway aimed at the heart of the Middle South. The notorious shoals and obstructions began too far south to impede an amphibious offensive spearheaded by the gunboat flotillas of the North. With an apprehensive eye the Confederate generals began early to prepare a defensive system embracing the great navigable rivers of the region. Foremost in their plans were Forts Henry and Donelson guarding the lower Tennessee and Cumberland rivers.

Early in 1862, following nearly a year of indecisive sparring, the great armies of the North and South began to prepare for important spring campaigns. Numerous bases of operations had been established, and most of the recruits were actively training in camp.

In the West the scattered Union and Confederate armies had spent much of the winter strengthening defenses and adapting the influx of volunteers to army life. Yet the military situation was that of stalemate, causing in some regions a false sense of security.

In mid-February this impasse was broken with an abruptness that stunned both North and South. Striking unexpectedly, a combined Union Army and Naval expedition attacked and captured the two key Confederate forts protecting the lower Tennessee and Cumberland rivers.

In a fortnight a major Confederate defensive network was decisively broken, causing it to be abandoned by the Southern armies. The vast Middle South's interior thus lay open to invasion, and what had once been a distant war quickly loomed over the inhabitants of southwestern Tennessee.

The Union advance up the Tennessee was the design of Henry Wager Halleck, one of the North's most prominent generals. Balding, forty-seven years old, the commander of the Department of the Missouri, Halleck was rapidly approaching the zenith of his career.

Despite his austere manner and frizzled appearance Halleck was then considered by many as the foremost exponent of the art of war in America. When the black shadow of civil war was cast across the nation, President Abraham Lincoln, acting upon General-in-Chief Winfield Scott's recommendation, had appointed Halleck, then engaged in a highly successful business and law career in California, to the rank of major general in the regular army. He thus was fourth on the list of ranking generals in the entire service.

A cautious, methodical man, Halleck was also a supremely adept administrator. His widely read book, *Elements of Military Art and Science,* revealed his dedication to the principles of Baron Henri Jomini, the noted Swiss military analyst. Known as "Old Brains" to his soldiers, who derisively noted his receding hairline and bulging eyes, Halleck came west in the winter of 1861 to take command of Major General John C. Frémont's troubled Department of the Missouri. After restoring order to a department plagued with corruption, fraudulent contracts, and inefficiency, Halleck turned his full attention to the military situation.

One night in January, 1862, prior to the initial movement up the Tennessee, General Halleck chatted informally at his St. Louis headquarters with Brigadier Generals George Cullum, his chief of staff, and William T. Sherman, his friend and admirer since their former days at West Point. When the conversation turned to the much-talked-of "advance," Halleck placed a large map on the table, took a pencil, and asked Cullum to draw a line across the map where the Confederate line lay. Cullum ran a pencil mark through Bowling Green, Forts Donelson and Henry, and on to Columbus, Kentucky.

"Now," Halleck asked, "where is the proper place to break it?"

Both Sherman and Cullum were aware that others were urging a movement down the Mississippi River, yet they were equally aware of the Confederate strength at Columbus, Kentucky, where General Leonidas Polk had fortified the river bluffs with tiers of heavy guns. After a moment's hesitation either Sherman or Cullum spoke up and said, "Naturally, the center."

Halleck then drew a line perpendicular to the other, through the middle of Cullum's line. It ran almost parallel with the course of the Tennessee River. "That," he announced, "is the true line of operations." *

* Although it has been claimed that Ulysses S. Grant conceived the plan of operations along the Tennessee, Grant's story, as written in his memoirs, is inconsistent with the record. Halleck's correspondence of January 20, 1862 (W of R I-8-509) reveals his overall strategy before the date of Grant's visit to department headquarters in late January, at which time Grant is said to have proposed an attack on Ft. Henry. (W of R I-7-534, 561, 562, 565). The real impetus for active operations, however, probably came from Abraham Lincoln, who had long been complaining about inactivity in the Western Theater (W of R I-7-533, 928).

MAJOR GENERAL HENRY W. HALLECK. Mastermind of the Tennessee expedition, Halleck was the influential department commander who sought to remove Grant. His friendship for Sherman did much to obscure the responsibility of that general for one of the war's costliest surprises. (LIBRARY OF CONGRESS)

On February 2 Brigadier General Ulysses S. Grant initiated the first phase of Halleck's strategy with a cautious advance up the Tennessee from Cairo, Illinois. Four days later he proudly announced to Halleck, "Fort Henry is ours." This electrifying news had hardly greeted Halleck's eyes when he was astounded to read in the same communique that Grant proposed to take and destroy nearby Fort Donelson on the Cumberland immediately.

Following ten fretful days during which Halleck lamented, "It is the crisis of the war in the West," Grant telegraphed triumphantly to his department commander, "We have taken Fort Donelson and from twelve to fifteen thousand prisoners."

Halleck was ecstatic. Praise poured in for him and his subordinates from a jubilant North. Secretary of War Edwin Stanton commented on the "brilliant results" and "energetic action" in the West. Another friend thought it not improbable that Halleck might be made the next Democratic nominee for President. "Give me command in the West," he urged. "I am not satisfied with present success. We must now prepare for a still more important movement." Nearly three weeks later Halleck had his wish. He was promoted to the command of several consolidated departments, becoming overall commander west of Knoxville, Tennessee.

Along the Tennessee Union gunboats now ranged as far as Florence, Alabama, destroying bridges and shipping, breaking up numerous militia camps, and capturing the dreaded Confederate gunboat *Eastport,* then under construction at Cerro Gordo, Tennessee.

Reporting on his successful expedition to clear the Tennessee, Lieutenant Commander S. L. Phelps of the Union Navy happened to mention very strong Union sentiment along the river, particularly at Savannah, Tennessee. Thus encouraged, Halleck now openly boasted that if sustained in authority, he would "split secession in two in one month."

On February 20 Halleck announced to the War Department that he would campaign along the Tennessee, with or without the co-operation of General D. C. Buell's Army of the Ohio, which he had requested. After waiting for the fall of Nashville, which occurred on February 25, Halleck was able to withdraw most of his troops from the Cumberland and organize for the "decisive movement" that he believed would end the war in the West.

Less than a week later Halleck was ready. He instructed Grant to begin the movement by leading an expedition up the Tennessee to destroy the railroad bridge over Bear Creek, near Eastport, Mississippi. Grant also was told to disrupt railroad communications at Corinth, Jackson, and Humboldt, if practicable. Although his transports would carry infantry supports, Grant was told to use detachments of cavalry and light artillery to strike the objectives swiftly before effective opposition could be mounted. "Avoid any general engagement with strong forces," added Halleck. "It will be better to retreat than to risk a general battle."

Grant's troops were issued marching orders on March 2, but when he suddenly was replaced as the field commander on March 4 because of alleged neglect and inefficiency, the expedition was delayed. It was necessary for Brigadier General C. F. Smith, Grant's replacement, to travel to Fort Henry from his post on the Cumberland. Because of high water on the Tennessee embarkation of the troops was further slowed.

Meanwhile Brigadier General William T. Sherman at Paducah had been authorized to join C. F. Smith's expedition. Sherman, having promised to send his own division on behalf of General Smith to Savannah, Tennessee, because of the strong Union sentiment there, was soon surprised to learn that his own troops were in the vanguard of the entire expedition. Following the occupation of Savannah on March 8 by a single regiment of Sherman's division most of Smith's flotilla appeared on the eleventh. "The weather was soft and fine," one officer wrote, "and one or more flags floated over every boat." The regimental bands were playing, and to the inhabitants the long, winding column of sixty-three transports seemed grand, overpowering, and somewhat terrifying.

Wasting little time, General Smith began tactical operations on the following evening. Smith had learned of sizable Confederate strength at Corinth, Mississippi, and he determined to break the enemy's rail communications on either side of Corinth. Two separate striking forces were selected for the purpose, one to attack north of Purdy, Tennessee, and the other to raid in the vicinity of Eastport, Mississippi.

The first was dispatched on the ill-fated night of March 12 to damage the Mobile & Ohio Railway. Its destination was Crump's Landing, in the vicinity of Purdy. Commanded by the mustachioed son of an ex-Indiana governor, Brigadier General Lew Wallace, who would later write *Ben Hur,* the column consisted of a full division, about five thousand troops, nearly all of whom had fought at Fort Donelson.

Late in the evening of March 12 General Smith was rowed in a small yawl to Wallace's transport, the *John J. Roe,* to give Wallace his instructions. The night was dark and the river choppy. When Smith terminated the conference and stooped to reboard his bobbing yawl he slipped and fell, skinning his leg from the ankle to the knee against the sharp edge of a seat. Although he scoffed at the injury, an infection and fever soon developed. By the end of the week the leg was so swollen and painful that he was confined to bed. His men later joked that their commander, who was tall and square-shouldered with a long, snow-white moustache, was suffering from "gout in his big toe."

Before departing for Crump's Landing on the night of March 12 Lew Wallace hurriedly penned a note to his wife. Although he was an author, scholar, lawyer, and soldier, Wallace was not yet thirty-five. His impending promotion to major general, the highest rank then authorized for the Army, was assured, based upon his service at Fort Donelson. In this letter home Wallace expressed much of the optimism then prevailing throughout the Union Expeditionary Corps. Terming his mission upriver a mere "errand," Wallace wrote that the enemy was disorganized and demoralized and that the war, if pushed, could not last long. "Still," he added somewhat as an afterthought, "they will fight."

In the early morning hours of March 13 Wallace disembarked his troops at Crump's Landing, an obscure riverboat landing place four miles upriver from Savannah, at the end of a wagon road from Bethel Station. Following Halleck's explicit instructions, Wallace occupied the riverbank with infantry and sent his cavalry off to raid the railroad, all without opposition. Moreover, as the troops landed, a Union flag was hoisted from a nearby house, a welcome omen to Wallace's men.

Only hours later General Wallace began to have misgivings. While one of his brigades marched to Adamsville along the Purdy road to watch for the enemy, Wallace camped at Linton's farm, about three miles west of the river. During the afternoon a citizen appeared with a report that fifteen to eighteen thousand Confederates under General Cheatham had marched in the same direction yesterday and were camped across a creek only four miles distant.

When his cavalry failed to return by 4:30 P.M., Wallace sent a dispatch to General Smith saying that he was "a little uneasy" about his situation. "The enemy can, I am told, throw a bridge across the creek in three hours, and by good roads get into my rear," said Wallace.

Although the cavalry strike force under Major Charles S. Hayes, 5th Ohio Cavalry, soon returned and reported the railroad damaged without opposition, Wallace remained wary. He confided to his wife several days later that his mission had turned out to be a hazardous affair. "Nothing saved me from attack but an exaggerated idea of my force; which exaggeration I kept up by such little tricks as changing my lines in the day and multiplying fires by night," Wallace wrote. After the cavalry returned, Wallace retreated with his entire command to Crump's Landing, arriving late that evening.

Because the landing site was "very difficult" it required most of the next day, March 14, to reembark his division. During the interim he again sent Major Hayes and the cavalry on a reconnaissance along a river road toward the suspected enemy concentration. Although a flooded creek and its treacherous banks discouraged Hayes from attempting more than a hasty patrol, he discovered that the enemy had deserted the neighborhood and had fallen back on Purdy after first learning of Wallace's nearby landing.

Despite Wallace's skittishness General Smith was pleased with the results of the raid. Major Hayes had succeeded in damaging about one hundred and fifty feet of trestle where the Mobile & Ohio Railroad crossed Beach Creek, between Bethel and Brown Station. A portion of the track had been torn up, the rails bent and then thrown into the creek. This, Hayes thought, would "preclude the passage of trains until the whole structure is taken down and rebuilt." *

Encouraged by the success of Wallace's first venture, C. F. Smith now embarked on the second phase of his plan. Brigadier General William T. Sherman, once an obscure West Point lieutenant of the 1840's and now commanding a new and untried division, was chosen to make this attempt—a raid on the railroad communications east of Corinth in the vicinity of Burnsville, Mississippi. At noon on a rainy Friday, March 14, Sherman marched his troops aboard nineteen army transports and sailed for the mouth of Yellow Creek, about thirty miles upriver from Savannah. Puffing great clouds of black coal smoke, the flotilla steamed up the Tennessee through a

---

* Confederate General Braxton Bragg reported this bridge repaired the next day.

continuous downpour. For most of Sherman's men this was their first military adventure, and the covered decks of the transports were crowded with onlookers despite the rain.

Along the west riverbank, nine miles south of Savannah, the high bluffs abruptly receded into an irregular, rolling hillside. This site, marked as Pittsburg Landing on the Union maps, lay just a few miles north of the Mississippi state line and about two hundred and fifty miles upriver from the main Union supply base at Cairo, Illinois. As a landmark Pittsburg Landing was hardly worthy of notice—a sloping hill with a small field cut by a rutted country road. Two small log buildings squatted in the field, along with the charred outline of a third. Beyond its drab history as a minor freight depot for river cargo shipped to and from nearby Corinth, Mississippi, Pittsburg Landing had already achieved a more important military significance.

On March 1 the reverberations of heavy guns had shaken the quiet countryside for miles around. Two Union gunboats, the *Tyler* and *Lexington,* making a patrol up the Tennessee had discovered Gibson's battery of Confederate field artillery and the 18th Louisiana Infantry camped at the landing. When the gunboats' big 8-inch naval guns opened fire, the Confederates were seen to withdraw hastily. A few sailors and two companies of the 32d Illinois Infantry then went ashore to burn the log house near which the enemy battery had been placed. Soon the Confederates reappeared, however, and following a brief fight the Union landing party returned to the gunboats, fearing that the enemy had been reinforced.

After making daily visits to Pittsburg to check for fortifications the *Tyler* again debarked troops at the landing on March 4. Proceeding under a flag of truce, the detachment traveled a mile inland before encountering enemy pickets. Learning from local residents that nine bodies had been counted in the enemy's camp and that their tents had been removed three miles from the river following the fight, the scouting party withdrew to the gunboats. Lieutenant William Gwin, the *Tyler's* commander, was satisfied that the Confederates would not attempt to refortify Pittsburg Landing, and he ordered his gunboat to return to Cairo, Illinois.

From midriver, ten days later, the landing again appeared to be unoccupied as Sherman's division sailed past. However, since Lew Wallace had reported Confederate Brigadier General Benjamin F. Cheatham camped in the vicinity with a large force, Sherman feared that the enemy might occupy the landing and embarrass his expedition's return from Yellow Creek. Accordingly, before departing that morning he had suggested to General Smith that one gunboat and another division be sent as a precautionary measure to hold Pittsburg Landing. Sherman's own destination lay nearly twenty miles farther upriver, at the mouth of Yellow Creek in northern Mississippi. From that point Sherman planned to launch his cavalry for a swift strike overland at the Memphis & Charleston Railroad, about nineteen miles distant.

At seven o'clock in the evening of March 14 the gunboat *Tyler,* leading Sherman's expedition, touched shore at Tyler's Landing, Mississippi, near the mouth of Yellow Creek. Six companies of the 5th Ohio Cavalry were ordered ashore, but since the rain continued to fall in torrents, it required four hours to disembark.

When the downpour ceased at 11:30 P.M., Major Elbridge G. Ricker ordered his four hundred Ohio troopers to begin the raid. Their instructions were to destroy a trestle and tear up as much of the railroad as possible in the vicinity of Burnsville, Mississippi. Packhorses carried the necessary axes, crowbars, and picks, and a local civilian guide went along to show the way.

Despite the wet weather the men set off in good spirits; the rain had stopped, and the cool night air was a refreshing change from the crowded confines of the army transport. Deep ravines and winding, rain-swollen creek bottoms cut across the line of march, forcing the column to make wide detours. By one o'clock in the morning the rain again was falling steadily. The weather had turned much colder, and soon snow mixed with driving rain blew out of the darkness. At one flooded creek bottom Major Ricker was forced to order his cavalrymen to swim a rushing torrent. Three troopers were unhorsed in midstream and narrowly escaped drowning. When the heavily laden packhorses also foundered in the current, all of the picks and axes were lost.

Though all of his men were thoroughly soaked, Ricker pushed on. At 4 A.M. the vanguard approached another treacherous and flooded creekbed. The log bridge was afloat, and the icy rain was still falling. After a hasty consultation with his officers, Ricker concluded that it was impossible to execute his orders to strike the railroad, and he reluctantly ordered a return to the riverboat landing.

Meanwhile General Sherman had landed several brigades of infantry. Planning to march halfway to the railroad in order to support the return of his cavalry, Sherman started at daylight. After wading through a knee-deep slough a half-mile wide before reaching high ground, Sherman's two brigades trudged for several miles through the mud along a narrow ridge road. Reports that the river was rising six inches per hour back at Tyler's Landing caused Sherman to order one of his two artillery batteries to return to the transports. The infantry pressed on. About four and a half miles inland General Sherman's advance came to an impassable creek at flood stage. Colonel Hicks of the 40th Illinois had his men chop down several large trees to make a bridge, but the waters soon rose above the emplaced timbers. A messenger from Major Ricker had already arrived, informing Sherman that the cavalry was returning.

Satisfied now that "no human energy could . . . overcome the difficulty" short of the slow process of bridging every stream, Sherman ordered the whole force back to the transports.

When the weary column neared the river about midmorning, they found that the big lowland slough was now a broad lake separating them from their transports. First the battery of field guns tried to dash across, but it became so badly mired that the gunners had to cut the harnesses in order to save their horses. After a number of unsuccessful attempts to retrieve the guns, they were finally disassembled and removed piece by piece in rowboats launched from the transports. It also was necessary to fashion a crude pontoon bridge from yawl boats in order to reembark the infantry.

While the artillerists labored with their guns, a few of Sherman's infantrymen huddled miserably on "a high spot" and built a fire to cook their rations. To their disgust the "encroaching river" soon covered the ground and extinguished the fire. Years later Major Ricker of the cavalry wrote that it was the consensus among many veterans of the expedition that this night's march was the most terrible endured during the entire war.

Realizing the importance of his mission and its unfulfilled objective, Sherman reboarded the *Tyler* for a look at conditions further upriver. At the mouth of Indian Creek, near the Chickasaw bluffs, he found the landing inaccessible—entirely under water. Again, after approaching to within easy cannon range of Confederate fortifications at Chickasaw, on the Mississippi–Alabama border, Sherman saw that an attempted landing upriver would be futile. The Tennessee had risen fifteen feet in less than twenty-four hours, and the entire shoreline for nearly fifty miles, from Chickasaw back into southwestern Tennessee, was under water.

The mighty Tennessee was again proving to be a formidable obstacle to the designs of man. General Lew Wallace wrote of the superstitious local residents' feelings about the river having risen so rapidly: "They think the Lord is keeping it up purposely." Privately he admitted that he thought so himself.

Having "no alternative" because of the flooded conditions along the river, Sherman's rain-drenched transports now cruised slowly downriver during the night of March 15, stopping at the first landing site above water—Pittsburg Landing, Tennessee.

CHAPTER II

To Wage an Offensive

For months the Federal Government had anticipated in vain the invasion of the South. "The purpose of this war is to attack, pursue, and destroy a rebellious enemy," Secretary of War Edwin Stanton had declared in January, 1862.

Even President Abraham Lincoln had become annoyed prior to the movement up the Tennessee and Cumberland rivers with the inactivity in the Western Theater. "Delay is ruining us," he had admonished the general commanding the Department of the Ohio, ". . . Please name as early a day as you safely can . . . be ready to move southward."

News of the successful operations in the Western Theater had an immediate effect. Several days following the capture of Fort Donelson, the War Department bustled with a new spirit of optimism. "Savannah is ours," wrote Thomas A. Scott, Assistant Secretary of War. "Norfolk will be in a few days. We then hope for Nashville, Columbus, Memphis, and the cities farther South," he added.

Even the cautious Halleck boldly stated with more truth than he then realized, "I shall soon fight a great battle on the Tennessee. . . . If successful it will settle the campaign in the West." He had caused the enlarged Federal army of Fort Donelson to mass at Fort Henry, on the Tennessee, and in early March, 1862, had it poised aboard transports for what Halleck considered "a golden opportunity to strike a fatal blow."

Numbering about twenty-five thousand men and twelve batteries of artillery, the Tennessee expedition seemed to one observer as though "we had men enough . . . to clean out the Confederacy and half of Europe."

Three of the five divisions were veteran, having campaigned at Forts Henry and Donelson. Commanded by Generals McClernand, C. F. Smith (before replacing Grant as commander of the expedition), and Lew Wallace, they were the proud victors of whom Grant

12

had written, "Fort Donelson will hereafter be marked in capitals on the maps of our united country, and the men who fought the battle will live in the memory of a grateful people."

Only two divisions with the Tennessee expedition were new. Sherman's division, known as the Fifth, had organized at Paducah, Kentucky, in late February. Composed of nearly all Ohio and Illinois recruits, it had embarked on March 7 and 8 for Fort Henry. The Fourth Division was largely an Illinois command, having formed at Fort Donelson immediately following the capture of that place. One of its three brigades had fought there and had lost heavily. The division commander, Stephen A. Hurlbut, was an Illinois politician and a lawyer who knew Abraham Lincoln well. During the antebellum controversy over Fort Sumter, Hurlbut had served as one of President Lincoln's emissaries to Charleston. His reward had been a brigadier general's star.

Hurlbut, a somber-looking man with flaring mustachios, was ordered on March 7 to embark his fledgling division at Fort Henry. Sailing in the midst of C. F. Smith's main column, his eight thousand-man division departed from Kirkman's Landing near Fort Henry on March 10.

One of Hurlbut's officers wrote at the time that he never expected to see a "grander sight than . . . when we swung out in midstream [to] . . . lead the fleet. . . . Dense volumes of smoke rolled to the sky, and decks were dark with blue coated soldiers. Bright brass cannon glittered on the foredeck, where the batteries were loaded, and the bands played their most soul-stirring airs."

Upon arrival at Savannah Hurlbut's men were impressed by the awesome size of the Tennessee expedition. "We tied up to the west shore where the boats are crowded for a mile . . . sometimes four and five deep," said the lieutenant colonel of the 14th Illinois Infantry, who was also amazed to observe that there were "many vessels on the town side."

For a time it all seemed terribly grand and inspiring. "The river is beautiful tonight," wrote a Federal officer, "with the many bright lights on either shore, like so many will-o'-the-wisps dancing over the water." Another officer wrote to his wife that "the most magnificent sight" he had ever seen was the procession of steamers moving up the Tennessee. "Say what you will," he added, "war has its attractions."

A few days later the mood had changed drastically. The crowded and unsanitary conditions aboard the steamboats by now had made life wretched for the men. While Lew Wallace's and Sherman's divisions sailed upriver to raid the Memphis & Charleston Railroad, C. F. Smith's main column languished at Savannah, awaiting their return.

"We have to use the muddy river water for drinking and cooking," complained an Illinois officer. Since some of the transports were jammed with nearly a thousand men and their equipment and horses, proper sanitation was impossible. A rash of illness broke out, followed by so many deaths that lumber for coffins ran in short supply. Surgeon J. H. Brinton with Smith's expedition soon reported "an epidemic [of] typhoid fever of the most aggravated form. . . . The town of Savannah became one vast hospital." Brinton also found that his supplies of drugs and medicine were inadequate. Only one steamboat, the *City of Memphis,* had been assigned as a hospital boat, and the entire lower deck of that vessel was occupied by the quartermaster's department.

Matters soon became so out of hand that Lew Wallace took it upon himself to send "a boatload of diseased and dying men" to Evansville, Indiana. Said Wallace, "I had no place to shelter them, but few doctors to tend them, and not enough plank to make coffins for them when dead."

It came as a welcome relief when a portion of Hurlbut's division was sent ahead to Pittsburg Landing on March 15. Sherman, before departing on his unsuccessful railroad raid the day before, had written to Smith suggesting "as a precautionary measure" that "one division, say Hurlbut's or Wallace's, move up to Pittsburg Landing and there await our return."

Smith chose Hurlbut, and when Sherman's weary division returned to Pittsburg Landing during the night of March 15, they found Hurlbut's men waiting there aboard a flotilla of flat-bottomed river transports. Although fatigued by the exposure and hard work of the past two days, Sherman completed his report that night and steamed downriver to Savannah to deliver it.

His report suggested that because of the unfavorable conditions upriver an attempt on the railroad was more feasible from Pittsburg Landing. "By seemingly advancing on Corinth with a well appointed [large] force," Sherman wrote, "and sending off a small party of cavalry to the left, by Farmington, it may be still that the interruption of the road without a general engagement could be successfully accomplished. I am willing to undertake it. . . ."

According to Sherman C. F. Smith "saw in the flooded Tennessee the full truth of my report."

Apparently he was able to convince General Smith of the plan's practicality. Sherman was duly instructed "to occupy Pittsburg strongly" and to reconnoiter the ground there. Returning to Pittsburg Landing with Lieutenant Colonel James B. McPherson, a military engineer temporarily attached to C. F. Smith's staff, Sherman made preparations for "a strong reconnaissance toward Corinth, which I will convert into a destruction of the telegraph and railroad lines if possible."

Before attempting this foray, Sherman cautiously rode three miles into the interior to look for signs of the enemy. Satisfied that Cheatham's force (reported by Wallace) had withdrawn farther inland, Sherman ordered the necessary troops debarked.

His plans conformed to Halleck's instructions to feint with the infantry and strike with his cavalry. The entire division was to move "slowly and deliberately" up the main Corinth road beginning at midnight—their progress not exceeding two miles per hour. Meanwhile Lieutenant Colonel Thomas Heath and a detachment of the 5th Ohio and 4th Illinois Cavalry would proceed along a separate road, acting as though they were about to picket a bridge across Lick Creek, before suddenly striking for the Memphis & Charleston Railroad east of Corinth.

Major W. D. Sanger, a former West Point cadet and now an officer of Sherman's staff, and Major Samuel Bowman, an Illinois cavalryman who had skirmished with a detachment of Rebel cavalry along the Purdy road that morning, would go along "to advise" Heath of the propriety of making the final dash at the railroad.

"Don't hesitate to make the attempt . . . unless you have strong evidence of its too hazardous character," Sherman wrote. "The object is worth a desperate effort."

At six o'clock in the evening of March 16 Heath's cavalrymen started for the interior. At midnight Sherman's First Brigade followed along the main Corinth road.

They had gone but a short distance when Heath and his cavalrymen suddenly returned. They had encountered about five companies of Tennessee cavalry and had withdrawn after a brief skirmish, losing a guide and three Illinois troopers wounded.

Said Sherman, "I saw that an attempt on the [rail] road was frustrated," and he ordered his infantry to bivouac in the frosty woods about three-quarters of a mile from the Landing.

The next morning Sherman made a reconnaissance to and beyond the scene of Heath's skirmish. He was surprised to find that the enemy had also fled, having dispersed "in utter confusion," leaving "horses loose and mired in the bottoms, saddles, sabers, [and] shotguns scattered through the woods." Sherman, however, was convinced that he would not be able to cut the Memphis & Charleston Railroad from Pittsburg Landing without a serious engagement. "I have tried it twice," he wrote. "[It] is impossible from here, because the ground is well watched and a dash cannot be made."

Yet March 17 became a notable day in the rapidly unfolding sequence of events—for several reasons. Sherman, advised by C. F.

Smith during their night conference of the sixteenth to reconnoiter the ground near the landing, was measuring the terrain as he rode along the Corinth Road that morning. "I . . . am strongly impressed with the importance of the position, both for its land advantages and its strategic position," he wrote. "The ground itself admits of easy defense by a small command, and yet affords admirable camping ground for a hundred thousand men. . . . The only drawback is that at this stage of water the space for landing is contracted too much for the immense fleet now here discharging."

Of equal significance was the man with whom Sherman was now corresponding. Captain John A. Rawlins was Ulysses S. Grant's adjutant general, and his presence marked the arrival at Savannah of the new Federal field commander.

Promoted to major general for his recent victories at Forts Henry and Donelson, U. S. Grant had subsequently fallen into serious difficulty with Army headquarters.

Halleck mistrusted Grant and perhaps sensed an emerging rival in the arena of popular esteem. When he learned about March 1 that Grant had gone to Nashville, beyond the limits of his command, he complained to General George B. McClellan, the Army's General-in-Chief, "I have had no communication with General Grant for more than a week. He left his command without my authority and went to Nashville. His army seems to be as much demoralized by the victory of Fort Donelson as was that of the Potomac by the defeat of Bull Run. It is hard to censure a successful general immediately after a victory, but I think he richly deserves it. I can get no returns, no reports, no information of any kind from him. Satisfied with his victory, he sits down and enjoys it without any regard to the future. I am worn out and tired with this neglect and inefficiency."

When McClellan telegraphed his reply, endorsed by Secretary of War Stanton's approval, Halleck was armed with the needed support. Said McClellan, "The future success of our cause demands that proceedings such as Grant's should at once be checked. Generals must observe discipline as well as private soldiers. Do not hesitate to arrest him at once if the good of the service requires it. . . . You are at liberty to regard this as a positive order. . . ."

Halleck acted the following day, March 4. He removed Grant from field command and chided him for not obeying orders to report the strength and location of his troops. To further justify his action Halleck advised McClellan on the same day that it was rumored Grant had returned to his old whiskey-drinking stupors. "If so," Halleck confided, "it will account for his neglect of my often repeated orders."

Grant was taken completely by surprise. At a loss to explain the sudden ire of his commanding general, he concluded that there were enemies in the chain of communications between the department commander at St. Louis and himself. The Army telegraph line then extended only as far south as Cairo, Illinois, and Grant was sending his dispatches by boat to Cairo for forwarding by telegraph to St. Louis. A considerable delay resulted, and according to Grant the telegraph operator at Cairo was a Confederate sympathizer who did not forward all dispatches.

When Halleck telegraphed on March 6 that he had been advised by Washington to arrest him, Grant bitterly asked to be relieved from further duty. To darken matters further Grant took sick and considered refusing any new assignment.

Halleck's coup lasted less than a week. On March 10 he learned that President Lincoln was involved and that he would be required to furnish the Army Adjutant General with specific information about his allegations against Grant.

Halleck backed down. Possibly he was unwilling to risk his own reputation by calling a court of inquiry against the only general in the Union Army who had won a major victory. On March 15 he advised Adjutant General Lorenzo Thomas that Grant had "acted from a praiseworthy although mistaken zeal for the public service in going to Nashville," and that the irregularities occurring at Fort Donelson were in violation of Grant's orders, who was absent at the time. "General Grant has made the proper explanations," said Halleck, who added that "all . . . irregularities have now been remedied."

Halleck meanwhile telegraphed to Grant that he would not be relieved of duty and that he was to take command of Smith's expedition upriver. "Instead of relieving you," Halleck wrote, "I wish you as soon as your new army is in the field to assume the immediate command and lead it on to new victories."

For the second time in less than two weeks, Grant was greatly surprised. On the sixteenth he boarded a steamboat and sailed for Savannah, arriving on the following day. Since Halleck had thoughtfully sent a copy of his exonerating letter to Fort Henry, Grant believed that the department commander had intervened with the Government on his behalf, and he remained "very grateful to him" for many years.

Although his name was now a popular byword, Grant had not been a man of important stature until recently. The son of an illiterate tanner, he had met with failure much of his life. Detesting the leather trade, young Hiram Ulysses Grant grew up with a love for horses and apparently little else. A poor student from rural southern Ohio, he had nonetheless been admitted to West Point at age seventeen, largely through the efforts of his father to see that his children were well educated.

Grant disliked military life from the beginning and had little desire to remain in the Army. Yet the Mexican War provided adventure with Taylor's army in Mexico, and he was commended on several occasions for gallantry under fire. Emerging from the war as a first lieutenant, Grant spent several dreary years in garrison duty in the East before going to the West Coast in 1852. His wife, the sister of a classmate at West Point, and his children remained in the East. Again he became disillusioned with the service and began to drink heavily. In 1854 he resigned, reportedly to avoid court-martial for excessive drinking.

Then nearly thirty-two, Ulysses Grant took up a new trade in Missouri, becoming a farmer. Poor health ended this attempt four years later, and he went to St. Louis as a real estate broker. When the brokerage failed in May, 1860, the distraught Grant returned to his father's leather-goods store in Galena, Illinois, becoming a clerk.

Luckily Grant met Illinois Governor Richard Yates in Springfield, following President Lincoln's call for seventy-five thousand volunteers to suppress the rebellion. Yates was eager to muster the influx of volunteers pouring into the capital, but he had few experienced officers to do so. Grant was placed on his staff for that purpose, but soon took command of the unruly 21st Illinois Regiment, which he quickly disciplined and made into an effective unit.

While commanding a subdistrict at Mexico, Missouri, Grant read with surprise in a St. Louis newspaper that he had been nominated by Congressman E. B. Washburne of Illinois to be a brigadier general. Washburne knew Grant only slightly, from a war meeting at Galena, but the volunteer army was being expanded and four new brigadiers were allotted to Illinois. Grant was placed first on the list.

National exposure followed three months later when Grant attacked Belmont, Missouri, opposite the Confederate stronghold at Columbus, Kentucky. The fighting lasted nearly an entire day but was indecisive. When enemy reinforcements were ferried across the Mississippi from Columbus, Grant was forced to withdraw. His horse was shot from under him, and he had several other narrow escapes, but Grant felt that he had won a great victory at Belmont. When the battle was criticized in the North as being unnecessary and barren of results, Grant was deeply offended.

Several days later Henry Halleck became Grant's new department commander. Although the aggressive Grant was rudely rebuffed by Halleck when he first proposed the idea, permission was granted on January 30, 1862, for a combined Army and Navy expedition against Fort Henry on the Tennessee River.

A week later Forts Henry and Heiman were in Union hands, the result almost entirely of the work of the Navy's gunboats.

Emboldened by his easy success, Grant marched overland to the Cumberland River and on February 12 laid siege to the Confederate garrison at Fort Donelson. Following a bitter fight on the fifteenth, the Confederates surrendered on the next day. The prisoners included several generals and nearly fifteen thousand troops, then the largest single capture in American history.

Grant became famous overnight. Made a full major general of volunteers for his victory, Grant now believed that the war was almost over. He was confident that but little resistance would be offered to the Federal Army's invasion of the Middle South. Known as "Sam" Grant to his fellow officers, who construed his adopted initials "U. S." to mean "Uncle Sam," Ulysses, perhaps for the first time in his life, had gained the self-assurance that follows great success.*

Grant arrived at Savannah and found the expedition's commander, C. F. Smith, stricken with a tetanus infection. According to Grant Smith welcomed him with enthusiasm and explained his troop dispositions. Before leaving Fort Henry, Grant had advised Halleck that Smith's troops had landed at Savannah. "Why, I do not know," said Grant, who reasoned that fortifications must have been encountered beyond that point.

Actually the occupation of Savannah seems to have been Halleck's idea. On March 4 Halleck mentioned Savannah as a possible place of rendezvous with Buell's Army of the Ohio. Again on the fifth he advised Grant that if successful, the expedition would encamp at Savannah. "We must pierce his [the enemy's] center at Savannah or Florence," wrote Halleck, who also confided to General McClellan, "As Savannah is near the railroad and between Corinth and Henderson, I have directed the landing to be made at that place, unless General Smith, from local information, should deem some other point preferable." Sherman's dispatch of the seventeenth explained the situation upriver to Grant's satisfaction.

Smith and Sherman were the only West Point officers commanding a division in the expedition. Smith had graduated from the Academy when Grant was three years old. Sherman had outranked Grant until the latter's recent promotion, and during the Donelson campaign had offered to waive seniority. Grant had not forgotten this gesture, and in fact he placed full confidence in both of these generals.

Going by Sherman's strong endorsement of Pittsburg Landing, Grant ordered the troops remaining aboard transports at Savannah

---

* Hiram Ulysses Grant had entered West Point as Ulysses S. Grant. Representative Thomas L. Hamer, who filled out Grant's application, knew him as Ulysses. Hamer forgot about the "Hiram" and added the boy's mother's initial, "S," for Simpson, on the application. The name stuck.

MAJOR GENERAL ULYSSES S. GRANT. The belatedly restored field commander of the Tennessee expedition had an overconfidence that the war was all but over that nearly led to a stunning disaster. Famous following his victories at Forts Henry and Donelson, Grant's fate hung by the narrowest of threads at Shiloh—yet he refused to panic. This photo taken in December, 1862. (U. S. SIGNAL CORPS PHOTO [BRADY COLLECTION], NATIONAL ARCHIVES)

to sail upriver immediately and debark at Pittsburg Landing. Only McClernand's division, which had encamped about the town, remained at Savannah.

Meanwhile Halleck was busy with a project of great personal importance. As far back as early February he had strongly urged the joint cooperation between his army and the troops in the Department of the Ohio under Brigadier General Don Carlos Buell. Buell, whose army of fifty-five thousand had occupied Nashville following the fall of Fort Donelson, did not formally disagree with Halleck's plan but was reluctant to commit his troops accordingly.

Buell, a bearded forty-four-year-old Regular with a stern countenance and a reputation for strict discipline, had progressively antagonized Halleck into some rather rash action. During the Fort Donelson campaign Halleck had repeatedly pleaded in vain with Buell for help. When it appeared that the Confederates might counterattack, Halleck even tried cajolery. "I have asked the President to make you a major general," Halleck wrote. "Help me, I beg of you. Throw all your troops in the direction of the Cumberland."

Buell, who was a close friend of Army General-in-Chief McClellan, procrastinated. "Tell me what reliable information you have . . . and definitely what you want," Buell replied.

Halleck quickly lost patience with Buell. Appealing to McClellan and then to Secretary of War Stanton, he implored, "I must have command of the armies in the West. Hesitation and delay are losing us the golden opportunity. . . . There still is [time] . . . to strike a fatal blow, but I can't do it unless I can control Buell's Army."

When President Lincoln decided not to alter assignments, Halleck was crestfallen. "If it is thought that the present arrangement is best for the public service, I have nothing to say," he glumly wrote on February 24.

Buell was soon nominated for major general, and Halleck could but rant at the Ohioan's indecision. "If Johnston has destroyed the railroad and bridges in his rear, he cannot return to attack you. Why not come to the Tennessee and operate with me to cut Johnston's line? . . ." Halleck asked.

Buell was wary of a Confederate counteroffensive along the Nashville front, however. "Their plan seems to be to get [in] the rear of the Tennessee, and in positions to concentrate either on Halleck or me," he wrote. "I will say more about this when my information is clearer, and until then I cannot well determine my movements."

In succeeding days, Halleck became increasingly bitter. "What a mistake that Buell did not send forces to move with us up the Tennessee . . ." Halleck wrote to Thomas A. Scott, the Assistant Secretary of War. "I cannot make Buell understand the importance of strategic points till it is too late."

Buell wrote a rather curt letter to Halleck on March 9, telling him that "The point I previously suggested [Florence, Alabama] is the only one from which we can operate centrally," and "otherwise I may detach too little to serve you, or else so much as to endanger Middle Tennessee."

Halleck was incensed. "I am surprised that General Buell should hesitate to reinforce me," he angrily wrote McClellan. "He [Buell] was too late at Fort Donelson, as Hunter has been in Arkansas. . . . Believe me, General, you make a serious mistake in having three independent commands in the West. There never will and never can be any cooperation at the critical moments. . . . You will regret your decision against me on this point. Your friendship for individuals has influenced your judgment. Be it so. I shall soon fight a great battle on the Tennessee unsupported, as it seems. . . ."

Amazingly Halleck had his way. The very next day, March 11, President Lincoln's War Order #3 consolidated the three departments west of Knoxville, Tennessee, into one, the Department of the Mississippi, under Halleck. McClellan, who had argued with Lincoln over plans on the Richmond front, was removed as General-in-Chief, enabling Halleck to report directly to the Secretary of War.

Stanton had been in favor of Halleck's overall command in the West and was regarded as friendly. For the first time Henry Halleck could now control operations in the all important Western Theater, where the war might be won by occupying the vast Mississippi Valley.

Halleck could afford to be magnanimous now that he had prevailed. "The new arrangement of departments will not interfere with your command," he told Buell, who had finally agreed in general terms to Halleck's joint offensive on March 10.

Even when Buell balked at Halleck's suggestion to move all available troops by river up the Tennessee, Halleck was unruffled. Buell thought it was fine to use the river to get supplies, but he wanted to march overland to reach the Tennessee. Said Buell, "I am decidedly of [the] opinion that my force should strike it by marching. It can move in less time, in better condition, and with more security to our operations than by the river."

Halleck consented and on March 16 sent Buell his orders: "Move your forces by land to the Tennessee as rapidly as possible. . . . Grant's army is concentrating at Savannah. You must direct your march on that point, so that the enemy cannot get between us."

Buell's army, which he reported on March 14 to number fifty thousand effective troops organized into eighteen brigades and six divisions, was still at Nashville. The necessary orders were immediately issued, and on March 16, General Alexander McCook's division broke camp, forming the advance of Buell's army.

Ahead lay a rugged, 122-mile march over a tortuous, muddied road with several deeply flooded rivers to cross.

CHAPTER III

A Campsite in the Wilderness

"Pittsburg Landing . . . excited nothing but disgust and ridicule. . . . A small, dilapidated storehouse was the only building there. . . . Up the bluff through a ravine ran the miserable road from the river, its course marked by the unfathomable yellow mud of that region," remembered an Illinois officer who came ashore with one of Sherman's brigades on the evening of March 16.

The steep bluffs jutted nearly one hundred feet above the river, and to another observer the region looked like a total wilderness. At the top of the bluff lay several half-buried bodies, the victims of the gunboat encounter of March 1, now exposed by the incessant rains. Sherman's troops filed past these rotting remains in awed silence during the afternoon of the sixteenth. Though the weather had turned clear and frosty, the men were made to bivouac in the open woods near the landing without shelter.

Although a portion of Sherman's division was still aboard their transports, the march inland was resumed the next morning. Stuart's brigade, following one of the country roads paralleling the river, marched nearly two miles south through what one officer described as "an uninteresting tract of country, cut up by rough ravines and ridges," and thickly covered with timber. Their destination lay along the Hamburg–Savannah road, at a point near the Lick Creek bridge, which Sherman had designated as one of the two approaches to Pittsburg Landing that he wished guarded.

The remaining troops ashore marched along the main Corinth road for slightly over two miles and camped near a one-room, hewn-log church, known locally as Shiloh Meeting House. Here they were to guard the direct route from Corinth, Mississippi, and another road crossing Owl Creek on their right, approaching from the direction of Purdy, Tennessee.

Sherman's decision to march several miles inland from Pittsburg

Landing had been of twofold purpose. According to Sherman C. F. Smith told him during the night of the fifteenth "to take positions well back" so as to leave room for the entire army. Moreover the peculiar topography of the region provided two main avenues of approach from the south. Sherman deployed his troops to watch both at a point distant from the landing. Grant, the new field commander, not only concurred in these dispositions but, being anxious to make a rapid lodgment on the enemy railroad, immediately ordered all of the troops waiting aboard transports at Savannah to move to Pittsburg Landing.

Because of his early presence there Sherman assumed the principal role in organizing the Federal army at Pittsburg Landing. Although he was one of the most controversial generals on the army rolls, good fortune had recently smiled on the wiry, forty-one-year-old West Pointer. Known as "Cump" to his close friends, Sherman at one time had been victimized by unfavorable publicity to the point of mental imbalance.

Less than six months earlier many Northern newspapers, led by the Cincinnati *Commercial,* had accused Sherman of being "crazy, insane, and mad" after he had asked for 200,000 men to put down the rebellion in the Mississippi Valley. When Adjutant General Lorenzo Thomas termed the request "insane," Sherman, then on unfriendly terms with many newspaper reporters for his refusal to grant interviews, was criticized severely by the press.

In November, 1861, he had been abruptly relieved from command of the Department of the Cumberland and transferred to Major General Halleck's Department of the Missouri, largely as a result of his alarmist behavior in Kentucky. When Halleck later sent Sherman into the Missouri interior on an inspection tour, Sherman compounded his difficulties by ordering troop movements without proper authority.

By his own admission he acted and spoke with imprudence. Halleck had Sherman recalled and sent him home to Ohio "for the benefit of his health," deeming him physically and mentally broken and temporarily "unfit for duty."

After he was restored to duty in late December, 1861, Sherman took command of Benton Barracks at St. Louis and, soon thereafter, the important river depot at Paducah, Kentucky. While there Sherman organized a new division for service under his own command, having earlier been promised this opportunity by Halleck.

Clouds still hung over Sherman's head, however. As the former superintendent of what is now Louisiana State University, he had even at one time been under suspicion of disloyalty. Rumors of his insanity were still circulating. Sherman's new recruits looked upon him with uncertainty.

Actually there was little in Sherman's background to inspire confidence. Born February 8, 1820, the sixth of eleven children, he had had a very difficult childhood. His father, Charles Robert Sherman of Lancaster, Ohio, a judge of the Ohio Supreme Court, died suddenly when William was nine, leaving little means of support. The family soon split up, and William was adopted by a close friend of his father's, United States Senator Thomas Ewing of Ohio.

Under Ewing's influence Sherman received an appointment to the U. S. Military Academy in 1836. While on recruiting duty in the East during the spring of 1846, Lieutenant Sherman learned of the war in Mexico. Eager for active service, he left a corporal in charge of his post in Zanesville, Ohio, and without authority took a steamboat to Cincinnati. Naïvely expecting that he would be sent on to join the army in Texas, he reported to Colonel Fanning, the officer in charge. When Fanning learned that Sherman had left his post without orders, he angrily sent the crestfallen young lieutenant back to his station.

Sherman was further disappointed in his efforts to see war service, soon being ordered to California on headquarters duty. Although he returned East in 1850 and married his adoptive sister, Ellen Boyle Ewing, Sherman found the monotony of Army life and insufficient pay enough cause for leaving the service in 1853.

A banking venture in San Francisco failed in 1857, and Sherman returned to New York to manage a Wall Street bank. Several months later that bank also closed its doors. Sherman, with a wife, four children, and no income, joined the law firm established by two of Thomas Ewing's sons in Leavenworth, Kansas. The income was meager, and Sherman, in despair, applied for the position of superintendent of a new military academy then being organized in Alexandria, Louisiana.

When the Louisiana State Seminary of Learning and Military Academy opened its doors on January 1, 1860, Sherman was its superintendent. Only a year later Sherman found his position untenable. When Louisiana prepared to secede from the Union, Sherman reluctantly resigned and left for the North.

Frustrated in his varied endeavors, Sherman "was extremely anxious about the future." His luck had been bad, and he had little reason to look forward with optimism.

Yet two letters were waiting for him in Ohio. An old Army friend, Major H. S. Turner, was trying to secure the presidency of the Fifth Street Railway in St. Louis for him at an annual salary of $2,500. Turner's letter offered the prospect of an appointment in March.

The other letter, from his brother John, Ohio's new U. S. Senator, asked that he come to Washington. Sherman did so, but following a disappointing interview with President Lincoln, he accepted the St. Louis offer.

Although he petitioned Secretary of War Simon Cameron for an Army appointment following the bombardment of Fort Sumter, his request apparently went unanswered. His influential brothers had not forgotten "Cump," however, and they worked actively in his behalf.

In mid-May Sherman received a dispatch from Washington announcing his appointment as colonel of the 13th U. S. [Regular] Infantry. Having witnessed as a bystander the street fighting in St. Louis following the capture of Southern sympathizers at Camp Jackson, Sherman departed for Washington. He was soon placed in command of a brigade in McDowell's army and fought with gallantry in his very first battle, Bull Run.

For a while it seemed that Sherman had at last found the success he had so ardently courted. Following a promotion to brigadier general, he was ordered west, to the Department of the Cumberland as second-in-command to Brigadier General Robert Anderson. When Anderson's health soon failed, Sherman succeeded him as department commander.

Yet during the following months the bright promise of mid-1861 was marred by frustration and ill temper. Even his brother Hoyt, who saw "Cump" for the first time in eleven years during the winter of 1860–61, was uncertain of his health. Gratefully Hoyt remarked to a friend after his visit: "Cump's all right; he isn't crazy."

Still, the adverse publicity had taken its toll, and Sherman approached the Tennessee campaign with a bitter resolve. Despite a service record of thirteen years in the Regular Army, he had been under fire on only two occasions, both occurring during the campaign of First Bull Run. Moreover his leadership in combat was unproven insofar as his Western troops were concerned. Although outwardly undaunted by the taunts of being "crazy," Sherman avidly sought an opportunity to silence his critics.

In the days following Grant's arrival at Savannah Sherman became more openly the informal camp commander at Pittsburg Landing. Grant told Sherman on March 17 that he had ordered the troops moving up from Savannah "to report to you," and to organize the unassigned regiments and assign them to divisions "as you deem best."

Sherman began the task with his usual energy. On the seventeenth he ordered Hurlbut's troops to disembark and encamp a mile inland along the Corinth road. Ample room existed across the vast expanse of timberland to encamp many thousands more, and only the limited landing area below the bluffs caused Sherman to hesitate in fully endorsing Pittsburg Landing as a base from which to launch the Federal offensive.

The ground across which Sherman directed deployment of his troops was of growing significance. Near the landing the topography was spectacular, if not admired by the Federal soldiers. Bold, deep ravines, often with small creeks rushing toward the Tennessee, cut through the undulating tableland. Two large and swollen creeks dominated the region, creating in effect a rough equilateral triangle of campground that extended for three miles before being interrupted by a range of two-hundred-foot-high hills south of the landing.

Lick Creek, running along the northern edge of these hills, joined the Tennessee about two miles south of the landing. Since the Tennessee at this point ran almost due north, the river nearly paralleled the high ground along the landing and formed the eastern side of the triangle. On the opposite shore the ground was relatively low and flat, in the spring often being marshy.

About a half-mile north of Pittsburg Landing the second large creek ran to a meeting with the Tennessee. Although Snake Creek continued to the west, its course was directed away from the landing. A large tributary, Owl Creek, cut across the rolling tableland from the southwest, however, forming the western boundary of Sherman's Pittsburg Landing campground. Both Lick and Snake creeks were treacherously deep in the spring; under flood conditions Owl Creek might reach a depth of thirty feet, although four feet was more normal.

Sherman saw in this triangle of land strategic position and "an admirable camping ground." The terrain, although noted by Sherman to be of "easy defense by a small command," was not chosen for its defensive value. Foremost in Sherman's mind was the establishment of an offensive base of operations. "I . . . acted on the supposition that we were an invading army," he wrote. "The position was naturally strong . . . we could have rendered this position impregnable in one night, but . . . we did not do it. . . . To have erected fortification would have been evidence of weakness and would have invited an attack."

Since Sherman's initial recommendation had led to the concentration at Pittsburg Landing, he, more than any other officer, was responsible for the army's presence there. More importantly, as the unofficial camp commander he was entrusted with the organization and defense of the encampments.

As the various divisions and unorganized regiments arrived, they were assigned sites throughout the triangle, most of the new units camping near the landing.

No fortifications were ordered built, however. Across the three-and-one-half-mile base of the triangle, from Lick Creek to Owl Creek, only Sherman's division guarded the outer perimeter. Between Stuart's brigade and Sherman's main encampment at Shiloh Church a gap of more than a mile existed, to be filled by a yet unorganized division. On each flank two swollen and treacherous creeks barred passage. In the army's rear the broad Tennessee swirled wildly by, and rapid evacuation or reinforcement was hindered by the limited landing space below the bluffs.

Twenty-two miles distant, at Corinth, Mississippi, a large Confederate Army was rapidly organizing. Sherman, despite his calculating plans, had inadvertently placed the Federal army in a natural trap.

To the men going ashore from the cramped confines of an Army transport the encampment at Pittsburg Landing was a welcome sight. The weather, which had been cold and rainy, briefly turned very warm toward the end of March.

One Michigan private wrote home that he anticipated warm weather in Tennessee but he "didn't expect to see it so very hot." "It seems to me," he continued, "that it is nearly as warm here now, as it is there [in Michigan] in the middle of summer; but I suppose that it is on account of coming from as cold a place into a warm one, without getting broke in by degrees."

The vegetation was rapidly responding to the warm weather. The grass was green but not very tall. Many of the trees bore tiny leaflets, and the fruit trees were in blossom.

One of Sherman's Illinois officers thought their camp along Locust Grove Branch of Lick Creek was "a sort of tropical revelation." A beautiful peach orchard, fragrant with dainty pink blossoms, became the campsite of the 55th Illinois in Stuart's brigade. The surrounding scenery, wrote an officer, "abounded in deep ravines, sparkling waters, rugged bluffs and beautiful foliage."

Very soon the unseasoned troops began to regard their camp-sites as a sort of martial picnic ground. Although Sherman's special orders prescribed that "each brigade must encamp looking west," so as to be in line of battle when called to arms, and that "the interval between regiments must not exceed twenty-two paces," in practice these orders were disregarded. Hildebrand's brigade, adjacent to Sherman's headquarters at Shiloh Church, numbered three regiments, each fronting in a different direction. Intervals ran as much as one hundred paces between regiments in Stuart's brigade, while the brigade itself sprawled over a half-mile from one end to the other.

According to Sherman's orders convenience of fresh water might "be considered" but was not to determine the location of the camps. Yet the 53d Ohio in Hildebrand's brigade pitched its tents about four hundred yards in advance of and across a stream from their nearest neighbor so as to be near a clear spring.

Soon so many high-ranking officers were found to be inhabiting private dwellings that General Grant issued orders that all regimental officers would be required to live in tents and brigade commanders would not be allowed to occupy houses at government expense.

Most of the Federal soldiers found their regimental camps to be quite comfortable and well equipped. Each company was provided with five large Sibley tents, pitched close together in a row. For the officers a smaller square tent was erected at the head of each row. Ovens fashioned of dried clay were set up to bake fresh bread. Numerous hospital tents were erected, as was a quartermaster's tent for the storage of regimental supplies. Some regiments even had potbellied stoves made of sheet metal to heat their tents.

Throughout the first week in camp most of the time was consumed in clearing campsites, bringing up supplies from the Landing, and embellishing the camps with such refinements as elevated bunks made from tree poles, in order that the men might sleep off the ground.

The task of unloading troops and their equipment and supplies at Pittsburg Landing proved to be more difficult than at first anticipated. High water so restricted the landing area along the bank that Sherman had to back his boats away in order to allow Hurlbut's troops to disembark on the eighteenth. When other Federal troops arrived, they found the landing area hopelessly jammed. One commander observed that Pittsburg Landing was "occupied with boats for its entire length, five deep." By the time C. F. Smith's division arrived the landing area was so congested that one of his brigade commanders, Brigadier General John McArthur, carved out a separate landing area and road in order to speed the unloading process. So many thousands of troops were found crowding about the landing that it was necessary for Sherman to move Buckland's and Hildebrand's brigades out to the Purdy road camps on Thursday, March 20.

By the end of the week the weathered white tents of Sherman's division stretched for nearly a mile through the lightly timbered woods along the Purdy road. On their far right ran Owl Creek, rain-swollen and out of its banks, choking the adjacent ravines with backwater and ankle-deep mud. A long, dry ridge ran along the Purdy road before falling away into a lowland marsh near the Owl

Creek bridge. A little more than a mile east of this bridge, in the midst of Sherman's camps, the main Pittsburg–Corinth road intersected with the Purdy road.

Nearby, on the main Corinth road, a small group of Southern Methodists had erected a one-room cabin of sturdy logs, "chinked and daubed." It was named Shiloh Meeting House, after Shiloh, "A Place of Peace," from the Bible, First Book of Samuel.

For nearly ten years the local residents had gathered there to observe the Sabbath. Their little log chapel was built of oak with hewn walls and a clapboard roof, both of which had long since weathered and cracked.

Several hundred yards behind the Meeting House, south of the crossroads, Sherman established his headquarters tent. Hildebrand's Ohio brigade was camped nearby, east of the church on the same side of the main Corinth road. On Hildebrand's right, across the road, another all-Ohio unit, Buckland's brigade, was encamped. Still farther to the west, stretching to the Owl Creek overlook, was McDowell's brigade, composed of Iowa, Illinois, Ohio, and Indiana recruits. Stuart's detached brigade remained far to the left, guarding the bridge over Lick Creek. With an eloquent flair Sherman designated his encampment "Camp Shiloh" and soon established a daily routine of drill, inspection, and reviews.

Although C. F. Smith sailed to Pittsburg Landing with his division following Grant's arrival, he remained sick aboard the transport *Hiawatha*. Because of his incapacity he requested that Sherman continue to direct the encampment of the new arrivals, including that of his own Second Division.

Smith's troops were placed by Sherman about a mile west of the landing, on a line parallel with the Tennessee River. Stephen A. Hurlbut's Fourth Division had previously camped immediately south of Smith's location and was extended along the Hamburg–Savannah road. All three divisions already ashore at Pittsburg Landing numbered nearly twenty thousand troops during the fourth week in March.

Grant thus far had relied on the judgment of Generals Smith and Sherman in ordering the concentration at Pittsburg Landing. On the nineteenth, however, he steamed upriver to inspect personally the encampments at Crump's and Pittsburg landings.

Returning that night to Savannah, Grant was well satisfied and reported to district headquarters in St. Louis that the two sites were "the only ones where a landing can be well effected on the west bank . . ." so far as was known. He was careful to add, however, that this only applied "to the present stage of water."

Of greater importance to Grant was the dispatch from Halleck

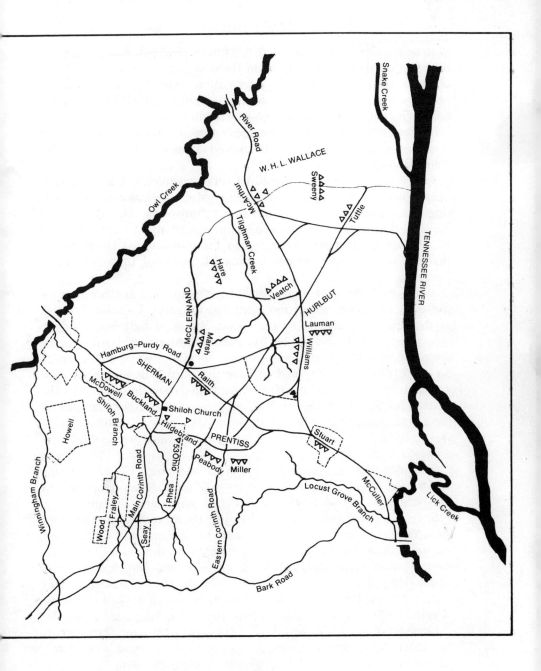

MAP 2
Union Camps at Pittsburg Landing
(Chapters 3–4, 8–9)

that was waiting for him upon his return. Halleck had received a telegram on the seventeenth from Buell in Nashville in which Buell claimed to have "reliable" information that the Confederates, twenty-six thousand strong, were marching "to strike the river below Savannah, to cut off transportation."

Halleck's deceptively ambiguous note to Grant said that if this was true, "General Smith should immediately destroy [the] railroad connection at Corinth."

Grant realized that the flooded rivers prevented extensive enemy operations and dismissed the possibility of Confederate artillery getting close enough to annoy the river transports. He telegraphed Halleck, however, that "immediate preparations" would be made to advance on Corinth according to his instructions. Grant added that he would go in person, leaving McClernand in command at Savannah.

When told the next morning that it would take another four or five days to debark all of the troops at Pittsburg Landing because of the restricted landing space, Grant estimated that he would be able to begin his advance by the twenty-third or twenty-fourth. In anticipation McClernand was ordered to send two of his brigades on to Pittsburg Landing and to have the third follow as soon as a garrison could be organized at Savannah from the new arrivals. Grant also had C. F. Smith hold all troops at Pittsburg subject to immediate marching orders, with three days' rations in their haversacks. Even Lew Wallace, at Crump's Landing, was told to be ready to march at a moment's notice.

The morning of March 21 was clear and cold. General Grant, anxious to organize an advance on Corinth, steamed upriver to Pittsburg Landing to confer with C. F. Smith and Sherman.

Several Confederate deserters had just been brought in, and from them Grant learned "that thirteen cars [had] arrived at Corinth on the nineteenth" with enemy reinforcements. Noting as well that the roads were almost impassable for artillery and baggage wagons, Grant delayed his plans to advance. Yet the Confederate deserters convinced him that Rebel morale was poor and that when attacked, "Corinth will fall much more easily than Donelson did. . . ."

Because of the delay in relaying dispatches by river transport to and from the telegraph terminal head at Fort Henry it was March 22 before Grant received Halleck's curt telegram of the twentieth. Halleck suspected that Grant had misinterpreted his dispatch about Buell's news of the Confederates marching on Savannah. Fearing that Grant was about to advance without waiting for Buell's reinforcements or for Halleck's own arrival, Halleck warned, "Don't let the enemy draw you into an engagement now. Wait until you are properly fortified and receive orders."

Grant was somewhat shaken. He had just experienced serious difficulty with Halleck, and he wanted no further trouble. Grant telegraphed immediately that he was making "no movement . . . except to advance General Sherman's division, to prevent Rebels from fortifying" a nearby village.

Privately "Sam" Grant disagreed with Halleck's cautious strategy. The very next day he confided to C. F. Smith, "I am clearly of the opinion that the enemy are gathering strength at Corinth quite as rapidly as we are here, and the sooner we attack the easier . . . will be the task of taking the place." Complaining that "I do not hear one word from St. Louis [Halleck]" about future plans, Grant could merely authorize C. F. Smith to occupy Pea Ridge (Monterey) along the main road to Corinth.

Since Smith was sick aboard a steamboat at Pittsburg Landing, Sherman was given the assignment to go to Pea Ridge, a small village about ten miles from Shiloh Church. Instead of "occupying and partially fortifying" the village as Grant had contemplated, Sherman planned only a "strong reconnaissance."

Following the establishment of his Shiloh camps Sherman had come to look upon Corinth as the "new Manassas of this region." He was also of the opinion that the Confederates were at a loss to know the strength and intent of the Federal troops at the landing. When a slight skirmish occurred on the twentieth with about sixty enemy cavalry near Pea Ridge, Sherman felt the Rebel horsemen were there to reconnoiter the Federal camps and would "make desperate efforts to penetrate our lines to ascertain our approximate force."

Sherman's strong reconnaissance of March 24 was staged for the purpose of learning what troops, if any, the Confederates were moving to Pea Ridge. Two full brigades started along separate roads in "delightful" weather, but being unaccustomed to marching, they soon found the tramp over rough ridges and muddy creeks tiresome. When no Confederates were encountered, some of the men clamored to be led on to Corinth, yelling and shouting as Sherman passed the long blue column.

Amused, Sherman remarked that there were sixty thousand armed Rebels there and they might be too many for two Union brigades to fight. Although his recruits grumbled at the prospect of making a long hike without fighting the enemy, Sherman marched only as far as Pea Ridge. When he found no Confederate troops there, he ordered a return to the Shiloh camps after bivouacking at Chambers's plantation for the night.

Again Sherman's efforts had amounted to little result. In fact the only gain he was able to show for his first two weeks in camp was the acquisition of a captured Confederate racehorse. By Sherman's account a lone "Arkansas ranger" was brought into camp leading a fine sorrel mare. The man claimed his Union captor had tricked him, having on a white hat and asking him to "come over" in a deceptive manner. When brought before Sherman, he implored, "General, you are not going to take my horse, are you?"

"Certainly," Sherman responded, stating that the horse was captured property.

"But it is a racehorse," the man protested.

"All the better," remarked Sherman, who appropriated the steed for his own use.

Ironically, it was one of the few occasions at Camp Shiloh when Sherman would profit.

CHAPTER IV

Gathering of the Host

In the waning days of March, 1862, Pittsburg Landing bore little resemblance to the obscure riverboat landing site of a few weeks earlier. Supply steamboats and troop transports by the dozens vied for the limited landing space below the bluffs. Often, while a few vessels discharged their cargo at the riverbank, a sizable fleet of steamboats waited in midriver.

Atop the bluff the few dilapidated log cabins of two weeks ago had been overwhelmed by a vast and bustling tent city. Parked wagons, munitions, and boxes of commissary supplies were everywhere. To one impressionable young private seeing a large encampment for the first time it was a "wild scene." "Men were everywhere," he wrote, including some playing cards in a small enclosure where "in one corner . . . lay a dead infantryman, whose presence seemed unknown to the boys who were hazarding all they had on a . . . hand."

Another soldier, an officer, wrote that one might "march for miles and . . . see nothing but the white tents of infantry, cavalry, and artillery. . . . The sound of drums and the blowing of trumpets," he continued, "fill my ears from morning to night."

Inevitably where the Army moved the sutlers followed, and Pittsburg Landing was swiftly descended upon. Shortly after Sherman's troops went into camp, sutlers Ellison, McKeown, and Naylor arrived with a large supply of goods, including such luxuries as chewing and smoking tobacco, canned fruit, and newspapers. Although nearly a week old, daily Chicago papers were offered at the landing for fifteen cents each.

At the end of March the concentration of troops at Pittsburg Landing had grown to about thirty thousand men of all arms, including two new divisions.

Ordered up from Savannah on March 20, the veteran division of Major General John A. McClernand was among the last to

35

encamp at Pittsburg Landing. McClernand claimed strong political connections reaching all the way to President Lincoln, who
had appointed him a brigadier general in May, 1861. Although
a fiery and bombastic Democratic congressman, McClernand had
been a strong influence in holding the loyalty of the southern
Illinois Democrats. Lincoln's appointment thus seemed political.
The forty-nine-year old McClernand knew little of military science,
his only experience having been during the Black Hawk War of
1832, when he served for three months as a private.

Made a major general for his service at Fort Donelson, Mc-
Clernand basked in the glory of public acclaim. A gangling, bushy-
faced man with a violent temper and a disdain for West Pointers,
McClernand was also a blatant egotist. His ambitions were excessive, and his actions often impetuous and rude. McClernand was
not looked upon with favor by his fellow officers.

His division was composed of nearly all Illinois troops that had
fought in the front lines at Fort Donelson. Following their arrival
at Pittsburg Landing they were located west of Hurlbut's and north
of Sherman's divisions. One brigade, Ross's, camped less than a
half-mile from Shiloh Church.

The other organized troops then at Pittsburg Landing belonged
to an embryo division created by Grant's order of March 26. Commanded by Brigadier General Benjamin M. Prentiss, a forty-two-
year old Illinois lawyer-politician with a homespun militia background, the new division was designated the Sixth. Most of Prentiss's men, with the exception of several Missouri regiments, were
raw recruits, deficient in training and discipline. They were directed
to encamp in the gap existing between Stuart's and Hildebrand's
brigades of Sherman's division, thus forming a large portion of the
army's outer perimeter. When all of Prentiss's tents were erected,
an interval of more than a quarter-mile still existed between Prentiss's right and Hildebrand's outermost regiment, the 53d Ohio
Volunteers.

Since each division was assigned a complement of cavalry and
artillery, it was in effect operationally self-sufficient. Artillery batteries were distributed among the various brigades and were controlled by infantry as well as artillery orders. Following the common
practice of the day, cavalry regiments were split up into battalions
and assigned to duty with separate divisions. This structuring resulted in regiments such as the 4th Illinois, 5th Ohio, and 11th
Illinois Cavalry being divided among two or more divisions and
scattered from Crump's Landing to Lick Creek.

Because so many recruits and unseasoned regiments were in the
field for the first time discipline soon became a source of great

anxiety. Several regiments arrived in a rowdy and disorderly condition, their officers exerting little control over the men. One Missouri regiment, the 21st Volunteers, found it great fun to shoot
at chickens, civilians, and any other sporting target encountered
on their way upriver to Pittsburg Landing. Grant was so outraged
that he had the colonel tried by court-martial.

A few days later Grant learned from Halleck in St. Louis that
nearly two hundred men had gone to the North on sixty- and
ninety-day furloughs without valid authority. Said Halleck, "There
seems to be collusion between the officers and men to give sick
leaves to well and healthy men who wish to visit their homes. . . .
If this abuse of the furlough system is not promptly checked, half
of the army will be on furlough."

Grant immediately had several boats leaving for the North
stopped. On board were found a number of soldiers with passes
signed by regimental commanders, a brigadier general, and, in
one case, a captain. Grant, much embarrassed, hurriedly apologized
to Halleck, promising to "arrest all of the parties" and to prefer
charges.

Already on the defensive with Halleck, Grant was further plunged
into difficulty by the large number of sick accumulating at the
landing. Halleck warned on March 24 of "gross irregularities in
your district in regard to the disposition of the sick and wounded,"
reminding Grant that it was "impossible . . . to have proper pro-
vision for the sick and wounded when no regard was paid to my
orders."

Grant had earlier complained that "alternate days of rain and
sunshine, pleasant and very cool weather" had affected the health
of his men. Some regiments had remained cramped on board their
river transports for more than a week, waiting to disembark. At
least one regiment, the 7th Illinois in C. F. Smith's division, had
languished aboard the steamer *Fairchild* for eleven days before going
ashore. They had been forced to drink the polluted river water,
and nearly all were sick. One young Michigan private, stricken with
the ague aboard a transport, was left to his own devices. "When I
had the chills," he wrote, "I sat beside the smoke pipe on the upper
deck; and when the fever came . . . I lay upon the floor in the
sick room with my head upon my knapsack . . . sweat(ing) like
a butcher."

Ashore the illness continued. One Federal surgeon estimated in
late March that nearly one-third of the entire army was unfit for
duty. The 44th Indiana of Hurlbut's division was for a while completely immobilized by dysentery. Another unit, Taylor's Battery
A, Chicago Light Artillery, was so stricken by disease that one of

its privates thought that if it continued, "we shall not have men enough to run the battery." Home remedies such as "some blue pills and a good dose of castor oil" often compounded the problem and increased the suffering.

Regular medicines were scarce, and when Grant telegraphed for a quantity sufficient "for ten thousand sick," Halleck condemned Grant's medical staff, implying that requisitions were improperly made out. Lew Wallace's unauthorized shipment of a boatload of ill soldiers North brought a further outcry from Halleck. "By whose order were these sent to New Albany?" he demanded. To add to the dismal situation Halleck was greatly angered by the arrival of transports laden with Grant's sick at St. Louis, where the hospitals were already overflowing with casualties from Curtis's fight at Pea Ridge, Arkansas. Halleck had ordered Grant's sick sent to Cincinnati, and he again demanded to know why no one would follow his orders.

Grant put the blame on the district's medical director and told Halleck, "This army is mostly new to me, and it is impossible that I should correct all irregularities or know of them at once, especially as I receive such feeble support from many of the officers."

Meanwhile the number of sick continued to increase and began to overflow the regimental hospital tents. On the twenty-eighth Grant reported that his sick had been without "some important medicines" for a week. The only hospital boat with the army, the *Memphis,* moved from Savannah to Pittsburg Landing and took the severest cases aboard. Deaths occurred so frequently that one of the 11th Indiana's soldiers had to be buried in a coffin made of lumber taken from a steamboat berth, the regular coffin planks being completely used up. In another Indiana regiment eight men died of disease within two weeks. Grant finally became so exasperated that he sent Surgeon J. H. Brinton to St. Louis to plead with Halleck for more hospital boats.

Unhappily for Grant all of his army's ills were not confined to those of a physical nature.

Bickering among the Union generals over seniority was now widespread. Much of the trouble centered around fiery John McClernand, who had quarreled with nearly everyone. Just before the Tennessee expedition sailed, McClernand had complained to Grant about being compelled to serve under C. F. Smith, who had thirty-six years' experience in the regular army. Said McClernand, "I rank him [Smith] as a brigadier and cannot recognize his superiority without self-degradation, which no human power can constrain me to do." Even after Smith was bedridden with a tetanus infection aboard his transport at Pittsburg Landing, McClernand wrote to Smith telling him "while entertaining the highest respect for you both as an officer and as a man . . . as I understand my relation to Major General Grant, I only receive orders from him."

Grant, who held the highest regard for C. F. Smith, was thrust into the controversy. Both Smith and McClernand were major generals, promoted to that rank for their service at Fort Donelson, but it was not then known who had been appointed first. Grant advised Halleck on March 27 that since both had been made major generals "without the date of promotion of either . . . being known," it would be "necessary for me to move my headquarters from this place [Savannah] to Pittsburg," following Buell's arrival.

Beneficially for the army's morale, the task of setting up camps required much of each general's attention. Once the campsites had been cleared, there were other pressing matters, one of which was food.

The concentration of troops at Pittsburg Landing had been so rapid that it had outstripped the capacity of the subsistence department to provide adequate food for the men. "We have had nothing in the shape of [soft] bread since we left Paducah," one private in Sherman's division complained as late as March 23. Until the 55th Illinois received potatoes and flour on the same date, they were compelled to eat only hardtack.

Many of the officers at the same time, however, enjoyed delicacies from home. Colonel Jacob G. Lauman wrote of eating such savory

CAPTAIN RUSSELL B. KIN-SELL. This officer of Company G, 81st Ohio Volunteer Infantry, was photographed at St. Louis less than a month before Shiloh. His dashing, plumed hat and fancy dress sword depict much of the naïveté existing in the Federal army before the realities of war were known. (ALBUMEN PHOTOGRAPH, AUTHOR'S COLLECTION)

treats as canned tomatoes and cherries, homemade cake, and wine, all shipped by friends and relatives at home. Combined with the regular fare of "bacon & beans" the officers of Lauman's mess, at least, ate well.

Although many enlisted men went without such luxuries, they were soon treated to an ample ration of meat. Toward the end of March several local citizens came to Savannah and reported to Grant that a large quantity of Confederate bacon was stored on the Tennessee near Nichols Landing, forty miles downriver. Grant quickly ordered one of McClernand's officers, Major Melancthon Smith of the 45th Illinois, to go and get it. Smith put two companies each of infantry and cavalry aboard a steamboat and sailed for Nichols Landing on March 24.

Since Grant was concerned that Smith might be waylaid by the Confederate cavalry infesting the countryside, he cautioned him that if the enemy appeared in sufficient force to make a stand, Smith was to return without a fight.

Enlisting the aid of a Union sympathizer, Major Smith uncovered "from 100,000 to 120,000 pounds" of pork, loaded it aboard his steamer, and returned to Savannah about the twenty-seventh, all without incident. Grant had the pork distributed among the division commissaries, and for the next few weeks the aroma of frying bacon wafted about the Federal camps, courtesy of the Confederates.

As an added advantage the Federal penetration well below the Mason-Dixon line had insured a plentiful supply of captured cotton. The South's most valuable commodity was in such short supply in the North during 1862 that the price of middling upper cotton had already trebled its prewar price, selling at just under fifty cents a pound.

Several days after landing at Pittsburg Sherman suggested confiscating one hundred bales of cotton discovered in his front. "I think I should take it, [and] ship it, subject to the claim of the rightful owner. If he be in open rebellion, then of course it is forfeited," Sherman wrote. One of his brigade commanders was accordingly told to haul it within the Union lines when transportation could be spared from clearing campsites.

Even Grant became involved in the "exporting" of cotton to the North. During the last week in March he reported to Halleck that he had permitted a boatload of cotton to be shipped to Louisville on behalf of the owners. When he learned that the Confederates were burning all uncollected bales to prevent their loss to Union troops, Grant complained that under existing orders he "could not give all the protection to this species of property that seems needful." Although Halleck failed to give his approval, large quantities of cotton continued to be collected and hauled to the river landings during late March for shipment North.

Halleck intended to leave little to chance in his quest for a successful campaign. Despite the vast amount of war materiel that had arrived at Pittsburg Landing by late March, he had still other plans. On the twenty-second he had telegraphed Grant that he "proposed to fit out one or more heavy siege batteries to be drawn by oxen," which he would forward if Grant could supply the animals. .

When Grant sent word several days later that if enough oxen couldn't be found, "surplus mules" would be used, Halleck authorized shipment of the battery. It was soon transported up the Tennessee, unloaded at Pittsburg Landing, and parked on the bluff overlooking the river. The chance presence of these siege guns on April 6 was to have a profound effect on the fate of the Federal army.

For the 51,288 Union soldiers reported present at Pittsburg and Crump's landings March ended with an ominous upswing in activity. The skies had cleared, bringing a bright sun that warmed the air and dried the muddy roads.

In the vicinity of Crump's Landing Lew Wallace had comfortably settled his men in three primary locations. His Third Brigade, Colonel Charles R. Woods', was at Adamsville, little more than a cluster of log houses about five miles from the Tennessee River on the road to Purdy. Its mission there was to protect Wallace's road-corduroying and bridge-rebuilding crews under Major Charles S. Hayes of the cavalry. To further ensure their safety Lew Wallace had advanced Thayer's brigade two and a half miles to a fork in the Purdy road known as Stoney Lonesome. Being midway between Crump's Landing and Adamsville, Thayer's men served as a reserve for both the infantry and the road-construction detachment. Wallace's own headquarters and his First Brigade, Morgan L. Smith's, however, remained at Crump's Landing, on the Tennessee.

Since the army's main concentration lay four miles distant by river at Pittsburg Landing, Wallace thought it necessary that an overland means of communication and transit be established between the two forces.

Following a reconnaissance of the terrain, Lew Wallace made an important decision. Two roads twisted through backwoods forests, to the vicinity of Pittsburg Landing, both crossing heavily flooded Snake Creek. Though the roads followed widely divergent routes, each was under water near Snake Creek, with the bridges dismantled. The western route, known as the Shunpike, was an old farm road that led about seven miles from Stoney Lonesome across three creeks —Snake, Clear, and Owl—to join with the Purdy road nearly two miles from Sherman's headquarters at Shiloh Church.

The other road, called the River road, followed the general direction of the Tennessee River for about six miles, crossing only Snake Creek before it arrived at one of C. F. Smith's brigade camps, about a mile from Pittsburg Landing.

Wallace observed that both routes were in "deplorable" condition. According to Wallace his cavalry commander, Major Hayes, reported Snake Creek was "a sheet of dead backwater, its shores a bog of unknown depth." Yet Wallace regarded the Shunpike as the shorter route to the army camps near Pittsburg Landing. "It seemed logical that the going or the coming would be to or from the front [Sherman's camps] rather than to Pittsburg Landing, the base," he wrote.

Belatedly Wallace decided to repair the Shunpike connecting with Sherman's camps at Shiloh Church. His primary overland line of communication was thereby established with the outer perimeter of the army, rather than the depot at Pittsburg Landing. The decision was nigh disastrous.

During the last week in March Major Hayes reported the roadwork completed and the Shunpike open to Shiloh Church. Wallace and Hayes then rode over the entire route and returned, satisfied with Hayes's work.

Meanwhile the Confederate force in the vicinity of Purdy had been scouting Wallace's road construction. On March 31 a detachment of Rebel cavalry suddenly swooped out of the woods and charged some of Major Hayes's cavalry pickets along the Adamsville–Purdy road. The Federal officer in command, Lieutenant Charles H. Murray, said his men fired one volley before giving way under a "severe fire" from the enemy's "double barreled shotguns." The pursuit continued for a half-mile before the Confederates gave up the chase. Although the affair was nearly bloodless—none of the thirty-five Confederates and only one of the twenty-nine Federals were wounded—two Federal privates and a sergeant were captured.

Lieutenant Murray blamed the rout on skittish horses and his men's "spurious weapons," reporting that his company had only seven carbines and a few cast-iron pistols that would "neither cock nor revolve." Lew Wallace was displeased. He thought the fault was partly due to Murray's "bad management" and passed the report on to Grant's headquarters with a request that his cavalry be provided with better arms.

Despite the enemy's aggressiveness Grant apparently paid little attention to the skirmish. He was busy at the time with arrangements to send a sizable force of infantry, cavalry, and artillery upriver to destroy Rebel batteries near Chickasaw, Alabama. Grant considered it important to clear the Tennessee of enemy strongholds, and he had been awaiting the arrival of the armored gunboat *Cairo* for that purpose. Earlier, on March 25, the heavy Confederate batteries at Eastport had damaged at least one of the Navy's wooden gunboats operating on the Tennessee, compelling its withdrawal.

Since the *Cairo* was armored, it was thought capable of reducing the enemy batteries without undue danger. Following her arrival on the evening of the thirty-first Grant selected "Cump" Sherman, his trusted West Point professional, to lead the expedition.

Sherman took aboard only two battalions of infantry, one hundred and fifty cavalrymen, and a section of 12-pounder howitzers. Wasting little time, his two transports sailed at 6 A.M. on April 1 in the company of the gunboats *Lexington, Tyler,* and *Cairo.* Sherman was instructed to be exceedingly cautious. He was "not to engage any force that would likely make a stand against him. . . ," but to destroy all batteries, if possible.

At the mouth of Indian Creek, twenty-six miles beyond Pittsburg Landing, the *Cairo* shelled the enemy's earthworks but obtained no reply. Proceeding "steadily and cautiously" up the river, the gunboats threw shells at several old battery sites, but again there was no response.

At Eastport, five miles past Indian Creek, Sherman landed a portion of his troops after the gunboats had shelled the town. One of Sherman's infantrymen observed that "cannon balls from the gunboats had gone through several houses in a row. Not a human being was visible, man, woman, or child, the whole population having suddenly abandoned their homes and fled behind a hill for protection. . . . Meals were on the tables untouched. . . ."

Sherman then cruised three miles farther upriver, to the bluffs at Chickasaw. The old Indian mound there that had been converted by the Confederates into a parapet was partially washed away, and Sherman reported, in disgust, that Chickasaw as a military position was of "little importance."

Since the shoals beyond Chickasaw barred further passage south, Sherman soon ordered his flotilla back to Eastport. After making a personal inspection, Sherman noted that the landing there "is the best I have seen on the Tennessee River. The levee is clear of trees or snags, and a hundred boats could land there without confusion." Before ordering his expedition's return to Pittsburg Landing, Sherman learned that the road to the interior traversed "the hard gravel hills of the country" and had a firm base.

Following his arrival at Pittsburg late the same night Sherman reported the river "clear to and beyond Chickasaw." Yet the focal point of his report was to mention that Eastport would make an excellent base for operations against the Memphis & Charleston Railroad. Sherman emphasized that the railroad lay only eight miles from Eastport by a good road.

On the basis of Sherman's endorsement Grant immediately sent Colonel Joseph D. Webster, his chief of staff and a former Regular Army topographical engineer, back to Eastport to investigate with the gunboat *Tyler*. Webster soon returned to report that the enemy seemed to have permanently abandoned their battery positions and that the distance to the railroad was the shortest at that point. He noted, however, that the interior road passed through an abrupt range of hills that would afford the enemy "positions which could be readily defended by a small force." Moreover he reasoned that the Confederates, operating on interior lines, would utilize the railroad to concentrate troops at any threatened point faster than the Federal troops could be brought up. He further mentioned that the river was receding, and its shallow depth might not allow the heavy gunboats to pass upriver to cover a landing.

After reading Webster's report on April 3, Grant was discouraged from moving his base of operations. Thereafter he seems to have concerned himself only with improving the general condition and drill of his army at Pittsburg Landing. Furthermore he had been restricted by Halleck's orders to await the arrival of Buell's Army of the Ohio, en route from Nashville.

Buell's advance division under Alexander McCook had broken camp at Nashville on March 16. Advancing at the rate of fifteen miles a day through the fertile cotton belt in Central Tennessee, McCook's men seemed to enjoy their journey. Sprawling plantations and vast cottonfields lay along their path. Many of the soldiers were particularly amused by the numerous gangs of slaves who gawked in amazement as the long blue column passed.

On the eighteenth McCook's division marched to the vicinity of Columbia, Tennessee, where the Duck River flows through from the Cumberland Mountains, far to the east. Although Buell's cavalry were already there, they had been too late to prevent the burning of several important bridges without which any further advance was impossible. Both at Rutherford Creek, four miles from Columbia, and at the Duck River, just north of Columbia, the retreating Confederate cavalry had destroyed all bridges. The Duck River was at flood stage, and McCook had no choice but to halt, prepare campsites, and begin the construction of new bridges.

Buell, who had remained at Nashville, sent word to Halleck on the nineteenth that he had "three divisions at Columbia, or near there, working with all industry on bridges," and that he might be "delayed for four or five days. . . ."

While an inexperienced battalion of mechanics and engineers and a detail from an Indiana regiment labored to construct another bridge across the Duck River, Buell busied himself at Nashville. Besides making arrangements for the protection of the city and sending orders for the construction of a pontoon bridge to be utilized on the Tennessee, Buell worked on the final details of his forthcoming campaign.

He had in all six divisions in his department, roughly seventy-one thousand effectives. Allowing for detachments to guard several scattered locations in Tennessee, and the absence of other troops then operating against Cumberland Gap, Buell's remaining force consisted of about fifty thousand men present for duty. Because of his concern over a possible enemy counteroffensive from the vicinity of Huntsville, Alabama, Buell detached one of his divisions under Brigadier General Ormsby Mitchell and ordered it to Fayetteville, Tennessee. Mitchell was to deploy his nine thousand men there and either watch for an enemy advance from northern Alabama or cooperate with Halleck's offensive on the Tennessee, whichever the circumstances warranted. Meanwhile Buell and his remaining five divisions would advance along the Central Alabama Railroad to Columbia. There he would leave another division in reserve, to move wherever it was needed, before striking for the Tennessee with four divisions, numbering about thirty-five thousand men.

Unlike Grant at Savannah, who was just beginning to construct a line toward Columbia, Buell had direct telegraphic communication with Halleck at St. Louis. To Buell's annoyance, however, Halleck was utilizing the wire to prod him into greater action. Halleck anticipated a swift junction of the two armies; the Confederacy's vital railroads might be cut, enabling the isolation of the enemy garrison at Island No. 10, on the Mississippi.

Buell responded to the pressure by leaving Nashville on the twenty-fifth and traveling to Columbia, where his bridgebuilding operations were continuing with little success. Although a week had elapsed since McCook's arrival there, the river was still unfordable because of the heavy rains. Buell had expected the bridge to be nearly completed when he left Nashville, but following his arrival on the twenty-sixth he advised Halleck that the progress had been "much slower than expected" and the difficulties "greater than I supposed." The new Duck River bridge, he continued, would not be ready for use until Monday, March 31.

Although Buell had originally believed that Grant's army was concentrated at Savannah on the Tennessee's east bank, he learned no later than March 23 that Grant was "massing" his troops at Pittsburg Landing, on the west shore. Following Buell's arrival opposite Columbia on the twenty-sixth, his division commanders also learned that Grant's troops were at Pittsburg.

One of Buell's brigadiers, William Nelson, commanding the Fourth Division, allegedly became alarmed. Nelson, three hundred pounds and six feet four inches, was a towering bull of a man. Many felt that he had a temper to match. Although a congenial associate to his friends, when irritated Nelson could display the wrath of a madman. One war correspondent remarked that Nelson had placed so many incompetent officers under arrest that his headquarters resembled a secondhand sword store. Feared by troops of other commands but admired by his own men, Nelson had a presence that evoked respect.

As a soldier Nelson claimed an unusual background. A member of an old Kentucky family with intimate ties to many of that state's most prominent men, including Abraham Lincoln, he had been a lieutenant in the Navy before the War. Following Lincoln's inauguration Nelson was sent to Kentucky to survey the political sentiment. He later returned there to organize and arm the loyal Home Guard, and when hostilities finally broke out in Kentucky, Nelson was commissioned a brigadier general in the Army and placed in command of a division.

On March 27, when Nelson observed that construction on the bridge was lagging, he concluded that the Duck River was fordable. Riding over to Buell's headquarters, Nelson asked for permission to make the attempt with his division.

Buell was again being pressured by Halleck for a rapid linkup with Grant on the Tennessee. "We must be ready to attack the enemy as soon as the roads are passable," Halleck had written.

Buell, somewhat impatient with the slow progress on the bridge-building, agreed to let Nelson try.

It was important to Nelson that his division had the opportunity to take the lead. Later that night he told Colonel Jacob Ammen, one of his brigade commanders, ". . . the river is falling; and damn you, get over for we must have the advance and get the glory." Ammen was further told to make his preparations in secrecy, lest some other division take the advance.

On the following day, March 28, Colonel Ammen examined the ford and marked a crossing that ran to the depth of an army wagon bed. By evening Nelson had written a circular giving instructions for the crossing. Included were some unique directions: "On reaching the ford, the men will strip off their pantaloons, secure their cartridge boxes about their necks, and load knapsacks on the wagons; bayonets will be fixed, and the pantaloons, in a neat roll, will be carried on the point of the bayonet. A halt will be ordered on the other side of the ford, to allow the men to take off their drawers, wring them dry, and resume their clothing and knapsacks."

Promptly at six in the morning of a cold and raw March 29 the nearly naked Fourth Division snaked across the ford to the opposite shore. By stationing mounted cavalrymen in the river to break the strong current and mark the path, Ammen was able to get the infantry across without difficulty. After some trouble in hauling a number of Army wagons by hand up the slippery bank, most of Nelson's division was safely across before sunset. The following day Crittenden's division passed across, but it was not until April 2 that the final division, Thomas's, crossed.

It had taken Buell's army exactly two weeks to cross a river slightly more than two hundred yards wide.

After passing through Columbia, during which a Union sergeant observed, "The people looked upon us with sour faces, while our bands tickled their ears with [the] 'Star Spangled Banner,' 'Hail Columbia,' "Red, White, and Blue,' and 'John Brown's Body,' " Buell's army resumed its march along the narrow and rutted roadway to Savannah, about eighty miles away.

Intervals of six miles between divisions were specified in order to prevent clogging of the roadway. The long blue column of thirty-five thousand men soon stretched for nearly forty miles through the rough and sparsely settled countryside. Averaging thirteen miles a day, Nelson's division pushed on toward the Tenneseee despite recent word from Grant that Buell's troops were not wanted at Savannah until Monday, April 7. Buell and his headquarters remained at Columbia.

The days alternated dry and hot, and tropical with rain, and the march was difficult and tiresome. One Ohioan in Nelson's division remembered that "The road was heavy; an old worn stagecoach road, of a slippery, treacherous clay, which trampings of our advanced regiments speedily kneaded into a tough, stiff dough. . . ." The terrain was also hilly and cut by "rushing turbid, swollen streams, gorging and overflowing their banks," as another Federal noted.

By the third of April, Nelson's division was at Hardin Creek, five miles from Waynesboro. At Waynesboro the road forked to reach the Tennessee River at several different points.

Although Buell had understood as early as March 16 that Savannah was the point of rendezvous for both Federal armies, he now began to debate the matter. He had previously instructed his divisions to march to Savannah, but he suddenly wrote to Halleck on March 28 that he had studied every contingency and had "kept the object of concentration, wherever necessary, constantly in view." He then suggested that "Fayetteville is in as good a line for Decatur as Columbia is, and at the same time guards the route to Nashville from the East." Several days later Buell recommended to Halleck as an alternative that Waynesboro, some thirty-five miles from Savannah, be utilized for the concentration of his army. This, he said, would permit a more central line of operations and enable him to hasten to any threatened point in the vicinity of Ormsby Mitchell's detached division.

Amazingly Halleck approved the new plan, telegraphing on April 5 to Buell, "You are right about concentrating at Waynesboro. Future movements must depend upon those of the enemy." Simultaneously Halleck notified Grant of the change, telling him that Buell would be at Waynesboro and would "exercise his separate command" unless the enemy should attack, in which case Grant would assume the overall command.

The receipt of this news must have been puzzling to Grant. By April 5 Nelson's division was already at Savannah, and it was too late for Buell's army to concentrate at Waynesboro.

The delay in relaying communications and a mistaken interpretation by Grant had caused Nelson's men to hurry on to Savannah. A telegraph line was being constructed from Savannah to Waynesboro by Grant's men, and from Nashville to Waynesboro by Buell's engineers. Neither was completed, however, which necessitated both armies using couriers to transmit information.

Two cavalrymen from Buell's army had arrived at Grant's headquarters on March 31, bringing a dispatch from Halleck dated March 24. Halleck reported that the enemy had concentrated at Corinth and talked vaguely of severing the Confederate railroad at Jackson and Humboldt, Tennessee, without a serious engagement.

Grant inferred that an offensive movement was imminent as soon as the roads were dry, and he sent a return note the same evening to the commander of Buell's advance (Nelson). His dispatch read in part, "I have been looking for your column anxiously for several days, so as to report it to headquarters . . . thinking some move may depend on your arrival."

Nelson knew nothing of Buell's intended concentration at Waynesboro and hurried on in the pouring rain toward Savannah, arriving on the morning of the fifth. Buell had not left Columbia until April 3. Consequently he did not catch up with Nelson's advance division until his arrival at Savannah on the evening of the fifth.

Grant, after having urged Nelson to hurry on, however, learned from Halleck that many of the new troops assigned to his army would be delayed at St. Louis due to a shortage of transportation. Lacking the needed boats, Grant advised Nelson, in Buell's advance, on April 4 that he need not hasten his march, for he could not be put across the river before Tuesday, April 8.

Yet by that time Nelson was within a day's march of Savannah and he continued on, his troops arriving about midday on the fifth.

CHAPTER V

Storm Signals in the West

The loss of Forts Henry and Donelson had been a devastating blow to Confederate General Albert Sidney Johnston. In the short span of two weeks his entire middle-Kentucky line of defense had become militarily untenable.

From Columbus to Bowling Green, Kentucky, and beyond to the Cumberland Mountains, Johnston and his generals were compelled to order the Confederacy's armies withdrawn. Thereby two states, Kentucky and Tennessee, were virtually abandoned to the enemy, sending refugees streaming from the cities and clogging the roads. In their wake civil chaos erupted. News of the calamity not only cast a pall of gloom throughout the South, but in Richmond shocked legislators leveled strong accusations at President Jefferson Davis, the military, and Sidney Johnston in particular.

Shortly thereafter, when reports began to circulate of invading Federal armies marching deep into the Southern interior, the crisis was intensified. Action seemed to be demanded by an irate public, and since the onus fell on Johnston, his operations now came under close official scrutiny.

Despite his professed love for the Southwest, Johnston was a native Kentuckian, the fifth of six children born to a former New England doctor and his second wife. Notwithstanding the rustic frontier life in Mason County, Kentucky, Sidney Johnston had been a healthy, bright youngster knowledgeable in many of the more technical skills, including mathematics.

At the age of fifteen he went to study medicine at Transylvania University. Yet four years later, following a period of interrupted study, the impressionable Johnston decided instead to become a soldier. A half-brother, Josiah Stoddard Johnston, then a U. S. Congressman from Louisiana, arranged his appointment to the U. S. Military Academy in 1822.

Unhappily, much of Sidney Johnston's adult life had been marred

49

by a series of cruel tragedies. After serving with the 6th Infantry during the Black Hawk War, Johnston resigned when his wife Henrietta developed tuberculosis. Little more than a year later Henrietta was dead, and Johnston, with a young son and a tiny daughter to provide for, withdrew in despair to a farm near St. Louis.

Attracted by the Texas Revolution of 1836, the distraught Johnston left for Texas in midsummer, seeking fame and fortune. Although his success was rapid, an appointment as senior brigadier general in the Texas Army resulted in a quarrel with a jealous subordinate, Felix Huston, who aspired to command the army.

In a duel fought on February 5, 1837, Johnston fell on the fifth or sixth exchange of shots, a pistol ball in his right hip. A slow and painful recovery delayed Johnston's resuming Army command for several months, but his subsequent honors included the post of Secretary of War in the Texas Government.

The Mexican War that began nearly a half-dozen years later found Johnston a civilian struggling to succeed in an ill-advised cotton-plantation venture. Promising his second wife that he would not remain in the Army longer than six months, Johnston belatedly arrived in the war zone at the head of a Texas regiment of volunteers. Their enlistment soon expired, however, and Johnston became a colonel without a regiment. Although he was appointed inspector general and fought with gallantry at Monterrey, Johnston was denied a command in the army. Disappointed, he returned to Texas following the expiration of his term.

The years following the war seemed even more frustrating when Johnston's efforts to succeed as a planter ended in bankruptcy. Of necessity, he accepted an appointment in 1850 as paymaster in the U. S. Army with the rank of major. Five years of frequent trips to frontier posts in Texas followed, replete with privations of extreme weather and the dangers of the trail.

Finally in March, 1855, good fortune smiled on Sidney Johnston. His close friend and admirer since their days at Transylvania, Jefferson Davis, was Secretary of War in the Franklin Pierce administration. At the time two new mounted regiments were being organized for the Army, and Johnston was appointed colonel of the 2d Cavalry.

Two years later, having served with his regiment in Texas, Johnston turned the command over to his lieutenant colonel, Robert E. Lee, and reported to Washington for an important new assignment—leadership of the Utah expedition to suppress the Mormon Rebellion. Johnston and his army suffered through severe mountain blizzards that winter, but entered Salt Lake City in the summer of 1858 and reestablished Government authority without bloodshed.

Several years later the highly regarded Brevet Brigadier General Johnston was ordered to California to command the Department of the Pacific. Esteemed by many, he was considered by at least one prominent Federal officer to be one of the few men capable of saving the country during the secession crisis that followed. Three months following his arrival in San Francisco, however, he learned that his adopted state of Texas had seceded from the Union. Johnston resigned the same day, April 9, 1861.

After pondering the consequences, Johnston determined to join the Confederate cause. Although his second wife was momentarily expecting another child, Johnston began the long overland march from California with a company of Southerners in mid-June, 1861.

Avoiding Union garrisons and patrols ordered to arrest them, Johnston's party crossed eight hundred miles of scorching desert to reach El Paso, Texas, in August. His subsequent arrival in Richmond was greeted with unrestrained joy by Jefferson Davis, who assigned Johnston to command Confederate Department No. 2. Davis also had his friend appointed a full general with rank second only to Adjutant General Samuel Cooper, an administrative official.

Now the highest ranking field commander in the Confederacy, Johnston was regarded by many of the North's generals as their most formidable opponent. His department embraced a huge region of the South, stretching from the Appalachian Mountains on the east to Indian Territory on the west. Included were the states of Tennessee, Arkansas, Kentucky, Missouri, and portions of Alabama, Mississippi, and Louisiana.

Johnston went immediately to Nashville to assume his command. There a number of difficult issues awaited him, including the matter of occupying Kentucky.

In April Kentucky's legislature had declared the state to be neutral, but on September 3, 1861, only a few days before Johnston arrived in Nashville, Confederate Major General Leonidas Polk marched across the state line from Tennessee and seized Columbus, in southwestern Kentucky. Polk's advance was predicated on information that the Federal troops at Cairo, Illinois, were on the verge of occupying Columbus, a strategic river site on the Mississippi. This move ended the sham neutrality of Kentucky and precipitated an invasion of that state by both belligerents.

In the ensuing race to overrun the state much of eastern Kentucky was occupied by the Confederates, while Louisville, Covington, and Paducah were seized by Union troops.

Johnston's arrival at Nashville on September 14, 1861, was greeted with much enthusiasm. Terming the conflict a common war involving all of the people, Johnston moved rapidly to consolidate Confederate gains in Kentucky. Under his orders a spearhead of four thousand Kentucky and Tennessee troops advanced by railroad to occupy Bowling Green on September 18. Johnston thus established the Columbus–Bowling Green–Cumberland Ford line as his northern frontier. Here he would spend three months fortifying his positions.

West of Bowling Green, Fort Henry on the Tennessee River and Fort Donelson on the Cumberland River were key defensive bastions. Both had been surveyed shortly after the secession of Tennessee by Brigadier General Daniel S. Donelson of the militia. Donelson, a lean, sixty-year-old former West Pointer, class of 1825, was sent in mid-1861 by Governor Isham G. Harris of Tennessee to locate sites for the defense of both rivers as near the Kentucky state line as feasible.

Although Donelson reported a favorable site on the Cumberland within the boundaries of Tennessee, he found nothing of use along the Tennessee River close to the Kentucky line. He recommended instead that ground across the border, in Kentucky, be utilized.

Governor Harris refused to do this on the basis of Kentucky's declared neutrality. A site destined to become Fort Henry, on the Tennessee River, twelve miles opposite Fort Donelson, was finally selected as the best location in Tennessee, largely in recognition of the convenience of mutual support.

Fort Henry, a closed fieldwork mounting seventeen guns, was soon erected on low ground near the river's edge, while another fort was planned for the opposite, or west, bank.

Before either work was completed, however, the Confederates were surprised by the appearance of a Federal gunboat flotilla intent on bombarding the two forts. Advancing from Paducah, Kentucky, along one of several great river highways penetrating the South, the expedition under Ulysses Grant arrived below Fort Henry on February 4, 1862. While C. F. Smith's troops debarked on the west bank under orders to take the earthwork opposite Fort Henry, known as Fort Heiman, Grant with the main column of twelve thousand men landed on the east shore and advanced directly on Fort Henry.

Although Johnston had anticipated a Federal advance in this sector, detaching eight thousand troops under Floyd and Buckner from his Bowling Green army and sending them west as reinforcements, his luck was bad. Already precommitted by Government policy to defend a political rather than a strategic line, with positions based on geography more than topography, Johnston relied heavily on his generals' ability to conduct a static defense. Because of the critical shortage of men and materiel much of his effort had been expended on logistics and other basic details, such as obtaining heavy ordnance and arranging for the construction of fortifications.

His choice for the Fort Henry command had been Brigadier General Lloyd Tilghman, a civil engineer by profession and an 1836 graduate of West Point. Tilghman's reports were mostly optimistic, suggesting a high state of efficiency at the fort within several months of his assuming command.

When it was learned from a private source that Tilghman had delayed approval of the engineer's construction plans for six weeks, however, Johnston sent his chief engineer, Major J. F. Gilmer, to investigate. On February 3 Tilghman rode with Gilmer across the narrow twelve-mile neck of land to inspect the fortifications at Fort Donelson.

Early the following morning Tilghman was startled by the sound of heavy firing in the direction of Fort Henry. When he learned from Colonel Adolphus Heiman, his deputy commander, that the enemy was landing below the fort, Tilghman hastened to rejoin the embattled garrison.

During the night of the fourth an anxious Tilghman recalled the garrison of Fort Heiman, trusting that the "extremely bad roads" would prevent the Federals from moving heavy guns to that site. His suspicions that the enemy was being reinforced were intensified during a reconnaissance on February 5.

At midnight on the morning of the sixth Tilghman telegraphed for reinforcements, indicating that he had a "glorious chance" to overwhelm the enemy.

Fourteen hours later Tilghman surrendered Fort Henry after sending all but a handful of its three thousand-man garrison to Fort Donelson. The gunboats had advanced at 11:45 A.M. on the sixth, beginning a bombardment that lasted two hours and ten minutes. Tilghman's artillerists had fired their guns for only five minutes when a 24-pounder rifle burst, disabling every man at the piece. Then an enemy shell exploded at the muzzle of a 32-pounder gun, killing or wounding all of its crew. Later a priming wire jammed and broke in the vent of a 10-inch Columbiad, rendering the gun useless. By 1:30 P.M. only two of Tilghman's seventeen heavy cannon were still firing. Moreover his gunners were tired and discouraged from seeing their shots often bound harmlessly off the gunboats' armor. Tilghman tried to encourage his men by personally serving at a 32-pounder gun for fifteen minutes. Yet when the Federal cannon began to breach the fort, he was forced to surrender.

Johnston was stunned by news of the fort's fall. The Tennessee River lay open to the enemy clear into Alabama, and a flotilla of three Union gunboats soon cruised upriver destroying Confederate supplies and riverboats along the shore.

Worse still, across the narrow neck of land from Fort Henry Fort Donelson lay vulnerable to a Federal assault by land or water.

Johnston moved swiftly to prevent its loss. Brigadier General

Gideon J. Pillow's two thousand troops at Clarksville, Tennessee, already had been ordered to Donelson following news of the attack at Fort Henry. Now Generals Clark and Floyd, with a combined force of ten thousand men, were dispatched to Clarksville, within easy supporting distance.

Johnston, considering the recent success of the enemy's ironclad gunboats, soon began to have misgivings about his ability to hold Donelson. Anticipating that fort's fall, he ordered the evacuation of Bowling Green and a retreat to and beyond Nashville, hoping to prevent interception by Federal gunboats as his army crossed the Cumberland River.

Since Fort Donelson was the only fortification on the Cumberland between Nashville and the enemy, the fate of the city was linked to that of the fort. The capital of Tennessee and a major depot of supplies, Nashville was highly important to the Confederacy. Johnston's initial instructions to Pillow were explicit—to do all that was possible to protect the city and the rear of the main army by holding Donelson.

After escaping from Fort Henry, Major Gilmer of the engineers had remained at Donelson to help with preparations for its defense. Writing to Johnston on February 10, Gilmer expressed his belief that a successful resistance could be made at Donelson. This opinion was also shared by Pillow, who asked only for more heavy artillery and the continuation of existing troop dispositions.

Yet two important Confederate generals involved in the defense of Donelson opposed a stand there. Both Simon B. Buckner and John Floyd wished to withdraw all but Pillow's troops from the fort, believing the Union ironclads "nearly invulnerable."

Later, as the issue continued to be disputed among the three generals, Johnston was asked for instructions. Believing the decision must be made on the basis of changing circumstances, Johnston placed full trust in the judgment of his senior ranking commander at the scene, General Floyd. Johnston's telegram of February 12 to Floyd read: "I do not know the wants of General Pillow, nor yours, nor the position of General Buckner. You do. You have the dispatch. Decide. . . ."

Unfortunately for the South John Floyd was a poor choice for high military command. He had once been Johnston's peer as Secretary of War during the Buchanan Administration and was also a former governor of Virginia. Prior to his Tennessee assignment Floyd had commanded a brigade under Robert E. Lee in West Virginia. A lawyer by education but a politician by vocation, Floyd did not have the high military qualifications of his subordinate generals.

His second-in-command, Gideon J. Pillow, had fought as a general in the Mexican War, and at the outbreak of the Rebellion he commanded the Tennessee State Militia. Yet his quarrelsome and jealous disposition had earned him many enemies, and his appointment in the Confederate service had been delayed until July, 1861.

Pillow's relationship with the third-ranking Confederate general at Fort Donelson, Brigadier General Simon B. Buckner, was not at all friendly. Buckner had graduated in 1844 from the U. S. Military Academy, fought with distinction in the Mexican War, and at one time had refused general-officer commissions in both the Union and Confederate armies. Only when his native Kentucky was invaded by both antagonists was Sidney Johnston able to persuade Buckner to accept an appointment in the Southern Army. During the initial occupation of Bowling Green Johnston had entrusted Buckner with command of the army's advance.

Acting under the orders of Floyd, Buckner came to Fort Donelson on the night of February 11 to remove his division from the garrison and withdraw it to Cumberland City, Tennessee. Pillow refused to allow Buckner's men to depart, however, and telegraphed to Johnston at Bowling Green for authority to keep them. When Johnston's reply was delayed, Pillow left by steamboat for Cumberland City to plead his case in person with Floyd. At this point Johnston sent the fateful telegram to Floyd, asking him to make the crucial decision.

Yet Floyd was still uncertain of what to do. Prone to vacillation, he could not make up his mind. Finally, on Pillow's urging, he agreed to concentrate all of his command at Donelson. When Johnston learned later that night that a battle was imminent at the fort and sent word to send reinforcements, Floyd shrewdly replied that he had anticipated the order and was then transporting his troops to Donelson.

Meanwhile Grant had suddenly marched his army against Fort Donelson. Advancing with his main column from Fort Henry on the morning of February 12, by nightfall Grant had invested the Confederates in their trenches. Opposition had been minimal. Only Forrest's cavalry regiment offered token resistance, and Grant elatedly reported "all is well," saying that he had driven the enemy within their works.

It is ironic that Buckner, who had briefly come to Donelson to remove his men, was in charge at the time. Pillow had gone upriver to talk Floyd into defending Donelson, leaving instructions for Buckner not to bring on an engagement should the enemy approach in force—a prospect that he regarded as very unlikely. On the afternoon of the twelfth Pillow returned to Donelson in time to witness a sharp artillery duel with Federal troops deploying opposite his fortifications.

During the thirteenth Grant's infantry launched sporadic assaults against the Confederate left, all of which were repulsed with heavy loss. That night the Union gunboat flotilla arrived with heavy troop reinforcements. On the fourteenth the weather turned freezing cold, bringing a driving rain that turned to snow and sleet.

Flag Officer A. H. Foote, confidently expecting results similar to those of the Fort Henry fight, ordered a direct attack by his gunboats at 3 P.M. that afternoon. With his gunboats cleared for action, Foote boldly sailed into close range and began a heavy bombardment.

For his overconfidence Foote was badly surprised and nearly killed. The Confederate batteries, firing from a thirty-foot bluff, soon disabled all of the ironclads and wounded Foote in the leg. Following an hour-and-ten-minute fight the battered fleet was forced to withdraw and limp all the way back to Cairo for repairs.

Yet the growing pressure was beginning to wear on the nerves of the Confederate generals. Earlier that day they had agreed to open a line of retreat toward Nashville, fearing that the heavy enemy reinforcements brought by the gunboats during the previous night would ensure a Federal victory and capture of the fort. However, after ordering out his troops at noon, Pillow countermanded the order, saying only that it was too late in the day for the attempt.

That night Floyd, Pillow, and Buckner again met in conference. Once more it was decided to attack the Union right at dawn, hoping to clear an exit for withdrawal of the garrison. At 6 A.M. the following morning, February 15, the attack began. By ten o'clock Pillow's troops had forced McClernand's division back against its left flank, following a stubborn resistance. By now Lew Wallace's troops in the Federal center also had become engaged with Buckner's Confederates. At noon the Union Army was driven back beyond the Wynn's Ferry road, leaving the way open for a retreat to Nashville. Buckner then halted according to plan to allow the garrison to pass through, taking position to cover their retreat.

Pillow, however, thought that the enemy was making preparations to attack the Confederate entrenchments on the far right, where only a small force had been left to protect the works. Accordingly he ordered all of his own troops to return to their entrenchments and directed that Buckner also hasten the two miles back to his section of the works.

Buckner balked at the order, even going to Floyd to urge that the evacuation be completed as planned. Floyd agreed to this at first, telling Buckner to remain in position until Pillow could be located. Yet when Floyd confronted him, Pillow convinced his irresolute superior that the enemy was being reinforced and that an attack was imminent against the Confederate right. Of decisive importance at the time, Floyd remembered, was that Pillow's troops had nearly completed the reoccupation of their rifle pits on the Confederate left.

Buckner was hastily told to return as quickly as possible to his entrenchments on the extreme right, which were being threatened.

Late that morning U. S. Grant had returned from a conference with Flag Officer Foote to find that the enemy had attacked and overwhelmed McClernand's division. Yet by the time Grant arrived on the battlefield, Pillow had already begun withdrawing his men. Grant soon learned that the Confederate prisoners had knapsacks and haversacks filled with rations. He concluded that the Confederates in attempting to cut their way out had become demoralized and had fallen back.

From the sketchy reports he believed the Confederates so confused and dejected that an attack on the left would succeed before they could reoccupy their extensive works. C. F. Smith was ordered to charge the enemy breastworks in his front without delay, these being the rifle pits that had earlier been occupied by Buckner. Smith hastened to attack with six regiments, leading the assault in person.

As Smith's men rushed forward at the double-quick, Buckner was still in the process of returning to his trenches, being delayed by the long march across the entire Confederate front. Only a small portion of his men had reached their positions when C. F. Smith's column broke over the breastworks.

With only a single regiment, the 30th Tennessee, defending trenches three-quarters of a mile in length, Smith's troops easily pushed through the abatis and drove the outnumbered defenders before them. One of Buckner's Kentucky regiments, hurrying toward its old lines, also was thrown back in confusion. Although Buckner was later able to check the enemy advance atop an adjacent hill, he could not regain his lost entrenchments.

That night the senior Confederate generals met once again and decided to retreat at dawn if the enemy had not strongly reoccupied their former positions on the Confederate left. Nathan Bedford Forrest of the cavalry was told to send out several scouts to see if the Federals had returned. Although the scouts reported campfires burning in the vicinity, they allegedly encountered no enemy. Despite this report it was concluded by Floyd, Pillow, and Buckner that the enemy had indeed returned in force.

Following a long discussion that continued into the early-morning hours, it was decided to surrender the army. Buckner claimed he could not hold his lines for half an hour after daybreak, when it was felt the Federals would attack with overwhelming numbers of fresh troops. He further reasoned that to cut through the Union lines would involve a loss of about three-fourths of the army, and no commander, he thought, had a right to sacrifice so many men to save a few.

Floyd agreed with Buckner, consenting to the capitulation provided that he be allowed to escape. Floyd was currently under indictment by a grand jury at Washington for embezzlement of public funds and misconduct as Secretary of War under Buchanan.

Saying that there were no two persons in the Confederacy whom the Yankees would prefer to capture more than himself and Floyd, Pillow also announced that he would not surrender. Pillow then declared that the army should fight its way out or attempt to hold on for another day until the river transports, sent upriver with Federal prisoners, returned.

When Buckner insisted that this was impossible, Floyd agreed to turn over the command to Pillow, who in turn would pass it on to Buckner, who would then negotiate for a surrender at daylight.

When this news leaked out, there were many angry complaints. Bedford Forrest was astounded at the turn of events and allegedly told the generals he neither could nor would surrender his command. Pillow gave him permission to cut his way out, which he did, not by fighting but by leading his command of five hundred cavalry and about two hundred others mounted on artillery horses out by a partially flooded river road. Pillow, taking his staff and Major Gilmer of the engineers with him, crossed the river in a small skiff and escaped by the opposite shore.

Shortly before daylight two small steamers arrived at the landing, and Floyd appropriated both of them to carry off the four Virginia regiments of his old brigade. While the 20th Mississippi of Floyd's brigade guarded their embarkation, the Virginians filed on board. About sunrise Buckner sent word that further delay at the wharf would cause loss of the boats, and Floyd ordered their departure. Left behind was the embittered 20th Mississippi, which had been promised to go aboard with the Virginians.

Buckner surrendered unconditionally shortly before daylight, turning over about nine thousand prisoners, thirteen heavy cannon, and fifteen thousand small arms to the Federal army. Although some of these Confederates later escaped, including Brigadier General Bushrod Johnson, who merely walked away from his unguarded camp, it was apparent to all that a stunning disaster had befallen the Confederacy.

Albert Sidney Johnston went to bed about midnight on the fifteenth believing that a complete Confederate victory had been won at Donelson, belief based on Floyd's telegram of 11 P.M. that the enemy was driven from the field.

Before daybreak Johnston was awakened by a messenger with dispatches from Donelson. While half-asleep he listened to news of the surrender. Saying only that he must save his army, Johnston ordered all of his troops to cross the Cumberland River to the south shore. This would prevent their interception by Federal gunboats speeding up the river.

The Nashville morning papers were filled with the news of a glorious victory, but the truth was soon known and the city became panic-stricken. A large mob gathered in front of Johnston's headquarters in Nashville on Monday, February 17, to demand an explanation. Floyd, who had recently arrived with his Virginia troops aboard the small steamer, was compelled to make a speech, as was General Hardee and Major Munford, Johnston's aide-de-camp.

With the evacuation of the city and its occupation by the enemy imminent, Nashville fell under an ugly mood. The press bitterly denounced the Southern generals, damning the Government for entrusting the public safety to hands so feeble. Senators and Representatives from Tennessee in the Confederate Congress hurried to see Jefferson Davis, demanding the removal of Johnston. The House of Representatives quickly appointed a select committee to inquire into the conduct of the war in the West. Dissatisfaction was widespread, and the press began to seek a scapegoat. Davis was hard-pressed to defend his close friend Sidney Johnston, and finally had to ask for a personal explanation. Johnston delayed sending this while awaiting sufficient information from his subordinate generals.

Johnston at first believed that Floyd and Pillow had made a gallant defense in the face of overwhelming numbers. Floyd was placed in charge of Nashville prior to and during its evacuation. Although Johnston's telegram to Secretary of War J. P. Benjamin on the seventeenth announced the surrender of Fort Donelson "after a most gallant defense," the facts soon became known.

Benjamin's letter to Johnston three weeks later advised that both Floyd's and Pillow's reports were unsatisfactory, and they were to be relieved from command until further orders. It was another blow to Sidney Johnston's sagging prestige.

Johnston had already come under earlier criticism for another disaster in his department that occurred January 19, 1862, at Logan Cross Roads, Kentucky. In this fight the Confederates had lost most of an army committed to the defense of Cumberland Gap, on Johnston's right flank.

Brigadier General Felix K. Zollicoffer, an influential former U. S. Congressman from Tennessee, had been the field commander, operating under instructions to block the approaches to east Tennessee from central Kentucky with his nearly six thousand troops. After advancing to the Cumberland River in early December, Zollicoffer suddenly crossed to the north bank, occupying Beech Grove, Kentucky.

Although Johnston warned that the river should not be crossed, his dispatch arrived the day after the movement was made. Zollicoffer, who was afraid to recross in the face of the enemy, fortified his campsite near the river with the limited means available. Shortly thereafter the district commander, Major General George B. Crittenden, arrived at Zollicoffer's camp and assumed command.

Crittenden was of an old-line Kentucky family, now widely split apart by the war. His father, the elder statesman John J. Crittenden, had remained loyal to the Union and had worked relentlessly to to keep Kentucky from seceding. George's younger brother, Thomas L., was a Union brigadier general then commanding a division of Buell's army. George, however, had been one of the senior Regular officers to resign from the U. S. Army and join the Confederacy in 1861.

Although Crittenden ordered the construction of sufficient boats to withdraw the command to the south side of the Cumberland, Union Brigadier General George H. Thomas advanced to attack in cooperation with another Federal force under Brigadier General A. F. Schoepf. Crittenden then decided to fight. Thomas's advance had reached Logan Cross Roads, ten miles from the Confederate camp, on January 17. The rains, high water, and almost impassable roads had delayed several of Thomas's regiments, however, and he halted to await their arrival before attempting a further advance.

Crittenden, meanwhile, learned of Thomas's position. Anticipating that the rising waters of nearby Fishing Creek would separate Thomas from Schoepf's troops, Crittenden called a council of war, whereupon it was decided to attack.

Advancing in a driving rainstorm on January 19, the Confederates were hampered by bad roads and were badly strung out when their advance struck the Federal pickets. By the time the lead regiments approached the main Federal camp, Thomas's troops were waiting in line of battle.

The Confederate attack was uncoordinated, and much confusion existed as to identity of the troops. The nearsighted Felix Zollicoffer rode up to a Federal colonel, thinking him to be a Confederate officer whose troops were firing on Zollicoffer's men, and was killed.

Worse still, Thomas had been reinforced just before the fight by three regiments and a battery from Schoepf, without the knowledge of the Confederates. A counterattack by these troops against the Confederate left broke several of Zollicoffer's Tennessee regiments, whose antiquated flintlock muskets would not fire in the rain. The entire line soon fell back in disorder, and the Federals pursued Crittenden all the way to his entrenchments.

With Thomas and Schoepf preparing to assault his fortifications the next morning, Crittenden escaped across the river with most of his men that night. Abandoned were twelve pieces of artillery, a large quantity of small arms and ammunition, one hundred and fifty wagons, more than a thousand horses and mules, and an immense quantity of food and equipment.

The disaster was a serious reversal for the Confederacy. Crittenden, who was censured, later submitted his resignation. His troops were demoralized by the defeat, and many deserted. Two entire regiments that had been recruited in the vicinity of Crittenden's retreat quit and went home. The remainder marched with meager provisions through eastern Tennessee, finally joining Johnston's army following its withdrawal from Nashville.

The series of misfortunes, added to the loss of Kentucky and Tennessee, placed a heavy burden on Sidney Johnston. Although his Central Army of Kentucky had numbered about fourteen thousand men when the evacuation of Bowling Green began, before the army reached Nashville fifty-four hundred, or over a third, were reported sick and unfit for duty. A further difficulty was added when Johnston's army, having just reached the city, was compelled to evacuate Nashville because of the fall of Fort Donelson.

Once his army was safely across the Cumberland, Johnston reported to the Secretary of War that he had to retire a safe distance from Nashville until reinforcements arrived to drive the enemy back. It is evident from Johnston's correspondence that as late as February 18 his plans called for little more than to retire between the rivers, to hold the enemy in check, and when his forces were sufficiently increased, "to drive him back."

Reinforcement, however, was of critical importance, even to maintain a static defense, and Johnston was soon provided with this prospect. In addition to five or six regiments promised by General Lovell in New Orleans, eight regiments had been allocated to the department by Secretary of War Benjamin before the fall of Donelson. With these troops already on the way, Johnston's ranks were augmented by the fugitives from Fort Donelson and the remnant of Crittenden's army. By the time the Central Army reached Murfreesboro, its troop strength had increased to about seventeen thousand, enabling Johnston to detach twenty-five hundred men under Floyd to guard Chattanooga.

Despite Johnston's statement that his army was "in good condition," the mood of the troops by now was that of despair. The Kentuckians were particularly bitter and denounced Johnston as they sloshed through the pelting rain during the retreat to Murfreesboro. One high-ranking officer telegraphed to Richmond that if Johnston were not removed, the army would be fully demoralized. A member of the Confederate Congress traveling with Johnston's army wrote to Jefferson Davis that Johnston had committed inexcusable "errors of omission, commission, and delay." He concluded that Johnston could not possibly reorganize his army with any confidence and urged that Davis come in person to take command.

While the furor continued within the retreating army, panic reigned in Nashville. The city had been abandoned by the main army on February 18, with only a small rear-guard detachment under Floyd, and Forrest's and Morgan's cavalry remaining. Despite all efforts to stop it looting soon became widespread. One Confederate officer watched an old woman stagger under a load of meat that he "hardly thought a quartermaster's mule could carry." On another occasion Floyd watched helplessly as a mob took possession of boats loaded with government bacon and began throwing it ashore.

Torrents of rain fell on the city, adding to the misery. On the twenty-second one of the two railroad bridges washed away, leaving only the Tennessee and Alabama bridge by which to effect a complete removal of war materiel still on the north bank. When Floyd departed with his staff on the afternoon of the twentieth, the main suspension bridge was destroyed. Only Forrest and the cavalry remained to remove as many of the stores from the city as possible. Despite their exhausting efforts property estimated at millions of dollars, including twenty-four heavy cannon, had to be abandoned. Forrest later condemned the mass of frenzied citizens for obstructing an orderly evacuation, recalling that it had been necessary to charge the mob with drawn sabers in order to clear a path for his wagons.

On February 23 only a small detachment of cavalry remained in the city as Buell's advance appeared in Edgefield, opposite Nashville. The formal surrender occurred two days later, when a delegation of citizens headed by the mayor delivered the city to Buell. By that time Johnston's army was safely intact at Murfreesboro, nearly forty miles southeast. Because of the influx of scattered regiments from the Donelson and Logan Cross Roads fights Johnston spent nearly a week reorganizing his army.

While the infantry rested, the cavalry remained active in the vicinity of Nashville, staging several successful forays against Buell's troops. Here an emerging cavalry leader, John Hunt Morgan, began to attract the notice of friend and foe alike.

Then only a captain, Morgan led his men in an incessant series of raids. Pickets and outposts were ambushed at random, a Union steamer was set afire while anchored at Nashville, and a daring daylight occupation of a road between two enemy camps near the city netted nearly one hundred prisoners. Later, raiding north of Nashville, Morgan occupied Gallatin, Tennessee, for three days, burning a railroad engine and a few cars and learning the latest news of Buell's movements. The energetic Morgan not only provided Johnston with important intelligence, but he also disrupted communications and diverted troops that might have been utilized elsewhere. Shortly after rejoining the army in early April, Morgan was rewarded with a promotion to colonel.

The reorganization of Johnston's army was announced on February 23. Five days later he was again marching south in a movement of crucial importance. It involved a calculated risk on the part of Johnston, and it had been decided upon only after an agonizing assessment of the adverse military situation then confronting the Western Department.

Johnston termed this movement "a hazardous experiment" involving some risk that his army would be intercepted and destroyed in route. Largely a result of the influence of one of the South's most prominent generals, however, an all-out campaign to defend the Memphis & Charleston Railroad at Corinth, Mississippi, had been quickly agreed upon.

Pierre Gustave Toutant-Beauregard, the South's fifth-ranking general, had come west in February, 1862, amid widespread popular acclaim. Beauregard, the "Hero of Fort Sumter" and the tactical commander during the Confederate victory at First Bull Run, for which he had won huge praise, was thought by many of his admirers to be the reincarnation of one of Napoleon's marshals. A professional soldier since the age of sixteen, he was known as "Old Bory" to his men. A smallish, middle-aged general of Latin appearance, he had eyes that some said resembled a bloodhound's.

Of Louisiana Creole stock, Beauregard had been raised as a youth in New Orleans, tutored in New York, and formally educated at West Point, graduating second in his class in 1838. As an officer on General Winfield Scott's staff during the Mexican War, he was twice cited for gallantry and wounded twice. Although he briefly considered leaving the service following that war, Beauregard was persuaded to take charge of the military defenses of Louisiana, becoming a brevet major of engineers.

In November, 1860, Beauregard suddenly rose to prominence with his appointment as the new superintendent of the U. S. Military Academy. Although he actually assumed the position for a few days in January, 1861, Beauregard was swiftly removed by Secretary of War Holt for pro-Southern sympathies.

Resigning from the Federal Army soon afterward, he was placed in charge of the defenses of Charleston, South Carolina, and directed operations against Fort Sumter in Charleston Harbor. With the fort's fall, for which he received the Confederate Congress's vote of thanks, the popular brigadier general was ordered to Virginia, where he later directed much of the fighting at the Battle of Manassas.

Now a full general as a result of this latest victory, Beauregard was a national hero and his name a household byword. Yet his excessive ambitions soon resulted in political difficulty with the government. His request for a chief of ordnance brought about a bitter dispute with the Secretary of War over the independence of his command from that of Joseph E. Johnston in northern Virginia. President Davis finally had to admonish the persistent Beauregard that he was not outside the limits of the law. When Beauregard continued to insist on being treated as an independent commander, Davis transferred him to the West—but only after ascertaining that the assignment would be accepted.

Despite a severe bronchial infection Beauregard left for Bowling Green, Kentucky, on February 2, 1862. His arrival there several days later was welcomed with enthusiasm by the harried Johnston. Although Beauregard had agreed to assume command of the district of Columbus, Kentucky, including the troops there under Major General Leonidas Polk, when he learned that he had been misinformed by a representative of Congress about the number of troops in the Western Department and their offensive capability, he requested permission to return to Virginia. With some difficulty, Johnston was able to persuade Beauregard to remain, the final decision being based on the Creole general's usefulness in defending the Mississippi Valley.

During a conference held at the Covington House on February 7, Generals Hardee, Beauregard, and Johnston concluded that both Columbus, on the Mississippi River, and Bowling Green, in central Kentucky, should be abandoned by the main armies. Since Fort Henry had fallen to Grant's army the previous day, Fort Donelson was then thought to be untenable.

By now Beauregard's respiratory infection had become so acute that he was unable to leave for Columbus, via Nashville, until the thirteenth, when the evacuation of Bowling Green was completed. Before leaving, Beauregard said he thought it necessary to withdraw the Columbus garrison to Jackson, Tennessee, in order to guard the Memphis & Charleston and Mobile & Ohio railroads. Johnston agreed to the plan, contingent upon War Department approval. Since Johnston's anticipated retreat was to be along the Nashville & Stevenson Railroad in the direction of Chattanooga, he gave Beauregard authority to command independently in the Mississippi Valley.

The still-ailing Beauregard left Nashville by train on February 15, arriving the following day at Corinth. Awaiting him there were important dispatches with news of the loss of Fort Donelson. Johnston now reasoned that with the enemy controlling both rivers, the separation of the two Confederate armies was complete. Accordingly Beauregard was to act strictly on his own judgment.

Although complaining of "wretched" health, Beauregard was soon compelled to act. When Colonel Thomas Jordan, his trusted chief of staff brought from Virginia, reported to him at Jackson, Tennessee, the next day, Beauregard was further alarmed. Jordan had just inspected Columbus's defenses, and found them faulty and the troops poorly organized. Too weak and feverish to go there in person, Beauregard summoned Leonidas Polk, the garrison's commander. Then, following a conference in which Polk demurred, he ordered the evacuation of Columbus. The War Department telegraphed its consent on the nineteenth, and the evacuation began the following week, continuing until March 2.

A portion of the garrison, under Brigadier General John P. McCown, was sent to New Madrid to defend the Mississippi River, both at the big bend there and at Island No. 10, while permanent fortifications at Fort Pillow were being completed. The remainder of the troops, under Polk, were ordered to Humboldt, Tennessee, at the important intersection of the Memphis & Clarksville and Mobile & Ohio railroads.

Meanwhile a combined Union Army and Naval expedition organized for the conquest of the Mississippi River under Brigadier General John Pope was under way. Pope did not discover the evacuation of Columbus until March 4, however, and the Union gunboats under Commodore Foote failed to attack Island No. 10 and the batteries at New Madrid until preparations for their defense were nearly complete.

Beauregard, beset by ill health and a perplexing military situation, lamented to a friend in a letter sent East, "I am taking the helm when the ship is already in the breakers and with but few sailors to man it." Nonetheless he began the task, pledging "a bold front and stout hearts."

Foremost among the many pressing problems was the mobilization of all available manpower into a defensive army. Contemplating a "defensive, active" strategy that would give him maximum maneuverability to strike any invading column, Beauregard sought to concentrate his forces.

Acting under the independent authority granted by Johnston following the evacuation of Nashville, Beauregard met with Governor Isham G. Harris of Tennessee less than a week after the fall of Fort Donelson. Pressed by Beauregard for support, Harris promised that all state troops called out in west Tennessee would be quickly gathered at Jackson and Corinth. Unexpected help had already come from the Gulf, for Brigadier General Daniel Ruggles had arrived in

Corinth with a brigade of Louisiana volunteers the day following the Donelson surrender. Ruggles's department commander at New Orleans, Major General Mansfield Lovell, had sent the brigade at the request of the War Department, asking only that they be stationed at Corinth so that they might be returned quickly to the Gulf by rail, if needed.

Added to a small force under Brigadier General James R. Chalmers, camped at Iuka, twenty miles east of Corinth on the Memphis & Charleston Railroad, Beauregard now had about twenty-one thousand men to defend the vital Mississippi Valley.

Resorting to perhaps a little salesmanship, Beauregard left few means untapped in his quest for more troops. In a confidential letter to the governors of Tennessee, Mississippi, Louisiana, and Alabama, Beauregard proposed to march against Paducah, Kentucky, in order to "seize and close the mouths of the Tennessee and Cumberland rivers. . . . Aided by gunboats," continued the optimistic Beauregard, "I could also successfully assail Cairo, and threaten if not indeed take, Saint Louis itself."

In order to accomplish this ambitious program Beauregard asked for "from five to ten thousand men, armed and equipped," from each governor. Furthermore it was implied what must have been obvious considering the recent disasters, that the defense of the South's interior was at stake.

The series of Confederate disasters had so drastically influenced the political climate that a favorable response was quick in coming. Governor John Gill Shorter of Alabama issued a proclamation calling for twelve regiments despite a complete lack of weapons with which to arm the recruits. Governor T. O. Moore of Louisiana, who had been warned, "Let the people of Louisiana understand here is the proper place to defend Louisiana," promised to do everything possible, including the turning out of troops for ninety days' service. Isham G. Harris of Tennessee reported that he had not only ordered out every man in the state who was, and could be, armed, but he promised to serve with them himself.

Although it appears that Beauregard had again exceeded his authority by calling for levies without War Department approval, he received belated notice from Secretary of War Benjamin that his course of action was fully approved, provided the troops were armed and enlisted for twelve months. In the emergency, said Adjutant General Samuel Cooper, even certain troops would be accepted for ninety days' service.

As an added stroke of good fortune Beauregard now learned that other important reinforcements were coming from the Department of Alabama and West Florida. Braxton Bragg, the Confederacy's eighth-ranking general officer, had voluntarily pledged a large portion of his troops to the defense of the Valley.

Bragg's presence was regarded as so important by the ailing Beauregard that he had earlier telegraphed to the Adjutant General that he would "serve under him rather than not have him here." After Beauregard's aide, Lieutenant A. R. Chisolm, delivered the confidential appeal to Governor Shorter at Montgomery, he was directed to proceed to see Bragg at Mobile.

Chisolm arrived at Mobile on February 28 and was astounded to learn that Bragg was on the verge of leaving the following day to join Beauregard with ten regiments, four others having already been sent to east Tennessee for Johnston's command.

Bragg had long recognized the importance of a strong army along the northern frontier in order to protect the interior, and had readily agreed to send Brigadier General J. K. Jackson with the four regiments requested for Johnston by the War Department earlier that month. Furthermore, immediately following the loss of Fort Henry Bragg sent Brigadier General Leroy P. Walker to command in the district of North Alabama, looking to the defense of the upper Tennessee and the Memphis & Charleston Railroad. Fort Donelson's fall caused Bragg promptly to write to the War Department suggesting the concentration of his troops in the interior for the defense of the Mississippi Valley. This he considered vital, even at the risk of losing the seaboard. "We are being whipped in detail," wrote the aroused Bragg, "when a vigorous move with our resources concentrated would be infinitely more damaging to the enemy."

By the time Beauregard's emissary arrived on the twenty-eighth, the alarmed War Department had already authorized the move. Bragg hurried north, arriving in advance of his men on March 2 at Jackson, Tennessee, and was immediately placed in charge of the troops gathering at Corinth by the grateful Beauregard. Bragg's regiments began arriving at Corinth from Mobile and Pensacola on March 6. Within ten days nearly all of his ten thousand well-drilled troops were present.

By now Beauregard had learned of even greater good fortune: Sidney Johnston would attempt to unite his army with the combined forces under Beauregard for a bold defense of the Mississippi Valley.

Lieutenant Samuel W. Ferguson of Beauregard's staff had gone to Murfreesboro on February 22 with dispatches for Governor Harris of Tennessee, who was there conferring with Sidney Johnston. Harris had met with Beauregard on the twentieth at Jackson, Tennessee, while en route to Nashville and Murfreesboro, and knew in advance of Beauregard's confidential letter requesting additional troops from the Mississippi Valley governors.

Ferguson, however, also bore a dispatch for Johnston that over-shadowed the importance of the Harris message. Beauregard noted that Johnston's line of retreat toward Stevenson, Alabama, was taking him continually more distant from the concentration around Corinth. Beauregard suggested instead that Johnston turn toward Decatur, Alabama, where he would be in position to cooperate with or join the Mississippi Valley army.

Johnston, later said by Governor Harris to have been considering joint operations with Beauregard at the time, promptly decided to act. Going one step beyond Beauregard's suggestion, he announced in a dispatch to Jefferson Davis on February 24, "This army will move on [the] 26th, by Decatur, for the valley of the Mississippi."

Several days later Johnston wrote in detail of his decision to Secretary of War Benjamin: "I am compelled to elect whether he [the enemy] shall be permitted to occupy Middle Tennessee, or turn Columbus, take Memphis, and open the valley of the Mississippi. To me the defense of the valley seems of paramount importance, and consequently I will move this corps of the army . . . toward the left bank of the Tennessee, crossing the river near Decatur, in order to enable me to cooperate or unite with General Beauregard for the defense of Memphis and the Mississippi."

Johnston's decision was fraught with danger. Buell's army had just occupied Nashville, and the extent of the Federal pursuit was unknown. Buell's troops, estimated to be forty thousand strong, were believed fully capable of intercepting Johnston's march south. More-over there was strong opposition to the plan from within the army. Major General William J. Hardee, the army's second-in-command, Colonel W. W. Mackall, Johnston's adjutant general, and Major Gilmer, his chief engineer, believed the movement to defend the Mississippi Valley impossible. The distraught Hardee even believed that nothing could save the army short of Jefferson Davis's presence.

Johnston had undoubtedly been stung by the army's loss of faith in his command, but he remained resolute, confiding to his close friend the President, "If I join this corps to the forces of Beauregard (I confess a hazardous experiment), then those who are now de-claiming against me will be without an argument."

The reorganization of the army having been announced on the twenty-third, plans were made for the evacuation of Murfreesboro on February 26. Since a heavy rainstorm on the twenty-second had washed away the pike and railroad bridges, however, it was not until the twenty-eighth that the army withdrew.

Johnston optimistically reported his army "in good condition and increasing in numbers" before the march south. Even though a detachment of twenty-five hundred men commanded by Floyd had been sent east on the twenty-fifth to defend Chattanooga, the influx of troops from the armies that had fought at Fort Donelson and Mill Springs enabled Johnston to start for Decatur with about seventeen thousand men. Other reinforcements from Bragg under J. K. Jackson added nearly two thousand troops. Johnston soon revealed signs of growing confidence. Before leaving Murfreesboro, he told Adjutant General W. C. Whitthorne of Tennessee that "under the favor of Providence" he would return in less than ninety days and recover Nashville.

In order to reach Decatur Johnston chose to march by way of Shelbyville and Fayetteville. The railroad from Murfreesboro to Stevenson made a direct connection with the Memphis & Charleston Railroad at Stevenson, by which Johnston might move more rapidly. Yet the burden on the railroad was immense, considering the tons of war materiel and supplies being transferred from Bowling Green, Nashville, and Murfreesboro. Boxcars were in short supply, organization imperfect, and efficiency very poor. In the opinion of Major Gilmer of Johnston's staff the movement of the army by rail was impossible without the loss of vital supplies and munitions upon which it depended.

Mindful of the considerable time needed to march his army to the Mississippi Valley, Johnston was concerned that a Union column coming down the Tennessee River might intercept his movement along the railroad west of Decatur. Attempting to disguise the Confederate line of march, Johnston tried to create the impression that he was falling back on Chattanooga. Mail for the army was directed to Chattanooga, as were long trains of ordnance stores. Since Floyd and his detachment were already en route there, Johnston anticipated that enemy spies would report the direction of their movements.

The ruse proved to be successful. Grant reported on February 25 that the Confederates had fallen back to Chattanooga. Sherman repeated the same dispatch two days later, and Buell advised General-in-Chief McClellan on February 28 that the enemy was said to be concentrating in the direction of Chattanooga. Even by March 6, when Buell knew of Johnston's presence in the vicinity of Shelbyville, he said it had been rumored that Johnston was remaining in middle Tennessee, awaiting Beauregard's arrival for an advance on Nashville.

With Hindman's brigade of Hardee's division leading the march, the retreat from Murfreesboro began at sunrise on February 28. Hardee and most of the army's cavalry remained in the rear, destroying bridges after the troops had passed. While cavalry detachments under active leaders such as J. S. Scott, of the 1st Louisiana, and John Hunt Morgan screened their movements, the army continued south. Shelbyville was occupied on March 1 and evacuated on March 4. Marching orders specified an advance of fifteen miles a day, but

beyond Shelbyville the distance was reduced to a twelve-mile minimum because of bad roads.

While Johnston was at Shelbyville on March 3, he learned from
Beauregard that the enemy was advancing troops by steamboat along
the Mississippi. Curiously, Beauregard cited this information from
the *Memphis Appeal* newspaper of March 1, which had copied an
earlier report of the Cincinnati *Enquirer*. Anticipating an immediate
enemy offensive, Beauregard urged Johnston to hurry his troops by
rail to Corinth.

Johnston was rapidly approaching the point of no return. Once
beyond Decatur he would be committed to carry out his original
plans. Noting that there were no indications of an immediate enemy
movement from Nashville, Johnston proceeded to complete the
linkup, saying that Beauregard had been urging him "to come on,"
and he had no fears for the safety of Chattanooga.

It had been necessary to leave an infantry brigade and two cavalry
regiments behind at Shelbyville to remove a large stockpile of pork
and subsistence provisions. His army was now strung out, and inclement weather and bad roads further delayed Johnston's march.
It was not until March 10 that the advance reached Decatur.

At Decatur Johnston planned to expedite the crossing of his
artillery and baggage wagons by utilizing the railroad bridge across
the Tennessee. He ordered the entire two and a half mile embankment approaching the bridge planked for that purpose, but a wide
variation in axle lengths made it impractical to wheel the wagons and
guns across. Instead railroad platform cars had to be used, a slow
and laborious process.

By March 15 Johnston's army was concentrated in and beyond
Decatur. The vanguard had marched ahead to Courtland, nearly
halfway to Tuscumbia, but heavy rains continued to fall, delaying
Confederate movements.

Although Johnston again reported with confidence that his men
were "in good condition and fine spirits" and "anxious to meet the
enemy," indications of a disheartened army continued to filter from
within as the troops languished at Decatur. Once more the favorite
target of criticism was Johnston.

Basil W. Duke, brother-in-law of John Hunt Morgan, confided that
both officers and men openly denounced Johnston's leadership, placing the whole burden of blame on him during the retreat from Murfreesboro. Hardee continued to have little confidence in Johnston
and looked only to Bragg and Beauregard to restore Confederate
fortunes. Newspapers added to the furor, reporting that many soldiers
were enlisting only on condition that they not be made to serve under
Johnston.

The pressure on Jefferson Davis to remove Johnston remained

constant. The public knew little of Johnston's plans, and many watched with remorse as his army continued their retreat into the Deep South. Following the loss of Nashville all but one of Tennessee's Congressmen called upon President Davis to demand Johnston's removal, terming him "no general." Davis's reply was curt; if Sidney Johnston was not a general, he said, they had better give up the war, for they had no general.

Yet by March 12 the strain became so great on Davis that he sent a private letter to Johnston asking for an explanation of the recent disasters in order to help appease public opinion.

Johnston, of course, was aware of his critics. He advised Davis that he had observed silence because the facts were not fully known, and he did not feel the cause would be served by condemnation of any person when every individual's services were needed during the present crisis. Major E. W. Munford, an aide-de-camp, heard Johnston speculate that the clamor caused by the army's retreat would turn to praise following a pitched battle. To a newspaper reporter Johnston offered no excuse for the defeats in his department, saying only that he could not "correspond" with the people—they wanted a battle and a victory.

Despite the growing controversy and adverse weather Johnston worked hard to increase the effectiveness of his army while at Decatur. Troop dispositions were altered in order to obtain intelligence and pave the way for the army's advance to Corinth. Railroad cars were requisitioned in quantity from Floyd in Chattanooga, providing added mobility. Even such minutiae as distributing provisions and the impressment of wagons to haul corn came under the general's scrutiny.

While waiting in camp for nearly a week, the troops were buffeted by severe rainstorms. On the night of March 14 high winds knocked down nearly every tent in a Kentucky brigade of the Reserve Corps. Amid the swirling hats, blankets, and camp debris a herd of frightened cattle bolted past, scattering the men. This experience proved so bewildering to many of the Kentuckians that several had to be rounded up in Decatur's "gin" houses the following day.

Although the weather remained inclement, Johnston was compelled to forward reinforcements to Beauregard following the receipt on the fourteenth of an urgent request for a brigade. Beauregard had just learned of an imminent raid on the Memphis & Charleston Railroad in the vicinity of Eastport, Mississippi, and he "expected battle."

Johnston dispatched Hindman's brigade on the fifteenth, although the creeks were so flooded that Hindman was obliged to leave his artillery behind. Despite recurring crises along the Mobile & Ohio and Memphis & Charleston railroads during the following week Johnston was unable to forward large numbers of troops because of a lack of adequate transportation. Bragg was particularly anxious for assistance at Corinth and kept urging Johnston on, but the muddy roads were nearly impassable and the creeks swollen beyond recognition.

Although the uneasy Johnston requested four hundred rail cars with engines from Beauregard at Jackson, Tennessee, he was promised only one hundred sixty. Consequently it was March 20 before Johnston's advance under S. A. M. Wood reached Corinth, which was only ninety-three miles from Decatur.

The military railroad, inefficient to begin with, was proving totally inadequate. Bragg condemned the entire system, complaining that wood and water stations were abandoned, that employees refused to work for want of pay, and that troops were molesting innkeepers along the route. Lieutenant John M. Otey of Beauregard's staff was sent to investigate the conditions and found "palpable dereliction of duty" on the part of military police along the Memphis & Charleston road and "gross misconduct" by troops aboard the trains.

Johnston patiently remained at Decatur until March 22, arriving the following day in Corinth. By now his troops were nearly united with Bragg's and Beauregard's, and held positions at Tuscumbia, Iuka, Burnsville, and Corinth. Satisfied that the movement deemed "too hazardous" by his staff had been accomplished, Johnston almost embraced Bragg when they met at Corinth, saying Bragg's presence had "saved me and saved the country."

Reflecting on the events of the past few months, Johnston had written to Jefferson Davis while at Decatur, "The test of merit in my profession with the people is success. It is a hard rule, but I think it right." To that task Sidney Johnston now devoted his full effort.

CHAPTER VI

A Most Difficult Task

While Johnston's army was en route from middle Tennessee, Beauregard was busily organizing his defenses against the expected Union thrust up the Tennessee. Too sick to assume command following his arrival at Jackson, Tennessee, on February 17, Beauregard could but ponder the wretched military situation he had inherited.

Immediately following the loss of Fort Henry on February 6 so few troops had been available that the vital Memphis & Charleston Railroad was virtually undefended along the Tennessee. Eight companies of Colonel James R. Chalmers's regiment, the 9th Mississippi, and a portion of the 38th Tennessee under Colonel R. F. Looney at the time were the only Southern troops present in northern Mississippi to defend the region.

When three Union gunboats steamed up the Tennessee to Florence, Alabama, on February 7 and 8, the Confederates were so few that citizens were called out to man several field guns in possession of the railroad at Huntsville. Sailing unopposed up the river, the Federal gunboats captured two steamers, one loaded with iron destined for Richmond, Virginia, and seized the half-completed 280-foot Confederate gunboat *Eastport*. Six other steamers were set afire by the Confederates to prevent their capture. Only impassable Muscle Shoals beyond Florence prevented further depredation upriver. With their prizes safely in tow, the Union expedition leisurely returned to Fort Henry on the tenth, stopping en route to break up a Confederate militia camp at Savannah, Tennessee.

The panic created by the appearance of Federal troops deep in Confederate territory was extensive. In some instances entire communities adjacent to the river had fled to the forests, spurred on by reports of burning and plundering by the gunboat crews. Farther south, Braxton Bragg had been among the first to react to the crisis, sending Brigadier General Leroy Pope Walker from Mobile to command in northern Alabama on February 10.

Walker was by vocation a politician, the Confederacy's original Secretary of War. Yet he had found his lack of experience such a handicap that he resigned the post under heavy criticism in September, 1861. Made a brigadier general in the Provisional Army the same month, the gangling, stone-faced Walker was not highly regarded as a military officer. Ironically it was Walker who clearly perceived the strategic situation and predicted with amazing accuracy the Federal campaign up the Tennessee. As a result of Walker's work the Confederacy early began to reinforce vital areas along the railroads.

Establishing his headquarters at Tuscumbia, Alabama, Walker, who was a native of the region, complained that he was expected to defend railroads that comprised "the vertebrae of the Confederacy" with a piddling force. Warning that the enemy would make "either Savannah or Hamburg in Tennessee, or Eastport, in Mississippi," the base of their operations, Walker demanded reinforcements, including engineering help.

Only a few days after Walker's request of February 14 additional reinforcements were forthcoming from the Gulf states, including a new interim commander, Brigadier General Daniel Ruggles of Virginia.

Ruggles arrived in Corinth from New Orleans on February 17, bringing with him a brigade of Louisiana volunteers. Authorized by Polk to take command of the district in the vicinity of the Memphis & Charleston Railroad, the crusty, fifty-two-year-old Ruggles established his headquarters at Corinth, nearly midway between Memphis and Decatur. Serving under his command was L. P. Walker, at Tuscumbia in northern Alabama, and Chalmers, guarding the important railroad bridge over Bear Creek near Iuka, twenty miles east of Corinth.

Ruggles had barely assumed command when he learned of another enemy incursion along the river. Although most of the Federal Navy had withdrawn from the Tennessee in order to support Grant's attack against Fort Donelson, a lone Federal gunboat, the *Tyler,* remained to carry out a thorough reconnaissance of the Tennessee. Realizing the importance of the Bear Creek railroad bridge, Lieutenant William Gwin, the *Tyler's* commander, secretly planned to destroy the bridge by launching a small cavalry strike force from the Tennessee.

On the morning of February 20 Confederate scouts sighted the *Tyler* moving upriver near Hamburg, Tennessee. Alerted to what was believed to be another raid on Florence, Alabama, Ruggles cautioned Chalmers to watch the river closely.

Landing at Eastport, north of Iuka, Gwin soon learned from residents that the Confederates had three or four thousand troops at Iuka and were actively guarding the Bear Creek bridge. Since Gwin had been unable to take the cavalry along because of the lack of space, having instead only fifty sharpshooters aboard, he concluded that the Bear Creek bridge was inaccessible. The *Tyler* then returned to Cairo on the twenty-second, bringing news of strong Union sentiment at Savannah, Tennessee. Gwin also recommended Corinth as an objective point for operations against the Confederate railroads.

Reflecting on the increased Union gunboat activity on the Tennessee, Beauregard, who was still convalescing, instructed Ruggles on February 24 to watch the river with "the utmost vigilance." Ruggles had already anticipated this suggestion and several days earlier had sent Confederate troops to observe the river from Savannah to Florence. Although troop dispositions were skeletal, a number of key points were under observation, including Pittsburg Landing, Tennessee. Here Ruggles had sent one of his own regiments, the 18th Louisiana Infantry, and Gibson's field battery with instructions "to attack the enemy's gunboats and transports in the event of his appearance."

Meanwhile Henry Halleck had been pondering the unsuccessful foray upriver by the *Tyler* in mid-February. Concluding that the meager results were due to the lack of sufficient strength, Halleck now ordered two gunboats with strong infantry detachments aboard to patrol the Tennessee.

Chosen for the work in addition to the *Tyler* was the converted river steamboat *Lexington,* refitted for gunboat duty by Commander John Rodgers at Cincinnati in 1861.

On March 1, 1862, the *Tyler* and *Lexington* rounded Diamond Island below Pittsburg Landing and sailed toward the bluffs along the west bank. Here it was found the Confederates had posted a regiment and a battery. The six-gun field battery of the Confederates was no match for the six-and eight-inch naval guns of the gunboats, however, and the fight was soon ended.

Although the losses on both sides were minimal—Federal, two killed, six wounded, and three missing; Confederate, nine allegedly killed—the devastation wrought by the heavy naval guns was sufficient to alarm the Confederate generals. Ruggles feared the powerful effect of the gunboat shells and ordered Chalmers's infantry not to expose themselves by fighting "under [the] gunboats."

Although Ruggles commended the 18th Louisiana for its "brilliant success" in the Pittsburg fight, its camp was soon withdrawn three miles from the river. The Tennessee now was kept only under distant surveillance at that point.

Despite the growing aggressiveness of Federal vessels along the Tennessee, Beauregard's activities continued to be limited, caused by "a nervous affection of the throat."

Following Bragg's arrival from Mobile on March 2 Beauregard

assigned him to full command of troops in northern Mississippi. Bragg now assumed from Ruggles the responsibility for defending the Memphis & Charleston Railroad. While Beauregard was dividing Polk's Columbus, Kentucky, army for the defense of Fort Pillow, Island No. 10, and the Tennessee River, Bragg ordered the concentration around Corinth of all his available forces. Taking a dim view of the "heterogeneous mass" of soldiers he was to command, the precise Bragg imposed a stern discipline on the army. All of the railroads were placed under military control, and an armed detail was ordered to go with each passenger train to arrest all persons traveling without proper authority. Liquor sales were forbidden around troop concentrations, and many saloons were closed. Bragg even declared martial law in Memphis, Tennessee, and had prisoners of war sent farther south.

Foremost in the Confederate general's mind remained the prospect of an enemy invasion using the Tennessee as a line of operations. On March 6 Bragg said he had information that a large Federal column would soon come up the Tennessee. He instructed Ruggles to have one hundred rounds of ammunition issued for each man and to keep two hundred artillery rounds per gun on hand. All baggage was to be sent south, along with the sick, because of the "impending danger."

With each passing day the apprehension continued to increase. On the seventh Confederate scouts reported to Polk that large bodies of Union troops were aboard transports lying at Fort Henry. A few days later Polk had news that sixty enemy transports had passed upriver, en route to Eastport.

At last the threatened Union invasion seemed to be under way. Bragg ordered Ruggles to begin entrenching at Corinth and sent Brigadier General Adley H. Gladden with infantry, cavalry, and artillery to Bethel Station, north of Corinth on the Mobile & Ohio Railroad. Ruggles immediately placed his troops on a combat-ready status, subject to two hours' notice. By March 11 the network of Confederate scouts had reported the occupation of Savannah, on the Tennessee's east bank. Yet the actual point of attack was still in doubt. When the gunboats Lexington and Tyler arrived in front of the Chickasaw fortifications near Eastport, Mississippi, on March 12, there was fear of an attack in that vicinity.

Chalmers, the regional commander, had caused a five-gun battery to be erected along the river bluffs a mile and a half above Eastport, including two 24-pounder guns originally assigned to L. P. Walker at Florence. Commanded by Captain S. S. Calhoun, two infantry companies trained as heavy artillery at Pensacola, Florida, had emplaced the artillery and constructed earthworks to defend the river.

Intent on uncovering the Confederate battery's strength, the gunboats shelled the works at long range, taking a plunging fire from the bluffs in return. After firing nearly a hundred rounds, the *Lexington* and *Tyler* dropped downriver to rejoin the vanguard of C. F. Smith's expedition. The Union naval officers were convinced that the long range of the Confederate guns would prevent the landing of troops at Eastport.

Despite the gunboat operations near Eastport, Chalmers had recently surveyed the river and knew it to be impassable for the heavy Federal warships between Eastport and Florence because of the falling water level. He reported this to Beauregard, and the Confederate high command now regarded Pittsburg Landing, Hamburg, and Eastport as the likely sites of a Union landing on the west bank.

By now Beauregard considered the crisis so grave that he assumed formal command of the Army of the Mississippi, even though his health was still poor. His general orders of March 5 decreed that the enemy must be made to atone for the recent Confederate reverses. "Our cause is as just and sacred as ever animated men to take up arms," proclaimed Beauregard, ". . . we must and shall triumph."

News of the expected Federal landing came on the day following the Eastport fight, March 13. The site chosen by the enemy, near Crump's Landing on the Savannah to Purdy road, had been anticipated only by Adley Gladden at Bethel Station.

Gladden had grown apprehensive when his scouts detected sixty-five boats at Savannah, fifty-seven of which had arrived on the eleventh. Having only two regiments of infantry, a few companies of cavalry, and a single light battery, Gladden complained that he was too weak to attack and without sufficient transportation to retreat in the event of a sudden Union advance.

During the night of March 12 Gladden's scouts observed the debarkation of Lew Wallace's division, thought to be eighteen thousand strong. By 2 A.M. the following morning this information was in Ruggles's hands at Corinth. Telegraphing to Beauregard and Bragg at Jackson, Ruggles quickly spread the alarm.

Convinced that the hour of crisis was at hand, the Confederate high command reacted hastily, ordering a full-scale troop concentration at Bethel Station without waiting for verification of the number of enemy landed. In the next few hours Confederate troops were dispatched from Eastport, Iuka, and Humboldt, all to rendezvous at Bethel Station. Even Colonel Alfred Mouton's 18th Louisiana was ordered to march to Purdy as fast as possible, stripping the river outpost near Pittsburg Landing of all but a small detachment.

James R. Chalmers was present at Eastport when an urgent telegram from Ruggles arrived on the thirteenth, asking him to hold his main force "in readiness at Iuka for an immediate movement to [Corinth] by railroad." Designating a sizable portion of his troops to remain at Eastport in order to watch that important river site, Chalmers ordered a night march to Iuka by the remainder of his force. While en route Chalmers received another dispatch signed "Daniel Ruggles," ordering him to entrain with his entire force for Bethel Station. "Don't change cars at Corinth," the telegram warned. "Celerity is all important."

Believing that a battle was raging or imminent because of Ruggles's previous dispatch, Chalmers sent back to Eastport for the remainder of his men. Unable to find sufficient railroad cars at Iuka, Chalmers's united force was compelled to wait until ten o'clock the following morning for transportation. Yet when his train finally arrived at Corinth on the fourteenth, Chalmers learned that there had been a serious mistake. Despite the fact that the dateline on the second dispatch was Jackson, Tennessee, he had failed to discover that the Iuka telegraph operator had mistakenly placed Ruggles's name on it rather than Bragg's, who had sent the order. Placing more urgency in the dispatch than was justified, Chalmers had inadvertently stripped Eastport of its garrison at a most critical moment.

While Chalmers was absent at Corinth, Sherman had gone upriver with a flotilla of gunboats and transports to destroy a bridge on the Memphis & Charleston Railroad near Burnsville. Landing at Yellow Creek, within ten miles of Eastport, Sherman launched his cavalry strike force on the evening of the fourteenth, only to run into foul weather. Forced to abort the attempt in the face of torrential rains, Sherman reboarded his transports on March 15 and, after briefly visiting Eastport, returned downriver to Pittsburg Landing. Chalmers hastened back to Iuka on the night of the fourteenth, much embarrassed over the telegraph fiasco and his "seeming abandonment of the guns at Eastport."

As further reports of Lew Wallace's initial landing near Crump's were received, Beauregard concluded the enemy's invasion was in earnest and continued to overreact. Polk was told to move most of his army to Bethel Station with the utmost speed. Johnston was asked by telegraph for a brigade, and Brigadier General Jones M. Withers, sent less than two weeks ago to Fort Pillow with several Alabama regiments, was ordered to Bethel via Memphis. Detailed battle orders were issued in Beauregard's name on the fourteenth, instructing the men to shoot at the feet of the enemy to avoid overshooting and thus create difficulty in evacuating the wounded. Officers were told they must be "cool and collected," requiring their men to single out a target. Bragg, having called in Chalmers's entire force from Iuka, went himself to Bethel Station in expectation of a fight.

In the midst of this invasion crisis communications between army headquarters and Corinth suddenly broke down. Ruggles reported the telegraph would not work during much of the fourteenth and fifteenth. He had not heard from Gladden since the fourteenth and feared to move for want of information. His artillery, already en route to Purdy, was caught in a driving rainstorm and had become mired. Plagued by disrupted communications and a shortage of transportation, Confederate headquarters remained in a quandary.

Bragg had meanwhile called off the emergency from Bethel Station at midnight on March 14. Scouts arrived with information that Wallace had retired to the river after destroying one bridge on the Mobile & Ohio Railroad. Bragg concluded that the enemy's strength had been exaggerated and that the bad roads had forced a change in their plans. With operations temporarily at a standstill because of inclement weather, Bragg now considered seizing the initiative— and even recommended a sudden advance to New Madrid on the Mississippi River, where Pope's army was besieging an outnumbered Confederate garrison.

Beauregard, however, was not convinced that the enemy had been thwarted in his attempt on the railroads. With communications finally restored, Polk was ordered to continue his concentration at Bethel.

Leonidas Polk, an Episcopal bishop and a Confederate major general, was a man of unique contrasts. Educated at West Point, where he had been a schoolmate of Jefferson Davis and the roommate of Sidney Johnston, Polk nonetheless had resigned from the Army six months after graduation to study for the ministry. Ordained in 1830, he had risen in the Church to become Bishop of Louisiana. With the outbreak of war in 1861 Polk went to Richmond on behalf of Governor Harris of Tennessee to urge strengthening of the Mississippi Valley defenses. Much to Polk's surprise, Davis offered him command in the Valley, pending Sidney Johnston's arrival from California. Commissioned a major general, Polk returned to Tennessee, ordering the occupation of Columbus, Kentucky, in September, 1861.

Polk was a study in contrasts. Tall and barrel-chested, with a massive jaw and a shock of flowing gray hair, he had been sickly much of his life. Although a close friend of Sidney Johnston, whose character he thought resembled that of George Washington, Polk was mistrustful of his superiors. When Beauregard ordered the evacuation of Columbus, Polk had objected, terming his citadel the "Gibraltar of the West." Citing the six months of hard labor required to fortify the city, Polk said he could hold it against any assault so long as his supplies lasted, and only begrudgingly agreed to withdraw. Less than two weeks after the evacuation of Columbus Polk complained to President Davis that the post had been "well-nigh impregnable," and having to abandon it had been trying.

When Columbus was evacuated on March 2, Polk had been among the last to depart. With flames from the fired buildings blazing in the background, Polk led his rear detachment south to Union City, Tennessee. He had managed to save nearly all of the military stores, including several trainloads of ammunition and over a hundred pieces of artillery. Although his army in effect had been divided, McCowan's eight-thousand-man division and A. P. Stewart's brigade being assigned to defend New Madrid and Island No. 10, Polk marched with the remainder toward the concentration near Corinth, satisfied that he had accomplished a most difficult undertaking.

By March 11 Polk had established his headquarters at Humboldt, Tennessee, sixteen miles north of Jackson. While there he deployed his approximately seven thousand troops as directed by Beauregard to protect the railroads in northwestern Tennessee. Among the troops previously dispatched by Polk to watch the river below Fort Henry was a detachment of mounted rifles at Paris, Tennessee, under Major H. C. King. King had reported important information on March 7, advising Polk of the heavy Federal concentration of transports lying about Fort Henry. However, when King was attacked and driven from the town on March 11 by a column sent by Grant to disrupt conscription activities, Beauregard was angered. Although the Federal troops soon withdrew following a minor skirmish, Polk had to explain why he had failed to post infantry at Paris, as ordered by Beauregard.

The lackluster Confederate performance of the past few days had also disillusioned Bragg, who thought it "entirely in the power of the enemy to cut the [rail] road at pleasure." Complaining that the "task is a most difficult one, especially with the mob we have, miscalled soldiers." Bragg pondered a Federal raid farther upriver, particularly at Iuka, which he considered "the most assailable point on the road."

Although news of the abortive Sherman expedition to Yellow Creek quickened his anxiety on March 15, Bragg was astounded and confused when he learned the following day of another Federal beachhead on the west bank.

On Saturday, March 15, Bragg, still at Bethel, had advised Beauregard's headquarters that because of the recent rains "the country people say no force of any size could now move on this point from Pittsburg or its vicinity." Accordingly when Ruggles telegraphed from Corinth at 2 A.M. on March 16 that the Federals, said to be thirty thousand strong, had landed at Pittsburg Landing, Bragg was puzzled. Saying his scouts had assured him that the enemy was not at Pittsburg "in any force" as late as the previous evening, Bragg refused to act upon "information so conflicting" other than to send out a strong reconnaissance.

Bragg delayed, but by 6 A.M. Ruggles had confirmed the Union landing at Pittsburg and had telegraphed an alert to Chalmers at Iuka and to L. P. Walker at Tuscumbia.

Meanwhile Bragg apparently learned from his own sources of the enemy's presence. Despite his disenchantment with the morale and discipline of the Confederate troops, Bragg now was "anxious . . . to strike a blow" as soon as possible and wired Ruggles of his intention to advance against the Pittsburg concentration.

Fortunately Beauregard had ignored Bragg's suggestion of March 14 that Polk's movement to Bethel be suspended. Polk's soldiers continued to arrive from Humboldt during the sixteenth, and Bragg quickly began organizing them for battle. His dispatch to Ruggles of March 16 outlined the plan; Bragg would advance from Bethel with Polk's army and unite with Ruggles at Adamsville, midway to Pittsburg. Together they would strike the enemy a crippling blow. Ruggles was asked for his combat status and means of transportation preparatory to an immediate advance.

By the time Bragg received a report from the reconnaissance ordered toward Pittsburg, he began to realize that mounting a prompt attack was a forlorn hope. Not only were the roads a hopeless quagmire, but the army was found to be in no condition to advance. "The troops arrived too slowly, were too poorly supplied, and too badly organized, instructed, and disciplined, to justify a hope of even carrying them to the point desired, much less a success against a well organized foe," complained Bragg.

Labeling these "radical defects," Bragg announced to Beauregard on March 18 that the army must remain on the defensive until these conditions could be corrected.

In this Beauregard entirely concurred. Having learned on the sixteenth of Bragg's intention to strike the Union beachhead at Pittsburg Landing, Beauregard had feared Bragg was about to act hastily. He quickly cautioned him against an "uncertain offensive." Although in favor of "entic[ing] the enemy into an engagement as soon as possible," Beauregard felt that Adamsville was too near the enemy's position to make a junction. He also regarded the nature of the terrain, the inferior quality of the troops, and the uncertainty of the enemy's intentions unfavorable for "purely offensive" operations. Believing that the Federal generals might launch their main effort farther upriver, toward Iuka or Eastport, Beauregard favored a "defensive-offensive" of waiting for the enemy to advance in force from the river, then striking quickly while he was in motion, cutting him off from his base of operations.

Largely because of the wet weather and bad roads the only troop movements ordered against the Union position at Pittsburg during the first few days were reconnaissance detachments of infantry and cavalry. Five Tennessee cavalry companies sent from Purdy on the afternoon of the sixteenth to picket the Pittsburg and Corinth road encountered Sherman's cavalry reconnaissance that night and were scattered.

The frequent Federal patrols during the first week following the landing led the Confederate generals to consider the enemy's aggressiveness a prelude to a movement in force. Beauregard's general orders of March 17 specified in minute detail the procedures for observing the enemy and warning of his advance. Pickets and reserves were ordered to stand to arms for an hour immediately before daybreak. Vedettes were warned never to take off their horses' bridles or saddles while near the enemy. Countersigns were established, and sentinels were instructed to conceal themselves. Prompted by the unruly character of many of his troops, Beauregard even went so far as to specify that "loud talking, singing, whistling, and fires" were strictly prohibited while on picket duty.

Bragg also was quick to gird his men for the coming contest. After only two weeks in the field he was so disgusted with the disorderly conduct of some of his command that he published orders threatening the death penalty for acts of pillage, plunder, and destruction of private property.

Beset by a variety of organizational, logistical, and operational problems, Bragg and Beauregard now looked to the arrival of Sidney Johnston's army for Corinth's security. On the eighteenth Bragg advised Johnston that the enemy was moving in force, their advance being only twelve miles away, and urged his immediate assistance. With the lack of transportation and inclement weather hindering Johnston's rapid transit, Bragg continued to chafe at the delay. On the nineteenth he warned that the Federals had pressed his pickets back to Purdy, ten miles distant. Complaining that for the want of cavalry he was unable to keep his entire front under observation, Bragg implied that only the mud was preventing an enemy march on Corinth.

Because of Beauregard's lingering illness Bragg formally assumed command on March 19 of all troops at and near Corinth. He also used the occasion to caution his men that a fight was expected at any moment—henceforth troops were to appear "under arms ready for action at reveille, retreat, and tattoo."

With the arrival of S. A. M. Wood's brigade of Johnston's army on the twentieth, Bragg was greatly relieved. Following Johnston's arrival in Corinth on the twenty-third, and his army's occupation of Corinth, Burnsville, Iuka, and Tuscumbia, the principal Confederate armies were united.

Beauregard was cheered by news of Johnston's approach and felt well enough to travel to Corinth to meet him on the twenty-third. Just one week earlier Beauregard had been able to speak only with great effort. When his physician warned that he must stop talking altogether Beauregard said exasperatedly, "They might as well tell a drowning man that he must not catch at a straw." The pressure of events rapidly drawing to a climax had frayed the nerves of the Confederate generals.

Immediately following Johnston's arrival the four ranking Confederate generals in the Mississippi Valley met for a summit conference at Corinth. Uppermost in importance was the marshaling of all available forces to resist the formidable Union offensive. With Johnston's thirteen thousand troops now present the only remaining untapped source was the Trans-Mississippi army of Major General Earl Van Dorn.

Van Dorn, a former major in Sidney Johnston's old 2d U. S. Cavalry regiment, was regarded as among the most promising officers of the army. His West Point background and wide experience in Mexican War and Indian-fighting campaigns had well qualified him for command of the Trans-Mississippi District in Johnston's department. Having assumed command of his district in January, 1862, Van Dorn had planned an offensive against St. Louis in early April, but had been thwarted by the advance during February of Union Brigadier General Samuel Curtis's Army of the Southwest. Van Dorn then hastened to western Arkansas, where the retreating Confederates under Ben McCulloch and Sterling Price were gathered. Immediately following news of Curtis's advance against Springfield, Missouri, Van Dorn received a letter from Beauregard dated February 21.

Although he had no authority to command Van Dorn, Beauregard urged him to join forces for an offensive east of the Mississippi River that would penetrate clear into Illinois. Despite Beauregard's self-proclaimed "brilliant programme," Van Dorn was preoccupied with Curtis's offensive in Arkansas.

Gathering Price's and McCulloch's forces along with Albert Pike's Cherokee and Creek Indians, he marched against Curtis's positions in early March. The Union army, although divided in two main columns, learned of the Confederate advance in time to concentrate in a strong defensive position fronting Little Sugar Creek. Although Van Dorn successfully attacked Curtis from the rear on March 7, a separate Confederate column under McCulloch was repulsed in a bloody assault on the Union right. Generals McCulloch and McIntosh were killed, Colonel Louis Hébert captured, and many other ranking officers shot.

Disorganized by the loss of their leaders, McCulloch's division fell into confusion and was scattered. Van Dorn, advancing with

Price's Missourians from the northeast, was soon met by reinforcements coming from the Federal right and was brought to a standstill near Elkhorn Tavern. At nightfall the Confederates lay across Curtis's line of communications atop a chain of hills known as Pea Ridge. Yet at daylight Curtis attacked, utilizing two divisions under Brigadier General Franz Sigel that had not seen heavy fighting the previous day. Van Dorn was routed and driven off with the loss of nearly a thousand men.

Following Van Dorn's disorderly retreat to Van Buren on the Arkansas River, Beauregard again appealed for a united defense of the Mississippi Valley. Instead Van Dorn preferred to advance through northeastern Arkansas against the Union army besieging New Madrid and Island No. 10. Once he learned that New Madrid had been evacuated on March 13, however, Van Dorn asked for further instructions.

Beauregard again did not hesitate. On March 22 he asked Van Dorn to move to Memphis, by river if possible. The request was followed the next day by formal orders from Johnston to accomplish this, based on the Corinth conference of the same date.

It was March 27 before Van Dorn received Johnston's dispatch at Little Rock. His army of nearly twenty thousand men was soon started overland for the White River, where transports would be sent to move the army to Memphis. On March 29 Van Dorn, accompanied by Colonel Dabney H. Maury of his staff, left by steamboat for Corinth. Conferring with Beauregard and Johnston at their headquarters about April 1, Van Dorn was instructed to hurry every available man to Corinth for an anticipated attack against the enemy. He then returned to Des Arc, on the White River, on April 5 to expedite his troops' departure. Little's brigade of Price's army was embarked on Monday, April 8. By the eleventh they were at Memphis.

Unfortunately for the Confederacy their movement was far too late; five days earlier the great battle for the Southwest had been fought. Arkansas and Missouri had been stripped of major Confederate armies in a vain effort to save the Mississippi Valley. As a result of Van Dorn's transfer about sixty thousand Union troops were soon withdrawn from the Trans-Mississippi and sent to Tennessee. Their added pressure would contribute significantly to the waning Confederate fortunes in the months ahead.

Following the Johnston-Beauregard-Bragg-Polk conference of March 23 the Confederate army was reorganized. Under orders published March 29 Johnston's Central Army of Kentucky was consolidated with Beauregard's command, to be known as the Army of the Mississippi. Three army corps were created, commanded by Polk, Bragg, and Hardee. In addition a Reserve Corps was established and assigned to Crittenden. The cavalry was apportioned among the various corps, one regiment to a division, with all remaining units being assigned to a cavalry reserve under Brigadier General J. M. Hawes. Overall army command was assumed by Sidney Johnston, and Beauregard became second-in-command. Bragg was designated chief of staff in addition to his duties as commander of the Second Corps.

This plan, although published in Johnston's name, actually was Beauregard's. Upon his arrival at Corinth Johnston generously offered Beauregard command of the army. Johnston was still under heavy condemnation for the recent disasters in the West, and neither the army nor his officers expressed much confidence in his leadership. He was willing to retire to Memphis or Holly Springs and act as administrator of the department. Beauregard, in contrast, was the popular hero of Fort Sumter and Manassas. He held not only the public trust but, most importantly, that of the Army.

Beauregard would not accept formal command, replying that he had come west to assist Johnston, not to supersede him. Yet in the days ahead Beauregard functioned much as the army's commander, drafting orders, planning organization, and directing active operations, all under Johnston's name. The matter of reorganization, for example, was handled by Beauregard, who drew up the plans, submitted them to Johnston, and witnessed their publication without any change or alteration.

Among the notable aspects of the new organization was Braxton Bragg's assignment as chief of staff. Although the creation of such a position was a departure from typical Confederate military organization, it provided an effective means to restore the army's morale. Bragg's reputation as a strict disciplinarian and talented organizer well qualified him for the position. Many of the troops concentrated about Corinth were unruly, and marauding bands of soldiers infested the countryside, pillaging indiscriminately. Officers were often ignored or abused. Bragg's background of nineteen years in the Regular Army and his strict attitude were effective in curbing such incidents. His irascible temper and harsh manner were already well known. During the Mexican War an attempt had been made to assassinate Bragg by exploding a 12-pounder shell at the foot of his bed. It was said that he had argued with nearly every officer encountered in the Old Army, earning numerous enemies. A further complication was that Bragg suffered from frequent migraine headaches. Feared by subordinates for his harsh methods, Bragg fully displayed his attitude in his publication of orders specifying summary punishment for the pillaging of private property. "Stern, dictatorial measures are necessary and as far as my influence goes, will be adopted," wrote Bragg shortly after Johnston's arrival.

Even generals were not spared Bragg's wrath. George B. Crittenden, already under indictment for the disaster at Logan's Cross Roads, learned on March 31 that Bragg had had him removed from his command. During his lengthy career in the U. S. Army Crittenden had resigned from the service on two occasions to avoid court-martial for drunkenness on duty. A third time he was tried, convicted, and dismissed before being reinstated by executive order. Bragg was a staunch believer in temperance and had no patience with those who drank heavily. On March 31 he sent William J. Hardee to Iuka to investigate reports of Crittenden's drunkenness and neglect of duty. Hardee found Crittenden and one of his brigadiers, William H. Carroll, drunk. Following Bragg's instructions Hardee arrested both and removed Crittenden from command of the Reserve Corps. Generals of higher rank then being in short supply, Brigadier General John C. Breckenridge was soon promoted to command of the reserves. Through Bragg's continuing efforts the Confederate army soon began to develop into a more manageable force.

Among the critical problems plaguing the army's high command was the shortage of general officers. As early as March 4 Beauregard had written to the War Department asking for two major generals and five brigadiers. When Adjutant General Samuel Cooper delayed in authorizing the appointments, Beauregard fumed at the inactivity. Complaining that "part of this army is in a state of chaos," Beauregard even threatened to request being relieved from command if his requests were not met. Cooper coolly replied the following day that only four generals were being nominated for Beauregard's command, the others being needed elsewhere. Writing to Confederate Congressman W. P. Miles, Beauregard revealed his bitterness: "What in the world shall I do . . . ? Will not Heaven open the eyes and senses of our rulers? Where in the world are we going to, if not to destruction?" Warning that the enemy would soon attack, Beauregard asked Miles to "wake up the authorities to the great danger," all due to a want of competent brigadiers to organize the army properly.

Cooper gradually relented, sending several officers from Virginia to act as bureau chiefs. Finally on March 21 he announced Senate confirmation of seven generals and the nomination of four others. Of the appointees only three were present at Corinth for active operations during the first week in April. Six brigade commanders remained in the army, holding the rank of colonel.

Even more distressing to the Confederate generals was the lack of suitable arms and ammunition. The new levies raised under Beauregard's call were generally unarmed, and the impoverished War Department could supply but few long arms and no sabers or pistols. Beauregard was forced by the emergency to appeal to the governors for shotguns "with bayonet attachments." Of those arms already in the hands of the troops many were obsolete and others were of so many varieties that ordnance officers were unable to maintain adequate supplies of ammunition. Hindman's brigade, one of Hardee's best units, had two regiments armed only with flintlock muskets. The soon-to-be-famous Kentucky Brigade of the Reserve Corps was handicapped by a serious logistical problem; their weapons were a mixture of Belgian rifles, flintlock muskets, squirrel rifles, and altered muskets, and each type required a different caliber of ammunition. Recognizing the critical deficiency in weapons, Ruggles was busily attempting to repair the dilapidated arms of the Corinth garrison as early as February 26.

Although Beauregard attempted to alleviate some of his ordnance difficulties by establishing a powder mill at Meridian and a percussion-cap manufactory at Columbus, Mississippi, both efforts failed.

The only significant success in arming the Confederate troops was achieved through the efforts of Sidney Johnston. When six thousand long Enfield rifles arrived through the blockade aboard the *Kate* in early February, over half (thirty-six hundred) were ordered to the West. Johnston then learned a few days later that the steamer *Victoria* had successfully run the blockade at New Orleans with fifteen thousand arms, and he asked for the entire cargo. Secretary of War Benjamin approved, and all were shipped to Tennessee. As late as the night of April 3 these Enfields were being received and distributed to the troops at Corinth. Ironically it was perhaps one of these Enfields that would play such a tragic part in the life of the man who had ardently sought them.

Since cannon also were lacking in the Army of the Mississippi, Beauregard was reduced to the necessity of issuing a proclamation on March 8, calling for plantation bells from the Mississippi Valley planters to be melted into field guns. The response was so favorable that by late March Beauregard advised Father Mullon of St. Patrick's Catholic Church in New Orleans that his offer of "the church going bell" was unnecessary. By that time Beauregard had a large number of plantation bells on hand at railroad stations and river depots. Plans were quickly made for their use in 12-pounder Napoleons and 6-pounder rifles, to be cast by the Natchez Foundry, and Leeds & Co., New Orleans. By April 1 eighteen batteries were serving with the army, apportioned among the various brigades. Nearly all of these batteries had six guns each, though most were of smoothbore pattern.

While the army was being reorganized for active service, the enemy failed to advance, making instead only infrequent reconnaissances. On March 20 and again on the twenty-fourth Union gunboats appeared at Eastport to exchange shots with the Confederate batteries. Although these encounters were reported, the generals at Corinth gave only passing notice. The growing Union concentration at Pittsburg Landing was of first importance.

From Bethel Station on March 24 Bushrod Johnson reported active road construction between the enemy camps at Pittsburg and Lew Wallace's position along the Purdy road. Except for their carrying off cotton and amassing artillery, the Union troops near Crump's Landing were remaining hidden in their camps. Johnson was concerned that preparations might be under way for a sudden attack on his position.

The same day, March 24, Sherman led a reconnaissance from Pittsburg Landing to Monterey. Sidney Johnston, showing his concern, included news of the movement in his dispatch to Richmond. Some of Forrest's cavalry were sent to investigate, and Major D. C. Kelly later reported that ten thousand infantry and eight hundred cavalry had encamped at Monterey that night.

Although Johnston soon learned that the enemy's numbers were exaggerated and that they had in fact returned to the river, it was felt that the Federals were surveying the terrain for an immediate offensive on Corinth. Johnston ordered reinforcements for his outpost at Burnsville and recalled the Eastport garrison to Iuka.

Despite the Union gunboat activity at Eastport, where a fight occurred as late as the twenty-fifth, Johnston correctly foresaw the impracticality of an enemy advance from that point. Spring rains had heavily mired the roads and flooded the creeks, imposing great obstacles to an invading army. The heavy 24-pounder guns were removed on the twenty-sixth, and the two regiments guarding Eastport abandoned the village that afternoon.

On Johnston's opposite flank, however, there was serious concern of an enemy thrust. Following Bushrod Johnson's report of a threatened attack in his sector, Benjamin F. Cheatham's brigade was sent as a reinforcement to Bethel Station. Beauregard considered this outpost so important that he sent detailed instructions for Cheatham's deployment. Included in the dispatch was some rather prophetic advice: ". . . be careful not to act on mere rumors and create false alarms." Unknowingly, Cheatham's presence at Bethel was to help precipitate the Battle of Shiloh.

As the final days of March passed there were renewed reports of Union reconnaissances. Although the Confederate high command was busily involved in reorganizing the army, strict measures were taken to prepare for an enemy advance. Martial law was declared along the Mobile & Ohio and Mississippi Central railroads on March 30.

When word was received of Sherman's naval expedition to Eastport, again there were fears of an attack on the Memphis & Charleston Railroad near Iuka. Despite preparations for active operations on the Corinth front, Braxton Bragg hastened two brigades to Iuka. Colonel B. H. Helm was ordered to burn the Florence bridge if the enemy passed Eastport. Much to everyone's relief it was learned on April 2 that the Federals had abandoned Eastport and sailed down-river.

Although Sidney Jonhston apparently did not regard the latest Eastport expedition as a serious threat, it was further evidence of an imminent Federal offensive. For nearly two weeks he had been burdened with administrative detail. His stated objective was to fight a battle and defeat the enemy, yet he seemed to be willing to await the enemy's movement.

That other, more aggressive plans were fermenting in Johnston's mind was soon to be demonstrated.

CHAPTER VII

A Rendezvous with Destiny

Among the most important units in Johnston's army during March, 1862, were two detached companies of shotgun-armed Louisiana cavalrymen. It was an unlikely prospect; their parent regiment, the 1st Louisiana Cavalry, although regarded as an effective unit, was torn by dissension. Less than three months later all but two of the regiment's captains were arrested for insubordination when they refused to serve under their commanding officer.

Following Johnston's retreat from Nashville in early March the 1st Louisiana was given a rather routine assignment. It was to take position on the army's left flank, watch for Buell's advance, and when it occurred, destroy bridges along the Central Alabama Railroad in the enemy's path. While waiting for Buell to move, the regiment's commander, Colonel John S. Scott, withdrew to Columbia, Tennessee, leaving two companies under Captain G. A. Scott of Company E in the vicinity of Nashville.

Captain Scott was a most effective officer.* His forty-man detachment routed a Federal scouting party on March 9, and he accurately estimated that thirty-two to thirty-five thousand enemy troops were occupying Nashville. Basing his action upon Captain Scott's able intelligence work, Colonel Scott fell back to Pulaski with his main column less than two weeks later. Before departing from Columbia, Scott burned the pike bridge over the Duck River.

The importance of this action was fully demonstrated when Scott learned in mid-March that Buell's troops had been unable to cross the Duck River. While his two detached companies watched Buell's

---

* Gustavius A. Scott was raised in Louisiana's East Feliciana Parish. His father, Alexander, was a prominent planter in the district, having over 640 acres under cultivation. Captain Scott commanded Company E of the 1st Louisiana Cavalry from September, 1861, to June 21, 1863. On that date he was killed in a skirmish near Clinch River, Tennessee.

90

ineffectual efforts to rebuild the bridge, Scott remained at Pulaski, forwarding government stores and rounding up the numerous stragglers from Johnston's army.

For a brief period Johnston overlooked the importance of Scott's intelligence operations. On March 20 he ordered Scott to retreat to Decatur, burning en route the railroad bridges in Tennessee. Several days later, following his arrival in Corinth, Johnston realized his mistake. Scott's men were providing such valuable information about enemy troop movements that on March 25 Johnston sent special instructions to Braxton Bragg not to interfere with the 1st Louisiana's deployment south of the Elk River. Accordingly when Nelson's troops forded the Duck River on March 29, Scott's two detached companies were nearby to observe their crossing. The news they reported was to have an important influence on Confederate destiny in the West.

Meanwhile, as the suspense involving enemy operations continued to intensify at Corinth, Sidney Johnston was in frequent communication with Richmond. Jefferson Davis, who had repeatedly expressed his confidence in Johnston's leadership, again offered encouragement. Lieutenant Thomas M. Jack, a member of the General's staff who had taken Johnston's personal explanation of the Fort Donelson disaster to Davis, returned about April 1, bringing important dispatches from Robert E. Lee and the president. Lee, acting as Davis's military adviser, assured Johnston that no one sympathized with his present difficulties more sincerely than he did. Lee's letter contained friendly, but specific advice: "I need not urge you, when your army is united, to deal a blow at the enemy in your front, if possible, before his rear gets up from Nashville."

Jefferson Davis's letter was even more significant and had a profound effect upon Johnston. Davis wrote: "If you can meet the division of the enemy moving from the Tennessee before it can make a junction with that advancing from Nashville the future will be brighter. If this cannot be done, our only hope is that the people of the Southwest will rally en masse . . . to oppose the vast army which will threaten the destruction of our country." Included in the Davis dispatch was an awesome reminder: "My confidence in you has never wavered, and I hope the public will soon give me credit for judgment rather than continue to arraign me for obstinacy. You have done wonderfully well. . . . I write in great haste, and feel that it would be worse than useless to point out to you how much depends upon you."

Johnston's course of action had been clearly defined. The faith that Lee and his close friend the President placed in him was more than a personal obligation; it was a matter of the deepest honor and the gravest responsibility. The Confederacy desperately needed a victory in this hour of crisis, and Sidney Johnston's personal behavior in the days ahead was to reflect this great burden.

Pittsburg Landing, Tennessee, lay nearly twenty-three miles north of Corinth. Yet prior to the Federal landing there little notice had been taken of the region. Daniel Ruggles had ordered a survey of the Tennessee River between Eastport and Pittsburg for possible defensive positions as late as March 7. The Louisiana captain, James Trezevant, who made the survey before March 11, did so without the benefit of a compass, square, or rule. His skeleton map was admittedly imperfect and his notes brief. Pittsburg Landing was portrayed as a good site from which to fight gunboats, though it offered few defensive positions along the interior roads as far south as Monterey.

Although preparations for an immediate offensive had been made following Johnston's arrival at Corinth, it was not until March 31 that a detailed reconnaissance of the country was ordered by headquarters. Chalmers was sent to Monterey as commander of the "advance" and instructed to make a thorough reconnaissance beyond Lick Creek with his brigade. Concurrently Bragg also ordered a second brigade under Colonel Randall Gibson to go to Monterey as a replacement for the lone regiment originally stationed there. Clanton's regiment of Alabama cavalry was sent along to screen the infantry.

That Johnston anticipated making an attack in the Pittsburg region as early as March 26 is evidenced by his correspondence of that date. Writing to Colonel James E. Mathews, Johnston directed that a "corps of at least twenty reliable citizens [be formed] who are familiar with this section of country, particularly that portion of it lying between the Memphis & Charleston and Mobile & Ohio Railroads and the Tennessee River." Urging prompt action and "judicious" selections, he informed Mathews that they would be "used as guides."

On April 1 Johnston issued special orders preparatory to active operations. Both the First and Third corps were to be "placed in readiness for a field movement and to meet the enemy within twenty-four hours." Bragg's corps would remain behind to counter the movement of Sherman's division, which was then threatening Eastport. On the same day Beauregard asked Polk for information about the enemy concentration at Pittsburg, adding "it would not be well to awaken the enemy's suspicions to any intention on our part of advancing in that direction." Only the prospect of Van Dorn's reinforcements arriving in time for the impending battle and the want of better organization apparently caused Johnston to delay an immediate advance.

Following a review of his troops on April 2, however, there was a

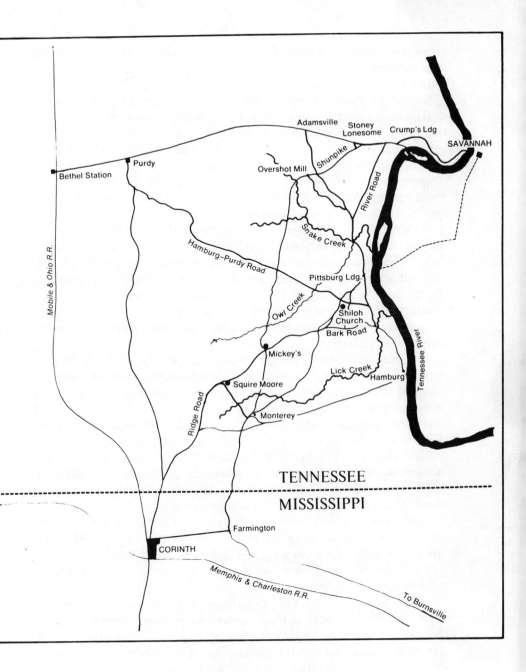

MAP 3
Campaign of Shiloh
March–April, 1862 (Chapters 6–7)

dramatic change in Johnston's plans as the result of several unforeseen developments.

At Bethel Station, twenty-three miles northwest of Corinth, the Confederate troop strength had remained heavy despite the false alarm occasioned by Lew Wallace's initial occupation of Crump's Landing. The vulnerability of the Mobile & Ohio Railroad had already been demonstrated, and the nearby enemy concentration along the Tennessee was continued cause for anxiety. Following Bushrod Johnson's arrival in mid-March and his subsequent report of a threatened enemy attack, Benjamin F. Cheatham had been ordered to Bethel Station to assume command.

Taking W. H. Stephens's brigade with him, Cheatham had to march overland from Corinth and did not arrive until about April 1. While Cheatham was en route, a clash of pickets occurred in Bushrod Johnson's front, which drew further attention to the area. At Purdy, four miles east of Bethel, Johnson maintained an outpost of infantry and cavalry. Here they were separated from the enemy by only eleven miles, Wood's 3d Brigade of Lew Wallace's division being at Adamsville.

On March 31 the post commander at Purdy, Colonel Preston Smith of the 154th (Senior) Tennessee Infantry, heard an unusual amount of drumming in the enemy camps. Attempting to learn what the enemy was up to, Smith sent out a detachment of Mississippi and Alabama cavalry under Lieutenant Colonel Richard H. Brewer. Brewer was told to reconnoiter as far as Adamsville, if practicable, before returning. Taking thirty-five men, Brewer soon met and routed a company of Federal cavalry pickets along the Purdy road. Sergeant E. T. Cook and two privates of the 5th Ohio Cavalry were taken prisoner and brought to Purdy for interrogation.

Smith soon learned from the prisoners that the Federals numbered at least three brigades in his front, commanded by Lew Wallace. Smith reported this to brigade headquarters and remarked that two of the enemy's brigades were on the near side of Adamsville and were said to be moving against Purdy.

When Cheatham arrived at Bethel shortly thereafter, his instructions concerned purely defensive operations. Beauregard's orders of March 27 asked that he station a strong outpost detachment at Purdy, consisting of "at least two regiments and two or four pieces of artillery." Moreover Cheatham was to "reconnoiter personally, immediately upon arrival at Bethel, the roads leading to and from that place to a distance of about five miles."

By April 1, with Confederate headquarters actively planning an offensive, Beauregard wanted detailed information about the roads leading to the Tennessee. Since he had not heard from Cheatham, Beauregard sent word on that date to Polk to make sure that Cheatham made the reconnaissance "as close to the enemy's position as safety to the reconnoitering officers and escort will permit." Cheatham, who had just arrived at Bethel, planned the mission for the next day.

Following Beauregard's instructions, Cheatham advanced on April 2 with the strong outpost detachment ordered for Purdy and apparently completed his personal reconnaissance.

The movement of this sizable force of Confederate troops was observed by Federal scouts lurking in the vicinity. Upon receipt of this information Colonel Charles R. Woods, commanding at Adamsville, feared an attack on his isolated brigade. He immediately sent a courier to Lew Wallace at Crump's Landing to warn that the Confederates were advancing in his front.

Wallace responded to the apparent crisis by promptly ordering his First and Second Brigades to go to Woods's relief.

Although it was evening when the men of the First Brigade were called to arms, the brigade, under Colonel Morgan L. Smith, set out in what Wallace later described as an incredibly short time. The Second Brigade at Stoney Lonesome fell in behind as Smith's column sped by. Wallace remembered with pride years later that his two brigades double-quicked the two and one half miles to Adamsville with only three short rests. Before midnight the whole division stood in line of battle, ready for an attack.

To the wary cavalry scouts of Cheatham's division, however, the sudden appearance of Wallace's entire division implied that an attack was imminent on the Confederate outpost at Purdy. It was simply a matter of error compounded by error. Cheatham learned of the large-scale enemy movements before 10 P.M. and sent an urgent telegram to Polk, his corps commander, warning that the enemy was marching in force along the Purdy road. Polk gave the dispatch top priority and sent it on to Beauregard without delay.

Beauregard, rather by an odd combination of circumstances, was now to make one of the truly crucial decisions of the war. He was aware that Jefferson Davis's letter of March 26 urged an attack before the two enemy columns were united. Moreover, by coincidence news had recently arrived of Buell's army crossing the Duck River. Mistakenly interpreting Lew Wallace's aggressiveness in Cheatham's front as a prelude to an advance, and that "the junction of the enemy's armies was near at hand," Beauregard endorsed Cheatham's telegram: "Now is the moment to advance and strike the enemy at Pittsburg Landing." The dispatch was promptly sent to the adjutant general's office with another annotation: "Colonel Jordan had better carry this in person to General Johnston and explain the military situation.—G. T. B."

Colonel Thomas Jordan had been announced as the army's adju-

COLONEL THOMAS JORDAN. A close friend of Beauregard's, Jordan was the army's newly appointed assistant adjutant general. Educated at West Point, where he was the roommate of William T. Sherman, he had a prominent role at Shiloh, if ill-fated. Acting as Beauregard's spokesman, Jordan argued successfully for an offensive commitment on the night of April 2, based upon Lew Wallace's defensive maneuvering in front of Cheatham near Bethel Station. His subsequent authorship of the Shiloh battle orders, requiring deployment of Hardee's, Bragg's, and Polk's corps in three tandem lines, was one of the battle's worst mistakes. On the battlefield Jordan roamed behind the lines, ordering inactive troops toward the sound of the heaviest firing. His peremptory order to Cheatham at 11:00 A.M. on Sunday to charge the enemy began the first of the piecemeal assaults on the Hornets' Nest. (LIBRARY OF CONGRESS)

tant general only two days earlier. A graduate of West Point and the former roommate of William Tecumseh Sherman, Jordan was an intimate friend of Beauregard's and his former chief of staff during the Bull Run Campaign. On March 29, following the loss of New Madrid, Brigadier General W. W. Mackall, Sidney Johnston's adjutant general, had been sent to command at Island No. 10. Upon Mackall's departure Jordan assumed the vacant position.

Jordan had been chatting with Colonel Jacob Thompson, the former U. S. Secretary of the Interior, when the Cheatham dispatch was brought in after 10 P.M. on April 2. After reading it to Thompson, Jordan took the note to Johnston's headquarters and handed it to the General in the presence of his staff. Johnston read the telegram and endorsements without comment. He then walked across the street to confer with Bragg at his quarters, Jordan following behind.

Bragg was found asleep and was roused out of bed in his nightshirt. When Bragg finished reading the dispatch, Jordan said a discussion followed in which Bragg agreed with Beauregard's conclusion. Yet Johnston, it was said, offered strong objections to the plan, stating that the army's offensive capability was diminished by inexperience and a lack of equipment. Furthermore he noted that the Reserve Corps was scattered at several locations along the Memphis & Charleston Railroad and would have to be assembled quickly. According to Jordan his own comments on behalf of Beauregard influenced the final decision. Jordan professed to have detailed knowledge of Beauregard's plans and argued that Beauregard felt it necessary to attack the Federals before they were ready to advance. He further estimated that the Reserve Corps could be quickly concentrated by rail at Burnsville for a march to Monterey.

Although other testimony is lacking, it is likely that Jordan's account is erroneous. Johnston had already decided to attack Pittsburg Landing prior to April 2.* Jordan's statement, written many years after the war, is inconsistent not only with Johnston's correspondence and character, but Bragg's as well.

Johnston habitually remained passive during critical discussions, often weighing each individual's remarks in silence despite strong personal convictions. Major E. W. Munford, an aide-de-camp, described Johnston as being "slow of speech" and unable to express his "high intellectual worth," a defect of which he was fully aware. Yet Johnston invariably displayed great self-control. He was a man of intense thought, and most often kept silence as to his own plans.

Bragg, on the other hand, was outspoken in his criticism of the army's lack of discipline. His contemporary documents consistently disparage the effectiveness of Johnston's army. Just two weeks earlier Bragg had refused to advance because of the army's poor condition.

It is quite possible that Jordan, following the passing of many years, may have attributed to Johnston what perhaps were derogatory remarks by Bragg. Indeed, there is significant evidence that the question in consideration during the Bragg-Jordan-Johnston midnight conference was actually the matter of timing—of when to attack.

That Johnston made the final decision to attack is acknowledged by all. Unquestionably Beauregard's suggestion that now was the time to advance was of influence. Johnston probably preferred to attempt the attack after Van Dorn's arrival. Yet Beauregard's estimate of urgency, as elaborated by Jordan, compelled a decision. That Johnston's final decision was based on the rapid approach of Buell's army to a junction with Grant's troops along the Tennessee is evidenced by his telegram to Jefferson Davis of the following day. According to Beauregard it was learned "from a reliable quarter" on the night of April 2 that the junction of the two enemy armies was near at hand. This information was probably received from the small but vital Confederate cavalry detachment north of the Tennessee under Captain G. A. Scott. Buell was said to be in motion, thirty thousand strong, from Columbia to Savannah, via Clifton, Tennessee.

* See pages 91–92.

There are no known records that provide the exact time this dispatch was received at Confederate headquarters, but the news of Lew Wallace's threatened attack near Purdy more or less coincided. Wallace's demonstration thus gave credibility to the prospect of an impending junction. Nelson's advance division of Buell's army had actually reached Proctor's Furnace, five miles from Waynesboro, on the evening of April 2, following a day's march of sixteen miles. At the time they were separated from Grant's base at Savannah by only thirty-five miles.

Following a lengthy conference Johnston ordered preparations for an immediate advance. Jordan sat at a table in Bragg's bedchamber and drafted a circular to Bragg, Polk, and Hardee. The corps commanders were to have their commands "in hand ready to advance" by 6 A.M. on April 3 with three days' cooked rations in haversacks and one hundred rounds of small arms ammunition issued. Couriers immediately were sent to the respective headquarters with the circulars, signed receipts for which were obtained from each general by 1:40 A.M. Only Breckenridge, commanding the Reserve Corps, was notified by telegraph.

After leaving Bragg's quarters, Jordan went directly to the tent of Captain A. R. Chisolm, Beauregard's aide-de-camp, and roused him from bed. Chisolm was instructed to waken Beauregard at about dawn (5 A.M.) and inform him of Johnston's decision to attack.

When Chisolm arrived at Beauregard's quarters the following morning, the general was already awake and displayed a number of notes he had made on the backs of telegrams and envelopes during the night. They were read to Chisolm, who made a copy before the originals were handed to Jordan about 7 A.M. Beauregard had anticipated Johnston's decision and had drafted a proposed plan of operations during the night. Jordan was instructed to use these notes as the basis for drawing up marching orders and a plan of attack.

When Jordan left soon thereafter, he took with him Beauregard's sketch of the roads leading to Pittsburg Landing so as to prepare the required orders accurately. On his way to have breakfast, Jordan met Johnston, who was on his way to Beauregard's quarters. Following a hasty breakfast Jordan rejoined the generals. A discussion was already in progress, and Jordan overheard Beauregard explaining his plan of operations to Johnston. Bragg came in soon thereafter, followed by Polk and Hardee about 10 A.M. According to Jordan Beauregard was required to explain his plans in detail before they were accepted by Johnston.

What Beauregard then proposed was far from one of the most decisive battles of the war. It was, in essence, merely a large-scale raid. The Confederate objective would be to "strike a sudden blow at the enemy. . . . By a rapid and vigorous attack on General Grant . . . " said Beauregard, "he would be beaten back to his transports and the river, or captured, in time to enable us to profit by the victory, and remove to the rear all the stores and munitions that would fall into our hands in such an event before the arrival of General Buell's army on the scene." Thereafter the Confederates would return to Corinth, the strategic point of the campaign, by pre-arranged plan, "[as] it was never intended to hold a position so near the river."

By the signed affidavit of Jordan, dated April 18, 1862, Johnston ultimately accepted Beauregard's plan of operations without a single modification. According to Beauregard it had been agreed following Johnston's arrival in Corinth that all orders relating to operations would be left in Beauregard's hands. Accordingly the rough notes Beauregard had made during the night were drawn up later that day as Special Orders No. 8 and formally signed by Johnston. Since Jordan had previously taken Beauregard's map of the area to his office, Beauregard drew a sketch of the country roads in pencil on the tabletop to explain his plans further. Several years later, when the table was sent as office furniture to Charleston, South Carolina, this pencil sketch was still visible.

As it was late morning when the plans were made final, and since the preparation of written orders had not yet been undertaken by Jordan, Beauregard gave verbal orders so that the movement could begin by noon. The routes were described to each general, and an order of march was designated.

Special Orders No. 8, issued by Adjutant General Jordan later that afternoon, specified that Hardee was to lead the advance from Corinth along the twenty-three-mile main road to Pittsburg, also known as the Ridge road. Bragg's Second Corps would take the lower road to Monterey, distant about twelve miles. Later Polk's First Corps would follow in the rear of Hardee's troops along the Ridge road. Breckenridge's Reserve Corps was to concentrate at Monterey "by the shortest and best routes" after Bragg's corps had moved on.

Unfortunately there was a mixup in communications, and the army did not move on time. Beauregard stated that he positively gave instructions for the leading corps to march by twelve noon without further orders. From the evidence it appears that the narrow streets of Corinth were jammed with Bragg's, Polk's, and Hardee's troops. The men of all three corps had been alerted during the early-morning hours of April 3, and most were ready to march soon thereafter. In the absence of written orders from the adjutant general's office Bragg, as chief of staff, had sent a directive to Hardee ordering him to march "as soon as practicable." Captain B. B. Waddell, aide-de-camp of General Beauregard, was told to report to Hardee with two guides. Although Waddell was soon on hand, Hardee had difficulty in organizing his corps after receiving Bragg's order. At least two of Polk's brigades were camped in the city, and it was said that these troops had clogged the Corinth streets ahead of some of Hardee's regiments and were slow in moving their wagons and artillery aside to let Hardee's men through. By Jordan's account Hardee had to ride to Beauregard's headquarters late on the afternoon of the third and report that his men could not pass. When Beauregard's aide located Polk, the gray-haired bishop-general reportedly was awaiting clarification by written order before moving.

It was almost 3 P.M. before some of the regiments in Brigadier General S. A. M. Wood's brigade began to march. One regiment had been ready and waiting nine hours earlier. Several units of Hardee's advance actually started about 11 A.M., causing the corps to be widely scattered along the Ridge road.

Despite the congestion most of Hardee's men cleared Corinth late in the afternoon of April 3, although at least one regiment did not leave until the evening of the following day. In order to make up for lost time the 44th Tennessee of Wood's brigade marched for nine hours before bivouacking en route after midnight. They were then several miles short of their intended destination, a farmhouse known as Mickey's.

Near day's end the guides accompanying Hardee's advance mentioned the proximity of a clear spring along a seldom-used road adjacent to the Confederate line of march. Without further consultation a portion of Hardee's corps was led off down the blind road to camp near the spring for the night. No one was sent to notify Polk's corps, however, which was marching in Hardee's rear, a half-hour behind.

When Polk's corps approached the blind cutoff, they found the main road ahead unoccupied and passed on, planning to bivouac after they reached Hardee's rear guard. Instead of finding the main column ahead, they ran into Hardee's advance picket a mile beyond his bivouac. It was already past midnight, and Polk's exhausted soldiers dropped along the roadside to sleep.

Early on the morning of the fourth Hardee's corps marched back to the Corinth and Pittsburg road and found it blocked with Polk's troops. The road was too narrow to permit the wagons and artillery of Hardee's command to pass. Teamsters, riflemen, and officers worked together to lift Polk's wagons aside and push Hardee's train through, but a lengthy delay resulted. When the road was finally cleared, Polk advanced only a short distance before stopping again, to await the arrival of one of Bragg's divisions, marching by the Monterey–Purdy road.

Braxton Bragg's troubles also had been many during the first day's march. According to Special Orders No. 8 Bragg was to split his corps after reaching Monterey and advance along two separate roads to arrive at the Ridge road before sunset on April 3. Bragg's troops were considered to be the best trained and disciplined in Johnston's army, and Beauregard had relied heavily on this factor in formulating his plans.

Bragg got off to a bad start when his assistant adjutant general, George G. Gardner, sent a communiqué to Daniel Ruggles ordering preparations for a movement "early tomorrow morning, 6 A.M." The dispatch was dated April 3, and Ruggles construed "tomorrow morning" to mean April 4. Gardner, of course, had sent the message by Bragg's direction shortly after midnight following the Bragg-Johnston-Jordan midnight conference of April 2. By "tomorrow morning" he meant April 3.

Since the actual orders to march were not given until late on the morning of April 3 (verbally by Beauregard), Ruggles was taken by surprise, and his division was apparently unready.

It was later that afternoon before Withers's division of Bragg's corps began the advance to Monterey along the lower road. This road was even narrower and in worse condition than the Ridge road taken by Hardee. Bragg's transportation was also slow in moving and was badly handled. The overloaded baggage wagons soon bogged down in the soft roads, and despite the short eleven-mile distance to Monterey the last of Withers's column did not arrive until late on the night of the third.

Bragg's other division, Ruggles's, was even later in starting and was forced to bivouac along the muddy road that night. Despite preparations for an early advance the following morning it was 11 A.M. before Ruggles's advance approached Monterey.

Bragg was greatly disappointed. His orders were to be in position at the junction of the Corinth–Pittsburg and Monterey–Purdy roads with Ruggles's division early on the morning of April 4. Withers's division was supposed to be even farther ahead, near Mickey's house, at the junction of the Ridge and Monterey–Savannah roads.

Bragg, blaming the ignorance of Ruggles's guide and having news of the Monterey–Purdy Road's poor condition, decided to change his route of march. Instead of sending Ruggles along the Monterey–Purdy road, as planned, he ordered that commander to follow Withers's troops marching up the Monterey–Savannah road to Mickey's. Since Polk's corps would be waiting at the intersection of the Ridge and Monterey–Purdy roads, however, Bragg sent a note to Polk at 10 A.M. on the fourth, notifying him of the change in plans.

Polk, however, had already arrived at the intersection and was awaiting the appearance of Ruggles's division before Bragg's courier arrived. The delay caused Polk's corps to bivouac along the Corinth–

Pittsburg road at nightfall of the fourth, after marching only six or seven miles during the entire day.

During the afternoon of the fourth a light rain began to fall, soaking the already soft roads. Ruggles, who was lagging behind Withers, fell even farther back. At nightfall his leading brigade bivouacked only several miles beyond Monterey. Ahead, Withers's division camped that night at their objective, Mickey's house, one full day behind schedule.

On the night of April 4 the Confederate troops were woefully dispersed. Hardee's corps was in advance along the Corinth–Pittsburg road about three miles from Shiloh Church. Polk was behind him on the same road within a few miles of Mickey's with two divisions under Clark and Cheatham. Bragg's advance division, Withers's, lay along the Monterey–Savannah road at its intersection with the Ridge road at Mickey's. Ruggles was between Monterey and Mickey's, and Breckenridge's Reserve Corps had finally reached the vicinity of Monterey after an all-day, twenty-three-mile march from Burnsville. Breckenridge's artillery, however, was stuck in mud along the treacherous road from Farmington, and before midnight word was received that his entire train was immobilized.

To the Confederate high command the delays of April 3 and 4 had not been entirely unexpected. Both Beauregard and Johnston spent the afternoon of April 3 at Corinth issuing orders and preparing for the advance. Their final preparations included notifying President Davis by ciphered telegram of the impending battle. "Buell is in motion, 30,000 strong . . . to [join Grant at] Savannah," wrote Johnston. "Hope engagement before Buell can form junction." From Confederate headquarters also came an address to the soldiers of the army urging them to do their duty: ". . . with the trust that God is with us your generals will lead you confidently to the combat, assured of success," announced the commanding general.

Because of the heavy administrative workload it was 11:15 A.M. on Friday, April 4, before Beauregard and his staff mounted their horses and started for the front. About three hours later they rode into Monterey and learned that Johnston had also just arrived.

Sidney Johnston's departure from Corinth at ten o'clock the same morning was well remembered by Mrs. William M. Inge nearly sixty years later. It was Mrs. Inge's "Rose Cottage" home that served as Johnston's headquarters during his stay in Corinth. Mrs. Inge later described how the general's blue eyes gleamed as he prepared to ride away. When she asked the general if she might fix him a couple of sandwiches and some cake, he politely refused, saying, "No, thank you, Mrs. Inge, we soldiers travel light." Without Johnston's knowledge, however, Mrs. Inge managed to slip two sandwiches and a piece of cake into his coat pocket before he rode off. As Johnston prepared to depart, a staff officer, Edward Munford, saw him pause on the door step of his headquarters, lost in thought. Finally looking up, Johnston was heard to mutter, "Yes, I believe I have overlooked nothing."

By one o'clock Johnston was at Monterey, believing that Hardee, Polk, and Bragg were nearing their designated positions. Although he soon learned of the costly delays, several Union prisoners were brought in during the evening of the fourth from whom it was learned that the Confederate approach was as yet unsuspected.

During the afternoon and evening of April 4 Johnston conferred with Beauregard, Bragg, and Breckenridge. Because of the meeting's obvious importance Breckenridge had galloped through the rain to Monterey, although his corps was still bogged down in the mud en route from Farmington.

After discussing the progress of the army, Johnston issued instructions for a full-scale attack early the following morning. Polk, who was not present at the conference, was notified to march with his command promptly at 3 A.M. in support of Bragg and Hardee. Polk later acknowledged receipt of this dispatch and promised to carry out his orders. According to Major Munford plans were made with the utmost care for the morning's attack on the enemy camps. Hours were prescribed for breaking camp, distances and marching times were calculated, and routes for proper deployment were described. By 7 A.M. the army was to be fully deployed. An hour later the battle was to begin.

Having made preparations for the army's rapid movement before dawn, Johnston and his generals lay down for a short night's rest. About 2 A.M. on the fifth the low-hanging clouds that had been sending intermittent showers during the previous day were displaced by huge storm clouds. The rain fell in torrents, and Johnston's army, exposed on the open ground without tents, was fully drenched.

At 3 A.M., with the storm still raging, the men were called into line, but Bragg and the other corps commanders were forced to postpone any movement until dawn. In the pitch darkness a movement over the flooded roads with the cold, driving rain beating down was impossible.

About five o'clock the storm subsided, but the roads had become vast quagmires of mud and standing water.

It was 7 A.M. before Bragg's troops were under way. Ruggles's march from the vicinity of Monterey was also delayed by the flooded road. At daylight Polk, after marching a short distance to the Mickey's house intersection, ran into Bragg's men and had to wait for them to pass. Hardee's corps had gone forward at dawn, and was within two miles of the enemy camps at Shiloh Church and in line of battle before 10 A.M. However, their wagons loaded with munitions and baggage remained behind on the Ridge road, clogging the narrow passageway.

By Jordan's original plan of operations the right flank of the Confederate army was to be extended to Lick Creek by either a brigade or division from Bragg's corps. The extent of open ground remaining after Hardee's corps had deployed would determine the size of the organization required. At Bragg's headquarters near Mickey's house on Friday night, April 4, Bragg decided to detach only a brigade for this purpose. Instructions were given to Brigadier General Adley H. Gladden of Withers's division to move his brigade in advance and take position on Hardee's right. Gladden, however, was well down the Monterey–Savannah road, behind Chalmers's brigade. In the sea of mud created by the heavy downpour it required a great amount of time for Gladden to pass Chalmers. Jackson's brigade, which was originally behind Gladden, was forced to wait for both brigades to clear its front. Ruggles's trailing division, meanwhile, was delayed when its advance brigade came up with Jackson's immobilized troops.

It was about 10 A.M. when Gladden began to file into line abreast of Hardee's battle line. Chalmers then followed, forming on the right rear of Gladden when it was found that an interval still existed between the Confederate right and Lick Creek. Chalmers deployed his brigade in echelon, extending to a fork in Lick Creek, thus becoming the extreme right of the Confederate army. Jackson, who followed Chalmers, deployed directly on his left, forming a second line about twelve noon.

Meanwhile Sidney Johnston had grown impatient with the delay. By Beauregard's original design the first line of battle was to have deployed early on the morning of April 4. When that became impossible, 8 A.M. on the fifth was agreed upon as a practical time to launch the attack. Four hours beyond that point Johnston was provoked into taking matters into his own hands.

Both Johnston and Beauregard had slept at Monterey on the night of the fourth. Leaving Monterey just after daylight, the two generals approached Bragg's position at Mickey's about 8:30 A.M. Bragg, who was awaiting improved weather conditions, was told to advance, and the generals passed on, arriving in the rear of Hardee's deployed line soon thereafter.

By late morning Johnston became concerned when Ruggles's division failed to follow Withers's three brigades into the second line of battle. Ruggles would form the entire left wing of the second line, and no movement could be initiated without his six thousand men. Major Munford of Johnston's staff was sent to Bragg to find out why the missing troops were not in position. Bragg could not explain their absence, and he sent to the rear for an explanation. Another hour passed, and Ruggles still had not been heard from. Johnston again sent Munford to Bragg for information. Again Bragg could not answer, and only repeated his earlier statement that information would be forwarded.

It was half past twelve o'clock, and Johnston was quite angry. Glancing first at his pocket watch, then at the towering sun, Johnston exclaimed, "This is perfectly puerile! This is not war!—Let us have our horses." In the company of Munford and two other staff officers Johnston rode back along the roadway until he found Ruggles's troops standing motionless in an open field.

Brigadier General Daniel Ruggles was a curious figure in the Confederate command structure. His stern New England background and domineering disposition made him unpopular with many of his subordinates. A former West Point regular, he was considered a strict disciplinarian who apparently held himself aloof from volunteers. His clerk was sometimes made to sleep at night on top of a writing table so as to be ready to write orders at a moment's notice.

According to Munford Ruggles's way was blocked by some of Polk's troops who had moved along the Ridge road after Bragg's First Division had passed. One of Ruggles's men recorded in his diary, however, that "tremendous" firing had been heard ahead, and his impression was that Ruggles ordered his brigade out of the narrow, wagon-cluttered roadway so as to find a way through the woods and come into position on the left in time to join in the fighting. Ruggles's scouts were sent out in several directions to learn if the entire army was engaged.

Johnston may have arrived while Ruggles was waiting for his scouts to report. By Johnston's orders the Ridge road was soon cleared, and Ruggles's troops were moved back into column. Polk had been instructed by Johnston when he passed Mickey's that morning to "move promptly in rear of General Bragg" so as to make room for Breckenridge's Reserve Corps, which was to follow. Thus it is possible that several regimental or brigade commanders in Polk's lead division, Clark's, may have been overzealous in carrying out these orders before Ruggles's tardy division appeared. A huge gap that had existed earlier in the day between Jackson's brigade of Bragg's First Division and Ruggles's division was probably contributory to the difficulty.

Regardless of responsibility, it was about 4 P.M. before Ruggles's three brigades were in position behind Hardee's front line. Gibson's brigade deployed on the immediate left of the Corinth and Pittsburg road, forming the division's right. Anderson's brigade comprised the center, and Pond's brigade the far left, stretching nearly to Winningham Branch of Owl Creek.

Once Ruggles's division had cleared the intersection at Mickey's,

Polk's command moved up quickly. The men of Clark's division, who had been under arms since 3 A.M., waited five hours at Mickey's for all of Bragg's corps to pass. It was nearly dark before they came forward on the Ridge road and bivouacked in column of brigades behind the center of Bragg's battle line. Cheatham's division of Polk's corps arrived after dark, having marched that morning from Purdy, a distance of about thirteen miles. Cheatham, whose fateful telegram on the night of April 2 had contributed to the decision to launch an attack, had been instructed to defend Bethel Station and Purdy if attacked, otherwise to march to Monterey and there join Polk's corps. Although Cheatham reported that the enemy was quiet in front of Purdy on April 3, he did not decide on an advance until Saturday morning, April 5.

Breckenridge's Reserve Corps was the last to file down the Ridge road, camping about a mile short of the Bark road intersection during the night. Breckenridge's march had covered twenty-three torturous miles from Burnsville to the vicinity of Monterey during the fourth. The roads had been far worse than those from Corinth. Breckenridge's artillery became stuck in the mud so many times along the way that they did not catch up with the infantry until just before dawn on April 5. When the weary Reserve Corps camped after nightfall on the fifth, they had marched farther than any other troops in Johnston's army, and in less time.

While Bragg's, Polk's, and Breckenridge's troops were floundering in the mud during the fifth, Hardee's men were waiting in line of battle, momentarily expecting orders to advance. When Johnston went to the rear to look for Ruggles, Beauregard had remained with the front line. Although still feeling the effects of his long illness, Beauregard talked with Hardee at noon and was asked to ride in front of the battle line so that the men would know he was with them in the field. Beauregard at first professed sickness, but later agreed to review the line provided there be no cheering, which might alert the enemy. The word was soon passed, and Beauregard briskly rode along the front, his staff trotting along behind.

By midafternoon Beauregard had returned to his temporary headquarters at the intersection of the Corinth–Pittsburg and Bark roads to await the arrival of Polk's corps. Bragg, whose troops were finally in position about 4 P.M., joined Beauregard at his temporary headquarters soon thereafter. Bragg apparently was in a surly mood. After discussing the extended delay in moving the army into position, the wanton disregard of secrecy on the part of the troops, and a lack of sufficient provisions, Bragg and Beauregard agreed that it would be best to withdraw the army to Corinth without a battle. Polk, whose troops were then moving forward on the Ridge road, was immediately sent for. When Polk arrived, he was treated rather harshly by Beauregard, who implied that his troops had been responsible for the delay. Polk had differed with Beauregard before, and he argued vigorously that he had been unable to move his corps until the troops ahead had cleared the intersection at Mickey's in midafternoon.

While this heated discussion was taking place, Johnston rode up, having passed among Bragg's troops to offer encouragement on his way back from looking for Ruggles. When he learned what had occurred, Johnston was shocked, especially by Beauregard's proposal of a withdrawal.

It was nearly 5 P.M. With Generals Bragg, Polk, Beauregard, and Johnston standing in the middle of the road and their respective staffs waiting nervously to the side, an informal council of war was held to decide if a battle should be fought at all. Beauregard apparently did much of the talking. It was his contention that the noise of the inexperienced troops and the delay in forming the army for attack had served notice to the enemy, who would be found "entrenched to the eyes" and ready for an attack. Moreover he stated that Bragg's men had consumed their five-day supply of rations in less than three days. For these reasons Beauregard urged that the attack be abandoned and the army returned to Corinth.

Johnston said little but asked for Polk's opinion. Polk's reply was that his troops were still in good condition, that they were eager for

GENERAL P. G. T. BEAUREGARD. The popular hero of Fort Sumter and First Bull Run, Beauregard had come west to command in the Mississippi Valley. Beauregard was afflicted with a chronic respiratory infection which impaired his effectiveness before Shiloh. Bold in his design to strike Grant's vulnerable camp at Pittsburg Landing, Beauregard suddenly lost his nerve the evening before the plan was to be carried out. His failure to obtain accurate information on front-line conditions following Johnston's death and his carelessness that night in not detecting the arrival of Buell's reinforcements were major factors contributing to the Confederate defeat on Monday. (U. S. SIGNAL CORPS PHOTO [BRADY COLLECTION], NATIONAL ARCHIVES)

the battle, and he thought the army should attack. The matter of provisions again being mentioned, Johnston summoned Colonel William Preston of his staff and asked him to find Breckenridge in order to learn the condition of the Reserve Corps. Before Preston departed, Breckinridge trotted up and reported to Johnston that his men had ample provisions.

Without display of emotion Johnston quietly but firmly remarked, "Gentlemen, we shall attack at daylight tomorrow." Abruptly the conference ended, and the generals went to their commands. Turning to leave, Johnston displayed his customary self-control. When out of earshot, he confided to Preston, his close friend and brother of his first wife, "I would fight them [the enemy] if they were a million. They can present no greater front between these two creeks than we can; and the more they crowd in there, the worse we can make it for them . . . Polk is a true soldier and a friend."

Major Munford, another close friend, also talked with Johnston just after the impromptu council of war. Munford knew that it was Johnston's nature not to betray emotion; yet he saw that despite Johnston's exterior calm, he was deeply aroused.

There is substantial evidence that at the time Sidney Johnston was greatly disappointed with Beauregard. After he had allowed the popular hero of Fort Sumter and Manassas to plan and direct much of the campaign, Beauregard had suddenly shown a lack of confidence on the very eve of battle. Such conduct was not understandable to the determined Johnston. According to Dr. D. W. Yandell, Johnston's personal physician, the General called him aside that evening for a private talk. Dr. Yandell stated that Beauregard was as yet a very sick man and that his opinions should be largely disregarded, implying that the illness had temporarily affected his mind. Beauregard's role on the following day may have been influenced accordingly. The next morning Johnston instructed General Beauregard to remain behind in the army's rear, sending forward reinforcements and directing munitions to the front.

As Johnston had once remarked, he would put his trust in the "iron dice of battle." The elaborate plans that had been made would not now be changed. The overall responsibility had always been Johnston's, but Beauregard's late-hour dissent placed the burden of fighting the coming battle solely on Sidney Johnston. Johnston revealed his great determination to his aide Munford. "I have ordered a battle for tomorrow at daylight, and I intend to 'hammer 'em'!" Preston wrote less than two weeks later that Johnston was anxious to attack that evening for fear the enemy would discover the Confederate army's presence. The fatigued condition of many of the troops dissuaded him, however, and he agreed to wait until morning.

To many of the troops the coming battle was a grand adventure. Most had never been in combat, although the war was nearly a year old. "I have a great anxiety to see and be in a great battle," Quartermaster Frank M. Gailer had written several weeks before. "If we do have one it will be one of the fiercest of the war. We have retreated as far South as we can go and if we don't fight now we might as well give up." On the morning of the fifth, when Beauregard and his staff had passed the waiting lines of infantry, a private in Ruggles's division described their "breathless anxiety" as Beauregard trotted by saying, "Fire low, boys, fire low." When firing was later heard ahead, the men could hardly be restrained from rushing forward, and they began laughing and shouting. Polk's new battle flags, ordered from Lovell at New Orleans, were unfurled and displayed to the men. There was much excitement.

By nightfall, after a day of marching and waiting, the ardor had diminished. The 38th Tennessee of Bragg's corps was by now without rations, and the men spread their blankets on the hard clay and went to sleep, supperless. Some of Breckenridge's Kentuckians were more fortunate. After consuming the last of their rain-soaked rations earlier in the day, they scared a rabbit out of the brush near camp and ran it down. That night the hungry soldiers dined on barbecued rabbit and ash cakes (cornmeal, salt, and water placed between two cabbage leaves and cooked in the red-hot ashes).

The lack of provisions was so widespread, however, that General Bragg and some of his staff spent much of the night trying to bring up the army's supply wagons. Their efforts proved unsuccessful, and one of Bragg's men later complained that the wagons never did arrive.

The Confederate army encamped for the night within two miles of Shiloh Church. By original estimate, Confederate headquarters on April 3 placed the Union lines about a mile in advance of Shiloh Church. Scouts and cavalry detachments had been ordered to observe the enemy's camps continually. By nightfall of the fifth it was known that the first line of enemy camps lay near the church site, running nearly east and west from Owl Creek toward Lick Creek.

James R. Chalmers of Bragg's corps had been given responsibility for much of the reconnaissance work, yet it was his cavalry that nearly betrayed the impending attack. Chalmers had been ordered to Monterey about March 31 as commander of the "advance." By Bragg's orders Chalmers was to reconnoiter thoroughly the country across Lick Creek in the direction of Pittsburg Landing. Chalmers reported on April 2 that a detachment of Roddey's Cavalry had thoroughly scouted the Lick Creek area and found the creek to be impassable by infantry along the Hamburg–Savannah road. Accordingly Chalmers felt that a flank attack from the direction of Hamburg was not practicable. Since this implied that such an attack was contemplated, it is possible that Johnston or Bragg originally considered making an assault from this direction.

On the morning of April 3 Chalmers, at Monterey, received an order from Bragg's assistant adjutant general to cook five days' rations and prepare for operations at a moment's notice. About the same time Chalmers learned from the commander of his cavalry, Colonel James H. Clanton, that the enemy had attacked his outer pickets. Chalmers promptly reported the incident to army headquarters, promising to forward details as soon as available.

The cavalrymen picketing the Monterey outpost at the time were of the 1st Alabama Cavalry, Clanton's own regiment. Two of his privates were said to have been captured by a sudden enemy dash, and Clanton hastened to investigate.

Although the Confederates advanced with infantry to meet the threat of an attack, the incident was merely the result of an attempt by William Tecumseh Sherman to snare some of the Confederate pickets frequently observed along the road to Corinth. Following his return from the gunboat expedition to Eastport on April 2 Sherman had ordered the 54th Ohio Infantry to advance along Lick Creek after dark and wait at Greer's house, where a backwoods road leading from the main Corinth road crossed the creek. Colonel W. H. H. Taylor was instructed to ride at midnight with a strong cavalry detachment along the Corinth road and drive any enemy pickets encountered down the backwoods road toward the 54th Ohio, waiting at Greer's.

Taylor left camp at midnight, taking with him four hundred troopers of his 5th Ohio Cavalry. The night was so dark, however, that Taylor halted four miles out to await daylight. At dawn on April 3 Taylor's command finally moved on, encountering soon thereafter nine Confederate vedettes. The advance detachment immediately charged, capturing one Rebel private, wounding another, and scattering the rest. After riding to the vicinity of Greer's without further incident, Taylor returned to camp, arresting on the way a Dr. Parker, who had allegedly given warning to other Confederate pickets.

When the details became known to the Confederates at Monterey, the aggressive Clanton planned revenge. A lawyer and an Alabama statesman before the war, the thirty-five-year-old Clanton was already considered by some as dangerously impetuous. Braxton Bragg had warned Ruggles less than a month earlier that Clanton was "gallant to rashness" and would require advice as to caution.

LIEUTENANT HENRY HOWE COOK. One of Bushrod Johnson's men from Company F, 44th Tennessee Infantry, Cook was eighteen years old at the time of the battle. Cook and his single-shot percussion pistol personify the youth and improvised equipment of many of the Confederates at Shiloh. (PHOTOGRAPHIC HISTORY OF THE CIVIL WAR)

This appraisal was well founded. As the advance cavalry screening Hardee's front on April 4, Clanton's regiment nearly started the Battle of Shiloh prematurely.

It was well known to Clanton that the Union division camped about Shiloh Church regularly stationed picket companies at farmhouses along the various roads in their front. At 2:30 P.M. on the fourth, with a light rain falling, some of Clanton's gray cavalry swept out of the woods and surrounded the advance pickets of Buckland's brigade. One lieutenant and six men were captured following an exchange of shots.

Although Clanton's men apparently withdrew to within a quarter-mile of Hardee's advance, then marching north along the Ridge road, they were soon discovered by a lone company of Federal infantry sent to investigate the picket's disappearance. Clanton was hampered by the falling rain and unfavorable terrain, but he soon surrounded the outnumbered Federals. When a second enemy detachment appeared, they too were attacked.

According to a Federal participant Clanton was about to charge the isolated infantry detachments when a strong column of blue cavalry appeared. The Confederates, taken by surprise, fled at the enemy's approach, losing many prisoners in a running fight through the woodlands.

Hardee's infantry was formed in line of battle behind a prominent knoll when the retreating cavalry swept past. Hard on their heels came the 5th Ohio Cavalry, which suddenly was confronted by infantry and artillery of Cleburne's brigade. As the infantry and artillery opened fire, the surprised Federals broke ranks and escaped as best they could. Soon thereafter scouts learned that the Federals had returned to camp, apparently unaware that they had uncovered the advance strike force of the Confederate army.

Among the three officers and eight men taken prisoner by the Confederates during the skirmish was Major LeRoy Crockett of the 72d Ohio Infantry. That evening Crockett was brought by his captors to Monterey for interrogation. As he passed the long lines of gray infantry, Adjutant General Jordan heard Crockett remark, "This means a battle," and "They don't expect anything of this kind back yonder." Together with Major Gilmer of Johnston's staff Jordan questioned Crockett at length "in an informal manner." From him they learned that Grant's army had no entrenchments in their front and numbered about thirty-two regiments of infantry and twelve batteries of artillery, in all not over twenty-five thousand men.

On the following day, April 5, while the army was moving into position, cavalry units such as Avery's Georgia Mountain Dragoons scouted the Union lines. By Hardee's orders Avery's company made a close reconnaissance of the Federal camps, getting to within two hundred yards of a column of infantry marching to their drill ground with drums beating. Though they were shot at on several occasions by Federal pickets, the Georgia Dragoons returned to Hardee's headquarters about dark and confirmed the location of the enemy camps.

Following the many acts of carelessness and indiscretion on the part of the raw Confederate troops there was much concern among ranking officers that the advance from Corinth had been discovered by the enemy. After the heavy rain on the morning of the fifth many of the men in Hardee's corps fired their muskets "to see if they would go off." Later they sent up a lusty cheer as a frightened deer bolted from cover along the roadside. All during the day there was indiscriminate firing along the front lines despite the attempts to stop it. Roaming Confederate cavalrymen also attacked and scattered several Federal outposts stationed in advance of the Shiloh Church camps. At 7 A.M. on the fifth Union pickets were driven from the Widow Howell's house, only three-quarters of a mile from the Union camps. Many of the Confederate regiments in Hardee's line were beating drums and blowing bugles as they moved into position. That evening, when Beauregard again heard drumming nearby, he sent a staff officer to silence it. Much to Beauregard's surprise the staff officer soon reappeared and reported that the noise was coming from the enemy's camp.

Despite widespread carelessness on the part of many Southern troops there was still no indication that the enemy expected an attack. An unsuspecting Federal assistant surgeon and his orderly who took the wrong road were captured by Hardee's pickets during the night of the fifth. Confederate headquarters learned from them that Grant had returned to Savannah for the night, an event that could hardly be expected of a commander anticipating a fight.

During the evening the plans for the morning's battle were reviewed by the ranking Confederate generals at Johnston's headquarters. Johnston's original concept appears to have been an attack with corps abreast, each corps being assigned a sector of the front. His telegram to Jefferson Davis of April 3, 1862, implied that the attack formation would consist of "Polk, left; Hardee, center; Bragg, right wing; Breckenridge, reserve." Later the same day, however, Jordan had drawn up the army's marching orders utilizing Beauregard's notes and "Napoleon's order for the Battle of Waterloo," such being considered a proper model for operational detail. This concept called for an attack by succeeding waves of infantry, with each corps aligned one behind the other across the entire front. The basic premise, said a staff officer, was that "no force the enemy could [amass] could cut through three double lines of Confederates." It was a fatal flaw, as events would later demonstrate.

By accepting these plans and witnessing their publication in his own name, Johnston must bear full responsibility for their use. On the evening of April 5, when the Confederate army was fully deployed in this unwieldy battle formation, Johnston ordered only a few last-minute changes. The army was committed as designated in Special Orders No. 8, except that a single regiment in Bragg's corps was transferred to Polk's command in order that Colonel George Maney of Tennessee might command a brigade.

Prominent among the varied subjects discussed by the Confederate generals that night was the tactical plan of attack. By Johnston's order the enemy's left flank was to be turned "so as to cut off his line of retreat to the Tennessee River, and throw him back on Owl Creek, where he will be obliged to surrender." The plan called for a simple envelopment of the Federal left. No one then knew, however, where the enemy's left flank rested or what strength would be required to break it. Information on the Federal camps along the Bark road toward the river was so meager that Bragg instructed his chief engineer to make a reconnaissance in that direction before daylight and report by courier as soon as possible.

While the generals talked in low, earnest tones, the troops prepared for the coming battle with considerable, if ill-judged, enthusiasm. Campfires, strictly forbidden by orders, were ablaze in a long line throughout scattered sections of the forest. An occasional drum roll sounded, often mixed with bugle sounds and shouting.

Before the soldiers slept that night there was excited discussion of the great fight that was certain to occur in the morning. The battle orders of Johnston, read to every regiment while on the march from Corinth, urged resolution, discipline, and valor. The army, Johnston warned, would be fighting with "the eyes and hopes of eight millions of people" resting upon them. Copies of Beauregard's General Orders #3, prepared in mid-March following the first enemy landing, were still in circulation and were avidly read in many regiments. Again the men were reminded to fire at the feet of the enemy so as to avoid overshooting. Soldiers would not be permitted to break ranks "to strip or rob the dead" or assist in removing the wounded. Anyone abandoning his regiment under pretense of such would be "shot on the spot." They were hard words, but the full meaning would not become evident until the morrow. For now it seemed to many only the prospect of a grand adventure.

When the army at last bedded down for a brief night's rest, Jordan, the imperious adjutant general, found Johnston bivouacking in the open air. The night was cool, and Johnston had spread his blankets under a large tree. With the embers of a small campfire glowing nearby, they talked of the past. Jordan had served eight years in the Old Army on the Pacific Coast. When Johnston was secretly relieved as commander of the Department of the Pacific in April, 1861, the Federal Government had sent his replacement, Colonel E. V. Sumner, by steamer under an assumed name. Johnston spoke of the occasion with great emotion. He had been deeply offended by the War Department's stealth in the matter, feeling that his conduct as a man of honor should have been above suspicion.

Johnston also may have remembered the night before he left California for the South. There had been a farewell party at Captain Winfield Hancock's. As the hour of midnight approached and the resigned officers prepared to leave, Johnston asked his wife to sing some of the old songs they used to sing. When Mrs. Johnston sang "Mary of Argyle" and "Kathleen Mavourneen," tears filled the eyes of all at the party.

At last the embers burned lower and the bittersweet memories of long ago faded. Again the gravity of the present crisis loomed in full perspective. Tomorrow was an opportunity that Sidney Johnston had long awaited.

CHAPTER VIII

The Unsuspecting Sherman

Pittsburg Landing, Tennessee, had been Indian country forty-five years before. The vine-tangled oak forests then were a vast hunting ground abundant with game of all varieties. Black bear, wolf, beaver, wild turkey, geese, duck, deer, and even panther inhabited the dense canebreak and woodlands.

However, following the War of 1812, the white man began to encroach upon the vast southwest Tennessee wilderness. In 1815 Colonel Joseph Hardin, a Revolutionary War veteran with a land warrant for two thousand acres, came to survey land on the east bank of the Tennessee River. Hardin's survey resulted in the arrival during the following spring of two parties of settlers, totaling forty-eight men, women, and children.

They found cane so dense at the mouth of the creeks that it seemed impossible to pass. Huge oaks of six species stood in towering groves, as they had for centuries. At night the howl of the wolf and the blood-chilling scream of the panther were familiar sounds to the settlers camped on Hardin Creek.

Within four years the wilderness had yielded to such mainstays of civilization as a flour mill, a blacksmith store, and a carpenter shop. Yet the busy pioneers also suffered their first death by violence—a white man killed by Indians in a quarrel over fur pelts.

The west side of the river, where the soil was relatively poor, re-mained an Indian hunting ground for many years. The inexorable pressure of civilization finally drove the Indians away, however, and settlers slowly began to cross to the west bank.

In the decade before the Civil War the great coffee-colored sand bluff rising high above the Tennessee became the site of a general store operated by two brothers. Later Pitts Tucker moved his family upriver and built a rude log cabin below the great river bend north of the Mississippi state line. His trade was in hard liquor, and Pitts Tucker's Landing soon became a popular stopping spot for frontier

115

river craft. When more than one family moved to this location, the site became known as Pittsburg Landing.

Despite the many hardships and drawbacks—so many snakes were killed along the creek north of Pitts Tucker's liquor shop that it was named Snake Creek—the population of Hardin County numbered 11,217 in 1860. Only about 15 percent of the population was slave, and the people were quite religious, many being Methodists.

The populace's sincere and staunch political sentiments proved of more than passing significance in the Great Rebellion of 1861. It was well known to authorities on both sides that a large portion of Hardin County's residents were pro-Union, especially in the more populous eastern region. The county had voted against secession in 1861, and more recently three-fourths of the voters had cast their ballots for a Union candidate. Moreover, following the arrival of Union naval vessels at Savannah, Lieutenant William Gwin of the *Tyler* was able to enlist a large number of recruits for his gunboat.

By far the most notable hotbed of Union sentiment in Hardin County was at Savannah, the county seat. William H. Cherry, a wealthy planter of considerable local influence, was among the more prominent Union men. Cherry donated his large house as a head-quarters for the Union commanders following the occupation of Savannah and sent servants into the interior to gather information on Rebel troop movements. In reprisal the Confederates attempted to burn as many of Mr. Cherry's cotton bales as they could find.

Despite the prevailing Union sentiment in Savannah the local Confederate militia attempted to draft all the able-bodied male residents on Thursday, March 6, 1862. These new draftees were to be mustered in on the following Monday, March 10. However, word soon spread upriver to the Union army at Fort Henry, causing a Federal gunboat to return. The occupation of the town by a detachment of the 40th Illinois Infantry on March 7 prevented any further attempt at induction. When the 46th Ohio Volunteers arrived aboard the transport *Adams* on the following day, Savannah was secured for the Federal forces.

One Confederate regiment already had been recruited in the vicinity, and when about forty refugees from the Confederate draft enlisted in the 46th Ohio, both armies had men from Hardin County in their ranks.

On the west side of the river Southern sentiment was much stronger. In midsummer, 1861, the Confederates had organized "a grand barbeque and parade" at Shady Grove Church, near Saltillo. Following a patriotic oration and perhaps a little "jug tipping," many recruits signed up to fight for the "Sunny South." All the volunteers, old and new, then galloped in a circle around the meeting arbor with tiny Confederate flags tied to their horses' heads. As an observer later remembered that it was one of the last gala occasions in Hardin County for a long while. Less than a year later many of the participants were dead.

Because of this partisan Confederate sentiment, when the Federal army occupied the west bank in March, 1862, the farmers in the vicinity of Crump's and Pittsburg landings became a valuable source of information to Confederate headquarters. As late as April 2 citizens living within the Union lines slipped through to the Confederate outpost at Monterey with information that "the enemy have no fortifications . . . [and] are suffering terribly from sickness." Another citizen's warning enabled Confederate vedettes to escape a Federal cavalry patrol in the early morning of April 3. The citizen involved, Dr. Parker, was arrested, however, and was held by the Union authorities.

In contrast to the considerable flow of information passing to the Confederate army, the Union commanders received little help from farmers on the west bank. Despite the fact that the protracted three-day march of the Confederates from Corinth must have been seen by many, there is no record of any citizen having warned of their approach. The citizens, one observer later noted, even if of Union sentiment, could not easily be brought "to the point of asserting their manhood," if for no other reason than that the Confederates had occupied the region for nearly a year, and reprisals were certain to be swift if they returned.

The result was a serious gap in Union intelligence operations, causing the Federal generals to rely entirely on military sources.

Ironically, word of a threatened Confederate attack allegedly was received from agents utilized by Lew Wallace, but was discredited.

Wallace, fearing an attack upon his isolated division at Crump's Landing, said he had recruited three scouts to operate as spies in the vicinity of Corinth and Purdy. One of these scouts, Horace Bell, whom Wallace regarded as an unsavory sort, came into Wallace's headquarters at sunset on April 4 and reported, "The whole Rebel army is on the way up from Corinth," fifty thousand strong, marching on Pittsburg Landing. Bell said he had ridden from Corinth along "with some friends in Hardee's corps" and learned that the Confederates were advancing in four columns.

Wallace was skeptical, however, and questioned his scout closely. Previously he had heard that Bell was a double agent, and this raised further doubt in his mind. Yet when another scout, named Carpenter, came into camp and corroborated Bell's story, Wallace said he wrote a dispatch to Grant, reporting what the two spies had seen. Since Grant's boat had earlier passed upriver to Pittsburg Landing and had not yet returned en route to Savannah, Wallace told his trusted orderly, Private Thomas W. Simpson, Company I, 4th U. S. Cavalry, to deliver the note to General Grant if he was at Pittsburg Landing, otherwise to leave it with the postmaster there for forwarding by boat in the morning.

Simpson traveled the partially flooded river road, plunging through backwater that ran belly-deep on his horse before arriving at Pittsburg Landing. There he learned that Grant had already returned to Savannah. Although it was then late at night, he awoke the postmaster and placed the dispatch in his hands for delivery to Grant early the following morning. Returning to Crump's Landing at 2 A.M., Simpson reported to Wallace what had occurred.

Nothing further was heard from army headquarters on the following day, and Wallace believed that his message had been given due consideration and put aside. He later admitted, "it never entered my head that a force from Corinth meaning battle . . . could close in upon our divisions south of Snake Creek without full knowledge of it at headquarters." Furthermore he feared being considered pretentious in pressing the matter. McClernand had earlier earned Grant's animosity by his overbearing recommendations, and Wallace remembered the lesson well. As an added complication the reliability of his two scouts was suspect, a consideration that was intensified when Wallace had to break up an impending duel between the two men shortly after they delivered news of the enemy's advance.

Although there is no positive record of it, the story of the Wallace dispatch does have some credibility. Grant sent a note to Sherman on the morning of April 5 that inquired about a threatened enemy attack. Sherman's reply was negative, and Wallace's dispatch, if received, was promptly disregarded.

Although McClernand was now present at Pittsburg Landing, and as the ranking officer there should have assumed command in Grant's absence, Sherman continued to be the "informal" camp commander. C. F. Smith's tetanus infection had worsened, causing him to return to Savannah about the first week in April, there to wither in a sick bed at Mr. Cherry's brick house.

Following Sherman's return from the naval expedition to Eastport on April 2 he was asked by Grant to snare some of the Confederate pickets observed in the direction of Monterey.

At department headquarters in St. Louis Halleck was clamoring to know what the enemy's strength and positions were. On March 31 he wrote to Grant demanding, "Give me more information about enemy's number and positions. Your scouts and spies ought by this time to have given you something approximately to the facts of the case."

Grant again was embarrassed. As a result of the intelligence gap stemming from a lack of local cooperation on the west side of the river, he had to rely entirely on military sources. Sherman apparently had not sent spies to Corinth, as did Wallace. Although several Confederate deserters had come in with vague information on the growing enemy concentration at Corinth, Grant considered their reports unreliable.

Sherman's midnight patrol on the evening of April 2 was staged for the purpose of taking prisoners from whom it was hoped some news could be learned. The only military prisoner taken, Private Lammon of the 1st Alabama Cavalry—considered by Sherman to be "pretty intelligent"—was soon sent under guard to Grant for questioning. Grant, however, failed to learn much. He reported to Halleck on April 4 that nothing very reliable could be learned of the enemy except that they had a "large and increasing" force at Corinth and that their morale was low.

In contrast to the situation reported in the enemy's camps, the status of Grant's men was found to be "excellent." During Grant's field inspection of April 2 and 3 even Sherman paraded his division for a formal "review and inspection" by the commander. Sherman's regimental bands played, the colors dipped in salute, and the troops stood at shoulder arms. Grant seemed favorably impressed; his only critical remark was that some of the troops still wore gray uniforms.

As the warm April sun continued to shine, the health of the troops greatly improved. One of Sherman's privates observed on April 4 that the "sick boys are all getting well and the doctors have scarcely anything to do." The bright sunshine and warm temperatures had also sent spirits soaring, causing a young Illinois artillerist to write jubilantly that it was so warm "we go in our shirt sleeves." Another soldier thought it was so hot as to be uncomfortable in the daytime, "but the nights," he added, "are delicious, just cool enough to sleep well."

About the only general basis for complaint from the ranks seems to have been the monotony of camp life. An Illinois infantryman found cause to grumble that he had "nothing to do," saying, "It will be two weeks tomorrow since I done anything but eat and lay around the encampment." Other troops, notably Sherman's, began to chafe at the constant drill and inspections. A bugler in the 4th Illinois Cavalry complained on April 3 that his battalion had been reviewed "three times in the last three days," and that it all was "very tiresome and seems to me to be useless."

Sherman was a strong advocate of drill and instruction. Most of his men were recruits, new to Army ways and discipline. By Sherman's order there was daily drill and fatigue duty.

On April 3 he issued permission for Buckland's brigade to march three miles out the Corinth road for "drill and instructions." One of the 70th Ohio's soldiers remembered that the men regarded it as "a kind of picnic excursion." After marching several miles, his regiment halted and stacked arms for dinner, sending a small detachment farther down the road as pickets.

The pickets were proceeding to their places when they were suddenly challenged: "Halt! Who comes there?" The officer in charge then yelled out, "It is the advance guard of the . . . Army of the United States!"

"The hell you say!" came the reply, followed by a volley of gunfire. Buckland's pickets made a hasty retreat to their brigade, and a long drum roll was heard in the direction of the enemy. According to an Ohio private, "A short council was held by our officers, resulting in a speedy retreat to our camp at Shiloh Church."

Sherman regarded the affair as minor and apparently made no report to Grant. He knew that the Confederate cavalry made patrols in the vicinity and attached little importance to their presence. Furthermore he was involved in the details of a widespread reorganization of the army's artillery and cavalry, and was then busy planning the transfer of men and materiel.

Grant, intending that his artillery and cavalry should be controlled at the divisional level, reassigned all such units among the various divisions on April 2, thereby relieving them from duty with brigades. In the course of the reassignment, however, units that had served with a brigade in one division were generally transferred out of their old division and reattached to a new and unfamiliar command.

Sherman's division lost the veteran 5th Ohio Cavalry, including Major Elbridge G. Ricker, who knew the ground in front of Sherman's camps. In their place Sherman received two battalions of the 4th Illinois Cavalry from C. F. Smith's and Hurlbut's divisions. The loss of Ricker's men was particularly damaging. During the midnight patrol of April 2 Ricker had learned that the Confederate cavalry had visited the various fords on Lick Creek the day before and also that they had reinforced and advanced their picket line. This and other evidence, said Ricker, caused the 5th's officers to consider the possibility of an attack.

Sherman's artillery was also involved in the reorganization. Stone's battery, with Stuart near the mouth of Lick Creek, was ordered to join C. F. Smith's division, and Captain Emil Munch's 1st Minnesota Battery went to Benjamin Prentiss's newly formed Sixth Division. Only Waterhouse's and Behr's batteries remained with Sherman, being joined by the well-known Taylor's Battery B, Chicago Light Artillery.

Although Grant's orders were dated April 2 and were announced the following day, most of the division commanders were in no hurry to effect the transfer. By Sherman's order the exchanges involving his division were to occur on Saturday, April 5.

Only one Union general, Lew Wallace, requested that the exchange be expedited. Wallace feared that the enemy was massing troops for an attack on his division in the vicinity of Adamsville. Colonel Charles R. Woods's alarm on the afternoon of the second, which in turn had caused the Confederates to fear a Union advance, led Wallace to think his troops at Adamsville threatened. Claiming on April 4 that "news of the reinforcement of the Rebel troops at Purdy is confirmed" and "the object of the movement is not known," Wallace asked "as a measure of precaution" for Stone's and Markgraf's batteries to be hastened to Crump's Landing.

Grant responded the same day, ordering both batteries to join Wallace on the following morning. Grant also told W. H. L. Wallace, the new commander of C. F. Smith's division, that "it may be necessary to reinforce General Wallace to avoid his being attacked by a superior force. Should you find danger of this sort, reinforce him at once with your entire division." Grant later admitted, "My apprehension was much greater for the safety of Crump's Landing than it was for Pittsburg. . . . I feared it was possible that he might make a rapid dash upon Crump's and destroy our transports and stores . . ." This concern was fully evidenced two days later when, hearing firing upriver, Grant believed that Crump's Landing might have been attacked.

Other transfers in the army, occurring at the same time, involved changes in the high command. Because of C. F. Smith's protracted illness Grant found it expedient to transfer newly appointed Brigadier General W. H. L. Wallace from McClernand's to Smith's division. As the senior ranking officer, W. H. L. Wallace would have command of the division in Smith's absence. A man of tall, rangy physique with a ruddy complexion and a receding hairline, Wallace had won his general's star for gallantry at Fort Donelson.

Brigadier General Jacob G. Lauman, promoted at the same time as W. H. L. Wallace, was disappointed in being transferred from C. F. Smith's division to the command of only a brigade in Hurlbut's division. According to Lauman Grant told him "that he meant to take all the new brigadier generals away from their old commands, at least temporarily." Lauman accepted the disappointment graciously, thinking that Grant "will do the best he can for me." Earlier, however, Grant had intimated to W. H. L. Wallace, a fellow Illinois officer, "that he intended" to put him in command of a division. Wallace felt some embarrassment when placed in command of C. F. Smith's division on April 3, thinking it would be difficult "to fill the place of such a man as General Smith."

Beyond the changes in units and personnel during the first week in April there was a considerable amount of other confusion in the Union camp. One of Sherman's colonels, endeavoring to find clothing and axes at Pittsburg Landing, found everything there crowded and in disorder. Although Sherman later testified that the stores remained afloat so as to enable a shift in base, if necessary, the colonel said they remained on boats because they had no storehouses in which to put them. Finding that his requisitions would not be filled, the colonel felt that there was a great deal of danger in the disorder existing in the army at the time.

To Sherman, however, the events of the past several weeks merely demonstrated that his soldiers had "as much idea of war as children." Their need for drill and instruction was cause for constant training, and he worked hard to improve their discipline.

On Friday, April 4, several incidents occurred that caused Sherman to doubt further the efficiency of his division. Sergeant C. J. Eagler of the 77th Ohio was one of the outpost pickets for Hildebrand's brigade that morning. It had rained all night, but the sun was now shining brightly and Eagler and his captain, W. B. Mason, decided to take a walk to the edge of a "plantation" in their front. When they reached the wooden fence bordering Seay field, they saw that along the far edge of timber, about a quarter-mile away, enemy troops were apparently eating breakfast.

Mason turned to Eagler and told him to report to regimental headquarters "that the enemy was in our front in full force." Eagler double-quicked to headquarters and related to Major B. D. Fearing what he had seen. While Fearing promptly went to see Sherman, Eagler returned to his picket post.

About an hour later a detail of ten men and a captain came out to the picket line and handed Captain Mason a paper. Mason read it, then said he would take care of it himself. As Eagler later learned, the paper was an order for his arrest, signed by Sherman, for bringing a false alarm into camp. Mason promptly dropped the matter, knowing that he too would meet with Sherman's ire.

That same afternoon one of Sherman's inexperienced regiments, the 72d Ohio, was drilling in the fields near their brigade's outpost pickets. About 2:30 P.M. they were startled by a sharp firing in the woods nearby. Colonel Ralph P. Buckland, the 72d's brigade commander who had ridden out to see his former regiment drill, immediately went to investigate. He soon found that one of his picket outposts consisting of a lieutenant and six men had been captured by Confederate cavalry. Buckland remained at the house where the outposts were captured while his acting aide went back to camp with a report.

Meanwhile Major LeRoy Crockett and the remainder of the 72d Ohio arrived at the outpost. Crockett had detached a single company and sent it into the woods on his right as skirmishers, intending them to parallel his main column's march. Buckland told Crockett that this was a mistake; the men were inexperienced and would get lost. Yet Buckland quickly compounded the error by ordering Crockett to take another company out to find the detached skirmishers while the main portion of the regiment remained at the outpost.

When Buckland's aide returned and reported that Sherman was sending out a cavalry detachment to look for the captured pickets, Buckland rode back to camp, believing that the 72d would return shortly.

After a short wait in camp during which time he saw no sign of the returning infantry, Buckland again went to the picket line, where he found the Ohio infantry still awaiting Crockett's return. Hearing constant firing in the direction the major had taken, Buckland selected three more companies and started for their relief. They were soon stopped, however, by what Buckland described as "one of the severest rain and thunder storms" he had ever witnessed. According to Buckland the rain soon filled his exposed boots so full of water that it ran over the tops. After the storm subsided, Buckland pushed on.

Following in Buckland's path, Major Ricker and about one hundred fifty men of the 2d Battalion, 5th Ohio Cavalry, galloped along the Corinth road under Sherman's order to investigate the pickets' disappearance. About two miles from camp Ricker split his command and trotted through the woods toward the sound of heavy firing.

His main column soon came up with Buckland's detachment, which he found engaged with a large force of Confederate cavalry. Buckland, having attempted to rescue one of his separated companies, was being menaced by a full enemy regiment, the 1st Alabama Cavalry. Picking their way through a strip of fallen timber, Ricker's men made a dash at the gray cavalry, who scattered at their unexpected approach.

With a shout the Ohioans pursued the scattering Confederates, felling horses and riders with carbine fire and capturing about thirty prisoners. For nearly a quarter-mile the chase continued, the Union cavalrymen pressing hard to catch the fleeing enemy atop a nearby hill.

Suddenly, as they passed over the crest of a knoll, Ricker's men came face to face with a Confederate battle line bristling with at least four pieces of artillery and a long row of burnished muskets. The enemy loomed so close that one of Ricker's privates was unable to stop before being carried within their lines and captured. Another Federal escaped by shooting a cannoneer at point-blank range. Amid a volley of musketry and three resounding cannon shots, Ricker's men dashed for cover, losing many of their prisoners in their retreat.

Unknowingly they had encountered the advance elements of Hardee's corps, en route from Monterey.

As Ricker re-formed his force behind a small hill, Buckland's men came up on the run. Following a hasty conference Buckland and Ricker thought it "prudent to retire to our own lines with as little delay as possible." They took with them ten prisoners and several trophies, including the saddle and mountings from the dead mount of the 1st Alabama's lieutenant colonel. Two other badly wounded prisoners were carried to the Widow Howell's farmhouse and left there.

It was already dark, although the rain had subsided, when Ricker and Buckland returned to their division's line of outposts. Here they found Sherman impatiently waiting, with two regiments of infantry drawn up in line of battle. As they approached, Buckland observed from Sherman's manner "that he was not pleased."

Sherman had been in his tent near Shiloh Church when the three cannon shots sounded. Riding with his staff to the picket line, he had awaited Buckland's and Ricker's return in the pouring rain. Buckland tried to explain his admittedly "irregular proceedings" by saying that he "had accidentally got into a little fight," and, pointing to the prisoners, added that these were "some of the fruits."

Sherman angrily told him that he might have drawn the whole army into a battle and gruffly ordered Buckland back to camp.

When Ricker volunteered that the enemy force was strong, "at least two regiments of infantry and a large cavalry force," Sherman chided him, saying, "Oh!—tut; tut. You militia officers get scared too easily." He also remarked to Ricker that he thought it was simply a reconnaissance in force. In his official report Sherman concluded that the enemy occupied Monterey "in some considerable force" and that the troops encountered were a brigade of infantry, cavalry, and artillery. No important significance was attached to their presence, however.

Despite Sherman's insouciance the affair had already caused considerable alarm throughout the Pittsburg Landing area. The long roll had sounded in several camps, sending Sherman's and McClernand's divisions into line of battle. Even W. H. L. Wallace's division, near the Landing, was alerted. Wallace noted that the incident "caused a good deal of excitement in camp"; he had his division ready to turn out, but it had not been necessary.

At one point both Generals Sherman and McClernand had sent notes through their staffs to Grant at Savannah, saying that the outposts had been attacked by Confederate cavalry, "apparently in considerable force." Thereafter Grant had hurried to Pittsburg Landing by steamboat.

When he arrived, it was late at night, and another storm was raging across the countryside. The night was so dark that Grant had difficulty finding his way along the muddy road to Shiloh Church. About halfway to Sherman's camp he met W. H. L. Wallace and Lieutenant Colonel McPherson, of his own staff, returning from a visit to Sherman's headquarters. They reported everything quiet at the front. Because of the intensity of the storm, then, Grant returned to the landing without seeing Sherman.

On the way back Grant's mount slipped in the treacherous footing and fell heavily, pinning the General's leg. The rain-soaked ground was soft, preventing a fracture, but Grant's ankle soon became so swollen that his boot had to be cut off. For the next several days he was unable to walk without crutches.

W. H. L. Wallace's and McPherson's visit to Sherman's camp had been prompted by the skirmish of that afternoon. Riding out to Shiloh Church about 11 P.M., they found "everything quiet and the general in fine spirits." Sherman boasted that "he had driven the enemy back some three or four miles" and had "lost no men killed, three or four wounded, and ten taken prisoners or missing." The enemy was said to have lost many dead and wounded and "some ten or twelve prisoners."

Although Sherman apparently expressed satisfaction with the day's events during his chat with Wallace and McPherson, other evidence implies that he was somewhat displeased with his division's performance.

Immediately following his return from the front that evening he had his adjutant general issue orders that were a rather demeaning critique: In case of alarm regiments were to form on their parade grounds and await orders instead of advancing to the front, as had several of Buckland's units. He also admonished the brigade commanders that "in no event should a brigadier go beyond his advance pickets without orders of the division commander." Even details such as the men's attire were faulted, Sherman pointing out that the 72d Ohio "went out in gray flannel shirts, which . . . resembled the secession uniform." Finally Sherman warned that no detachments were to be made on the flank of a marching column. This he considered more dangerous "than in receiving the fire of a regiment."

In a private letter, Sherman confided that he had a low opinion of his volunteer troops. He thought his volunteer officers "afraid of the men" and careless in the extreme. Said Sherman, "I will do all I can with my division, but regret that I have not better discipline and more reliable men."

Sherman's attitude was considerably influenced by his relationships with several regimental commanders within his division. Sherman's troubles with Colonel Thomas W. Worthington dated back to early March, when Worthington had taken his transport up the Tennessee to Savannah without permission, arriving several days ahead of C. F. Smith's main flotilla. Although a graduate of West Point, Class of 1827, Worthington was an eccentric whom Sherman termed "a strange character." Worthington was older than Halleck, Grant, and Sherman, and according to Sherman, claimed to know more about the war than all three put together.

Sherman had arrived at Savannah on March 11 to find Worthington's regiment, the 46th Ohio Infantry, comfortably billeted in private residences and Worthington stalking about "giving orders as though he were commander-in-chief." When Sherman ordered some of Worthington's men out of a citizen's home, Worthington clutched the General's arm and asked him to be quiet as they already had been told to leave. Sherman exploded with rage and had a Missouri regiment bodily turn the supposedly "sick" Ohioans out.

In camp at Pittsburg Landing Worthington further earned Sherman's wrath by his alarmist behavior. As early as March 26 Worthington was convinced that the enemy was about to attack the Union camps. On the twenty-ninth he became so alarmed that he requested seventy-two axes from Sherman in order to build an abatis.

Sherman reduced his requisition to twenty-two, believing a large

BRIGADIER GENERAL WILLIAM TECUMSEH SHERMAN. Often nervous and irritable in camp, with a low regard for his volunteer troops, Sherman nominally commanded the Fifth Division. Yet, as the informal camp commander in Grant's absence, Sherman became the eyes and ears of the army. Beginning with his recommendations that led to the establishment of a weak beachhead in close proximity to the enemy and continuing with a complete lack of basic defensive preparations, Sherman made many serious mistakes before Shiloh. His lack of vigilance nearly resulted in a major disaster, and almost claimed his life. Only in the fiery crisis of battle, where Sherman's icy nerve steadied his men, did his great potential as combat commander emerge. Photographed at Memphis in August, 1862. (PHOTOGRAPHIC HISTORY OF THE CIVIL WAR)

number of axes could not be had. Furthermore he saw no need for the construction of fortifications.

Worthington continued to complain about the lack of necessary tools. On March 31, three days before the Confederates marched from Corinth, Worthington became convinced that an attack was imminent and gathered over one hundred rounds of ammunition for each man in his regiment. His repeated outcries had already become so offensive that Sherman said he was threatened by C. F. Smith with arrest if he allowed Worthington to come on board his boat again.

By April 3, the day the Confederates actually did advance, Worthington had so angered his superiors that they paid no attention to his "constant prognostications." Worthington already considered himself snubbed and confined his observations thereafter to his war diary, where he took great care to chastise Sherman.

Another source of trouble for Sherman was Colonel Jesse J. Appler of the 53d Ohio Volunteers. Like Worthington, Appler was elderly, but he had neither formal education nor Army experience. Appler's lack of even the most basic military knowledge resulted in his regiment's arriving in camp without ever having been drilled. His men thought he had "much general intelligence," yet Appler's skittishness also was well known throughout the regiment.

On April 5, the day after Sherman's outposts were captured, Appler was particularly nervous. Rumors of all sorts were circulating through camp, and when a party of mounted men was sighted at the far end of the field from his isolated campsite, Appler sent a detachment to investigate. Soon several shots were heard, and the officer in charge returned to report that he had been fired on by "what appeared to be a picket line of men in butternut clothes."

Appler ordered his regiment to turn out and sent his quartermaster to alert Sherman. About the time the regiment formed, the quartermaster returned and reported in a loud voice, "Colonel Appler, General Sherman says: 'Take your damned regiment to Ohio. There is no enemy nearer than Corinth!' "

A loud laugh erupted from the men, and the regiment hastily broke ranks without waiting for an order.

Several others among the division's ranking officers also lacked the professional skill that Sherman had known in the Regular Army. Colonel Jesse Hildebrand, commander of the Third Brigade, was past sixty and knew little of modern tactics. Although commanding a brigade, he insisted on retaining personal command of his regiment, the 77th Ohio. Hildebrand had no staff, not even a mounted orderly, to assist in his brigade duties.

Portly Colonel John A. McDowell of the First Brigade was the younger brother of General Irvin McDowell, leader of the Union army at First Bull Run. Yet John had only served briefly as a captain of an independent militia company about fifteen years earlier, and knew more about railroading than fighting. He held a low opinion of artillery and was fond of asking, "Whoever heard of a dead or wounded artilleryman?"

This unwieldy gathering of citizen-soldiers caused Sherman to complain nearly a month later, "I have not really one thorough soldier in my whole army. They are all green and raw. . . ."

Sherman's disdainful attitude was reflected in the events of April 5, a day that later became the source of much embarrassment to him. Despite his indifference some of his men had become alarmed over the enemy's activities during the past week. Rumors persisted that the Confederates were in heavy force in the woods nearby.

The ten Confederate prisoners taken during the skirmish of the fourth and confined that night in Shiloh Church allegedly taunted their guards with stories that they were the advance of a great army that would drive the Yankees into the river the next day. One particularly defiant Confederate, when asked if there were enough "graybacks" left in the woods "to make interesting hunting," replied, "Yes, more than you'ns have ever seen, . . . and if you ain't mighty careful, they'll run you into hell or the river before tomorrow night."

Thereafter several of Sherman's brigades strengthened their outposts. Stuart's brigade, some two miles from Sherman's main camp, sent out strong reinforcements to its pickets on the night of April 4. During the heavy rainstorm that struck about midnight both officers and men huddled miserably under the tossing trees, vainly watching for the enemy.

On the morning of the fifth further trouble occurred in front of Buckland's and McDowell's brigades. At 7 A.M. the pickets located at Widow Howell's house, less than a mile from Shiloh Church, were attacked and driven in. The lieutenant in charge promptly abandoned the post, leaving behind the bodies of two wounded Confederate cavalrymen who had died during the night. Although Buckland and McDowell were notified, no attempt was made to reoccupy the dwelling. According to Buckland the pickets "fell back" without his orders.

Sherman was probably advised, but spent much of the morning writing reports and other correspondence. Since Grant had not been able to reach Sherman's headquarters in the terrific downpour of the night before, he sent a note on the morning of the fifth, asking Sherman about the extent of enemy activity in the army's front.

Sherman's reply was short and assured. "I have no doubt that nothing will occur today more than some picket firing. The enemy is saucy, but got the worst of it yesterday, and will not press our pickets far. I will not be drawn out far unless with certainty of advantage, and I do not apprehend anything like an attack on our position."

Earlier the same morning Sherman had advised Grant "all is quiet along my lines now." He thought the enemy had cavalry, two regiments of infantry, and a battery of artillery "about two miles out."

Although unconcerned by their absence, Sherman was temporarily hampered in his assessment of the situation along his front by the transfer of cavalry ordered by Grant on April 2. Two battalions of the 4th Illinois Cavalry, transferred to Sherman's division, failed to arrive until the evening of April 5. His old cavalry, a portion of the 5th Ohio, departed early the same morning, leaving Sherman without cavalry during the daylight hours.

Sherman's lack of vigilance was apparently rooted in his conviction that the Confederate generals would not give up the advantage of operating on the defensive in order to attack the Union base. His appraisal of Confederate sightings was influenced accordingly.

On the afternoon of April 5 several of the 40th Illinois pickets thought they saw several pieces of artillery in the woods beyond Widow Howell's house. They told an officer, who reported this to a captain on McDowell's staff, but no one from headquarters evidently bothered to investigate. Later, when some of Buckland's pickets noticed the glimmer of a brass field gun in their front, Buckland went out to look for himself. "I looked but could see nothing of the kind," said Buckland, who then went back to Sherman's headquarters and reported the result.

About 5 P.M. Captain A. G. Sharp of the 46th Ohio, commanding a picket outpost, made a positive identification of an enemy cannon beyond the Widow Howell's. Sharp later testified that he told both McDowell and Sherman, but the General reassured him and nothing further came of the matter.

At Seay's house in Hildebrand's front, the pickets had to withdraw when threatened by a large force of gray cavalry. Hildebrand sent additional pickets to reoccupy the house, but they were unable to do so.

By nightfall of the fifth Sherman apparently was more mindful of the enemy's presence in his front. Two young officers of W. H. L. Wallace's division, out for a Saturday-afternoon ride, were cautioned by some of Sherman's pickets to go no farther. Looking across a field, they saw a party of Confederate cavalry intently watching them. They then rode back to Sherman's camp and remarked to friends in Barrett's battery that they might have a chance to use their guns without even hitching up. Leaving for their own camp soon thereafter, they met Colonel T. Lyle Dickey of the 4th Illinois Cavalry, newly transferred to Sherman's division. When Dickey heard their story, he asked them to return and tell Sherman.

Sherman was found in his tent, and "in his quick, nervous manner" informed the officers that the enemy had been up three times on the right and had fired on McDowell's pickets. He added, however, that his orders from Grant were to do nothing that would tend to "bring on a general engagement until Buell arrives." As an afterthought he remarked that Buell's troops should have arrived ten days ago, later repeating the statement several times as he pored over his map.

Later that evening Sherman went to Hildebrand's tent to discuss his plans to send the division's cavalry out the following morning to "drive away or capture" the enemy force observed in the woods in front. Hildebrand was instructed to march the 77th Ohio Infantry out to the Seay house at 6:30 A.M. in order to support this movement.

Although many of Sherman's troops seemed genuinely worried by the enemy's presence, the majority discounted the frequent alarms. Lieutenant Patrick H. White of Barrett's battery chatted with one of Sherman's brigade commanders, David Stuart, on Saturday afternoon about the possibility of an enemy attack. Stuart said he had just returned from a scouting trip that had taken him clear to the Tennessee River, and he had not seen any sign of the enemy.

According to another lieutenant of one of Stuart's regiments the entire day passed without any alarm or suspicion in their camp. Even the 70th Ohio, drilling in a field near their camp, paid no attention to a party of Confederate cavalry who sat watching their maneuvers.

The day was very bright and warm, and the soldiers enjoyed themselves immensely. The woods surrounding the Union camps were filled with "Johnny-jump-ups," as the men termed the familiar wildflowers, and hunting for wild onions and "turkey peas" was a favorite pastime. At a nearby camp in Prentiss's division a redbird appeared, as he had daily, to serenade the regiment from his perch in a black oak tree. It was a standing joke among the men that the bird was a Union cardinal and had enlisted in the regiment to sound reveille.

In his camp at Pittsburg Landing, W. H. L. Wallace sat down to write an affectionate letter to his wife. He observed that the weather was delightful and that the vegetation was growing rapidly, although the leaves were "not yet fully developed." He thought this must be "a great ways" ahead of spring back in Illinois. Still Wallace was homesick. He missed his wife's love and longed for his "quiet, pleasant home," which was "the place of all others on earth the most desirable."

For the volunteers who had left home and family far behind letter-writing was a popular, almost essential outlet for their pent-up emotions. One soldier said that over two hundred letters were mailed every day in his regiment. News from home was so eagerly sought that when one soldier observed that "not half" the outgoing mail was received each day, he felt that the Army was intercepting their letters home for fear of giving information to the enemy.

For the past two weeks the soldiers had had little to do but eat, sleep, and drill. Although several details were sent out to repair bridges in the army's front, duty was light on April 4 and 5. One young volunteer assigned to Sherman's division wrote home at the time, "Nothing of interest is going on except reviews." To another, camp life was "dull and monotonous without a little prospect of doing work."

At army headquarters, nine miles distant in Savannah, April 5 proved to be far more of an eventful day. The arrival of Buell's Army of the Ohio had been anticipated for days, and finally news arrived of its approach.

Following the fording of the Duck River by Nelson's division on March 29, Grant had been in frequent communication with the advance column. Buell had written on Friday, April 4, that he would arrive at Savannah the next day with at least one division, but the courier did not arrive at Grant's headquarters until April 5. Since Grant had already planned a trip to Pittsburg Landing for that afternoon, he sent a reply to Buell saying that he would meet him tomorrow, April 6.

Since a few of Buell's advance elements had already reached Savannah, some arriving as early as April 3, the presence on April 5 of Nelson's entire division was not unexpected. By 1 P.M. the last units of Nelson's advance brigade had arrived and were pitching their tents near town. Nelson rode in himself about noon and found Grant at Mr. Cherry's brick house along with the bedridden C. F. Smith. An aide overheard the ensuing conversation. When Nelson asked where the enemy was and what they were up to, C. F. Smith replied rather nonchalantly, "They're all back in Corinth, and, when our transportation arrives, we have got to go there and draw them out, as you would draw a badger out of his hole."

Later in the afternoon Grant and Nelson rode over to see one of Nelson's brigade commanders, Jacob Ammen. Grant declined to dismount as he was about to leave for Pittsburg Landing, but he talked with Ammen for a few minutes. Ammen remarked that his troops were not fatigued and could march on to Pittsburg Landing, but Grant was reassuring. "You cannot march through the swamps," he said. "Make the troops comfortable; I will send boats for you Monday or Tuesday, or some time early in the week. There will be no fight at Pittsburg Landing; we will have to go to Corinth, where the Rebels are fortified. . . ."

That evening Buell arrived at Savannah, wearied after a thirty-five-mile horseback ride over rough roads. Grant had gone upriver to Pittsburg Landing aboard his steamer *Tigress* and was not expected back until late that night. Buell then went to bed, sleeping in Nelson's tent. His headquarters staff had camped more than five miles from Savannah, and his own baggage had not yet arrived.

CHAPTER IX

Some Queer Generals

At Pittsburg Landing Grant met with his engineer, McPherson, who that day had surveyed the land near Hamburg, Tennessee. McPherson had been sent rather belatedly "to examine the defensibility of the ground" and to lay out campsites for Buell's army, "if advisable to occupy that place." From Hamburg, about four miles beyond Pittsburg Landing along the Tennessee, the road was good to Corinth, and was even a few miles shorter.

McPherson was considered by Grant to be highly competent, one of the few professional military engineers on Grant's staff. With an escort of six infantry companies under David Stuart and a squadron of McClernand's cavalry, McPherson had gone to Hamburg on the morning of April 5. Ironically, the route taken by McPherson and Stuart had been along the River road, which led away from the concentration of Confederates advancing from Monterey. Accordingly they saw no sign of the enemy.

Lame from his fall the night before, Grant received McPherson's report aboard the *Tigress* at Pittsburg Landing. After taking aboard the ten prisoners captured by Buckland and Ricker on the fourth, Grant's steamer then returned to Savannah about 11 P.M. According to the officer in charge of the prisoners Grant remained on board all night, being up with other officers "to a very late hour." Another eyewitness found Grant and his staff up after midnight. This, so one observer thought, caused Grant to be "very late" in rising on Sunday morning, April 6.

During the fifth Grant dispatched several letters to Halleck in St. Louis, giving the latest information on enemy activities. Grant's correspondence reflected the status at his headquarters as night fell on April 5. Said Grant: "The main force of the enemy is at Corinth, with troops at different points east; . . . I have scarcely the faintest idea of an attack [general one] being made upon us, but will be prepared should such a thing take place."

133

* * *

To the now-slumbering army at Pittsburg and Crump's landings the events of the past few days had resulted in some foreboding of trouble. Although Lew Wallace seemed more concerned about an attack on his isolated division near Crump's Landing than on the main camps at Pittsburg, he sent a dispatch to W. H. L. Wallace on April 5, asking that the cavalry of their respective commands "familiarize themselves" with the route between the two camps. This he considered important since new units had been assigned and they did not know the road to use "in case of [an] emergency."

One of Hurlbut's officers, Lieutenant Colonel William Camm of the 14th Illinois Infantry, wrote in his diary on April 4 that his men believed they would be attacked. Nearly a week earlier Camm had learned from a citizen whose house was being used for a court-martial that the Confederates had placed two field guns and "several hundred soldiers" at a fork in the Purdy road, about five miles distant.

When he reported this to Hurlbut, he was told to ready four companies for a patrol at dusk that evening. At the designated hour Camm found Hurlbut sitting on a log near his headquarters, visibly dejected. Hurlbut told him to go back to camp, that "they have no use for soldiers here," saying that Sherman had refused to allow the patrol to leave. Camm, who had bathed at a ford on Owl Creek on several occasions and failed to observe any Federal pickets guarding the approaches, noted in his diary that the army must have some "queer generals."

Camm was not alone in his opinion. Nearby, in the army's brand-new Sixth Division, considerable controversy had arisen between the commander and his subordinates over the prospect of a threatened enemy attack.

Brigadier General Benjamin Mayberry Prentiss, a direct descendant of settlers who had crossed on the *Mayflower,* had taken command on March 26 of the Sixth Division, newly created from unassigned troops then arriving at Pittsburg Landing. Prentiss, who had been a captain of Illinois volunteers during the Mexican War, was a mediocre lawyer who had campaigned unsuccessfully for Congress in 1860. From an inconspicuous beginning in 1861 as the elected captain of a Quincy, Illinois, infantry company, the forty-two-year-old Prentiss had, in the short span of four months, risen to be a brigadier general.

A rather somber-looking man with a full, Mennonite-style beard, Prentiss had already run afoul of Army politics. His relationship with Grant was unfriendly, resulting from their service in Missouri, where the two had clashed over seniority. Initially Prentiss had replaced Grant as commander of a district near Ironton, Missouri. Grant, then a brigadier, believed himself the senior, however, basing this on his previous Regular Army service despite a common date of rank for both. In a huff he refused to serve under Prentiss and reported to headquarters at St. Louis.

A few days later Grant was reassigned to command of the district of Southeast Missouri, including troops ordered to Cape Girardeau under Prentiss. When Prentiss arrived in advance of his troops, Grant was there to give him orders. A quarrel over seniority again followed, and Prentiss angrily left for St. Louis. The ensuing confusion served to break up a planned expedition to capture Jeff Thompson's partisan band, and for months Grant regarded Prentiss with disdain.

Although his contemporaries considered him quarrelsome, Prentiss was regarded as a sincere and dedicated soldier.

In April, 1862, his division had been assembled for less than two weeks, and many of Prentiss's men had not yet formed an opinion of him. Most of them were recruits, unfamiliar with army life. Of the ten regiments assigned to the Sixth Division, only four had served in the field and only one had been in battle. Three of the division's regiments were not yet in camp; they were still at Pittsburg Landing, waiting for orders.

Prentiss's men found camp life "kind of loose." In contrast to Sherman's camps guard duty was light, drills were not yet a regular routine, and the food was excellent—one soldier found plenty of

BRIGADIER GENERAL BENJAMIN M. PRENTISS. Grant's old antagonist, newly assigned to the embryo Sixth Division, Prentiss emerged from Shiloh with considerable laurels —many of which were unjustified. Although taken totally by surprise on the morning of April 6, Prentiss later claimed credit for discovery of the Confederates, a discovery that he inadvertently impeded. After the breakup of his division, Prentiss's chance presence at a small but critical sector of the W. H. L. Wallace–Hurlbut line earned him lasting fame as the defender of the Hornets' Nest. Reinforced by fresh regiments and units from other commands, Prentiss defended a portion of the sunken road, yet his position was totally dependent upon the main segments of this perimeter—Hurlbut's and W. H. L Wallace's commands. Six months a prisoner of war, Prentiss returned thereafter to active service but failed to obtain important results. (CARTE-DE-VISTE, AUTHOR'S COLLECTION)

"fried sowbelly," steaming "flapjacks," and good strong coffee to satisfy his appetite.

Although the men were generally raw, many of the Sixth Division's officers were veterans, some having served as volunteers in three months' regiments. Lieutenant Colonel William H. Graves of the 12th Michigan Infantry had been with the 1st Michigan at Bull Run, where he was severely wounded. Others, like Alexander Chambers, colonel of the 6th Iowa, were former regulars. Chambers was a West Point graduate, class of '53, and held a Regular Army captain's commission. Men such as Colonel Madison Miller, 18th Missouri, boasted Mexican War experience, Miller having taken a wound at Buena Vista. Even the new regiments, which were arriving at the rate of two a day and slated for the Sixth Division, were sprinkled with veterans. Both the colonel and lieutenant colonel of the 15th Michigan, coming ashore on April 5, had fought in other regiments during the past year.

Despite this there was only one regiment in Prentiss's division that had thoroughly combat-experienced officers and men, the 25th Missouri Volunteer Infantry. All of the 25th's field officers were battle-tested, the regiment having fought at the siege of Lexington, Missouri, where it was finally captured after three days of hard fighting. Then known as the 13th Missouri Infantry, its designation was changed to the 25th Regiment following a prisoner exchange and their reorganization in the fall of 1861. The regiment had been greatly chastened by its capture, but several days after arriving at Pittsburg Landing on March 28 their colonel wrote home that the boys had "a very pleasant camp" and were "as lively as crickets. . . . The enemy is supposed to be about eighteen miles from us," he added, saying "we expect rough work."

Since Prentiss's division was the last to encamp, it had been allocated, by McPherson's survey, ground on the immediate left of Sherman's troops, in the gap between Stuart's and Hildebrand's brigades. As a part of the army's outer perimeter, outposts and pickets were routinely established. Yet it was common knowledge that Sherman's division was located in advance, along the road to Corinth. It was presumed that this would result in Sherman's detection of any enemy buildup along the front. Prentiss's pickets, stationed only about three hundred yards beyond their campsites, had, by the afternoon of April 5, become accustomed to seeing Confederate cavalry in the woods nearby. Yet to many of Prentiss's experienced officers the sharp skirmish of April 4 and the enemy's proximity were cause for concern.

An intended review of the Sixth Division by Grant was postponed from Saturday, April 5, to the following Tuesday. Prentiss, however, conducted the review himself during the afternoon of the fifth, parading his regiments in a nearby clearing known as Spain field. Immediately after the review an officer of the 25th Missouri, Major James E. Powell, approached the division's officer of the day and said he had seen about a dozen "butternuts" looking through the underbrush at the parade.

Both Powell and the officer of the day, Lieutenant Colonel W. H. Graves, had already witnessed several stunning Union defeats. Powell's regiment had fought at Wilson's Creek, Missouri, and Graves had been at Bull Run. Powell's lengthy service in the Regular Army, beginning as an enlisted man during the Mexican War, gave his observations considerable weight.

"After my experience at Bull Run," said Graves, "I felt ill at ease." Together the two officers went to see Prentiss. Following a brief conference with the General it was decided to send out a reconnaissance patrol and strengthen the outpost pickets. Colonel David Moore, with three companies of the 21st Missouri, and Powell, with two of his companies, were told to make the patrol.

In the heavy timber and deep ravines beyond Prentiss's front Moore apparently lost perspective. He returned to camp after dark, stating that "a thorough reconnaissance over the extent of three miles failed to discover the enemy." According to another account the patrol traveled only about a mile to "an old cottonfield" where some Negroes said about two hundred Rebel cavalry had been seen that afternoon. This discrepancy suggests a failed mission and a faked report.

Moore's route must have been diagonally to the southwest, across the front of Sherman's division. He evidently did not penetrate deeply into the woods. About 7 P.M. Moore advised Prentiss that the results of his reconnaissance were negative. This was to have a profound effect on Prentiss's reasoning later that night.

About an hour and a half later Captain Gilbert D. Johnson, who had gone out with Company H of the 12th Michigan to strengthen the outer pickets, came back to camp and told Officer of the Day Graves that "he could see long lines of camp fires" and "hear bugle sounds and drums."

Graves went to Prentiss with the report, but he was instructed only to withdraw Captain Johnson's company. Said Graves, "He [Prentiss] remarked that the company would be taken if left there, that it was merely a reconnaissance of the enemy in force, and [he] ordered the company in, which was obeyed."

Captain Johnson returned to camp with his men about 10 P.M. His account was so convincing, however, that Graves again returned to Prentiss's tent, this time taking Johnson with him. Prentiss merely told the officers not to be alarmed, that everything was "all right." In the opinion of the two officers everything did not seem to be "all right." Joining Major Powell of the 25th Missouri, they went to the tent of Colonel Everett Peabody, their brigade commander, and told him what had occurred.

Ironically, there were few men more capable of handling this situation in the entire army than Peabody. Known for his competence and strong will, this second child of a Springfield, Massachusetts, preacher, had graduated from Harvard in 1849 as an engineer. For nearly ten years Peabody had labored to construct the Western railroads, becoming the Chief Engineer of the Memphis & Ohio road in the mid-1850's. When he settled in St. Joseph, Missouri, shortly before the war to build the Platte County Railroad, Peabody had already acquired a reputation as the "best field engineer in the West."

Following the beginning of hostilities one of his friends wrote to James H. Lane of Kansas that there was no man in northern Missouri who could be more useful to the Union cause than Everett Peabody. Originally commissioned a major of volunteers, he took a battalion that became the nucleus of the 13th Missouri Infantry. When the regiment was formally mustered into service, Peabody was promoted to colonel.

During the siege of Lexington in September, 1861, Peabody was struck in the chest by a spent musket ball. He was so paralyzed by the blow that his men attempted to carry him to the hospital. On the way Peabody took another wound, a rifle ball in the ankle, and was captured. Unable to walk without crutches for three months, he was paroled by Price's Missourians. Following his exchange and the reorganization of his old regiment, Peabody joined the Tennessee River expedition, becoming senior colonel of Prentiss's 1st Brigade and an acting brigadier general.

Yet Peabody's rise in the military had been marred by controversy. He was often short-tempered and headstrong, and his outspoken manner had involved him in many violent arguments. On one occasion he attempted to impress a Missouri cavalry battalion into his regiment at gunpoint, for which he was charged with "exciting mutiny," although never brought to trial. During the siege of Lexington he exchanged some hot words with a captain of Mulligan's Irish Regiment. The two had actually drawn swords when another officer intervened.

Although he was not particularly handsome, Peabody's large physique commanded great respect. He stood six feet one inch tall and weighed two hundred and forty pounds, his stern countenance added import to his actions. Not yet thirty-two, Peabody was plagued with an inner belief that he would soon be killed. Yet his outlook remained calm. Writing home shortly after joining the Army, he talked freely of his death: "I have a sort of presentiment that I shall go under. If I do, it shall be in a manner that the old family shall feel proud of it." His most recent letter, written to his brother on March 31, again mentioned the possibility of a violent death and closed with an ominous remark: "Say to them all at home, that if we have good luck, I shall win my spurs."

On the night of April 5 Peabody was much closer than he realized to fulfilling this prophecy. After talking with Graves, Powell, and Johnson, he was further convinced the Confederates were in force along the army's front.

Earlier in the evening Peabody had been to see Prentiss with a suggestion that the division be put in condition to resist an attack. Preparations to meet anything more than an enemy patrol were lacking, and Peabody wanted to redeploy at least one artillery battery, then in park, to a position in front of the 25th Missouri's camp. According to one of the 25th's officers Prentiss "hooted" at the idea of an attack by the enemy and failed to give Peabody's ideas serious consideration.

About midnight Peabody went to the tent of his close friend, Captain Simon S. Eveans, and woke him, saying that he had not slept yet and did not intend to do so, "as there was business to attend to." In Peabody's estimation the army was exposed to a powerful enemy in a very careless and unguarded manner, and was likely to be surprised at any time.

Captain Eveans and his tentmate, Acting Lieutenant James Newhard, dressed and took out some cigars. As the officers talked, Peabody seemed to ponder the alternatives. Finally he remarked that he did not intend to be taken by surprise and would act upon his own judgment.

Lieutenant Newhard was sent to find Powell, who, when he arrived, was told to take a patrol and reconnoiter in front of the army's pickets.

In the opinion of many of the Sixth Division's officers this decisive action was responsible for saving the Union army from certain destruction. Upon his own responsibility, and without regard to censure, Peabody ordered Powell to take three companies of the 25th Missouri out at 3 A.M. and look for the enemy observed by Johnson. His instructions to Powell if he encountered the enemy were to "drive in the guard and open up on the reserve, develop the force, hold the ground as long as possible, then fall back."

Powell, the veteran Regular Army officer, soon had his patrol organized. Three of the 25th's best captains, Schmitz of Company B, Dill of Company H, and Eveans of Company E, were summoned and told to turn out their men quickly and quietly, seeing that each man had forty rounds in his cartridge box. Somehow, probably because of Graves's and Johnson's involvement, two companies of the 12th Michigan Infantry were included in the patrol.

In a short while the men were ready, and they started for the woods in front. Peabody was there to shake the hands of his officers and bid them good-bye. Later that day, so he said, he would be killed.

Led by their tough little major the patrol filed down an old wagon trail and disappeared into the darkness. Ahead the trail led for a mile through thick forests to an obscure cottonfield and a rendezvous with destiny.

CHAPTER X

The Sun of Austerlitz

Today Fraley field seems little more than a dull, undistinguished plot of ground. Its drab appearance and gentle contours are unimpressive, much as they were in 1862. Only a small brook bisects what used to be the middle of the field, leisurely wandering northwest toward Shiloh Branch of Owl Creek. The surrounding woods are thick and brushy and seem overpowering in their abundance. Some of the soldiers who camped nearby in April, 1862, described the Fraley land as merely "an open spot" in the timber. Like other woodland plots it was probably overgrown with heavy patches of thistles and cockleburs, and had a scattering of small trees and saplings.

From a military standpoint Fraley field was of little significance, except that it was generally open over an expanse of nearly forty acres. To the deployed Confederate corps of William J. Hardee, the Fraley ground provided a good point of observation, causing the skirmishers of S. A. M. Wood's brigade to occupy it during the early morning of April 5. Having patiently waited in line of battle for the entire day while the various corps gradually moved into position, the men of Wood's brigade finally were told to camp where they stood. As night fell Wood recalled his advance pickets, sending out in their place the 3d Mississippi Infantry Battalion, commanded by Major A. B. Hardcastle.

Hardcastle's men, like many others of the Confederates, were newcomers to the service, having been recruited at Grenada, Mississippi, during the past winter. Numbering about two hundred and eighty men, the battalion deployed at nightfall across the front of Wood's brigade. Hardcastle selected a slight rise of ground in the southwest corner of Fraley field for his main picket line. Here the clearing abutted with another farm field, Wood's, which combined to form a rough hourglass pattern of cleared ground.

Posted in advance of this line and extended into Fraley field were two detachments of less than a dozen men each, the most advanced being within a hundred yards of the main Corinth and Pittsburg road. Beyond them only a few mounted cavalry vedettes watched in the direction of the enemy's camps, the closest of which lay about a half-mile distant.

Unlike the previous evening, when a heavy rainstorm had soaked the exposed Confederates, the night of April 5 was clear, cool, and unusually quiet as daylight approached. Just before daybreak Hardcastle's outposts were startled to hear "singular beats on the drum" in the vicinity of the enemy's camps. Alerted by this nearby enemy activity, the advanced pickets watched through the half-light of approaching dawn for its significance.

Following one of the numerous, seldom-used wagon trails traversing the countryside, Powell and his patrol of five companies of Missouri and Michigan infantry probed through the semidarkness east of Fraley field. After an uneventful hike through the woods past a clearing where only the "crowing of a barnyard rooster" disturbed their march, Powell's patrol had nearly fallen victim to a self-inflicted disaster. Powell had unwisely divided his force into three separate columns after passing beyond his picket line. When the detachment on the right suddenly stumbled across another's path in the pitch-dark forest, each had mistaken the other for the enemy. Only at the last instant were the men prevented from firing into one another.

Everyone's nerves seemed on edge, and the most advanced of the three squads halted after reaching the Pittsburg and Corinth road to await better visibility.

As the first streaks of light gathered on the horizon, an enemy horseman was discovered in their front. Promptly the Federal captain in charge ordered his men to withdraw. They had just started to leave, hoping to join Powell's other detachments, when three sudden shots rang out. Making a hasty retreat, the squad soon found and rejoined Powell, who summoned the other detachments. In the dim morning light Powell formed his men into a long skirmish line and sent them forward across the road into Fraley field. It was now about 4:55 A.M.

After firing three warning shots, the Confederate vedettes had wheeled and retreated to their main picket line. Lieutenant F. W. Hammock of Major Hardcastle's advanced pickets next saw what he believed was about one thousand soldiers in a line three hundred and fifty yards long advancing upon him.

Having only seven riflemen, the Confederate lieutenant ordered his men to fire when the enemy was ninety yards away. At the sound of Hammock's fire the startled Federals raised their muskets and returned the fire. Hammock's men were thereby forced to fall back under a shower of musket balls to the battalion line, passing through the second detachment of advanced pickets on their way.

When Powell's infantry approached midfield, they were again fired on by the second picket detachment, which then also gave way and quickly fell back.

It was nearing dawn. Ahead the ground gradually ascended to a brushy knoll at the border of an adjacent field. Through the haze a line of kneeling soldiers was observed awaiting their approach. Powell's men, already jumpy from having been shot at, opened fire with their smoothbore muskets at a range of nearly two hundred yards.

According to Hardcastle this first enemy volley was too high—"most of the shots passed over us," he said. When his Mississippians returned the fire, however, Second Lieutenant Frederick Klinger of Company B, 25th Missouri Infantry, was struck by one of the bullets. Klinger thus became the first item on what would soon become a dreadful butcher's bill. Powell, following his instructions, continued to fight from the middle of the first clearing. More soldiers were soon hit, and blood began to flow freely on both sides.

Amid a drab, weed-thatched farm field in an obscure, backwoods section of Tennessee one of the bloodiest chapters in American military history was about to begin. Although most of the participants were as yet unaware, the Battle of Shiloh was now joined.

Fortunately for Powell's command there was scattered cover in Fraley field. After the first few volleys Powell's men deployed behind saplings and brush wherever possible and opened a brisk fire on the Confederate line. One of Powell's men noted that the incoming fire was particularly accurate. Several bullets soon struck at head height the small tree behind which he was standing, and another clipped his right ear. Private Franklin H. Bailey of the 12th Michigan Infantry considered the fight to be a "sharp" one. A lad of barely seventeen, he had been so anxious to go with Powell's reconnoitering party despite the fact that he was recovering from a "severe case of the ague" that he had deceived his captain when refused permission. Enlisting the aid of his orderly sergeant, Bailey had been able to obtain a supply of ammunition although an officer refused to issue him any. Then, with the darkness concealing his identity, he went along. As he stood in the middle of Fraley field, loading and firing his ponderous Austrian musket, Bailey suddenly saw the man next to him fall. Although so enraged that he "could have tore the heart out of the Rebel" who had fired the shot, he later "shuddered to think of ever having to go into another battle."

The toll in Hardcastle's line, meanwhile, included several sergeants and a corporal wounded and at least two privates killed.

Despite these mounting losses Hardcastle's Mississippians also doggedly held their ground in this, their first fight.

As there were nearly three hundred Confederates and several hundred Federals involved in the skirmish, much tumult was emanating from Fraley field. Alerted by the sound of gunfire, a number of Confederate officers now sprang into action.

Sidney Johnston was eating a breakfast of coffee and cold biscuits at a small campfire with his staff when he heard the firing. Asking his staff to note the hour in their notebooks, he prepared to ride to the front. Edward W. Munford recorded the time as 5:14 A.M. With the sharp rattle of musketry as their guide, Johnston and his staff mounted and departed for the front just before sunrise.

Brigadier General S. A. M. Wood had also heard the firing. Noting that it came from his picket line, he sent a staff officer to instruct Hardcastle to hold his ground until the brigade could advance. By the time this messenger arrived Hardcastle's men already had been fighting for about a half-hour. Encouraged by the staff officer to continue the contest, Hardcastle's Mississippians found that the enemy refused to retreat. Volley for volley was fired and received.

Another half-hour passed with little change except for the steady exodus from both sides of an increasing number of wounded. As there was no sign of Wood's advancing brigade, some of the Confederates became discouraged. The sun had climbed above the treetops, and as the sharp rattle of musketry continued, billowing clouds of white smoke drifted high into a cloudless sky.

In Prentiss's camp a trickle of casualties had begun to arrive shortly before 6 A.M. Fraley field being distant about three-quarters of a mile, the sound of gunfire was deadened by the thick forests. Peabody, however, learning from Powell's wounded that a sharp fight was in progress, ordered out "a sustaining force" from his brigade. Apparently there was some question as to the extent of fighting and the number of enemy troops encountered. Peabody sent only five companies of the 21st Missouri to Powell's relief. Ironically the officer in charge, Colonel David Moore, was the man who had conducted the unsuccessful reconnaissance of the previous afternoon. In Moore's opinion there was no large enemy force nearby, and he confidently marched from camp about 6:15 A.M., fully expecting to encounter "only a skirmishing party."

About the same time Powell noticed a change in the opposing Confederate skirmish line in Fraley field. With their colors departing first, the Confederates had begun to pull back, one company at a time. In their place, however, another line of gray infantry soon appeared, the new line being stronger than the first. One of Powell's Michigan privates soon saw a body of Rebel cavalry working its way

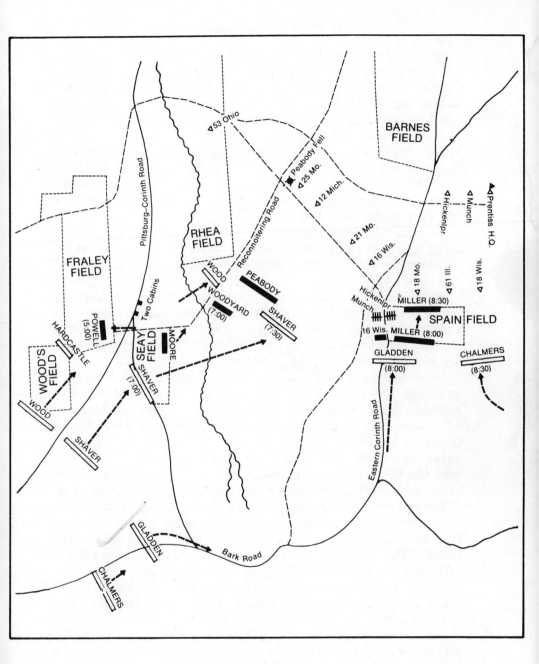

MAP 4
Assault on Prentiss
5 A.M.–9 A.M., April 6 (Chapter 10)

around the Union left flank. Powell's attention was directed to this, and after a brief pause he had his bugler sound retreat.

The long-awaited advance of S. A. M. Wood's brigade finally had materialized at about 6:30 A.M. With Wood's deployed battle lines marching across the open field in Hardcastle's rear, the Mississippians had fallen back to take their place in the brigade line. Having suffered nearly two dozen casualties in the morning's fight, the 3rd Mississippi Battalion now formed on the right of Wood's brigade, which halted briefly while a new line of skirmishers went out. Lying dead in the grass nearby were four privates of Major Hardcastle's battalion, the first Confederates killed at Shiloh.

As the new skirmish line of two Arkansas infantry units rushed across the rise of ground at the corner of Fraley field, they exchanged several sharp volleys with Powell before the Federals disappeared into the woods beyond.

Powell's men looking to their rear, now witnessed an awesome sight. Moving behind the onrushing line of Arkansas skirmishers was a seemingly endless battle line of men in "butternut." Slowly they marched across Farmer Fraley's field, their rifled muskets glimmering in the soft morning light.

Beauregard later aptly described the Confederate advance as "like an Alpine avalanche." The front line alone consisted of twenty-two regiments and two battalions of infantry divided into four brigades, in all over nine thousand effective troops. With the exception of Gladden's brigade, which was added to the front line to fill the interval between the Third Corps right and Lick Creek, these men were Hardee's—veterans of several months' service in central Kentucky, although inexperienced in drawn battle. They were the core of Sidney Johnston's Kentucky army, however, and accordingly had earned the dubious honor of making the initial assault. Hardee's men were typically backwoodsmen and rural, lower-middle-class farmers. His Arkansans were an especially rough-and-tumble lot, many of them appearing with gigantic Bowie-type knives and an assortment of revolvers thrust through their belts. Though inexperienced, their commanders were some of the most promising officers to be found in the army.

William Joseph Hardee himself was among the more prominent generals of the South. His name was a byword in military circles on both sides, and his textbook, *Rifle and Light Infantry Tactics,* published in 1853, was the standard of its day. A graduate of West Point, 1838, he had twice been brevetted for gallantry during the Mexican War. Before serving as commandant of cadets at the U. S. Military Academy, Hardee had reached the rank of brevet lieutenant colonel in the Old Army. When his native Georgia seceded from the Union, Hardee resigned his commission and soon became a Confederate brigadier general, serving in Arkansas until the fall of 1861. A rather tall and wiry man with the correct and upright bearing expected of West Pointers, he had been promoted to major general when ordered to Kentucky in October, 1861. As a former major in Sidney Johnston's old 2d U. S. Cavalry Regiment, Hardee had come to be regarded by Johnston as his right arm. In the order of battle for April 6 Hardee commanded the front line, three-fourths of which was made up of men from his own Third Corps.

For brigadiers Hardee relied on such men as Thomas C. Hindman and Patrick Ronayne Cleburne. Cleburne later would become one of the most dashing and aggressive fighters in all of the Confederacy, earning a reputation as "the Stonewall Jackson of the West." Hindman was an eminently successful citizen-soldier, a decorated veteran of the war with Mexico and an influential Congressman of his adopted state, Arkansas. Even the lesser-known commanders were men of some distinction. Sterling A. M. Wood was an Alabama state legislator and a prominent newspaper editor before the war. Colonel R. G. Shaver had led an Arkansas regiment before earning command of a full brigade in late 1861. With such men in the forefront the Confederate army had confidently awaited the order to advance on the morning of April 6.

According to the official battle reports of Hardee's regimental commanders the men were called into line at daylight. Allowing for the time necessary to form ranks and distribute orders to advance nearly an hour passed before Hardee's entire line was in motion. There were obvious reasons for this delay. Once Hardee had been notified to begin the advance, couriers had to be sent to advise the brigade commanders, who in turn passed the word along to the regimental commanders. Considering the irregularity of the line, the roughness of the terrain, and the early morning hour it was a considerable task for the couriers to distribute Hardee's orders.

Shaver's brigade was among the first to go forward. Before sunrise this nearly all-Arkansas brigade was marching through the timberland with its old flintlock muskets at the ready. According to a Confederate staff officer a heavy white mist hung in the air, shrouding the trees in an eerie fog.

As daylight filled the woodlands a mile southwest of Fraley field, Johnston and his staff rode forward on the Pittsburg and Corinth road. Arriving at the Y in the road, where the Bark Road made a a junction, Johnston dismounted to set up his headquarters. Soon thereafter Beauregard rode up, having spent the night in an ambulance nearby. Beauregard found General Johnston sipping coffee— Johnston was particularly fond of coffee, once having complained when compelled to drink a substitute brew made from scorched sweet potatoes and cooked wheat and rye. According to Beauregard they discussed the general plan of operations. Beauregard was to remain in the rear, following the movements of the army and sending the reserves forward when needed. Johnston would go to the front and lead the attack.

As the minutes passed, several other generals joined in the conversation around a small campfire. Inevitably the question of whether to proceed with the attack again was discussed, it being learned that an enemy patrol had fired on Hardee's skirmish line. According to Bragg Beauregard once more urged a retreat to Corinth. Since the firing in front had nearly died out, uncertainty about the enemy's design intensified. Suddenly the sharp rattle of musketry again broke out in the woods nearby. Johnston calmly remarked, "The battle has opened, gentlemen; it is too late to change our dispositions." He then proposed to move immediately to the front.

As his subordinates scattered to their respective commands, Johnston summoned his staff. The general's thoroughbred bay, Fire-eater, was brought forward. Johnston's appearance as a horseman excited great admiration. One of his staff officers later remembered that, like a cavalier, Johnston sat upon a horse as if it had grown up a part of him. Another soldier remembered Johnston, mounted upon a magnificent steed, his face "aflame with a fighting spirit," to be "the ideal embodiment of the fiery essence of war."

Johnston, in buoyant spirits, turned to his staff and exclaimed, "Tonight we will water our horses in the Tennessee River." Precisely at 6:40 A.M. Johnston, accompanied by his staff, rode to the front, leaving Beauregard in charge at Headquarters No. 1. It was a markedly unorthodox arrangement, considering Beauregard's earlier role.

Overhead a dazzlingly brilliant sun had begun to climb in a cloudless sky. Some of the Confederate officers looked up and remarked that it must be another "sun of Austerlitz."

About halfway back to camp on the narrow trail now known as Reconnoitering road, Major Powell's men were surprised to see Colonel David Moore and five companies of the 21st Missouri advancing toward them. Although Powell had many dead and wounded, Moore berated him for retreating and insisted that he turn about and join the 21st's column. Together they would finish them (the Confederates) up in no time, said Moore. Despite Powell's warning that the enemy was advancing in force, Moore would not listen. Those able to fight among Powell's men were compelled to return to duty. Moore's only concession was to send a lieutenant back to camp to bring up the remainder of the 21st Missouri. While the lieutenant dashed away on this errand, Moore reorganized the two commands into several columns preparatory to a further advance.

Upon returning to camp, Moore's lieutenant found Prentiss there, talking with the 21st's lieutenant colonel, Humphrey Woodyard. Prentiss had belatedly learned of the events occurring within his division, traceable, so he believed, to the unauthorized and irresponsible action of Peabody. Becoming increasingly irate as the story unraveled, Prentiss ordered Woodyard to join Moore, but talked of taking strong disciplinary action against Peabody.

A few minutes before 7 A.M. Woodyard joined with Moore and Powell in the woods about a half-mile northeast of Fraley field. Advancing by right flank in several ranks, the combined units again followed the wagon trail leading to Fraley field. Several hundred yards ahead they came to a fork in the road, where the path earlier taken by Powell's reconnoitering party made an abrupt turn to the right. In the roadway awaiting their approach was Company A of the 16th Wisconsin Volunteers.

As the brigade pickets stationed on the extreme right, Company A had heard the distant firing at daybreak and by coincidence had moved westward along a country road that crossed Moore's route. Led by their captain, Edward Saxe, they fell in with Moore's command, taking position at the head of the column. Earlier some of Saxe's men had observed Powell's patrol leaving camp and had laughed at them for going through the motions, confident there were no Rebels within ten miles. As Saxe made ready to march along with Moore, he threw off his coat and remarked, "Boys, we will fall in on the right and lead them."

A few minutes later the head of Moore's column, led by Captain Saxe, came to an old cottonfield past which Powell had earlier marched. Visible across the field on their left were several lines of enemy infantry screened by cavalry.

Saxe continued on.

A few paces more, and then, from behind a fence along the roadside, a volley of musketry blazed in their faces. Saxe and Sergeant John J. Williams were instantly killed. The men immediately behind them went flat in the road and opened fire on the fencerow, soon causing the Confederates to fall back.

Seeing the trouble ahead, Moore promptly ordered his Missourians to file to the left and form in the open field so as to flank the enemy's position. Unknown to Moore, however, the troops he had encountered were the advance skirmishers of Shaver's brigade, which at the very moment was advancing from its bivouac area less than a half-mile away.

The cottonfield, Seay's, was the site of a farmhouse from which Sherman's outpost pickets had been driven the day before. Behind a second split-rail fence that ran along the western edge of this field at least two companies of Arkansas infantry were strongly posted.

As Moore's men marched into the open field, they came under a brisk fire from this fencerow, distant about a hundred yards. Moore, standing in front, was forming his men when a musket ball the size of a concord grape struck him in the right leg, shattering the bone below the knee. Next Lieutenant Henry Menn, Moore's messenger, was shot in the head. Having quickly lost several officers including their commander, Moore's skittish line fired a ragged volley and then began to draw back.

Rather than see his men butchered in the open field, Powell also told the 25th Missouri to cease firing and fall back. They promptly marched for camp at the double-quick, vanishing down Reconnoitering road and leaving the 21st Missouri to decide its own fate. Soon thereafter Captain Saxe's men also started for camp, believing as the firing died down that the skirmish was over. Wrapping the bodies of Saxe and Williams in rubber blankets, they marched rapidly through the woods. Less than a half-hour later they were back in camp, eating breakfast.

With Lieutenant Colonel Woodyard now in command, the 21st Missouri drifted out of effective range of the Rebel muskets. Before going to the rear, however, Moore had sent a soldier to Sherman's nearby line of pickets, warning that the enemy was moving in their front.

Yet Woodyard withdrew only a short distance, halting his men along a knoll on the eastern edge of Seay field. Now uncertain of the enemy's intentions, he held his ground, maintaining a desultory fire until about 7:15 A.M. At that time the Confederate infantry occupying the opposite fencerow began to withdraw.

Woodyard soon learned the reason for this. Leading the advance of Hardee's front line, Shaver's brigade swept from the southern fringe of Seay field in seemingly endless numbers. Woodyard realized that he would soon be outflanked and ordered his men to withdraw to the northeastern corner of the field. Here they were joined by three other companies of the 16th Wisconsin Infantry that also had been on picket duty. Learning that Company A had gone to the front, these companies had marched off "like a lot of school boys," said one of the men, to help Company A. Nearly all were green. The night before, as they were going out on picket duty, they had received live ammunition for the first time since their enlistment.

Placing these three companies under his command, Woodyard sent them farther to the left, where they deployed along a timbered rise overlooking a small ravine. Then, as the Confederates continued to appear in increasing numbers from the opposite tree line, Woodyard again ordered a retreat, soon rejoining the three Wisconsin companies with his own command. His men were barely in position before their thin line was struck by Shaver's skirmishers. Loading and firing from behind an incline, these few soldiers were, to their surprise, momentarily able to hold the enemy in check.

Marching for the first time under enemy fire, Shaver's brigade now began to show its inexperience. Although it was unscathed by the ineffective Union fire, a halt was ordered to allow the skirmishers to go forward and "feel the ground." Following a delay of some minutes Shaver's two-thousand-man brigade hesitantly pushed forward and engaged the Federals at close range.

In Woodyard's line one of the Wisconsin privates agreed with his captain, who thought discretion was the better part of valor. When a hasty retreat was ordered, there was no hesitation about compliance. Soon a mad scramble occurred as the larger Confederate force enveloped both flanks and poured several volleys into the fleeing Federals. Firing wildly, Woodyard's Missourians also fell back. In their footsteps Shaver's Arkansas infantry swept across the vacated ridge, advancing at "quick time."

About 7 A.M. the sharp volleys issuing from Seay field had alerted Everett Peabody of further trouble. At the time he was eating breakfast with a civilian visitor. Taking care not to alarm his guest, Peabody excused himself and went to locate his officers.

Having had no orders from Prentiss's headquarters, and with the rattle of musketry less than a thousand yards away, Peabody now made another important decision, again solely on his own responsibility. Summoning the 25th's drummer, he had the boy sound "the long roll," the army's urgent call to arms. Since a large portion of the 25th and all of the 21st Missouri regiments were already engaged, there were but two other regiments now in camp. Of these the 16th Wisconsin was on the extreme left, about six hundred yards distant, and did not respond to the long roll.

According to a private in Peabody's brigade, their colonel had already ordered most of the 25th Missouri to form in their camp streets after daybreak, when the wounded first began to arrive. As the 12th Michigan and remainder of the 25th Missouri raced for their guns and formed on the color line, Prentiss came riding rapidly down the line. Reining his horse in front of Peabody, who was just preparing to mount, Prentiss angrily demanded to know if he had provoked an attack by sending out a force without orders. Peabody answered that he had sent out a reconnaissance patrol after attempting to notify Prentiss of his intention.

This further infuriated Prentiss, who shouted within hearing of a number of witnesses, "Colonel Peabody, I will hold you personally responsible for bringing on this engagement."

Peabody glared back at him. With obvious contempt he remarked that he was personally responsible for all of his actions. He then mounted his horse and rode away. Prentiss never forgave him. In his official report he mentioned Everett Peabody only once, and then merely to list him as a brigade commander.

About 7:30 A.M. Peabody led his two regiments forward into the south woods. Numbering about eleven hundred men, they moved swiftly toward the sound of the firing. Many of his men's lives could now be measured in the span of a few minutes.

A short distance into the woods Peabody met Powell, limping back to camp with the survivors of the original reconnaissance patrol. Peabody learned from Powell that the enemy occupied Seay field. Adding Powell's able men to his ranks, Peabody advanced in line of battle, soon finding himself in the vicinity of Woodyard's running fight with Shaver's brigade.

According to Woodyard, he asked Peabody to position his men along a ridge in the rear, where Woodyard might rally his rapidly retiring command. Moving the 25th Missouri and 12th Michigan onto the crest of high ground, Peabody deployed his troops in a battle line about four hundred yards long under the shade of towering oaks. Forward of this line lay a ravine, its slopes thick with briars and thornbushes.

It was shortly after 7:30 A.M. Peabody's men were standing at rest, looking to the front but unable to see much, when Woodyard's men drifted back on the left and formed an extension of their line.

Suddenly the Confederates broke over the crest of the opposite ridge, seventy-five yards away. The sight was unforgettable. With massed ranks many lines deep the Confederates came through the oaks in seemingly endless numbers. One of Peabody's privates thought it was the "grandest scene he had ever witnessed." To the colonel of the 12th Michigan the spectacle was staggering; every hilltop in his sight was nigh instantly covered with Confederates. Shouting to his men, Lieutenant Colonel Robert T. Van Horn of the 25th Missouri gave the commands: "Attention, battalion, ready —aim—fire!" There was a flash of fire and a tremendous roar. For those several thousand Americans battle was at last a reality.

Advancing in the Confederate line was a young soldier, Henry M. Stanley, aged nineteen. Later to become Sir Henry Morton Stanley, the famous journalist and explorer, he was experiencing at Shiloh his first test of manhood. As a private in the "Dixie Grays," Company E of the 6th Arkansas Infantry, Stanley had set out that morning in buoyant spirits. At dawn, while waiting for the line to advance, he and a companion had plucked a bunch of violets and jauntily stuffed them in their caps. Gaily they joked that perhaps the Yanks wouldn't shoot them if they saw the flowers, a sign of peace.

To Stanley, advancing at the double-quick into the ravine, the first enemy volley was an appalling crash of sound. It was as if a "mountain had been upheaved, with huge rocks tumbling down a slope." Then he heard a shout—"There they are!"—and the Confederates blazed away with leveled muskets. Again and again the sequence was repeated; loud explosions and violent sounds in all directions. When the man behind him fired too close to the side of his head, Stanley felt like punching him, though he was blinded by the smoke and nearly deafened. Too soon he was thoroughly frightened, yet he continued to work his musket with nervous haste, mindful that others were doing so.

Shaver's brigade, momentarily stunned by the heavy Federal musketry, failed to press its attack. Instead the two opposing battle lines stood in place, firing volley after volley into one another across the wooded ravine.

As the Federal fire found its mark, at least one Confederate regiment, the 7th Arkansas, was ordered to flatten. Although Shaver's brigade overlapped the Union left by the length of nearly a full regiment, its own left was outflanked by Peabody's line, causing the Confederate regiments on the right to halt until the whole line could again go forward. Division, brigade, and regimental commanders were active in prodding the men to move on, however, and when Wood's brigade appeared on Shaver's left, Shaver again prepared to charge.

The men of Wood's brigade, advancing through heavy timber on Shaver's left, earlier had watched with concern as the rough ground created a wide interval between their lines. Four regiments on Wood's right flank had finally veered in the direction of Shaver's command, although this resulted in a gap within their own brigade. Since the path taken by Shaver's brigade in its pursuit of Woodyard was obliquely to the northeast rather than toward Sherman's camps directly north of the Confederate staging area, Hardee's front line was split into segments.

Communications and tactical coordination, never good enough under ideal conditions, were all but lost in the rough timberland south of the enemy's camps. Wood's two right-flank regiments, the 55th Tennessee and 3d Mississippi, moving at a slower pace than Shaver, belatedly arrived in advance of Shaver's left with their flank exposed to Peabody's waiting infantry. At the first discharge of the Federal guns both of these regiments were taken by surprise and stampeded.

The 55th Tennessee was a new regiment, having been organized for less than ninety days, and was sadly under strength. Of such raw Tennessee recruits the wife of Braxton Bragg had earlier warned her husband, "Do not trust the Tennessee troops. . . . Put the Tennesseans where your batteries can fire upon them if they attempt to run." Yet the 3d Mississippi Battalion also was in difficulty. Of these Mississippians Elise Bragg had confidently written, "They will never fail you." The 3d was now without its commander, Major Hard-castle, who had been separated in the tangled thickets and had wandered to the left when his battalion had gone to the right. Leaderless, the Mississippians also fell easy victim to Peabody's short-range musketry.

Side by side the Tennesseans and Mississippians ran to the rear shouting, "Retreat, retreat." The effect was wildly contagious. Major James T. Martin of the 7th Arkansas Infantry, on Shaver's left, was slowly advancing with his men when the 55th Tennessee burst through their line in complete disorder. Martin saw his regiment suddenly melt away before his eyes. The 7th's nearly eight hundred men began running to the rear in the wildest confusion, and only the determined effort of a number of officers stopped some of them. Lieutenant Colonel John M. Dean, commanding the regiment, Martin, and several company officers ran among the fleeing men, ordering them to halt. S. A. M. Wood and his entire staff arrived at a gallop and dashed among the men to help. General Hindman also was present, actively rallying the fugitives. By their concerted effort they were finally able to re-form the lines.

Although the regiments forming Shaver's right did not break, they had suffered severe losses during the stand-up, short-range fire fight. Captain Charles Swett's battery, having unlimbered on Shaver's right, found many targets within easy range, and their blasts of grapeshot and canister had shaken the Federal line. Yet Swett's position was exposed, and Shaver noted with alarm that gunners were falling so fast that the battery would soon be useless. Upon reporting the situation to Hindman, Shaver was ordered immediately to charge the enemy's line.

About 8:15 A.M. the order "Fix bayonets!—On the double-quick!" ran along the lines in Shaver's brigade. Moving forward at a trot and supported by Wood's four regiments, Shaver's troops rushed through the trees at Peabody's line. Here Private Stanley first heard the bloodcurdling, high-pitched Rebel yell that rose all along the line. According to Stanley it "drove all sanity and order" from the attackers, released their pent-up emotions, and electrified the charging line with the wildest enthusiasm.

To Peabody's waiting infantry it seemed, indeed, as if an avalanche had broken loose. The Confederates swarmed across the shallow ravine, their flanks overlapping the Federal line. "In a few minutes," one veteran sadly commented, "all was chaos."

Two brothers, privates in the 25th Missouri, had been fighting side by side just as a battery appeared from the left at full speed. Pointing out the battery to his brother, one said, "We will give them hell now. . . ." His brother watched, first with hope, then in despair as the battery halted, unlimbered, and opened fire on the Federal line. As the first brother remarked, "We couldn't help it, we had to let go."

Woodyard, who reported a deadly cross fire coming from both right and left, promptly fell back. To one thoroughly confused private of the 16th Wisconsin the so-called retreat was "a mad scramble to the rear." He soon became so disoriented that he fell in with some Missourians and continued to fight with them.

By 8:30 A.M. the remnants of Peabody's line were streaming back through camp, their officers desperately attempting to rally the men among the standing tents. Everett Peabody, bleeding from several wounds but still mounted on his big horse, hurriedly galloped to the left to look for Prentiss. He was nowhere to be found.

Prentiss had learned shortly after 7 A.M. of the enemy's advance, getting the news from a messenger dispatched by the wounded David Moore. Following his stormy exchange with Peabody, Prentiss had galloped among the Sixth Division's camps to spread the alarm. Among the first in his path was the camp of the 18th Missouri. Its colonel, Madison Miller, was also commander of the understrength Second Brigade, consisting of the 18th Missouri, 61st Illinois, and, temporarily, 18th Wisconsin regiments.

Miller at the time was breakfasting with his regiment's field and staff officers on cold sliced beef, baked chicken, hot biscuits, butter, and coffee. Prentiss suddenly dashed up to the officers' mess and shouted for Miller to get his brigade in line—they were already fighting on the right. Miller leaped up, meat and mess tins flying, and ordered a youthful private to beat the long roll. Officers raced to join their companies. One officer hastily stuffed breakfast meat inside his shirt as he dashed off, reasoning with a good amount of common sense that it might be a long while before he had another meal.

Next in line was the camp of the 61st Illinois Volunteers. About 7:30 A.M. they heard the long roll in the adjoining camp of the 18th Missouri. This resulted in what an eighteen-year-old Illinois private described as a scene of "desperate haste," as the long roll was taken up in the 61st's camps. While the men were buckling on their cartridge boxes, an unidentified staff officer galloped rapidly down the line from the right. Halting abruptly in the middle of a company street, he cast a hurried glance about him. The horse was flecked with foam, and its eyes and nostrils were "red as blood." The mount whirled nervously about, knocking over tin mess plates, and the officer shouted, "My God! This regiment's not in line yet! They have been fighting on the right over an hour!" In an instant he was again off, leaving the 61st in a state of near shock.

Although the 16th Wisconsin was actually a part of Peabody's brigade, it was out of earshot of the 61st's drum roll, and Prentiss himself had to order the regiment into line. All but Company A of the four picket companies by this time had returned to camp. Most were leisurely eating breakfast when their company officers called roll to see who was missing from the Seay field fight. The remainder of the regiment was about to have breakfast when the long roll suddenly sounded and the order "Fall in!" spread through camp.

According to the 16th Wisconsin's colonel, Benjamin Allen, Prentiss now ordered him to advance upon the enemy. Deploying his men in line of battle, Allen promptly marched to the front and took position in a thicket two hundred yards from camp. On their extreme left lay the southwestern corner of Spain field, where Prentiss had reviewed his division on April 5. Allen's men were not pleased with what they saw. The brush was so thick in front that they could see only a short distance. In their left rear the center of Spain field sloped upward to a gentle crown. Some of the men foresaw that the enemy's bullets would do terrible damage if they had to retreat in that direction. Already one of the 16th's lieutenants suspected that Allen was unreasonably ambitious for promotion and had advanced the regiment into a position of danger in order to get personal recognition. Although heavy firing was heard ahead and to the right, nothing could be seen through the woods in front, so Allen had his men stand idly by, awaiting developments.

As Peabody had warned, Prentiss's division, especially Miller's brigade, was sadly unprepared for battle. The 18th Wisconsin, newly arrived on the fifth, had reported without equipment and had consumed the last of its rations before coming ashore. The men had not been fed for a full day and, worse yet, were short of ammunition. Nervously the 18th Wisconsin formed in heavy brush on Prentiss's left flank, a short distance in front of their camp.

This unexpected sequence of events was a trying ordeal for twenty-year-old Private Jeremiah W. Baldock of Company K, 18th Wisconsin Infantry. He had been detailed on picket duty the night before and was so tired when he was relieved at about sunrise that he remarked to his orderly sergeant that he was "going to sleep today, even if Abe Lincoln comes." Baldock was in the process of removing his uniform when the long roll sounded and orders came to fall in. Since his accouterments were nearby, Baldock found that instead of enjoying a lengthy nap, he was the first man of his company to form for battle.

Miller's initial position was along the north edge of Spain field, behind a natural cover of stumps and fallen timber that fronted the open ground. When Prentiss rode by, however, he ordered Miller to advance the brigade south across the field and form in the timber—this conformed with the location of Allen's 16th Wisconsin. Moving out from behind their cover, Miller's three regiments inclined slightly to the right as they crossed Spain field. When the movement was completed at about 8 A.M., Miller's regiments dressed on their colors, ordered arms, and stood awaiting the enemy's appearance.

Prentiss now had nearly three thousand men in the immediate vicinity of Spain field, including two batteries of field artillery posted to support the infantry. One of these units, Captain Andrew Hickenlooper's 5th Ohio Independent Battery, had just arrived from duty in Missouri, setting up camp on April 5 in a picturesque cedar grove adjacent to Prentiss's headquarters. When the long roll had sounded, the men knew the battery would be going into its first fight.

John H. Hollenshade, the 5th Ohio's senior first lieutenant, having earlier tendered his resignation when the battery was ordered to field duty, now decided it was time to leave. While the battery galloped to the front, Hollenshade headed for Pittsburg Landing and the first steamer north.

Maneuvering his six bronze guns—four rifled 6-pounders and two 6-pounder smoothbores—into Spain field, Hickenlooper came into battery east of the eastern Corinth road. Across the road to his right Captain Emil Munch's 1st Minnesota Battery unlimbered four 6-pounder rifles and two 12-pounder howitzers. For a few minutes Prentiss's new line stood idle, the men and their officers waiting quietly.

"Everything," wrote an eyewitness, "seemed as still as death."

Advancing on the extreme right of the right of the first Confederate battle line, the brigade of Brigadier General Adley H. Gladden had been delayed and disarranged by the rough terrain. Shortly after the advance began Shaver's brigade had inclined to the left, causing Gladden's men also to execute a pronounced "left wheel." This resulted in further difficulty for Brigadier General Jones M. Withers, Gladden's division commander, who was responsible for closing on Lick Greek and guarding the Confederate right. Not only did the gap widen between the creek and Gladden's right because of the gradual swing to the left, but the creek itself ran diagonally to the right, increasing the front to be covered by about a half-mile. This was also observed by another Confederate brigadier, James R. Chalmers, who had been deployed in echelon on Gladden's right. Although Chalmers promptly moved up on Gladden's right, a large gap still remained, and it increased as the Confederates progressed. Hastily Withers detached Clanton's Alabama cavalry, recently reassigned, and ordered them to patrol the ground along Lick Creek so as to protect the exposed Confederate flank.

As a result of this left-wheel movement Chalmers was thrown out of alignment. He was somewhat in the rear of the front line, when Gladden approached Spain field shortly after 8 A.M. Through the trees ahead Gladden's skirmishers sighted a line of blue-clad soldiers. Immediately there was firing. The 1st Lousiana Infantry now rushed ahead from its position on Gladden's left, getting ahead of the 26th Alabama Regiment, still hampered in crossing a marsh. When the 26th emerged from the swamp, the 1st Louisiana was directly in its front, creating great confusion and causing the 26th to wander across the brigade's rear, belatedly occupying the first available space in line, which was on the extreme right. So eager were the Confederates to attack that other regiments also advanced on their own initiative, little attention being paid to alignment in the dense underbrush.

These confused moments completely ruined the coordination of Gladden's attack. Prentiss's men were standing quietly in line, listening to the terrific din and watching "blue rings of smoke" that curled upward on the right where Peabody was engaged. Suddenly they came to full alert.

Like the "sweep of a mid-summer thunder head rolling across the stubble field," as one veteran put it, the roar of battle came rumbling down the line from the right. Simultaneously a wave of bright light flashed through the woods in front. It was sunlight glinting from hundreds of gun barrels. In a long brown line, with muskets at right-shoulder shift, the Confederates came through the woods.

The 61st Illinois, a new regiment mustered in barely two months before, was so nervous about "seeing the elephant" * for the first time that most of the men had loaded their guns even before forming that morning. Catching sight of the Confederates, they began firing without orders. "From one end of the regiment to the other leaped a sheet of red flame," wrote an awed Illinois private.

Some of the Illinoisans by now were so excited that they could not comprehend orders. Private Leander Stillwell of Company D looked around to see his second lieutenant, Bob Wylder, "fairly wild with excitement, jumping up and down like a hen on a hot griddle." Stillwell, who was unable to see a target through the billowing gun smoke, was trying to peer underneath it when Wylder

---

* "Seeing the elephant" was Civil War slang for the experience of having been shot at in battle. The term derived from the common practice of small boys watering the awesome circus elephants in order to get into the show free. As one battle-tested veteran commented, it was the same with being in combat, "You won't like it a damn bit."

shouted, "Stillwell! Shoot! Shoot! Why don't you shoot!" Although he protested that he couldn't see, Wylder told him to "shoot anyhow," and Stillwell pulled the trigger, shooting blindly into the smoke.

Despite widespread Federal confusion the Confederates were momentarily staggered, and they drew back. When Gladden's slower regiments came up, they too began firing from a fixed location, about one hundred and fifty yards distant.

Much to nearly everyone's surprise the Federal troops now were ordered to fall back across Spain field. Prentiss, who apparently was observing from the right of his line, had already noted the heavy pressure brought to bear against Peabody. As the firing became heavier beyond his right and moved closer, Prentiss ordered a "change front to the right."

By doing so, Prentiss evidently planned to protect his flank and to present a solid front to Shaver's Confederates, then driving Peabody. Even before the appearance of Gladden's men orders to change front had been passed to the 16th Wisconsin on Prentiss's right. As they began to execute the maneuver, Gladden's and a portion of Shaver's brigade had simultaneously appeared in their front. One of the 16th's lieutenants remembered that the change of front was effected under a sharp fire. Several volleys were exchanged with the Confederates, which seemed to check their advance, before Prentiss again ordered the 16th Wisconsin to fall back. When the roar of musketry along the left of his line announced that the Confederates had also appeared in front of Miller, the bewildered Prentiss told Miller to retreat with his entire brigade to the north side of Spain field.

One of the 61st Illinois's privates remembered that he had fired but two or three rounds when the order came to fall back. As they recrossed the open ground, Prentiss's ragged line fell into more confusion, coming under a heavy Confederate fire from several directions. Their inexperience was proving costly.

Perhaps the sorriest confusion involved the 15th Michigan Infantry, which had belatedly arrived to fight alongside the 18th Wisconsin. Following its arrival at Pittsburg Landing on the previous afternoon, the 15th had been ordered to join Prentiss's division. After bivouacking near the landing that night, the regiment had started along the eastern Corinth road before 7 A.M. on the sixth. When they heard firing ahead, some of the men asked Hurlbut's troops, whose camps were along the road, what the shooting was about. Hurlbut's men told the greenhorns that some of the pickets must be "shooting squirrels."

A short distance ahead the 15th met a wounded man being helped to the rear. When they asked him about the pickets "shooting squirrels," he held up a bloody hand and said that they were the "funniest squirrels" he ever saw.

By the time the 15th Michigan approached Prentiss's camps, Miller's brigade had already formed along the north side of Spain field. An officer ordered them to file to the left, designating a position on the left of the 18th Wisconsin, which they soon found was Miller's extreme left flank.

"We unslung knapsacks . . . fixed bayonets, and stood to attention at order arms," wrote a private of the 15th. Soon "there appeared over the ridge in front a column of men, some of them dressed in blue, some in gray. . . ."

When the approaching line opened fire, the 15th immediately suffered losses. Yet not a shot was fired in reply. Incredibly, the regiment had marched to the front without ammunition and now stood with empty Austrian rifles, unable to shoot back. "We [merely] stood at order arms and looked at them as they shot," grumbled a private.

Soon the regiment was ordered to about-face and fall back. Thereafter the 15th marched to the rear, staying out of the fight until much later in the day.

In the nearby 18th Wisconsin Infantry the order to "about-face and fall back" had not been heard by all. Those who did hear soon joined the headlong rout, to the chagrin of the 18th's lieutenant colonel, Samuel W. Beal. Still firing both of his revolvers at the advancing enemy, Beal was swearing furiously at his men, calling them cowards for running away. They paid no attention to him, however, and most ran back over a hill into camp.

When a lull later occurred in the fighting and one of the 18th's privates had a chance to look about him, he estimated that only 150 of the regiment's original 862 men were still in line. Most of Miller's other regiments also had experienced trouble. A soldier heard the voice of the lieutenant colonel commanding the 18th Missouri tremble and crack as he gave the order to withdraw. When the Missourians got up and ran toward their campground, they were raked by a "terrific enfilading fire" from the west, costing the lives of many officers and men.

As the remnants of Miller's brigade hastily re-formed as best they could in dense timber along the north edge of the field, the Missourians took cover behind trees and opened fire on the heavy masses of gray infantry emerging onto the field.

According to brigade commander Miller, his men were now "thoroughly aroused." The 61st Illinois was also behind cover, with many of its men protected by logs and stumps. Only the 16th Wisconsin on the brigade right had become separated, causing it to wage an isolated, retrograde fight as it stumbled through the timberland toward its campground.

Already the linchpin of Prentiss's new line, Hickenlooper's and Munch's batteries began spraying canister and shell across the nearly one hundred and fifty-yard width of Spain field as rapidly as their guns could be served. Although the gunners were subjected to heavy musketry fire, they worked their bronze guns with devastating effect.

In the forefront of the Confederate advance was portly Brigadier General Adley H. Gladden, fifty-one, whose men were now serving with Hardee's front line because of the need for additional manpower. A cotton broker and postmaster in Columbia, South Carolina, before the Mexican War, Gladden had fought as a young man with the Palmetto Regiment at Belen Gate, where he was wounded. When Gladden again donned a uniform, it was to fight with a Southern regiment in 1861. After serving briefly as colonel of the 1st Louisiana Infantry under Braxton Bragg at Pensacola, Florida, he was rewarded with a promotion to brigadier general in September, 1861.

A politician of influence in New Orleans, Gladden was also a man of some humor who had once joked that all it took to make a Zouave was an Irishman and two yards of red flannel.

On the morning of April 6 Gladden was not in a good humor. When informed by one of Bragg's couriers that Chalmers's brigade would move up and advance on his right flank, Gladden apparently considered it an affront. One of Chalmers's privates overheard his remark: "Tell General Bragg that I have as keen a scent for Yankees as General Chalmers has."

As his brigade swept into Spain field, Gladden was with them, mounted and accompanied by his staff. A thin haze of smoke hung low over the field, obscuring the enemy line. Gladden apparently galloped ahead to obtain a better view. With an ear-shattering roar the Federal cannon loosed their projectiles.

In one instant Gladden was sitting erect upon his horse; in the next he was gone, knocked from the saddle and flung heavily to the ground. Startled staff officers glanced at the prostrate form. An exploding shell had nearly torn off his left arm.

As blood streamed from the gaping wound, staff officers rushed to his aid. Although a desperate attempt was made to save Gladden's life, including amputation of his arm on the battlefield, he was later taken to Beauregard's headquarters in Corinth, where he died on April 12. It was only the beginning of Shiloh's scything of high-ranking officers.

Following the wounding of Gladden Colonel Daniel W. Adams

assumed command of the brigade. A Kentuckian by birth and a Lousiana lawyer when the war began, the pugnacious Adams had once killed a man in a duel. His older brother Wirt was also at Shiloh, in command of a Mississippi cavalry regiment. Both would later become Confederate brigadier generals.

About 8:20 A.M., a few minutes after Gladden fell, Adams saw that the brigade was suffering severely as it formed along the southern edge of Spain field. He ordered an immediate advance. With ranks closed and banners flying the Confederates swept across the open ground. Hickenlooper's battery now changed to canister: twenty-seven iron balls, each over an inch in diameter, packed in a tin case. When a cannon was fired the tin case ripped open at the muzzle, spraying the iron balls in the pattern of a gigantic shotgun.

Hickenlooper's guns were firing about every thirty seconds, and they punished the Confederate battle line with terrible effect. As Adams's men approached midfield, the Union gunners began using double charges of canister. The Confederate battle line was seen to shake from one end to the other.

"The fire became so very severe," said Colonel Daniel Adams, "that . . . the whole brigade began to falter and . . . fall back."

With Prentiss's infantry delivering a rapid small-arms fire, the Confederates ran back across the field, leaving behind a carpet of dead and wounded. Adams, with the smoke of battle surrounding him, rode to his own regiment, the 1st Louisiana Infantry, seized its blue battle flag emblazoned with a pelican, and began waving it to rally his men.

Despite the repulse of Gladden's brigade, Prentiss's tactical situation continued to deteriorate. Many stragglers were wandering through his camps, creating panic and mass confusion. Moreover a general exodus had already begun in the direction of Pittsburg Landing. The close proximity of the fighting had so frightened a large number of noncombatants that rumors of a disaster were beginning to spread rapidly. The quartermaster of the 18th Missouri, laboring desperately to evacuate his regiment's bedding and knapsacks, was finally able to get one wagon moving despite the skittishness of his mule team. When he did so, he found that he could not make speed because the road to the landing was already choked with stragglers and wounded men.

By now so many men were drifting away from the line of battle that Captain Henry P. Stults of Company B, 18th Missouri, angrily told some of Prentiss's Illinois Cavalry, patrolling nearby, that if anyone from his company tried to run by them, to "cut his damned head off!"

About 7:30 A.M. Prentiss had dispatched couriers to Hurlbut and C. F. Smith with news of an attack in force. Help had not yet arrived, however, and shortly after 8:30 A.M., following the repulse of Gladden, Prentiss began to realize the extent of his jeopardy. Meanwhile his First Brigade commander, Everett Peabody, was then furiously galloping about the camp of the 18th Missouri looking for Prentiss. Peabody's plight was desperate. His lone brigade had already been shattered by the combined assault of Shaver's and Wood's brigades, and his line of camps was about to be overrun.

Peabody wanted artillery. If he cursed Prentiss for refusing to allow a battery to be parked in front of his brigade the night before, his anger was to be understood.

Peabody and Prentiss apparently never did meet, and when Peabody galloped back to his brigade, he found the Confederates on the outskirts of his camps, closely pressing his men. Clusters of Federals were firing from behind whatever cover they could improvise. Regimental organization, disrupted during the earlier fighting, was now nonexistent. His men were scattered about, fighting as individuals without any control. Peabody himself was alone. His aide had gone off to find the colonel of the 12th Michigan. Some of his men were firing from behind hay bales intended as forage for the officers' horses. Others were shooting from behind trees and logs.

Yet the enemy had hesitated briefly on approaching Peabody's camp. A private of the 25th Missouri thought this was due to sight of their Dutch ovens, fashioned of mud and used by the cooks to bake bread, which the enemy seemed to fear were masked batteries. Because of the diminished volume of Federal fire the respite was brief. Again the enemy came on at a "dogtrot." Volleys of musket fire swept through the camp, knocking over tents and equipment.

Peabody, riding among the officers' tents on the right of the 25th Missouri's camp, was gesturing and shouting to his men to "stand to it yet!"

Already bleeding from four wounds—in the hand, thigh, neck, and body—his large physique presented an inviting target, and again he was shot. This time a musket ball struck him in the upper lip and passed out the back of his head, killing him instantly. His body tumbled backward and came to rest, his legs across a log and his head and shoulders on the ground. In terror Peabody's mount bolted to the rear, its stirrups flapping wildly as it raced past a knot of Missouri soldiers forming for another stand.

Not yet thirty-two, Everett Peabody met death that day, just as he had predicted.

Private Joseph Ruff of the 12th Michigan Volunteers by now had realized that this was "not going to be a normal day." Ruff had been with Powell's reconnaissance patrol earlier that morning and had returned to camp carrying a wounded soldier before the fight at Seay field. Leaving the wounded man in camp, Ruff picked up his pail and walked a half-mile to Rhea Spring, near Sherman's camp, for water. Ruff presumed the fighting would soon be over, and since he was company cook that week, he went about his duties.

While on his way to the spring Ruff was startled by the sight of Confederates marching across the fields against Sherman's camps. Hastily dipping his bucket full of spring water, he started back to camp. Soon bullets were whistling about his ears as he struggled with the heavy pail. Once back at his camp he found it in a turmoil. The brigade was in line of battle, and a short distance away were the Confederates. Many soldiers, including wounded, were falling back through the tents, shouting and screaming. Ruff dropped his pail of water, "for it did not look as though there would be any breakfast," and ran to get his musket and equipment. He emerged just in time to see Peabody's line waver and break. A few minutes later he was engulfed in the headlong retreat through his camp.

Another of Peabody's privates said that he, like the others, ran through the 25th Missouri's camp, crossed a small creek, and scampered up a steep incline, supposing that the "Johnnies" were close after him.

Not everybody ran, however. An attempt was made by Colonel Francis Quinn of the 12th Michigan Infantry to rally a portion of his men behind their encampment. Here one of the 12th's riflemen, a youth of seventeen, found himself so thoroughly engrossed in the fighting that he thought no more of seeing a man shot down by his side than of a dumb beast being killed. "The more men I saw killed," he wrote, "the more reckless I became."

Side by side a mixture of soldiers from all four regiments of Peabody's brigade fought desperately to hold their color line. Outnumbered, fighting as small detachments rather than as organized units, they were unable to halt the onrushing Confederates. The lieutenant colonel of the 21st Missouri found that his men were so scattered by the ensuing retreat through camp that he was unable to detail their actions from that time on. Like others, his regiment literally ceased to exist during the remainder of the battle. Some of its men fought with other commands, while others clogged the roads leading to the river landing.

In the camp of the 16th Wisconsin the situation was equally dismal. Although actually a part of Peabody's brigade, the regiment had been fighting mostly on its own since Prentiss's first retreat from the Spain field line. Gradually falling back under simultaneous pressure from the left of Gladden's and the right of Shaver's brigades, the 16th had reached its camp in some disorder, although still intact as a fighting unit. When Colonel Allen ordered a stand in front of his camp, the Confederates closed to short range, and Allen was soon in the midst of a "desperate conflict."

COLONEL EVERETT PEA-BODY. Headstrong, capable, and quick in temper, this Harvard-educated brigade commander's decisive action may have saved Grant's army. Convinced that the army was about to be attacked, he warned Prentiss, but to no avail. Taking matters into his own hands, Peabody ordered the dawn reconnaissance patrol that uncovered the Confederate army. Angered by Peabody's disobedience of orders, Prentiss threatened to court-martial him. A few hours later Peabody was shot in the head and instantly killed. Although he was denied much of the recognition due him, Peabody's men long remembered his important contribution. (MISSOURI HISTORICAL SOCIETY)

First Cassius Fairchild, the 16th's lieutenant colonel, was shot in the thigh and carried from the field. Then Allen had his own horse shot from under him. As he began to mount another, it too was shot dead. The Confederates were lying on the ground in the regiment's front, many of them having thrown off their blankets, which were tangled in the surrounding brush. This was noticed by the Wisconsin soldiers, who thought it was a ruse to draw their fire. They soon passed the word to shoot low, but not at the blankets.

Despite the 16th's spirited resistance they were soon outflanked on their right by the collapse of Peabody's line. Although orders to fall back came directly from Allen, many of the 16th's officers and men failed to hear them. Lieutenant D. F. Vail of Company K suddenly looked about and found that nearly all his men had drifted away. The shocking thought ran through his mind that he was practically alone. He too decided to retreat. Running to his tent to save a tintype of his fiancée, he rummaged through a trunk, found the picture, and dashed outside, spurred on by a hail of bullets that whizzed close about his ears.

Amazingly, there were many like Lieutenant Vail who risked their lives to save valued keepsakes. George W. Graves of Company A, 16th Wisconsin, ran into his tent to save a memento just as several Confederate bullets tore through the canvas. Thoroughly frightened, Graves bolted out the entrance, convinced that the Confederates were right behind him. "By that time everybody was running," he later wrote, ". . . so I ran too."

By 8:45 A.M. all of Peabody's camps were in Confederate hands. Prentiss, with his battle line still resting along the northern edge of Spain field, was badly outflanked. His orders were to fall back, take to the trees, and hold the enemy in check as long as possible until reinforcements arrived. Again couriers galloped to the commanding generals of the Second and Fourth divisions, reporting that Prentiss was falling back and needed reinforcement.

As to be expected, most of Prentiss's untrained men had become completely bewildered and nervously excited by this, their first battle. Colonel Madison Miller later admitted that he was so overwrought that Prentiss "had to reiterate his order [to withdraw] before I could comprehend." Some units had difficulty in getting any orders at all. Hickenlooper's 5th Ohio Battery had been supported by the 16th Wisconsin on its right, but the advancing Confederates finally forced these supports to give way.

Again Spain field was filled with Gladden's Confederates, led by their new brigade commander Daniel Adams in a second attack. Adams, still grasping the 1st Louisiana's pelican battle flag, advanced his men close to the Union line and ordered a charge. Here Hickenlooper's men again heard the Rebel yell as hundreds of Confederates ran at the Union line. "[It] caused an involuntary thrill of terror to pass like an electric shock through even the bravest hearts," wrote the plucky Hickenlooper.

Yet all of the battery's guns were still in action, pouring double charges of canister into the oncoming ranks as fast as the 6-pounders could be served. Each blast tore great gaps in the Confederate ranks, costing the lives of many officers, including the popular Major Robert B. Armistead of the 22d Alabama.

Meanwhile Captain F. H. Robertson's battery of 12-pounder Napoleon guns had been wheeled into position to support the Confederate attack. Their fire added to the storm of lead whizzing about Hickenlooper's battery.

The Confederate infantry loomed only a few yards distant when Hickenlooper, mounted on his white horse, Gray Eagle, gave orders to limber to the rear. Yet, before the left section, which was under a junior second lieutenant, could hitch up its guns, a point-blank volley of musketry swept through its ranks.

Every horse in the section, twenty-four in all, went down in a frenzied mass of struggling animals.* Hickenlooper's own mount was struck three times in the neck and sank to its knees. Briefly strug-

---

* Each gun was drawn by six horses, hitched in pairs, as was the caisson, one caisson per gun.

gling to its feet, the horse trembled, failed to maintain its balance, and plunged to the ground, throwing its rider.

Stunned by the fall, Hickenlooper glanced up in time to see the Confederates dash among his disabled guns, their faces blackened with powder smoke. Drawing his revolvers, Hickenlooper sprinted for safety as the remnant of the battery pulled away. Having already abandoned two bronze 6-pounders to the 22d Alabama Infantry, Hickenlooper's cannoneers desperately attempted to get the remainder of their battery away. It was a wild ride across ditches, over logs, between trees, and through the underbrush, but the guns somehow made it.

When the shattered battery finally halted beyond Prentiss's line of camps, Hickenlooper learned that fifty-nine of the battery's eighty horses had been shot in their harnesses. Lieutenant Blackburn, who had lost his section, was crying like a child.

Captain Emil Munch's Minnesota Battery also had been bloodied and disabled. His gunners had first come under fire while the battery was unlimbering on the right of the eastern Corinth road. Here one private was killed and three men wounded by musketry before the guns could be deployed. At the first roar of Munch's guns the trail of a bronze 6-pounder broke at the elevation screw and had to be withdrawn. When the Confederates attacked for the second time, Munch, like Hickenlooper, saw his infantry supports break, and he gave the order to retreat. Beginning from the left, the gunners rehitched their guns and dashed to safety. Munch was about to follow when his horse was struck and killed. When he lingered to unbuckle and save his saddle, Munch also was shot and had to be carried from the field with a musket ball in his thigh.

By now Munch's gunners had to run a heavy gauntlet of fire in order to escape. When the lead driver of the last gun was struck by a glancing bullet, he veered between two trees and his gun became struck. With the Confederates running after them, the Union gunners wheeled the piece from between the trees, jumped back on the limber, and grimly hung on as gun and horses bounded away.

Returning to their camp, Munch's artillerymen found that all was chaos. Sick and wounded were running in all directions. Some had blankets wrapped around them, others were clad only in underclothes. To one of the battery's lieutenants the scene was "perfectly awful." When the pursuing Confederates began firing into the camp, their bullets struck into the sick and wounded. "Their groans," he wrote, "were almost sickening."

The renewed attack of Gladden's brigade also had routed Prentiss's remaining infantry. Eighteen-year-old Private Leander Stillwell of the 61st Illinois then jumped up from behind a log with several others and ran back to camp.

"I saw men in gray and brown clothes, with trailed muskets, running through the camp on our right," Stillwell said, "and I saw something else, too, that sent a chill all through me. It was a gaudy sort of thing, with red bars. It flashed over me in a second that that thing was a Rebel flag. . . . It was going fast, with a jerky motion, which told me that the bearer was on a double quick. . . . The main thing was to get out of there as quick as we could."

As Stillwell ran down his company street, he thought to save a packet of letters from his knapsack. Yet, "one quick backward glance" changed his mind. The Confederates were pursuing so rapidly that many of Prentiss's men were trapped among their tents. Lieutenant Daniel R. Hudson of the 18th Missouri was helping with the removal of the sick and wounded when he was captured. Fifteen men of the 18th were taken prisoner along with him.

The retreat through camp was so disorderly that Prentiss's Second Brigade commander, Madison Miller, found that many of his men had lost all self-control. The anguished cries of the wounded were drowned out by the pandemonium.

One badly wounded youth of the 18th Missouri desperately called to his chaplain, then passing in an Army wagon. Although the reverend got to his side, he was horrified to find that a musket ball had punctured a hole in the boy's abdomen. A foot-and-a-half-long section of intestine was protruding, yet the wound had contracted and was squeezing the bowel tightly. "I feel as if my bowels are in boiling water," screamed the soldier.

Taking a small knife from his pocket, the chaplain widened the wound and pressed the intestine back in place. Beyond that he could only offer spiritual consolation, saying that he must put his "trust in Christ for strength and salvation." He knew that the boy must die.

On Prentiss's extreme left the 18th Wisconsin had rallied in front of its camp for a brief stand. Like Prentiss's other regiments, the men of the 18th sensed imminent disaster. Advancing in their front were two thousand Confederates led by Brigadier General James R. Chalmers.

Chalmers, having swung in a wider arc in order to close with Gladden, pushed through the oak forests east of Spain field, arriving on Gladden's right flank while the fight with Prentiss was in progress. Because he had swung too sharply to his left, Chalmers's entire brigade was misaligned with the Union front when the camps of the enemy were sighted.

Hastily correcting the alignment, Chalmers marched to within one hundred and fifty yards of the enemy line, halted his men, and opened fire. Only two or three volleys were exchanged with the Wisconsin regiment before Chalmers ordered a bayonet charge. To his great surprise only the 10th Mississippi Regiment, about 360 men strong, responded. In the noise and confusion Chalmers's order had been heard only by this regiment, toward the brigade's extreme right. Led by their bold colonel, R. A. Smith, whose "clarion voice" sounded above the din, the 10th Mississippi ran up an incline, straight at the camp of the 18th Wisconsin.

The reaction in the Union line was spontaneous.

Already shaken by their earlier retreat from Prentiss's advanced line, the remnant of a regiment nearly one thousand strong got up and ran. With the fiercely yelling Confederates close on their heels, the 18th streamed back through their camp in disorder.

Private Jeremiah Baldock of Company K ran into his tent to retrieve a Bible from his knapsack, believing that his body would then be properly identified should he be killed. When he stepped outside, three Confederates were coming down the company street at him. Firing his musket in their faces, he ran as fast as his legs would carry him. Never had he felt so alone. Terrified at the sight of Confederates bayoneting a wounded member of his own company, Baldock sped from camp in a state of shock. Behind him swarms of the enemy were already looting and pillaging the regiment's tents.

Prentiss's Sixth Division was now a total wreck. Of the two brigades numbering seven regiments and nearly five thousand fighting men, only two or three regiments retained some effective strength. The 21st Missouri Infantry was completely gone; the men remaining fell in with other commands and fought as individuals. The 12th Michigan and 25th Missouri were reduced to a mere handful, yet these two units stuck together throughout the long and bloody day.

Other regiments such as the 61st Illinois and 16th Wisconsin drifted out of the fighting but later saw service with other divisions. Of Miller's brigade only the 18th Missouri and a handful of the 18th Wisconsin were intact as the victorious Confederates swept through the last of their camps. Already being flaunted as trophies in the hands of Gladden's Louisianans were seven stands of colors.

Somehow a few of the tents in the 12th Michigan's camp were set afire. As the regiment's survivors scampered to safety, many suddenly realized that they had lost everything. Private Bailey of Company D looked back and saw the camp afire. His knapsack, haversack, canteen, overcoat, fatigue blouse, and blanket were obviously lost, but what made Bailey most downcast was the loss of a long letter he had intended to mail to his sweetheart in Michigan. Later it was discovered that there were other, more tragic losses in the raging fire. Some of the 12th Michigan's sick and wounded had not been evacuated during the hasty retreat. The next day their charred bodies were found among the camp ruins.

By 9 A.M. Prentiss's routed division was streaming north in full flight toward Pittsburg Landing. The men were panicky and near exhaustion. One sickened private who had been in the fighting from the very beginning had so lost track of the time that he thought it was now about noon.

As the weary rear elements retreated down the eastern Corinth road, a riderless white horse appeared from the pall of smoke engulfing Prentiss's camps and trotted among the men. It was Gray Eagle, Captain Hickenlooper's supposedly dead charger.

Although his back, neck, and forelegs were covered with blood, he had followed the retreating lines looking for his master. With a loud neigh the horse halted in front of the surprised Hickenlooper. Cheered by his horse's pluck, he mounted Gray Eagle and rode off to regather his broken battery.

As the rout continued, however, the problems seemed to multiply for Prentiss's division. Many of the men by now were out of ammunition, including nearly all of the 18th Missouri's riflemen. Furthermore Prentiss's division had been soundly defeated and the men knew it. Morale was at nadir. Having turned his back and fled for a half-mile, one of Prentiss's privates was convinced that they were forever disgraced. As he ran he kept thinking to himself, "What will they say about this at home?"

CHAPTER XI

Sherman Will Be Shot!

The Sabbath, April 6, 1862, had dawned as another routine day for most of William Tecumseh Sherman's Fifth Division. Reveille sounded at 5:30 A.M., and despite the muffled rumble of musketry distant about a mile to the south, camp routine proceeded as usual. Sherman himself was up and had breakfasted by 6:30. Many of his troops, however, were busily preparing for the regular Sunday-morning inspection and were as yet unfed.

Only in the camp of the 53d Ohio Volunteers was there unusual activity. Isolated in Rhea field about four hundred yards south of the 57th Ohio's encampment, the 53d had been in a state of turmoil since daylight. Their colonel, Jesse J. Appler, although the butt of Sherman's joke for his timorous behaviour on Saturday, once again feared an attack. Being in disfavor, Appler was confused and uncertain of what to do.

About daylight, when Powell's reconnaissance patrol fired on Hardcastle's pickets in Fraley field, Appler had heard the shots. He promptly went to the tent of his adjutant, Ephraim C. Dawes, saying, "Adjutant, get up quick!" Dawes, a young lieutenant not yet a year out of Marietta College, dressed and hurried to beyond the left of their camp with his colonel. There the two listened to the sporadic firing about a half-mile distant, puzzled as to its meaning.

Appler said he had been up all night and had heard constant gunfire in the woods nearby. According to Dawes Appler was unsatisfied with Sherman's routine disposition of pickets along the division's front and had sent sixteen men to watch the far end of Rhea field during the previous evening. Their orders had been to report any movement of troops in their front, but not to fire unless attacked.

While Appler was standing on the edge of camp talking with Dawes, this special picket detachment suddenly returned from the south end of the field and reported with obvious excitement that they had also heard heavy firing and were sure that a large enemy force was on the army's front.

171

Appler was highly alarmed. At first he sent his adjutant to form the regiment; then, remembering Sherman's caustic remarks, he called him back.

Next he decided to alert Colonel Hildebrand, his brigade commander. Adjutant Dawes again started to leave, but he was called back a second time. Following another delay Appler agreed to send an enlisted man to the brigade picket line, about three hundred yards southwest, to learn what the pickets had observed. Before the man left camp a wounded soldier of the 25th Missouri appeared from the south woods and moved rapidly toward Appler's regiment. Clutching a bloody arm, the man hurried past, crying out, "Get into line; the Rebels are coming!"

Appler had heard enough. He immediately ordered the long roll sounded and his regiment formed on the color line.

It was now shortly after 6 A.M., and several of the 53d's officers came running into line half-dressed. Only two of the regiment's officers were mounted, the lieutenant colonel and the quartermaster, and Appler sent each to warn brigade and division headquarters, respectively.

By the time the quartermaster returned, the 53d was standing along their color line facing west, toward the Pittsburg and Corinth Road. Remembering yesterday's false alarm, the quartermaster leaned over and whispered to Appler, "General Sherman says you must be badly scared over there."

Soon thereafter the 53d's lieutenant colonel returned, bringing instructions from brigade commander Hildebrand to send out two companies to reinforce the brigade pickets. Appler sent them off, then began stalking up and down the line and pondering his next move.

When one of the half-dressed officers on the left of the 53d's line thought he saw Rebels crossing the far end of Rhea field, he shouted a warning. Appler immediately ordered his regiment to file to the left and deploy in line of battle a few yards south of camp. As the regiment swung into motion, one of the two detached companies sent to support the pickets came back through the brush, its captain reporting, "The Rebels out there are thicker than fleas on a dog's back."

Adjutant Dawes, having led Appler's column to its new position, now looked to the right. "The sun had arisen in a clear sky, and the bright gun barrels of the advancing line shone through the green leaves," said Dawes. ". . . The Confederate line of battle [was] apparently within musket shot, and moving directly toward our right flank."

Dawes ran to Appler, who was just behind the center of his line, and gasped, "Colonel, look to the right!"

Appler whirled about, a look of astonishment on his face. Sighting the Confederates, he blurted out, "This is no place for us," and ordered his "regiment to about face and right wheel."

Back through their standing tents streamed the 53d Ohio, Appler leading the retreat. According to one of the 53d's officers, it was not yet 7 A.M. and the noncombatants were still in camp performing their normal Sunday duties. "Officer's servants and company cooks were preparing breakfast, sentinels were pacing their beats, details for brigade guard and fatigue duty were marching to their posts, and . . . the sutler shop was open," he reported.

As the regiment hastily withdrew through camp, Appler shouted in a shrill voice, "Sick men to the rear!" causing instant turmoil among the 53d's numerous hospital cases.

Then, from the bushes west of the campsite, a scattered volley of shots rang out. The Confederate skirmishers, closing in from the west, were firing at Appler's retreating column. Although no one was hit, the 53d hurried past the line of officers' tents and swept out into the open, halting on the brow of a small knoll behind their camp. Deploying a few paces beyond the crest, Appler's men lay down amid light brush covering the reverse slope to await developments.

Appler's long roll had already created a stir in the adjacent Federal camps. By chance the closest encampment was that of an artillery unit, Captain A. C. Waterhouse's Battery E, First Illinois Light Artillery. Waterhouse's men were new to the service—they had been in camp just one week, had drilled only three times, and were still in the process of training their recently arrived horses to artillery harness.

Before 7 A.M. the battery's guns, four 3½-inch (3.67) and two 4½-inch (3.80) James rifled cannon, had been limbered, and the horses harnessed in preparation for the routine Sunday-morning inspection. When the drum roll sounded and Appler's men were seen countermarching through camp, Waterhouse's battery was ready for action.

Major Ezra Taylor, Sherman's Irish-born chief of artillery, had taken an early breakfast and was preparing to ride along the division's front to survey the ground. His horse was already saddled, and Taylor hastily galloped to Waterhouse's camp, ordering the battery's deployment.

Under Taylor's orders one section of 3½-inch James rifles went forward about one hundred and fifty yards across a small stream to the edge of a country lane near Appler's position. The remaining four guns came into battery on the crown of a nearby hill overlooking Rhea field. This disposition, although made in haste, was most significant.

At 7 A.M. Waterhouse's advance section unlimbered among scattered trees to the right and rear of the 53d Ohio. The two guns were quickly loaded, and the gunners stood by their pieces, looking uncertainly into the field ahead.

Riding the "beautiful sorrel race mare," captured from the Confederates several weeks earlier, General Sherman, accompanied by his staff, trotted into Rhea field shortly after 7 A.M. Close by his side rode his orderly, Thomas D. Holliday of Company H, 2d Illinois Cavalry, his carbine at the ready. Slowly moving in advance of Appler's line, Sherman reined to a halt in front of Company E, near the regiment's right.

A body of troops was observed marching diagonally across the far end of Rhea field, nearly a half-mile distant. Sherman uncased his field glass to study their movements.

About fifty yards distant a small stream fringed with brush ran across the front of Appler's camp, forming the western boundry of Rhea field. Having fired on Appler's retreating men, Cleburne's advance skirmishers continued to press north through marshland adjacent to the Pittsburg and Corinth road. While Sherman and his staff were looking to the left, toward the opposite end of Rhea field, these skirmishers emerged from the brush on Sherman's right, within easy musket range.

Sighting the party of mounted Federals, the men of the 15th

PRIVATE THOMAS D. HOLLIDAY. A member of Company H, 2d Illinois Cavalry, Sherman's orderly was killed at his general's side in Rhea field at the first fire, morning of April 6. (SHILOH NATIONAL MILITARY PARK)

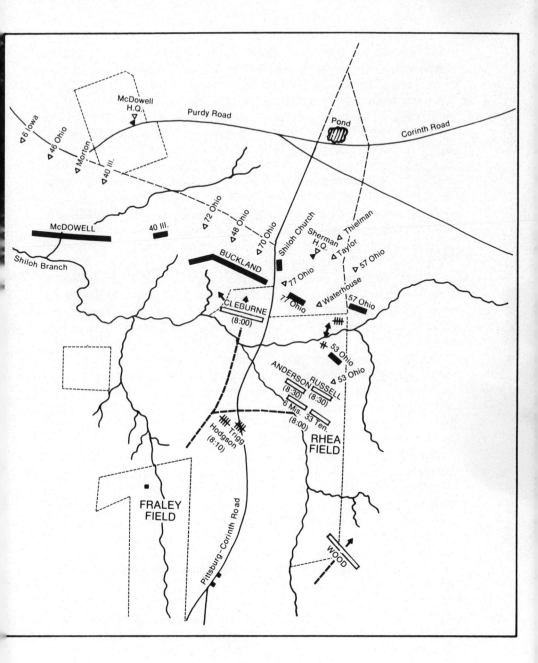

6 Iowa
46 Ohio
Morton
40 Ill.
McDowell H.Q.
Purdy Road
Pond
Corinth Road
72 Ohio
48 Ohio
70 Ohio
Shiloh Church
Sherman H.Q.
Thielman
Taylor
57 Ohio
McDOWELL
40 Ill.
Shiloh Branch
BUCKLAND
77 Ohio
CLEBURNE
(8:00)
77 Ohio
Waterhouse
57 Ohio
53 Ohio
53 Ohio
ANDERSON
(8:30)
RUSSELL
(8:30)
6 Mis.
33 Ten.
(8:00)
Hodgson
(8:10)
Trigg
RHEA
FIELD
FRALEY
FIELD
Pittsburg-Corinth Road
WOOD

MAP 5
Initial Assault on Sherman
7 A.M.–9 A.M., April 6 (Chapter 11)

Arkansas halted and raised their muskets. In their sights loomed what was obviously an important Federal officer.

Adjutant Dawes of the 53d Ohio was standing with several officers on high ground toward the regiment's left when he saw the Confederate skirmishers emerge on Sherman's right. Realizing that he could not warn Sherman in time, Dawes glanced down the line and saw Lieutenant Eustace H. Ball of Company E walking in front of the right flank. "I called to him: 'Ball, Sherman will be shot!'," said Dawes. "[Ball then] ran towards the general crying out: 'General, look to your right!' "

Sherman dropped his telescope and whirled about. The skirmishers stood with leveled muskets, barely fifty yards away. "My God, we are attacked!" were his only words, and he threw up his hand as if to ward off the shots.

It was too late. The enemy muskets flashed, and a deadly volley ripped through the cluster of mounted Federals. Close by Sherman's side Private Holliday was struck and instantly killed. "The shot that killed him was meant for me," Sherman tersely wrote less than a week later.

Probably it was here that Sherman was struck in the hand by a single buckshot from an enemy musket. Many of the Confederates were armed with .69 caliber smoothbore muskets firing "buck and ball," a paper cartridge containing a ball and three buckshot. Effective only at short range, the buckshot penetrated Sherman's right hand but did no serious damage.

Wheeling his horse rapidly about, Sherman dashed to safety, followed by his staff. As he passed the astonished Appler he shouted, "Appler, hold your position; I will support you." Appler's men again looked to the front. It was a sight "never to be forgotten," wrote one of his officers. "The steadily advancing lines of Hardee's Corps . . . extended until lost to sight in the timber on either flank. . . . Directly in front of the spot where General Sherman's orderly lay dead there was a group of mounted officers and a peculiar flag—dark blue, with a white center."

Patrick Ronayne Cleburne, the thirty-four-year-old daredevil commander of Hardee's left flank, had emerged from the nearby woods covered from head to foot with mud. Of Irish stock, the son of a Cork County doctor and an 1849 emigrant to the United States, Cleburne was about to experience his baptism of fire as a Confederate general.

Although striking in appearance, Cleburne was not considered handsome. His alert, gray-blue eyes disguised an introverted personality. Yet Cleburne was one of the Confederacy's most aggressive fighters. His considerable military reputation was founded, so he said, on lessons learned while an enlisted man in the British Army. To those who knew him best Cleburne's most distinguished characteristic was outstanding personal courage.

Scraping the mud from his uniform, Cleburne looked about him. "An almost impassable morass" adjacent to the Corinth and Pittsburg road spanned about forty acres in front of the Union-held high ground. Cleburne had unwisely attempted to lead most of his brigade through the middle of it. When his horse bogged down and became unmanageable, he had been thrown off. "It was with great difficulty I got out," Cleburne later remembered.

His troops had struggled only a short distance into this marsh overgrown with tangled vines before splitting apart, two regiments veering to the right and four going to the left. The result was a quarter of a mile gap that now existed within his brigade. On the right, where Cleburne confronted Appler's vacated campsite, he could muster only two regiments for an attack—the 6th Mississippi and 23d Tennessee, numbering about one thousand men. Though Bragg's second wave was not yet in sight, the aggressive Cleburne decided to advance anyway.

Trigg's Arkansas battery, trailing Cleburne's right wing, had unlimbered nearby. Following Cleburne's instructions to "wake up" the enemy with a few shells from a howitzer, it opened fire.

In quick succession the two Federal guns on the right of Appler's campsite responded, causing the sound of cannon fire to reverberate for miles. Yet almost immediately after firing, these two Federal guns were limbered to the rear, Major Taylor having ordered their withdrawal to the hilltop held by the main section of Waterhouse's battery because of the enemy's proximity.

Although Trigg's battery continued to fire, most of the shots went wild. The lush spring foliage restricted vision, and the gunners were unable to see properly to adjust their fire. Trigg's first shot reportedly cut off a treetop near the 53d Ohio's position and sent it crashing to the ground. Little other damage was reported in the Union lines, although at least one young Ohioan was suddenly overcome by fear that he might be killed by a falling limb.

Meanwhile Cleburne had formed his two regiments and sent them up the incline toward the waiting enemy line about 7:45 A.M. Interposed between the advancing Confederates and Appler's infantrymen were the standing tents of the 53d Ohio's vacant camp.

A Confederate officer observed, "He [the enemy] was very advantageously posted. . . . His line was lying down behind the rising ground on which his tents were pitched, and opposite my right he had made a breastwork of logs and bales of hay."

Waiting with their Austrian muskets at full cock, the 53d Ohio watched the Confederate line sweep through the vacant row of officers' tents. Then at a distance of fifty yards, "There was a tremendous crash of musketry," said Adjutant Dawes.

The effect was plainly visible in the Confederate ranks. Cleburne reported: "Musketry and artillery at short range swept the open spaces between the tents . . . with an iron storm that threatened certain destruction to every living thing that would dare to cross. . . . A quick and bloody repulse was the consequence."

Their battle line broken by the standing tents, the frightening noise and confusion accentuated by the shrieks of the wounded and dying, the 6th Mississippi and 23d Tennessee broke in disorder down the slope.

Portly Colonel Mat Martin, the former commander of the 23d Tennessee, arrived on the field just as his old regiment broke. Along with Cleburne, Martin galloped among the frightened Tennesseans and ordered them to stop. Some did, but most continued to run away. It "was with difficulty," said Cleburne that about half the regiment was rallied a hundred yards in the rear.

Meanwhile the 6th Mississippi had rallied under the urging of their field officers and again re-formed in line of battle below the line of enemy tents. A small regiment four hundred twenty-five men strong before the first charge, they now numbered probably not more than three hundred officers and men. Led by their colonel, J. J. Thornton, and major, Robert Lowry, the 6th Mississippi started once more up the gradual incline, their battle flags waving alone in the morning breeze.

Watching from the high ground in front were about six hundred Federal infantry, posted under cover and supported by a battery of six rifled guns.

When the Federal cannon opened fire, the Confederate ranks were blown apart. Waterhouse's battery of 4½-inch and 3½-inch James rifles were firing downhill at a range of less than five hundred yards with shell and canister. Appler's men also delivered another deadly volley of musketry, again catching the Mississippians amid the standing tents. Bullets seemed to be everywhere and both Thornton and Lowry were severely wounded. After enduring several minutes of futile ordeal, the surviving Confederates recoiled in disorder over their dead and dying.

The 6th Mississippi was reduced to a burial squad. In the short span of less than a half-hour it had suffered losses of three hundred officers and men killed and wounded (70.5 percent) from an aggregate of four hundred twenty-five. Sixty men led by a captain were all that re-formed following the charge. During the entire war only three Southern regiments suffered heavier casualties in a single battle.

Curiously, the bloody repulse also had created a convulsion in

PRIVATES WILLIAM H. LANDIS AND J. A. LANDIS. Armed with outdated flintlock muskets, these two brothers from Company A, 23d Tennessee Infantry, face the camera before Shiloh. On Sunday William lost an arm in the bloody fighting participated in by Cleburne's brigade. (CONFEDERATE VETERAN, AUGUST, 1915)

the Federal line. Colonel Jesse Appler, his nerves at the breaking point, had cried out at the height of the attack, "Retreat and save yourselves!" Promptly the entire left flank of the 53d Ohio, where Appler was standing, got up and ran to the rear in disorder. Two or three companies on the right, which did not hear the order, hesitated momentarily before following their comrades' example. Much to the chagrin of their brigade commander, Hildebrand, the 53d Ohio was soon streaming back through the rear woods in full flight.

Earlier, Hildebrand had formed his two remaining regiments, the 57th and 7th Ohio, on their color line and advanced in support of Appler. Yet they saw Cleburne's Confederates moving in their front and decided to go no farther than the downslope fronting a creek less than three hundred yards from camp. Hildebrand later cited a lack of artillery support as the reason for this.

Out of confusion, Waterhouse's guns had remained silent during the initial advance of Confederate troops across the south end of Rhea field. Major Taylor, who was directing the battery's redeployment, had hesitated to open fire because he saw a body of troops emerge onto the field carrying what seemed to be an American flag and wearing dark uniform jackets. Thereby a portion of Wood's brigade escaped bombardment on their oblique march across the open field to attack Peabody's brigade. Soon thereafter Taylor noticed that "[They] were followed by other troops who wore a uniform not to be mistaken. . . . I ordered the firing to commence."

At least three of S. A. M. Wood's regiments were then shelled at a range of about seven hundred yards by the six James rifles. Several privates and a captain of the 27th Tennessee were instantly killed. Only a slight depression in the ground saved the 16th Alabama, marching on the 27th's right, from a serious loss.

As the Confederates reached the skirt of woods east of Rhea field, Wood's two right-flank regiments halted in anticipation of swinging to the left against the battery. The 16th Alabama had actually changed front, filing into column in order to facilitate a march through the woods, when Peabody's battle line was discovered in the timber ahead and to the right. Both of Wood's flank regiments promptly deployed to engage Peabody, leaving Waterhouse's battery to fire unmolested.

Elsewhere matters were also going poorly for the Confederates.

Much to Cleburne's anger Waterhouse's guns, in shredding the 6th Mississippi's and 23d Tennessee's unsupported attack on Appler's camp, had done so without harassment by Confederate counterbattery fire. Trigg's battery had already gone to another location, since the thick leaves and spring vegetation enabled them to "only see in one direction" while enduring a severe cross fire from several Federal batteries. Cleburne, thereafter, had no artillery under his command the remainder of the day.

Unaware of the 53d Ohio's stampede to the rear, Cleburne was still without sufficient support to press an attack against Waterhouse's battery. Braxton Bragg's second Confederate line, slowly moving up through the rough ridgeland to the south, was yet a half-hour away. Shortly after 8 A.M., while the survivors of his two shattered regiments were re-forming, Cleburne galloped around the swamp, separating his brigade in order to observe the progress on his left flank.

Ralph Pomeroy Buckland, a fifty-year-old former lawyer and state senator from Ohio, had been at breakfast when he discovered between six and seven o'clock that the Union pickets had been fired upon. Mounting his horse, Colonel Buckland rode toward the Federal picket line, after ordering that his brigade of three Ohio regiments be formed on the color line.

As he approached the outpost pickets, there was skirmishing in the vicinity of Widow Howell's field, about a half-mile distant, toward the front of McDowell's brigade. The picket reserve already had fallen back across a small log bridge, now being only about a quarter of a mile from the line of Union camps. Through the trees ahead Buckland could see the outermost pickets slowly retiring. Buckland, fully alarmed, ordered the reserve pickets to defend the bridge across Shiloh Branch of Owl Creek as long as possible, then galloped off to alert Sherman at division headquarters.

When Buckland arrived at Sherman's tent, about 7 A.M., he was told merely to reinforce the pickets with a single regiment and "to keep the enemy back." Following these uninspired orders, Buckland returned and selected the 48th Ohio, his center regiment in the brigade line, for this duty since both the colonel and lieutenant colonel had volunteered to go.

Colonel Peter Sullivan, a jaunty Irishman with Mexican War and militia experience, soon led the 48th Ohio off through rough timberland toward a muddy little creek that meandered across the front of Sherman's division, not four hundred yards distant.

Sullivan's men were edgy. They had hurried from breakfast when the long roll sounded only to stand and wait for nearly a half-hour, listening to the ominous crash of musketry rolling from the woodlands a mile to the left. Marching in column, the head of the regiment had nearly reached the little creek bottom when, said an officer, "we discovered the enemy by their glistening bayonets, forming in line of battle on our side of the creek."

Sullivan halted his men in their tracks. Hastily ordering a countermarch, he sent word to Buckland that he was returning; the enemy was in force and forming on the north side of the creek. Buckland hesitated momentarily, pondering what to do. Finally he sent two companies ahead as skirmishers from his right-flank regiment, the 72d Ohio. Then, about 7:45 A.M., he ordered the entire brigade to march a short distance into the woods and form in line of battle.

As the returning 48th Ohio hurried back and fell in on the left of the 72d regiment, the Confederates swept into view, not more than a hundred yards distant. "They came upon us so suddenly that for a short time our men wavered," admitted the 48th's lieutenant colonel.

The Confederates fired first, their volley killing and wounding a large number of men. At the sight of this carnage the 48th's color-bearer, Sergeant Theodore D. Jones, became so frightened that he "shamefully deserted us," said his disgusted regimental commander.

Yet the 48th scored too.

Simultaneous with the first enemy fire, the 48th's front rank had discharged their Austrian muskets, followed by those in the rear. The crashing volley from Buckland's van quickly drove the

Confederates to cover in the hollow of a ravine in front. There they crouched behind trees and logs and returned the Federal fire with "unabating fury," noted a Union soldier.

This attack by Cleburne's main column had been launched with an effective strength of about fifteen hundred officers and men. Yet they were blithely unaware that 2,234 Federals were deployed in their front in wooded terrain with a favorable field of fire. Moreover the ground was conducive to an ambush.

A narrow ravine ran toward the Federal right, beyond which the ground widened into a flatland at Owl Creek. In Buckland's extended battle line his right-flank regiment, the 72d Ohio, overlapped the Confederate left by a wide margin. Oblivious to this the 2d Tennessee was marching as a reserve behind Cleburne's left wing of three regiments when the Federal battle line loomed in front. Rushing ahead on the Confederate left, the 2d Tennessee angled into this narrow ravine and dashed up the defile toward the Federal flank. Buckland saw them coming just in time and rushed the 72d Ohio forward to the edge of the ravine. Throwing one company across the narrow neck to fire point-blank into the face of the approaching column, Buckland soon had the Confederates at his mercy.

"A murderous crossfire," so called by Cleburne, swept through the Confederate ranks, bowling over nearly a third of the 2d Tennessee's 365 men. Nearly a dozen officers were hit, including the 2d's major and all company commanders. The bloodletting was so profuse that a member of the regiment later thought, "The fire encountered was the worst the regiment suffered during the war, with one exception." After enduring three sharp volleys, the Tennesseans broke and ran in wild disorder.

All along Buckland's battle line the crash of musketry swelled. Most of the Ohioans were fighting well, although badly frightened in this, their maiden battle.

Jesse Nelson, a drummer with the 48th Ohio and not yet nineteen, laid aside his drum as the battle began to fight in the ranks. He was on his knees in the act of firing when a musket ball struck him in the head and killed him.

Other strangelings were caught in the fighting as well. The 48th's band had volunteered to go into the fight when the long roll sounded, and hastily arming themselves, they marched into battle with their regiment. At the first fire two of the musicians fell fatally wounded.

Protected by the natural cover in their front, the left wing of Cleburne's brigade and Buckland's brigade fought each other with stubborn determination. Mounted officers, riding up and down the lines to encourage their men in the formal tradition were shot with appalling rapidity. Early in the fighting Lieutenant Colonel Herman Canfield, commanding the 72d Ohio, silhouetted himself along the crown of the Federal ridge and was shot from his horse.

Here, along the 72d's front, the fighting grew particularly bloody. In the span of about forty-five minutes, the Ohioans lost twelve dead and sixty-eight wounded, nearly 12 percent of their effective strength. When their lieutenant colonel fell, the 72d was without field officers, Major Crockett having been taken prisoner the previous Friday.

Brigade commander Buckland now deemed the situation so critical that he took command of this regiment in person, unwisely leaving his other two regiments to "maintain their parts of the line" on their own.

Toward the left of Buckland's line the 70th Ohio was in the midst of a sharp fire fight with several of Cleburne's regiments. One of Cleburne's colonels, Benjamin Hill, of the 5th * (35th) Tennessee, here described the incoming Federal fire as terrific. A battery of light artillery, Barrett's Battery B, 1st Illinois, had taken position just to the right of Shiloh Church. Although some distance away from the main battle, it supported Buckland's line by firing shell and canister. Hill's Tennesseans had been shooting and yelling loudly when first struck by the shower of canister. "Both the yelling and firing of the enemy . . . cease[d] for a time" observed a Federal artillery officer.

Thus pinned down, Hill's men stood the unfamiliar stress of combat like many other raw and inexperienced recruits both North and South, evidencing extremes of bravery and cowardice. Hill noted that one of his privates was so scared that he was unable to fire his musket even when ordered repeatedly to do so. Yet another soldier, a mere lad of fifteen, remained well in advance of his company, fighting recklessly. He was twice knocked down by spent balls and finally had his musket shattered by a bullet. One private of Company C was struck by a musket ball that passed through both cheeks. Although the blood ran from his mouth, he refused to go to the rear.

Yet, many of the 35th Tennessee went to the rear under the slightest pretense, including several lieutenants and a sergeant. When Hill twice found one of his captains sulking in the rear, he drew his revolver and threatened to shoot the man.

Because of the disparity in numbers and the rugged terrain, Cleburne's four regiments were unable to advance. Whenever they rallied and attempted to charge, the Federal volleys stopped them before they began. About 8:30 A.M., after thirty minutes of continuous

---

* There were two 5th Tennessee Regiments in the Confederate Army. Hill's regiment was later known as the 35th.

fighting, Hardee's first line of attack west of Shiloh Church was temporarily stalled.

Peering across the smoke-fringed landscape at the Federal line nearby, Brigadier General Patton Anderson of Bragg's second assault wave observed the difficult tactical situation confronting him. "A battery of his field pieces [Waterhouse's] was in position on the height of a domineering hill, from four hundred to six hundred yards in front of our lines, commanding his camp and the approaches to it. Immediately in our front and between us and his battery, ran a boggy ravine, the narrow swamp of which was so thickly overgrown with various species of shrubs, saplings and vines, so densely interwoven as to sometimes require the use of the knife to enable the footman to pass. Over this the enemy's battery had a full field of fire upon our whole lines as we descended the declivity terminating in the swamp. . . . on the opposite skirts of the swamp his infantry [Buckland's] had all the advantages presented by such shelter. . . ."

Marching in a direct line from their staging area south of the Widow Howell's field, Anderson's brigade was one of the first units of Bragg's line to make an appearance. Advancing over the crown of a wooded ridge west of Rhea field shortly after 8 A.M., Anderson's men boldly swept into full view of the Federal lines.

One Federal officer breathlessly wrote that this sight was one never to be forgotten. Behind Anderson's men another mass of Confederates swept through the woods, their gun barrels glinting in the sunlight.

Although the fighting had been continuous for more than an hour, Sherman now looked up and "saw the glistening bayonets of heavy masses of infantry to our left front in the woods beyond the small stream. . . . It was a beautiful and dreadful sight . . . to see them approach with banners fluttering, bayonets glistening and lines dressed on the centre," said Sherman. For the first time he regarded the enemy attack as more than just a foray against his own camp.

Nearby, riding his horse along a wooded crest, Confederate General Braxton Bragg confidently watched his men march into action. Commanding the second battle line, five brigades and 10,731 men, Bragg had boasted less than two weeks earlier that his troops were "far superior" to Polk's and Johnston's (Hardee's) undisciplined volunteers. Although his corps had been assigned a vital role, because of the Confederate battle orders Bragg was unable to fight his troops as a consolidated unit. Instead of advancing in a massed column of attack, Bragg's corps was strung out across the rough timberland in an extended line. Many of his brigades were already struggling to maintain alignment and proper distance from Hardee's first line. The inevitable intermingling and confusion led Bragg to reflect bitterly years later about the "faulty arrangement of troops" and to name "Beauregard, or his man Jordan . . . [as] entitled to all the blunderings of those details."

As required by Adjutant General Jordan's battle orders, Bragg's corps had deployed about a thousand yards in rear of the first line. When the advance occurred, about 5:30 A.M., Bragg's brigadiers adjusted their pace and direction by guiding on the right.

Anderson's brigade, assigned as a reserve to Gibson's and Pond's brigades, had marched about a quarter of a mile before its officers discovered they had closed to within three hundred yards of Hardee's front line. A halt was immediately ordered to allow Hardee's men to regain a proper interval.

Although the rattle of musketry had already sounded in the woods ahead, Bragg's men remained halted for about a half-hour. During this interim Gibson, marching on the left of the Pittsburg–Corinth road, was ordered by Bragg to cross over to the right, his left flank then resting on the roadway. When the advance was resumed, Bragg again changed its position, ordering the brigade back to the eastern side of the road. As a result of this constant shuffling, Gibson's brigade lagged behind and did not arrive in the vicinity of Rhea field until about 8:30 A.M. A further delay occurred when Pond, on Bragg's extreme left, failed to advance concurrently with the other units. These wide gaps and staggered fronts not only disrupted Bragg's parallel line, but his progress was so delayed by the rough ground that his leading brigade, Anderson's, had advanced only a mile in two and one-half hours.

The elaboration of the Confederate plan of attack was "simply execrable," Bragg later wrote. Although he had anticipated that his entire corps would attack along an extended front, only Anderson's brigade appeared in the vicinity of Sherman's camps about 8 A.M.— entirely unsupported.

For this reason Patton Anderson decided to await additional help before ordering an attack. A halt of "some time" occurred, although his troops were exposed to a heavy shelling from the Federal artillery. During this delay only the deployment of Hodgson's soon-to-be famous battery of light artillery, the 5th Company, Washington Artillery of New Orleans, occurred.

Wheeling into battery about 8:10 A.M., Hodgson's Louisiana gunners immediately opened fire with shell and spherical case from their six rifled and smoothbore guns, aiming deliberately at Waterhouse's battery atop the hill overlooking Rhea field. Composed of many of the young bluebloods of New Orleans, Hodgson's artillery

MEN OF THE FAMOUS WASHINGTON ARTILLERY OF NEW ORLEANS. Dressed in blue uniforms and high boots, shortly before Shiloh, this relaxed group of enlisted men knew little of what they would face a few weeks later. Following the heavy fighting in the vicinity of the Hornets' Nest, a member of the battery wrote: "I had no idea of war until then, and would have given anything in the world if I could have been away." (PHOTOGRAPHIC HISTORY OF THE CIVIL WAR)

had been hurried forward by Ruggles to the crest of a ridge overlooking the "boggy thicket." Here they were joined by two guns under Captain Shoup belonging to Hardee's corps.

To the accompanying thunder of Hodgson's guns, Colonel R. M. Russell and a brigade of about twenty-five hundred Tennessee and Louisiana infantry swept into view shortly before 8:30 A.M. A component of Polk's corps, they supposedly were part of the third Confederate line of attack. Yet, marching along the line of the main Corinth road, they had made more rapid progress than many of Bragg's brigades.

After Polk's leading brigade, Stewart's, was sent to the right, Russell's men had momentarily halted near the south end of Rhea field to await orders. Much to their disgust they were compelled to endure a rain of solid shot and shell from Waterhouse's battery at the far end of the long field. Here Lieutenant John Crowley of the 11th Louisiana Infantry was struck by an exploding shell that ripped off his left arm. Since his right arm had been amputated on the field of Belmont the preceding November, Crowley was now armless.

Following "a few minutes" of shelling, said Brigadier General Charles Clark, Russell's division commander, "I was ordered to move to the edge of the open field in front, and was there met by Major General Bragg, who informed me that the battery on the left and front of my line was enfilading his troops. . . ." Russell was instructed to "charge through the enemy's encampment and take it at all hazards."

Provided with their awaited support, Anderson's brigade now advanced on the left into the swamp that Cleburne had found impassable. Numerically the weakest of Bragg's brigades, a scant 1,633 strong, Anderson's command marched with ranks fairly intact to the edge of the thicket under a heavy bombardment.

A few minutes later Colonel August Reichard of the 20th Louisiana found himself surrounded by "a dense undergrowth in which it was impossible to see five paces ahead." Word soon came that his right-flank company had lost contact with the brigade, and Reichard ordered a halt. He was about to extricate the regiment by retracing his steps when the 2d Tennessee of Hardee's first line suddenly appeared "in full retreat" and swept through the 20th's line, turning it into a rabble.

Although both regiments were soon rallied, the 20th Louisiana had been completely separated from its brigade, further fragmenting Bragg's battle line. The 2d Tennessee, having re-formed about forty yards behind the 20th Louisiana, was found to be so severely cut up that second lieutenants, and in one instance a sergeant, commanded its companies. "Some wept, some cursed, others lamented the death of some of our bravest officers and men, and not a few drifted to the rear," candidly wrote a member of the regiment.

By the time Reichard's 20th Louisiana again forced its way across the swamp under a heavy fire, the fighting along much of Buckland's front had slackened.

Although Reichard brought fewer than 226 officers and men into Buckland's sector, the arrival of these Confederates had been observed in the Union lines. This was promptly overestimated as a serious threat to Buckland's flank. "I [now] feared the enemy would turn my right," said Buckland, who sent an officer along the Hamburg–Purdy road to find McDowell and bring up help.

Portly Colonel John A. McDowell, like most of his men, was about to enter his very first battle. Thus far his brigade had not been engaged, merely having listened in awe to the heavy firing on their left for about forty-five minutes. Occupying the outermost camp on the right of Sherman's division, McDowell's brigade of three regiments was responsible for guarding the Purdy road bridge over Owl Creek, it being the main route of communication with Lew Wallace's division in the vicinity of Adamsville.

As early as sunrise one of McDowell's officers had been to the brigade picket line and observed the enemy "advancing past the Howell house." Soon thereafter a picket of the 40th Illinois was shot through the heart at long range. The officer, Colonel Thomas Worthington, then rode back to brigade headquarters and learned that McDowell was not yet up. Already regarded by Sherman as an alarmist, Worthington said he "made no further effort to alert the camp," but rode back to the picket line again to observe the enemy's movements.

About 7:30 A.M. McDowell's brigade responded to the general alarm and formed on their color line, finally advancing some fifty yards to the brow of a ridge overlooking the Owl Creek flatlands. Here they awaited in vain the appearance of the enemy.

McDowell, who had ignored the storm signals gathering in his front for the past few days, already was so thoroughly confused that he was uncertain where all of his brigade pickets were stationed. As his 2,358-man brigade advanced to a ridge overlooking the Shiloh Branch of Owl Creek, McDowell found that an awkward gap of about two hundred yards separated his left flank from Buckland's right. His overall strength had been reduced by the detachment of several companies of the 6th Iowa and one of the Morton Battery's 12-pounder howitzers, sent to guard the bridge crossing Owl Creek.

When Buckland's aide arrived to warn McDowell that the enemy would pour into the gap existing between the two brigades, Mc-Dowell reluctantly allowed the 40th Illinois to go to Buckland's support. He cautioned them, however, to take position on the right, in the rear of Buckland's flank, where they were to take no part in the fighting unless attacked.

Buckland, who was grateful to have their help, had been convinced by the renewed pressure on the 72d Ohio's front that the Confederates were bringing up heavy reinforcements. His horse had been wounded in front of the saddle and was bleeding profusely. When one of Sherman's aides had earlier asked if he could hold his position, Buckland had confidently replied, "My men are fighting bravely and I will hold my position."

Suddenly drained of his confidence by the appearance of Confederate troops, principally Reichard's 20th Louisiana, Buckland sent word to Sherman that the enemy was being heavily reinforced, and he "would need help."

Less than a week later Sherman was to muse, "Sunday we caught thunder." By midmorning Sherman had narrowly escaped death so frequently that it is difficult to keep track of each incident. Leaving his quiet headquarters tent among the budding trees near Shiloh Church, Sherman had ridden to the front shortly after seven o'clock. His first warning of unusual enemy activity had been from Appler's quartermaster, followed by a terse dispatch from Peabody's brigade, then a personal visit by Buckland.

When he was nearly killed by the volley fired from the bushes near Appler's camp, Sherman was sufficiently alarmed to send staff officers to Generals McClernand, Hurlbut, and Prentiss to report that his division had been attacked and that he desired support. Yet Sherman failed to perceive that the enemy planned a general attack on the entire Pittsburg Landing camps. "I confess I did not think Beauregard would abandon his railroads to attack us on our base when he knew that by waiting a short time we should be forced to advance . . ." Sherman admitted a month later.

Only when he saw the "glistening bayonets" of Bragg's second battle line advancing in his front about eight o'clock did Sherman become "satisfied for the first time that the enemy designed a determined attack on our whole camp."

Sherman had reached the crossroads of his military career. He had been the victim of one of the greatest strategic surprises in the annals of war, and his behavior under the stress of fighting at great disadvantage would provide fair measure of the man as a leader in combat.

Twenty-one-year-old Lieutenant John T. Taylor, Sherman's aide-de-camp, had for several days asked his general why they did not march out to fight the Rebels. Sherman's answer had always been, "Never mind, young man, you will have all the fighting you want before this war is over. . . ." As Taylor trotted along behind Sherman that Sunday morning, he realized "that I did not want to see a battle fought as much as I had supposed. The roar of cannon, the shriek of shells, the . . . wounded and dying men," wrote Taylor, filled him with "absolute fear."

Looking to his general for succor, he saw Sherman astride his "sorrel race mare," smoking a cigar, cool and unperturbed. A short, scraggly red beard masked a stern expression. "General Sherman's conduct," said Taylor, "soon instilled . . . a feeling that it was grand to be there with him."

Often nervous and sometimes irascible in camp, Sherman on the battlefield acted as though ice water ran through his veins. "Many wondered, thinking me indifferent and nonchalant," Sherman later wrote, but "knowing beforehand what to expect," he paid no attention to the bullets flying about and refused to panic when some of his troops fled their positions.

About eight o'clock, when Appler's 53d Ohio ran to the rear, Sherman had only two other regiments in line east of the Corinth road. The 57th Ohio, without its sick colonel, had taken position on the left of Waterhouse's battery near the edge of Rhea field. The 77th Ohio, Hildebrand's former regiment, was on the right, near Shiloh Church and across the road from Captain Barrett's battery, the Chicago Light Artillery.

Under command of Major Benjamin D. Fearing, the 77th Ohio had started from camp about 6:30 A.M. to reinforce the brigade picket line. Some of Fearing's men, on duty as outpost pickets that morning, were stationed near the Corinth Road, about three hundred yards beyond the camp of the 53d Ohio. Being in advance, they had heard from one of Peabody's Missourians that the Confederates in "formidable force" were moving toward Sherman's camps. Yet when Fearing went to Sherman with this information, he was ordered merely to advance to the picket line with his regiment. By the time the 77th was formed and had marched a few hundred yards from camp, Cleburne's Confederates were observed advancing to attack Appler's regiment. Deploying along the gentle downslope leading from their tents to the small creek in front, Fearing's Ohioans had knelt in line of battle fifty yards east of Shiloh Church. Here they waited as a great panoply of the enemy's troops paraded before their eyes.

CHAPTER XII

Seeing the Elephant

Even as Cleburne's men had discovered, Russell's and Anderson's Confederates of Bragg's second line found the boggy ravine tough going. Anderson's brigade, marching on the left, had the shorter distance to travel and was slightly in advance when pandemonium ran through the entire line. The undergrowth here was "almost impenetrable," thought one Confederate. Battle lines became jumbled, regiments lost their way or were unable to advance at all, and the repeated bursts of enemy shells struck terror into the men. When the 20th Louisiana became entangled in the brush and was separated, only four regiments remained in Anderson's line. Immediately thereafter the 17th Louisiana, on the extreme flank, wandered too far to the east, reducing Anderson's regiments in line to three.

Russell's brigade fared even worse. Split into two segments by faulty communications when first ordered to charge, Russell's battle line was decimated by the lowland swamp. "Instead of two regiments advancing [on our left]," Russell bitterly recorded, "but seven companies . . . succeeded in passing the almost impenetrable undergrowth. . . ."

Just beyond the swamp lay the bullet-riddled camp of the 53d Ohio. With fixed bayonets four companies of the 11th Louisiana and three of the 22d Tennessee dashed up the slope about 8:45 A.M., sheltered momentarily by the low crown of the hill in front.

At that moment Lieutenant Patrick H. White of Barrett's battery, Chicago Light Artillery, looked to the left from his battery's position near Shiloh Church. An open space ran to the crest of the ridge near the 53d Ohio's camp. "We saw a line of troops marching with their flank toward us," White wrote, ". . . but we were not sure whether they were our own or the enemy." Although White's gunners aimed their pieces at this exposed line and stood waiting to pull the lanyards, the battery's officers hesitated to give the order. "Just then General Sherman called out, 'Don't fire! Those are our own men,'" said White. But as the unidentified line reached the crest of the hill,

191

White recognized the "Rebel flag of the 11th Louisiana Tigers." He gave the order to open fire.

These blasts of canister tore into the Confederate ranks with terrible effect, reported Russell. Immediately afterward the ground was swept by a withering volley of musketry from the 57th and 77th Ohio regiments. "The enemy . . . opened such a deadly and well aimed fire as to make it impossible to hold the point gained . . ." confided one of the 11th Louisiana's officers. As his regiment raced for cover at the bottom of the hill, only the color sergeant stood fast, waving his flag in the face of the enemy until he was ordered to fall back. Miraculously he was not hit.

Once begun the chaos spread like wildfire to other advancing Confederate troops. Anderson's three regiments, having fallen slightly behind Russell's 22d Tennessee and 11th Louisiana, also were caught up in the confusion and came rushing back. With them were a handful of the 6th Mississippians who had survived Cleburne's assaults and had bravely joined Anderson's attack.

Here Anderson's 17th Louisiana nearly went to pieces. Having wandered too far to the right, it was marching up the hill close behind two of Russell's regiments when the 22d Tennessee suddenly broke and ran back through its line. Pausing only to fire several volleys, the 17th also went to the rear in disorder, many of its companies becoming mixed during the retreat.

At the bottom of the hill officers attempted to rally their men as best they could in the smoke and deafening noise. "Owing to the hurried manner and the fire under which we were compelled to re-form the regiment," said a harried Confederate, "many of the men were not even in their own companies or regiments."

All the while, Braxton Bragg had calmly watched Anderson's and Russell's attack from a location near the main Corinth road. According to Bragg his spirited charger was "proudly surveying the field" when a Minie ball fired by a sharpshooter struck the animal in the middle of the forehead. Horse and rider went down in a heap, and Bragg had to be pulled from beneath the carcass, his right leg badly bruised by the fall. "[The bullet was] intended for me and nothing but the head of the noble animal saved me," Bragg later remarked.

Although he complained about being compelled to ride an "inferior animal," Bragg soon remounted a staff officer's horse and dashed after a regiment to his left, then in full retreat. "To my dismay," Bragg confided, "[I] found Mark's [11th] Louisiana regiment disgraced.—They belonged to Polk's mob."

Bragg, who had earlier instructed Brigadier General Charles Clark, Russell's division commander, to lead the charge against Waterhouse's battery, later begrudgingly admitted that Clark's soldiers (Polk's corps) had opportunely come up to fill a large void in

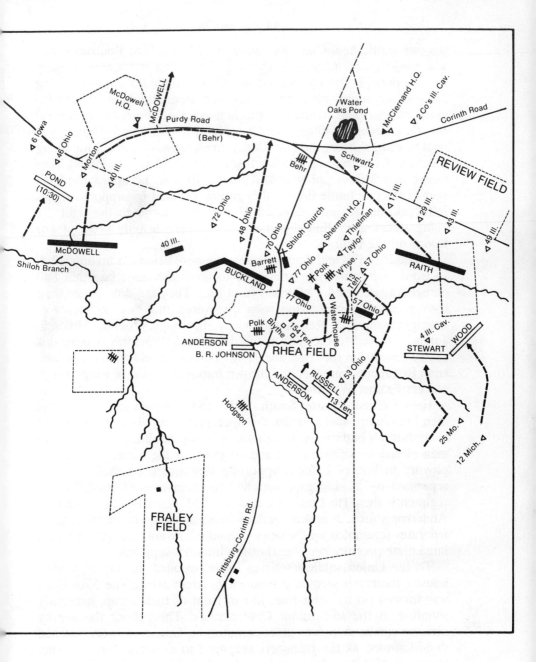

MAP 6
Collapse of Sherman's Line
9 A.M.–11 A.M., April 6 (Chapter 12)

his own battle line. Clark had gone in with the 11th Louisiana, and following that regiment's repulse he dashed about re-forming as many men as possible for another assault. Clark's difficulties in organizing for another attack were many, however, stemming from the confusion and disorder created by the first attempt. Fortunately several other Confederate officers were nearby to lend a helping hand.

Bushrod Johnson, the Fort Donelson escapee, was marching along the main Corinth road with his brigade of about two thousand Tennessee and Mississippi troops. About 8:30 A.M. he approached the rear of Bragg's battle line. Although first ordered to support Bragg's left flank, he was now directed to move his troops to the right, "it being stated . . . that the enemy . . . were heavily pressing our troops on the right."

While Russell's and Anderson's troops were being cut up on the hill in front, Johnson's men attempted to cross the same bog that had earlier fragmentized Cleburne's front line. They fared no better than their predecessors. Johnson soon discovered that two regiments of his right wing had been separated by the rough ground. Although Johnson veered to the left, in the direction of Barrett's battery, his two regiments on the right, the 154th Tennessee and Blythe's Mississippi Regiment, were met and thrown into line by one of Bragg's staff officers against Waterhouse.

Here Colonel Preston Smith of the 154th Tennessee, leading his men in column, swept across the open ground of Rhea field toward Waterhouse's battery. Although under heavy small-arms fire, Smith's men closed to within three hundred yards of the battery before deploying in line of battle. Supporting this attack on their left, but separated by a wide gap, marched the remnants of Russell's two regiments, the 11th Louisiana and the 22d Tennessee, and some of Anderson's men. Jumbled together in an unwieldy mass, these Confederates scrambled up the slope behind Clark and Russell, applying immediate pressure on Waterhouse's infantry supports.

To the Union soldiers waiting in the wooded vicinity of Waterhouse's battery it seemed a moment of great crisis. The 57th Ohio was formed on its color line, just in front of their camp, nervously shooting at the still-distant Confederates. Throughout the nearby division camps there was great commotion. One eyewitness watched dumbfounded as the teamsters prepared to evacuate his campsite; "teams were put to the wagons in double quick time, then they were off like lightning, leaving tents, provisions, and forage all to the mercy of the Secesh. . . . Some of the drivers were scared so bad that they cut the horses loose from the wagons and mounted them," wrote the man, a private of the 4th Illinois Cavalry.

By the time the 154th Tennessee approached to within easy musket range, the 57th Ohio already had begun to break up. A few minutes later they fell back through the rows of standing tents despite the frantic efforts of Lieutenant Colonel A. V. Rice to stop them.

The remnant of the 53d Ohio, now rallied by officers after its retreat in disorder from Rhea field, was watching from a hillock near Sherman's headquarters.

"I saw the 57th Ohio . . . falling back through its camp, its ranks broken by the standing tents," said Adjutant Dawes of the 53d. "It seemed to me we could help them by moving the length of a regiment to our right and perhaps save the line. I ran to where Colonel Appler was lying on the ground behind a tree, and . . . said, 'Colonel, let us go and help the 57th. They are falling back.' "

Appler looked up. "His face was like ashes" and flushed with the "awful fear of death," said Dawes. Pointing over his shoulder in an indefinite direction, Appler "squeaked out" in a trembling voice, "No, form the men back here."

Dawes was astounded. "Our miserable positions flashed upon me. We were in the front of a great battle. Our regiment never had a battalion drill. Some men in it had never fired a gun. Our lieutenant colonel had become lost in the confusion of the first retreat, the major was in the hospital, and our colonel was a coward."

Dawes, in a rage, swore at Appler and said he would not do it. Appler jumped to his feet and "literally ran away"—according to another officer—again shouting, "Fall back and save yourselves!" Promptly all but two companies of the 53d abandoned their position, joining the growing number of refugees streaming along the Corinth road back to Pittsburg Landing.

Waterhouse's blazing guns by now had swung around and were firing down the ravine between the camp of the 53d and 57th Ohio with such rapidity that it seemed to one participant that "all the furies of hell broke loose at once could not have made more din."

Here the Confederates were attacking from several sides, even wheeling a section of field guns ahead of their battle line in Rhea field. Under the command of Captain Marshall T. Polk, these two guns already were firing canister into the wavering 57th Ohio and Waterhouse's battery with good effect.

Although Captain Polk's gunners suffered terribly in the open field, losing many men including Polk, who was shot in the leg, their fire contributed to the chaos that spread through the Union lines.

About seven rounds had been fired by Polk when one of Bragg's staff officers delivered an urgent appeal to Preston Smith to push his stalled regiment forward. "The order was promptly executed," said Smith, whose left-flank companies jumped up and sprinted for Waterhouse's guns immediately in their front.

At this point Captain A. C. Waterhouse, standing amid his guns to direct their fire, was suddenly cut down by a volley of musketry from the flank. Seeing that the Confederates were closing from the left, where the 57th Ohio had originally supported him, Waterhouse gave the order to limber up and retire, just before being carried off the field covered with blood.

Because of Waterhouse's drivers and horses "not having sufficient, drill," observed a nearby Federal officer, "they were unable to limber up all their pieces in time." When a frightened team bolted, the rear wheel of a caisson became jammed between several trees, and the rig had to be abandoned. The rest of the battery was drawing off when Major Ezra Taylor, Sherman's chief of artillery, came galloping across from Barrett's battery, believing Waterhouse's retreat was too hasty.

"I ordered him to unlimber and contest every foot of ground," said Taylor, who merely sent a messenger to look for another battery to come up and help out in the face of the growing attack.

Waterhouse's guns had withdrawn only about one hundred yards before being halted. Again they unlimbered and swung into action. Since the 57th Ohio had already gone to the rear, Waterhouse's battery was unsupported except for two frightened companies of Illinois infantry, just up from McClernand's nearby camps. Firing canister at point-blank range into the mass of Confederates swarming up the hill, some of Waterhouse's cannon were now turned so completely about that they were shooting both in front and in rear of their battery's new position.

Incredibly, much of Waterhouse's difficulty was caused by a single regiment of Tennesseans led by an unlikely commander. Colonel Alfred J. Vaughan, Jr., a native Virginian and a graduate of V.M.I. who had joined a Tennessee regiment when he was unable to obtain arms for his own company raised in Mississippi, was one of the few Virginians at Shiloh. Vaughan had become separated from Russell's brigade at the onset of the advance across the swamp, causing his regiment, the 13th Tennessee Infantry, to go farther to the east, where it fell under Bragg's eye. Seizing any regiment for the purpose at hand, Bragg ordered the 13th to march by the right flank and take the enemy's battery "at all hazards."

Vaughan first attempted this by going in a wide circle, planning to come up in rear of the enemy battery. Having passed through one Federal camp where the fire was particularly heavy, Vaughan suddenly changed direction and swung sharply to the left, coming down the ravine between the abandoned tents of the 53d and 57th Ohio.

Vaughan's charging men thus helped put the 57th Ohio to flight and caused Waterhouse's hasty withdrawal. Moreover his Tennesseans, veterans of the fight at Belmont, quickly began to work around the repositioned battery's left flank, again attempting to take it from behind. This action, added to the pressure of troops under Russell and Clark, represented a serious threat to Waterhouse's battery.

One of Bragg's staff officers, Captain William O. Williams, appeared in Russell's front. Waving his sword, he galloped ahead of the surging Rebel line and was the first man to reach the crown of the hill. Yet as Russell's men charged into full view close behind, Waterhouse's guns temporarily brought them to a standstill, aided by the 77th Ohio, which raked the Confederate flank with musketry.

This proved to be only a brief respite, however. As Waterhouse's gunners now realized, the fate of their battery was sealed. Approaching from the left, Vaughan's 13th Tennessee was within fifty yards and closing rapidly. By the time one of Waterhouse's lieutenants, John A. Fitch, finally ordered a retreat, his men and horses were falling so fast that the guns could not be rehitched. Three cannon were abandoned to the enemy. A few passing infantrymen tried to drag one of the guns away, but the ground proved too soft and the slope too steep. What remained of the battery hastened to the rear about 9:30 A.M., making a desperate effort to escape the Confederates. Later, when the drivers brought their teams under control, it was found that all the iron axle trees had broken, disabling the remaining three guns. Since the battery was a complete wreck and both the captain and the senior lieutenant were wounded, the men of Waterhouse's battery despondently marched for Pittsburg Landing, abandoning another of their disabled James rifled guns along the way.

Along the ridge near Waterhouse's camp Vaughan's 13th Tennessee regiment burst through the three deserted guns with a shout of triumph. A nearby Union officer watched with disgust as the Confederates took possession of the cannon. "They swarmed around them like bees. They jumped upon the guns, and on the hay bales in the battery camp, and yelled like crazy men," he said.

Another Federal lieutenant was so overcome with anger that he seized a rifle from one of his men and fired it at the Confederate color-bearer, who had just planted his flag over one of the guns. Although nearly two hundred yards distant, the man toppled over. To the Federal officer's dismay, however, "the colors were soon replaced, and the enemy continued slowly to advance."

The 13th Tennessee was nearly out of ammunition, however, and was missing four companies that had been separated during the charge. Therefore they soon paused amid some abandoned Federal tents to rummage through the debris for musket cartridges. Here Colonel Vaughan observed a dead Union officer with a large pointer dog standing guard over the body. According to Vaughan the dog refused to allow the Confederates to approach his dead master.

Matters were already proceeding from bad to worse for Sherman in this sector when the Confederate attack resumed. Only one of Sherman's regiments was still intact east of the main Corinth road. Doggedly fighting alongside Shiloh Church, the 77th Ohio continued to hold its first position, enduring what one private termed a "long series of sledge hammer blows." At one time following Cleburne's initial attack, many of the 77th had thought the battle over, and several men including a sergeant-major ran down to the creek in front to "secure some trophies." They were soon chased back to their line on the run as first Bragg's and then Polk's soldiers attacked in their front.

When the 57th Ohio was flanked and went to the rear, the 77th alone comprised the extreme left of Sherman's line. Without being told to do so, the regiment promptly swung around to meet the new threat. "The men in the left companies . . . left faced in their tracks," said one of the 77th's privates, "and were firing at the enemy in the rear of the position first occupied by the 57th Ohio . . ." Soon more Confederate regiments appeared, including the 154th Tennessee. The fighting became desperate and bloody.

Private Robert H. Fleming of the 77th Ohio, a clerk at brigade headquarters, had been compiling the daily report that morning when the colonel first ordered his regiment into line. After the fighting began, it ran through Fleming's mind that "the boys would be writing home that they were all in it except 'Little Bob,' . . . clerking at headquarters."

Borrowing an Austrian rifle from a sick private, he ran to join his regiment, falling into line in time to be wounded following the collapse of Hildebrand's left. "I thought I was done for," wrote Fleming who as he fell "felt that deathly shiver . . . and the warm blood spurting out." After struggling to his feet, his first impulse was to save the gun and accouterments that he had borrowed. Deciding that "discretion was the better part of valor," however, he threw away the weapon and painfully made his way to a field hospital. As he went, he saw that the 77th was gradually breaking up on the left, with men singly and in squads passing to the rear as the Confederates worked around their flank.

Colonel Jesse Hildebrand, riding an enormous black horse and appearing to one observer "as cool and collected as if leading a parade," was galloping about with almost "reckless gallantry," urging the 77th to continue the fight. At one point he had ridden his horse between the opposing battle lines to steady his men. Yet it was of no use—the brigade continued to disintegrate before his eyes.

Finally he dashed about, ordering the remnant of the 53d and 57th Ohio back to the road. The men did not understand which of several roads he meant. They soon became confused, and many continued to the rear, some going all the way to Pittsburg Landing.

By now the enlarging crisis had attracted Sherman, who rode among the wavering Union infantry near Shiloh Church, vainly attempting to shore up his line. Bullets were whizzing about, many now coming in from beyond the left flank. Staff officers were seen to gallop up, bending low in their saddles as if Sherman were in the midst of a swarm of hornets.

By midmorning Sherman's sorrel race mare had been wounded, although the general continued to ride her. The Confederates were now so close in front that another bullet intended for Sherman killed the animal outright. Sherman jumped up from beneath the carcass. "The firing . . . was terrific," he said, "and I had no time to save the saddle, holster, or valise."

Seeing his aide John T. Taylor nearby, Sherman had him dismount, then took his horse. As he again swung into the saddle, Sherman jested with his young aide, saying, "Well, my boy, didn't I promise you all the fighting you could do?" Taylor agreed, confiding before he went off to find another mount that this obligation was more than fulfilled.

Although the crisis continued to worsen in front of Sherman, help was nearby. The camps of a large Federal brigade stood less than a quarter of a mile from Hildebrand's campsite, having been haphazardly placed there several weeks earlier, during the initial occupation of the Shiloh Church area. Actually a part of Major General John A. McClernand's First Division, the all-Illinois Brigade of Colonel Leonard F. Ross had previously formed and advanced to Sherman's support, arriving in the vicinity of Waterhouse's battery nearly an hour before the capture of that battery.

Although composed of veteran regiments, three of whom had fought at Fort Donelson, the brigade was burdened this morning with sickness and confusion. The commanding officer, Ross, was absent from the brigade, leaving Colonel James S. Reardon of the 29th Illinois in charge. Reardon was ill, however, and when the brigade was called out, the third senior colonel, Julius Raith, was told to take command. Although a veteran officer with Mexican War experience, Raith was taken by surprise by the assignment. He had no regular aides and only one mounted staff officer to assist him. Of the four regiments in his brigade at least one thought the firing in front was a joke when ordered to form in line about 7:30 A.M.

When Raith sent Lieutenant Colonel Adolph Englemann to turn out the 49th Illinois Infantry, he found that his orders to form for battle were scoffed at. The 49th thought that the gunfire in front was nothing more than the brigade pickets "firing off their pieces."

Indeed, Englemann's own men had been emptying their guns that morning when the distant rumble of musketry was first heard. His regiment had been called into line on April 4, whereupon the weapons were loaded in anticipation of an engagement. Finally on Sunday morning the regiment had received McClernand's permission to fire off these rounds so as to clear the weapons. This, added to the guffaws of the 49th, so confused Englemann that he decided to ride in the direction of the firing to see if the enemy was actually present.

He was back in a flash, having gone only a short distance before encountering Hildebrand's embattled regiments. The 49th was "speedily paraded" to their color line, said Englemann, who then hurried back to his own regiment.

By eight o'clock all of Raith's regiments had formed and stood awaiting orders in front of their camp. Yet Raith decided that this location was "a poor position to await the enemy in," and he ordered his brigade forward to the sheltered brow of a hill, about a hundred yards distant.

Their new position was several hundred yards behind and to the left of Waterhouse's battery, and Raith's men soon observed the Confederates deploying on the opposite hill in heavy columns of regiments. Unfortunately for Sherman Raith chose to remain there. When the final overwhelming attack came, Raith was too far in the rear to prevent Hildebrand's brigade from being flanked on the left. Most of Raith's infantrymen remained mere spectators of the fighting in their front. Only the 17th Illinois, on Raith's right, was within proper supporting distance of Sherman's line east of Shiloh Church. Even it was forced to fire at long range, however, as the Confederates swarmed over Waterhouse's guns.

Adjutant Dawes of the 53d Ohio was near Raith's line with the remaining two companies of his regiment. They were obviously near to breaking from the repeated enemy attacks. Recognizing a soldier of the 17th who he knew had been at Donelson, Dawes went to an officer and asked if the private might come over and help his men. It was agreed, and Private A. C. Voris of the 17th Illinois soon passed among the 53d Ohio, "telling the men he had seen the elephant before, and had learned that the way to meet him was to keep cool, shoot slow, and aim low. 'Why, it's just like shooting squirrels,' he said, 'only these squirrels have guns, that's all.'" Their courage bolstered, this handful of Ohioans joined with another mixed squad and, according to Dawes, drove back a disorderly line that was pursuing them.

Still, their efforts did little to halt the combined Confederate onslaught. Waterhouse's guns were gone, and the 77th Ohio had broken up. Sherman had no remaining units east of the Corinth Road to prevent the enemy from rolling up his entire line.

Most opportunely Raith and his men were there, blocking the path of the exultant Confederates and causing them to pause in their rapid pursuit of Sherman's broken line.

Although Sherman's left was shattered, the obstinate stand made by Waterhouse's battery was of much importance, having caused the Confederates to redeploy large numbers of troops. Bragg's staff officers, scouring the field for all available regiments to help break Sherman's line, now sent nearly eight thousand additional Confederates in the direction of Raith's Illinois brigade.

Led by Alexander P. Stewart, a brigadier under Charles Clark in Polk's corps, a mixed brigade of Arkansas and Tennessee infantry advanced from the southeast. On their right came more reinforcements—two already bloodied brigades of Hardee's front line, Wood's and Shaver's—summoned to the left following the rout of Prentiss.

It was an invitation to chaos. Despite these overwhelming numbers the Confederates were able to make little progress. Muddled communications and poor attack coordination ruined what might have been a decisive attack in the crucial Shiloh Church sector.

Stewart's men had been brought forward from reserve by Sidney Johnston and led toward the camps of Peabody's brigade. They arrived there after the enemy had been driven off, and no one was present to give Stewart orders. After he passed through the debris-strewn camp, Stewart met a staff officer who told him "to move to the left." Going in that direction, Stewart belatedly discovered that one of his regiments, the 4th Tennessee, somehow had not received this order and was separated from the main body. Halting his brigade along the incline of an enemy-held hill, Stewart ordered his men to lie down while he went back to find the 4th Tennessee.

Returning soon thereafter, he found to his great surprise that his brigade had moved away. Later Stewart learned that one regiment, the 33d Tennessee, had been detached by an aide of General Polk who brought it to the vicinity of an abandoned enemy camp—that of the 4th Illinois Cavalry. Here they came under fire of Federal artillery, positioned three-quarters of a mile north, and long-range musketry from Raith's brigade. By chance another Confederate regiment, the 12th Tennessee of Russell's brigade, had taken cover in the same encampment and was lying on the ground to avoid the rain of Federal projectiles.

In the smoke and confusion the 12th Tennessee mistook the approaching 33d for the enemy and fired in their faces, wounding seven men. The 33d, believing they had been deceived by a Federal regiment, "returned the fire with spirit," said their colonel. This of course produced great confusion among the 12th, and they fell back about fifty yards. By the time proper identification was made the storm of Federal artillery fire had become so severe that both regiments had to take cover in the midst of the disordered Union camp.

Following close on the heels of the 33d, Stewart's other two regiments also had moved up without their commander. They too were greeted at the top of the knoll by a blast of Federal grapeshot, compelling them to retreat to the foot of the hill. Next S. A. M. Wood's brigade, marching behind and to the right of Stewart, also came under the "galling fire of shell, shot, and grape." Wood was unable through the billowing battle smoke to see any of Stewart's troops, whom he thought to be on his near left. He continued ahead. Stewart's regiments, however, having halted, were actually poised tangent to Wood's flank and stood fronting the ground across which these men were marching. In the general confusion of the left-wheel movement, the intensity of the enemy's artillery fire, and the inexperience of the Confederates there was ample opportunity for the serious mistake that occurred.

"As my brigade advanced," wrote Wood, ". . . two regiments of troops came up in our rear. As they reached the crest of a hill the men, without orders, fired into us, killing at the first fire five in Major Kelly's battalion (9th Arkansas), a lieutenant in the 8th Arkansas, and wounding many others."

Probably responsible for this fire were Stewart's two missing regiments, the 5th Tennessee and 13th Arkansas. Private Edwin H. Rennolds of the 5th Tennessee remembered that his unit "came up with a regiment . . . formed at an angle with the line of advance. . . . Our regiment extending further to the left than it," said Rennolds, "three or four companies of ours were uncovered, and [they] commenced firing in front, no enemy being visable to me however. . . . Many of the men fired with their guns elevated at an angle of about 45 degrees." Sighting an enemy camp, "among which we could see a line of soldiers, which was taken for the enemy," continued Rennolds, ". . . fire was opened on them." According to several Confederate officers this fire struck among at least three of Wood's regiments moving obliquely across their front.

Wood, and some of his staff quickly acted to avert further trouble, riding toward the erring Confederate regiments and shouting for them not to fire. He was close in their front when they again opened fire at him, wounding his horse. The animal leaped and twisted in terror, throwing Wood, whose leg became caught in the stirrups. As the horse plunged away, Wood was roughly dragged through a nearby abandoned Union camp, leaving him nearly senseless for three hours.

"The whole of our force on the left fell back a short distance," observed one of Wood's officers from a spot beyond the deadly cross-fire zone. Soon the regiments on the right also went back to a ravine. Finally a color-bearer ran out in front of the lines and waved his flag. "[It] was recognized as a Confederate one and the firing ceased," remembered one of the 5th Tennessee's privates.

By now it was after ten o'clock. Wood's attack had been stalled and his brigade badly disorganized. It was temporarily unable to advance beyond the hill fronting Raith's camps.

Colonel R. G. Shaver of Arkansas, leading Hindman's old brigade, managed to avoid a similar fate by mere chance. Shaver also had advanced by the left flank following the defeat of Prentiss, but starting later than Wood, he was prevented from reaching his destination. Said Shaver, "Before making any considerable advance I was ordered to make a flank movement . . . and dislodge the enemy, who were in strong force in a woods some 300 yards in front. . . ." Swinging to the right to attack other Federal reinforcements formed in the vicinity of Sherman's review field, Shaver thus was prevented from closing with Raith.

By their own mistakes the Confederates had squandered another opportunity to crush the Federal right decisively.

Despite the numerous tactical mishaps hindering the Confederates Raith's brigade had already fallen into a state of turmoil approaching panic. Again faulty communications were to blame.

McClernand, whose headquarters lay about a half-mile northeast of Shiloh Church, had formed his two rear-most brigades on their regimental parade grounds about 7:30 A.M. About a half-hour later, following a brief reconnaissance by Captain Warren Stewart of his staff, McClernand ordered these brigades to move to the Corinth road ridge that ran in front of his headquarters. A considerable amount of time elapsed before these brigades, moving by column, were able to march into position along the main Corinth road north of Sherman's review field.

During this interval Raith's brigade had come under fire a quarter of a mile ahead. Lieutenant Abram H. Ryan, acting as Raith's assistant adjutant general, then had been told to go to the rear and find Marsh's brigade, which Raith believed would be found in a position now proper for his own brigade. Riding a bloody horse that had already been struck by a musket ball in the neck, Ryan found Marsh and his men near the sharp bend in the Corinth road. McClernand was with them, supervising their movements. When he heard Ryan's report, McClernand sent orders for Raith's brigade to fall back and form on the right of Marsh. Ryan dashed off, only to discover when he returned that in the confusion of the fighting Raith had gone among his men and could not be found. The entire brigade was actively firing at the heavy columns of Confederates that were plainly visible as they "crowded" in from the left. Ryan decided to act on McClernand's authority and ordered a general retreat beginning with the left-flank regiments and gradually extending to the right. Sadly not everyone got the word to fall back at the same time.

The 43d Illinois, near Raith's left, already had found that the enemy was "passing beyond our right and left flanks" and about ten o'clock gave way without orders, falling back upon Schwartz's battery in the direction of the main Corinth road.

Although Wood's and Stewart's Confederates were soon stalled in the vicinity of Raith's encampment, where many of their men were pillaging the abandoned tents, Russell's, Bushrod Johnson's, and some of Anderson's soldiers had already begun to press on following the capture of Waterhouse's battery.

At least one gun of Captain Marshall Polk's battery that had accompanied the 154th Tennessee into Rhea field was now brought into position near Waterhouse's captured cannon. Here General Clark, advancing with several regiments of Russell's brigade, reported a brisk fire fight of about fifteen minutes' duration with Raith's line.

Said one weary Union officer, "There was a good deal of disorder here. Everybody wanted cartridges. There were three kinds of firearms in our brigade and six different types in the division, all requiring ammunition of different caliber. . . . [Our] line was soon broken; bullets came from too many points of the compass."

During this fighting a soldier was struck on the shin by a glancing ball, and he screamed in pain. His captain ordered him to go to the rear, but as the line broke and began to drift away, the soldier came limping back and said, "Cap, give me a gun, this blamed fight ain't got any rear."

At last Raith's 17th Illinois, "pouring a terrific fire on the advancing foe," fell back, belatedly having received the order to withdraw and form a continuous line with McClernand's division.

Already the situation had so thoroughly deteriorated east of Shiloh Church that Colonel Jesse Hildebrand believed his brigade had been lost. Despondently he rode away, tendering his services to McClernand although a handful of his men as yet were fighting nearby.

Sherman remained in the midst of a vicious cross fire. His left flank had all but disappeared. Confederate artillery was firing from the rear of Hildebrand's camps, enfilading his line. As Sherman now admitted, "some change became absolutely necessary."

Although Sherman regarded the position at Shiloh Church as being so important that he gave it his personal attention throughout the morning, he had also sent staff officers to brigade commanders McDowell and Buckland, renewing his orders to hold their ground. Buckland, however, had already learned from the reaction to his earlier request that Sherman was unable to send him reinforcements. "This," said Buckland, "convinced me that matters were going wrong somewhere, and that sooner or later I would be compelled to fall back. . . ."

The Confederates in Buckland's front then numbered about five regiments, in all not more than two thousand men. Like the troops in front of Raith, they were confused and disorganized, although maintaining a desultory fire.

At one point the 72d Ohio, after effectively ambushing Cleburne's men at the head of a narrow ravine, had run low on ammunition. Finding that the 40th Illinois, sent by McDowell to support the 72d, would not advance into line since they had been told "not to engage in the fight unless attacked," and that it was impossible to distribute a resupply of cartridges along the firing line, Buckland ordered the 72d to fall back. Although the position was temporarily abandoned, the Confederates obligingly failed to advance. Soon thereafter Buckland was able to move his men back to the same position, having refilled their cartridge boxes.

Matters quickly began to change for the worse, however. Before the 72d could renew the fight with the Confederates, word was received of trouble farther to the left.

Barrett's battery, firing into Rhea field from their position near Shiloh Church, had been hammering all morning at the Confederates forming in the vicinity of the 53d Ohio's abandoned camp. When Bragg's combined assault on Waterhouse's battery began about 9 A.M., three of Patton Anderson's regiments had gone to the left, around the base of the hill to attack Barrett. Led by Bushrod Johnson two Tennessee regiments and four guns of Captain Marshall Polk's battery joined in the attack, their route nearly paralleling the main Corinth road.

Barrett's cannon roared in defiance, the gunners double-shotting their pieces as the Confederates approached a small creek one hundred fifty yards in front. "After our first discharge they gave us a volley which passed over our heads," said one of Barrett's officers. The ground in front sloped down to the creek, and seeing that their own fire was carrying high, Barrett's gunners depressed the muzzles. "At the second discharge three of their field officers' horses came [galloping] into our line . . ." wrote Lieutenant Patrick White, who estimated that nearly four hundred of the enemy were killed here.

Much to White's anger the 77th Ohio, which had been supporting Barrett's battery from across the road, then jumped up and retreated from the field. "They ran like sheep, threw away their guns, and did not stop until they reached the landing," said White in disgust.

Though now virtually unsupported, Barrett's guns continued to fire into the advancing Confederate ranks. Their blasts of canister knocked down so many gray infantry that Colonel W. A. Stanley, commanding one of Anderson's regiments, the 9th Texas, felt it "almost impossible to withstand the heavy fire." Along with the 17th Louisiana and the 1st Florida Battalion, Stanley's regiment retreated in disorder, finally re-forming in the rear as a support to the Washington Artillery of New Orleans.

Bushrod Johnson's men fared little better. At Barrett's first fire an officer of the 15th Tennessee reported a momentary wavering in the ranks, during which their lieutenant colonel had to draw his revolver to restore order. J. Knox Walker's regiment, the 2d Tennessee, was then some two hundred yards in the rear, behind Polk's battery, which was posted in the open along the road. Many of the 2d's riflemen had already drifted away, and the regiment was skittish under the incoming Federal fire. In their front Polk's battery was taking a terrible beating from a cross fire of Barrett's canister and the 70th Ohio's musketry. Bushrod Johnson twice tried to get the 2d to move up and provide better support to Polk's gunners, but each time the Tennesseans broke and ran.

By now Polk's battery was nearly helpless. "More than half the battery was disabled," said Johnson, and only one gun continued to be fired. Moreover Tyler's regiment, the 15th Tennessee, was also in trouble, having lost their commander after his horse had been shot three times.

Hastily Johnson ordered Polk's battery withdrawn and made a third attempt to lead the remnant of the 2d Tennessee past the battery. Prodding his men on, Johnson had nearly reached Polk's guns when he was shot down, seemingly mortally wounded. As he was borne from the field, his men scattered to the rear. "Their object was to cross our creek, but I am proud to say they did not do so . . ." wrote a jubilant Federal artillerist.

The Confederate batteries along the crest of the opposite ridge continued to shell Barrett's guns, but their fire went high, caused by the ascending smoke and Barrett's midslope position, so one Federal thought.

For the sweating Union artillerists the respite was brief. Having re-formed from the ravine ambush in Buckland's front, another 2d Tennessee Regiment, Bate's (Provisional), appeared from the east and suddenly drew fire from Barrett's cannon. Colonel Bate promptly led his men toward the Federal battery, moving "briskly to the charge" without informing his second-in-command what was intended. A few minutes later Bate's left leg was broken by a Minie ball, and he was hurriedly carried from the field. Bate's lieutenant colonel, who was on the opposite flank, then halted the regiment. Not having understood what the movement was about, he ordered a retreat.

In front of the smoking Union guns the Confederates lay in windrows. Their attacks, isolated and uncoordinated, had failed to dislodge a weakened Federal brigade half their overall strength. Even Bushrod Johnson found cause to apologize. "I was prevented from bringing the whole brigade together . . . into action. . . . Had I accomplished my purpose, I am convinced I would . . . report much more satisfactory results," he later wrote.

There was bitter irony here; the series of bloody attacks had been unnecessary. As the fighting abated in Barrett's front, the Federal gunners saw that their left flank was turned. Their support had gone, and the Confederates who had driven off Hildebrand's brigade were in their rear, advancing at almost right angles to Barrett's line.

Sherman at last sent word for Barrett's battery to fall back—he hoped to form a new line along the Purdy–Hamburg road, some five hundred yards in the rear. Lieutenant Patrick White stood among Barrett's guns and observed the growing chaos. "I knew it was time to retreat as we saw our troops falling back on the right and left," said the troubled White.

Except for two caissons for which there were no horses, the guns were rehitched to the teams and the battery sped away, just in time to avoid a Confederate regiment that emerged in front and fired a parting volley.

Five hours after the battle began the Shiloh Church area finally had been cleared of Federal troops. The last remaining regiment, the 70th Ohio on Buckland's left, had gone to the rear when their colonel feared the Confederates might fall on his flank and roll up the line.

It was ten minutes past ten. Sherman's staff officers raced along the division's line with orders for Buckland's and McDowell's troops to fall back to the Purdy road and organize a second line.

Captain J. H. Hammond of Sherman's staff galloped up to the 48th Ohio of Buckland's brigade and repeated Sherman's order. The 48th also had fallen back to its color line after witnessing the 70th Ohio's retreat. "We about-faced and retreated through our camp," said one of the 48th's officers. Already the Confederates were seen to be maneuvering dense columns from the east. For the time being each regiment seemed to be left to its own means.

The 70th Ohio, having retreated to its camp, was shelled there by the Confederate batteries along the opposite ridge. Belatedly they took shelter in a ravine nearby. One of Cleburne's pursuing regiments, the 35th Tennessee, soon moved up to attack.

"The Rebels raised their cornbread yelp, and making a desperate charge, captured our camp; taking full possession of our tents, and blankets, knapsacks and all our love letters," lamented one of the 70th's privates. At this point Captain Hammond dashed by, ordering Colonel Cockerill back to the Purdy road. As the 70th Ohio again streamed to the rear, they could hear the Confederate taunts of "Bull Run, Bull Run" shouted after them.

Farther to the right Buckland received word to retreat just as his 72d Ohio riflemen were returning with filled cartridge boxes. After leading them in good order back to the designated position, Buckland had his men form a new line in the middle of the road—just before disaster struck.

All morning long Colonel John A. McDowell's brigade had stood in line on the far right, listening to the fighting toward Shiloh Church without firing a musket. Of his three regiments only the 40th Illinois, sent to support Buckland's right, had become slightly engaged when the 72d fell back toward the Purdy road.

When McDowell received Sherman's order to fall back and form on the Purdy road, he had difficulty in speedily complying. His line extended three-quarters of a mile through a broken and wooded ridgeland, and his brigade camps already had been evacuated, causing the Purdy road to be choked with quartermaster's wagons and teams.

Apparently the lieutenant colonel of McDowell's former regiment, the 6th Iowa, had utilized the morning's long wait to shore up his nerves with a bottle of whiskey. When McDowell ordered his brigade to fall back, the lieutenant colonel "about-faced the left wing and marched it back to the field fence, leaving the other four companies standing in line in the woods," reported a member of the regiment. McDowell then galloped up and asked an officer what this meant. "It means, sir, that the colonel is drunk," came the reply. McDowell, in a huff, ordered the 6th Iowa's adjutant to relieve the intoxicated lieutenant colonel of his sword and to place him under arrest.

For McDowell it was only the beginning of much bad luck. As his infantry fell back through its camps, a battery of artillery attached to his brigade, Behr's 6th Indiana Battery, came dashing along the Purdy road, heading for Sherman's left flank.

Having fired only several shots at distant enemy columns that morning, they had been ordered about 9:30 A.M. by Captain Hammond of Sherman's staff to replace Barrett's battery at Shiloh Church, which was said to be running low on ammunition. Only one gun, a 12-pounder howitzer, was to remain with McDowell, this piece having been detached earlier to guard the Owl Creek bridge.

Meanwhile Buckland's men had rallied and formed in the middle of the Purdy road, probably because of the limited visibility in the brush along this roadway. This chance combination of circumstances nearly lost the battle. "We . . . were ready to renew the fight," said Buckland, "when we were shoved out of the road and thrown into confusion by Behr's battery of artillery, which came rushing along the road at full speed from the right. . . ." Simultaneously "a mass of flying men from Hildebrand's brigade" came up the road from the opposite direction. Buckland's brigade simply disintegrated.

". . . The fleeing mass from the left broke through our lines, and many of our men . . . fled with the crowd," remembered an irate officer. Moreover Buckland found that "the enemy was so close upon us that it was impossible to form again on the Purdy road." Another Federal witnessed the Rebels pressing his regiment heavily, shouting in derision, "Get up there, you damn Yankee sons of bitches, and fight like men."

In this chaos and confusion Sherman cut across the angle of the Corinth and Purdy roads to meet Behr's battery, coming from the right. "I . . . met Behr's battery at the crossroads," said Sherman, "and ordered it immediately to unlimber and come into battery, action right." Behr turned and quickly gave the order. Evidently his men were just unhitching the fields guns when Behr was shot from his horse by the advancing Confederates.

To Sherman's ire the drivers and gunners became panic-striken when Behr fell, and they fled in disorder, abandoning the five cannon without so much as firing a shot. Here Sherman lost another horse. Lieutenant John Taylor, who had just captured another mount to replace the one he had lent to Sherman, was nearby. "Riding over to where I had left the General," said Taylor, "[I again found] he was dismounted.—My horse had been killed." Taylor helped Sherman catch a stray battery horse, which the general then mounted. Less than twenty minutes later that mount was struck by a solid shot and instantly killed.

Sherman seemed at the time the very essence of the embattled warrior. His stubby red beard was smudged by battle smoke, and his shirt collar was twisted askew, the front resting under his ear. His hand was still bleeding, and his coat had been torn in several places by bullets. Lieutenant Patrick White of Barrett's battery also observed Sherman and thought that he was "the coolest man I saw that day."

The enemy approached rapidly on Sherman's left flank, dashing in among Behr's abandoned guns to overrun the handful of Federals there. An officer of the 53d Ohio, mixed in with Buckland's men, looked about him. "Here was more confusion than I saw at any time during the day. . . . There were many disorganized men; the road was almost blocked with teams hurrying from the battle line . . . [again] the Confederates charged, there was a brisk fire for a few moments.—Our line gave way at all points."

As the routed Federals scattered into the heavy underbrush north of the Purdy road, Adjutant Dawes of the 53d Ohio saw a brass field gun "stuck between two small trees . . . abandoned by all but one man, who sat on the wheel horse crying." Although he ran to the gun with a handful of men and broke down the saplings to release the wheels, they were too late. The Confederates soon poured in from several directions and captured the gun.

It seemed that Sherman's division was about to break up altogether. On his left Hildebrand's brigade "had substantially disappeared from the field." Buckland's brigade was so badly scattered that its colonel admitted: "We made every effort to rally our men but with very poor success. They had become scattered in all directions." Only McDowell's brigade, marching up from the far right flank, still remained intact.

Fortunately for Sherman the Confederates proved to be equally confused by their success. The brigade of Preston Pond, Jr., sent from Bragg's corps to guard the extreme Confederate left, had, like McDowell's brigade on Sherman's right, remained unengaged all morning. First Pond's brigade was weakened by the detachment of two regiments and its only battery of artillery to watch the Owl Creek bridge, "where it was thought the enemy would attempt to get through on our flank." The remaining troops then sat for several hours listening to the distant firing, which at times seemed "awfully grand." Finally they were ordered into the fight by General Hardee. Pond delayed, however, until about ten o'clock, waiting for his artillery to return from the vicinity of Owl Creek.

As Pond belatedly approached McDowell's camps, a few shells from one of his howitzers dispersed a handful of enemy soldiers from a log house nearby. Pond's three regiments then cautiously advanced, only to find McDowell's camps abandoned. Pond's protracted advance was more costly than at first realized, for he had unknowingly allowed a sizable Federal brigade to escape intact. In the hours that followed the effect upon the Confederate cause would be nigh disastrous.

Yet other Confederate mistakes also impeded the rapid pursuit of Raith's and Sherman's battered line. Charles Clark, Polk's senior division commander, had led a portion of Russell's and Anderson's brigades up the hill where Waterhouse's guns had been taken. Here they fought Raith's men for about fifteen minutes before the Federals retreated. Only small clusters of Union infantry were still in front, firing sporadically, when Clark ordered his men to cease firing. All did not comply, however, and Clark galloped "along the line to enforce the order." He was soon shot in the right shoulder by an unknown marksman and had to leave the field, causing some unsteadiness among his men.

More serious than many of the other difficulties hampering the Confederates was the widespread looting and pillaging of the captured Federal camps. All three of Sherman's Shiloh Church camps and one of McClernand's were now in Southern hands. One Confederate private, whose regiment had halted momentarily near a captured enemy camp, was told to rummage through the tents and bring out as much food as he could carry. "We found plenty of cooked food in the tents," said the soldier, "and . . . I carried them as much of it as the limited halt would permit. [By now] some [men had] found their way into a sutler's tent, and the pillaging commenced. . . ."

Soon so many soldiers were found plundering Sherman's captured tents that Beauregard sent most of his personal cavalry escort to clear the camps. In addition to stragglers many other healthy soldiers were leaving the battlefield by assisting wounded men. Beauregard's entire staff was at one point ordered to rally all loiterers and send them back into battle.

Even Braxton Bragg was so perplexed by the need of "superior and staff officers [to be] constantly engaged in the duty of file closers" that he thought the Confederates' failures were "due entirely to a want of discipline and . . . officers."

Through the agony of watching his division crumble under repeated Confederate attacks, Sherman had kept his composure. Yet in his front the crisis continued. His men were scattered, disorganized, and as he admitted in a letter home, "at least half" had run away. Only McDowell's brigade and a confused mass of companies, squads, and individuals remained.

The burden was now on McClernand to protect the vast network of Union camps north of the Corinth road and to prevent the enemy's approach thereby to Pittsburg Landing.

Sherman would remain with his handful of men, "struggling to maintain this line," unmindful of personal danger. Indeed, he may have considered that his troops no longer could influence the outcome of the battle. Yet Sherman's presence counted for much. His leadership on the field of battle fired men's souls. It inspired bravery and it steadied their nerves. When the fighting was over, they would speak in awe of Sherman's valor.

His was the genius born of crisis.

CHAPTER XIII

Roots of Despair

The town of Savannah, Tennessee, wrote a Union officer, "is a quiet, sober looking old town with a single street, a square brick court house, a number of buildings scattered along the street, with some pretty and rather stylish residences in the suburbs."

On the morning of April 6 Savannah was choked with wagons and war materiel destined for shipment to the army at Pittsburg Landing. The congestion was compounded by Nelson's division of Buell's army, which had camped during the previous evening in McClernand's old campsite on the outskirts of town.

When Nelson's men awoke that morning, they found the weather "beautifully clear and calm," a bright, pleasant morning. At least one of Nelson's brigade commanders, Jacob Ammen, had ordered a review and inspection for 9 A.M., and many of the men were astir before sunrise.

Lieutenant Horace N. Fisher of Nelson's staff, the headquarters officer of the day, had risen at 4 A.M. to attend to his duties. When Fisher completed his rounds, he started back to his tent to dress for the review. As he climbed the little knoll where the headquarters tents overlooking a small meadow, Fisher heard the sound of "skirmish fire" up the river. Standing in front of the tents, he listened intently to the distant rumble and concluded mistakenly that it was artillery. He said he looked at his watch; it was 5:20 A.M.

Later, when the firing continued, Fisher went to Nelson's tent and awoke him. Buell was there, and soon Fisher observed that "all the headquarters officers were in front of the tents, in their underclothes and stocking feet, with their hands to their ears. . . ."

Nearby in Ammen's brigade the men were busily polishing their guns and brass accouterments with ashes from the still smoldering breakfast fires. Ammen's orderly was methodically shining his colonel's spurs, and the regimental officers were preparing for the impending inspection.

212

At first the men paid little attention to the distant noise; the sound of occasional gunfire was "not an uncommon occurrence when near a large army," said one officer. Yet when the reports became more numerous, the sound of artillery being almost continuous after 7 A.M., many of Ammen's men began to realize that a battle was at hand. Ammen recorded that his men quickly abandoned preparations for the review and began to prepare for action.

Meanwhile Nelson had been stalking about his headquarters tent, impatient for orders. An aide had already gone to the river to see if transports had arrived during the night, and Nelson fumed about the lack of information. Said a member of the 6th Ohio, "Nelson . . . chafed like a lion caged, he ate no breakfast, paced up and down before his tent, could not be pacified, and would not be pleased with anything or anybody. . . ."

When the firing of cannon became louder and louder, Nelson turned to a friend and exclaimed violently, "By God, Bradford, if I get no orders by twelve o'clock, I will move without them. . . ." He then mounted his horse and galloped in the direction of Grant's headquarters, passing through Ammen's camp on the way. Ammen said Nelson came "dashing" into the camp with orders to get ready to go to Pittsburg Landing, either by boat or "through the swamp." He then galloped off again, heading for Grant's headquarters.

Grant had been sleeping in an upstairs bedroom of the Cherry house when his adjutant general and close friend, John A. Rawlins, went into the general's private office to read the mail, just arrived by steamboat from Cairo. Before breakfast was announced Grant came downstairs and began scanning his mail, also talking with Brigadier General John Cook of Illinois.

While breakfast was being served, between 7 and 7:30 A.M., Private Edward N. Trembly, a headquarters orderly, came in and reported the sound of artillery coming from the direction of Pittsburg Landing. Grant left his breakfast unfinished and went outside on the back porch, where he heard "heavy firing." Immediately summoning his staff, he walked the few steps down to the river and boarded the *Tigress,* giving orders to start upriver at once.

Since the *Tigress* had been lying idle at the riverbank, steam pressure had to be generated before the boat could proceed. Grant used the time to dictate several messages to Buell and his subordinate, Nelson. The latter was advised, "An attack having been made on our forces you will move your entire command to the river opposite Pittsburg. You can obtain a guide easily in the village." Grant then dashed off a note to Buell saying, "Heavy firing is heard up the river, indicating plainly that an attack has been made upon our most advanced positions." He also apologized for not meeting with

Buell as planned that day and mentioned having given orders to Nelson.

By the time Nelson arrived at Grant's headquarters, the *Tigress* had already departed. Following Grant's suggestion as outlined in his note, Nelson sent his staff into Savannah to find a guide who knew an overland route to Pittsburg Landing.

They soon learned that the few citizens available had no specific knowledge of a feasible route to Pittsburg Landing. "All knew there were wagon paths up through the woods and swamps . . . but the recent high waters had flooded the bottoms, and the prevailing impression seemed to be that those routes were still impassable," wrote one of Nelson's men.

Nelson's adjutant general, Captain J. Mills Kendrick, learned that the village doctor knew the back roads to Pittsburg Landing as a result of his professional rounds. The doctor, however, had been called away to attend to a patient, and he was not supposed to return until noon. With Nelson waiting impatiently, Kendrick and a cavalry escort went to examine the roads through the swamps. During their absence Nelson maintained a sharp watch for the arrival of transports, not knowing if Grant would dispatch empty boats from Pittsburg Landing.

By now Nelson's entire division had been readied for a rapid march. Ammen's brigade was prepared to leave by 10 A.M., each man's weapon having been inspected and all cartridge boxes filled. When another hour passed and nothing further was heard from headquarters, Ammen decided to seek Nelson and learn what was planned. He found both Nelson and Buell at the Cherry house, the two generals being "very impatient" because no boats had appeared from upriver to transport their troops. The rumble of the cannon continued amid rumors of a Federal rout. Some of the staff officers sent to find a way through the swamps returned and reported having had no success. Said the worried Ammen, "The boats [now] appeared to be the only means of our reaching our companions in arms."

While Buell and Nelson continued to fume about their predicament, Ammen went upstairs to see his friend, the bedridden C. F. Smith. "He was in fine spirits," said Ammen. "[He] laughed at me for thinking that a great battle was raging, [and] said it was only a skirmish of pickets. . . ." The two continued to talk for nearly an hour. Finally, "as there was no cessation, no diminution, and the sounds [of artillery] appeared to be coming nearer and growing more distinct," said Ammen, Smith admitted that "a part of the army might be engaged."

About noon Captain Kendrick and his cavalry escort returned to report that the road along the river bank was impassable, it being inundated by swollen streams. Kendrick had with him, however, "a large, fine-looking Tennessean who professed to be a strong Union man." He was said to be the local doctor who had been away that morning. According to Ammen the man indicated that he knew every path through the swamp. He said that infantry and horsemen could get through but that wagons and artillery would bog down in the deep mud.

A small steamer had just appeared from downriver and put in at the landing, and Buell commandeered the boat for his own use. Before proceeding upriver, Buell told Nelson to march overland through the swamp if the long-expected boats did not soon arrive. Caught up in the sudden excitement Ammen hurried back to his camp with Nelson's order to be "ready to march either by boat or by land."

Although Ammen's men had been ready and waiting for two hours, it was another hour, about 1 or 1:30 P.M., before orders came. They were finally instructed to march through the swamp, leaving their artillery and baggage behind, as no boats were yet in sight. "To the music of the cannon's roar," said Ammen, "Forward" was sounded and the column started along the dry ridge.

As the men stepped off, Nelson was there to observe their appearance. One of his men remembered that he rode slowly down the line telling his soldiers, "Now, gentlemen, keep the column well closed up." Later he would find cause to use stronger language.

Although Grant's steamboat, the *Tigress*, had to move against the current, its boilers were fully stoked and the small, twin-stacked transport had approached Crump's Landing by 8 or 8:30 A.M.

"Up to that time," said Grant, "I . . . felt by no means certain that Crump's Landing might not be the point of attack." This was corroborated by many witnesses including one of Lew Wallace's brigade commanders, Charles Whittlesey, who said he learned from Wallace that Grant feared "the real attack would be made on us, because we had a large stock of provisions."

Grant found Lew Wallace waiting aboard a transport lying at Crump's Landing. As Grant's boat swung in to shore and ran alongside Wallace's transport, Grant was observed on the second deck along with some of his staff. Soon the boats were lashed together, and the *Tigress's* engines were stopped. Grant leaned over to talk with Wallace, standing on the hurricane deck of his boat.

According to Wallace the ensuing conversation revealed Grant's bewilderment. He asked if Wallace had heard the firing. "Yes, sir, since daybreak," came the reply.

"What do you think of it?"

"It's undoubtedly a general engagement," said Wallace.

"Well, hold yourself in readiness to march upon orders received."

Another witness remembered that Grant said he would send Wallace orders when he got to Pittsburg Landing and learned "where the attack was." Grant himself said less than a week later that his orders to Wallace were "to hold his division in readiness to be moved in any direction to which it might be ordered." There is no significant difference.

Following this brief conversation Wallace wrote that the lashings were untied, a small bell tinkled on the *Tigress,* and she moved off, swiftly disappearing in the direction of Pittsburg Landing.

Wallace, although perplexed by the situation, told an officer who had been conducting a court-martial to break up the court and go to his command, that it was felt an attack might be made on their own division.

Earlier that morning, about 6 A.M. according to Wallace, a sentinel had woken him saying he could "hear guns up the river." Following a discussion with some of his officers, Wallace decided to concentrate his division at Stoney Lonesome, since he was uncertain of an attack from the direction of Purdy and could fight or march to Pittsburg Landing more easily from that point.

Wallace gave the necessary orders to an aide, Lieutenant John W. Ross, telling him to carry these instructions to Colonels Thayer at Stoney Lonesome and Woods at Adamsville. Wallace then went aboard his transport for breakfast with Whitelaw Reid, a Cincinnati newspaper correspondent, expecting momentarily to receive orders from Grant.

Following his boat-to-boat conference with Grant after 8:30 A.M., Wallace mounted his favorite horse, John, and rode with his staff to Adamsville. Before departing, he had a spare horse saddled and tied to an elm tree at Crump's Landing. This was to be for the use of Grant's courier, who, it was presumed, would arrive by steamboat to bring Wallace his orders.

When Wallace arrived at Adamsville about midmorning, the firing appeared to be progressing toward the river. Colonel Whittlesey, who had just arrived to resume command of his brigade from Charles R. Woods, said that this "diminished the chances of an attack on us, but did not authorize the abandonment of our stores and a movement without orders."

According to another officer a reconnaissance was made toward Purdy, but it was found that there was no enemy in this direction. Wallace then rode back to Stoney Lonesome, leaving Whittlesey's Third Brigade at Adamsville to await orders.

The scene at Stoney Lonesome was alive with excitement and

GRANT'S STEAMBOAT *TIGRESS* AT PITTSBURG LANDING. In this photograph taken a few weeks after the battle the *Tigress* is moored in the middle. Grant hastened to the battlefield aboard the *Tigress* on the morning of April 6, arriving at about 9 A.M. The wooden gunboat *Tyler* is visible in the background. (PHOTOGRAPHIC HISTORY OF THE CIVIL WAR)

interest, Wallace remembered. "The men stood in dense groups about their stacked arms. The musketry ruffled the air distinctly, while the guns [cannon] were subjects of exclamation—'There! Hear that! Now they're at it! Just listen!'"

"Officers crowded around men," Wallace continued, ". . . we all agreed that the coming of an order depended upon the fortunes of the fight. . . ."

Wallace and his troops waited as patiently as possible.

Ten-thirty had already passed, and no order was yet received. Both the First and Second brigades were now present, nearly four thousand men.

Eleven o'clock. "Still the pounding of the guns . . . but no order," Wallace wrote. "The impatience of [those] . . . around me was continually bubbling over." Finally an aide, Lieutenant Ross, was sent to Crump's Landing to see if Grant's courier had been delayed there.

Grant's boat probably reached Pittsburg Landing about 9 A.M. On its way up it passed the steamer *Warner,* which, so one officer reported, had been dispatched by W. H. L. Wallace to Savannah to advise Grant that a battle was in progress. The *Warner* "rounded to" and followed the *Tigress* back to Pittsburg Landing, having provided Grant with the first positive information of a battle.

As soon as the *Tigress* touched the bank, a plank was run out and Grant's horse was brought off. Riding up the steep bank, Grant started immediately for the front, his staff riding closely behind.

About a half-mile inland Captain John A. Rawlins, Grant's adjutant general, said they met W. H. L. Wallace and learned from him "the particulars of the attack and how matters stood. . . ." Grant now became convinced for the first time that the Pittsburg Landing camps were the true point of attack. He told Rawlins to ride back to the landing and send Captain A. S. Baxter, his chief quartermaster, to Crump's Landing on board the *Tigress*. Baxter would take orders to Lew Wallace to move his division up to Pittsburg Landing.

Grant's orders were verbal. Considering the confusion and excitement of the moment, in all probability they were brief and general in nature. Grant insisted many years later that his instructions were for Wallace to march by the "road nearest the river." Much evidence is to the contrary, however. It seems likely that Grant did not specify any route, merely saying to Rawlins that Wallace should "come up."

Grant was unfamiliar with the roads between the two points, had never traveled them, and he later said, "I . . . do not see why any order was necessary further than to direct him to come to Pittsburg Landing, without specifying by what route."

When Rawlins returned to the river, he found Baxter near the *Tigress* and verbally gave him his orders. Baxter was afraid he might "make some mistake" in delivering them, however, and he asked Rawlins to give him a written copy.

In order to do this Rawlins had to go on board the *Tigress* and obtain "some writing materials." Then, with Rawlins dictating and Baxter writing, the orders were composed.

Wallace said the orders were written in pencil, "on a half sheet of common foolscap, ruled." Although a great amount of controversy followed over its context, some of the principals agreed that the order read substantially as follows: "You will leave a sufficient force at Crump's Landing to guard the public property there, and come up and take position on the right of the army. Form a line of battle at a right angle with the river, and be governed by circumstances."

It was after 11 A.M. by the time the *Tigress* had steamed down to Crump's Landing and Baxter had found the waiting horse there, and Lieutenant Ross, who escorted him to Wallace at Stoney Lonesome.

Wallace said Ross and Baxter drew rein and dismounted, following a hard ride, at 11:30 A.M. Baxter handed the note to Wallace, who quickly read it. According to Baxter Wallace said he was ready to move his command immediately and knew the road, as he had put it in good order. The conversation was brief; Baxter said he did not stay longer than three minutes before returning to the river to reboard the *Tigress*.

After passing the note around to several officers, Wallace said the paper fell into the hands of his adjutant general, Captain Frederick Knefler, who thrust it under his sword belt. Soon forgetting it was there, he later lost it.

Despite Grant's urgent orders, Wallace delayed his march for a half-hour while his troops had "dinner." The march began about noon, with Major Hayes's cavalry in advance. They were followed by Smith's First Brigade, then Thayer's brigade. Both batteries of artillery went along, reducing the pace of the march. Wallace also detached two full regiments to remain behind and "prevent an approach of the enemy by [the] Adamsville road."

The going was "swift and without incident," according to Wallace, who estimated he had six miles to travel. "The cannonading, distinctly audible, quickened the steps of [my] men," he said.

But Wallace had chosen the wrong road.

Instead of marching directly to Pittsburg Landing, which Grant had presumed, Wallace was moving along the Shunpike connecting with Sherman's right, near Shiloh Church. The error probably resulted from ignorance of the actual distances involved, though Wallace felt certain he had chosen the shorter route. The Shunpike crossed Snake, Graham, Clear, and Owl creeks and required a march of about eight miles to reach Wallace's planned destination. The River road, which Wallace had never traveled, involved a distance of only about five miles to the point where Grant wanted him.

Worse still, Sherman's division had been routed and driven from its Shiloh Church camps two hours before Wallace even began his march. Wallace's men thus were heading toward the rear of the Confederate army, likely to be isolated and cut off, perhaps even captured.

"Every step was in hearing of the fight," wrote Wallace, "for now we were nearing the [battle]. . . ."

Several hours earlier Douglas Putnam, Jr., a paymaster Grant had allowed to board the *Tigress* that morning as a volunteer aide, had been looking for a horse near Pittsburg Landing. Finding a mount at about the time Adjutant Rawlins was ready to return to the battlefield after sending Baxter to Crump's Landing, Putnam joined Rawlins for the ride back to the front.

While en route Putnam asked Rawlins where they would find Grant. Without hesitating Rawlins responded, "We'll find him where the firing is the heaviest."

The two riders galloped on. Putnam heard a peculiar sound, like the patter of raindrops on the leaves. He looked up and asked Rawlins if it were raining. "Those are bullets, Douglas," came Rawlins's terse reply.

Down the road staggered a bloody horse, terrified and dragging its bowels, which a cannonball had ripped from its stomach. Ahead the billowing smoke clouds marked the line of battle.

Grant was found in the thick of the fighting, conversing with his division commanders, one by one. Putnam observed that he wore "his full uniform, with the major general's buff sash, making him very conspicuous. . . ." Although staff officers McPherson and Rawlins pleaded with him not to expose himself, Grant insisted he must see and know what was going on, and he rode just in rear of the battle line.

About eleven o'clock, so one officer estimated, Grant met with Sherman near Jones field, holding a brief conference "with but few words." Sherman, haggard and begrimed with blood and smoke, looked the part of a warrior. Bullets were zipping about, making it difficult to converse. Sherman told Grant that he had lost several horses killed under him, and he also displayed several bullet holes in his uniform. After asking about matters on Sherman's left, Grant moved on.

It was plainly evident to Grant that things were going badly for the Union troops. He already had dispatched another courier to Lew Wallace about 10:30 A.M. with a verbal message, "Hurry forward with all possible dispatch." The courier, a lieutenant of the 2d Illinois Cavalry in W. H. L. Wallace's division, was said to know the road well.

He found Lew Wallace at Stoney Lonesome, apparently while Wallace's troops were having their dinner, before noon. Wallace later denied that he refused to march to Pittsburg Landing without written orders, but the lieutenant came away with this impression. Probably Wallace asked the courier if he had written orders, and when the lieutenant said he did not, Wallace merely brushed him off, saying, "I . . . will be up shortly."

Following Grant's brief chat with Sherman, his aide Douglas Putnam went with him to another part of the battlefield. They were riding along the road when Grant looked up and saw a column of troops coming up from the rear. Thinking these were Wallace's troops, he exclaimed with great delight, "Now we are all right, all right—there's Wallace."

Grant soon discovered his mistake. Disappointed, he rode on toward the Federal left, where three divisions were struggling to hold their position. The situation was critical. Grant told one of his brigadiers that he had to hold his position "at all hazards."

About 11:30 Grant got off a message to the "Commanding Officer Advanced Forces [Buell's Army], near Pittsburg." Grant presumed that Buell's troops were already approaching Pittsburg Landing, along the opposite shore. His message decreed urgency. "The attack on my forces has been very spirited from early this morning. The appearance of fresh troops on the field now would have a powerful effect. . . . If you will get upon the field, leaving all your baggage on the east bank . . . it will be more to our advantage, and possibly save the day to us. The Rebel forces are estimated at over 100,000 men. My headquarters will be in the log building on top of the hill. . . ."

Since Buell had not as yet begun to march, the officer dispatched failed to find his advance, and the letter was finally put on a steamboat for transit to Savannah.

Meanwhile conditions continued to worsen. At Pittsburg Landing a vast mob of wounded and stragglers had gathered, many huddling miserably under the protection of the river bluff. These men were so "panic-stricken," said Grant, that most "would have been shot where they lay, without resistance, before they would have taken muskets and marched to the front. . . ."

So many wounded were continually arriving that the surgeons found their tents overflowing. Their patients were placed on steamboats, and all available space utilized. Soon so many wounded soldiers were aboard the vessels that one private, hobbling back to the landing about noon, found that there was no room for him on the lower deck. He was taken up to the hurricane deck and there exposed to the glaring sun, which caused him undue misery. Moreover the sanitary conditions at the landing were wretched, and everywhere there was the cry for "water, water, water!" To one observer the confusion and pandemonium here made it seem as if the "army [was] verging upon a collapse."

Albert Sidney Johnston, his manner reflecting "coolness, confidence, and determination," had ridden to the front in the company of most of his staff before 7 A.M. Up and down the Corinth road the Confederate troops were massed, waiting for orders to advance.

Randall Lee Gibson, an intimate friend of Johnston's son, and commander of a brigade in Bragg's corps, observed the general's approach and ordered his brigade to salute. Johnston paused for a moment to shake Gibson's hand, telling him, "Randall, I never see you but I think of William [his son]. I hope you may get through safely today, but we must win a victory."

Continuing on, Johnston came up with Hardee's front line shortly after seven. Sharp skirmishing had already begun in the vicinity of Seay field, and Johnston rode to the edge of the woods to observe the action. Several companies of Arkansas infantry were engaged with a sizable detachment of Federals. One of Johnston's staff reported that the firing was heavy, and many men were seen breaking ranks. Riding into the field, Johnston rallied the men himself. When they had regrouped, he addressed their regiment: "Men of Arkansas! They say you boast of your prowess with the bowie knife. Today you wield a nobler weapon—the bayonet. Employ it well."

Turning to a young officer whom he had known in the Old Army, Johnston placed his hand on the man's shoulder, looked him in the eye, and said, "My son, we must this day conquer or perish!" The officer, Colonel John S. Marmaduke, said he felt nerved "tenfold."

Following the advance and engagement of Hindman's division, Johnston had ordered Bragg's troops forward. Hardee reported the presence of a heavy force in the woods three-quarters of a mile to the northeast (Sherman's division). Cannon had already sounded from that direction. Johnston rode to two small cabins near Rhea field, where he watched Cleburne's brigade attack Appler's camp.

For nearly a half-hour Johnston chatted with his staff while watching the action in front. Finally word came that Bragg's line was hotly pressed and that he would need support on his right. Johnston quickly pulled a full brigade, Alexander P. Stewart's, out of Polk's battle line and led it personally to the right.

Stewart's brigade, although moving in compact formation, was unable to keep pace with Johnston, who heard heavy firing ahead and galloped on to learn the situation on his crucial right flank. Coming up with Gladden's brigade shortly before 9 A.M., Johnston ordered a bayonet attack, which swept through Spain field just as Prentiss's line was withdrawing.

As the victorious Confederates poured through the captured camps of Madison Miller's brigade, they found "breakfast . . . on the table, officer's baggage and apparel left in the tents, and every evidence . . . of unexpected conflict and sudden rout."

Colonel William Preston, Johnston's aide-de-camp, learned from several Federal wounded that the camp they were riding through was that of the 18th Wisconsin. Going to the colonel's tent, Preston took a stand of colors, which he later sent to Beauregard.

Johnston, observing a Confederate officer emerge from a captured tent with an armload of trophies, sharply censured the man, saying, "None of that, sir; we are not here for plunder!" Then, seeing the disappointment in the man's eyes, Johnston picked up a little tin cup and said, "Let this be my share of the spoils today."

There were many Federal prisoners being collected in small groups at the time, and those who could walk were being sent rapidly to the rear. Some, mostly German immigrants who spoke only broken

English, feared that they would be killed. As they filed past, they grabbed at Johnston's boots, desperately begging for mercy. Johnston said to them, "Why, men, you don't suppose we kill prisoners, do you? Go to the rear and you will be safe there."

Johnston's magnanimity may have proved costly. Seeing many wounded and suffering soldiers amid the captured camp, including a large proportion of Federal officers, he turned to his personal physician, Dr. D. W. Yandell, and said, "Doctor, send some couriers to the rear for medical officers. Meantime, look after these wounded people, the Yankees among the rest. They were our enemies a moment ago, [but] they are our prisoners now."

Although Yandell protested, saying that he should remain with Johnston as his place was with him, Johnston said no, he would advise the doctor when he was ready to move on. Yandell then dismounted and went to work. He was never to see Johnston alive again.

Shortly after nine o'clock Johnston met with the commander of his front line, Hardee, at the 18th Wisconsin's camp. They soon galloped ahead to reconnoiter a second enemy camp, Stuart's, in the direction of the river.

By this time Union troops had begun to re-form at the south end of a clearing where a large grove of peach trees was in full blossom. A Federal battery, Willard's Battery A, First Illinois Light Artillery, was in action near the corner of the field, behind one of Stuart's camps.

Since both Johnston and Hardee had their staffs with them, a large cluster of mounted officers was gathered in one spot. Lieutenant P. P. Wood, commanding Willard's battery, quickly trained his guns on them. The distance was considerable, about six to eight hundred yards, but several accurately aimed shells burst in close proximity to Johnston, scattering the gathering of officers and persuading Johnston to move down the hill to escape this fire.

About the same time, near 9:30 A.M., a courier came up with what was to become a dispatch of great importance, Captain Lockett's report of the situation on the army's extreme right. Captain S. H. Lockett, a member of Braxton Bragg's staff and the assistant chief engineer of the army, had been sent personally by Bragg to scout the Federal left flank at 4 A.M. that morning. Lockett was told to take a squad of cavalry and ride along the Bark road to reconnoiter the enemy's camps, getting "all the information possible" about the Federal positions and activity.

Taking with him Lieutenant S. M. Steel, an engineer who had surveyed the area before the war and knew it thoroughly, Lockett crept past the Federal pickets and observed David Stuart's sleepy camp before dawn. Twice Lockett and Steel scouted the Union camps and returned to the waiting squad of cavalry, sending reports of drowsy Union sentinels and normal camp routine back to Confederate headquarters on each occasion.

About 7 A.M. Lockett made a third trip, farther to the right, and observed Stuart's Federal troops cleaning their guns and accouterments for the usual Sunday-morning inspection. Firing had already begun on the left, however, and soon officers began to come out of their tents, not understanding what the noise was about.

Finally, as the firing grew louder and closer, couriers began to arrive. Lockett watched wide-eyed as the long roll was sounded and Stuart's men raced to fall in. "The whole party in front of me was so thoroughly awake and alarmed," said Lockett, "that I thought my safest course was to retreat."

Lockett then "began to fear that the division in front of me would swing around and take our forces in flank, as it was manifest that the Federal line extended farther in that direction than ours." Drawing a hasty sketch of the ground, he sent a courier to the rear with his report, urging "the importance of having our right flank protected."

Lockett was mistaken. The Federal troops in his front were not a division; they comprised only the isolated and badly frightened brigade of David Stuart, intent simply on holding their ground.

After receiving Lockett's report, Johnston briefly pondered the consequences before making a major decision to commit his reserves. According to Johnston's battle plan the right flank was critical; if the Federal army was to be driven back against Owl Creek resistance must first be overcome here. He decided to act immediately.

Colonel Preston and Captain Wickliffe of his staff were sent to guide Breckenridge's Reserve Corps forward to the extreme Confederate right. In addition two frontline brigades, Chalmers's and Jackson's, having just swept through Prentiss's camps, were halted and ordered to the right, being told that the enemy was "attempting to turn our flank."

David Stuart, a somewhat overambitious Chicago lawyer, had led his regiment of volunteers to war in late 1861. His notorious civil reputation cast a cloud over his military activities. Involved in a scandalous Chicago divorce case, Stuart had met with widespread popular disapproval. This not only hampered his recruiting but ultimately led to serious political difficulty with the Senate, which refused to confirm Stuart's appointment as a brigadier general.

A proud man but an autocratic and unscrupulously ambitious commander, Stuart had set up his headquarters at Noah Cantrill's white frame house along the Hamburg–Savannah road. According to returns dated April 5 Stuart had 2,811 men present for duty in his

brigade. On the same day the four pieces of artillery previously assigned to him had been transferred to W. H. L. Wallace's division.

There had been firing since dawn on April 6 in the direction of
Shiloh Church, providing the first inkling of trouble to Stuart's
men. About 7:30 A.M. Stuart had learned from one of Prentiss's
officers that the enemy was in his front in force.

Since Stuart's primary assignment was to guard the approach from
Lick Creek, he ordered his brigade formed east of their camps, immediately under the bluffs rising across Locust Grove Branch. Several companies of skirmishers were pushed forward to Locust Branch,
while two others went to the small bridge spanning Lick Creek.
While his three regiments shuffled from position to position, not
knowing from what direction an attack would come, the skirmishers
poked about in the brush.

Stuart's men already had noticed that the firing continued to roll
farther and farther north. One private of the 55th Illinois Regiment
now believed "that the Rebels were being drawn into a trap" and
that they would all be taken prisoners before his regiment could get
into the fight. "We enlisted to fight; why not let us at them?" he
thought.

When a civilian appeared from the brush, badly frightened and
with tears running down his cheeks, a picket heard him say that he
had been in the rear of the Confederate army and that they were
killing men by the thousands. The masses of enemy, he said, were
"a powerful sight."

Soon there was a signal from another picket to rally on the reserve.
Confederate cavalry were thought to be in the woods nearby. The
two companies of advanced skirmishers lay down behind a knoll,
Locust Branch in their front. As one picket remembered, they did
not have long to wait.

James Ronald Chalmers, thirty-one years old and a brigade commander in Bragg's corps, had just regrouped his command following
the capture of Prentiss's camps. He was preparing to reengage the
enemy about 9:30 A.M. when Sidney Johnston's orders came to fall
back.

Following a delay of about a half-hour while a citizen-guide,
Lafayette Veal of McNairy County, Tennessee, was obtained, Chalmers began to march to the right, making a wide circuit over two
miles of rough ground bordering on Locust Grove Branch.

About 10:30 A.M. Chalmers's troops were brought to a halt. Brigadier General Jones M. Withers, Chalmers's division commander,
had ordered the halt "until the cavalry should ascertain whether the
enemy still outflanked us." Clanton's 1st Alabama Cavalry galloped
ahead, riding in column of fours, while Chalmers's infantry grounded

their muskets. It was their second half-hour delay since being ordered to the right to engage "an advancing enemy."

When the Confederate cavalrymen approached Locust Creek, one of Stuart's Illinois buglers, armed with a Colt revolving rifle, fired a single shot at them. The cavalry quickly scattered, but soon some of Chalmers's infantry appeared in line of battle. The captain commanding the Illinois skirmishers ordered his men to fire, and the fighting began in earnest.

Chalmers later reported that although there were only a few of Stuart's skirmishers, they had caught his 52d Tennessee Volunteers unaware. This regiment "broke and fled in most shameful confusion," wrote Chalmers, who tried repeatedly to rally the fleeing men. Finally he became so disgusted that he ordered the remainder of the regiment removed from his line. Only two companies were allowed to fight with another regiment. At last Withers sent word to move on, now being satisfied that there were no enemy concentrations beyond his right. Chalmers's nearly two thousand men again pressed forward, causing Stuart's skirmishers to give ground, firing as they went.

Ironically much of Stuart's brigade already had fled, even though they had not yet been engaged.

The 55th Illinois, not having been under fire before, had formed along the edge of timber fronting McCuller's field about a quarter-mile east of their encampment. Commanded by Swedish-born Lieutenant Colonel Oscar Malmborg, the 55th was ordered to "half left wheel" just as a few stray bullets whizzed overhead from the skirmish line.

The 55th was nervous, and its commander uncertain of what direction to face his men. "The companies began to crowd and overlap each other," said an officer, "and a wild stampede followed."

Stuart, who had been anxiously watching the enemy's movements through his field glasses, rode ahead of the flying mass. Whirling his horse about, he "faced the throng . . . with eyes flashing, and [in a] voice . . . like a trumpet, commanded them to halt," said an eyewitness. Fortunately for Stuart his stand worked. The Illinois officers were soon able to halt and re-form their men about two hundred yards to the right rear, along a ridge bordering a deep ravine.

Meanwhile the Confederates had succeeded in planting several batteries of field guns along the high bluffs overlooking Stuart's camp. These batteries, Gage's Alabama and Girardey's Georgia, began shelling the exposed Federal line, including the 71st Ohio on Stuart's right flank.

The 71st was a new regiment, commanded by the former Adjutant General of Ohio and one of her prominent citizens, Rodney Mason. As soon as the enemy's shells began bursting in their midst,

MAP 7
Redeployment to Confront Stuart
9 A.M.–12 noon, April 6 (Chapter 13)

Mason and his regiment went to pieces. "I regret that the regiment did not bear themselves with greater steadiness . . ." Mason later admitted. His brigade commander, Stuart, charitably wrote that he "could not find" Mason thereafter, reporting only that he saw "nothing more" on the 71st throughout the fight. Grant was sympathetic at first, but later in the war concluded that Mason had a "constitutional weakness" when that officer surrendered Clarksville, Tennessee, to an inferior enemy force.

On Stuart's left only the 54th Ohio's Zouaves remained in line. The 54th occupied a fencerow fronting McCuller's field, having stood for several hours waiting for the Confederates to approach through an old orchard. Colonel T. Kilby Smith said he had less than four hundred men in line to resist what looked like a force of ten thousand Confederates advancing toward him.

Chalmers's troops, skirmishers of the 9th Mississippi Infantry in advance, swept through the orchard in what seemed to be perfect order. "To my great surprise, not a shot was fired until we came within about forty yards of the fence," reported Chalmers. When the 54th's muskets blazed in their faces, the Confederates suffered heavy losses.

Yet, from the commanding bluffs nearby, Gage's field guns began pounding Smith's line, enabling Chalmers to charge and drive the Ohioans back after a hard fight.

CONFEDERATE OFFICERS BEFORE THE BATTLE OF SHILOH. These officers are of the 9th Mississippi Infantry, Chalmers's brigade, Bragg's corps. After assisting in the capture of Prentiss's camps, the 9th was withdrawn by Johnston's order and sent with the remainder of their brigade to confront Stuart's infantry on the extreme eastern flank. Visible within the tent are M1855 rifles, an improved-pattern rifle. (PHOTOGRAPHIC HISTORY OF THE CIVIL WAR)

It was now after eleven o'clock. The way had been cleared, a path being open deep into the Federal rear along the river. Two of Stuart's regiments had fled, almost without firing a shot. The other unit was in full retreat. Stuart, who had ridden to the right to bring up Willard's battery, only to learn that it had been moved, returned to find that he had not more than eight hundred men in line with their back to a rugged ravine. The 55th Illinois was so unnerved by reports that Confederate cavalry were advancing from the direction of Lick Creek that they had formed in a hollow square. Stuart also seemed shaken and began to worry that a body of cavalry had been sent around his flank "to harass or cut off our retreat." When another enemy column was observed approaching from the left, Stuart detached four companies from the 54th Ohio, further weakening his small force.

"Fortunately," a Union officer later reflected, "no aggressive movement of the enemy [occurred]. . . ." Chalmers's troops, although only briefly engaged in two separate fights, had allegedly run out of ammunition. As his wagons were some distance behind, according to Chalmers his brigade lost more than a half-hour before a fresh supply was brought up.

Of further embarrassment to the Confederates was the slow progress of Brigadier General John K. Jackson's brigade, sent to follow Chalmers along the ridges bordering Locust Creek. Jackson had been in the second Confederate assault wave when Prentiss's camps were captured. Ordered at first to the left, where heavy firing was heard in the direction of Sherman's camps, Jackson had been called back by Sidney Johnston's order and moved to the right.

Coming up on Chalmers's left, Jackson's troops had found skirmishers from the 71st Ohio in their front. Girardey's battery, taking position on a bluff overlooking Stuart's camps, was soon in action and drove the skirmishers back with blasts of canister. Following standard procedure, Jackson, before advancing against Stuart, sent his skirmishers out "to feel" the enemy.

Meanwhile Girardey's gunners began bombarding the Federal camp. Soon thereafter Sidney Johnston appeared and personally ordered some of Jackson's men to charge the camp in front. Although this camp (that of the 55th Illinois) appeared abandoned, Rodney Mason's 71st Ohio Regiment was in line just to the east. Mason had already sent one company of skirmishers under Captain Thomas W. Bown into the 55th's camp to occupy a long house normally used as a hospital.

By the time Jackson's Confederates advanced under the cover of Girardey's artillery, Mason's regiment had prematurely fled in disorder. Captain Bown's company was substantially all that remained between Jackson's men and Stuart's camps.

The 2d Texas Infantry, Colonel John C. Moore commanding, was one of the first units to appear in Bown's front, advancing through an open field south of the log house. The 2d was a hard-luck regiment. It had endured a grueling three-week march from Houston, Texas, to Corinth, arriving on April 1 with many of its men nearly barefoot. Immediately thereafter they had been ordered into the field.

Moore's men, ordered to "double-quick" from the bottom of a ravine through the open field, were nearly exhausted by the time they reached the top of the hill. Moore ordered a halt, but seeing that his right was "suffering severely" from the fire coming from the log house, he shouted for his men to charge.

Bown's men put up a desperate fight but were soon overwhelmed and compelled to surrender. Here more than half of his company was killed or wounded in the few minutes of fighting.

In the following confusion a small knot of the 71st Ohio that had not gone with their colonel to the rear attempted to make a stand. Their lieutenant colonel, Barton S. Kyle, was with them, "trying to stem the wild wave of fugitives." Kyle was soon shot, however, and the handful of remaining Ohioans drifted away, later to join the ranks of the 55th Illinois.

Unknown to the battered survivors of Stuart's left, their skeletal resistance had bought a precious amount of time.

Earlier, when David Stuart observed the pelican flag of Gladden's 1st Louisiana Regiment "advancing in the rear of General Prentiss's headquarters," he correctly assumed that his right flank had been turned. Stuart sent his adjutant to the rear for reinforcements, and soon had the promise of immediate help from Hurlbut. Instead of Hurlbut's troops advancing, however, only two regiments and a battery appeared, led by the colorful Scotsman, Brigadier General John A. McArthur of W. H. L. Wallace's division.

Advancing about 9 A.M. with Willard's battery well in advance, McArthur had marched down the Hamburg–Savannah road until he ran into the mass of men streaming north from Prentiss's camps. First putting Willard into battery along the road in rear of the 71st Ohio's camp, McArthur hastened to return for his infantry, then some distance behind. As his men came up about 11 A.M., McArthur sheltered them in a ravine east of the road for protection from the enemy's artillery.

Yet McArthur's dispositions soon proved to be faulty. Willard's battery, exposed along the open road, took some quick losses—a sergeant and three horses were killed before they could engage the enemy. Moreover McArthur's infantry found their bushy ravine to be a deadly trap. Although they were protected from the distant Confederate field guns, when a body of troops earlier observed near the

71st Ohio's camp advanced in McArthur's front, the visibility was so poor that at least one Federal officer could not establish their identity.

This officer, Lieutenant Colonel Augustus Chetlain of the 12th Illinois, had risen from a sick bed to command his regiment that morning. Now as he rode forward in a weakened condition to learn their identity, one of Jackson's marksmen put a bullet through his horse. Chetlain was thrown off and severely injured. A devastating fire poured down from the ridge above; Chetlain feebly got to his feet and ordered his regiment to fall back about seventy-five yards to high ground.

"My new position was more favorable," said Chetlain, who had already lost a disabling number of casualties in the ravine. Fortunately for McArthur his small command already had been reinforced by another Illinois regiment from ground west of the Hamburg–Savannah road. This unit, the 50th Illinois—numbering about six hundred men—filed into line about 11:30 A.M., extending McArthur's flank to the east.

Three full regiments strong, McArthur's force presented a solid front to Jackson's attacking infantry. Confronted here by strong resistance, the Confederates were content to lie down and snipe at long range, waiting for their artillery to move up over the rugged terrain.

In David Stuart's immediate front Chalmers failed to resume his advance until about twelve o'clock. After marching about a quarter-mile, Chalmers came upon the enemy strongly positioned on a hill with a deep ravine in front. "A very stubborn fight ensued," he said.

Stuart had wisely decided to move his men back through a fifty-foot-deep ravine to the crown of an opposite hill, where about one hundred fifty yards separated the two battle lines. According to Stuart Chalmers's troops came up deliberately, taking "fully fifteen minutes" to deploy.

Although outnumbered by Chalmers nearly two to one, Stuart had recent word from McArthur that if he could hold his ground, that general would support his right flank. Stuart, moreover, held the advantage of terrain—one Confederate commander described the ravine in front as "almost impassable" and noted that it was bordered by a morass.

Soon heavy volleys of musketry crashed along the Federal line, staggering the advancing Confederates and causing them to dodge behind trees and brush.

Here one young lieutenant of the 55th knelt on one knee to give instructions to a corporal who was lying on the ground loading his Dresden rifle. Thrusting the point of his sword into the ground, the officer began to speak—and was shot in the head. With the corporal looking on in horror, the lieutenant reeled backward, his hand still grasping the hilt of his sword until the blade bent double. When his quivering fingers released their grasp, the sword bounded high into the air. It was such a ghastly spectacle that the corporal shuddered to think of it twenty-five years later.

With each exchange of volleys the bloodshed continued. One Federal private, not yet seventeen, was hit seven times before he died. A comrade who looked at the boy's body said he "was as red as if he had been dipped in a barrel of blood."

Many of the Federal riflemen already had begun to drift to the rear. The 55th Illinois's chaplain, Milton Haney, on his way to the front with a detail of litter-bearers, ran into a captain of his regiment running in the opposite direction. When asked if he was wounded, the officer shrieked, "Oh! Oh!! Oh!!! The regiment is all broken to pieces!" The astonished chaplain could but watch with disgust as the man sped "on like a racehorse" in the direction of the landing.*

A few minutes later Chaplain Haney learned that the captain was mistaken; the 55th Illinois had not been routed. As he came to the front, minus four of his six litter-bearers who had joined the captain in his flight, he found the 55th fighting along a wooded ridge.

Haney was among the luckier men in Stuart's line that day, already having escaped capture by the narrowest of margins. At the first sound of the long roll Chaplain Haney had been busily polishing his leather boots for Sunday inspection. They were heavily muddied from crossing a small stream during his return from a special service at the camp of the 12th Michigan on the previous evening.

As the fighting began, Haney had just finished polishing one boot. Looking at the great contrast between the two, he decided that he must also shine the other, although his regiment was already vacating the camp. Hurriedly the chaplain began to black the second boot, determined to keep a proper appearance. He completed the task, piled his equipment into an Army wagon, and finally ran from camp "just in time to escape capture." Chaplain Haney was more fortunate than a Confederate counterpart, Reverend M. L. Weller of the 9th Mississippi. As Weller urged the Mississippians on, one of Stuart's riflemen put a bullet through him, inflicting a mortal wound.

Despite their greater numbers, Chalmers's Mississippians were unable to drive Stuart's men from the ridge. Still, some worked their way to within a few feet of the Federal line. "We fought like Indians, behind trees, logs, and lying down behind the ridge or hills," wrote one of Chalmers's men, who later boasted: "The yanks were within twenty feet of us . . . I gave it to one old blue belly about where his suspenders crossed, sending him to eternity."

* This officer was probably Captain Joseph Clay of Company G, who was arrested for cowardice after Shiloh and later dismissed from the service.

Chalmers's own losses were staggering, particularly in the 5th Mississippi Regiment, toward the Confederate right. Most of the brigade's 425 casualties occurred here, forcing Chalmers to cling to the opposite ridge and await the arrival of Gage's battery.

"It was some time before it [the battery] could be brought into position," reported Chalmers, who noted that Gage's men had to cut their way "through a thickly wooded country over ravines and hills almost impassable to ordinary wagons."

Nearly two hours had elapsed since the beginning of the fight along the ridges. Gage's battery, although joining Chalmers's line "in a commanding position" to enfilade the Federal line, "was . . . employed with little beyond threatening effect, the firing being too high," said Stuart.

Stuart, however, was apprehensive of an all-out attack by Chalmers's infantry. His own troops were running so low on ammunition that they had to rummage through the cartridge boxes of the dead and wounded in order to keep firing. No support had come up on the right, where McArthur had promised to help. Furthermore Stuart had no artillery to counter the enemy's battery. Believing, perhaps, that he was somewhat forgotten while fighting an isolated and remote battle, Stuart began to consider a retreat.

Unknowingly Stuart's and McArthur's troops were anchoring the entire left flank of Grant's line. Should they retreat, the way would be open for a Confederate envelopment of the entire line. The fate of many men hung in the balance, perhaps that of Grant's army.

CHAPTER XIV

A Swarm of Hornets

Benjamin Mayberry Prentiss, Grant's old antagonist, found himself floundering in the midst of a great crisis following the loss of his division's camps about 9 A.M. His two brigades had been worse than decimated, "by reason of casualties and because of the falling back of many of the men to the river, they being panic stricken," said Prentiss.

Along the roads, through the thickets, and across the ravines Prentiss's routed troops streamed northward by the hundreds, working their way toward Pittsburg Landing. A postmaster of an Illinois regiment, having taken a parcel of letters to the Landing for safekeeping, observed Prentiss's demoralized soldiers on his return. Here one battle-shocked sergeant of the 16th Wisconsin Infantry cried out to the postmaster that it was "no use, the day is lost!" This sergeant was so shaken that he even handed over his musket and cartridge box, saying only that he "had fired ten rounds and had thirty left."

Another eyewitness, advancing along the Wheatfield road, saw "Prentiss's regiments rushing back from the front pell-mell, holding up their gory hands, shouting, 'You'll catch it!—we are all cut to pieces—the Rebels are coming.'"

Although all seemed lost to the mass of fleeing men, help was then rapidly approaching from the direction of the landing. Marching at the head of two brigades, Stephen A. Hurlbut, Lincoln's close friend and Prentiss's fellow Illinois brigadier, swept from the woods hurrying to Prentiss's relief.* The sudden appearance of Hurlbut's troops along the Wheatfield road was an incredible stroke of good fortune for Prentiss and the entire Union army. They were the only Federals in position to halt what by now was a general stampede, and to block a Confederate advance directly to the river landing.

Hurlbut's men had risen that morning to a bright and beautiful

---

* Hurlbut and Prentiss were appointed to rank from the same date.

sunrise. "It was a morning for doves to coo and lambs to gambol on," said one of Hurlbut's officers. "The balmy air, the bright new foliage glimmering in the rising sun, [and] the gentle treble of the blue birds in the overhanging boughs seemed . . . to awaken . . . regard for . . . God," said another.

"As we were preparing for our usual Sunday morning inspection," wrote the lieutenant colonel of the 14th Illinois Infantry, "some of the soldiers still had their pieces [muskets] apart for cleaning, and the officers in their best uniforms. . . were waiting for the proper signals to form, when the harsh sound of irregular firing was heard to the Southwest."

Most of Hurlbut's brigade commanders alertly ordered their men into line without waiting for orders from division headquarters. About the same time, near 7:30 A.M., Hurlbut received an urgent message from Sherman, who advised that "he was attacked in force, and heavily, upon his left."

Hurlbut's aide immediately went to Colonel James C. Veatch with orders to take his twenty-eight-hundred man brigade to Sherman's support. "In ten minutes," Hurlbut proudly wrote, "this brigade . . . was in march . . ." Hurlbut's two remaining brigades, numbering about forty-five hundred officers and men, then formed in line of battle in front of their camp, listening in awe to the distant "rapid volleys of musketry."

Again, shortly before 8 A.M., Hurlbut said he received "a pressing request for aid"—this time from Prentiss. Ordering his entire command to advance to Prentiss's support, Hurlbut rushed his infantry, artillery, and cavalry down the Hamburg–Savannah road as rapidly as they could be formed in column.

Colonel Nelson G. Williams' First Brigade was in the van, followed by Jacob Lauman's Third Brigade. According to Lauman his troops started for the front twenty minutes after receiving Hurlbut's orders.

By 8:30 A.M., as Hurlbut's soldiers advanced along the road to the front, Prentiss's men "in broken masses" drifted to the rear. With each few yards the routed soldiers seemed to become more numerous. The roadway was soon so choked with them that some of the fugitives began to break through Hurlbut's column.

Hurlbut's men were shocked by this sight. One of his officers termed Prentiss's soldiers "panic-striken wretches," and feared that their fright was unnerving his own troops. A lieutenant of the 44th Indiana, advancing with Lauman's brigade, was so enraged by this spectacle that he grabbed the bridle of a passing horse and, drawing his revolver, threatened to shoot the rider, a colonel, who was shouting, "We're whipped, we're whipped; we're all cut to pieces!"

By the time Hurlbut's advance reached a large open field about a half-mile in the rear of Prentiss's camps, it was apparent that Prentiss's entire division had broken up. Hurlbut, in order to defend as much ground as possible, deployed his two brigades here, each fronting separate sides of the field, one south and the other west.

Lauman's infantry occupied the western side, their line being nearly perpendicular to the Wheatfield road and running from the corner of the open field across to the roadway. Here it terminated in brush and heavy timber beyond the road.

Williams's brigade had formed at almost a forty-five-degree angle to Lauman's line, fronting the southern edge of the field and extending nearly to the Hamburg–Savannah road. In William's rear was a rather large and sprawling peach orchard, the pink blossoms brightly fluttering in the sunlight.

At the angle of these two lines Hurlbut placed the most experienced of his field batteries, Mann's Missouri Light Artillery. Of the other two batteries, Hurlbut sent Ross's 2d Michigan to support Williams and put Meyers's 13th Ohio in on the right, in front of Lauman. He also used his cavalry, two battalions of the 5th Ohio, Sherman's former command, deploying them in an extended line in rear of the infantry.

According to an officer of Ross's battery the Confederate battle lines "could be seen very distinctly" as his battery wheeled into position. Moreover, north of Prentiss's camps the enemy soon unlimbered several batteries that began firing before all of Hurlbut's infantry were in position.

One of their first rounds, probably fired by Robertson's battery of Gladden's brigade, struck the horse of Colonel Williams of the First Brigade. The animal was instantly killed, and Williams was so severely shocked by the concussion that he had to leave the field. Another plunging Confederate shell found an open caisson of Meyers's 13th Ohio Battery. An onlooker watched with amazement as the caisson was "shivered to pieces," the ammunition chest exploding.

Meyers, who had been slow in coming up, was in position about one hundred fifty yards in advance of Lauman's infantry, on the crest of a knoll in an open woods. Hurlbut later said that Meyers had unlimbered his guns too far forward and had lost the protection of the reverse slope. Unfortunately for Meyers the exploding caisson frightened the battery's horses, causing one team to break loose and run wildly through Hurlbut's lines.

With more enemy shells bursting nearby and the terrified horses bucking and neighing, Meyers's inexperienced gunners panicked. "All then left the battery without having fired a shot," wrote a nearby Federal officer. Hurlbut saw the fleeing officers and men, termed it "disgraceful cowardice," and asked for volunteers to go

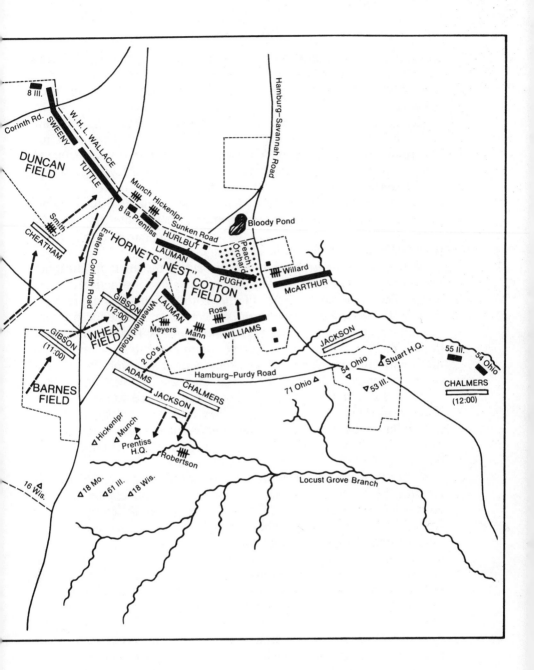

MAP 8
Formation of the Hornets' Nest Line
8:30 A.M.–3 P.M., April 6 (Chapter 14)

and spike the abandoned guns. A handful of artillerists from Mann's and Ross's batteries responded. Led by several sergeants they rushed forward to spike the guns and cut the plunging horses free from their harnesses.

Yet Meyers's abandoned guns could not be removed. Tantalizingly, they were parked in clear view of both sides, but the cross fire of artillery and musketry made them mere pawns in the forthcoming contest. Hurlbut was so enraged that he later had Meyers dismissed from the service and the battery disbanded.

Along Williams's front the Federal infantry was told to lie down for protection against the incoming enemy shells. Soon the advance elements of Gladden's Confederates began to appear, sweeping north from the rear of Prentiss's headquarters.

As the oncoming gray infantry approached the angle in Hurlbut's line, nearly everyone on the left of Lauman's line instinctively began firing. The lieutenant colonel of the 25th Kentucky soon realized that the Confederates were distant some four or five hundred yards, far beyond effective range of his muskets, and he had his men cease firing. Yet the 17th Kentucky, on Lauman's extreme left, found the enemy close in their front, and they poured a galling fire into the column, causing it to veer sharply to the east. As they passed, the 17th's colonel noticed that the Confederate force numbered only "two small regiments," and he said they took tremendous losses.

Moving in close column at the double-quick, these Confederates disappeared in the direction of Williams's waiting infantry, where they were about to run the gauntlet of his fire.

Yet in their anxiety some of Williams's Iowans along the right of the line began firing too soon, causing the Confederates to turn away. Here too was the 32d Illinois Infantry commanded by Colonel John Logan.* Seeing that the retiring enemy column was out of range, Logan forbade his regiment to fire.

Suddenly, to Logan's chagrin, the entire left wing of his regiment began shooting wildly. Running over to this flank, Logan ordered the firing stopped. He later learned that his men had begun firing simply because the regiment on their left had done so. In the midst of this confusion Colonel Isaac Pugh, who had taken over for the wounded Williams, feared that another body of Confederates was attempting to flank his brigade on the left. Pugh promptly ordered one of his regiments back "about one hundred paces" into the peach orchard.

Hurlbut, seeing his left withdrawing, followed with orders for all

---

* Another Logan, the famous John A. (Black Jack) Logan, later prominent as a soldier and statesman, was absent from Shiloh, having taken a severe wound at Fort Donelson.

of his troops to retire to the same line. A few minutes later the right of Hurlbut's division was withdrawn, taking position behind an old fence along the edge of the woods.

All of Hurlbut's troops now fronted on moderately open ground. Along the left his line sprawled through the peach orchard, fragrant with its candy-sweet pink blossoms. On his right the trampled remnant of a cottonfield lay in front.

This improvised change in position was to prove of crucial importance. Not only were Hurlbut's soldiers provided a favorable field of fire, but they had good protection under cover of the orchard and a heavy split-rail fence. A Confederate force attacking this front would be compelled to cross a minimum of three hundred yards of moderately open ground, exposed to a concentrated fire of infantry and artillery.

According to the Confederates the "two small regiments" observed by the Federals attacking their line were actually only two companies of skirmishers. Colonel Daniel Adams of Gladden's brigade had deployed these troops merely "to see if the enemy were really in front of us in large force. . . ."

When Adams observed Hurlbut's troops advancing to Prentiss's aid, he began to worry that the Federal reinforcements were about to move against him. Ordering his brigade to form in a square—an outmoded defensive formation used in the Napoleonic Wars—Adams merely waited while Robertson's battery of field guns dueled with the enemy batteries supporting Hurlbut's line.

After Robertson's fire stampeded Meyers's 13th Ohio Battery, Adams continued to remain inactive, still being wary of a Federal attack. General Hardee and his staff rode by, however, and saw Adams halted. Not knowing the extent of the enemy's strength, Hardee also ordered a reconnaissance by several of Adams's companies. Dutifully they advanced as directed, only to be driven off by several of Lauman's and Pugh's regiments posted near the angle in the cottonfield. According to Adams this patrol returned and reaffirmed previous reports that the enemy "was being reinforced and advancing on our position." Adams thereafter refused to advance, believing that the Federals would soon attack. He was, of course, mistaken. Hurlbut's troops were soon seen withdrawing into the peach orchard.

Along with Adams's (Gladden's) troops two other Confederate brigades had originally confronted Hurlbut's division but now were gone. Chalmers's brigade, having aided Adams in the final assault on Prentiss's camps, had been scattered in passing through them. Yet Chalmers hastily reorganized his men for a further advance. Finding Pugh's brigade of Hurlbut's division in his front, Chalmers said, "We were about to engage them . . . , when we were ordered by General Johnston to fall back. . . ." Soon thereafter they were ordered to the right, to attack Stuart.

Jackson's brigade also had come up following the capture of Prentiss's camps. His men were about to march into action when they too were recalled by Johnston's order.

As Chalmers and Jackson withdrew, the Confederate right was stripped of most of its strength. Chalmers paused only once to face about and return Hurlbut's fire. Incredibly, this strange maneuvering apparently caused Isaac Pugh to fear Chalmers was attempting to turn Hurlbut's left flank, leading to the withdrawal of most of Hurlbut's First Brigade to the north side of the peach orchard.

Following this blundering the firing in Hurlbut's front became desultory. The Confederates had made a serious error following Captain Lockett's report of a Union "division" threatening to attack their extreme right flank. Johnston, having pulled two relatively fresh brigades out of line in front of Hurlbut, all but wasted them on a wide, time-consuming flank march to the east. Here they squandered more precious time in sparring with Stuart's brigade before pressing an attack in that sector.

Meanwhile Wood's and Shaver's brigades, having captured Peabody's camp on the western side of Prentiss's encampment, had gone to the left to help Bragg and Polk attack Sherman's and McClernand's divisions. At this point the only Confederate troops remaining in front of Hurlbut were Adams's, whose brigade had already been hard hit in the Spain field fight. Although Johnston dispatched several staff officers about 9:30 A.M. to bring Breckenridge's Reserve Corps to this front, they were more than two hours' distant.

Johnston meanwhile patiently sat his horse along a bluff to the east of the 18th Wisconsin's camp, watching the artillery duel between Robertson and Hurlbut's two remaining batteries. Here he received another report from Captain Lockett, who had become "very uneasy about the state of affairs" on the extreme right. Lockett said he reported in person about 11 A.M., warning Johnston that the right flank was still in jeopardy. Johnston related that he had already ordered Breckenridge up and asked Lockett to ride back and help guide Breckenridge into action. "Tell him to drive the enemy he may find in his front into the river," added Johnston as Lockett galloped off.

The long delay in procuring enough Confederate troops to mount an attack in Hurlbut's front was to become one of the decisive factors in the battle. Hurlbut utilized the lengthy pause to calm his jittery troops and reorganize his battle line. Ross's battery, the 2d Michigan, was pulled out of line, having suffered casualties in both men and horses in its fight with Robertson. Mann's battery was easily able to keep Robertson occupied, and Hurlbut's regimental officers passed up and down the lines, giving instructions to steady the infantry and arrange for a resupply of ammunition, if needed.

Perhaps the most significant result of the delay, however, was the recovery and return to the front of a part of Prentiss's division. Hurlbut wrote that "General Prentiss having succeeded in rallying a considerable portion of his command, I permitted him to pass to the front of the right of my Third Brigade. . . ."

Prentiss had found that some of his regiments still retained a semblance of organization following their disorderly retreat, and he gathered them in Hurlbut's rear. Among these units were the 18th Missouri and 18th Wisconsin of Miller's brigade, and the 12th Michigan and 25th Missouri of Peabody's brigade. Although "nearly exhausted," the men were replenished with ammunition and led back to the front about 10 A.M. Here they took position in "an old roadway" that had been progressively worn into the landscape by many years' use as a wagon trail.

Yet Prentiss's men seemed rather skittish when they returned to the front. One of Lauman's officers said they "acted like a flock of frightened sheep, ready to start in any direction." He noticed that their line "was like the tail of a kite, extended back some thirty or forty feet," and that "their Captain walked hurriedly up and down near them, unable to control himself, much less them.

"I talked with him quietly," he continued, "[and] asked him if he could not get his men to use their muskets on the enemy; that if they became engaged [again] they would forget their fear. [It seemed] to no purpose."

Even Prentiss was described by Colonel Hugh Reed of the 44th Indiana as "clamoring for he knew not what—the line to be pushed forward to his former position, etc. He was as demoralized as his troops."

Undoubtedly Prentiss was nervous, excited, and probably somewhat dazed. He told the colonel of the 12th Michigan Infantry that his troops should fight their way back to their tents—considering the circumstances, a rather impractical suggestion. Fortunately for Prentiss and his handful of men they were soon bolstered by the arrival of a fresh regiment from Pittsburg Landing. The 23d Missouri Infantry had started about 7 A.M. that morning to join Prentiss, having only recently arrived at Pittsburg Landing, where they were being assigned to the Sixth Division.

These Missourians had marched about two miles, listening to the sound of heavy firing toward the front, when they met one of Prentiss's regiments, the 15th Michigan, returning without ammunition. After sharing some of their Austrian rifled-musket cartridges with them, the 23rd continued on, meeting one of Prentiss's staff officers farther along the Corinth road.

Soon they were led into line, forming on the left of Prentiss's position in the sunken road. About seven hundred strong they probably numbered more than the remnant of Prentiss's entire division.

Although Prentiss's infantry seemed shaken, his two batteries of artillery were still full of fight. Hickenlooper's battery had lost two of its guns in Spain field, but the remaining four pieces were brought into position on a gentle knoll along the sunken road. Munch's Minnesota Battery was deployed farther to the right, near the edge of Duncan field. Munch also had only four guns in service; a shell had lodged while being rammed down the fifth gun's tube, causing the piece to be sent to the Landing.

By chance Prentiss's men had occupied one of the critical sectors in the Union line. Beyond his right were two brigades of infantry recently brought to the front by W. H. L. Wallace, commanding the Second Division. As luck would have it, Prentiss's command provided the means of connecting Hurlbut's and Wallace's troops. Moreover, by plugging the gap between these two divisions, Prentiss also became the hinge upon which the two extended battle lines rested. Although the road that they defended was sunken for only a short distance, it ran in a convex path over a distance of more than a half-mile. Here the Union battle lines extended in a great semicircle, with Prentiss occupying the angle where the pressure was sure to be severe.

W. H. L. Wallace had nearly reached the age of forty-one. A lawyer and an Illinois volunteer during the Mexican War, Wallace had unexpectedly risen to the command of a full division, having been appointed a brigadier general only a few weeks earlier. He was a deeply religious man who looked at war with a calm and rather fatalistic attitude. Less than a month earlier Wallace had cautioned his wife, "Our Father who art in Heaven will take care of His children and do with them whatever is best." Known as "the other Wallace" to an army that was more familiar with Lew Wallace of Indiana, W. H. L. Wallace had been at breakfast that morning when the roar of musketry and artillery alerted his men to an attack.

Wallace, like Hurlbut, had ordered his division under arms as the roar of battle continued and grew louder. Forming a line about 8 A.M., W. H. L. Wallace's division was then far in the rear, its camps being in the immediate vicinity of Pittsburg Landing. About an hour elapsed before he ordered his men to the front. First one brigade under John McArthur was sent to the left, along the Hamburg–Savannah road, to support Stuart. Then, with his two remaining brigades, Tuttle's and Sweeny's, Wallace marched out the main Corinth road, taking position on Hurlbut's right about 10 A.M.

Along the way Wallace's men had also encountered many of Prentiss's fugitives making their way to the rear. "They were panic-stricken and . . . report[ed] their regiments 'all cut to pieces,' " said an officer of the 2d Iowa. Another was appalled at the sight of the refugees along the road. "We were met by stragglers . . . , some bare headed—some without guns—some powder begrimed and wounded, and some helping off others that were wounded," he noted. "Army wagons loaded with baggage, and scattered parts of two or three batteries . . . were mixed up promiscuously with the crowd of flying fugitives."

Among the debris streaming northward was a wagon containing a few Confederate prisoners. An Iowa soldier heard them curse his regiment as they marched past, calling them "damned Yankees" and shouting that the Northerners would catch enough of "Dixie's land" before the day was through. "I never felt more like shooting a Rebel," admitted the soldier.

Like Prentiss's men Wallace's troops, largely by chance, occupied a strong defensive position. Tuttle's brigade was on the left, partially deployed along the extension of the sunken road in the midst of an open woods. His two right-flank regiments, the 7th and 2d Iowa, extended beyond this woods along the edge of an old field to the Corinth road. The clearing in their front, a large cotton farm known as Duncan field, was found to be occupied on the opposite side by Confederate artillery.

Sweeny's brigade, which had gone to the right of the Corinth road, was also deployed along the edge of Duncan field. Along a ridge in Sweeny's rear three batteries of Missouri Light Artillery unlimbered to sweep the open ground.

Although their lines were loosely tied together, with several bulges and gaps therein, the Union sunken-road perimeter was formed of three main segments. Hurlbut with about forty-five hundred men held the peach orchard sector. Prentiss and approximately a thousand troops were in the sunken road at the angle. W. H. L. Wallace and two brigades totaling fifty-eight hundred men formed the right flank along Duncan field. In support of this irregular line numbering more than eleven thousand men and curving over an arc of more than a half-mile, were seven batteries of artillery totaling thirty-eight guns.

The Confederates through their protracted delay in the pursuit of Prentiss had allowed a formidable Federal line to form. Their efforts to dislodge it would prove extremely costly.

* * *

Following one of the maxims of his Napoleonic studies, General G. T. Beauregard had instructed his officers that when they went into a fight without specific directions, they should march toward the sound of the heaviest fighting. Brigadier General Benjamin F. Cheatham, commanding the 2d Division of Polk's corps, had been in the rear of Bragg's corps since early morning, awaiting orders to go to the front. Finally, when the Confederates had been hard-pressed in the vicinity of Shiloh Church about 8:30 A.M., Cheatham sent his First Brigade under Bushrod Johnson along the Corinth road to attack Sherman.

Cheatham, however, had remained behind with his Second Brigade, under Colonel William H. Stephens. About 9 A.M. Cheatham met one of Beauregard's staff officers, who bore orders for the movement of reinforcements to the right.

Beauregard, still at Headquarters No. 1 near the junction of the Bark and Corinth roads, had just learned from Major Numa Augustin of his staff that a "brisk engagement" was in progress along the extreme Confederate right. Augustin thought there was danger that the enemy (Prentiss) might flank the Confederate troops there, and he recommended sending troops to the right.

Beauregard seized upon Cheatham's remaining brigade, sending an aide to tell Cheatham to go to the extreme right "to ascertain the point where the firing was the heaviest and there engage the enemy. . . ."

Cheatham's men soon marched down Reconnoitering road, but the fight with Prentiss was over before their arrival at the abandoned Federal camps. Continuing along the road, Cheatham approached Duncan field about 10 A.M., just as the last of W. H. L. Wallace's men were filing into position alongside Prentiss.

Cheatham was in his early forties, with a bushy moustache and long, wavy hair that curled in ringlets over his ears. Cautious in his approach, he soon saw that his understrength brigade of three regiments was no match for the "strong force" of Federals posted across the field. Cheatham bade his men wait while he brought up Captain Melancthon Smith's Mississippi Battery of six field guns.

Before Smith could unlimber, Munch's Federal battery opened fire from along the sunken road ridge, killing several battery horses. Yet Smith's guns soon were in action, shelling the fencerow occupied by Prentiss's and Wallace's infantry.

Adams had Gladden's bloodied brigade about four hundred yards distant, awaiting ammunition, but Cheatham, being unsupported, was unable to advance. For about an hour the artillery exchange continued.

In Wallace's line the shells burst overhead with a terrifying din.

At first most of the inexperienced Federal infantry stood behind the fencerow, where they took some unnecessary losses. One of Wallace's Iowans even stuck out his foot to stop a bounding artillery shell that he thought had spent its force. His foot was so horribly mangled that it later had to be amputated.

Another soldier with the 2d Iowa graphically described the incoming artillery fire. "I am lying so close to Captain Bob Littler that I could touch him by putting out my hand when a shell bursts directly in our front and a jagged piece of iron tears his arm so nearly off that it hangs by a slender bit of flesh and muscle . . . He jumps to his feet, and crazy with the shock and pain, shouts, 'Here, boys! here!' and drops to the ground insensible. A rabbit, trembling with fear, rushes out of the brush in which the Rebel battery is hidden and snuggles up close to a soldier, his natural terror of man entirely subdued by the dreadful [din]."

When a late-arriving Missouri battery unlimbered and joined in the contest from the ridge in Wallace's rear, the fury of the guns was intensified. By now the air was heavy with the sulphurous smell of burned powder.

About 11 A.M. Colonel Thomas Jordan, the Confederate adjutant general, happened to pass along the rear of Cheatham's soldiers. Jordan had been disappointed when left behind at rear headquarters during First Bull Run in order to hurry reinforcements into action. Reminding Beauregard of this, he had obtained special permission to go into action with the troops at Shiloh. Now, with several other staff officers, Jordan was roaming the battlefield on behalf of Johnston, yet following Beauregard's maxim by ordering the troops "repeatedly found halted for want of orders . . . toward the heaviest firing." Accordingly, when Jordan met the stalled Cheatham, he directed him to "charge the battery" opposite his front.

Although Cheatham's men as yet were the only troops immediately confronting the long, convex Federal line, Cheatham observed what he thought was Breckenridge's Reserve Corps coming up on his right rear. Probably this was only Gibson's brigade of Bragg's corps, a rather small command of four regiments, marching under instructions to remain behind the front line as a support, so Gibson later stated. Gibson's men, however, halted in Barnes field behind Cheatham's line and stood awaiting orders.

With banners flying Cheatham's lone brigade, led by Colonel William H. Stephens, advanced toward the angle at the corner of Lauman's and W. H. L. Wallace's lines. Only three regiments strong, the Confederates rushed "at double-quick time" across about three hundred yards of open ground. Only their right regiment, the 9th

Tennessee, extended into the woods at the edge of the field. In their immediate front several thousand Federal infantry watched the oncoming gray lines with nervous excitement.

Surprisingly, Cheatham's soldiers reached midfield without difficulty, although they were fired on by artillery and some musketry. At this point Colonel William T. Shaw of the 14th Iowa realized that his segment of the Union battle line ran at an unfavorable angle to the Confederate front. Shaw's regiment held the left of W. H. L. Wallace's line, and a gap of more than two hundred yards existed between his flank and Prentiss's right, which lay in the rear.

Fearing that the Confederates would enfilade his line, Shaw had his men quickly move back to a new position paralleling that of Prentiss. Here the entire line occupied the reverse slope of the sunken road ridge. Shaw instructed his men to lie down and to hold their fire until the enemy, advancing in two separate lines, closed within thirty paces. "[We then] opened directly in their faces," Shaw wrote, "[and] the enemy's first line was completely destroyed."

Directly in front of the Duncan field fencerow the carnage was appalling; the Confederate losses were so severe that Shaw noticed only a few of the enemy bothered to return the Federal fire. Cheatham, brought to a halt by the "terrific fire" in front, was further staggered by "a murderous cross-fire" from the far edge of the field on his left.

Ironically, one of McClernand's routed regiments, the 8th Illinois of Hare's brigade, had rallied in the course of its disorderly retreat along the northern edge of Duncan field. They were resting here, awaiting orders behind a fencerow, when Cheatham's men appeared from the west woods. Shooting at the Confederates' exposed flank together with the 7th Illinois of Sweeny's brigade, the 8th helped drive the Southerners back across the field.

In the woods on Cheatham's right, however, the Confederates had suceeded in closing with Lauman's infantry. Here their advance had been so screened by a heavy growth of underbrush that Lauman had difficulty in following their approach. Finally Lauman judged from the gleam of their bayonets that the enemy was about a hundred yards distant, and he ordered his men to fire. "Soon the whole line was one blaze of fire," wrote an eyewitness.

Still the Confederates surged ahead, protected by the brush. In front of the 31st Indiana they charged to within ten yards of the Federal line. Here "the slaughter among the enemy . . . was terrible," wrote the 31st's colonel. After a fight of nearly a half-hour and the expenditure of about thirty rounds per man, the Confederates were driven off. So many of Cheatham's men had been killed that Lauman was sickened when he saw the ground "literally covered with their dead." Stephens, who had led Cheatham's attack, had been thrown from his wounded horse and was so overcome by exhaustion that he left the field. The first Confederate attempt to break the sunken-road line had decisively failed, yet it was only the beginning.

Seeing that the enemy was now at a disadvantage, Colonel Shaw of the 14th Iowa quickly had his men pursue the retreating Confederates. They were soon joined by a portion of the 12th Iowa. Spread out in a thin blue line, the two regiments rapidly swept through the woods south of Duncan field, meeting with little opposition. Significantly, it was the first Federal counterattack of the day.

Yet Shaw's aggressiveness amounted to little. Gibson's Confederates were nearby in Barnes field, and as Shaw's line approached, they opened fire at extreme range. Shaw's men returned the fire, wounding a few soldiers of the 1st Arkansas Infantry. Then, as rapidly as they had advanced, Shaw's men turned and fell back. Shaw said that since Prentiss's troops had failed to advance, he feared the enemy would turn his flank and attack in the rear. Taking several prisoners along, Shaw's men hurriedly returned to their original line. The fighting momentarily ceased in the vicinity of the sunken road.

Elsewhere the Confederate high command was struggling to overcome what obviously had been a serious flaw in Adjutant General Jordan's battle plans. By midmorning the three Confederate battle lines had become hopelessly intermingled. Bragg was so exasperated with the confusion and costly delays that he felt compelled to work out a makeshift arrangement in order to retain some control. There were no clearly defined sectors of command, and seeing his, Polk's, and Hardee's troops so thoroughly mixed together as to be unmanageable, Bragg told Polk when that general came up about 11 A.M. that "if you will take care of the center, I will go to the right." This plan was agreed to by Polk, it being "understood" that Hardee would have the extreme left.

Following the battle Bragg bitterly condemned the initial tactical arrangement. "The want of proper organization," said Bragg, caused the Confederates to be "without system or order" and was, he thought, among the main reasons for the lack of total success.

To further Bragg's ill temper, about this time he had another horse shot from under him by a "shower of grapeshot." Bragg obtained another mount and rode off to the right, where he found Gibson's brigade standing idle in Barnes field. Bragg was immediately incensed. In his official report he wrote that Gibson's brigade "was in rear of its true position." To his wife Bragg was more candid. "I had not been able to force him [Gibson] into battle up to twelve o'clock," he wrote.

Greeting Gibson with what must have been harsh words, Bragg "commanded" him to go to the right and attack the enemy.

Randall Lee Gibson was not yet thirty years old. A dapper, well-bred Louisianan with a wealthy family background, Gibson was a law graduate of Yale University and already a man of influence. Although his brigade had not as yet been seriously engaged with the enemy, Gibson said this was because "I had received instructions . . . to move more slowly, and keep at a greater distance from the front line"—this following the capture of Prentiss's camps. Gibson had "presumed," should Bragg want his troops thrown in the front, "I would be directed accordingly."

Thus far Gibson's four regiments had sustained only a few casualties from a cannonade by Federal batteries near Rhea field. As Gibson's men marched to the right under Bragg's orders, they crossed the Hamburg–Purdy road, filing through a small wheatfield where they briefly halted and formed in line of battle.

Henry W. Allen, colonel of the 4th Louisiana Infantry, here occupied the extreme left of Gibson's line. A Harvard-educated lawyer, planter, schoolteacher, and legislator, Allen had his men in line and was awaiting orders to advance when suddenly they were fired into from the rear. At this the regiment nearly broke up.

The culprits proved to be some of Cheatham's soldiers who had followed Gibson's brigade in their movement to the right. One of Cheatham's Tennessee regiments, on edge following their encounter with Lauman and Wallace along the sunken road ridge, had appeared and mistakenly poured a close-range volley into the Louisianans.

A private in Allen's regiment recalled the circumstances: "Young Vertner, an aide of General Hardee's, galloped in front of our ranks with the 'Stars and Stripes' around his waist. Some one cried out, 'Here's your Yankee,' and immediately a hundred guns were levelled at him and he and his horse fell riddled with balls. The 4th [probably 9th] Tennessee seeing this, thought that we were the enemy and opened upon us with terrible effect, killing and wounding 105 of our regiment."

"This was a terrible blow to the regiment," wrote Colonel Allen, who had difficulty in rallying his frightened troops.

Soon thereafter, about noon, the order came to advance. Gibson's brigade, now re-formed, pushed forward through heavy underbrush, its right regiment, the 19th Louisiana, crossing into "a small farm." A log cabin stood in the middle of this field, and a split-rail fence bordered its northern edge. Marching toward the fence, the 19th colonel saw that beyond the fencerow the brush was so dense and tangled that it seemed impenetrable.

On Gibson's left his soldiers also found the going tough. "[The ground] was covered with the thickest undergrowth of blackjack [scrub oak] I ever saw," wrote a Louisiana private. "It was almost impossible for a man to walk through it."

Unknowingly Gibson's men were marching straight into the jaws of one of the deadliest ambuscades of the battle.

Portions of Lauman's, Prentiss's and W. H. L. Wallace's troops were posted in front, their center being protected by the sunken road. Prentiss's fresh regiment, the 23d Missouri, having earlier formed on the left, was hastily moved toward the center in order to confront the advancing Confederates. On Prentiss's right a gap of several hundred yards remained unprotected between his and Wallace's commands. Following Cheatham's attack, Prentiss had asked Wallace for troops to fill the opening. The 8th Iowa of Sweeny's brigade, having been detached for this purpose, now hurried to its new position. Numbering about seven hundred men armed with rifles, the 8th was led by a Scotsman, Colonel James L. Geddes. Shortly before noon Geddes's troops filed into line alongside the 14th Iowa, barely getting into position before the expected onslaught came.

As Gibson's men were poking through the underbrush, unable to see far ahead, the ground in front seemed to explode in their faces. "We were first apprised of their [the Federals'] proximity by a shower of musketry sweeping through our ranks," reported a surprised captain of the 13th Louisiana Infantry.

Prentiss's troops and portions of Lauman's and Wallace's had opened up at almost point-blank range. "[It was] a perfect rain of bullets, shot and shell," wrote one of Gibson's colonels. Firing from a knoll in the rear of Prentiss's infantry, two brass 6-pounders of Welker's battery, Missouri Light Artillery, joined in the conflict, their blasts of canister and case shot tearing into Gibson's infantry with deadly accuracy.

This storm of gunfire was so severe, and seemed to come from so many directions, that the colonel of the 1st Arkansas soon sent word to the Confederate regiment on his left, "For God's sake cease firing!"—he believed that they were killing his men and he was killing theirs.

On Gibson's right the 19th Louisiana had been caught in the middle of the open field. Rushing ahead to the fencerow, the Confederates opened fire, only to discover they were shooting blindly into the underbrush. "From the manner of the men looking through the bushes, as if hunting an object for their aim, it was apparent that they . . . were unable to [see] the concealed foe, and were only firing at the flash of the enemy's pieces," said their colonel. His men were falling at such a rate and seemed so bewildered by the invisible Union position that Colonel B. L. Hodge of the 19th ordered his men to cease firing and to charge with fixed bayonets.

Hodge's men rushed about twenty or thirty steps into the brush, but found the going so rough and the fire so severe that they broke and ran back to the fence row.

Try as they might, Gibson's men could not stand up to the deadly sunken road fire. Valiantly Colonel Henry Allen, later to be Governor of Louisiana, tried to restore order in his regiment, the 4th Louisiana. Gibson was nearby, as was Braxton Bragg. Seeing Gibson's Louisianans quitting the field, Bragg thought it disgraceful and sent his staff officers and escort to rally them.

All along the sunken-road periphery the Confederates had met with heartbreaking losses. The ground was so covered with their dead and wounded that it seemed to one Confederate a "valley of death." In a few minutes the 19th Louisiana had lost nearly fifty men out of less than three hundred. Officers and men had fallen alike under the "murderous fire of grape and canister" that Gibson felt was primarily responsible for the repulse. Gibson, who had lost his horse during the attack, was now on foot, rounding up his men. Although he had tried, his attack against the sunken road had fared no better than Cheatham's.

Beneath the smoking guns in Prentiss's line the Federal infantry lay down to snatch a moment's rest. The brunt of the fighting had fallen on the newly arrived 8th Iowa, plugging the gap between Prentiss's and Wallace's lines. Many of its men, especially officers, had been shot despite the good natural cover. The losses might have been heavier if Colonel Madison Miller of Prentiss's command had not been nearby to help out. Miller had observed the 8th Iowa standing up, awaiting the enemy's attack. Riding up to them, he insisted that they lie down. The line officers to whom he spoke refused to obey, however, not knowing who Miller was. Finally a captain recognized Miller and told the reluctant officers to follow the colonel's orders. This they did, just in time to receive Gibson's attack.

By now Prentiss was fully aware of the important position his improvised command was holding. Following Gibson's attack, General Grant and his escort, a detachment of the 5th Ohio Cavalry, came up to visit the sunken road line. Grant examined Prentiss's line and told his brigadier that he must "maintain that position at all hazards," adding that Lew Wallace would soon be up.

This news was quickly passed among the waiting Federal infantrymen. Two guns from Hickenlooper's Ohio Battery were hastily rolled forward and placed in front of the 8th Iowa to sweep an old side trail. Hickenlooper, still riding his bloody white horse, looked up with amazement to see his sixty-five-year old father, who he assumed was back home in Ohio. Later he learned that his father had enlisted the aid of a friend to join an Ohio cavalry regiment and thus be near his son. He had arrived at Pittsburg Landing unannounced and had been detailed to go with Grant's escort that morning. Father and son had only a brief moment together before they were called to their duty.

According to Hickenlooper the lull in the fighting was of sufficient duration to allow the heavy pall of smoke to clear away and provide a clear view of the ground in front. About 1 P.M. his brass field guns were in position, loaded and ready. The 8th Iowa was immediately behind, in the sunken road, with instructions to defend the guns to the last. Soon it was apparent to all that the struggle was about to be renewed.

Braxton Bragg had been known for his terrible disposition in the Old Army. In the disorder and confusion plaguing the Confederates following Gibson's repulse there is little to suggest that Bragg kept an even temper. Riding up to some of Gibson's men, Bragg said that he "gave them a talk." He was particularly disturbed by the brigade's leadership, and he later blamed Gibson's bloody repulse entirely on the "want of proper handling."

According to Gibson, who did not see Bragg, one of his civilian

MAJOR GENERAL BRAXTON BRAGG. The Army of the Mississippi's chief of staff and commander of the second assault wave, Bragg was one of the strictest disciplinarians in the Confederacy. He was also regarded by many as one of the South's best generals. Notorious for his ill-temper and quarrelsome disposition, Bragg expressed little confidence in troops other than his own. At Shiloh his blundering tactics and piecemeal frontal assaults cost the Confederates severely. Although an adept organizer and administrator, as a combat general there were few worse. (SIGNAL CORPS PHOTO [BRADY COLLECTION], NATIONAL ARCHIVES)

aides, Robert Pugh, was sent to Bragg with a request for artillery. Gibson's own battery, Bain's Mississippi, was absent on detached duty, and Gibson feared the result of another attack if he was unsupported by artillery. Yet Gibson was frustrated in this attempt. "The request was not granted," Gibson later complained, "and in place of it he [Pugh] brought me orders to advance again on the enemy."

Bragg also sent one of his own staff officers along the line to prod the troops forward. Colonel Hodge, on Gibson's right, protested strongly when told to attack the same position. "I thought it impossible to force the enemy from this strong position by a charge in front," Hodge later wrote. "Of course the order was obeyed without delay."

Gibson's brigade was soon pushing through the underbrush, striking for the same angle in the sunken road line.

Alerted by the ear-piercing Rebel yell, the Federals girded for their approach. "On came the enemy, yelling and yelping, and for about ten minutes [they] kept up a dreadful and incessant firing, with but little effect, for our men were flat on the ground," said one of Prentiss's colonels. "Not so with our [bullets]," he continued, "for the groans and shricks in the bushes told [of] the destructiveness of our fire."

Nearby, Hickenlooper's brass 6-pounders were firing as fast as they could be served. Changing from shrapnel to canister and finally to double canister, these cannon were firing so rapidly it seemed to Hickenlooper their discharges were one continuous roar.

Still the Confederates came on. When they were about twenty yards distant, the Federal infantry jumped up and "sent forth a sheet of flame."

Men were struck down in sheaves. A Confederate private looked around and saw so many men shot he thought he was in a "slaughter pen." "[They] mow[ed] us down at every volley," he wrote. "We still pressed on . . . I cannot imagine how I escaped being killed as I was in the front rank all the time."

Up to the very muzzles of the guns charged Gibson's men. The fighting was desperate, and became hand to hand.

"Our men were killed at the guns, the horses were shot in [their] harness," said a Federal colonel. Another officer watched in horror as "almost every man and horse belonging to the battery was killed." Finally the guns fell silent, and for a moment it seemed they would be engulfed by the onrushing enemy.

"The crisis was upon us," observed a captain of the 8th Iowa. Colonel Geddes of the 8th rode forward and in his shrill Scottish brogue called for volunteers to go and save the guns. "In an instant," said Captain C. P. Searle of the 8th, "men, mostly from companies H and C, sprang forward. . . ."

The fight among the guns was "short but desperate." Colonel

Geddes's mount was shot from under him, and he took a wound in the leg. A hundred men of his regiment were killed and wounded. Some of the troops on Prentiss's left fired so many times that they were fast running out of ammunition.

Yet the Confederate line was near chaos. Colonel Allen of the 4th Louisiana had been shot in the face with a rifle ball, the missile passing through both cheeks. The surrounding brush was so thick that his Louisianans were unable to maneuver, and, as a soldier admitted, "they were uncontrollably excited." "Our men in the rear killed a great many of those in the front," he later confided.

Blasted by canister and close-range musketry from three directions, Gibson's men could not hold on. For the third time the gray infantry recoiled from the sunken road line.

When the smoke cleared away, the Federal defenders were amazed at the extent of devastation along their front. One Indiana colonel was sickened to see not only that the ground was covered with the dead and wounded, but that the bodies lay in piles. The dead lay in grotesque poses, some headless, some disemboweled, others cut half in two. "It was a most hideous and revolting sight," noted Andrew Hickenlooper.

For hundreds of yards the brush had been chopped to pieces by the heavy storm of projectiles. "It somewhat [had] the appearance of a Southern corn field that had been topped," observed an eyewitness.

To the Confederate survivors of Gibson's brigade the stinging blasts of missiles had seemed like facing a swarm of hornets, and they termed the enemy stronghold "the Hornets' Nest."

To add to the horrors of the scene, the woods caught fire, and the dead and dying were quickly enveloped in the raging conflagration. Soon the pitiful screams of the wounded were audible above the crackling roar of the fire.

The detachment of infantry sent from the 8th Iowa to rescue Hickenlooper's two guns hurriedly wheeled the battered cannon by hand back to the sunken road. Here they were hitched to ammunition wagons by order of Colonel Miller and hauled to the rear. Hickenlooper's other two guns remained in place, however, and a new fire zone rapidly was cleared in front, in case the enemy should attack again.

From the weight of evidence it appears that Braxton Bragg was again greatly displeased with Gibson's efforts. "[They] moved to the attack, only to be driven back by the enemy's sharpshooters occupying the thick cover," Bragg wrote in derision less than a month later. This remark caused such heavy resentment among Gibson and his officers that Gibson, in a rage, petitioned the adjutant general for a formal court of inquiry.

Long before the last assault Gibson's officers already had formed an opinion that they were being sacrificed needlessly by Bragg's frontal attacks. As a result, when Bragg ordered still another attack by Gibson against the Hornets' Nest, some heated verbal exchanges followed.

Captain S. H. Lockett, recently returned from an errand to find and bring up Breckenridge, was in front of the Hornets' Nest with Bragg. Bragg was angered by the sight of Gibson's men streaming back from their second unsuccessful assault. Turning to Lockett, he told him to take the colors of the 4th Louisiana and carry them forward. "The flag must not fall back again," he warned.

Lockett dashed through the line of battle, then under fire, seized the flag from the color-bearer, and told him, "General Bragg says these colors must not go to the rear." A few minutes later the color sergeant was shot down, and Lockett thought he alone was confronting the enemy.

Out of the battle smoke strode an officer "with a bullet hole in each cheek, the blood streaming from his mouth." Angrily he asked, "What are you doing with my colors, sir?" Lockett replied that he was only following Bragg's order to hold them in place.

"Let me have them," the wounded officer demanded. "If any man but my color bearer carries these colors, I am the man. Tell General Bragg . . . he must attack this position in flank; we can never

COLONEL RANDALL LEE GIBSON. A Yale graduate and son of a wealthy Louisiana planter, Gibson was not yet thirty at the time of Shiloh. Called upon by Bragg to lead his brigade in three separate unsupported charges on the Hornets' Nest, Gibson saw his brigade decimated in the terrible storm of fire. Angered by Gibson's inability to make still another attack, Bragg termed him "an arrant coward." It was not until 1864 that Gibson finally won promotion to brigadier general. (CARTE-DE-VISTE, HERB PECK, JR., COLLECTION)

carry it alone from the front." It was Colonel Henry W. Allen of Louisiana.

Unfortunately Allen did not have his way. A few minutes later Bragg rode up to say he thought the enemy might be advancing. Allen was promptly ordered to take two regiments forward and ambush the Federals. "Serve them as they have served you," were Bragg's instructions. When Allen objected and asked if he must charge again, Bragg impatiently replied, "Colonel Allen, I want no faltering now." Stung by Bragg's reply, Allen whirled about without saying a word and went to lead his regiment forward.

Gibson received Bragg's order for yet another attack while with Colonel J. F. Fagan's 1st Arkansas. The 1st Arkansas was a large regiment, and Gibson personally led them back into the fight. On Gibson's right Colonel Hodge's 19th Louisiana made it to the fence fronting the sunken road ridge before being driven to cover by a devastating fire. "Here we remained exposed to his merciless fire for over half an hour, without the power to inflict any injury upon the hidden foe," wrote the bitter Hodges.

Yet Fagan's regiment, braving "a perfect rain of bullets, shot, and shell," again got to within close range of the Federal line. For a few minutes the fighting was furious.

Prentiss's line had been adjusted to bring more firepower into the Hornets' Nest angle by moving the 14th Iowa into the position formerly held by the 8th Iowa. The 8th had thus been squeezed to the left, compacting the line and intensifying the volume of fire coming from the angle.

Gibson's men had inclined more to their right in their latest attack and were striking in the direction of what once had been Lauman's position. Since Prentiss had shifted to the left, however, the brunt of fighting again fell on his troops.

Major James E. Powell, the former Army Regular who had led the dawn reconnaissance patrol that began the battle, was urging a handful of the 25th Missouri's soldiers to do their duty when he was struck and mortally wounded. Near his side the 25th's color-bearer was shot and killed. Yet with a dying grasp he clung to the staff so tightly that it had to be pried from his hands by the sergeant who took his place.

In a few minutes the fighting ended as abruptly as it had begun. "In justice to my command, I again ordered them to fall back," wrote a Confederate colonel. "It would . . . have been madness to have kept my command there longer." Spurred on by the blasts of canister and volleys of musketry, Gibson's men raced for cover. Their repulse marked the fourth failure of a Confederate assault against the Hornets' Nest.

A Union officer later wrote that the Hornets' Nest "was not very large and could, from . . . horseback, be at times surveyed tolerably well." Yet in front of this angle in the sunken road the fighting had been so severe as to earn a lasting place in the national history.

The Confederate survivors were embittered for years. "The result was inevitable," said the adjutant of the 13th Louisiana. Colonel Fagan harshly reported that the attacks had been a forlorn hope, that his men lay in "heaps of killed and wounded." The blood-soaked Colonel Henry Allen was even more emphatic. "The brigade was sacrificed by three separate charges . . . without the aid of any artillery whatever, although we had it at hand. . . ."

Gibson's brigade had been terribly cut to pieces. The 4th Louisiana had lost nearly four out of every ten men taken into action. Gibson later wrote that his loss exceeded that "of nearly any brigade at Shiloh." Despite these tragic losses, Bragg was unconvinced of Gibson's worth. He bluntly wrote to his wife two days later that Gibson's troops "were demoralized and nothing would induce them to go [forward]. A want of confidence in their leader, Gibson, destroyed them. Entre nous, he is an arrant coward. . . ."

As Gibson's men streamed back to Barnes field to re-form and to replenish their ammunition, Bragg gave up on them. "Finding I could do nothing with this force," Bragg wrote, "and that our extreme right under Withers, Cheatham, and Breckenridge was holding back, undecided what to do, I stationed the crowd under Gibson to hold its ground, and I moved to the extreme right. . . ."

It was now nearly 3 P.M. On the right Bragg would find a mixed assortment of Confederates gathering for a death grapple with Hurlbut's waiting infantry. There he would also learn some rather shocking news.

CHAPTER XV

Into the Mouth of Hell

A little more than a year before the Battle of Shiloh John Cabell Breckenridge had been Vice President of the United States.

A political moderate, Breckenridge then had been looked upon by many as the man to save the nation. In 1860 nearly a million citizens had voted for him to be President of the United States. "The Constitution and the equality of the States," Breckenridge had proclaimed, ". . . are symbols of everlasting union." As late as December, 1861, technically he was carried on the rolls as a United States Congressman.

Yet on April 6, 1862, dressed in "a well fitting blouse of dark colored Kentucky jeans," the swarthy Breckenridge prepared to launch a powerful attack against his former countrymen that, if successful, might alter the course of the war.

Breckenridge, whose impressive appearance was enhanced by long flaring mustachios, commanded the Confederate Reserve Corps —more than six thousand infantry and four batteries of artillery, largely made up of Arkansas, Kentucky, and Tennessee troops. Early that morning, about 7:30 A.M., he had led his men forward, deploying them in a column of brigades at the intersection of the main Corinth and Bark roads.

Although the battle raged in front, Breckenridge's men were told merely to sit and await further orders. Slowly the battle dragged on. At one point, when scattered firing erupted nearby, the men in Statham's brigade hurriedly loaded their guns. Yet word soon came that it was only another of Breckenridge's brigades firing off their weapons to see if the charges were dry.

When nearly an hour passed and no orders had arrived, the men began to grumble. Occasional word was passed along the line that the enemy was retreating and that many of their camps were in Confederate hands. Loud cheers greeted this news. Finally, about 8:30 A.M., the long-awaited orders came. Breckenridge was ap-

257

proached by one of Beauregard's staff officers and told to march into action. Sidney Johnston, having learned of Sherman's infantry west of Shiloh Church, had just sent word that "strong reinforcements" should go to the left.

"Under this advice two of General Breckenridge's brigades were started to the support of the left," wrote Colonel Jacob Thompson of Beauregard's staff. "But before he proceeded far, I bore a message to General Breckenridge to send but one to the left, and to order two brigades to the right, on Lick Creek." This change was due to the arrival of another courier with news that the enemy "was not strong" on the left and had fallen back. Moreover Beauregard had learned from his roving aide, Major Numa Augustin, that a brisk fight was in progress on the right, in front of Prentiss's camps. Augustin recommended sending troops to the right so as to extend the Confederate line toward Lick Creek.

Shortly before 9 A.M. Breckenridge halted Bowen's and Statham's brigades and, accompanied by Augustin, countermarched along the Bark road, which led eastward in a winding path for nearly three miles to the field of battle. Only Trabue's Kentucky Brigade continued its advance down the Corinth road. Ironically, when these two segments were reunited later in the day, they would have marched in a complete circle, meeting at the bottom of their respective arcs.

Meanwhile, General Johnston, unaware of Beauregard's orders, had also decided to order Breckenridge's corps into battle on the extreme Confederate right. Captain Lockett's report having warned of a threatening Federal column toward Lick Creek, about 9:30 A.M. Johnston sent Captain Nathaniel Wickliffe and Colonel Preston of his staff to locate Breckenridge and bring his troops into line at the desired point.

On their way to the rear about 10:20 A.M. the two officers were surprised to meet Bowen's brigade advancing along the Bark road. From Bowen they learned that Breckenridge already had been on the march toward the Confederate right for more than an hour.

Soon thereafter, about 11 A.M., the advance elements of Breckenridge's corps began to emerge in the Confederate rear. The heavy forests masked their movements, and Bowen's brigade moved up to within eight hundred yards of the Confederate right, where Chalmers and Jackson were confronting Stuart and McArthur. Behind Bowen Statham's brigade of Mississippi and Tennessee troops swung into position, deploying eight hundred yards to the left and rear of Bowen. The Confederate battle line was thus staggered, extending in echelon to the west. When the movements were completed, a massed line of eight thousand infantry stood poised to break the Federal left.

* * *

As Statham's men moved up through the wreckage of Prentiss's camps, hundreds of mangled bodies lying amid the debris of battle caught their sight. "Some [were] torn to mincemeat by cannon balls," wrote A. H. Mecklin, a soldier in Statham's 15th Mississippi Regiment, "[and] some [were] still writhing in the agonies of death." When a cannonball came crashing through a tree nearly a foot in diameter, Mecklin saw the man behind it torn "into a thousand pieces."

The battlefield, he observed, was a revolting sight. Nearby trees were riddled with bullets. Even the branches and tops had been shorn of their young leaflets by the heavy volleys. "On all sides lay the dead and dying," said Mecklin. "It was very warm. The sky was clear and but for the horrible monster death . . . this might have been . . . a [pleasant] Sabbath morn."

Amid this ghastly scene Statham's men had been allowed to rest momentarily. Just before they marched off in a northerly direction toward the peach orchard, a general officer came galloping down the line. The men supposed it was Beauregard, and they "greeted his appearance with deafening cheers," yet it was Albert Sidney Johnston.

About twelve o'clock, reported Johnston's aide-de-camp Colonel Preston, Statham's brigade moved forward to occupy an enemy camp about a half-mile in advance along a high ridge.* Moving obliquely to the right, Statham's men approached the deserted camp of the 71st Ohio. Beyond this camp lay the Sarah Bell peach orchard, where Hurlbut's men were waiting.

"Our movements became more brisk and our officers more excited," wrote one of Statham's young riflemen. "It was evident from all [of] these indications that we were near the scene of action. . . ."

The 15th Mississippi rushed forward at the double-quick, yet several accidents revealed their inexperience. A pistol shot rang out, and it was discovered a lieutenant had accidentally shot himself in the hand with his own revolver. Almost at the same moment the regiment's adjutant was accidentally stabbed in the thigh by a bayonet. Soon thereafter the advance slowed and was finally brought to a halt in a stand of woods.

---

* Breckenridge's corps was put in motion by Adjutant General Jordan, who had received word from Braxton Bragg that help was needed on the right to "turn and capture" several Federal batteries in front of Prentiss's position. Jordan had hesitated to commit the Reserve Corps without authority from Johnston. Yet Colonel Preston, Johnston's aide-de-camp, was with him. Both Jordan and Preston agreed that the reserve should be deployed.

Riding up to General Breckenridge, whose troops were standing idle, Jordan told him it was "Johnston's order" that he advance and take the batteries. Straightening himself in his stirrups, Breckenridge then gave the necessary orders.

As Statham's men re-formed and dressed in line of battle, they heard heavy firing toward the right. In this direction the fight between Stuart and portions of Chalmers and Jackson had just been renewed. Although Stuart doggedly continued to hold his ground for more than two hours, the critical sector on his right—just to the east of the peach orchard—now would be severely tested. The troops here were McArthur's, a scant three regiments of Illinois infantry numbering less than two thousand men, to oppose the combined onslaught of John Bowen's, John K. Jackson's, and William S. Statham's Confederate infantry.

Bowen's men were nearly all from the trans-Mississippi states. Their commander, a rather somber-looking man who seemed considerably older than his thirty-two years, had served as a Regular Army officer on the frontier and was a graduate of the U. S. Military Academy. Throughout the Army Bowen was known as a highly competent fighter, a reputation that he was determined to enhance this day.

Bowen advanced his four regiments in a column of two abreast, the 1st Missouri and 2d Confederate Infantry marching together in an almost northerly direction toward the deeply ravined ground just to the east of the peach orchard.

Sidney Johnston rode with them for several hundred yards in order to put them in at the proper place. "A few more charges," he urged, "and the day [is] ours."

Bowen's advance was cautious. When the 1st Missouri and 2d Confederate halted momentarily to allow Bowen's other two regiments to catch up, Brigadier General Withers appeared and ordered them to resume their attack; the enemy was just in front, he said.

Farther to the east Withers's own troops under Jackson were encountering heavy opposition from McArthur's Federal infantry. A portion of Jackson's brigade, the 19th Alabama and 2d Texas, had been compelled to go to the right to help Chalmers in his fight with Stuart. Since Jackson's remaining two regiments had merely stood in front of McArthur sniping at long range, it was these troops that Withers wished to aid.

Despite the presence of Bowen and Statham the Confederates were held in check for about an hour, their seven regiments merely maneuvering cautiously in McArthur's front. The 20th Tennessee, on Statham's right flank, directly confronted the 9th Illinois, which was on McArthur's right. The 20th had come under fire while crossing what one of the regiment's sergeants described as "a mule lot of about three or four acres," bordered by "staked and ridered" fences. Pressing on about one hundred yards, they had encountered McArthur's men along a thinly wooded ridge. "After the first volley they dropped back to a deep ravine parallel with our line, and right here was the slaughter for both sides," wrote Sergeant W. J. Mc-Murray of the 20th.

Terrified by the heavy firing about them, a small herd of goats led by an aged "billy" ran between the two battle lines. In a matter of minutes the herd was annihilated. "Only one or two of them [were] left," sadly noted a Confederate soldier as he later passed the spot.

The Federals continued to fight desperately to hold their ground. At one point the 9th threatened to overlap the 20th's exposed flank. Yet another Confederate regiment, probably one of Bowen's Arkansas units, came up and restored the line.

In the rugged terrain cut up by deep ravines and overgrown ridges Breckenridge's Confederates were unable to mount a coordinated attack. Out of this confusion came a staggering loss to the Southern Confederacy.

Albert Sidney Johnston, astride his big bay, Fire-eater, had been in the forefront of the fighting all morning. His restless energy in pushing the troops forward had been the source of admiration from all around him. On several occasions he had been under heavy fire. An officer of Beauregard's staff had observed Johnston near Rhea field earlier that morning: "General Johnston was sitting on his horse where the bullets were flying like hail stones. I galloped up to him amid the fire, and found him cool, collected, and self-possessed, but still animated and in fine spirits."

Another staff officer observed Johnston's ardor and his great determination: ". . . His countenance gleamed with the enthusiasm of a great man who was conscious that he was achieving a great success. . . ."

As Chalmers swept across the rough ground beyond David Stuart's camps about midday, Johnston seemed almost ecstatic. A volunteer aide, Edward W. Munford, sat by his side at the time, watching Chalmers's colors as they dipped out of sight beyond a nearby ridge. Johnston, in a joking mood, remarked, "That checkmates them." Munford replied that he appreciated Johnston's remark, but that "he must excuse so poor a [chess] player for saying he could not see it." Johnston laughed and said, "Yes, sir, that mates them."

When Bowen's brigade went forward against McArthur, Johnston rode with them for a short distance. Meeting stiff resistance, Bowen's men halted along a ridge confronting the enemy. Johnston, who had remained in the rear observing the fight, was exposed to a scattered fire from the line in front. Governor Isham G. Harris of Tennessee, a middle-aged politician who knew Johnston well and had volunteered to serve on his staff as an aide-de-camp, was with him.

Although the firing continued in front of Bowen, heavy gunfire was also heard in the direction of Statham's brigade, on the left near the 71st Ohio's camp. Accompanied by his staff Johnston galloped toward the west, coming up in the rear of Statham's brigade, then engaged in a long range fire fight with Hurlbut's troops in the vicinity of the peach orchard.

At the time Statham's men were in a shallow ravine between the 71st Ohio's camp and the Sarah Bell clearing, described by the Confederates as "a mule lot." Taking cover in the ravine about thirty yards behind the front line, Johnston was able to observe more than half of Statham's line. Edward Munford, who was with Johnston, described the scene. "I saw our line beginning to stagger,—not give back, but waver along its whole length like small grain when struck by a breeze. The general passed his eye from the right of the line to his extreme point of vision in the direction of the left, and slowly back again, when he remarked to Governor Harris, who was by his side, 'Those fellows are making a stubborn stand here. I'll have to put the bayonet to them.' "

Soon thereafter Breckenridge galloped up, apparently in a foul mood. For more than an hour he had been struggling unsuccessfully with Statham's, Bowen's, and a portion of Stephens's command in a vain effort to break Hurlbut's and McArthur's line.

Finding Johnston present in the vicinity of the peach orchard, Breckenridge heatedly spoke out, "General, I have a Tennessee regiment that won't fight."

Governor Harris, who overheard the remark, was shocked. Without waiting for Johnston's reply Harris interjected, "General Breckenridge, show me that regiment!"

Breckenridge in his preoccupation had not noticed Harris. Now, somewhat apologetically, he designated the regiment. Johnston spoke up, saying, "Let the Governor go to them."

The regiment was the 45th Tennessee Volunteer Infantry, Lieutenant Colonel Ephaim F. Lytle commanding. A new regiment, raised in the Wilson and Rutherford county regions during the past winter, the 45th was little trained. According to Captain George B. Hodge, Breckenridge's adjutant general, the 45th was posted toward the right of Statham's line next to the 20th Tennessee, which was on the extreme right. The 20th had pushed forward along the edge of a ravine, in wooded ground just east of the "mule lot." The 45th, never having been under fire before, had become disorganized by the double row of fences along the edge of the clearing where Mrs. Bell's two log cabins stood. They were then "a little in the rear and to the left" of the 20th Tennessee.

Mistaking the 20th for the enemy, they "poured a very destructive fire into us," angrily reported one of the 20th's men. Furthermore the 45th, according to Hodge, "delivered its fire at random, and inefficiently; became disordered, and retired in confusion. . . ."

BRIGADIER GENERAL JOHN C. BRECK-
ENRIDGE. Former Vice President of the
U. S. and unsuccessful Presidential candidate
of the Southern Democrats in 1860, Breckenridge was a political moderate who had originally opposed secession. Assigned to command
of the Reserve Corps only a few days before
Shiloh, Breckenridge was called on to lead
what was to be the decisive assault against the
Federal left in the vicinity of the peach orchard.
His inability to get Statham's brigade to advance caused Sidney Johnston to participate in
the charge, which led to that general's fatal
wounding. (LIBRARY OF CONGRESS)

Aided by their lieutenant colonel and major, the 45th was rallied
several times (Hodge said three) and was brought back to the edge
of the clearing, only to be again driven back in disorder.

Harris found the 45th protected by the crest of a knoll. Some of
its men were firing irresolutely from behind the rail fence, while
others lay out of the fighting in a ravine below. With difficulty he
prodded these up to the firing line.

Meanwhile Breckenridge had galloped among Statham's men to
order the bayonet charge called for by Johnston. In a few minutes he
returned, obviously upset, and said he could not get the brigade to
make the charge.

Johnston, still in good spirits, replied, "Oh, yes, General, I think
you can."

Breckenridge nearly broke down. "With an emotion unusual to
his controlled . . . temper," later related Johnston's son, he said
he had tried and failed.

Johnston's reply was curt but kind. "Then I will help you, we can
get them to make the charge."

Turning Fire-eater down the line of the ravine, Johnston galloped
among Statham's troops, passing slowly along their battle line. His
hat was off, his sword was still sheathed in its scabbard. In his right
hand he held the little tin cup he had taken from the captured enemy
camp that morning. Twirling it between his fingers, Johnston ges-
tured to the men.

Describing the scene, Johnston's son wrote the following. "His presence was full of inspiration. . . . His voice was persuasive, encouraging, and compelling. It was inviting men to death, but they obeyed it. But, most of all, it was the light in his gray eyes, and his splendid presence . . . that wrought upon them."

Johnston's words were few. He touched their bayonets with the tin cup and said, "Men, they are stubborn; we must use the bayonet."

Reaching the center of the brigade line, he turned and shouted, "I will lead you!"

Governor Harris again was nearby, having returned from his former assignment. Seeing Harris, Johnston told him to go to the right and lead "the Tennessee regiment." Harris complied, galloping back to the 45th Tennessee's position, where, "pistol in hand," he led them up to their alignment.

Elsewhere, in front of Statham's brigade, General Breckenridge, also riding a magnificent bay horse, appealed to his soldiers to do their duty and stationed himself at their head. Close by his side was his seventeen-year-old son, Joseph. Turning to an officer of the 20th Tennessee, Breckenridge yelled, ". . . charge and they [the enemy] will run." The officer pulled off his cap, placed it on the point of his sword, and raised it high in the air.

Down the line to the right the word had spread to Bowen's brigade, and they prepared to support the charge east of the Hamburg–Savannah road.

On the left a soldier in Stephens's brigade watched impatiently as Johnston sat astride Fire-eater, awaiting the signal to charge. Statham's men were excited—the line was said to be trembling with "irresistible ardor." Waiting in front to lead them was the highest ranking field general in the Confederacy, the former Vice President of the United States, and the Confederate Governor of Tennessee— an impressive array.

It was a few minutes before 2 P.M. With a wild shout, "which rose high above the din of battle," the line swept forward.

On the opposite side of the field Stephen A. Hurlbut's First Brigade suddenly saw the Confederates emerge from the woods, moving at the double-quick, with bayonets flashing.

Hurlbut's men were posted in a long semicircle across nearly three hundred yards of mostly cleared ground. Hurlbut's left flank was anchored by Willard's Battery A, Chicago Light Artillery, in position along the forward slope of a knoll just east of the Hamburg–Savannah road. Along the same prominent knoll, beginning at the edge of this road and extending west through the peach orchard, were two Illinois infantry regiments, the 41st and 28th. Since the knoll curved and flattened into a gradual rise at the northwest corner

MAP 9
Envelopment of the Federal Left
12 P.M.–3 P.M., April 6 (Chapter 15)

of the field, Hurlbut's remaining two First Brigade regiments were strung out in a line west of the peach orchard, extending back into the brush at the northwest corner of the field. Two batteries of field guns swept the ground in front, Mann's Missouri Battery being at the western edge of the peach orchard and Ross's Michigan Light Artillery standing in the open field near the small log cabin occupied by Manse George. Ross's infantry support, the 3d Iowa Volunteers, was behind a rail fence along the edge of this field. Hurlbut's First Brigade was now commanded by Colonel Isaac Pugh of the 41st Illinois, following the wounding of Nelson Williams. They had already taken sharp losses under a sustained fire, mostly when Stephens's brigade, moving to the right following its repulse at Duncan field, had joined with Statham's brigade about 12:30 P.M. in sniping at Pugh's brigade across the old cottonfield.

In the peach orchard Pugh's left flank also had been warmly engaged for more than two hours. Here the 41st and 28th Illinois had fought with Statham's men at long range, and although Statham's troops balked at making a charge, the firing had been prolonged. The two Illinois regiments had kept up such a heavy volume of fire that the 41st was nearly out of ammunition just before Johnston's bayonet charge. By this time all the trees about them had been so stripped of pink blossoms by the hail of bullets that it looked as if the orchard had been hit by a hurricane.

As Johnston's attacking infantry swept out of the south woods toward Hurlbut, the Federal left flank under McArthur first began to show signs of crumbling. Here the Confederate attack was spearheaded by Bowen, joined by two of Jackson's regiments on the right, although they had shot away the nearly fifty rounds of cartridges originally issued to them.

Ahead, near the crown of a bold ridge, McArthur's three Illinois regiments momentarily held their fire. The 50th Illinois, considered a veteran regiment following its service at Forts Henry and Donelson, was on McArthur's left flank. Actually a part of Sweeny's brigade of W. H. L. Wallace's division, the 50th earlier had been sent to bolster McArthur's thin line east of the Hamburg and Savannah road.

"The Rebels came on us before we knew it," wrote one of the 50th Illinois's sergeants. "The undergrowth [was] so thick we could not see them until they got within twenty yards of us." At the roar of the Confederate guns the 50th's line reeled under the heavy impact. Desperately the Illinois soldiers fought back. Although they poured several volleys into the Confederate ranks, striking down many, it seemed that the enemy numbered four times their own strength and that the entire regiment would soon be taken prisoner.

Because of Bowen's and Jackson's overwhelming numbers, the

50th Illinois soon broke and retreated, some of the bolder riflemen sullenly dodging behind trees and firing as they went back. The fighting had not lasted long, only about fifteen minutes according to one participant, yet seventy-nine of the regiment's 530 soldiers had been killed or wounded and many captured. The Union line east of the Hamburg–Savannah road was now dangerously fragmentized.

The 12th Illinois was next in line, just west of the 50th's position. When the 12th's colonel observed the rout beyond his left flank, he had his men fall back a short distance to the crown of the same ridge. As the Confederates appeared over the top of the opposite ridge they were greeted by a blinding flash of flame, causing the ragged gray line to halt momentarily. Apparently the left of Bowen's brigade was in the 12th's front. Colonel John D. Martin of the 2d Confederate regiment said that twelve of his men were struck down by this first volley, and his men instinctively halted to return the Federal fire. Yet Martin was supported on his left by two Arkansas regiments that surged ahead, raising the Rebel yell as they closely pressed the Federal line.

The 12th Illinois saw that they were about to be overwhelmed and fell back, withdrawing nearly a quarter of a mile to a point beyond the 5th Ohio Cavalry's abandoned camp.

The 9th Illinois, McArthur's last regiment, vainly tried to meet the enveloping enemy column by swinging two flank companies quickly to the left. It was a futile effort. "A most murderous crossfire poured into our ranks from the left which we were unable to silence . . ." said Colonel August Mersy of the 9th. Mersy could see the long lines of Bowen's infantry rushing alongside Statham's men, and knowing that his own men were nearly out of ammunition, he hurriedly gave orders to retreat. Yet he had not acted soon enough. Although the 9th had been fighting on this front for more than an hour and a half, when they attempted to escape across a ravine in their rear, the Confederates already had occupied the neck of the same defile, and were firing down the gap.

Now all became the wildest confusion. A shell exploded in the midst of the flying mass, killing a Kentucky thoroughbred belonging to General John McArthur. McArthur pleaded with an aide to save the saddle, but in his anxiety to get away, the aide came off without it. The cruel accuracy of the Confederate riflemen took such fearful toll that more than 365 casualties occurred among the 9th Illinois' 617 men, a loss of 59 percent—the highest loss of any Federal unit in the battle.

Back past "a level, burnt" clearing ran the 9th's survivors, with the 20th Tennessee in close pursuit. "[We] drove them pell mell for five hundred yards . . . to another ravine," jubilantly remembered one of the 20th's soldiers.

By 2 P.M. McArthur's command had broken up, and McArthur

himself had been severely wounded in the foot. All the ground adjacent to the peach orchard had been lost. Hurlbut's left flank was turned, and a gap of nearly a half-mile separated Stuart from what remained of the Federal left.

From the peach orchard large masses of Confederates could be seen sweeping across the ground east of the Hamburg–Savannah road, where McArthur's men had stood. As a result of their presence Mann's battery had already changed front, firing with canister at the oncoming Confederates, about five hundred yards distant.

Worse still, Johnston's bayonet attack was aimed squarely at the thin line in the peach orchard. From the Union lines an officer breathlessly described their advance. "On they came with a quick step, in gallant style, without firing a gun, the Stars and Bars flaunting jauntily in the breeze . . . [which was] as bold and defiant a battle flag as one could wish to meet in battle's stern array. . . . It seemed almost barbarous to fire on brave men pressing forward so heroically to the mouth of Hell."

Willard's Battery, opening fire from an angle east of the Hamburg–Savannah road, punished the Confederate lines severely. "[We made] our Bull Dogs bark at the most rapid rate that was practicable," said an excited cannoneer. Then, when the infantry opened fire, an officer wrote of the enemy that "his front rank went down, leaving a line of dead across his front. . . ."

Clear across the peach orchard, and beyond through the cottonfield, the Union line was a sheet of flame.

The Confederates pressed on.

Before the serried ranks of gray infantry could close with the Union line, the 41st Illinois got up and ran. Their commanding officer later offered the excuse that Hurlbut ordered his regiment to withdraw because of a lack of ammunition. Yet one of Willard's artillerists thought they were "deserted" by their infantry supports. Soon Willard's guns were in imminent danger of being captured. The battery was nearly out of ammunition, many dead horses were tangled in their harnesses, and a cross fire swept through the battery with terrible effect. One young Illinois cannoneer was suddenly stunned by a sharp blow in the seat of his pants. Angrily whirling about, he demanded an explanation from a nearby lieutenant. "What did you let your horse kick me for?" he asked. When informed that no horse had kicked him, the man grabbed his pants and, feeling the warm blood, screamed hysterically that he was wounded.

On Willard's left several of Breckenridge's regiments were closing rapidly, firing into the battery from the flank. In the midst of the smoke and deafening noise, Private Enoch Colby, Jr., looked up to see the enemy "within a hundred yards in plain view, four of their accursed flags flying, and four lines of battle deep. . . ."

The battery hurried to get away. With difficulty the four 6-pounder guns and two 12-pounder howitzers were brought off the field, all except the left gun. Every horse hitched to the gun had been shot except one, and that horse in its fright balked at moving in any direction. Seven cannoneers desperately grasped the trail and began pulling the cannon slowly to the rear. "Minie balls were falling like hail" about them. Soon five of the seven men had been hit, and it looked as if the gun might be captured.

"Just then a Minie ball struck the horse at the root of the tail, and he began pulling like six horses, and the gun came off flying," Colby later wrote.

With their line broken the remaining units of Pugh's brigade retreated from the peach orchard as rapidly as they could go. The colonel of the 28th Illinois received orders to fall back after five officers and about a hundred men had been killed or wounded. On his right the lieutenant commanding Mann's four-gun battery withdrew under a heavy cross fire when the infantry began to depart. Yet two wheel-horses and a driver of one of his 6-pounder guns were soon wounded, and the cannon rolled to a stop and had to be abandoned. By now so many gun horses had been shot that other horses had to be taken from caissons in order to draw off the remaining cannon. Two empty caissons were left behind among the dead and wounded.

As the Confederates swept through the south end of the orchard and overran the knoll in the middle of the planting, Federal resistance was light. Yet when Statham's men crossed this knoll, they found that the Federal infantry had regrouped along a wooded ridge at the north edge of the orchard. The fire now became so intense, and the Confederates were so winded by their charge, that they took cover behind the knoll and returned the fire.

Behind the line Albert Sidney Johnston sat on his horse and watched the firing. Miraculously, he seemed to have passed through the ordeal unhurt. Around him the dead and dying littered the ground.

Grant later remembered the spot as "so covered with dead that it would have been possible to walk across the clearing in any direction, stepping on dead bodies, without a foot touching the ground. . . ." Breckenridge's adjutant general and his own son, Joseph, had their horses shot from under them. The major of the 45th Tennessee had been wounded in the face. Here the gunfire had been so deafening that one of Statham's privates wrote in awe, "Never was [there] such firing."

From his location on the right, with the 45th Tennessee, Governor Harris noticed Johnston to the left, "about [in] the center of his line," he said. Riding over to Johnston, he found the general elated. Other members of his staff also observed Johnston's gleeful mood. Lieutenant Thomas M. Jack, an aide-de-camp, saw Johnston smile and slap his thigh, jesting about a spent ball that had stung him.

When Harris arrived, Johnston gaily kicked up his left foot and said, "Governor, they came very near putting me hors de combat in that charge." Looking down, Harris saw that a projectile had "struck the edge of the sole of his boot, cutting the sole clear across, and ripping it off to the toe."

Anxious about Johnston's narrow escape, Harris asked, "Did the ball touch your foot?"

Johnston said, "No," and was about to make added remarks when a Federal battery opened fire to the west, from a position that enfiladed the Confederate's new peach orchard line.

This battery, perhaps a section of 20-pounder Parrotts under Lieutenant Cyrus L. Edwards of Welker's Battery H, 1st Missouri Light Artillery, had just been sent to the left to help Hurlbut. Its threatening position now occupied Johnston's full attention. Lieutenant Jack was sent to move a Confederate battery to the left to play on the spot. Quickly Harris was told, "Order Colonel Statham to wheel his regiment to the left, charge and take that battery." As Harris galloped away on his mission, Captain Theodore O'Hara of Johnston's staff also was sent on another task. Only Captain W. L. Wickham remained with Johnston. The general remarked, "We must go to the left, where the firing is heaviest."

Amazingly, in the aftermath of the charge everyone near the commanding general failed to notice the crisis then unfolding.

Albert Sidney Johnston was desperately wounded.

During the assault on the peach orchard Johnston had been struck perhaps four times, although only one projectile had broken the skin. Fire-eater was later found to have been hit in two places.

In the excitement generated by the successful action no one, perhaps not even Johnston, noticed the profusely bleeding wound behind the knee joint in his right leg. A cylindroconodial lead ball more than a half-inch in diameter had struck "the outer and hinder portion of the calf, cut the large artery just above its bifurcation, and lodged against the shin bone in front."

This projectile, commonly known as a Minie ball, had been fired from Johnston's right rear by a rifled weapon, such as a .577 caliber Enfield rifle, at an extreme range, the ball not having enough energy to pass through the leg. In its path it had "torn without severing the popliteal artery, just where it divides into the anterior and posterior tibial arteries."

The wound, known in army jargon as a "bleeder," was serious but not necessarily fatal. In Johnston's pocket was a field tourniquet that could easily stanch the flow.

Wickham sat nearby, unaware of the dangerous wound. The minutes ticked away. Harris returned to report that he had delivered the order to Statham and it was being executed.

Riding up to the general's right, Harris spoke, but he saw Johnston sink down in the saddle and droop slowly to the left. Reaching out with his left arm, he grasped the collar of the general's coat and pulled him upright in the saddle. Harris looked into his face. It was "deadly pale." "General, are you wounded?" he asked.

Johnston, speaking with a deliberate tone, replied, "Yes, and I fear seriously."

By now Wickham was close by the general's left side. The rein dropped from Johnston's hand. Helping Harris prop Johnston up in the saddle, the two guided Fire-eater from the crest of the knoll, out of the range of small-arms fire coming from the distant tree line.

The exact location and direction of this move has since been a source of controversy. Many years after the battle an aged Harris identified a site near the corner of the Hamburg–Savannah and Hamburg–Purdy roads as the spot where he found Johnston reeling in the saddle. The hollow immediately in the rear was said to have been the ravine to which they guided him.

On the basis of contemporary documents and a thorough examination of the ground, it seems more likely that Johnston collapsed in the vicinity of the peach orchard and was guided by Harris and Wickham along the knoll nearly east across the Hamburg–Savannah road, to a small ravine in front of the ground where Willard's battery had stood. Here they were sheltered from the Federal fire coming primarily from the northwest.

Wickham helped Harris lift Johnston from his horse, and they laid him on the ground. Aware that the situation was serious, Harris told Wickham to "go with all possible speed for a surgeon." Doctor Yandell had been left behind by Johnston to care for the wounded at the 18th Wisconsin's camp, and was thus unavailable. The only other person in sight, "a soldier resting under a tree," was sent to bring any staff officer he could find to the ravine.

Harris took Johnston's head in his lap. "With eager anxiety I asked many questions about his wounds, to which he gave no answer, not even a look of intelligence," Harris said.

Among the first to arrive in the ravine was Captain O'Hara. Harris was attempting to pour some brandy down Johnston's throat. He swallowed once. O'Hara dashed off for help.

Harris later said he thought Johnston had a more serious wound than the one he noticed in the right leg. He accordingly "untied his

cravat, unbuttoned his collar and vest, and tore his shirt open . . ."
yet he could find no body wound.

From a location near the two cabins in Sarah Bell's clearing Colonel William Preston, Johnston's former brother-in-law, was watching a Confederate battery duel with the Federal artillery diagonally across the old cotton field. In great haste Captain O'Hara galloped up and said that Johnston was wounded and lying in a ravine nearby. O'Hara led the way. Joined by Dudley Hayden, they galloped to "a ravine about a hundred yards to the north of the cabins."

Preston found Johnston still breathing. Harris said about ten or fifteen minutes had elapsed since they had brought Johnston to the ravine.

"Johnston, do you know me?" Preston cried. There was no response. Desperately Preston also looked for a body wound, but could find none. Hayden took out a flask of whiskey; they tried to pour some down the General's throat. Johnston made no effort to swallow it. The liquid gurgled in his throat and ran down his chin.

It had been nearly thirty minutes since Harris and Wickham had led the general to the quiet ravine. Johnston ceased to breathe. It was 2:30 P.M. Governor Harris remarked that it was all over. Hayden felt Johnston's chest and said the heart had ceased to beat. The awful truth dawned on Preston. "My God, Hayden, is it so?" he gasped.

One of the highest ranking American generals ever to die on the battlefield, past or present, lay at their feet. Cause of death had been exsanguination (an acute loss of blood) following a wound inflicted perhaps by his own men.*

Gathering their wits about them, the small group of officers began to react. Preston and Harris agreed that Beauregard should be notified that he was now in command. Preston hastily scrawled a note to that effect and apparently handed it to Harris. Since the governor's horse had run off, he mounted Fire-eater. Harris found him so badly crippled that he got off and examined the animal. According to Harris the horse was wounded in three legs. Another staff officer later noted the animal had been shot through both hams. Nonetheless, Harris used Fire-eater to carry him to the rear, where he found a fresh horse.

Meanwhile Preston wrapped the body in a blanket and, secreting its identity from prying eyes, took it back to Johnston's headquarters of that morning. Most of Johnston's staff accompanied him on the sad journey.

Word of Johnston's death soon spread like an electric shock

---

* See Appendix A.

among a few of the General's intimate friends and ranking Confederate officers.

Captain Hodge of Breckenridge's staff was shocked to the point of tears when he heard the fatal news. Riding forth to notify Bragg and Beauregard, he met Captain Edward Munford of Johnston's staff, who was looking for his general, unaware of his death.

Although stunned, Munford located Bragg for the near-sighted Hodge, then galloped off to find Beauregard.

Farther to the west David Stuart had been perplexed by the heavy firing immediately beyond his right flank. Although Stuart apparently did not know of the fate that had befallen McArthur, the heavy volleys seemed to be rolling farther toward his rear. Both the 54th Ohio and 55th Illinois were running short of ammunition, and many of Stuart's men had already stripped the cartridge boxes of the dead and wounded. Two Confederate batteries were now firing in his front, and although their fire was high, the added pressure was beginning to wear on the men.

One of Stuart's Illinois riflemen at first had thought that shooting at the enemy was like hunting deer. As the fighting progressed, he changed his mind. "They were a good deal worse [than deer], for while I was looking for them, they were firing at me. . . . [Soon] it was every man for himself," he wrote.

Belatedly, Stuart consulted with the colonels of his two regiments. All agreed that it would be best to retreat, and about 2:15 P.M. Stuart gave the order to fall back through a ravine and form on a hill toward the right. As they turned to go back, Stuart's men found a gorge nearly a hundred feet deep confronting them. Undaunted, they made a hasty rush for the safety of the opposite ridge. Here, as they ran through the deep gorge, they were caught in a cross fire coming from the same ravine to the west and from the ground that they had just vacated.

Years after the war two veterans, one blue and the other gray, stood on this site reminiscing about the fight here. The Confederate, Major F. E. Whitfield of the 9th Mississippi, Chalmers's brigade, remarked that his men had been nearly on top of the fleeing Federal infantry. "It was like shooting into a flock of sheep," he remarked. "I never saw such cruel work during the war." The Federal officer, Lieutenant Lucien B. Crooker of the 55th Illinois, agreed, remembering the ravine as a "valley of death." "The merciless fire [here] was a veritable cyclone," he added.

Crooker had an interesting story to tell. He was wounded just before the retreat began. As he stumbled down the ravine, he collapsed at the foot of a towering elm tree. Sergeant Parker Bagley of his

GENERAL ALBERT SIDNEY JOHN-STON. The Confederacy's highest rank-ing field general at the time of Shiloh had been stung by heavy criticism fol-lowing the disasters at Forts Henry and Donelson in his department. Johnston concentrated his troops at Corinth, de-termined to strike a devastating blow at the Federal column invading the Missis-sippi Valley. Although a man of high character and great dignity, Johnston was overtrustful of subordinates and be-came obsessed with a need to achieve an important victory at any cost. His ill-advised exposure of his person in leading a charge at the peach orchard led to his tragic death, perhaps at the hands of his own men. The great void in army com-mand created by his death was felt not only at Shiloh, but in subsequent years as one after another of his successors failed to achieve victory in the West. (PHOTOGRAPHIC HISTORY OF THE CIVIL WAR)

GOVERNOR ISHAM G. HARRIS. The Confederate Governor of Tennessee was a volunteer aide-de-camp on Sidney Johnston's staff. Harris's inability to dis-cover Johnston's fatal leg wound quickly was an unfortunate aspect of the battle for the Confederacy. Later serving on Beauregard's staff, Harris was present at Shiloh Church when the final withdrawal order was given. (LIBRARY OF CONGRESS)

ENFIELD SHORT PATTERN RIFLE (officer's model), marked TOWER—1860
—.577 caliber. This rifle was of the same type run through the blockade aboard
the *Kate* and *Victoria* and issued to Confederate troops, including Breckenridge's
corps, immediately before the Battle of Shiloh. A stray Minie ball fired from one
of these Enfields possibly inflicted the leg wound that claimed the life of Albert
Sidney Johnston. The Minie ball depicted (actual size) is of Confederate type and
is a battlefield recovery. (AUTHOR'S COLLECTION—UNIVERSITY OF MICHIGAN PHOTO-
GRAPHIC SERVICE)

regiment, who had been wounded in the left arm, was nearby. Parker
grabbed Crooker with his good right arm, and the two painfully
dragged their way toward the rear. As they stumbled along, Crooker
noticed a bloody bandage around Parker's arm and realized for the
first time that his benefactor nad also been wounded. Exclaiming,
"Good God! Bagley, are you hit?" Crooker heard him reply that it
was all right; "That doesn't amount to anything; lean on me as
heavily as you have a mind to. . . ." At that instant there was the
sharp crack of a rifle from the edge of the ravine, and Crooker felt
a burning sensation across his back. Looking into Bagley's face, he
saw that his companion also had been shot. "I could feel his hot
blood run down my side, and [heard] his dying groan," said Crooker.
The bullet had struck Crooker crosswise under the shoulder and
had passed on, killing Bagley.

As was to be expected, the 55th suffered terrible losses in its disorderly retreat. One officer estimated the regiment had only about
512 men in line during the fight. Of these the regiment lost 275 men,
more than half its effective strength.

When scattered survivors reached the opposite hill, Stuart tried
to rally them but had little success. Girardey's Georgia Battery was
emplaced on a commanding knoll about a quarter of a mile away,
and their shells began bursting nearby, so that Stuart couldn't steady
his men.

* * *

The handful of Ohio and Illinois infantry that remained together now streamed back across the rugged terrain as rapidly as they could go, keeping to the ravine for as much protection as possible. When the remnant of Stuart's command finally re-formed near the camp of the 5th Ohio Cavalry, Stuart found that his men had an average of less than two rounds of ammunition per man. He had been wounded himself, in the shoulder, and it seemed obvious that they must again withdraw. Leading his men along the Hamburg–Savannah road, Stuart turned his back and marched for Pittsburg Landing.

From the banks of the Tennessee three-quarters of a mile inland to the north side of the Sarah Bell peach orchard all organized Federal resistance had been overcome. A mile and a half north along this open corridor lay Pittsburg Landing, the vital inner core of the Federal encampments. All of Bowen's, Jackson's, and Chalmers's infantry was now concentrated in easy position for a direct thrust due north to the landing. The key to the battle, and perhaps destruction of the Federal army, at last lay within their grasp. One of the most spectacular victories in military history loomed in the offing. Perhaps the complexion of the war might be altered in a single stroke.

But Albert Sidney Johnston had died, and after his death there came a lull in the battle. No one now seemed to be in control of the situation on the extreme Confederate right.

CHAPTER XVI

Surrender in the Thickets

Braxton Bragg appears to have been shocked, if not grief-stricken, when he learned from Hodge that the commanding general had been killed in "leading back some retreating troops." Galloping toward the right about 3 P.M., Bragg found "a strong force, consisting of three parts, without a common head. . . ." He said they were "holding back, undecided what to do," in the absence of instructions from higher command. Later Bragg wrote that ". . . No one cause probably contributed so largely to our loss of time—which was the loss of success, as the fall of the commanding general."

Bragg learned that the Confederates west of the peach orchard had been repulsed by the right of Hurlbut's line concurrently with Johnston's charge. The fighting here had been particularly bloody.

Two regiments, the 32d Illinois and the 3d Iowa, had held the contested ground, aided by Ross's Battery B, 1st Michigan Light Artillery. One of the 3d Iowa's soldiers, his heart beating rapidly, had watched as an enemy brigade "leaped the fence, line after line, and formed on the opposite side of the field. . . . It was a splendid sight," he said, "those men in the face of death closing and dressing their ranks, hedges of bayonets gleaming above them, and their proud banners waving in the breeze . . . we could not repress [our] exclamations of admiration."

Another soldier with the 3d, a corporal, remembered that their major had commanded them to lie down, saying, "Boys, lay low—don't fire a gun until you can see the whites of their eyes—then rise and give 'em hell!" Soon one of Stephens's regiments, probably the 6th Tennessee, was seen in the 3d's front, marching directly for Ross's battery. "On they came, confident they could take our battery," wrote the corporal.

The 3d Iowa, nearly seven hundred strong, opened fire with their smoothbore muskets and caused the Confederate line to waver, then give way. Colonel John Logan of the 32d Illinois jubilantly wrote that his men also "gave them such a dose of blue pills that they sickened at the stomach, and changed their course toward the left of our brigade."

On the 3d Iowa's right portions of three regiments of Lauman's brigade had pivoted to the left along the west edge of the cottonfield in order to flank the attacking Confederates. Firing "point-blank" into Stephens's men, Lauman's soldiers watched the Confederates melt away under their terrible crossfire. Stephens's men soon broke and fled in confusion to the woods at the south side of the clearing, leaving their dead and wounded strewn across the old cottonfield.

When the smoke cleared, an Iowa infantryman observed that the Confederates "lay so thickly upon the field . . . that they looked like a line of troops lying down to receive our fire. . . . It was some time before we could believe that such was not the case."

Yet the repulse had not occurred without some Federal loss. Ross's battery had found the enemy fire so hot that it had been forced to retire. Many horses and gunners had been shot, and the 3d Iowa's flag was riddled with bullets.

Worse still the respite was brief. Statham's regiment, the 15th Mississippi, had been put in motion by Johnston's last order, delivered by Governor Harris.

"On they came at a charge of bayonets . . ." said one of Hurlbut's 3d Iowa riflemen. "When they were within about a hundred yards of us, we arose and poured volley after volley into them. They delivered their fire at us, killing many of our brave boys, but those who survived our fire, fled. Of the whole Rebel regiment, I do not believe more than 200 escaped unharmed."

Despite the stubborn resistance of the Federal troops west of the peach orchard the opposite, or eastern, end of Hurlbut's line was obviously in turmoil. Here McArthur and Stuart had proved unequal to the task of holding back Breckenridge and Withers.

Bowen, Jackson, and Chalmers already were turning in a wide arc east of the Hamburg–Savannah road, using the peach orchard as an axis, their objective being Hurlbut's exposed flank, where only the 41st and 28th Illinois remained to contest an attack.

Hurlbut was apprised of the imminent crisis when a messenger from David Stuart galloped up and reported that Stuart "was driven in," and Hurlbut "would be flanked on the left in a few moments."

Hurlbut already had been under fire almost continuously for about four hours. Riding his favorite gray charger, he seemed to bear a charmed life, and had had several narrow escapes. A spent musket ball had struck him on the left arm, and an officer of his staff observed Hurlbut's cool indifference when a Minie ball hit a tree within a few feet of his head.

Compelled to make a decision either to abandon the left flank entirely or dangerously weaken his present line, Hurlbut boldly acted to shore up McArthur's routed left flank. Lauman's brigade was pulled out of line from the sector adjacent to Prentiss, west of the old cottonfield and about 2:30 P.M. was sent to the extreme left.

This followed by only a short while the dispatch of John Logan's regiment, the 32d Illinois. Logan had been ordered by Hurlbut in person to rush to the left and help the battered 41st Illinois during the crisis immediately following the loss of the peach orchard. Logan's regiment was thrown into confusion by the movement. His three left-flank companies outdistanced the balance of the command, and for a moment the bulk of Logan's regiment did not know where to go. Since a lull had occurred in the fighting, however, Logan was able to reunite his command and move close to the left of the 28th Illinois, in the vicinity of a small pool of still water soon to be known as the "Bloody Pond."

In Johnston's absence the command void on the extreme Confederate right was greatly felt. Breckenridge attempted to renew the stalled attack against Hurlbut by going to the right, among Bowen's and Jackson's men, and seeking help. Locating Brigadier General John K. Jackson, he asked that officer to come to his relief. Breckenridge also ordered the colonel of one of Bowen's regiments, the 2d Confederate Infantry, "to wheel to the left and march upon the enemy."

Ironically, many of the troops on the Confederate right had already begun turning to the northwest, following Beauregard's maxim of marching toward the sound of the heaviest firing. Jackson told Breckenridge that he already was moving in the desired direction, and his brigade would be up as soon as the ground could be cleared in front.

Jones M. Withers, Jackson's division commander, also said the "heavy and continuous firing" had convinced him the enemy was in heavy force on the left, causing him to order his division to wheel in that direction. This was confirmed by one of Jackson's colonels, Joseph Wheeler of the 18th Alabama, later a renowned cavalry commander, who said he was told about 3 P.M. to march to the left toward the sound of heavy firing.

Withers believed that he was acting in accordance with Johnston's battle plan, to push the enemy's left back against Snake Creek.

What Withers, Breckenridge, and the others failed to exploit, however, was the open corridor that lay directly to their front, now cleared all the way to Pittsburg Landing. By turning to the northwest they sacrificed the opportunity of capturing the Landing without heavy opposition. Moreover their turning movement was squarely in the path of Lauman's advance, ordered by Hurlbut to restore the broken Federal left flank.

The ponderous movement of a large segment of the Confederate army over the rough terrain required much time and further resulted in a lack of coordination among attacking units as they came up to meet the new Federal line under Hurlbut.

Among the first units to engage the enveloping column of Confederates was John Logan's 32d Illinois. According to Logan's brigade commander the Confederates advanced "cautiously and slowly."

The 20th Tennessee of Statham's brigade had run short of ammunition for their Enfield rifles following their last attack. Having fallen back to replenish their supply, they now moved "a little to the left" and advanced toward Logan's position on a low, wooded ridge. Colonel Statham led the attack, waving his sword and urging his men on. "[Our] line gave the yell and dashed forward wildly," wrote a Tennessee sergeant.

Although the 32d and 28th Illinois smothered their attack with rifle fire, the Confederates saw that there was no resistance beyond the 32d's left flank. Quickly they began working their way north. Logan, having "no support on the left whatever" and realizing that his flank was about to be turned, hurriedly swung a single company about so as to fire in that direction. Further adding to the crisis, the regiment in Logan's right front, probably the 28th Illinois, suddenly jumped up and ran away, many of the men fleeing through the 32d's ranks.

Logan was desperate. His men still held, but their ammunition was nearly gone. Logan rode along the line. Cries of "we are out of cartridges" greeted him. "I then ordered my command to fix bayonets, being determined to fight them in every way possible," Logan wrote. Realizing that his lone regiment would soon be captured should it remain there, however, Logan reluctantly gave the order to retreat.

The Confederates were within forty feet and closing rapidly as Logan, the last man to leave the position, began to fall back. First the regiment's lieutenant colonel was mortally wounded. Then Logan took a wound in the left shoulder. The 32d began to break up into fragments, and the men were soon out of control.

Hurlbut was nearby and saw the rout. Later he allegedly condemned the 32d's conduct, which earned him much disfavor with the regiment.

While Logan was withdrawing, Hurlbut attempted to fashion a patchwork line of defense in the middle of a nearby ten-acre clearing known as Wicker field. The situation was critical but not hope-

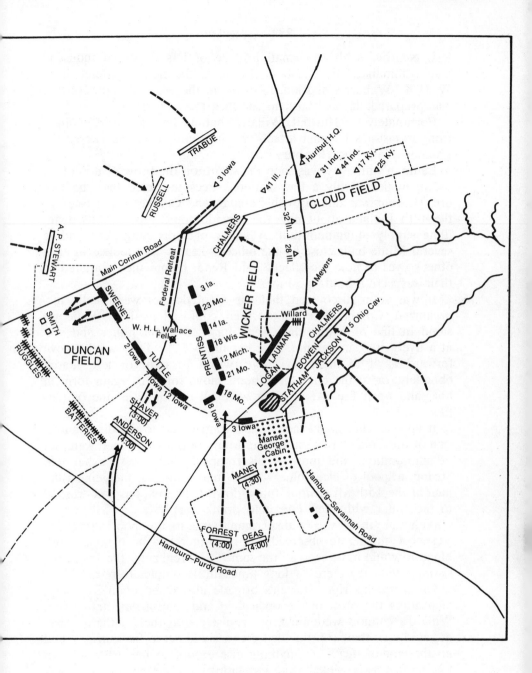

MAP 10
Collapse of the Hornets' Nest
3 P.M.–5:30 P.M., April 6 (Chapter 16)

less. Nearby, he had a small brigade of less than two thousand men commanded by Jacob G. Lauman, the new transferee from W. H. L. Wallace's division, to throw in the enemy's path. Hurlbut was prepared, if necessary, to sacrifice the brigade.

Fortunately for Hurlbut, Willard's battery had halted in its flight from Johnston's bayonet attack and had unlimbered in support of Lauman along the Hamburg road.

Lauman's infantry was soon drawn up on the brow of a knoll in the open field. Only a few scattered trees restricted their field of fire. Hurlbut was talking with Lauman and Colonel Hugh Reed of the 44th Indiana about how the brigade could replenish its dwindling supply of ammunition. A volley of shots rang out, sending several Minie balls close by the officers' heads. "We looked in each other's eyes to note the effect," said Reed, before they scattered to their respective battle positions.

It was soon discovered that the Confederates were badly disorganized. Colonel Reed noted their confused tactics. "While we stood in line of battle, they were marched about hither and yon at a lively step, in column, by companies. . . . They would move forward as if to make a charge, wheel to right or left, march obliquely, or to the rear, face about, move forward, again form in line, and open fire. At no time were all deployed in line of battle. . . ."

It appears that many factors had contributed to the disorganization of the Confederate battle line. Many of Statham's men were out of ammunition, and most of his troops by now were exhausted. Spying a "pool of clear blue water," many soldiers, including riflemen of the 15th Mississippi, threw down their weapons and "rushed to the water with their cups and drank deeply."

Although there was a dead man lying in the pool along one edge, a Confederate observed, "If the water had been mixed with blood it would have been all the same." His regiment, the 15th Mississippi, then lay there "a long time, until completely rested."

On Statham's right Bowen's brigade also came upon Lauman's men along the brow of the open field and took a devastating fire. Willard's cannon were throwing canister into the Southern ranks as rapidly as their shorthanded crews could serve the guns. "I had no thought of death or anything else except to hear the old gun talk as fast as possible," said a sweating cannoneer who was working his gun with only one other man to help him.

Their herculean effort paid off. "At this point we lost about 100 men, and would have been annihilated had not the enemy greatly overshot us," admitted one of Bowen's colonels.

The third Confederate column, Jackson's brigade on Bowen's

right, had been delayed by a burning woods. They also met resistance from the 12th Illinois of McArthur's brigade, which had retreated only about a quarter of a mile following Johnston's attack. As a result Jackson's progress had been so slow as to allow Chalmers's brigade to get in their front before they approached Wicker field.

On the far Confederate right Chalmers, meeting with little opposition following Stuart's withdrawal, had hastened "toward the center, where the battle seemed to be raging fiercely." Meeting a staff officer, probably of Breckenridge's staff, he was soon led toward the ground where Lauman was deployed.

As Chalmers's troops made their way forward, they heard the thunderous crash of big-bore artillery in the direction of the river. Precisely at 2:50 P.M the wooden gunboat U.S.S. *Tyler* had opened fire with her 8-inch naval guns, throwing heavy 53-pound shells in the direction of Breckenridge's advance. Lieutenant William Gwin, commanding the *Tyler,* had been anxious to join in the fight since early morning. Becoming impatient at the lack of instructions, Gwin had sent an officer ashore about 1:30 P.M. to request permission to open fire on Confederates seen advancing near the river. Meeting Hurlbut, the officer was told that the *Tyler*'s help would be gratefully appreciated—in fact, Hurlbut said that

BRIGADIER GENERAL STEPHEN A. HURLBUT. The hard-drinking, hard-fighting Hurlbut, a former South Carolinian, commanded the Fourth Division. Although an important Illinois Republican and friend of Abraham Lincoln, Hurlbut later proved to be a corrupt administrator. As a leader in combat he was more adept. At Shiloh, while defending the sector most critical to the Confederate plan of attack, Hurlbut had the misfortune to all but lose his division. Yet his obstinate stand significantly delayed the enemy's approach to Pittsburg Landing. (LIBRARY OF CONGRESS)

THE U. S. GUNBOAT *TYLER*. An important participant in the Shiloh campaign, commanded by Lieutenant William Gwin, the *Tyler* led several of Sherman's unsuccessful raids up the Tennessee. At 2:50 P.M. on April 6 the *Tyler* opened fire on Confederates advancing in the vicinity of the Hornets' Nest. At Nelson's suggestion this gunboat later maintained a harassing fire at ten-minute intervals throughout the night. (PHOTOGRAPHIC HISTORY OF THE CIVIL WAR)

without added support he would be unable to hold his present line for more than an hour.

Just as the Confederates began to close in on Lauman, the *Tyler* opened fire. Although her shells overshot the mark by a wide margin, the din added to the general confusion existing at the time.

Chalmers soon collided with Lauman and, meeting stiff resistance, tried to work around his flank. A Federal colonel observed that the fight here was "the most hotly contested of the day. . . . Our flag was a target at which they fired persistently, and it was riddled with balls," he later wrote. Several officers and soldiers of his regiment, the 44th Indiana, tried to keep the flag flying. All were either killed or wounded.

The fighting was so furious that in a short while the 44th and other regiments along Lauman's front had expended their ammunition.

Help was badly needed on Hurlbut's extreme left, where more of Chalmers's soldiers were maneuvering. Here one of Hurlbut's colonels was awed by the sight he beheld. "Regiment after regiment marched up from a large ravine to the left, moving in echelon, in compact lines, with Confederate flags flying, in perfect order, as if on parade . . ." he wrote.

Hurlbut, in desperation, called for his left to advance so as to counter the Confederate envelopment. Lauman's only reserve regiment, the 31st Indiana, supporting Willard's battery near the Hamburg road, was rushed into the woods east of the road and told to attack the Confederates. The 57th Illinois, having recently been sent from Sweeny's brigade of W. H. L. Wallace's division to reinforce the extreme Federal left, fell in beside the 31st Indiana for the attack.

Aided by Willard's cannon, the small Federal force bravely charged ahead. They were met by gunfire from Chalmers's entire brigade. At the first fire the major of the 57th Illinois was mortally wounded. Although the 31st Indiana fought valiantly, they were unable to make headway and began to lose heavily in commissioned officers.

"It was soon evident that the advance could not be sustained . . ." wrote Colonel Charles Cruft of the 31st. When the 57th Illinois fell back, Cruft also ordered his Indianans to withdraw.

Just as Hurlbut had anticipated, the unexpected attack had a disrupting effect on the Confederate advance. Chalmers was so dismayed by the stubborn resistance that he rode back to find help, meanwhile ordering his brigade to "lie down and rest."

On his way to the rear he came upon Colonel Joe Wheeler of Jackson's brigade. Chalmers told him his men were "worn out and overpowered by superior numbers" and that he would need immediate help. Wheeler, then advancing with the 19th Alabama, soon came up and found several of Chalmers's Mississippi regiments under fire. "I was impressed that this was a persistent effort on the part of the enemy to penetrate our line, and I determined to resist and prevent it at all hazards," Wheeler wrote.

Leading his regiment against the enemy near Wicker field, Wheeler found the Federals behind a fence, protected by a long, sloping ridge. "Both lines fought at close range, as severely as is ever experienced in a battle," he thought. Wheeler's opinions were well founded; in the span of less than an hour, his regiment suffered more than one hundred fifty casualties.

As the rest of Jackson's brigade came up and joined in the fight, the 2d Texas, on Wheeler's right, found the going particularly tough. The incoming fire was so heavy that Colonel Moore had his men lie down. An incessant rain of artillery projectiles continued. Moore's left flank, unable to return a fire they could not see, was thrown into confusion and went back. Even Hurlbut noted the "great effect" of Willard's guns on the "Lone Star flags" flying in Jackson's front. Jackson in his official report reported that this was a "murderous fire" and that the fight in the woods near Wicker field was "the hottest of the day."

Despite the courageous resistance of many of his men the great pressure was beginning to weaken Hurlbut's line. Masses of Confederates were crowding in front, including most of Chalmers's brigade. Led by the 9th Mississippi, they pressed on without Chalmers's knowledge, although ordered to rest. Their renewed efforts, coupled with the opening of a Confederate battery in close proximity to the Federal line, caused Hurlbut to order a retreat about 3:30 P.M.

The Federal left flank again was on the brink of disaster. Hurlbut feared that a heavy force of the enemy was already between his line and the river. Several regiments, including the 44th Indiana, had twice run out of ammunition and had had to be pulled out of line each time. Other units had disappeared entirely from the field.

By 4 P.M. the last groups of Lauman's men were heading back through the woods toward Pittsburg Landing. Hurlbut hoped to make another stand along the line of his encampments, but here he found the Rebels "pressing rapidly on each flank." With the resulting disorder only a single regiment, the 44th Indiana, remained to cover the withdrawal. Drawn up in line across the Hamburg–Savannah road by Lauman's order, the 44th was given the unwelcome assignment of presenting a bold front to the enemy. "[This] was done, thus demonstrating to them that it was not a rout," the 44th's colonel wrote with pride many years later.

The Confederates, presented with an opportunity virtually to annihilate a large segment of Grant's army, again were hampered by faulty communications. When one of Jackson's regiments ran out of ammunition, it simply left the line, and was next seen marching to the rear. Jackson discovered this and promptly "sent them back into the contest with orders to use the bayonet."

Another regiment, the 2d Texas, found an unexpected number of Federals in their left front, causing their colonel to suppose that "it was their intention to try to turn our left flank and cut us off from our forces on that side . . ." Accordingly he gave the order to fall back.

Following the collapse of Hurlbut's line the situation was so confused that even mistakes in identity were commonplace. A Federal officer, believed to be a colonel, dashed up to a Confederate regiment and shouted, "Boys, for God's sake stop firing, you are killing your friends." Discovering his mistake, he attempted to gallop away but was shot and killed. Another Federal officer was flushed from an encampment driving a horse and buggy. Although driving "at a furious rate," he too was shot and fell backward from his buggy.

Totally unaware of what they had accomplished, Breckenridge and other troops on the Confederate right by 4 P.M. had outflanked a large segment of the Hurlbut-Prentiss-Wallace sunken road line. The Federal troops later encountered toward the west by the pursuing Confederates were what had once been the center of this stout Federal line.

Bent backward in the shape of an elongated U the Federal sunken road line already was stretched to the breaking point. Hurlbut was virtually out of the fighting now; only one of Pugh's regiments remained in the vicinity of the old cottonfield. The remnant of the original sunken road line, under Prentiss and W. H. L. Wallace, was soon confronted on three sides by an increasing number of Confederates. As they closed in on the Federals, it was apparent to many that the sunken road perimeter had become a deadly trap.

In the vicinity of the old cottonfield Braxton Bragg had resorted to bombast in order to get the stalled Confederate attack moving again. Finding Gladden's brigade, under Colonel Deas, "lying down a half mile behind our line," he "gave them a talk" and ordered them forward into the fight. "Let everything be forward, and nothing but forward," said Bragg.

Although Colonel Deas was awaiting the arrival of a battery of field guns and a missing regiment, he marched his brigade obliquely to the left and soon came up against the remnant of Hurlbut's line near the Manse George cabin.

Alone in their immediate front were the 3d Iowa Volunteers under Major William M. Stone. Just before the Confederates appeared, Hurlbut galloped up and warned Stone that his line had been broken on the left. To Hurlbut it seemed "miraculous" that the 3d had not already been made prisoners. Stone was told to take his men to the rear.

After retreating about three hundred yards through the woods, the 3d turned about and again faced the enemy. "Looking forward to our old position," an Iowan wrote, "we beheld the enemy's hated flag floating above the house [Manse George log cabin.] behind which we had rested most of the day." In a few minutes the Confederates charged and "came so near that our officers used their revolvers against them," he related.

Although the number of Federals was few, Deas's brigade had become separated, and only two regiments, both decimated by the morning's fight, were pressing the attack. The Iowans held them at bay until the Confederates, being reinforced and "crowding past our right," said one of the 3d's soldiers, "forced us [in]to another retreat."

During their second retreat, about 4:30 P.M., the 3d Iowa ran into Prentiss's makeshift line, formed at a right angle in the woods, protecting what had once been the rear of the sunken road perimeter. By one account Prentiss told Stone that he hoped to hold the Confederates back until the army could re-form in the rear or night put an end to the battle. He urgently asked Stone to form on his extreme left. This was done, extending Prentiss's line.

Prentiss's men occupied the crown of a low knoll within a dense thicket. Having learned of Lauman's retreat and the breakup of Hurlbut's line, Prentiss about 4 P.M. had withdrawn his small command of less than one thousand a short distance north. Here they had taken position back-to-back with several of W. H. L. Wallace's regiments, and only about one hundred fifty yards distant.

According to a newspaper correspondent Prentiss was in the process of lighting a cigar from the pipe of one of his soldiers when he learned that his original sunken road line was outflanked to the east. Conferring with W. H. L. Wallace about that time, Prentiss expressed his opinion that the right wing of the army was still firm and that his position in the thicket could be held.

Later, when one of his colonels came to him and pleaded that their position was untenable, Prentiss replied that the colonel must

MANSE GEORGE WAR CABIN. A postwar photograph shows the rude cabin that stood just west of the peach orchard. The man in the door is believed to be Manse George, the tenant at the time of the battle. (SHILOH NATIONAL MILITARY PARK)

hold his ground, he had "positive information" that Lew Wallace's division would soon be up, and he, said Prentiss, intended to sleep in his own quarters that night.

Prentiss was under a delusion. Grant had earlier informed him of Lew Wallace's imminent arrival and stated that he must hold his ground at all hazards. Beyond this Prentiss had received no new instructions or information. At 4 P.M. Lew Wallace was still miles away. Furthermore the army's right wing under Sherman and McClernand had been driven back beyond W. H. L. Wallace's flank, allowing the Confederates nearly to encircle Prentiss and W. H. L. Wallace.

Although Prentiss, in his official report written more than seven months later, implied that he knew about 4 P.M. that the rest of the army "had fallen back to the vicinity of the river" and that he felt "we could thus save the army from destruction," it appears that this is a misrepresentation. W. H. L. Wallace's assistant adjutant general, Captain William McMichael, provided a different account upon his return from captivity in June, 1862. According to Mc-Michael Prentiss not only believed the ground tenable but had no knowledge of McClernand's and Sherman's withdrawal. This general dearth of information was shared by W. H. L. Wallace, thus setting the stage for a forlorn, although vital, last stand.

Only yesterday W. H. L. Wallace had written to his wife in Illinois about the arrival of spring in Tennessee. He told her about the delicate young leaves that were forming and how pleasant it would be to be with her and share her love. "I must not think of it now," said Wallace, "I trust in God that it may not be long ere we are again united. . . ."

At the very time he was writing this letter his wife was nearby, steaming up the Tennessee River for a surprise visit. Wallace recently had been sick, and his wife wrote that " I knew he would not think it consistent with his duty to send for me, though I found it mine to go to him."

Enlisting the aid of an army contractor, Ann Wallace had boarded a steamboat for the long trip up the Tennessee. Her presence was an unexpected pleasure for many of the soldiers returning to the army, and they kept her cabin gaily decorated with bunches of wildflowers.

About midnight on April 5 Mrs. Wallace's steamer, the *Minnehaha*, arrived at Savannah.

Being careful to let several officers of Grant's staff know that she had come without her husband's knowledge, for fear he would be blamed for her presence, Ann learned that her "Will" was at

Pittsburg Landing, in command of C. F. Smith's former division.

The *Minnehaha* arrived at Pittsburg Landing before daylight on the sixth. Not having a horse to ride, Ann Wallace remained on board, dressed in her Sunday finery while an officer went to see how far it was to camp. Soon the sound of gunfire was heard, and word came that a big battle was in progress. ". . . My husband had moved with his command to the front, so it was impossible for me to reach him," Mrs. Wallace wrote. "The only thing then for me to do was to wait where I was. . . ."

As the day wore on Ann became increasingly anxious for the safety of her family. Besides her husband, her father and two brothers were also present on the battlefield. "That long day on that steamboat, its scenes and sensations are beyond any description," she later wrote. "The wounded were brought by hundreds onto the boat. Some could sit and stand about and talk, others [were] helpless and pallid. . . . I passed from place to place holding water and bandages for the surgeons until it became so crowded that I felt I was in the way and I went on the upper deck and sat there instead of in the cabin."

About 4 P.M. Ann Wallace sat on the deck of the *Minnehaha*, appalled at the carnage about her. "The roar of cannon and musketry was almost deafening," she wrote. ". . . The floor of the cabin was covered by men in tiers, like bricks in the brickyard—all the staterooms, . . . even many on the upper deck [were filled. They were] suffering, dying—but brave and uncomplaining soldiers—still, waiting their turn, as the overtaxed surgeons went their fearful rounds."

At that very time, several miles distant, her husband was struggling to hold his ground amid a growing crisis.

Shortly after 4 P.M. one of Wallace's aides returned from the right, having just discovered that McClernand's troops were fighting "half a mile to the rear of Wallace's right." The aide, Lieutenant I. P. Rumsey, said he had pleaded with McClernand to throw his left forward, so as to protect Wallace's exposed flank, but McClernand had refused to do so. As a result Wallace's own right under Colonel Thomas W. Sweeny, a one-armed Irishman and an old Indian fighter with an impressive record in the Mexican War, was now in jeopardy.

Although Sweeny had not taken the sustained attacks that fell on Hurlbut's and Prentiss's troops, his brigade had been under artillery fire throughout the day. Much of his strength had been drawn away by numerous detachments to other parts of the field. By 4 P.M. only two of Sweeny's six original regiments remained in line along the Duncan field perimeter. The rest had been pulled out of line, one at a time, to meet various emergencies. On Sweeny's left, however, several of Tuttle's regiments, the 7th and 2d Iowa, lay in close support.

About 3 P.M., when a lull occurred in the fighting Sweeny ordered a reconnaissance by one of his two remaining regiments, the 7th Illinois. Crossing Duncan field, they "ascertained that the enemy on our front was now in very large force, . . . with lines extending far beyond our flanks. . . ."

The aggressive Sweeny soon ordered his two-regiment brigade forward into midfield, where they occupied the log house along the main Corinth road. Here his men had protection from numerous cotton bales lying about the Joseph Duncan farmyard.

Yet sections of two Confederate batteries, Ketchum's Alabama and Hubbard's Arkansas, soon began firing from across the field. Their fire was so accurate that an Iowa captain said his men were forced to lie down.

Along the Federal line to the left W. H. L. Wallace's other troops also were under bombardment. The enemy guns "played over us at a furous rate . . . with all styles of ammunition . . ." wrote one of Tuttle's officers. Another of his men said they were shot at with "solid shot, grape, canister, and bursting shell," which wounded eighty-seven men in his regiment, the 2d Iowa.

Looking, with his flowing white beard, more like an elder patriarch than a Confederate brigadier general, Daniel Ruggles was presently amassing the largest concentration of field artillery yet seen on the North American continent. Ruggles had been roaming the battlefield after advancing from the vicinity of McClernand's captured camps, advising idle batteries and regiments "to go wherever [they] heard the most firing." Approaching the western end of the Hornets' Nest line, Ruggles found the Federals drawn up in a thicket with their guns sweeping "a large circuit around."

One of his staff officers had brought up the first field guns to open against the Duncan farm, a section of Hubbard's Arkansas Battery. When it appeared that the Federals were in heavier numbers in the thicket toward the Confederate right, Ruggles sent these guns forward, only to have the Arkansas section nearly annihilated. A Federal battery of rifled guns, probably Stone's Battery K, 1st Missouri, consisting of four 10-pounder Parrott rifles, forced the Confederate lieutenant in command to retire his two smoothbore guns after firing only "three or four rounds." "It [was] a little more than I felt disposed to contend with," admitted the Confederate officer.

About this time it must have been evident to Ruggles that the

Hornets' Nest thicket would require more than the charge of massed infantry columns before it could be taken. Summoning all his available staff officers, Ruggles told them to "bring forward all the field guns they could collect from the left toward the right as rapidly as possible. . . ."

The result was, beginning about 4 P.M., an irregular and disconnected line of batteries that, as they arrived, ran from the main Corinth road south, then southeast, along the edge of Duncan field. Two separate concentrations seem to have developed. In front of the Hornets' Nest thicket five batteries and one section ultimately gathered. The line here was composed of Cobb's Kentucky, Byrne's Kentucky, Thrall's section of Hubbard's Arkansas, Swett's Mississippi, Trigg's Arkansas, and Robert's Arkansas batteries.

To their left, in front of the Duncan farm and the cotton bales, six batteries numbering about thirty-six cannon unlimbered: Rutledge's Tennessee, Robertson's Alabama, Stanford's Mississippi, Bankhead's Tennessee, Hodgson's Washington Artillery of Louisiana, and Ketchum's Alabama batteries.

In all, eleven batteries and one section—a total of sixty-two field guns—were bombarding Prentiss's and W. H. L. Wallace's troops before 5 P.M.

The effect was awesome. One Federal lieutenant with the 2d Iowa wrote that "it seemed like a mighty hurricane sweeping everything before it. . . . The great storm of cannon balls made the forest in places fall before its sweep, . . . men and horses were dying, and a blaze of unearthly fire lit up the scene. [Yet] at this moment of horror, when our regiment was lying close to the ground to avoid the storm of balls, the little birds were singing in the green trees over our heads!" Another Iowa officer long remembered the "galling fire of canister, grape, and shell" that did great execution among his men.

To a frightened captain of the 2d Iowa, "the shells and shot [that] passed over us terrifically at about the height of a man's head from the ground while setting down . . . continued so long that it was a relief when the Rebels began to advance upon us."

Marching from ground toward the right of Ruggles's batteries, a brigade of about one thousand men under Patton Anderson finally began working their way through the thick underbrush south of the Duncan clearing. Anderson had come up about 4 P.M., after meeting one of Bragg's aides. When he remarked that instead of being in reserve, the position originally assigned to him, he had found his way into the front line, the aide replied, "No difference; the general desires you to go wherever the fight is thickest."

A former physician, legislator, and Mexican War volunteer, Anderson was an aggressive though strict soldier whom his commander, Bragg, highly regarded.

Meeting Colonel Marshall J. Smith of the Crescent (Louisiana) Infantry, detached from Pond's brigade and also ordered into battle by one of Bragg's aides, Anderson and Smith agreed to conduct a simultaneous attack on the Federal stronghold. Smith would go to the left with his regiment and attack the Union infantry in the vicinity of the Duncan farmhouse. Anderson was to assault the Hornets' Nest thicket just south of the Duncan field. Their columns were formed even before Ruggles' batteries were fully deployed.

Across the Duncan clearing the Federal lines were thrown into momentary confusion. Anderson's advancing Confederates were mistaken by a few soldiers for Federal troops, and someone shouted that they were "our men." An Iowa captain borrowed a field glass to study the oncoming ranks. He was soon convinced that they were the enemy, and Wallace's troops girded for yet another attack.

Only an hour ago the fifth sustained attack against the Hornets' Nest had been driven off with an immense loss in life. The Confederate brigade of R. G. Shaver, after replenishing its stock of ammunition in one of Peabody's captured camps, had been brought

RUTLEDGE'S CONFEDERATE BATTERY. Dressed in an assortment of uniforms frequently found in the Confederate Army, a group of officers and men of Battery A, 1st Tennessee Light Artillery, pose for a portrait before Shiloh. During that battle Rutledge served with Statham's brigade, Breckenridge's corps, and was present as a part of Ruggles's artillery concentration in front of the Hornets' Nest. (PHOTOGRAPHIC HISTORY OF THE CIVIL WAR)

down a wagon road past Barnes field by one of Bragg's busy staff officers.

Advancing in the wake of Gibson's shattered brigade, Shaver was told only to dislodge the enemy in a thicket.* Plunging blindly ahead, he had encountered W. H. L. Wallace's troops at a distance of about fifty yards and suffered under a "terrific and murderous fire." A masked section of Munch's battery had opened from nearly point-blank range, taking the Confederates completely by surprise. The 7th Arkansas, Lieutenant Colonel John M. Dean commanding, was on the brigade left in front of the cannon. Shouting "Forward!" Dean got to within thirty yards of the guns before he was shot through the neck by a Minie ball and fell dead. On Dean's right the undergrowth was so thick that Shaver's men found it "impossible to charge." After a short but bloody fire fight the Confederates "fled about one-quarter of a mile," according to one of their officers, before they could be rallied.

Shaver's brigade, bloodied from fights with Prentiss, McClernand, and finally W. H. L. Wallace, withdrew entirely from the battle. A Federal officer who had witnessed the attack wrote that the Confederates had been mowed down with canister at close range and virtually annihilated.

Yet the Hornets' Nest line was to be tested again. The bodies of their comrades-in-arms were strewn throughout the tangled underbrush as Anderson's men came rushing into the thicket. A Federal soldier reported what occurred: "We lay in wait for the approaching force till they were in good range, when we rose and fired a volley into them, and kept it up at will. . . ."

Staggered by the galling small-arms fire, Anderson found that the Federals were also shooting canister from several howitzers, which tore through his ranks with deadly effect.

Although a lingering Louisiana officer from Gibson's brigade had warned him that he could not get through the thicket, Anderson had disregarded this advice. Pushing doggedly ahead, Anderson found that "the thicket was so dense that it was impossible for a company officer to be seen at platoon distance." Here one of his

---

* In Bragg's official report, dated more than three weeks after the battle, he wrote of Hindman's command (Shaver) attacking the Hornets' Nest prior to Gibson's three assaults. From other battle reports written soon after the fight, it appears that Bragg's sequence is wrong. Shaver said it was "between 1 and 2 o'clock in the afternoon" when he was ordered to withdraw to the enemy camp (Prentiss's) and resupply his men with ammunition. This was prior to his advance against the Hornets' Nest. One of Shaver's colonels reported they rested in the enemy's camp about an hour before being ordered forward. Accordingly, the time of Shaver's advance would be fixed at about 3 P.M., coinciding with Bragg's movement farther to the right. Gibson's brigade is reported by several eyewitnesses, including Bragg himself, to have attacked the Hornets' Nest about noon, thus placing Shaver's advance at a later hour.

colonels had his regiment so cut up by a cross fire and "a hail storm of canister" that the subordinate thought the Federals were firing from rifle pits.

Anderson's brigade had to fall back, fighting as they went, to a slight elevation about a hundred yards distant, where some protection was afforded from the storm of projectiles. At least one of his regiments had been separated in the attack, and Anderson galloped about rallying his men. Soon thereafter he sent word to Ruggles that artillery would be needed in front of the thicket to counter the enemy's battery, "which was the main obstacle to our onward movement."

Toward the north, where Smith's Louisianans were carrying out the other phase of the two-pronged attack, the Confederates met with greater success. Along with Smith's Crescent regiment, the 38th Tennessee, Colonel Robert F. Looney commanding, advanced from the vicinity of Owl Creek to take part in their first encounter of the day. On their way forward they had passed General Beauregard near Shiloh Church. Beauregard told them, "Go on, my brave boys. Charge them and the victory is ours," adding, "shoot low, shoot low," as they rushed out of sight.

Smith's and Looney's objective was the Duncan farmyard, where the 7th and 58th Illinois of Sweeny's brigade were posted.

Although about a thousand Federals were present, probably being equal to, or greater than, the two Confederate regiments moving against them, Sweeny's men were uneasy. The 7th Illinois was nearly out of ammunition for their .69 caliber muskets. Moreover, their position was too far advanced, being in the middle of the field with no immediate support on either flank. In the face of this Confederate attack the two Federal regiments opened a "steady and rapid" fire, and the Confederate ranks were said to have been visibly thinned. Although the fighting here lasted only about fifteen minutes, "the field was literally strewn with dead and dying," wrote a Confederate private. "[Still] we charged on."

The 7th Illinois, on Sweeny's right, was the first to break. ". . . To avoid being outflanked and surrounded it became necessary to retire to the position . . . originally assigned us . . ." said the 7th's commander. Once the 7th began to pull out, the 58th regiment also had to withdraw. Abandoning the Duncan farmyard, the two regiments fell back across the open field, fighting as they went. When they reached the eastern boundary of Duncan field, however, they found a new danger threatening them.

Instead of advancing directly across the open field in a frontal attack on Sweeny's position, other Confederates were filing off to the Federal right, passing through the underbrush north of the clearing in an obvious attempt to turn the Federal flank. Directing this attack was General Leonidas Polk, who had arrived north of the clearing with several regiments of Russell's brigade in time to order the Crescent Regiment and the 38th Tennessee to "charge the battery and camp under cover of the woods. . . ."

Moving in conjunction with Polk's troops, Smith's two regiments were soon beyond the Federal flank, then fronting the western side of the Duncan plot.

Sweeny's demibrigade now began to break up. The major commanding the 7th Illinois said he saw what the Confederates were up to, and he ran his men out to the northeast before the enemy could cut him off.

The 58th Illinois, on Sweeny's left, was not so fortunate. Before their commander recognized the danger the Confederates were on their flank, harrying their retreat. Falling back about a quarter-mile, the 58th was brought to bay near the camps of Hurlbut's First brigade. Here the 58th fought from behind a knoll, not knowing which way to move.

Colonel Thomas W. Sweeny had lost his right arm during the Mexican War. In the midst of the heavy fighting for Duncan field he had been shot with a Minie ball in the other arm, and his horse was riddled with seven balls. "Almost fainting from loss of blood," wrote a newspaper correspondent, "he was lifted upon another horse and remained on the field. . . ."

Just before his line broke up Sweeny had ridden into the Hornets' Nest to find Wallace and warn him of the imminent crisis. Soon thereafter a staff officer galloped up to Wallace with information that Sweeny's brigade was in "great disorder."

"General Wallace could not believe or understand my report, for he had great confidence in General Sweeny and his brigade," said the staff officer. Yet Wallace acted immediately. He knew the left flank under Hurlbut had given way and that Prentiss was under heavy attack, unlikely to hold the enemy back much longer. Since McClernand had been unable to come up to protect Sweeny's flank, Wallace realized that after nearly six hours of hard fighting, his line had become untenable.

His remaining troops, four Iowa regiments under James M. Tuttle, a tough volunteer officer who had been wounded at Fort Donelson yet remained on that battlefield, were scattered along the Duncan field perimeter extending toward the sunken road. Wallace's urgent order went out for the whole brigade to withdraw immediately.

In the confusion of the moment the orders were garbled. An aide galloped up to the colonel of the 12th Iowa and told him to fall back. When questioned where they should go, the aide had no idea, only that the colonel would receive further orders where to re-form.

Word of the impending disaster ran through Tuttle's ranks like an electric shock. In the sudden rush to get away each regiment was left to its own devices. "We fought on our own hook," was the way an Iowa soldier put it.

Wallace personally gave orders to the lieutenant commanding a section of Munch's battery near the 14th Iowa to try and get his guns through. Bleeding from a wound in the jaw, the Minnesota lieutenant took his two James rifles out at a gallop.

Bullets had already begun to come in from the rear before Munch's guns were underway. Following close behind, two regiments on Tuttle's right, the 2d and 7th Iowa, were among the first to vacate the Duncan field line. In the immediate vicinity was W. H. L. Wallace with most of his staff, riding slowly toward the rear.

A low ridge ran diagonally to the north, paralleling the relatively open ravine through which most of the 2d division was escaping. Coming over the crown of the ridge just as Wallace's party galloped past, the skirmishers of Anderson's brigade found a mass of fleeing Federals in their front.

Apparently Wallace's brother-in-law and aide, Lieutenant Cyrus E. Dickey, noticed the nearby enemy line and called the general's attention to it. Wallace, still riding slowly, rose in his stirrups, evidently to get a better view.

A moment later he uttered a short, agonized groan, jerked upward in the saddle, and fell on his face to the ground. A musket ball had struck him just above and behind the left ear, slanted through the skull, and passed out the left eye socket, destroying the eye in its path.

Dickey and an orderly quickly dismounted and ran to Wallace's side. The gaping wound in the side of his head convinced them that he was dead. With the help of several other orderlies they lifted him up and carried him away as rapidly as possible. Soon thereafter the Confederate fire became so hot that the orderlies dropped their cumbersome load and ran away.

Dickey was now alone. Quickly he dragged Wallace's body to the side of the road and placed it beside several ammunition boxes. Then he ran off, just ahead of the pursuing Confederates.

Meanwhile the cross fire had intensified along the route taken by Wallace's men. An Iowa soldier saw that the men were crowding in on one another and that all discipline was lost in the "mad race" for the Landing. Sighting a riderless horse standing nearby, he ran to get him and thus "gain greater speed in escaping. . . . Before

I can seize the bridle a man dashes in front of me, evidently bent on the same purpose, when a rifle ball crushes through the back of his head and he pitches forward in the dust," said the soldier.

Behind the 7th and 2d Iowa, most of whom had escaped through the angle, Colonel Joseph Woods's regiment, the 12th Iowa, was hurrying to extricate itself. Woods came up to the high ground near Hurlbut's camps and "discovered that we were already surrounded by the enemy . . ."

On Woods's left Anderson's Confederates had again advanced in a frontal attack following a bombardment of less than five minutes by the batteries massed by Ruggles to shell the Hornets' Nest. In Woods's rear the Crescent Regiment and the 38th Tennessee had swung around to block the only avenue of escape—the main Corinth Road.

Woods saw that his only chance was to try to force his way through, and he had his men open a "brisk fire" on the two Confederate regiments. Their fire was so effective it caused the Southerners to lie down on the opposite side of the hill. Woods felt he might have been able to break through if it hadn't been for the sudden arrival of more Confederate troops, coming from the direction of McClernand's former line.

Earlier Ruggles's staff officers had been sent to procure help from any available source. Two regiments from A. P. Stewart's

BRIGADIER GENERAL WILLIAM H. L. WALLACE. Newly promoted to command the ailing C. F. Smith's Second Division, the deeply religious Wallace was suddenly thrust into a crucial role on April 6. While escaping from the vicinity of the Hornets' Nest after six hours of desperate fighting, Wallace was shot through the head. His fate and the ordeal of his wife, Ann, who by chance was present, are among the most poignant of Shiloh's personal stories (NATIONAL ARCHIVES)

brigade of Polk's corps had responded, and came forward at an opportune moment under the personal orders of General Polk to charge the enemy's camp. As these onrushing Confederates swept over the top of the hill, the Crescent Regiment and 38th Tennessee jumped up and joined in the attack.

Sweeping around the knoll on their right, the 38th Tennessee came face to face with the 12th Iowa. "We gave them one murderous round of musketry," remembered a Tennessee infantryman, "then they threw down their arms and surrendered." Colonel Woods of the 12th had taken two wounds; only a captain remained to surrender the regiment. When the white flag went up, the Confederates were so close on several sides that Woods reported "their balls which missed our men took effect in their ranks beyond us."

Nearby, the 58th Illinois was also in a desperate plight. Its colonel, William F. Lynch, had just risen in his saddle and shouted to his men to "cut their way through" when a white flag went up in another regiment, apparently the 12th Iowa. Immediately thereafter a white flag was displayed among the 58th's ranks. Lynch rode to the spot and, with his sword, struck it to the ground. Yet he soon discovered this was of no avail; other Confederates were advancing from McClernand's sector in heavy force. Among them were portions of Russell's brigade of Polk's corps and Trabue's brigade of Breckenridge's corps, closing rapidly from the north, while Chalmers's brigade advanced from the east.

The 58th Illinois, numbering 327 men, surrendered as prisoners of war.

Nearly two hours earlier, about 4 P.M., Benjamin Prentiss had begun to prepare for another desperate struggle in his front. Following his conference with W. H. L. Wallace, Prentiss anticipated a Confederate assault on his left flank. He accordingly ordered the withdrawal of his battle line about two hundred yards north, to high ground within another dense thicket.

Prentiss was convinced he could hold this ground, yet he requested further help from W. H. L. Wallace—this although the 8th Iowa of Tuttle's brigade was already fighting on the right as a part of his command. Tuttle obliged by ordering Colonel William T. Shaw of the 14th Iowa to go to Prentiss's relief—just before Sweeny had been attacked and outflanked on Wallace's right.

Shaw, marching on an oblique angle past the 18th Wisconsin, had moved from the western side of the Hornets' Nest across the rear of Prentiss's line. As they approached the designated position, Shaw saw before him a regiment retreating in confusion and learned to his dismay that they were Prentiss's men.

Prentiss's timing in ordering a change of front had been most unfortunate, for just at that time the stalled Confederate offensive west of the Sarah Bell peach orchard was resuming.

Among the more unlikely aspects of the battle, an obscure colonel of cavalry, soon to become one of the Confederacy's most brilliant cavalrymen, had been instrumental in organizing this attack. Only a few hours before, Nathan Bedford Forrest, the antebellum Memphis businessman and slave trader, had been stationed three miles distant, entirely out of the battle. That morning Forrest had been detached with a portion of two infantry regiments under Colonel George Maney to watch the approaches to the Confederate right flank in the direction of Hamburg, Tennessee.

Crossing Lick Creek, Maney's force had deployed as ordered, but had observed no Federals in their front. About 11 A.M. Maney, who said he had authority to "recross the creek and join in the main battle" should no enemy appear, left Forrest and the 19th Tennessee behind and marched for the battlefield.*

Soon thereafter Forrest, anxious to get into the fight, formed his regiment and rode along the line. One of his officers reported the conversation.

" 'Boys,' said Forrest, 'do you hear that rattle of musketry and the roar of artillery?'—A yell, 'Yes, yes.' 'Do you know what it means? It means our friends and brothers are falling by [the] hundreds at the hands of the enemy and we are here guarding a damn creek. We did not enter the service for such work . . . we are needed elsewhere. Let's go and help them. What do you say?'—A yell, 'Yes, yes.' "

Galloping toward the battlefield, Forrest came up about mid-afternoon on the right of Gladden's brigade, then under Colonel Zachariah Deas. General Cheatham was nearby, and Forrest complained to him that his regiment was under artillery fire along the Hamburg–Purdy road. Forrest immediately asked for permission to charge.

Cheatham hesitated. In front lay the Hornets' Nest with the enemy's artillery sweeping the open field. Cheatham had already witnessed several bloody repulses here. He told Forrest he could not give the order. When Forrest persisted, Cheatham refused to accept any responsibility, saying ". . . if you make the charge, it will be under your own orders."

This was all the authority Forrest required. Offering to support Deas on the right, who was awaiting help of some means before

---

* Maney later apologized for this, reporting that he was advised (apparently by Forrest) that Beauregard had sent orders for all troops "to be brought to the scene of action."

attempting an attack against the 3d Iowa near the Manse George cabin, Forrest ordered his regiment forward into the open field.

Changing front from a column of fours into an extended line, then back again, as they charged across the open ground, Forrest's horsemen managed to elude most of the Federal volleys. Apparently they fell on the 23d Missouri Infantry just after Prentiss's order had gone out to fall back.

". . . The bugle sounded to charge, and we rushed over them," wrote one of Forrest's officers. Although the "black jack thicket" was so dense that the charge soon slowed to a walk, the cavalrymen continued on, "riding and firing," said a Confederate.

The attackers succeeded in throwing the 23rd regiment into confusion. As the Missourians streamed back through the underbrush, Colonel Shaw's regiment was coming up in the opposite direction from the old sunken road line. Shaw said that he rode among the retreating ranks and helped rally them on his left flank, just as Prentiss rode up.

Forrest's cavalrymen by now had found the thicket nearly impenetrable on horseback and had halted their pursuit. "We were unable to go further and were ordered to fall back," said an officer.

According to Shaw it was now about 4:55 P.M. Noting the confusion and disorder among Prentiss's troops, Shaw said he saw the general and "asked him what was to be done." Before Prentiss could answer, the enemy opened fire on the right, and the two Federal officers parted company, not to meet again that day.

This new Confederate attack was hard evidence of the deepening crisis in which Prentiss was ensnarled. About the same time Prentiss learned from Captain William McMichael of W. H. L. Wallace's staff of the collapse of Tuttle's brigade and the apparent death of Wallace. Realizing that he "was about to be surrounded," Prentiss acted to protect what remained of the Hornets' Nest defenders. An aide, Lieutenant Edwin Moore, was sent for reinforcements and presumably went to the Landing.

Prentiss, however, must have soon realized that this was a forlorn hope. He had portions of eight regiments in an L-shaped line, fighting to hold about three hundred yards of terrain. In all about two thousand men were present. Of these only about three hundred were of Prentiss's original command that had fought early that morning. Most of his troops were actually W. H. L. Wallace's and Hurlbut's, present merely by battlefield circumstance. The battle line was irregular, fields of fire were limited, and communications were practically nonexistent. Moving against this front were Breckenridge's, Withers's, and Stephens's combined forces. As one of Prentiss's Iowans later remarked, "We were completely surrounded and whipped, but did not know it."

It was not long before their commander learned the hard truth. "I found him [the enemy] advancing in mass, completely encircling my command," said Prentiss, "and nothing was left but to harass him and retard his progress so long as might be possible."

Although Prentiss's situation was desperate, the Confederates were also experiencing difficulty. Lacking command coordination, their attacks were organized in a haphazard manner.

When Forrest's cavalry dashed into the thicket, Deas's brigade, on their right, advanced against the Federals near the Manse George cabin. Although the 3d Iowa was driven from the position, a Confederate colonel complained that Forrest's troopers were unable to support the infantry effectively because of the "tangled wood." After firing about ten volleys and suffering under "the most terrific fire from the enemy," including artillery, Deas's men, streamed back across the open field, at about 4:30 P.M., abandoning the cabin where they had taken shelter.

As they went back, another Confederate brigade was seen attacking across the field. Cheatham, apparently noting the success of Deas and Forrest in closing with the enemy, had told the newly arrived Colonel George Maney to "prepare for action." Maney said Cheatham gave him "the privilege of selecting my command for the purpose" and advised him "of it being a difficult position, and of the failure of several previous efforts by our troops to carry it."

Taking command of Stephens's brigade, but selecting for the assault only three regiments, the 19th, 9th, and 1st Tennessee, because the brigade had already sustained heavy losses, Maney moved to the attack. Good fortune was with him that day. As his men rushed across the open field, they were not fired upon. "I was so fortunate as to pass the field and gain the cover of the woods before the enemy's attention seemed fairly directed to me," said Maney. Deas's brigade, retreating in front, was taking the full brunt of the Federal fire and soon rushed back through Maney's ranks in disorder. A Tennessee private noted that some men of his regiment derisively chided Deas's Alabamas for running, shouting "flicker! flicker! flicker!" after the bird known as the yellowhammer. Maney now had his command lie down, just before the Federals fired a volley that went over their heads.

Jumping up, Maney's men resumed their advance and saw that the Federals were beginning to waver under their return fire. "I . . . ordered the 1st and 9th [regiments] to . . . charge," said Maney, ". . . and both regiments sprang forward. . . ."

It was the beginning of the end for Prentiss.

James Geddes, colonel of the 8th Iowa, had in the absence of orders "considered it my duty to hold the position I was assigned to defend at all hazards." In the face of a "frightful assault from three directions," said one of his officers, ". . . the order came to retire, but too late."

With Maney, Anderson, and Chalmers rushing toward their position from different directions, Geddes, "to prevent annihilation," gave the order to fall back. "We started back under a most galling fire," said a captain, ". . . [that seemed] to come from every direction." All discipline and order was lost, and it soon became every man for himself. Most were pursued by the Confederates as they ran through the small ravine behind the Hornets' Nest. For many it was a terrifying experience.

Captain C. P. Searle of the 8th was running just behind one of his men when the man was shot and fell. Searle was so close that he inadvertently fell over him. "At the same time a spent ball struck my left arm and another went through my canteen," said Searle. "My arm tingled with pain, and the little water left in my canteen was warm and running over me as I fell to the ground. I thought it was my life blood. In fact, I was sure I was killed, but spying a 'Reb' close by, . . . I made one grand desperate effort to gain my feet, and much to my surprise, succeeded without trouble. I assure you I was a pretty lively corpse, for I left old 'Butternut' far in the rear. . . ."

Not all of the Hornets' Nest defenders were as fortunate in the sudden effort to escape. A short distance north a private of the 1st Tennessee saw a Union officer riding a "fine gray mare . . . sitting on his horse looking at our advance as if we were on review." Watching from a distance and almost spellbound by the event, the private saw his friend try to capture the officer, thought to be a colonel.

"W. H. [probably Private William A. Hughes, 1st Tennessee Infantry] rushed forward and grabbed his horse by the bridle, telling him at the same time to surrender. The Yankee seized the reins, sat himself back in the saddle, put the muzzle of his pistol in W. H.'s face, and fired. About the time he pulled the trigger, a stray ball from some direction struck him in the side and he fell off dead. His horse, becoming frightened galloped off, dragging him through the Confederate lines. His pistol had missed its aim."

The Union officer, possibly Colonel J. T. Tindall of the 23d Missouri, had been helpless to prevent the fragmentation of his regiment. As a part of Prentiss's line extending north toward the crossroads, Tindall's regiment had come under a "terrible shower of shot and shell," and soon broke.

Although the concentration of Ruggles's batteries continued to shell the thickets from a distance, at least one Confederate battery was rolled forward into the brush to shoot at the broken Federal line.

One of Forrest's cavalrymen said this was a portion of Captain Marshall Polk's battery, which they helped to move up following their recent charge.

Prentiss was desperate. All about him was chaos. He told his remaining artillery under Hickenlooper to limber up and escape if possible; it was too late to withdraw the infantry. The handful of his own original command was in disorder, and he ordered an officer to go and rally them. Beyond this there was little that could be done.

Colonel Madison Miller, who had earlier been rebuffed when he pleaded with Prentiss that their position was untenable, now decided it was time to leave. ". . . Without waiting or looking for a commander, I ordered a retreat by a left flank movement . . ." said Miller.

With Polk's battery spraying canister into their rear, the men in the angle got up and ran. One of W. H. L. Wallace's men, who was also running in this direction, was startled when he suddenly came over a rise and saw General Prentiss, "holding aloft the white flag."

Prentiss, in attempting to get away from Confederates closing from the south and east, had run straight into Leonidas Polk's infantry, blocking the main Corinth road near the 3d Iowa's camp.

Among the first Confederates to rush through Hurlbut's bullet-torn encampments here were Lieutenant J. C. Horne and Private T. M. Simms of the 22d Tennessee Infantry, Russell's brigade. Simms must have been surprised to find Prentiss his captive, yet he quickly brought the general out at gun point and delivered him to Colonel Russell.

Nearby, the Crescent (Louisiana) Infantry surrounded a large group of Federals who had surrendered about the same time. Included in the bag were Lieutenant Colonel Quin Morton of the 23d Missouri and Captain McMichael of W. H. L. Wallace's staff. With the surrendered swords of the Federal officers already in his possession, Colonel Smith of the Crescent Regiment attempted to prevent other prisoners from escaping in the growing confusion.

Just as Prentiss had raised the white flag in surrender, Colonel Miller, leading a remnant of the Sixth Division that had fought since sunrise that morning, came rushing onto the scene. Miller observed that Prentiss and his men were without arms, but was stunned when he belatedly realized that they had surrendered. Having no alternative, Miller also surrendered his men. In his diary he recorded the time as 5:26 P.M. Only one other large segment of the Hornets' Nest defenders yet remained to come out of the cul-de-sac.

Led by their colonel, William T. Shaw, the 14th Iowa was also attempting to extricate itself from the tangled thicket and their Confederate pursuers. At one point Shaw ran into the branch of a tree, lost his hat, and staggered on, dazed. When he finally regained his

CAPTURED FEDERALS TAKEN AT THE HORNETS' NEST. These officers and men of the 14th Iowa Infantry, W. H. L. Wallace's division, were allegedly still in Confederate hands at the time of the photograph. Survivors of some of the most desperate fighting of the war, these men had been prisoners for six months when this photograph was supposedly taken at Richmond, Virginia, just prior to their exchange. (PHOTOGRAPHIC HISTORY OF THE CIVIL WAR)

senses, he found himself within a few feet of a Confederate officer who was standing with his regiment in line along the Corinth road.

The Confederate, Major F. E. Whitfield of the 9th Mississippi, Chalmers's brigade, spoke first. "Colonel," said Whitfield, "I think you will have to surrender as you are entirely surrounded and the rest of your troops have already surrendered."

Shaw, noting the crowd of Union and Confederate soldiers mingled together near a few cabins, replied, "Well, Major, it looks that way." Taking out his watch, Shaw remarked that it was 5:45 P.M. Then he ordered the 14th to stack arms.

Just as Shaw's men surrendered, the quartermaster of the 12th Iowa came running up and excitedly asked Shaw what he was going to do. Saying that there was "no help for it," Shaw told him that they had to surrender.

It was all over. The 18th Missouri and 58th Illinois also surrendered to the 9th Mississippi. The few other Hornets' Nest troops, a portion of the 3d Iowa under Major Stone, had already been captured near the camp of the 41st Illinois following a brief stand there.

Although organized resistance had halted, the bloodshed continued. Many of the Federal prisoners of war refused to surrender their arms. The 8th and 14th Iowa had rifles, and rather than give them up intact, many of the men smashed them against trees. When the Confederates saw what was going on, they began shooting again, killing a few men of the 8th who were still trying to destroy their rifles.

Colonel Miller said some of his Missourians came up to him with tears in their eyes and begged to be allowed to break through the Rebel line or die in the attempt.

As was to be expected, the long day of bloodshed had frayed many of the men's nerves. Despite the settled issue, bitterness and hatred spilled over anew. When a burly Confederate captain stepped up to an Iowa officer and said, "You damned Yankee, give me your sword!" the Federal captive said he almost gave it to him point first. Another Federal prisoner, a sergeant of the 8th Iowa, was incensed to watch several Confederate cavalrymen drag the silk colors of the 12th Iowa behind their horses. "They rode back and forth along a path through a puddle of water and mud, and dragged those colors through the filth," the man bitterly wrote. His own regimental flag, a cotton banner, was then "torn to pieces and trampled into the mud."

Yet acts of magnamimity were equally common. Colonel Madison Miller tried twice to surrender his sword. General Leonidas Polk refused to take it, saying, "No man who has fought as you have should be deprived of his side arms." Even General Breckenridge would not accept the weapon when offered.

At a staggering cost of men and material the Hornets' Nest and sunken-road perimeter had been overwhelmed. The carnage had been appalling. Never in the history of warfare had the effectiveness of rifled arms been so visibly demonstrated. Given only the cover of natural rifle pits, the Federal defenders, many of whom were armed with Enfield rifles, had shot so accurately that nearly a dozen separate charges had been repulsed over a span of seven hours.

The Confederates had more than two thousand prisoners to show for their efforts. Prentiss admitted to the loss of two thousand two hundred, but Colonel Shaw, who had returns made the following day in order to draw rations, said there were only 1,558. Allowing for a discrepancy in accounting and the number of wounded prisoners reported, Shaw's figures can generally be regarded as incomplete. The 3rd Iowa, for instance, is not included in Shaw's total. A compilation of men listed as captured or missing in all regiments surrendered in whole or part at the Hornets' Nest amounts to 2,320.

In fact this was the largest capture yet made by the Confederacy and was quickly regarded as an outstanding achievement. One impressionable young Confederate was convinced that ten thousand prisoners had surrendered. Another jubilant Southerner thought that the entire Federal army had been captured.

The Northern soldiers, of course, held a different view. An Iowa soldier thought that Prentiss's stand had "delayed the enemy an hour" and prevented the capture of the entire army. "His fault consisted alone in not knowing when to retreat . . ." thought the man. Yet another participant believed that the Iowa regiments captured in the Hornet's Nest had been unnecessarily wasted. "Where . . . were the troops who ought to have stood by the Iowa boys? Away down at the steamboat landing huddled together like frightened sheep, to the number of thousands!" were his bitter comments.

In truth the result had been a series of pluses and minuses for both sides. Significantly, many hard lessons were learned by the Hornets' Nest fighting. Perhaps a Federal infantry captain provided the best epitaph on the desperate fighting there when he wrote to his brother a few days later: "It is time our people were getting rid of the idea that the courage is all on our side; it is a mistake. The enemy seemed to fight determinedly and I know they fell back steadily when forced to, contesting every step of the way . . ."

It was a sentiment equally appropriate for the soldiers both North and South who had fought at the Hornets' Nest.

CHAPTER XVII

At a Heavy Cost in Life

Early on the morning of April 6, 1862, the camps of General John A. McClernand had bustled with the usual routine of Army life. Following breakfast, the men began preparing for inspection, tidying their tents and polishing their brass-adorned equipment with fine ashes. There was the prospect of a clear, balmy day, and many of the men were in a good mood.

"It is good to be here," wrote an Iowa soldier, who considered "what money many would gladly spend to be able to witness the magnificent view our encampment present[s]."

The surroundings seemed a little more pleasant this morning; a number of visitors were in camp, including the wife of Colonel William Hall of the 11th Iowa. In an Illinois regiment the young son of a captain had just arrived for a visit. For many it seemed that a fine, leisurely Sabbath was in the offing.

The calm was first broken by the harsh rattle of musketry far in the distance. Soon began the "blood curdling sounds," so one soldier thought, of the "long roll." In a little while several cannon shot passed over the camps, followed by others that plowed up the ground and tore through the tents. Trees were splintered nearby, and a shell struck a horse in the hind leg, mangling its hoof. Men scattered in all directions and wagons, and teams were seen hurrying to the rear. When a projectile from a rifled cannon whistled close above an Iowa volunteer, it seemed to warn of an impending disaster.

McClernand's first reaction had been to send a courier to Sherman asking what all the firing was about. Then, as most of his division listened with growing concern to the roar of the guns, McClernand went to see for himself.

About 8 A.M., Raith, commanding the more advanced Third Brigade, moved forward to a more defensible position along a ridge in the rear of Sherman's hard-pressed line. Acting independently, Raith soon marched his men to within several hundred yards of

MAJOR GENERAL JOHN A. Mc-CLERNAND. Vain and egotistical, the commander of the First Division had political connections that earned him high military command despite a lack of experience. Quarrelsome, distrustful of West Point officers, McClernand claimed much of the credit for the repulse of the Confederates at Shiloh, which earned him further disfavor with many of his colleagues. (LIBRARY OF CONGRESS)

Waterhouse's battery. Hare's and Marsh's brigades, being camped farther to the rear, were at the time still formed on their parade grounds awaiting orders.

Soon thereafter McClernand hurriedly sent orders for these remaining brigades to advance to the front—Sherman was said to have been heavily attacked. Marsh's brigade, being camped nearest to the front, was the first to advance, marching in direct support of Sherman. After approaching the right rear of Sherman's camps, they were halted, and orders soon came to countermarch. The men later learned that McClernand had belatedly decided to put his two brigades into line farther to the east, along the ridge that ran in front of his headquarters.

Here the main Corinth road paralleled the ridge after making a sharp turn to the northeast about a quarter-mile north of Shiloh Church. A short distance south of the Corinth road lay an open field, used for reviews, spanning about twenty acres. Marsh's brigade had already taken its designated position along the road when Hare's men came up. Since McClernand wanted Hare formed on his left, his men had to pass behind the already deployed line to reach their destination.

Ahead, Raith's brigade was in trouble. Its commander had already anticipated a withdrawal to the division line, having sent an aide to locate Marsh's brigade in order to fall back in the proper position.

Unfortunately the aide had found Marsh's troops behind Sherman's right flank, before they had countermarched to their present position near McClernand's headquarters. Following a talk with McClernand, the aide returned with instructions to have Raith fall back on the division's right flank. A serious Federal mishap was in the offing.

Raith, meanwhile, had observed heavy columns of Confederates approaching from the left, causing him to change front by throwing his left flank back to clear a field of fire along a ravine. Broken fragments of Sherman's and Prentiss's divisions already were streaming past, and a growing uneasiness gripped Raith's men.

At the height of this confusion the Confederates moved to attack. The onslaught was led by a mixed force of Russell's, Bushrod Johnson's, and Anderson's troops in front and by Wood's and A. P. Stewart's brigades from the southeast. Raith's left flank immediately gave way in disorder. The aide who had been sent to locate Marsh's troops was unable to find Raith in the turmoil upon his return, and he told several nervous regiments to fall back toward the right. Raith's brigade, fragmentized and hard-pressed by the enemy, was soon seen streaming northwest, line officers and colonels desperately attempting to rally their men.

McClernand, about a quarter-mile in the rear, was warned of the enemy's approach by Captain Warren Stewart of his staff, who had made a hasty reconnaissance and escaped under a heavy fire to deliver his report. Hare's brigade was just then moving along the edge of the review field south of the Corinth road, coming up to take position on McClernand's left. As they filed along the skirt of woods, the Confederates, advancing along the opposite side of the field, opened fire. The range was considerable, about two hundred yards, but a few Federals were hit, including the two senior captains commanding the 18th Illinois. Quickly Hare's line was formed, the men standing in tense anticipation of an attack.

Down the line to the right cannon were roaring, enveloping McClernand's battle line in smoke. Marsh's brigade was defending this sector, a three-hundred-yard front bordering on the main Corinth Road. Here four regiments totaling 1,514 officers and men had deployed along a ridge, supported by three full batteries of field guns, the artillery forming the backbone of Marsh's line.

Plugging the gap between Hare and Marsh stood McAllister's battery of four 24-pounder howitzers. Burrows's 14th Ohio Battery was unlimbered near the center of Marsh's position, while Dresser's six-gun battery protected Marsh's right, near Water Oaks Pond. Farther to the right another Illinois battery, Schwartz's, was firing from near the crossroads in support of Sherman's line. In appearance McClernand's line was formidable, but the men were nervous.

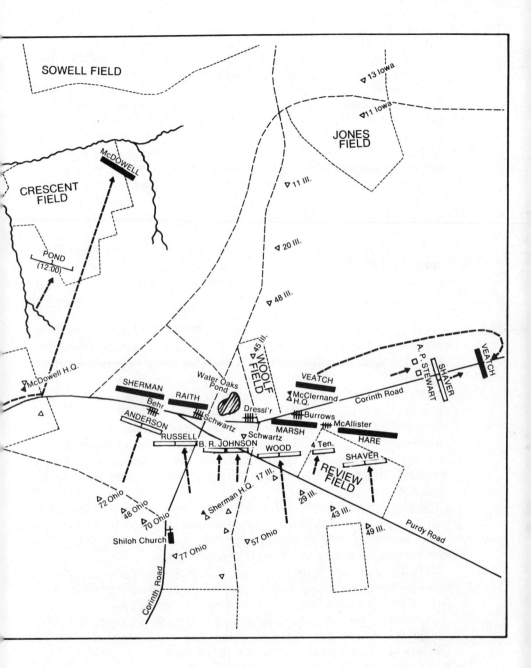

MAP 11
Defeat of the Federal Right
10:30 A.M.–12 noon, April 6 (Chapter 17)

The attack began at the strong point, on Marsh's front. "The enemy were seen approaching in large force and fine style, column after column moving on us with a steadiness and precision which I had hardly anticipated," wrote the breathless Marsh. The Confederate brigade of S. A. M. Wood, continuing its turning movement following the rout of Prentiss, was first to appear despite the severe punishment it had taken in the advance toward this new Federal front. Although Raith's brigade had broken up at the approach of these heavy columns, including Wood's, A. P. Stewart's, and Shaver's troops, numerous tactical mishaps had already fragmentized the Confederate battle line.

Following the wounding of Wood by his own men, his staff officers hastily attempted to re-form the brigade. Much of the trouble occurred on the brigade's left flank, where the Confederates were so disorganized that at least one regimental commander had his men fall down behind cover on the side fronting the enemy to avoid a fire from "friendly" troops in the rear.

Although the left remained stalled, the Confederate right flank now began to press onward. Their attack was supported by several batteries, including Bankhead's Tennessee, firing opposite Burrow's position. Not far from these cannon lay the 4th Tennessee of A. P. Stewart's brigade, hugging the ground for protection. When their general came up, he was inspired. Stewart said he had just talked with one of Bragg's staff officers, who pleaded that the battery in front must be taken. "I turned to the 4th; told them what was wanted; [and] asked if they would take the battery . . ." Stewart recalled with pride. Back came the reply, "Show us where it is; we will try."

Going forward under the eye of Stewart, the 4th Tennessee sprinted unsupported into the blasts of canister. Men fell right and left. According to their commander thirty-one men were killed and 160 wounded during this fateful charge.

"If you ever heard the little yellow dogs [brass field guns] bark," said an excited Federal participant, ". . . [I] guess they did some of it there. The fire flew out of their mouths in clouds."

Crossing from the open field into a growth of light timber to avoid this deadly fire, the 4th approached the Federal line at the double-quick. "We were within 30 paces of the enemy's guns when we halted, fired one round, [and] rushed forward with a yell . . ." wrote an officer.

Ahead, the 45th and 48th Illinois were in the edge of the woods on Marsh's extreme left, supporting McAllister's battery. The men were standing in line, apparently unable to see very well through the billowing battle smoke, when the 4th Tennessee suddenly loomed in front. The enemy came nearer, but no one gave the order to shoot.

"What does it mean? Why don't our officers give the command to fire?" stammered a private.

With the two lines only pistol range part, the strain became unbearable. Several infantrymen raised their muskets and fired into the oncoming ranks. "Cease firing!" shouted an officer as he rushed along the line. "Those are our troops."

Realizing that the flag of the Tennessee regiment had been mistaken for a Federal flag, some of the men pleaded with their officers that it was a mistake. The officers still insisted they were Federal troops. "The hell they are!" roared an excited private. "You will find out pretty damned soon. . . ."

By now it was too late. The Confederates were within a stone's throw, and they threw up their muskets and fired a point-blank volley.

"Our men fell like autumn leaves," wrote an embittered private. Another eyewitness, a Federal colonel, later said this fire was so devastating he thought it unequaled during the entire battle for destructiveness. "During the first five minutes I lost more in killed and wounded than in all the other actions," commented a saddened Marsh in his official report.

The 48th Illinois was the first to break. Both the colonel and lieutenant colonel were hit, and the entire regiment went to the rear in confusion. "In spite of my efforts to compel them to stand they fell back . . ." said Marsh, who became further alarmed when he saw that the panic was spreading to his remaining regiments.

Other Confederate battle lines were now seen approaching in successive waves. Some of Wood's troops, including the 16th Alabama and 27th Tennessee, began to head for Burrows's guns.

The break up of the Federal line was spontaneous.

McAllister's guns were uncovered by the retreat of their supports, allowing the 4th Tennessee to approach on their right flank. The Rebels were about to surround his battery when McAllister gave the order to limber up. Yet so many horses had already been killed that one gun had to be abandoned. McAllister took four slight wounds, but he got his three remaining howitzers rolling, just before the 4th Tennessee swept through his battery. One 24-pounder howitzer and two soldiers, "who did not have time to escape nor courage to fight," said a Confederate officer, fell into the enemy's hands.

Burrows's battery of 6- and 12-pounder Wiard rifles was next to take a pummeling. Their infantry supports also had become panic-stricken by the growing chaos and already had gone to the rear. Burrows's cannoneers were confronted by Wood's troops, among them the 16th Alabama and 27th Tennessee, who raised a yell and charged for the guns. Seventy horses went down amid the battery. The underbrush and trees were chopped to pieces in front. Mc-

Clernand, who watched nearby, saw his orderly shot down. When Burrows and several of his officers fell, the battery became helpless and was captured in entirety.

The last of Marsh's regiments, the 11th Illinois, had been fighting only ten minutes when they saw the sudden rout taking place on their left. Immediately the 11th's line also disintegrated. "[They] fell back, I regret to add, without my order," wrote Colonel Thomas Ransom of the 11th.

Nearby stood McClernand's third battery, (Dresser's) Battery D, 2d Illinois Light Artillery, commanded by Captain James P. Timony. Their guns had been positioned by Major Taylor of Sherman's staff just to the east of a small pool known as Water Oaks Pond, with the 11th Iowa in close support. Their opponents proved to be several of Bushrod Johnson's detached regiments, the 154th Tennessee and Blythe's Mississippi Regiment, coming up from the vicinity of Waterhouse's captured battery. The Tennessee regiment was directly in the 11th's front, moving at a measured pace. Here an Iowa sergeant watched wide-eyed as they approached. "The regiment that was advancing against us was evidently an A No. 1. One look at them was enough to convince a man that courage and discipline are virtues peculiar to neither North or South," said the sergeant. "Without a waver the long line of glittering steel moved steadily forward, while, over all, the silken folds of the Confederate flag floated gracefully on the morning air."

The fighting opened with a roar from the artillery. Timony's guns were served so well that they later earned the praise of Sherman's chief of artillery. "[The fire here was] the most terrific . . . that occurred at any point or at any time during the fight," said Major Ezra Taylor. Indeed, so many horses were shot in their harnesses that all the guns could not be moved in the emergency that followed.

With a determined effort the Confederates forced their way among the battery, enduring terrific losses at every step. Several intact teams that had just been hitched to the guns now bounded off without their drivers, the frightened horses dashing through the lines of infantry and scattering the men. Nearby, the 11th Iowa's major had been shot in the head, and its commanding officer unhorsed. The Confederates were threatening to surround the regiment on the right when the 11th Iowa hastily scattered, three of its companies becoming separated in the chaos. Four guns of Timony's battery were overrun where they stood, completing the near-destruction of McClernand's artillery.

A great disaster now seemed in the offing. Marsh's brigade was a shambles. McClernand's line was pierced in the center, and his whole line had begun to break up.

On Hare's front the Confederates had simultaneously advanced in a massed attack. The dapper, five-foot-one-inch-tall Hindman, inspired by Johnston's promise of another star, had ordered an immediate advance when he came up and found the Federals posted along the ridge across Review field. Hindman led in person, at the head of Shaver's brigade and one of Russell's regiments, the 12th Tennessee. When some of Shaver's men protested that nearly all of their ammunition had been expended during their recent fight with Prentiss, Hindman stopped them short. "You have your bayonets," he said.

The charge carried directly across the open field at Hare's troops, and the field was soon strewn with dead and wounded.

Before Hindman's men could close with Hare's infantry, this Federal line also began to crumble. "We gave them one round of musketry and [we] gave way," later wrote a Federal colonel. One of Hare's regiments fell back without firing a single volley. Even the 8th Illinois, on Hare's extreme left, was thrown into disorder, caused by the stampede on their right. The brigade, already weakened by the detachment of the 11th Iowa, was further fragmentized during the retreat when the 8th fell back in a different direction. The situation by now was desperate, and only circumstance intervened to save McClernand's division.

Following Sherman's urgent request for reinforcements about 7:30 A.M., Hurlbut had detached Colonel James C. Veatch with nearly three thousand infantry to go to Sherman's support. Veatch's brigade was soon started along the main Corinth road for the front, the men marching "with unusual briskness," wrote an officer.

As they approached Review field shortly after 9 A.M., an officer rode up in great haste and directed them to move behind Marsh's brigade, already formed in the woods beyond the Corinth road. Veatch's men quickly moved behind the deployed line, supporting Burrows's battery from the rear. A few minutes later the enemy attacked, and Marsh's troops were routed. Burrows's battery was "belching like a volcano" noted an officer, who watched spellbound as a tall sergeant stood alone to double-shot a cannon and fire it into the faces of the onrushing enemy. Then the battery had been engulfed by a swarm of Confederates. In the ensuing panic, loose battery horses and mules bolted through Veatch's line throwing the 14th Illinois into disorder.

An officer of the regiment, Lieutenant Colonel William Camm, looked up. "I could see the Johnnies running from tree to tree, and popping away at us as they came," said Camm. Volleys crashed along the regiment's front, but the 14th's colonel thought he saw an approaching line of men dressed in blue uniforms. Fearing that they were his own men, he gave the order to cease firing. A moment later the mistake was recognized and the fighting resumed.

"What [horror] followed no man could well describe . . ." said Camm. "I saw our handsome orderly of Company G fall with blood spurting from both temples. Color Sergeant John R. Kirkman rolled the body of his dead comrade off the national colors and rose with both flags in his hands. As he did so a shot passed through [the] folds of the stars and stripes, cutting . . . the staff, then passing through Kirkman's cap, grazing his head."

"The enemy [was momentarily] checked but was very stubborn, and we murdered each other . . . at close range," Camm continued. "Our brigade commander, General Veatch, rode down the line and I asked him to turn us loose with the bayonet. 'No, no,' he said, 'you would lose every man.' My horse was struck behind the saddle and lunged among the men so that I let him go. Throwing myself in front of the colors, [I] tried to get the men to charge, but between us was a struggling mass of wild and wounded battery horses, many of them harnessed to the dead, and I could not get them started."

Much of the burden had already fallen on Veatch's right flank, where the 15th Illinois had been uncovered by the rout of Dresser's battery and its supports. "Everything was confusion around us . . ." wrote an Illinois captain, who saw his regiment suffer severely under "a perfect storm of shell and bullets." The 15th's lieutenant colonel, Edward Ellis, already bleeding from a wound in the arm, was shouting for his regiment to stand firm when a bullet hit him in the chest and killed him. His major was shot through the head, and all but two captains were down when the regiment went to the rear in disorder.

The next regiment in line, the 46th Illinois, fared little better. So many retreating men ran through its ranks that the 46th's colonel attempted to dress the line under fire. A few minutes later "a raking crossfire" claimed nearly 50 percent of those companies formed on the right, including eight line officers, two color-bearers, and the 46th's major. The 46th also fell back in confusion, soon being separated from Veatch's other regiments.

With half his brigade routed, Veatch struggled to preserve his line. The 14th Illinois and 25th Indiana were thrown back on the right to confront the oncoming enemy and were told to lie down. When the Confederates fired over their heads, the 25th's commander had his men jump up and deliver successive volleys. Their efforts were unavailing; the enemy was too many and the Federals too few. "Back, back," shouted an officer. Only when the 25th's major jammed his colors against a fallen tree in the thick undergrowth some distance north along the Corinth road did the regiment stop to re-form.

Veatch now commanded only two regiments. His men were scattered, confused, and frightened. Officers' casualties had been particularly heavy, causing a critical leadership void. Yet Veatch's stand had been most significant. The delay of the enemy was to prove of vital importance, and it was later found that they had inflicted so many casualties upon the Confederates that effective pursuit was disrupted. Moreover, when the enemy hesitated to advance, the Federals began to regain their composure.

Down the road staggered an Illinois sergeant with tears running off his cheeks. Half-choking, he passed among his men telling them that they must die where they stood rather than break again. This seemed to encourage Veatch's men. By the time a few of Wood's and Shaver's Confederates swung to the northeast and moved up the Corinth road, several of McAllister's 24-pounder howitzers had been wheeled among the 14th Illinois line to sweep the road.

For a few minutes the cannon and rifles blazed again.

The fighting was so spirited that some of the men said the powder seemed to melt when poured down the barrels of their overheated muskets. When a corporal held up his smashed gunstock and screamed, "What in hell shall I do?" an officer calmly pointed to another weapon lying on the ground. Up the road through a rift in the smoke Lieutenant Colonel Camm of the 14th Illinois saw a mounted Confederate officer in front of his colors, "waving a bright sword, leading his men on."

"Before the smoke hid them again," said Camm, "officer, horse and color all went down." In a few minutes the firing abated. With help of the artillery the Confederates were beaten off, apparently demoralized.

Indeed, when the smoke cleared Veatch's men were so encouraged they even discussed advancing, "thinking all was going well."

A Confederate private who had participated in the Review field attack remembered this, his first battle, as a painful experience. The fighting, he thought, "was an awful thing. . . . It terrified my mind to hear the guns . . ." and he reflected that he had not words strong enough to describe the conflict. "Oh, God," was his prayer, "forever keep me out of such another fight."

The private was not mistaken—the volume of Federal fire had been tremendous and the carnage dismaying. Wood's brigade was inoperative following the charge. Its commander had been knocked senseless when dragged by his runaway horse through a captured camp. His staff attempted to handle the brigade in his absence, but the regiments were so wasted as to be unmanageable.

The 27th Tennessee, near Wood's right, had suffered as much as any regiment in the brigade. Its colonel had been shot in the chest and killed, just as some of his men were struck from behind by a volley fired by other attacking regiments. A captain was put in command, and when the casualties were counted, the losses amounted to half the regiment. The brigade was so scattered that when the 16th Alabama advanced to the right to attack Veatch following the replenishment of their ammunition, they found no support and had to await the arrival of Shaver's brigade.

Shaver's command had also suffered heavily in the frontal attack across the open field. In the pursuit of Veatch's two regiments along the Corinth road, one of Wood's Tennessee regiments sped in advance. They soon threw Shaver's men into disorder by rushing back pell-mell, having met McAllister's heavy cannon posted along the road. "They were in such great haste to get behind us that they ran over and trampled in the mud our brave color bearer," said an irate Arkansas field officer.

Shaver's troops also took a beating from the heavy blasts of shell and canister coming from Veatch's front. Shaver was unhorsed by the fire, and Hindman, aggressively leading in the front ranks, had his mount killed under him, the concussion of the shell temporarily disabling him.

Most of the Confederate regiments led by Hindman had already been so bloodied that there was little further incentive to resume the advance until compelled to do so. About fifty minutes had been consumed by the attack, and it was now nearly eleven o'clock.

Some of the regimental commanders, left to their own devices, ordered a halt and rested in the captured camps while "awaiting orders." One of Wood's colonels reckoned that his men had been fighting for five hours, and he ordered them to rest. Others marched their men to the rear to find ammunition and stayed there until ordered back to the front.

Even Shaver regarded his men as too exhausted to continue. His ammunition was running low, and he received permission to fall back to Raith's captured camps, to "supply my men with ammunition, rest my men, and await further orders."

Worse still, for a while no one seemed to be in command in this sector. Hardee had been there, along with Bragg, but just before Hindman was disabled, Hardee had gone to the right, satisfied that Hindman was "conducting operations . . . to my satisfaction."

Bragg also had departed following Hindman's attack on Veatch, considering that the brigade could do no more. He already had told Polk to take charge of "the center" and assumed Polk would press on, regarding the enemy resistance here "less strong" than toward the right.

Polk was dismayed to find only three brigades in position to fight following the impromptu transfer of command. Moreover the troops were so scattered that none of these brigades was intact, some being reduced to two regiments in line. The Federals had fled in several directions following the breakup of McClernand's line, complicating the tactical problem of pursuit. Moreover logistical problems continued to disrupt serious attempts to mount an attack. Not only was ammunition in short supply, but regiments such as the 4th Tennessee found their muskets so fouled by powder residue that they could not be loaded.

The result was a disjointed, spasmodic effort on the part of some Confederate units to resume the offensive, while others went to the rear for a rest. A. P. Stewart took two regiments, one of which belonged to another brigade, and swung to the northeast along the Corinth Road. Attacking Veatch's position soon thereafter, this weakened column was unable to make headway. Russell, too, found his troops badly scattered. With only two regiments he went in the opposite direction against Raith, their path carrying them northwest toward the "crossroads." Here they joined a portion of Bushrod Johnson's and Anderson's brigade in a bloody struggle for the important intersection of the Hamburg–Purdy and Corinth roads.

Adolph Englemann, lieutenant colonel of the 43d Illinois Infantry, had considered the weather so warm that morning that he had taken off his brand-new frock coat and buckled it behind his expensive saddle. When the 43d, with the rest of Raith's routed brigade, had withdrawn to the vicinity of the crossroads, Englemann found the fire so hot that he got down from his horse, Peet, and led his regiment on foot. He had just given Peet to a bugler to hold when the animal was struck and killed. "With him went my $50 saddle [and] my new coat," lamented Englemann.

In the confusion of the backward movement the brigade had been disorganized. One Illinois colonel stood out in their midst, rallying the men. As they staggered to a halt, the colonel put them in line near three field guns, still smoking from a recent fight. The colonel proved to be Raith and the guns were Schwartz's, both destined for important service in the minutes ahead.

Raith was among the best liked men in the division because of his pleasant disposition. Yet his life had been unhappy. His lovely wife had died several years before the war, leaving Raith with two young sons to raise. Although a prosperous owner of a flour mill in Illinois, he had chosen the life of a soldier, and became colonel of the 43d Illinois Infantry. When called unexpectedly to command the brigade that morning, Raith rose to the occasion.

Schwartz's battery, originally a Missouri unit with strong German ties, had been organized at St. Louis the preceding summer. Their namesake was a good friend of McClernand's who had been promoted and appointed as division chief of staff.

Schwartz had sent his battery to Sherman's support before eight o'clock that morning. Taking position toward Buckland's right, it had fought a prolonged duel with part of Bragg's artillery, losing several men and horses. Then, when Sherman's line had given way, Schwartz's guns had gone back with them, all except a single gun with a broken trail which had been abandoned.

Schwartz's three cannon, 6- and 12-pounder field guns, finally had been halted at the crossroads and loaded with canister, ready for another fight at close range. Raith used the guns as a rallying point. Two regiments, the 49th and 43d, were formed on the left, while the 17th and 29th eventually went to the right, there joining with Sherman's scattered regiments.

Raith's adjutant, Abram Ryan, had expected to find McClernand's division in the vicinity, having earlier been instructed to fall back and take position here alongside Marsh. But Marsh's brigade was n here to be found, and Ryan was stunned to learn that it had changed its position unannounced. As a result Raith had fallen back farther to the right to join with Sherman, rather than to connect with McClernand.

This development was significant. Following the disaster that befell Sherman along the Purdy road, Raith and Schwartz bought a precious amount of time at a heavy cost in life. In fact their sacrifice may well have saved the entire Federal right flank.

Raith had time only for a short pause before his hastily re-formed brigade was attacked near the crossroads. Among the first troops to approach was a Mississippi regiment of Bushrod Johnson's command. They were led by a mounted Confederate officer, the popular former U. S. Consul to Havana, Colonel A. K. Blythe. Schwartz's cannon greeted the Mississippians with a blast of canister, and Blythe went down in the billowing smoke. When some of his men reached the colonel's side, they found that he had been pierced through the heart by an iron ball more than an inch in diameter.

Anderson's brigade was on Blythe's left, almost in front of Sherman's position, when they noticed the nearby Confederate line wavering and about to give way. The noise was so loud that shouted commands could not be heard. Anderson took off his hat and waved it over his head. "[This gesture] seemed well understood," said Anderson, "and the command, 'Forward,' which it implied was most gallantly executed."

Although Sherman's infantry were so disorganized by the milling mass of runaways along the Purdy road that their fire was ineffectual, Schwartz's battery began to play on Anderson's troops, temporarily bringing them to a halt. After a few minutes, however, a Confederate battery was rolled forward and began to fire with effect against Schwartz. Anderson, provided with the needed support, again led his men to the attack. Their charge fell on Sherman's unsteady line, which broke into fragments and vanished into the thick underbrush north of the Purdy road. As Anderson's men ran in among Behr's abandoned guns, Schwartz's battery prepared to limber up.

The 29th Illinois, on Raith's right, had already fallen back with Sherman's infantry, just as another Illinois regiment on the brigade's left had gone to the rear for ammunition. Raith had only two regiments, the 17th and 43d Illinois, with which to cover Schwartz's withdrawal.

The crisis was extreme, and Schwartz acted boldly to save his guns. While the first section of his battery galloped off, Schwartz led his infantry supports forward to obtain a more favorable field of fire. The 17th moved up about twenty or thirty yards to meet the advancing Confederates before pouring a well-aimed volley into the attacking line. Confederate Colonel R. M. Russell observed that the Federal fire rapidly thinned his ranks, and he later commended the enemy's resistance as "most obstinate and determined."

Schwartz, in the forefront of the fighting, was shot in the leg. The 17th, fearing that they were unsupported and finding their ammunition nearly gone, began to retreat. By now Schwartz's lone remaining gun was in difficulty. So many of its horses had been shot that it could not be removed. When the onrushing Confederates fired into the battery, the few remaining horses went down, tossing the gun on its side. "Our whole line was falling back," wrote Lieutenant George Nispel of Schwartz's battery, " . . . and we were between our troops and the enemy." With five artillerymen Nispel ran to the gun, heaved it upright, and slowly began to drag the heavy cannon off by hand.

During the attack Raith had been holding his 43d regiment in place by sheer determination. By now they were the last Federal troops in line at the crossroads, being just to the left of Schwartz's position. The men of the 43d had been fighting well and were holding their ground when Raith fell. Soon it was discovered that a Minie ball had struck him in the right thigh, inflicting an ugly wound that shattered and exposed the bone. Four soldiers ran to Raith's side and tried to carry him away, just as the regiment fell back in the face of Anderson's flank attack.

They had gone but a short distance, with Raith screaming from the intense pain, when he asked to be left behind. The soldiers, he insisted, could be of more value in the ranks than by carrying off a disabled officer. When he again demanded that they stop, Raith was placed against a tree at the bottom of a ravine, near a small stream. He would lie there unattended for nearly twenty-four hours.

Nearby, Schwartz's remaining gun was being shoved by hand to the rear, some of the 43d Illinois's riflemen having paused to lend their help. Yet the incoming fire was terrific, and the soft ground impeded rapid progress. When Lieutenant Nispel saw that the Confederates were gaining, he rammed a steel spike into the gun's vent tube and abandoned it.

By now Raith's brigade had all but disappeared as an organized unit. Most of the regiments drifted north along the camp road, passing McClernand's encampments before finally rallying among the tents of Hare's brigade. Many of the men were out of ammunition, and their morale was at nadir.

"[The scene] was fearful," wrote one of McClernand's Illinois officers. "[I saw] artillery horses cut loose from the guns [and] cavalry horses, with saddles under instead of on their backs [running wild]. [There were] men with arms, and men without arms; wagons hitched with six mules, the drivers cussing and whipping. . . . All [were] rushing for the rear. . . . Still the muskets volleyed and the cannon thundered, while the smoke rolling up among the trees hid the lines at times, then drifted away."

Ironically, the scene was nearly as chaotic within the Confederate lines. The heavy Federal fire from the crossroads had taken its toll in courage as in lives. Many ranking officers had fallen, among them Clark and Blythe, and it required "nearly an hour" for one of Russell's regiments to rally its scattered men. "I had no idea of war until then," wrote an artillerist of the crack Washington Battery of Artillery, "and would have given anything in the world if I could have been away."

As soon as the fighting abated, entire regiments flung themselves down to rest or went to the rear seeking ammunition. As other troops began pillaging the nearby Federal camps, the entire battleground seemed to be in chaos. The surgeon of the 11th Louisiana remembered with anger that "the sight of all these objects [trophies] lying about in such abundance was too much for our men." They were soon loaded down with "belts, sashes, swords, officer's uniforms, Yankee letters, [and] daguerreotypes of Yankee sweethearts . . ." while others were drunk on "Cincinnati whiskey" and "Philadelphia claret."

In the few Confederate units that went in pursuit of the Raith-Sherman line there was further disorder. Russell was so confused by the appearance of some troops in the brush ahead that he halted his line after overtaking Schwartz's abandoned cannon. "Fearing they were some of our Louisiana troops," said Russell, "I caused the firing to cease and . . . sent forward to ascertain their true character." Conflicting reports were brought back.

Nearby, a scattering of Confederate troops had advanced to the edge of Woolf field and were firing at some of Raith's men. Here the 154th Tennessee, joined by a single gun of Polk's battery, had taken cover behind a fence to shoot at the retreating enemy. Although they were supported by portions of three regiments of A. P. Stewart's brigade, this entire force was soon thrown into disorder and began to retreat.

Here Preston Smith, the 154th's colonel, had attempted to advance across the small field with his mixed command. Once exposed in the open field, they were shot into by two staunch Illinois regiments that had rallied in their front: the 46th of Veatch's brigade and the 49th, originally a part of Raith's command.

Smith's men scattered under this fire, causing their commander to lose control and fall back behind the fencerow. When Barrett's cannon and several remaining guns of Schwartz's battery opened a long-range barrage from the camp of Hare's brigade, the awed Smith ordered a retreat. All of the horses and most of the men with Polk's detached gun were lying in a pool of blood. The sergeant commanding, J. J. Pritle, continued to fire his gun from the fencerow until all hope of saving it was lost. A detachment of infantry sent to retrieve the cannon was driven back, and Smith went to the rear, carrying with him the three regiments from Stewart's brigade.

Russell, who was immediately behind, was also caught in the tumult and had to fall back. A Confederate private felt that the fighting here was so confused that it was impossible later to tell his wife what had happened. "I wish to God that I could tell you all about it but I can't do it," he wrote.

In the disorder that followed, the several regiments that had fought at Woolf field were further scattered. Since nearly all of Wood's and Shaver's brigade had gone to the northeast in pursuit of Veatch, there were few Confederate reinforcements available. Even a large portion of Anderson's brigade had withdrawn from this sector following its easy capture of Behr's guns from Sherman, their commander believing that the diminishing volume of enemy fire indicated an abatement in resistance. Accordingly, when Anderson heard heavy firing toward Duncan field, he turned to the northeast and marched in that direction, having only an aide's advice "to go wherever the fight is thickest."

Crippled by heavy losses and plagued by a breakdown in command and communications, the Confederate left wing was temporarily unable to resume the offensive.

William Tecumseh Sherman had found little solace in the chaos existing amid McClernand's camps as he fell back about 11 A.M. A few troops of Buckland's brigade were still with him, and he told them "to avail themselves of every cover—trees, fallen timber, and a wooded valley . . ." anticipating the necessity of a desperate resistance.

Two regiments, the 46th and 49th Illinois, were observed in front, sniping at the enemy across Woolf field. But their position hindered the deployment of artillery, and they were soon ordered back. Once a fire zone had been cleared, Sherman began to pass among his men, reorganizing a battle line.

Riding through the pall of smoke nearby was "Sam" Grant, resplendent in his major general's uniform. He soon found Sherman, and the two generals here met face to face for the first time on any battlefield. There was a marked contrast in their appearance. Sherman, his uniform torn and a bloody handkerchief wrapped tightly around his hand, was gaunt and disheveled. His wound was inflamed from constant riding, and the pain had begun to numb his fingers.

The thought may have crossed Sherman's mind that Grant would be angry. He had predicted "no attack" at the very time when Grant was relying on him for the utmost vigilance. In consequence the army had been surprised, and presently was in danger of being destroyed. His own division, moreover, had been routed and his camps captured.

Sherman, speaking first, mentioned that he had had several horses killed under him, and he displayed his torn uniform rent by bullets. This attempt to sway Grant's opinion, if such, was unnecessary.

Grant said he thought Sherman was doing well in stubbornly resisting the Confederate attack. Then, indicating that his presence was more needed on the Federal left, he departed following a brief chat. About all Sherman learned from the conversation was that Grant had ordered up a resupply of ammunition and that Lew Wallace was coming from Crump's Landing with his division.

Grant's display of confidence hardly eased Sherman's immediate problem—how to halt the Confederate attack on his front. Placing Barrett's battery at the southern end of Jones field, he sent new orders for his only intact brigade, McDowell's, to move to the left and join with a new defensive line then forming at the camps of Hare's brigade.

McDowell had been only slightly engaged up to this point. His three regiments had run headlong into the Confederates blocking the Purdy road when first ordered to fall back, which had caused McDowell to drift north into Crescent field. After taking position along the edge of the woods fronting the open field, McDowell's men had the satisfaction of driving off Pond's Confederates, aided by a few rounds of canister thrown from a lone howitzer detached from Behr's battery.

Major Sanger of Sherman's staff soon came up with the order for McDowell to move to the northeast. Accordingly McDowell's men were led through Sowell field, en route to join Sherman. When they reached the farm buildings along the eastern edge of the field, McDowell deployed his regiments in an open woods, fronting nearly south.

Since the artillery of both armies was firing nearby, shells began to crash among the trees, exploding above the infantry's heads. "[It caused] us to hug [the] dear earth in earnest," remembered one of McDowell's Illinois soldiers.

On their left Sherman had finally formed a bedraggled collection of mixed troops, including the 70th Ohio of Buckland's brigade. Close by, Barrett's battery was firing repeatedly at a conspicuous target—Confederate artillery placed among the tents of the 45th Illinois in Woolf field. Even a howitzer of Schwartz's battery had been rolled forward to fire alongside Barrett, and their shells were seen to take effect in the distant lines, driving the Confederate troops to cover.

Sherman's men began to take heart. More importantly Sherman, apparently sensing the disorder in the Confederate ranks, began to reassess his situation.

Quite spontaneously an irregular though formidable line had gathered on his left. Men from Marsh's brigade stood alongside those from Raith's and Veatch's commands, all under McClernand's critical eye. Also of significance was the recent arrival of a fresh regiment earlier sent to guard a bridge over Owl Creek. Carrying common hunting rifles, with bullet pouches slung over their shoulders and squirrel tails bobbing gaily as they walked, the 13th Missouri Infantry, known as Birge's Sharpshooters, filed among Sherman's men. "We felt sorry for them," wrote a powder-grimed Illinois officer, who wondered if they could stand a charge without bayonets on their guns.

Already an hour had passed since the Confederates had overrun the Purdy road line. Although cannon were firing from within their position, the Rebels made no attempt to attack. Sherman conferred with McClernand. It was decided to advance and recapture Marsh's camps.

Sherman's staff officers galloped among the mixed commands and ordered them to advance. McClernand, assisted by three of his staff, also rode among his men and gave the order, "Forward." About twelve noon a long, ragged line of soldiers in Federal blue got up and began to move cautiously toward the Confederate positions near McClernand's captured headquarters.

Marsh's troops, in the van, soon came under a brisk fire from the Confederate cannon near the 45th Illinois's camp. As their line marched over the brow of a knoll, the Federal troops halted and delivered a volley before resuming their gradual advance. In this manner they fought their way past the camps of the 11th and 20th Illinois at the north end of Hare's encampment.

By now the Confederate cannon were within easy musket range, and the concentrated Federal fire felled so many men and horses that the survivors abandoned their guns and fled for cover.

On Marsh's right Sherman's mixed command was also moving up, although unsteady under the incoming small-arms fire. They were soon joined by McDowell's brigade, advancing west of McClernand's camp road. "We moved in line of battle up the hill about fifty yards," wrote one of McDowell's men, "when we came into a narrow open space, in plain view of the enemy. . . . [Our troops] were firing rapidly, and when they saw us they cheered loudly, waved their hands, and welcomed us to their relief."

Once on top the ridge the Federals, encountering stiff opposition, learned that the Confederates had been reinforced, just at the critical moment. Try as they might, McDowell, Sherman, Marsh, and Mc-Clernand were unable to make further headway. The Confederate troops stubbornly stood their ground, taking heavy losses in a fire fight that lasted more than three-quarters of an hour. Here the blood flowed so freely that McClernand later found enemy bodies so thickly strewn over a radius of two hundred yards from his head-quarters tent that the ground was nearly covered.

The man who had restored the Confederate lines was an obscure Kentucky lawyer in his later thirties, a descendant of a Revolutionary War veteran who had once served under George Rogers Clark, Colonel Robert Paxton Trabue of Breckenridge's Reserve Corps. Trabue had been following in the rear of Bragg's troops earlier that morning when Beauregard detached nearly half of his brigade to go to Anderson's support.

Taking his four remaining regiments and Cobb's battery of artil-lery on a line due north, Trabue had approached Crescent field following the arrival of McDowell. Here his troops came under fire from McDowell's howitzer, which cost the provisional governor of Kentucky, George W. Johnson, his horse. Johnson was determined to take part in the fighting, however, so he found a musket and joined the ranks of the 4th Kentucky as a private.

While Trabue reconnoitered the ground in front, Cobb's battery was removed to the east, apparently by a staff officer, where they un-limbered in the 45th Illinois's captured camp. Here, in a matter of minutes, they lost nearly all of their horses, and thirty-seven men killed and wounded. Ultimately the battery had to be abandoned in the face of Marsh's advance.

Trabue, pressing on without his missing battery, moved through the open woods and met McDowell's troops, just as they advanced to Marsh's support near the 20th Illinois camps. The Confederates fired first, their officers shouting drill-field commands to steady the men. "By this means . . . their aim was not a mere mockery of the word," reported an officer of the 4th Kentucky.

The 46th Ohio, Colonel Tom Worthington's regiment, was in their immediate front. Worthington was excited, and he kept yelling,

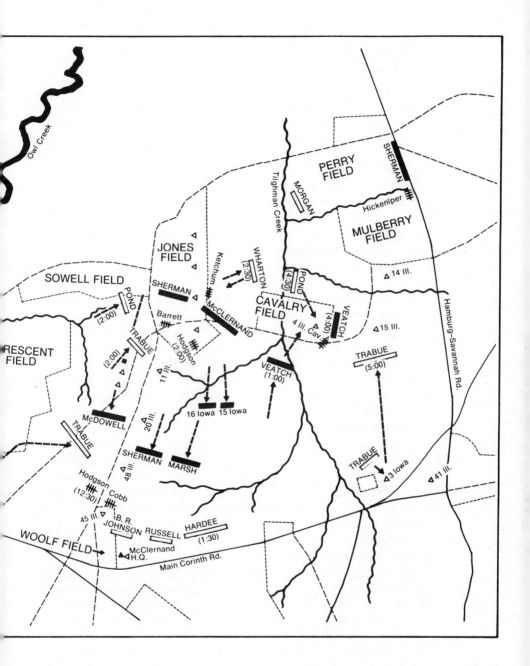

MAP 12
Action on the Federal Right
12 noon–5 P.M., April 6 (Chapter 17)

"Squat, boys! Squat! Damn you, squat for your lives . . ." as they changed front to meet Trabue's Kentuckians.

Worthington's advice was of little consequence. The 46th took heavy casualties, being fired into from the front and flank. After returning the volley, the 46th broke for the rear in disorder. In the melee Worthington's horse was shot twice and dropped to its knees, throwing its rider. Worthington had to chase after his men on foot and finally succeeded in rallying them behind a nearby knoll.

Although the entire Federal line was wavering, Trabue hesitated to attack. "Ignorant of the topography . . . and not knowing his force, I was . . . reluctant to charge," Trabue said later. Given this opportunity, McDowell's troops re-formed behind the crest of a ridge and settled doggedly in place, fighting Trabue's Confederates for an hour and a quarter.

The appearance of Trabue's troops proved to be a harbinger of still greater difficulty for McClernand and Sherman. Although portions of Russell's, A. P. Stewart's, Anderson's, and Bushrod Johnson's brigades had moved up to fight Marsh, the most damaging development proved to be the arrival of Hodgson's battery of the Washington Artillery. These young bluebloods of New Orleans already had seen spirited fighting against Barrett's battery at Shiloh Church. About 12:30 P.M. Hodgson's field guns were unlimbered in the middle of Hare's camp. Some Federal infantry at the time were only fifty yards distant, and Hodgson opened with canister, spraying the tents where a line of sharpshooters lay. "Here we suffered terribly," wrote one of the Louisiana cannoneers, ". . . we were placed face to face with [the enemy], and . . . found out the danger of sharpshooters. . . . The balls hissed around our heads and struck at our feet. I shall never forget my feelings when I saw the first man killed, he was within 20 feet . . . and [when] struck in front of the ear, fell backward, expiring without a groan."

Soon the fight became "too hot for us," confessed the cannoneer, and at least one gun was limbered up and run to the rear. The Federal fire was so accurate that Hodgson thought the sharpshooters were using "white powder, or some other preparation which discharged their arms without report."

Still the battery continued to fight off its attackers. "[I] saw his cannoneers stand to their pieces under a deadly fire when there was no support at hand," wrote an admiring Confederate officer. ". . . To have retired [then] would have left part of the field to the enemy."

Moreover, Hodgson's fire played havoc in the Federal ranks. Colonel Hicks of the 40th Illinois was directing an attack on the battery when his horse was shot from under him. As he jumped to his feet, a ball hit him in the left shoulder, again knocking him down. By now the 40th had approached to within two hundred yards of the bellowing guns, but here they were driven to cover, the men falling flat on the ground to escape the storm of canister.

In front of Cobb's disabled battery Marsh's men also had been unable to fight their way closer than two hundred yards of the abandoned cannon. McClernand was nearby, attempting to prod the men forward. By his urging the Federal line again crept forward, moving a few yards at a time. Here the 46th Illinois, separated from Veatch's brigade, saw their colonel plant the regimental colors in front of their battle line. The 11th Iowa, also close by, was fighting stand-up fashion, with closed ranks. Even the 11th Illinois, reduced to 115 men, made its presence felt.

Their effort fell short, however, when a regiment on Marsh's right, probably the 11th Iowa, retired. The Iowans were low on ammunition and were about to pull out when a green regiment coming up to take their place gave way, throwing both regiments into disorder. Thereafter Marsh's regiments were exposed on the flank and, one by one, went to the rear, re-forming in the timber near Jones field.

It was now nearly 1 P.M. McDowell's brigade was still fighting in the open woods west of the Camp Road, and McClernand, undaunted by the repulse, determined to return to their support. Moreover he had reinforcements—two fresh Iowa regiments and a portion of Hare's brigade, which now extended his line to the southeast.

Although some regiments had already dropped out of line (the colonel of the 46th Illinois thought his men tired, hungry, and out of cartridges, and finding himself within one-half mile of his regimental encampment, he marched them there and got dinner), McClernand's second battle line was even stronger than his first.

Spearheading the attack were the two Iowa regiments, newly arrived at Pittsburg Landing, having been issued ammunition for the first time that morning.

The 15th Iowa had been aboard the *Minnehaha* waiting to disembark when the distant guns sounded about 7 A.M. Amid the growing turmoil at the Landing, the 15th formed and started for the front nearly three hours later, their orders being to advance to the support of Dresser's battery at Water Oaks Pond. On their way forward along the Camp road they met the shattered remnant of Dresser's battery returning to the Landing—the gunners were out of ammunition, so they said. "This looked rather awkward," thought one of the 15th's officers. Back at the Landing the 15th had witnessed "great numbers of stragglers" milling about while "officers of all grades rode and walked around, praying, cursing, and imploring the men to form again." The men of the 15th Iowa began to fret that they were in for a severe baptism of fire.

On their right flank marched the 16th Iowa, equally raw and also assigned to Prentiss's division, although unable to join that command at the beginning of the fighting.

Together the two regiments approached Jones field and filed into line of battle, taking a beating from the Confederate guns as they advanced across the open ground. Passing into the timber, an officer assessed the difficult situation confronting them: "In front of us on a gently sloping hill, very thinly timbered, lay the enemy behind tents, which in their advance they had previously captured from our forces. They were almost hidden from our view, the tents, logs, and stumps affording them a good screen." Another Iowan, a lieutenant colonel, thought "it promised to be a clear case of butchery," and he bade his men lie down, telling them to half-rise when ready to fire. In this manner the Iowans, aided by another regiment on the right, maintained their line until nearly half of the 15th's commissioned officers were casualties. Included in this total was their colonel, who took a bullet through the neck and fell from his horse, temporarily paralyzed.

During the advance of the two Iowa regiments, McClernand had succeeded in pushing forward some mixed troops commanded by Marsh and others. Their charge was led by Major Mason Brayman, a former lawyer and newspaper editor, now McClernand's acting adjutant. Brayman led his men straight at the muzzles of the waiting Confederate artillery. When the 18th Illinois's line wavered, Brayman grasped their flagstaff and carried the colors forward. Along with the blasts of canister, Brayman's troops had to contend with two new Confederate regiments, the 2d and 15th Tennessee, ordered up to replace the 154th regiment, then out of ammunition.

Again the Federals were brought to a halt, though still maintaining a heavy fire. And the inadequately supplied troops were using ammunition faster than anticipated. "[My] men gathered a scant supply [of cartridges] from the killed and wounded of the enemy, who here covered the ground thickly," wrote an embattled Federal lieutenant colonel. When the few Enfield rifle cartridges found were expended, his troops were without ammunition, and they had to retire.

Other regiments, including the 11th Iowa, found not only that their ammunition supply was dwindling, but that the few cartridges they possessed were of poor quality. "One of our greatest misfortunes was the want of suitable cartridges," complained a sergeant. "The powder used in them was of such a poor quality that after firing the first few shots the guns were so dirty that it was almost impossible to load them, the bullet being forced down with the greatest difficulty."

The fighting during the second assault lasted only about a half-hour, according to one account. Several regiments having gone to the rear for ammunition, McClernand found that he could not maintain his advanced position. Reluctantly he rode down the line and told the troops still fighting to fall back.

The two Iowa regiments were among the last to retreat because of a delay in communicating the order. By now so many troops were running back that the Iowans became disorganized and soon scattered to the rear in confusion.

More than merely an interested spectator of this fighting was Confederate Major General William J. Hardee, the renowned military authority. Hardee had been to the right, where he found Sidney Johnston directing the battle, and had passed back toward the crossroads, arriving in the midst of the fight with McClernand in Marsh's camp.

Observing that "the enemy in front was much shaken," Hardee now put four regiments under cover of a ravine where they outflanked McClernand's line and ordered them forward. One of the colonels involved, Alexander Campbell of the 33d Tennessee, said he called to the regiments in advance to charge the Federals, "which they declined doing." Campbell's regiment had already moved to the top of the knoll and was exposed to a severe fire. "Knowing that I must advance or retire," said Campbell, "I ordered the 5th and 33d Tennessee to charge, which was done in most gallant style. . . ."

McClernand's and Sherman's determined defense of their last remaining camps here came to an abrupt end. With Hardee watching, the Confederates charged at a run through the residue of McClernand's line, which "gave way in tumultuous rout," said Hardee.

The sudden relief in pressure must have been noticed by Trabue, fighting just across the Camp road against McDowell. Joined by a portion of A. P. Stewart's, Anderson's and Russell's command, Trabue shouted orders to fix bayonets and advance at the double-quick.

McDowell had already gone to the rear, being disabled by a fall from his horse. His brigade was now caught in a cross fire and fell back. In the terrible smoke and confusion some of the Federals were trapped, among them an eighteen-year-old drummer boy with the 6th Iowa. He had lost his drum during the earlier retreat from camp and was angry with himself. "They took my drum, but I did not care for that," he wrote. "I got a gun and went in for life or death." When captured, he apparently had a small pistol concealed in his belt. "They took me prisoner and put one man over me, [but] I shot him, then ran for my regiment." Others were not as fortunate, however. When a count was taken following the battle, it was found that nearly forty men of the 6th Iowa had been captured.

Although converging zones of fire, mistakes in identity, and the thick undergrowth hampered Trabue's pursuit, the Washington Artillery continued to fire on Sherman's artillery in Jones field. Barrett's battery soon began to take heavy losses. "The fight between the enemy and the battery [Barrett's] in our front soon became quite exciting," said a Federal eyewitness, "but our battery seemed to get the worst of it. . . . They were compelled to fall back and leave one of their guns, which was promptly . . . brought off by our boys."

Like many of the blue-uniformed troops in the vicinity of Hare's camps, Barrett's battery soon went to the rear, quitting the fight for the remainder of the day. Among the regiments and fragments thereof that remained there was great disorder.

Some troops called for cartridges, but there were few to be had. The 11th Iowa had fought hard in front of Cobb's battery, which they had nearly taken, and still retained a captured Confederate battle flag picked up in the fighting. When they streamed back to their tents to get a resupply of ammunition, they found that it had been hauled to the river a half-hour earlier. After searching in vain for more, they marched to the river with empty rifles. Their experience was typical. The battered 43d Illinois had been promised a resupply at Hare's camp by Colonel Marsh, but when it could not be found, the men had to retreat. Although Grant had told Sherman that ammunition had been ordered up, the wagons were nowhere to be found. Officers were so desperate for cartridges that some paused to search Hare's deserted camps on their way to the rear. Even more disconcerting was the fact that once munitions were located, they were not always of the correct caliber, since a variety of weapons were in use within the army. "Searching through the encampment of the 8th Illinois Regiment, I found ammunition and carried it to the brigade," wrote an exhausted Federal adjutant, "but it proved to be of a wrong caliber." Desperately he galloped to the rear, seeking an ammunition train. When he returned, he found to his dismay that the needy regiments had scattered.

Elsewhere amid the debris-strewn woods, an aide found a dispirited regiment lying on the ground, distant from the fighting. "What regiment is that?" he demanded. When told the 40th Illinois, he shouted, "In the name of God, why are you not moving against the enemy?" The reply was that the men had spent all of their ammunition. The aide fairly exploded: "Then fix bayonets and you can meet them when they come; for they are massing their forces in our front and will evidently press us. . . ."

Ironically the aide was wrong. Although Sherman's and many of McClernand's regiments were scattered and disorganized, thus being vulnerable to an attack, the Confederate offensive was slowly sputtering to a halt in the rugged area north of Hare's camps.

Trabue's infantry went cautiously forward, not north in the direction of Hare's camp, but nearly east, along the camp road, toward the cavalry field. When they met some troops dressed in blue uniforms, later found to be Pond's Louisianans, they both came to a standstill.

Hardee's few cooperating regiments were plagued by an ammunition shortage. When they were belatedly supplied, they also went east, in the vicinity of Duncan field. Only the Washington Artillery of New Orleans seemed to continue their fire into the retreating Federals, streaming northeast toward Perry field. It was about 2 P.M. when Hodgson's Louisianans moved up and opened fire from Hare's abandoned camps, throwing their shells into some of Veatch's and Hare's troops near the cavalry field.

About the only positive action Hardee was able to take was to throw some cavalry in the direction of the Federal retreat. Beauregard, who was nearby, told Hardee to "push forward" the cavalry, noticing Wharton's Texas Ranger Regiment dismounted and standing idle in support of a nearby battery. Hardee summoned Wharton and ordered him to mount his regiment and intercept the enemy retreat. This soon proved to be another ill-fated venture.

Wharton, a boyish-appearing Texas lawyer, went forward with his regiment into boggy Tilghman Ravine, where some of McClernand's troops were concealed on the opposite ridge. Wharton's men were strung out, proceeding in single file, when they were fired into by the supposedly "routed" enemy. Wharton was hit, and his regiment, being unable to deploy in the marshy ravine, fled to the rear.

Only Captain John Hunt Morgan's squadron of Kentucky horse was later able to close with the enemy. Riding forward under Hardee's orders to "charge the first enemy he saw," Morgan took his men northeast, in the direction of Sherman's broken line. Coming up with a line of skirmishers across an open field, Morgan at once ordered an attack. In his front was Hickenlooper's Ohio Battery, which had fought much of the day with Prentiss but had recently joined with Sherman for further duty. An Illinois regiment, said to be the 29th, was in close support. McClernand was with them.

As Morgan's cavalrymen dashed at a full gallop across the open field, Hickenlooper's canister raked their already thin line. The Kentuckians were well mounted, however, and chased the skirmishers back through an open woods until they suddenly came face to face with the 29th's entire line. "They delivered one stunning volley," wrote one of Morgan's men, "the blaze almost reaching our faces,

CAPTAIN JOHN HUNT MORGAN. "The Thunderbolt of the Confederacy," Morgan served as a captain at Shiloh (was later promoted to colonel retroactive to April 4). He led the unsuccessful cavalry attack on Sherman's last line near Mulberry field on Sunday afternoon. (HUNT-MORGAN HOUSE, BLUEGRASS TRUST, LEXINGTON, KENTUCKY)

and the roar rang in our ears like thunder." Morgan saw that his small squadron was no match for infantry and artillery, and his men scattered in disorder to the rear.

Although Sherman did not realize it, the serious fighting on the extreme Federal right flank had already ended.

McClernand and Sherman had agreed during the afternoon to fall back to the Hamburg–Savannah Road, near Perry field. Sherman wanted to protect the bridge across Snake Creek that Lew Wallace would use in marching to the battlefield, but when he got there, he had trouble advancing the remnant of one of his regiments to a forward ravine where it could protect artillery re-forming along the road. When a one-armed Illinois officer belonging to another division, Colonel Thomas W. Sweeny, volunteered to go forward, Sherman agreed, saying he wanted the ravine converted into "a regular bastion."

Sherman's anxiety proved unfounded. When Grant came forward about 3 P.M., he speculated that the enemy had expended the "furor" of his attack in this sector, although things did not look bright on the Federal left. Sherman, with a mixed command of bedraggled but resolute infantry, then stood along the roadway behind McArthur's drill field, watching the enemy's "cautious approach" for the remainder of the day.

Only toward the left, where McClernand's prolonged and irregular line was anchored in Cavalry field, was there spirited action.

Fortunately for the Army of the Tennessee James C. Veatch's brigade had not been entirely scattered during the breakup of Mc-Clernand's initial line near Review field. Veatch had been able to keep two regiments together during the ensuing chaos, and he put them in line along the Corinth Road east of McClernand's subsequent position.

After repulsing Shaver's and a portion of A. P. Stewart's attack along the Corinth road, the 14th Illinois and 25th Indiana had gone north, to a ridge on the west side of Tilghman's Branch of Owl Creek. Here Veatch was able to link up with some of Hare's infantry and form a substantial line. "Our guns cooled and we got a new supply of ammunition," later recalled one of Veatch's officers. "There was only a skirmish fire on our right and front, but to the left in the direction of Prentiss's division, the battle still made a loud, overpowering roar."

Several hours later this line still had not been attacked. Yet someone thought it best to withdraw across the creek valley and occupy a new position just west of the 15th Illinois's camp. Here, along much of this new front, lay Cavalry field, with the deserted tents of a cavalry battalion standing stark against a rugged backdrop of timber.

About 4 P.M., just as Veatch's line was settling in place, a Confederate regiment dressed in blue came up and occupied the former Union position. This unit was Pond's 18th Louisiana Infantry, commanded by the bantam-sized former railroad engineer, Jean Jacques Alexandre Alfred Mouton. Mouton was French, like many of his men, and his volatile temper was already aflame.

As Pond's brigade had gone forward against McDowell's abandoned camps earlier that morning, only half of the brigade was present. Pond characterized his advance as extremely cautious. Since he was posted on the army's extreme left flank he thought it necessary "to keep my force in hand to hold Owl Creek against any and every contingency." Because of going slowly, his two regiments and a battalion had not seen significant action prior to the Federal retreat from Jones field, about 2 P.M.

At that time the 18th Louisiana Infantry, coming up on the left of Trabue's Kentuckians, somehow got in front, and as a nearby Confederate officer observed, their blue uniforms cost them dearly. Mouton noticed about five hundred of Sherman's men in full retreat from Hare's camps and he rushed his regiment "at double-quick" to cut them off.

Trabue's men were then close to the 18th's flank, but were unnoticed. Seeing the blue uniforms ahead, they opened fire, immediately throwing Mouton's regiment into disorder. When the artillery joined in, the shaken Louisianans became angry. Shouting "we fire at anybody that fires at us, God damn," the 18th returned the fire. Finally a staff officer went to investigate and signaled both parties to cease firing. Only then did the bloodshed stop.

Pond had become thoroughly confused by the exchange. Not knowing where the fire came from, he imagined that he had bypassed a large enemy force. After halting his brigade, Pond ordered a retreat back to the edge of the woods. There was much delay before the 18th warily advanced into Hare's vacant camps and rounded up twenty Federal prisoners, who apparently had been too sick to run away.

Not only was Trabue's advance disrupted; the entire Confederate offensive in this sector stalled when Pond further procrastinated. Although his line had quickly re-formed, Pond decided to await the arrival of Ketchum's battery before proceeding to the front. In all, nearly two hours elapsed before Pond received "a peremptory" order from Lieutenant Colonel Ferguson of Beauregard's staff to move his brigade forward.

All this time McAllister's battery of 24-pounder howitzers had been shelling the Confederates from a ridge east of Tilghman Creek. When Ketchum's guns finally came up to join Hodgson in Jones field, the two batteries began firing shell and spherical case into Cavalry field, driving some of Veatch's Federals from the abandoned camps back into the woods.

The prospect for a successful charge now seemed good, if it was supported by Ketchum's field guns, which were gradually being advanced by half battery. Yet here occurred another of the tactical blunders that had been plaguing the Confederate attack since morning.

Lieutenant Colonel Samuel W. Ferguson, U.S.M.A. 1857, was an aide-de-camp on Beauregard's staff. Sent by that general to assume command of a brigade "without a commander," Ferguson was led to the wrong portion of Pond's command, that consisting of the 16th and 18th Louisiana and the Orleans Guards Battalion, which Pond still led.

On his way forward Ferguson had encountered General Hardee. Hardee told him to lead Pond's troops "by the left flank as far as possible to the rear of a camp of the enemy . . . and, if possible, to take it in reverse."

Ferguson and Pond thus inevitably collided. Pond resisted turning over command to a junior officer, and when Ferguson made a reconnaissance and ordered a charge, there was a dispute. Both attempted to command.

Unknown to Pond and Ferguson, an aide from General Hardee's staff had just approached Ketchum's battery and ordered it further to the left, where some of Sherman's infantrymen were believed to be re-forming.

Deprived of half their artillery support, Pond's Louisianans filed into the ravine of Tilghman's Creek and moved haltingly forward. Ahead another ravine bisected the creek valley, running east between the camps of the 14th and 15th Illinois. Pond hoped to use the second ravine to cover his approach to the enemy's open-field perimeter. But when only halfway along this ravine, Ferguson ordered a direct assault. Although McAllister's battery was immediately in front, the distance was great—about three hundred yards.

Pond thought it a mistake. So did Mouton, but they ordered their men up the slope, the several regiments still being in column. Three of McClernand's regiments, the 8th and 18th Illinois and the 13th Iowa, together with two of Veatch's units, the 14th Illinois and 25th Indiana, held the timber that skirted Cavalry field in front.

Running over the rim and onto the open ground came the blue-coated Louisianans, their advance being closely watched by one of Veatch's Illinois officers.

"[They] dashed up the slope . . . with a loud yell, square in the face of McClernand's men, and in front of two [24] pounder [guns]," observed the officer.

Veatch had planned a warm reception, already having swung the 14th Illinois obliquely to the front so as to fire into the Confederate flank. A crossfire of artillery and musketry now swept through the 18th Louisiana's ranks, and a quick and bloody repulse was the result.

"The yell was . . . taken out of them," wrote a jubilant Federal officer, "but they right faced and went off in such good order that a shell from one of the [cannon] cut the same thigh off a file of four, and then cut a file closer—a sergeant, nearly in two."

Having taken losses that amounted to 207 officers and men, or about 40 percent of those present, the 18th Louisiana staggered away to the north and out of the fighting for the day. Although their brigade confronted Sherman during the early-evening hours, they posed no serious threat to the vital Hamburg–Savannah Road line. "I was alone with my brigade," wrote Pond, "without any . . . support." As a result he merely moved up to within three hundred yards of the roadway and opened a desultory fire with artillery, which was suspended at nightfall.

Pond and his men had been thoroughly shocked by the debacle they had witnessed. "The order to charge the battery was prematurely given," they later protested. Had they understood that the attack itself was unnecessary, there would have been even greater despair.

*   *   *

Emboldened by their success against Pond, McClernand's and Veatch's men were about to organize a countercharge when the bright prospect of triumph suddenly turned to impending disaster.

The 25th Indiana and 14th Illinois were still firing at Pond's retreating troops, just as the broken fragments of Federal troops retreating from the Hornets' Nest line began to appear in wild disorder through the woods. Close behind moved Trabue's Confederates.

The breakup of the Federal line was so rapid that Veatch's two regiments were separated and threatened with being entirely cut off. "I saw nothing left for me to do but reluctantly to withdraw from the advantageous ground occupied," said the shocked commander of the 25th Indiana. Nearby, a dazed Federal officer looked up into a line of gray infantry, halting only a few yards away. "Run, Colonel, run," shouted a sergeant as he dashed by. "In an instant the air seemed full of bullets," said the officer, who began running sideways, fearing that he would be shot in the back.

Passing through a hollow near Hurlbut's headquarters, Lieutenant Colonel Camm of the 14th Illinois found a young soldier running alongside him. "I heard a bullet 'thug' against him," said Camm, "his head fell upon my shoulder and I caught but one word, 'Mother.' "

Continuing his hasty retreat in the direction of the landing, Camm approached his regiment's camp and ran to the nearby spring to quench his burning thirst. "[Here I] found a Rebel soldier, one of the 18th Louisiana, laid full length, spread out and arms downward in the water," Camm recalled. "I pulled the body out and turned it over. . . . He had several bright colored woolen shirts on, evidently intended to resist bullets, but one had struck him in the breast and passed through clothing and body."

Shocked at the sight, Camm passed on to ghastly scenes of carnage as he stumbled toward the Landing. War was no longer the grand adventure that it had once seemed. It was a grisly, deadly earnest business, suddenly abhorrent to nearly all who beheld it.

The faces of the beaten Federal troops streaming north to the Landing reflected the agony of their ordeal. Among them an Illinois lieutenant under McClernand studied the faces of the men of his regiment. "No one ran," he noted, "they just walked on sullen . . . their terrors hidden under the cloud of smoke."

Another officer also regarded the massive pall of smoke. "The clouds of smoke rising all over the field made the day seem like night," he wrote. To many it seemed fitting. The black mood of despair then hanging over the Federal army proclaimed that the battle was all but lost.

CHAPTER XVIII

Brink of Disaster

"As far as the eye could reach," wrote a dispirited Iowa volunteer, "through the woods and over the fields [for] at least a mile, our line of battle [was] in full retreat. Infantry, artillery, wagons, ambulances, [were] all rushing to the rear. [It was] a scene of confusion and dismay—an army degenerating into a rout."

There were many eyewitnesses to the unfolding disaster. Following the collapse of the Hornets' Nest line, the situation seemed so dismal that many thought it would take a miracle to save the Union army. "Everybody for himself!" shouted a soldier as his regiment broke up in the rush to the rear. The confusion was contagious; a growing panic gripped the fleeing men. A frightened young Federal rifleman, cut off from his company, encountered a forlorn Irishman from an Iowa regiment hurrying along the road to Pittsburg Landing. When he asked the man where he was going, the Irishman replied, "Back, bejabers!"—there was too much mixing of the gray with the blue at the front for him.

Another routed Federal, one of Tuttle's soldiers, was running as fast as he could toward the river when a single field gun dashed past, going in the same direction. The gunners sat in their places, and the drivers were lashing the horses for greater speed. Suddenly the gun was halted, unlimbered, and swung around to fire into the mass of fleeing men. Shocked beyond comprehension, the man belatedly realized that they were Confederates. Although, as he put it, "enough Union soldiers rushed by them . . . to pick up gun, carriage, caisson, and horses and hurl them into the Tennessee," no effort was made to capture the gun or shoot the gunners.

To a nearby sixteen-year-old private of a Michigan regiment, the sharp, cutting sounds of Minie balls ripping through the Sibley tents of the camp that he was running past were especially terrifying. Concerned only with a "desire to get out of there," he dashed on with all speed for the landing. "The hair now commenced to rise on the back of my head, and was soon standing up," said the private. "I felt sure that a cannon ball was close behind me, giving me chase as I started for the river. In my mind it was a race between me and that cannon ball. . . . I was never so frightened before . . . [and] I never ran so fast before."

Fortunately for the Union army there were some survivors of the Hurlbut-Prentiss-Wallace line still willing to fight. Munch's battery, escaping from the vicinity of the "crossroads," had found the Confederates rushing through a ravine, attempting to cut off their retreat. "To prevent our being captured," wrote one of Munch's officers, ". . . the guns were once more brought into position." Firing canister at almost point-blank range, Munch's 6-pounder rifles were able momentarily to drive back their would-be captors. Yet immediately thereafter the battery withdrew "amid a terrible crossfire which threatened to kill every man and horse," said an officer. Soon the battery was engulfed in the debris of the Federal left wing streaming back toward the Landing.

Again there was a brief respite. Coming up the road in the opposite direction was an Ohio regiment, personally ordered by General Grant to reinforce what had been the Hornets' Nest line. The 81st Ohio had been detached to guard the bridge over Snake Creek early that morning, and were the only fresh troops available to throw into the contest as the crisis intensified in Prentiss's sector.

The 81st's colonel later wrote that when they got to within close proximity of Hurlbut's headquarters he found a deployed Confederate battle line, flying what he thought were Federal colors. Following the exchange of a few volleys, the 81st drew back to avoid being flanked by a column of Confederate cavalry.

Again the crisis intensified.

Pittsburg Landing had been the focal point upon which the broken and retreating Federal troops had converged throughout the day. By midafternoon the landing area was jammed with thousands of milling, bewildered Federal troops. "Here the scene was humiliating in the extreme," wrote one of the survivors of the Hornets' Nest. "All was an immense mob," he continued, "—a great rout, halting because it could retreat no further."

Another eyewitness, an officer of Grant's staff, was disgusted to find that "the space under the bank was literally packed by thousands . . . of men who from inexperience and fright [had] lost their grip!" At one time he saw a mounted officer waving a United States flag, "riding back and forth on top of the bank, pleading and entreating . . . 'Men, for God's sake, for your country's sake, for your own sake, come up here, form a line, and make one more stand.' "

"The appeal fell on listless ears," he wrote. "No one seemed to respond, and the only reply I heard was someone saying, 'That man talks well, don't he?' " Moreover, when some of the battle-weary fighting men retreating to the landing were also harassed by officers attempting to rally the sulkers, there was a backlash.

To an exhausted private who was suddenly accosted by an officer and chastised for running away, the incident smacked of hypocrisy. "A man on horseback with the cleanest uniform and the brightest sword I saw that day," he wrote, "rode pell mell upon us, and in a loud voice called us cowards, cravens, and the like. He was out of reach of either bullets [or] cannon shot. He ordered us to fall in with his men. We did not, but suggested to him that if he would move to the front he would find something that would take the brightness off his sword. He let us pass."

When many of the soldiers who had fought throughout the day reached the Landing, they were embittered by the spectacle they saw before them. A wounded Iowa corporal, after painfully making his way to the rear, revealed his disgust. "At the Landing I saw those miserable cowards who had run away in the morning. Their officers were vainly trying to rally them and form them in line . . . but many utterly refused to fight."

Another worn-out volunteer, having ridden over much of the battlefield that day, looked about him as he neared Pittsburg Landing late in the afternoon. "All appeared lost," he wrote, "and it seemed . . . [that] it was Bull Run over again."

Nearly a mile away Braxton Bragg sat upon his third war horse of the day and looked at the descending sun. "It was now nearly sunset," Bragg wrote. "[This warned us] to press our advantage and finish the work before night should compel us to desist."

Bragg's orders were urgent and explicit: "Sweep everything forward . . . drive the enemy into the river."

With the mass of Confederate soldiers gathered in the vicinity of the crossroads were three corps commanders, Generals Bragg, Breckenridge, and Polk.

Polk was exuberant. Noting that there was "one hour or more of daylight still left," Polk appraised the situation: "The field was clear . . . the forces of the enemy were driven to the river and under its bank. . . . Nothing seemed wanting to complete the most brilliant victory of the war but to press forward and make a vigorous assault on the demoralized remnant of his forces."

Immediately following Prentiss's surrender Colonel A. J. Lindsay with his regiment, the 1st Mississippi Cavalry, had galloped up to Polk and reported for orders. Lindsay's men had been in the army's rear most of the day and thus far had merely witnessed some of the fighting. Polk promptly seized upon the opportunity to use his cavalry effectively. He told Lindsay "to take command of all the cavalry and go [toward] the river to cut off the enemy's retreat."

While Lindsay went to collect such cavalry as he could find, the 1st Mississippi's lieutenant colonel, John H. Miller, led his regiment forward.

After pushing through underbrush a short distance north, Miller dismounted, apparently to get his bearings. Just then one of his men shouted, "Look, colonel . . . Yankees!"

About three hundred yards ahead Ross's Battery B, 1st Michigan Light Artillery, was attempting to escape with its five remaining guns, having fought most of the day in front of the old cottonfield near the Manse George cabin.

Instantly Miller sprang back into the saddle and shouted, "Charge, boys, charge! For God's sake, charge!" With Miller leading the way, the 1st Mississippi thundered across the intervening ground, "yelling like devils incarnate."

Ross' gunners, however, had also observed the oncoming Confederates. Desperately they halted the battery, unlimbered, and hastened to swing their guns about.

Yet Miller's Mississippians were on top of them before they were ready. "We came upon them so rapidly that they could neither fire nor escape," said one of Miller's men.

The entire battery of four 10-pounder Parrotts and one brass 6-pounder Napoleon was surrendered outright. Under the watchful eyes of their captors, the Federal gunners were made to limber the guns, remount the caissons, and march to the rear, officers and men riding in their places. Soon thereafter the battery was delivered to General Bragg, who was greatly impressed. "It was a sight rarely seen," said Bragg. "[They] were marched to the rear as if on parade."

Although only a small portion of the Mississippi cavalry continued ahead, other commands now galloped forth to pursue the Federals. Forrest's men dashed past Breckenridge, who tipped his hat in salute as they rode by. Soon they charged down the Corinth road, "running through the enemy's lines . . . cutting [many of] them off from the river."

A little later a portion of the 1st Mississippi Cavalry worked its way to the Tennessee. There the men led their horses down the embankment and watered them in the river. Albert Sidney Johnston's boast had at last come true.

Among the trampled and bullet torn tents of Hurlbut's encampment, however, the Confederates were experiencing unforeseen difficulties in capitalizing on their victory. So many troops had been directed toward the rear of the Hornets' Nest from all parts of the field that widespread confusion was evident. Union and Confederate soldiers were mingled together in a large crowd near the crossroads, inviting a mishap. As Polk's troops, comprising the extreme Confederate left, came up to meet Chalmers's men, then on the army's far right, they saw a mass of milling, blue-uniformed soldiers and they opened fire. The bullets struck down so many of the disarmed prisoners that a sergeant of the 14th Iowa said a Confederate officer told them to crawl inside the tents to hide their uniforms. "We did so," he wrote, "but just after there [again] came a heavy fire upon us. . . . One of the most dismal sounds in the world is bullets piercing the tents in which you are, and no chance to see where they come from. We went out of the tents again."

By the time the Confederate officers were able to get the firing stopped, many casualties had occurred, including several among their own troops. A further delay resulted when the prisoners were re-formed and divided into two lines. Finally the captives were turned over to Colonel Eli Shorter of the 18th Alabama, who was ordered to march them to Corinth. According to one of Withers's colonels this processing of the prisoners required about a half-hour.

Since several regiments were nearly out of ammunition another twenty minutes was passed in arranging for a resupply. Many of the Confederates thought the battle had ended and thus began plundering the captured Union camps. "We all helped ourselves to whatever we could find," wrote a thoroughly engrossed Confederate

MAJOR GENERAL LEONIDAS POLK. An Episcopal bishop (Louisiana) and the Confederacy's seventh-ranking general at the time of Shiloh, Polk had been at odds with Beauregard over the withdrawal of his Columbus, Kentucky, garrison. During the roadside conference on the afternoon of April 5, Polk sided with his friend Sidney Johnston. As commander of the third Confederate line of attack, Polk helped outflank W. H. L. Wallace in the Hornets' Nest and attempted to reorganize the milling Confederates following Prentiss's surrender. Yet a portion of his command withdrew to their Saturday-night bivouac that evening and were out of position when Monday's fight began. (LIBRARY OF CONGRESS)

private. "I took a fine carpet sack and filled it with useful trinkets; [I] took pants, cap, drawers, books, blankets, knives, forks, India rubber, knapsacks, haversacks, etc. . . . We [also] found apples, cheese, ham and good things, and ate all we could."

Adding to the disorder among the Confederates near Hurlbut's camps were the terrifying bursts of the heavy gunboat shells—soon to become an increasingly important factor in the battle. "There is nothing a soldier dreads so much as shell!" said one of Bragg's privates, who admitted he sought shelter behind a hill for fear that he would be "cut to pieces." At 5:35 P.M. the *Lexington* and the *Tyler* had taken position just north of the Landing and there opened fire with their big-bore naval guns. The explosions were so loud that an Ohio corporal, crouched on the riverbank beside the gunboats, wrote that the blasts came near "taking our hats off at every discharge." The jarring reports continued with such rapidity that two weeks after the battle the corporal's ears were still "playing tricks" on him.

Their effect in the Confederate ranks was even more pronounced. One of Polk's soldiers, never having heard naval gunfire, "expected to see our troops exterminated . . ." and was terrified as the shells, "striking in the trees mostly in our rear, tumbled them in every direction."

Yet among the Confederates subjected to the shelling there were a few, mostly professional soldiers, who recognized that the danger from the gunboat shells was actually small. Leonidas Polk in his official report commented, "The height of the plain on which we were above the level of the water was about 100 feet, so that it was necessary to give great elevation to his guns to enable him to fire over the bank. The consequence was that shot could take effect only at points remote from the river's edge. They were comparatively harmless to our troops nearest the bank, and became increasingly so as we drew near the enemy. . . ."

Polk was in fact among those most active in attempting to follow up the Hornets' Nest victory. Together with Bragg he helped reorganize the entangled Confederate brigades for the final push toward the Landing.

Bragg was emphatic. His order, "Drive the enemy into the river!" was quickly promulgated. Ruggles, commanding the First Division, was instructed to advance with all the troops he could find, while Withers, Bragg's other division commander, was told to "sweep everything forward."

Slowly, ponderously, the Confederate troops began to move. Chalmers's brigade had just distributed a fresh supply of cartridges, but Jackson's men were mostly without ammunition. Although forced to rely on the bayonet, Jackson's men were also sent forward. Robert P. Trabue's Kentucky brigade had found Enfield rifles among the stacked Federal arms, and two of its regiments were busy exchanging muskets for rifles when ordered to move forward.

"The sun was now near the western horizon," wrote a Confederate general. Infused with renewed ardor, the Confederate brigades filed into Cloud field, near Hurlbut's ransacked headquarters, and formed a new line of battle.

In advance were Jackson's and Chalmers's brigades, the latter being on the right. Behind Jackson's troops portions of Breckenridge's, Polk's, Bragg's, and Hardee's commands were brought up in close support. Advancing through the abandoned camps of Hurlbut's Third Brigade, the Confederates marched onward meeting little opposition, although an increasingly rugged terrain, broken by numerous ravines, slowed their progress.

About 6 P.M. Chalmers's and Jackson's troops cleared a ridge overlooking a gigantic chasm known as Dill Branch and swept down into the deep, vine-tangled ravine. Ahead on the opposite ridge, where the high bluff at Pittsburg Landing overlooked the river, a long line of batteries supported by infantry was drawn up awaiting their approach.

To the somewhat somber though still hopeful U. S. Grant, the events of the afternoon were cause for anxiety. Since midmorning Grant had anticipated the arrival of Lew Wallace's division from the vicinity of Crump's Landing. Following the dispatch of a second courier urging Wallace to make all speed, Grant had gone toward the left, where Hurlbut, Prentiss, and W. H. L. Wallace were deployed along the sunken-road perimeter. Convinced of the urgent need for Wallace's reinforcements following his talk with Prentiss, Grant "became very anxious as the tide of battle was setting against us," observed one of his staff officers. Still, Grant was expecting Lew Wallace to arrive momentarily. That prospect had changed shortly after noon, however, when the cavalry lieutenant sent about 10:30 A.M. to urge Wallace forward returned and reported that Wallace would not march without written orders. Grant fairly burned with anger. He turned to an aide, Captain W. R. Rowley, and told him to go to Wallace and give him written orders if necessary, but to get him to come up with all haste. ". . . See that you do not spare horse flesh," warned Grant as Rowley and several orderlies galloped off.

Meanwhile Lew Wallace had just begun his overland march to the battlefield from Stoney Lonesome, via the Shunpike. Rowley and his escort, traveling by the River road, later arrived at Lew Wallace's Crump's Landing camp only to find it almost deserted. A teamster, just departing with a baggage wagon, was the only source of information. He told Rowley that Wallace had gone up the Purdy road earlier.

Puzzled as to Wallace's route, Rowley hurried on, finally coming up with the rear of Wallace's column on the Shunpike about 2 P.M., following a circuitous ride of six miles.

According to Rowley Wallace's column was found halted with the men taking a rest by the roadside, some regiments having stacked arms in the middle of the road. Galloping past the long column, Rowley soon came up to Wallace, whom he found with the vanguard, "sitting upon his horse, surrounded by his staff, some of whom were dismounted and holding their horses by the bridles." Rowley angered Wallace by saying bluntly that it had been reported to Grant that Wallace had refused to march without written orders. "[That's] a damned lie!" replied the indignant Wallace, pointing out that he was already on the road to the battlefield.

Rowley answered that he hardly thought the road in question led to Pittsburg Landing; that he had already traveled farther since leaving Wallace's camp than in coming from the battlefield to the camp. Wallace replied that this was the only road he knew about and that it led to the Shiloh camps near Sherman's and McClernand's positions.

Rowley was astounded. "Great God!" he cried. "Don't you know Sherman has been driven back? Why, the whole army is within half a mile of the river, and it's a question if we are not all going to be driven into it."

The news fell on Wallace like a thunderbolt. By his own admission he became "rattled."

Then, according to Rowley, Wallace refused to act upon the information until he had checked with his cavalry advance. Riding forward to meet the cavalry, who were already returning, Wallace learned that they had heard musketry in the direction of the river, and it was presumed Rowley's report was correct.

Noting that his command would be "in danger of being entirely cut off" should he continue down the Shunpike, Wallace decided to countermarch.

At the time his advance was within a half-mile of Clear Creek but about four miles from Owl Creek. Only two of Wallace's brigades were present, Whittlesey's Third Brigade having belatedly marched from Adamsville at 2 P.M., following a delay in the receipt of orders.

From end to end Lew Wallace's two brigades were stretched over nearly three miles on the Shunpike, the rear of the column being at Overshot Mill, north of Snake Creek.

Wallace next decided that, rather than reverse the order of march, he would countermarch with his First Brigade, Morgan Smith's, doubling back through the entire length of Thayer's Second Brigade

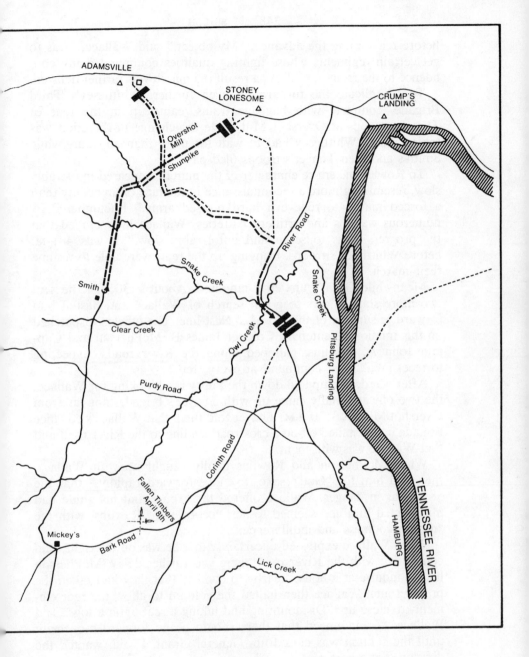

MAP 13
Lew Wallace's March to Shiloh
12 noon–7:30 P.M., April 6 (Chapter 18)

before reassuming the advance. "My object," said Wallace, "was to get certain regiments whose fighting qualities commanded my confidence to the front. . . ." As a result the march was further delayed.

To complicate the turnaround even further, Whittlesey's Third Brigade, complete with baggage trains, came up in the rear of Thayer's troops at Overshot Mill while the change of direction was taking place. Whittlesey had to wait for more than an hour, while Smith's and then Thayer's troops filed past.

To Rowley the entire character of the march "appeared intolerably slow, resembling more a reconnaissance in the face of an enemy than a forced march to relieve a hard pressed army." Encumbered by numerous wagons and artillery batteries, Wallace later agreed that the progress "was toilsome and untolerably slow." It was 4 P.M. before Whittlesey's troops, bringing up the rear, were able to resume their march.

Meanwhile Grant's anxieties mounted. About 2:30 P.M. he sent two more staff officers to go in search of Wallace and hasten him forward in support of the Hornets' Nest line. The officers dispatched on this mission, Lieutenant Colonel James B. McPherson and Captain John A. Rawlins, galloped along the River road, "expecting to meet [Wallace's] command at every step."

After wandering up and down the Purdy road looking for Wallace, the two officers finally came up with Thayer's brigade, not far from Overshot Mill, at 3:30 P.M. Thayer told them that Wallace's advance brigade had just filed off on a crossroad leading to the River road and that Wallace was with them.

When McPherson and Rawlins finally caught up with Wallace, they told him for "God's sake, to move forward rapidly," that the army was in danger. Wallace offered the excuse that his guide had misdirected him and seemed to act, according to Rawlins, with the "utmost coolness and indifference."

When Wallace expressed uncertainty that he was on the right road connecting with the River road, there was further delay. McPherson had to inquire at a house nearby to confirm that they had taken the proper route. Wallace then halted the column to allow the rear elements to close up. "Dismounting and taking a seat upon a log," said Wallace, "I announced that there should be no forward movement until the column was closed up. General Grant, I said, wanted the division, not a part of it. . . ."

Rawlins, McPherson, and Rowley fumed at the delay. According to McPherson the sun was yet three-quarters of an hour high. "I told him [Wallace] to hurry on and we might yet be there in time," said McPherson.

By the hour Wallace's advance finally reached the River road, McPherson was so impatient to get to the battlefield he suggested to

MAJOR GENERAL LEW WALLACE. A dashing thirty-four-year-old lawyer, politician, author, and soldier, Wallace commanded the Third Division. Recently promoted to major general for his service at Fort Donelson, Wallace's star was on the rise before Shiloh. His dilatory march to the battlefield from the vicinity of Crump's Landing earned severe criticism from Grant, however, and began a bitter controversy that continued into postwar years. After Shiloh Wallace's tarnished military career was never fully recovered. Even subsequent fame as the author of *Ben Hur: A Tale of the Christ* did not end his lifelong quest to clear his name. (LEW WALLACE, AN AUTOBIOGRAPHY)

Wallace that the artillery, "which was immediately in the rear of the advance brigade," pull to the side so as to facilitate the march. Wallace agreed, and the men marched briskly on.

Yet when the advance reached the bottomlands near Snake Creek, Wallace met several residents who informed him "that the bridge across Snake Creek was in possession of the enemy." Again the column was halted while the cavalry went to investigate. By now the artillery firing in the direction of Pittsburg Landing was terrific. "We . . . knew that it was our heavy guns, and that the enemy had attained a nearness to the river that filled our minds . . . with terrible apprehension," wrote Rawlins.

When further delays occurred in closing up the column and in reconnoitering the ground, Grant's staff officers watched the sun sink slowly out of sight. It was now plain that Wallace's troops would not arrive on the battlefield in time to be of use that day.

Following the dispatch of Captain Rowley to Wallace about 12:30 P.M., Grant had gone to his headquarters, the little log cabin atop the hill at Pittsburg Landing. On his way there he was nearly killed.

In the company of his staff officers, Grant had just started for the Landing, and was passing along the northern edge of Duncan field to reach the Pittsburg–Corinth road.

Across the field Captain Melancthon Smith's Mississippi battery had unlimbered under orders from General Cheatham to shell the Federals in the vicinity of the Duncan farmhouse. Spying the large gathering of Federal officers, the battery opened fire.

Grant and his staff were slowly moving along when the artillery blasts suddenly took them by surprise. "The shells and balls whistled about our ears very fast for about a minute," remembered Grant, as he and his staff dashed for cover. A few moments later, under the cover of the woods, they heard McPherson's horse "panting as if ready to drop." On examination it was discovered that a ball had passed entirely through the animal just behind the saddle. In a few minutes the horse fell dead.

Grant soon realized how close he had come to being hit. Looking at his sword he found that a missile had "struck the metal scabbard . . . just below the belt, and broken it nearly off." *

Pausing only to allow McPherson to mount Putnam's horse, Grant and his party then galloped on.

Arriving at his Pittsburg Landing headquarters soon thereafter, Grant learned that no word had yet been received from Nelson's division of Buell's army, expected to arrive at any time on the opposite bank of the river. Going down to the *Tigress,* Grant went on board, taking several staff officers with him, apparently to have lunch.

Shortly thereafter, or about 1 P.M., General Buell, having commandeered a small steamer at Savannah, arrived at Pittsburg Landing, where his boat tied up next to Grant's steamer. Informed that Grant was aboard the *Tigress,* Buell immediately went to see him. According to Buell Grant was found at the door of the ladies' cabin, where he had conferred with some of his staff, and appeared to be much worried. "Certainly there was none of that masterly confidence which has since been assumed . . ." wrote Buell.

Contrary to that report, several of Grant's staff officers testified to Grant's calm deportment at the time. Rawlins wrote an account nearly a year later that said Grant responded to Buell's inquiry of what preparations had been made for retreating by saying, "I have not yet despaired of whipping them, General." According to Rawlins this was based upon the expected early arrival of Wallace and of Nelson's division of Buell's army.

By most accounts Grant's conference with Buell was short. Buell said Grant merely displayed his broken sword, briefly discussed the battle, and made arrangements to send steamers to Savannah to bring up Crittenden's division. The two generals then went ashore.

As they left the boat, Buell's attention was attracted to the crowd of stragglers gathered under the riverbank, most of them frightened

---

* In his memoirs Grant wrote that this incident occurred on Monday. Yet Buell, and more convincingly, Putnam, who yielded his horse to McPherson, described the incident as taking place on Sunday.

and panic-stricken. Earlier, on his way up the Tennessee, Buell had observed "a stream of fugitives that poured in a constantly swelling current along the west bank. . . . The mouth of Snake Creek was full of them swimming across," he observed.

As Grant mounted his horse and prepared to ride up the hill, Buell, shocked by what he estimated were five thousand stragglers cowering nearby, began berating them in the strongest language. Finding that his words had no effect, the infuriated Buell next threatened to open fire upon them with the gunboats. When he finally saw that it was of no use, he angrily walked away.

Atop the hill Buell found that "all was confusion." "Men, mounted and on foot, and wagons with their teams and excited drivers, all struggling to force their way closer to the river," wrote Buell, "were mixed up in apparently inextricable confusion with a battery of artillery which was standing in park without men or horses to man or move it." Collaring the quartermaster of an Ohio regiment "who preserved his senses," Buell had the man lead the teams, one at a time, down the hill and park them on the narrow bottom below the landing. Eventually the hilltop was relieved of some of the congestion.

Grant, smoking his "inevitable" cigar, was keeping a calm exterior through it all. Yet there is evidence that he was genuinely shaken. Staff officer McPherson said that during the afternoon Grant was "very anxious," as evidenced by his sending McPherson and Rawlins to find Lew Wallace and hurry him up.

On the other hand a sick and exhausted colonel returning to the Landing later that afternoon found his friend Grant confident and reassuring. "The enemy has done all he can do today," Grant advised. "Tomorrow morning, with General Lew Wallace's division and the fresh troops of the army of the Ohio . . . we will soon finish him up."

To another staff officer Grant "appeared as cool and collected as if all were going as he would have planned."

Despite Grant's composure the battle situation was in no sense under control as the afternoon wore on. "Reports of the capture of the division of General Prentiss were rife [and] spreading like wild fire," wrote a volunteer aide, and it seemed to him that a great disaster was imminent.

Another soldier close to Grant, in fact one of his escort, said that about 4 P.M. "all appeared lost." Shells had already begun passing above the landing area and were falling near the transports. Accordingly the steamer *Rocket,* loaded with munitions, was ordered out of range down the river.

Even Grant was appalled by the deafening roar of musketry and artillery, which he said was "the most continuous . . . ever heard on this continent." As darkness approached, he realized that the enemy was preparing to make a "desperate effort" to capture the Landing and scatter his army.

Out on the battlefield, about 5 P.M., Colonel James Tuttle had rallied the remnants of W. H. L. Wallace's division to form a new line in the timber across the angle formed by McArthur's Camp road and the Hamburg–Savannah road. It was only a tentative, stopgap measure. As senior colonel Tuttle now commanded the Second division, reduced to a few fragments of Iowa and Illinois infantry. Their stand here had been prompted by the proximity of Tuttle's First Brigade encampments, strung out along the secondary paths cleared weeks ago by McArthur's troops on the high ground near the landing.

Tuttle's position was a scant half-mile west of Pittsburg Landing, and his defensive perimeter extended along the outer boundary of the 14th Iowa's camp. This makeshift line had seemed in danger of collapsing at any moment, should the enemy mount an attack.

Yet, as an Iowa soldier wryly noted, the enemy was unable to take advantage of the confusion that followed the collapse of the Hornets' Nest. "When we got out from between them," he wrote, "they pitched into each other, [while] at the same time a battery of ours commenced peppering them. . . ."

The lengthy delay in pursuit that followed was a reprieve to the Federals. Tuttle, able to realign his men and replenish their ammunition, was soon joined by fractions of several regiments that had been separated from their parent organizations.

One of McClernand's units, the 13th Iowa, having re-formed following the breakup of their division's last line, came up and attached itself to Tuttle's command. Two of McArthur's regiments, the 9th and 12th Illinois, having gone to their camps to clean their guns and obtain ammunition, also appeared and joined the line. What had recently been a precarious and uncertain position soon became an extended line, stretching toward Pittsburg Landing along the high ground.

Nearer the Landing Grant's chief of staff, Colonel Joseph D. Webster, a Chicago manufacturer and engineer, had been busily moving Madison's Battery B, 2d Illinois Light Artillery, into position during the later afternoon. Madison's guns were 24-pounder siege cannon, the same five-gun battery that Halleck proposed to draw by oxen for use in besieging Corinth. Shipped from St. Louis on April 1, it had arrived at Pittsburg Landing three days later, where it was parked on the bluff amid the vast quantity of war materiel accumulating for the Corinth offensive.

By Webster's efforts the monster 24-pounders were manhandled into a line facing south, about a quarter-mile from the river. As the broken remnants of Hurlbut's, McClernand's, Prentiss's, and W. H. L. Wallace's commands reached the Landing, other batteries were replenished and added to the line. Major John S. Cavender, commanding a three-battery battalion of Missouri artillery, put Welker's and Richardson's batteries of mostly 20-pounder Parrott guns in line on the right of the siege guns. Stone's battery of 10-pounder Parrotts went in south of the siege guns, taking position near its own camp, where their cannon could enfilade the ravine in front.

Soon other artillery units came up, among them McAllister's and Nispel's batteries from McClernand's division, Brotzmann's from Hurlbut's, and Lieutenant Peter P. Wood's field guns of W. H. L. Wallace's command.

On the extreme left, overlooking the ravine through which Dill Branch ran, was more heavy artillery—several 30-pounder Parrott rifles under Captain Louis Markgraf of the 8th Ohio Battery. Together with two sections of Munch's Minnesota Battery that had fought in the Hornets' Nest, these cannon were pointed straight down the ravine, across which any Confederate attack from the south would have to pass.

From end to end the Federal concentration of artillery spanned nearly a half-mile. Crowded into this space by 6 P.M. were at least ten batteries and their infantry supports, presenting a formidable barrier to the approaching Confederates.

In addition to Tuttle's enlarged command Hurlbut's relatively intact division was present. Its three brigades, although scattered, had been rallied near the Landing and moved back into line along the main Corinth road where they connected with Tuttle. Hurlbut had been told by Grant to take command of the broken and disorganized troops as they arrived at the Landing. He soon had elements of several divisions in line amid the siege guns, including some of Sherman's and McClernand's troops.

Although the majority of McClernand's men had formed along the Hamburg–Savannah road following the collapse of their last line about 4:30 P.M., this prolonged line had quickly been flanked from the south. Veatch's brigade, cooperating with McClernand's division, briefly halted on the extreme left flank near Hurlbut's headquarters. Here the debris of the Hornets' Nest line had descended upon them. "A dense mass of baggage wagons and artillery crowded upon our ranks," wrote Veatch, who was soon bodily unhorsed and separated from his men. The Confederates were rapidly closing in their rear, and Veatch's officers hastily had to give orders to fall back. Taking a severe cross fire, Veatch's and the left of McClernand's line retreated in disorder. ". . . We were run into by the retreating artillery, cavalry, and rabble, which very much scattered my command," wrote one angry regimental commander.

Another of Veatch's officers, caught up in the rout, observed the growing panic. "Cavalry, infantry, and teamsters came running by us at the same time, reporting that the Landing was in possession of the enemy," he wrote. The rumor spread and further dispirited the exhausted troops, who scattered in all directions, seeking safety.

Amid this pandemonium McClernand acted to restore his line. His First Brigade had just begun to fall back when its commander, Colonel A. M. Hare, was shot in the hand and arm. In the ensuing confusion many of the regiments became separated. Hare's replacement, Colonel Marcellus Crocker, led most of his brigade almost due east toward the Landing, where they eventually rallied and fought under Tuttle and Hurlbut.

Yet by the energetic action of their regimental officers the right of McClernand's division had largely remained intact. Using this portion of his division as a base, McClernand soon adjusted the center of his line by ordering it to withdraw a short distance. Colonel C. Carroll Marsh, one of McClernand's best officers, was told to detain all stragglers and put them into the new line.

After a few delays, including a nasty altercation with the colonel of the 13th Missouri whom Marsh threatened with arrest, the new line was formed. "I . . . gathered quite a force and formed a line near the camp of the 2d Division, concealing my men in the timber facing an open field," wrote Marsh.

Meanwhile McClernand was laboring to restore his routed left flank. Again the delay in the enemy's pursuit was instrumental in allowing his scattered units to re-form. McClernand began utilizing any and all oddments to plug the gap, including several Ohio regiments (probably the 81st and 53d Ohio), a portion of Veatch's brigade, and a few Illinois units from his own division. When formed, this line ran at nearly a right angle with Marsh's troops and extended east to Tuttle's position. One of McClernand's officers reported, much to his relief, that they were now able to take the time to obtain a much needed supply of ammunition and provisions from the nearby camps.

With Sherman's mixed command extending McClernand's line along the Hamburg–Savannah road toward the Snake Creek bridge, a compacted Federal line guarding a perimeter hardly more than a mile in length stood between the Confederates and final victory.

Among the exhausted Federal ranks there were those who fully understood that the fate of the army hinged on their efforts during

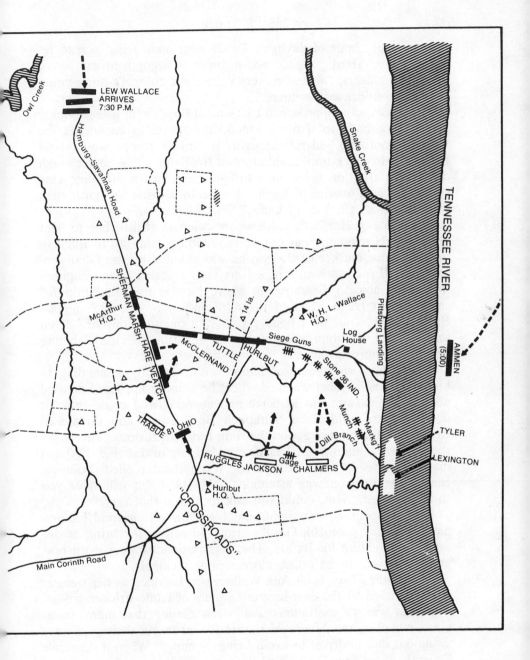

MAP 14
Grant's Last Line
4:30 P.M.–6:30 P.M., April 6 (Chapter 18)

the remaining hour of daylight. Tuttle went among his men to re-assure them. "[His] presence was a tower of strength to us," wrote one of his officers, "and wherever 'Yaller,' the colonel's horse could be seen, confidence was there."

Tuttle was soon approached by General Buell, who was galloping about, apparently in a black mood, attempting to encourage the mass of confused Federals to fight. If Grant's troops would hold the enemy in check until nightfall, said Buell, he would have enough of his own army on the ground to fight alone in the morning. One of Tuttle's men overheard Buell ask his colonel what the battle plan was. "By God, sir, I don't know," Tuttle lamented.

When one of Hurlbut's battle-weary colonels, still willing to fight although his regiment was out of ammunition, rode up to Buell to inquire about musket cartridges, he was stunned by the Ohio general's ire. "I rode to him, touched my visor reverently, and inquired if he were able to direct me to where I could find ammunition," said Colonel Hugh Reed of the 44th Indiana. "No, sir," replied Buell fiercely, "nor do I believe you want ammunition, sir." Reed said he "looked at him in astonishment, doubting his sanity," before turning his horse away.

When Buell spurred after him in close pursuit, demanding to know who the colonel was and where he came from, Reed whirled about. "My answer was as fierce and insulting as I could make it in my anger," said Reed. Although Buell swore and threatened Reed with disciplinary action, he soon rode off, furious. The 44th's surgeon was standing nearby, his eyes bulging in disbelief. "Who is that?—Who is he?" he stammered. When Reed replied, "General Buell," the surgeon was astounded. "My God, he will have you shot," he cried. "How could you talk to him in that way?"

Reed's encounter was significant; the crisis was beyond require-ments of army protocol. Grant's army, pushed to the brink of dis-aster, was fighting for its life. The men's emotions were worn raw, and there were to be other, more serious incidents.

Aboard the *Minnehaha* Ann Wallace was horrified as her steamer was inundated by the ever-increasing mass of panic-stricken troops. The rush was so continuous and overwhelming that many trans-ports, including the *Minnehaha,* were forced to cut their ropes and swing out into midriver to avoid being swamped. When a desperate Federal officer crawled aboard with a revolver and threatened to shoot the pilot if he refused to land and take on his routed men, a disaster was averted by only the narrowest of margins. The pilot pretended to obey but stalled until the officer could be persuaded to put down the loaded pistol.

Another eyewitness saw men plunge into the river in an effort to swim across, only to drown in the attempt. Others swam the mouth of Snake Creek, below the Landing, and hid in the woods beyond.

An Illinois chaplain, leading three ambulance wagons loaded with wounded back to the Landing, had come under artillery fire as his wagons rumbled up a hill near the river. When they halted beyond the fire zone, the chaplain was astounded to find that one of the three wagons was missing. He later learned from a few of the wounded survivors what had happened. The third driver, approaching the fire zone, had become terrified and cut his team loose, leaving the wounded to the mercy of the enemy while he escaped through the ravines. In desperation most of the abandoned men had stumbled from the wagon and painfully made their way to the Landing.

At the Landing the chaplain found the pandemonium so demoralizing that he was at the verge of collapse. Obtaining a drink of brandy from "General Grant's medical director, who by chance rode by," the chaplain felt "temporary strength" return to him. "This was all put forth in speeches to inspire the return to the front of the . . . stampeded soldiers," he said. "Never, perhaps, have I spoken with such power," thought the chaplain, who continued his harangue amid the clamor of the frightened, bewildered men.

Across the river from Pittsburg Landing the vanguard of Buell's army had already emerged from the woods following a grueling three-and-a-half-hour march along an obscure backwoods road from Savannah. Only one brigade was present, and their uniforms were wet and covered with mud. After traveling a good ridge road for three miles, Ammen's brigade had been led by their "fine looking guide" down into what one officer described as a "black mud swamp." "[He consoled] us by saying there was only about five more miles of it to the landing," said Colonel Jacob Ammen, who soon found his men sloshing through mud and water. "If there is a road, the subsiding waters leave but indistinct traces," recorded the weary Ammen in his diary.

Finally the pace of the march was so slowed that General Nelson galloped ahead with his staff and escort. As the roar of the guns became louder, couriers arrived with disheartening news from Nelson. "Colonel Ammen, the general sends his compliments to hurry up or all will be lost; the enemy is driving our men," reported one courier.

Ammen had several of his staff officers ride ahead to intercept any new messengers; he wanted no news of a disaster to reach his men. Riding among his troops, Ammen asked them if they could march faster, for they were needed at the front. Most agreed, expressing an anxiety that the fight would be over before they arrived on the battlefield. "You have seen the elephant often, we want to see him once, anyhow," they said.

Ammen observed the anxiousness of his inexperienced regiments. "The 36th Indiana and 6th Ohio Volunteer Infantry were eager for the fight," he said. "The 24th Ohio Volunteer Infantry had seen the elephant several times, and did not care about seeing him again unless necessary. All three regiments were cheerful, considerably excited, yet cool."

About 4:30 P.M. a portion of Ammen's leading regiment, the 36th Indiana, emerged from the woods and hurried across the meadow that bordered on the Tennessee. By now the noise from the battle was deafening; steam whistles shrieked in rapid sequence, and the shouts of the men could occasionally be heard above the roar of the guns.

"Signals [flashed] urging us to hurry over, which I could not understand," wrote Ammen, who thought the crowd of soldiers observed along the far riverbank were of the unengaged reserve.

While a detail of pioneers labored to cut a road wide enough for the men and their equipment to pass down the bank to the water's edge, the advance four companies of the 36th Indiana hurried to embark on the first transport, said to be a sutler's steamboat.

By knotting the halters of their horses, and then pushing them together over the riverbank, Nelson and his staff were able to take their mounts along. With nearly two hundred infantry and nine mounted officers aboard, the first steamboat churned across the Tennessee.

As they went across, Nelson and his men were appalled at the sight they beheld. Nelson estimated that from seven thousand to ten thousand men "frantic with fright and utterly demoralized" were cowering under the riverbank. As the boat churned through the muddy water, they saw men making their way to the opposite shore on logs. Among them were officers, identified by their shoulder straps, whom some of Nelson's men asked permission to shoot. "Such looks of terror, such confusion, I never saw before," wrote a disgusted officer, "and do not wish to see again."

As the small steamer approached the shore, but still well out from the riverbank, the captain rang the bell to stop. When asked why he did not proceed, the captain replied that he was afraid of running over some of the swimming men.

Nelson, his hot temper already roiled, exploded with anger. Swearing mightily, he told the reluctant captain what he thought of the swimming men. The boat went on.

As the prow touched the shore, the first company jumped off and cleared a small space at the point of the bayonet. They were greeted with cries from the mob. "We're whipped!" "The fight is lost!" "We're cut to pieces!"

When the gangplanks were run out, the second of the 36th Indiana's companies went ashore. Then the hulking Nelson, his six-foot, three-hundred-pound frame stretched to the fullest in an old fatigue coat and feathered hat, mounted Ned, his huge black horse, said to stand seventeen hands high. A staff officer watched in awe as Nelson ordered two aides positioned on each side of him and the other mounted officers in line immediately behind.

Turning to his escort, Nelson shouted, "Gentlemen, draw your sabers and trample these bastards into the mud!—Charge!"

As the mounted party sprang forward, the runaways in front "tumbled over each other in abject terror," observed the staff officer. With Nelson leading the way, the 36th Indiana dashed up the steep hillside shouting "Buell!" to encourage Grant's disheartened troops. It was about 5:20 P.M., and the big guns atop the bluff had already begun firing.

Perched near the crest of the hill was the log cabin formerly used by Grant's postmaster. Standing nearby were Generals Grant and Buell, soon to be joined by Nelson. By most accounts Grant was still cool and collected. As the four companies of the 36th Indiana came up, they were formed on the top of the hill near the log cabin.

BRIGADIER GENERAL WILLIAM "BULL" NELSON. Six feet four inches, three hundred pounds, with a temper to match his huge frame, Nelson led the Fourth Division of Buell's army. A former naval officer and a friend of President Lincoln, Nelson was highly regarded for his work in organizing recruits in Kentucky. Before Shiloh, his insistence on crossing the Duck River at the earliest moment was of crucial importance to the reinforcement of Grant's army at nightfall on April 6. Less than six months later Nelson was dead, the victim of an altercation with a fellow general officer, Jefferson C. Davis, whom he had slapped. (LIBRARY OF CONGRESS)

A vast array of men and materiel was everywhere in sight. Confusion was rampant, and stragglers began running through the 36th's line.

Ahead, the long semicircle of guns was belching flame; overhead, incoming shells were screeching. To one of Grant's staff it seemed the very crisis of the battle. Down at the Landing more of Buell's troops were hurriedly being transported across the river, including the balance of the 36th Indiana.

They, too, found the riverbank jammed with panic-stricken men who impeded their debarkation. In disgust one of the 36th's lieutenants told a demoralized officer on shore that if he was in that much misery he should jump in the river and drown himself. Nelson, who had found the sulkers "insensible to shame or sarcasm," after trying both, wanted to open fire on them.

As still another boat, loaded with three companies of the 6th Ohio, touched shore, they were rushed by a swarm of frightened men. "Some wading breast deep into the stream, were kept off [the boat] only at the point of the bayonet," wrote an Ohio private.

Clearing a path through the crowd, the 36th Indiana, followed by the 6th Ohio, rushed up the hillside. Although a few deserters taunted the new arrivals, there were other, more assuring cheers when they passed through the wounded, higher up the hill. "Give it to 'em, Buckeyes," shouted one of Grant's men as the 6th Ohio sped past. Nearby, an Ohio rifleman caught sight of "a little drummer boy . . . standing in his shirtsleeves pounding his drum furiously."

Throwing down their knapsacks, the new arrivals came into line with the first contingent, which was already formed near the log building. "Shout after shout rent the air, as they moved [into place]," wrote one of Hurlbut's men.

Nelson rode along the 36th Indiana's front "as unconcernedly as if on parade," noted one of his officers. Another of Nelson's aides, Horace N. Fisher, was also riding along the line with several officers, Graves and Carson, when he suddenly saw a cannonball whizzing through the air toward him. Fisher ducked just in time, but Carson, immediately behind, was struck. "I heard a thud and some dark object whizzed over my shoulder," said Fisher. "It was Captain Carson's head."

The incident was observed by the men of the 36th, and their ranks wavered for a moment. "Straighten up that line," shouted their colonel just as Grant ordered Colonel Ammen to take the regiment forward one hundred fifty yards to the support of Stone's battery, then firing across the deep ravine.

It was to be the 36th's first time in battle. The men moved toward the left of Stone's cannon at the double-quick. As they ascended the crest of a knoll, they saw the Confederates in front, advancing through the ravine in two lines. Colonel William Grose of the 36th intended to give the order, "Fire at will, fire!" but as soon as the opposing lines saw each other, they spontaneously opened up.

Throughout the afternoon the heavy siege cannon had stood poised to protect the vital Corinth road corridor to the Landing. Colonel Webster, who arranged their deployment, had foreseen the need for a last line of defense should the reverses of the day continue.

He had utilized the five large cannon as the backbone of his line. All were Model 1839 24-pounder siege and garrison guns mounted on heavy carriages, weighing nearly three tons each. The men had given appropriate names to the guns, including "Abe Lincoln" and "Dick Yates." When the great guns opened against Chalmers and Jackson about 5:30 P.M., the ground shook violently. Together with the continuous roar from the field batteries and the booming reports of the gunboat cannon, "the noise [was] not exceeded by anything I . . . heard afterward," wrote one of Grant's aides.

Jarred by the concussions, the nearby infantry supports crouched close to the ground. "It was nearing sundown," later wrote a tensed Michigan private, ". . . [and our] proud army of Donelson was crouching like whipped curs in a small circular line. . . ." Despite the threat of impending disaster the private considered the sight he now beheld spectacular beyond anything he had ever seen. "A grander sight no man ever saw than this coming of the Confederate army," he wrote. Just before the big guns opened, bright sunshine had filled the woods. The Federal line braced for an attack. ". . . Presenting the appearance of a huge monster clothed in folds of flashing steel," the enemy approached, said the private, "in perfect step, and with arms at right shoulder shift. . . . I live[d] an age in a moment."

With the thunder of the guns reverberating far across the countryside the scene also seemed "grand but fearful" to one of Hurlbut's Illinois officers. ". . . The sun looked like a ball of fire as it went out of sight, and the clouds of powder smoke hastened the glooming. . . . We could see the red flashes of our own and the enemy's guns, and shell burst all about us. One could not help wondering how man or living thing could escape wounds or death," he wrote.

In low, anxious tones word was passed among the Federal ranks; should the monster guns fail to halt the advancing enemy, the "last and only resource" would be the bayonet.

Little more than a quarter of a mile distant several Confederate generals stood watching the deployment of their advancing troops.

GRANT'S LAST LINE. Siege guns of Captain Relly Madison's battery stood in line on the afternoon of April 6. The heavy blasts from these guns helped drive off Chalmers's and Jackson's infantry at nightfall. This rare photograph was taken shortly after the battle. (PHOTOGRAPHIC HISTORY OF THE CIVIL WAR)

Braxton Bragg was encouraged by the movement. "[There] was every prospect of success," he wrote, despite the formidable line of enemy cannon drawn up in front. General Withers, commanding Bragg's Second Division, was busily engaged in sending staff officers to bring up all available reinforcements. It appeared to Withers that a concerted attack might drive the Federals into the river. His two brigades, Chalmers's and Jackson's, were moving rapidly to that purpose. Gage's battery of 12-pounder howitzers and 3-inch rifles had come up and was in position, shelling the Federal concentration. To an eyewitness the woods seemed alive with Confederate troops whose movements were precise and well executed.

The attack had begun earlier with a charge of cavalry. Lindsay's 1st Mississippi Cavalry, after capturing Ross's 2d Michigan Battery, had sped on, attacking Mann's Missouri Battery, then escaping from the double envelopment of the Hornets' Nest. Only a single company of cavalry went in pursuit of these cannon, most of Lindsay's men having escorted the captured Michigan battery to the rear. As they crossed a deep ravine, they swept by a single caisson that had been abandoned by the retreating Federals. The battery's commander, Lieutenant Edward Brotzmann, said the Confederates were so close and the terrain so rugged as to prevent his opening fire. Making a desperate effort to reach the safety of the Landing, the battery disappeared over the top of a hill at a full run.

As Lindsay's men cleared the top of this hill close behind, they suddenly saw in their front what appeared to be several brigades of Federal infantry drawn up in line. The lines were so close that General Buell, who was nearby, thought that the cavalry must be annihilated. "They fired at us," wrote one of Lindsay's men, "but from excitement they fired so wildly and so high in the air that we all escaped unharmed into the ravine. . . ."

Following the repulse of Lindsay's cavalry a brief lull occurred in the fighting. The stillness was oppressive, wrote a Federal infantryman awaiting the expected Confederate assault. Finally, as the gray ranks advanced in multiple lines, the shot and shell flew again amid a thunderous roar from the guns. It was apparent to nearly all that the high crisis of the day was at hand.

The advancing Confederates quickly found that the going was hard against the formidable line of enemy batteries. Chalmers's brigade, on the right near the riverbank, was beaten back in successive attacks. "[They] attacked from the southwest, the worst point they could have chosen," wrote one of Hurlbut's officers, "for it forced them to cross a hollow that opened into the river, and expose[d] them to the fire of the gunboats. . . ."

Gage's battery, firing from a prominent ridge in support of Chalmers's attack, was so severely hit by the Federal cannon fire that it had to withdraw.

On the Confederate left Jackson's brigade advanced only to the crest of the opposite ridge before it lay down along the reverse slope in the face of the heavy cannon fire. "[The men] could not be urged farther without support," said Jackson.

Withers was in the act of ordering up reinforcements and dispatching staff officers to press the attack when he was astonished to see some of Jackson's troops moving back from under fire and withdrawing from the field. "[I] sent [orders] to arrest the commanding officers and for the troops to be promptly placed in position for charging the batteries," said the indignant Withers. To his great surprise Withers soon learned that Jackson's men were retreating under orders to withdraw from the fighting.

Braxton Bragg was even more stunned by the movement. Over and over he had been repeating to the troops, "One more charge, my men, and we shall capture them all." Many years later Bragg said that what occurred here was one of the great mistakes of the war.

P. G. T. Beauregard was at his "headquarters No. 3," about a quarter-mile north of Shiloh Church, where the main Corinth road "takes an eastern direction." Shortly after 3 P.M. he was approached by Governor Isham G. Harris, who had been to the rear, at Beauregard's first headquarters near the intersection of the Bark and main Corinth roads. Learning that Beauregard had gone in the direction of Shiloh Church, Harris hastened on with news of Albert Sidney Johnston's death.

Beauregard was on horseback in a grove of trees when Harris rode up to tell him that Johnston was dead and that he, Beauregard, now commanded the army. When Munford, a member of Johnston's staff, later found Beauregard after an hour-and-thirty-five-minute ride, he was still in the same grove, talking with Captain Wickliffe, who had also come to advise Beauregard of Johnston's death. According to Munford, Beauregard "expressed the deepest regret" at Johnston's fate, then remarked that "everything else seems to be going . . . well." Munford turned aside into the woods, fell to the ground, and "wept like a child" over the loss of his friend Johnston.

Although Beauregard was less moved by Johnston's fate, he later reported "the responsibility [of commanding the army] was one which in my physical condition I would have gladly avoided. . . ." The lingering effects of Beauregard's respiratory infection had caused him to feel "greatly prostrated."

Some of Beauregard's staff officers soon were dispatched to the front to see how the battle was progressing. Meanwhile Beauregard seems to have become more and more concerned about the large amount of straggling taking place. Staff officers were detailed to round up the hundreds of aimlessly wandering men and "march them as reinforcements to General Bragg." One of Bragg's staff officers, David Urquhart, apparently reported to Beauregard about this time that "over one third of the army was scattered in different parts of the field, loading themselves with plunder from the abandoned Federal encampments." Beauregard had already personally rallied many stragglers and had seen for himself the widespread disorder in the Confederate rear.

Sometime during the afternoon an important communiqué arrived on the battlefield via Corinth. The dispatch, a telegram from Colonel B. H. Helm in the direction of Florence, Alabama, was delivered to Beauregard. Helm reported that his scouts had observed Buell's troops marching toward Decatur, Alabama. Since the message implied that all of Buell's troops were present, it was presumed that Buell could not possibly be marching to a rapid junction with Grant's army. Later, following the battle, it was learned that Helm's scouts had sighted only Ormsby Mitchell's division of Buell's army, then maneuvering in the vicinity of Fayetteville, Tennessee.

By 5:30 P.M. Beauregard had moved farther to the rear, taking position near Shiloh Church. The sun was still above the trees, and heavy, broken clouds were gathering in the western sky. Adding to the confusion throughout the rear area were the heavy bursts of gunboat shells, which seemed particularly to impress Beauregard. "[The gunboats] opened on our eager columns a fierce and annoying fire with shot and shell of the heaviest description," he later wrote.

Soon word was received of the capture of a large segment of the Federal army, followed by the arrival of Prentiss himself, brought to Beauregard's headquarters tent by Lieutenant A. R. Chisolm of Beauregard's staff. Prentiss was apparently in good spirits, and taunted his captors with the boast that Buell would reverse the fortunes of war in the morning, but this was regarded as "idle talk," said Colonel Thomas Jordan, the army's adjutant general.

Beauregard, obviously pleased with the day's work, directed that a telegram be sent to Richmond announcing "a complete victory, driving the enemy from every position," after a fight of ten hours. Then he made one of the eventful decisions of the day. Having observed the widespread disorder in the Confederate rear and believing that the victory was sufficiently complete, he ordered a halt to the fighting and a withdrawal by the army to the captured Federal camps.

It is obvious that Beauregard then had little knowledge of the events occurring at the front. Years after the war he candidly admitted to a former Federal officer why he had decided to stop the fighting. According to this source Beauregard said there were two reasons: "First, his men were, as he put it, 'out of hand.' [They] had

THE U. S. GUNBOAT *LEXINGTON*. Another of the wooden gunboats assigned to the Tennessee River, the *Lexington* was under Lieutenant James W. Shirk. Together with the *Tyler* she contributed to the disorder in the Confederate rear late in the afternoon of April 6. Her heavy 8-inch naval shells probably were of influence in Beauregard's decision not to press a final attack at twilight on Sunday. (PHOTOGRAPHIC HISTORY OF THE CIVIL WAR) been fighting since early morn; were worn out, and also demoralized by the flush of victory. . . . 'In the second place,' said Beauregard, 'I thought I had General Grant just where I wanted him, and could finish him up in the morning.' "

Major Numa Augustin, a volunteer aide-de-camp, was told to go to the front "to arrest the conflict and [order the troops to] fall back to the camps of the enemy for the night." Dressed in civilian clothes, Augustin galloped toward Pittsburg Landing about 6 P.M., soon coming up in the rear of the front lines. Here he found Ruggles "assembling a considerable force ready for immediate action" and told him that he must withdraw his troops. Augustin then rode on, quickly spreading the word among the troops to make no further pursuit and to fall back. Jackson, on his way to request support from Withers for a coordinated attack, was met by Augustin and told to retire. "This order . . . was promptly communicated to my command," said Jackson.

Augustin found Bragg observing Chalmers's repeated attacks in the vicinity of Dill Branch. Captain Lockett, of Bragg's staff, said Beauregard's staff officer came up to Bragg and told him, "The general directs that the pursuit be stopped; the victory is sufficiently complete; it is needless to expose our men to the fire of the gunboats."

Bragg's reaction was that of great surprise. "Have you given that order to anyone else?" he asked. When Augustin replied that he had and pointed out Jackson's troops, who were already retiring, Lockett said Bragg exclaimed, "My God, it is too late!" and ordered several of his staff to go and disengage the troops still fighting.

Out on the battlefield Colonel Joseph Wheeler, who was in advance of his brigade along the crest of a forward ridge, soon observed the change in plans. "Looking back, I saw the greater portion of [our] troops withdrawing to the rear," said Wheeler, who quickly followed with his own regiment.

Only a few of Chalmers's troops, closely engaged with Buell's infantry, failed to get the withdrawal order. As twilight crept across the land about 6:30 P.M. some desultory fighting continued, finally sputtering to a gradual halt when total darkness enshrouded the battlefield.

Just before the Confederate withdrawal U. S. Grant sat on his horse north of the siege-gun battery, watching the approaching Confederate troops. "Shells were screeching through the air and trees were breaking and casting their branches on the ground," wrote a frightened staff officer. "Nor were the bullets less vicious as they ripped around us. In a word, it was pandemonium broken loose. The enemy was advancing in lines of battle that reminded me of waves rolling in on the beach. Yet, in all this chaos . . . General Grant sat on his horse like a statue, watching the enemy's movement as the wreck of his army drifted by." To the impressionable young officer it seemed that within a short time the attacking Confederates would capture all.

On the left of the siege guns, where Buell had agreed to take charge of the troops and defend the line, the situation was grave. Stone's battery was nearly out of ammunition, and the captain commanding told the 36th Indiana's colonel that he would have to retire. That he soon did. Other nearby artillery units were so understrength that volunteers from the infantry manned the guns.

Behind the front line the 6th and 24th Ohio regiments were hastened up from the riverbank and ordered into line. "Don't stop to form, colonel, don't stop to form," shouted a staff officer as some of the 6th Ohio's companies went forward, "we shall all be massacred if you do! There isn't a man out yonder, on the left, between us and the Rebels!"

By now every man who could be coaxed into fighting was already in line, including drummer boys. "The belligerent little drummers nearly all preferred to fight," wrote an Illinois officer, "and were found along the line, gun in hand, as fierce as fighting cocks. . . ." When about a dozen Iowa soldiers from Grant's army volunteered to fight with the 36th Indiana, they were immediately sent to the firing line.

"Boys, fire low," shouted the 36th's colonel as Chalmers's Confederates approached for a second attack. The line erupted in a blaze of gunfire, and soon thereafter the Confederates were seen going to the rear. Although the Federal troops then did not realize it, the first day's fight had ended.

About fifteen rounds per man had been expended by Grose's 36th Indiana in the almost half an hour they had been on the battlefield. Only one private among them was killed. Three companies of the 6th Ohio that had formed on the 36th's left during the last attack had been too far away to join in the fighting. Despite their belated arrival there were many who were convinced that Buell's handful of troops had been instrumental in staving off certain defeat. "All feel that our salvation is due to him alone," wrote one of Grant's weary Iowa soldiers. Another eyewitness of the last attack, a Federal surgeon, thought the advance of Buell's reinforcements was "the most pleasant sight . . . I ever saw in my life."

When darkness made it apparent that the fighting was not to be renewed that day, the men at last began to relax. "All who had been engaged looked about and felt relieved," wrote a Federal officer. "Lines were re-aligned, guns wiped and swabbed, and congratulations exchanged."

As the last of Chalmers's Mississippians disappeared from the field,

Grant sat watching amid the line of smoking cannon. A nearby lieutenant, temporarily attached to his staff, heard Grant say something. "I rode forward, saluted, and waited for his order," said the officer. "He paid no attention. His eyes were fixed to the front. Again I heard him mutter something without turning. Then I saw that he was talking to himself, 'Not beaten yet by a damn sight' [he repeated]."

CHAPTER XIX

Night of Horrors

Ann Wallace had remained aboard the *Minnehaha* surrounded by wounded and dying men as the afternoon waned. Back and forth the steamer churned from shore to shore, ferrying Buell's troops to Grant's support.

The roar of cannon and musketry was almost deafening, and the groans of the wounded added an eerie and unearthly quality. Ann was watching from the upper deck, nearly spellbound by the wild scene, when a close friend, Elder Button, came up the steps, his face distorted with anguish. Button had been slightly wounded by a spent ball while helping with removal of the wounded from the battlefield and Ann felt compassionate, thinking his pained appearance was the result of his wound.

Approaching Mrs. Wallace from the rear, Button came near and spoke haltingly: "This is an awful battle." Without turning to look, Ann replied that she agreed, but that fresh troops were arriving and they might yet win the day and put an end to this "wicked war."

"You have a great many relations on that field. You cannot hope to see them all come in safe," continued Button.

Ann looked hard into the eyes of her friend and saw the expression of horror. In an instant she read the dreadful truth—her husband had been shot. "I was stunned, chilled, almost paralyzed!" she recalled.

A few minutes later one of Wallace's staff officers and Mrs. Wallace's brother, Cyrus Dickey, came aboard with details of the incident. "Will" had been leading his division back toward the Landing when shot in the head. Although they had tried to save his body, the enemy was pursuing too closely. They had laid him beside some ammunition boxes to protect him from being trampled before leaving him. Other than this, Dickey could say no more.

"My husband was dead!" wrote Ann Wallace, later, "and the enemy had possession of the ground where he lay. . . . The blow

MRS. ANN DICKEY WALLACE. This longing wife arrived unannounced for a surprise visit with her husband on the eve of the battle. Before they met, Ann had been thrust into the midst of a major battle and experienced the trauma of having her husband mortally wounded and abandoned on the battlefield. From a photograph taken about 1870. (ILLINOIS STATE HISTORICAL SOCIETY)

was too heavy to cause pain, suffering comes hours afterwards," she thought.

In a few minutes Dickey and the others left to see to wounded friends. Ann found herself alone, without anyone to comfort her, the entire night. All about her was pain and anguish. "The cabin floor was full of wounded, inside and out . . . laid close and in rows like bricks in a brickyard. . . . God gave me strength," she remembered, "and I spent much of [that awful] night bathing the fevered limbs and faces of [those] suffering about me."

Nearby lay the steamer *Continental*, crowded with wounded and no surgeons to attend to them. "Nearly every spot upon which a man could lie was occupied—on boxes, and under tables—the floor of the cabin was covered," wrote a painfully wounded Iowan of Hurlbut's division. "So numerous were the dead, dying, and wounded, that a person could scarcely move without stepping on them. . . . [They were] mangled in every conceivable way . . . some with arms, legs, and even their jaws shot off, bleeding to death, and no one to wait upon them or dress their wounds. . . . Hundreds would beg for a canteen of water to cool their intense thirst. . . . Some begged the captain to broach the commissary stores on the boat, but he would not allow them to be taken without a requisition. Many tried to buy when they could not beg food. . . . The gong sounded summoning the crew to their meals . . . but the captain replied that he had nothing to sell. I saw wounded men unable to move, and heard them praying for strength . . . to reach a musket to shoot the wretch!"

Ashore the suffering was even more intense. All of the Union camps with the exception of W. H. L. Wallace's were in Confederate hands. Many of the medical supplies and equipment had been abandoned in the captured camps. Medical stores, recently ordered from St. Louis, had not yet arrived. There were few surgeons and no place to put the wounded except for a single log hut, fifteen by thirty feet, perched atop the bluff, which was converted into a hospital. The medical staff had been overtaxed to care for the sick even before the battle, and the unexpected influx of thousands of wounded was simply overwhelming.

Finally a few tents were found and pitched near the log hut to shelter some of the more critical cases. When a small amount of hay was found aboard a transport, it was spread on the ground to serve as a bed for a few others. Several bullocks found at the Landing were slaughtered to feed the hungry men. Beyond this there was little that was done.

The only hospital boat, the *City of Memphis,* made trip after trip to Savannah and back, carrying as many wounded as could be crammed aboard. On board and on the battlefield the grisly work of the surgeons continued throughout the long and fearful night. There was no anesthetic, only an occasional sip of brandy or other spirits to alleviate suffering during operations. Amputations occurred so frequently that by morning a pile of severed arms and limbs had accumulated outside the log hospital. One exhausted drummer boy of an Illinois regiment finally flung himself down to sleep outside the log cabin. When he awoke he discovered to his horror that he had been mistaken for a corpse. Beside him lay a ghastly array of dead men piled in a long row, of which he was the head.

Because of the chaotic disarray about the Landing, incidents of lawlessness and violence were inevitable during the seemingly endless night. Amid the abandoned sutler stores a few soldiers found "brandy peaches," said to be fruit cans each containing a few peach slices and "a pint of miserable rotgut whiskey." An Irishman with one of Buell's regiments ingested the contents and in fifteen minutes became a "howling hoodlum," observed a sergeant. After more than a little hell-raising, the Irishman ran afoul of his colonel, who threatened to "buck and gag" him. Outraged by the reprimand, the drunken soldier snatched a musket from a stack and thrust the bayonet within a few inches of his colonel's chest. He was soon subdued and put under guard.

Elsewhere a few hungry soldiers descended upon a sutler's storehouse and ransacked the premises. A barrel of crackers, cheese, and smoking tobacco were among the items removed.

By late evening the moon had risen, casting a ghastly light across the battlefield. Most of the Confederate troops had withdrawn from close proximity to the Landing to bivouac amid the captured Federal camps. One of Polk's division's, Cheatham's, had marched about three miles from their most advanced position to camp and obtain rations at the spot where they had halted the night before. Although Beauregard had intended that his corps commanders should designate bivouac areas for their men, it was impossible to reassemble the troops that night. Most units camped where darkness found them.

Only Pond's brigade, in front of Sherman, remained in line of battle, within four hundred yards of the Federal perimeter.

Once they returned to the captured Federal encampments, the Confederates found a vast assortment of plunder. Little effort was exerted to control the pillaging, since it was felt by many in the ranks that the battle was over. The results were nigh disastrous. Several barrels of medicinal whiskey, including one found in the camp of the 13th Iowa, were quickly consumed. Soon so many disorderly soldiers were milling about that it seemed to a Louisiana surgeon that half the army was straggling back to Corinth, loaded down with trophies and drunk on "Cincinnati whiskey." One particularly jubilant Negro servant, taken along to cook for the officers of a Louisiana regiment, was last seen strutting through a plundered camp dressed in a Federal captain's uniform. Later it was supposed he had defected to the enemy.

To the inexperienced and often ill-equipped Confederate soldiers the profusion of personal luxuries that littered the enemy camps was irresistible. "Our boys say the Yankees lived like fighting cocks," reported a Tennessee officer, ". . . [They had] fine tents, fine clothing and fine eating. Everything that they could want."

One of Gibson's Louisiana privates was astounded by the variety of provisions he encountered—"fresh beef, coffee, sugar, rice, flour, crackers, corn meal, hams, cheese, apples, candy . . . sundries, and butter." Among the items of equipment eagerly snatched up were overcoats, blankets, oilcloths, and oilcloth haversacks.

"Not expecting battle [on the 7th] . . . we loaded ourselves with everything that we could lay our hands on," wrote one of Bragg's soldiers. "I had a fine blue cloth suit, entirely new . . . an oil cloth to spread over my blanket, a fine overcoat, and haversack full of parched coffee, one full of soda crackers, cheese and boiled ham, another filled with gilt edged paper, envelopes, two ambrotypes, love letters, a copy of McClellan's *Tactics* and all sorts of little mementos, a canteen, and a splendid Enfield rifle."

In one of Sherman's captured camps the Confederates found a bakery complete with ovens, flour, and commissary supplies. Several experienced cooks were detailed, and the bakery was soon turning out loaves of "fine soft bread" to feed the famished troops.

Yet there were those among the inexperienced Confederate army who apparently went hungry that night. Bragg disgustedly confided in a letter to his wife that many of his troops were "too lazy to hunt the enemy camps for provisions." Others feared being poisoned and ate nothing. Observing this, one young Confederate remarked after he had consumed a meal of captured food, "I would have eaten if it had been covered with Yankee blood."

While most of the Confederates feasted on captured provisions, many of their benefactors, having enjoyed similar meals the night before, now huddled miserably on the cold ground, supperless prisoners of war.

A captured Federal officer, having been marched about five miles from the battlefield and corraled in an old cornfield on the side of a hill, considered his plight: "We were hungry, tired, begrimed with the smoke of battle, discouraged, sick, and mad. I never saw so many long faces. . . . We lay between corn rows, too tired and out of sorts to sleep. . . . [The] night was growing chilly, and we had no blankets or overcoats."

Only a few blankets were distributed to officers during the night, and no food. A few soldiers tried to keep up their courage by singing "Hang Jeff Davis on a Sour Apple Tree," but most were too exhausted to do little more than ponder their fate. "I was thankful to the Almighty God that my wife was not left a widow, or my darling child an orphan; thankful, also, that they did not know my condition," wrote a sensitive prisoner.

Not so fortunate were those among the Federal wounded, lying on the battlefield, whose wits were their only means of survival. Corporal David Palmer of the 8th Iowa had been shot in the chest during the Hornets' Nest fighting. Alternately passing out and regaining consciousness while lying helpless he had been stripped of his coat and cap by several Confederates. When night came, Palmer was feverish and in shock. Yet he gulped a few swallows of liquor from a Confederate canteen and managed to drag himself into a nearby tent. It was occupied by a wounded Confederate soldier lying on a bed of straw. Desperately Palmer snatched at the straw, despite the protests of its occupant, until he had enough to fashion a bed. Again he lapsed into unconsciousness. When he awoke, there was a tremendous explosion nearby that turned night into day inside the tent. He soon realized what had occurred—the gunboats were shelling the Confederate positions. Palmer was horrified by the new danger.

As if to make the night more miserable, the Federal gunboats had been ordered to fire at short intervals throughout the night "to keep the Confederates from sleeping or resting."

The idea was "Bull" Nelson's. Lieutenant Gwin of the *Tyler* had been champing for an opportunity to be of service since his gunboat had ceased firing at 6:25 P.M. Having sent word to Nelson asking for instructions, Gwin was soon requested to "throw an 8-inch shell into the camp of the enemy every ten minutes during the night and thus prevent their sleeping."

Gwin opened fire from the *Tyler* at 9 P.M., throwing the heavy shells with five-second, ten-second, and fifteen-second fuses "and an occasional shrapnel from the howitzer." Every ten minutes a heavy detonation would shake the ground near the Landing, followed by an ascending howl as the shell arched high above the woodlands. At last the shell would burst in a distant sector, sending a shock wave and an eerie flash of light throughout the countryside.

By 1 A.M. the *Lexington* had returned from a trip to check on the safety of Crump's Landing. The *Lexington* relieved the *Tyler* and, by her commander's order, maintained the harassing fire at fifteen-minute intervals until daylight.

As was expected, the effect on the enemy proved to be mostly psychological. Throughout the night the Confederates cursed the "black rascals," as they termed the gunboats, and many were horrified by the air bursts that often sent huge tree limbs crashing down about them. To at least one group of Confederates the danger was more real than they imagined. Comfortably ensconcing themselves in a captured tent, they spread an oilcloth on the ground and thrust a bayonet into the soil to serve as a candle-holder. When a gunboat shell found them, they were in the act of playing cards. The next morning their bodies were discovered much as they had sat, each with cards still firmly grasped in his hand.

Yet the crowning touch of misery for those at Shiloh that night was added about midnight. During the evening the sky had grown overcast, and at about 10 P.M. a drizzling rain began. By midnight a severe thunderstorm was raging across the countryside, drenching both armies. The rain was falling in torrents, there were vivid flashes of lightning, and the roar of thunder was incessant. To one sensitive youth, "It seemed like the Lord was rubbing it in. . . ."

The rain was particularly disheartening. It was a cold, driving downpour that seemed to saturate everything. "I never saw it rain as it did that night," wrote a discouraged Wisconsin youth. "The thought came to me then, that this was the worst night I ever passed through." Another Wisconsin private, just ashore with Buell's troops, was unable to find shelter. "I put my blanket over my shoulder, stuck my bayonet in the ground, leaned my chin on the butt . . . and slept standing up," he wrote.

To a battle-sick Confederate awakened to go on a night patrol, the terrific storm was a source of horror. "Vivid flashings of lightning rent the heavens and . . . sickening sights fell before my eyes. . . . I saw a large piece of ground literally covered with dead heaped and piled upon each other. I shut my eyes upon the sickening sight. . . . Through the dark I heard the sound of hogs . . . quarreling over their carnival feast."

Another Confederate, one of Bragg's men, stood in the pouring rain, with flashes of lightning revealing the ghastly features of the dead about him. The groans and shrieks of the wounded were loud in his ears. "Oh, what a night of horrors. . . ." he thought. "It will haunt me to the grave."

Elsewhere the same tragic scene was reenacted within the Federal lines. "The night was dark and all through the woods we could hear the groans of wounded men begging for help. . . ." wrote a Union officer. Some considered that the rain had been brought on by the battle. When one of Buell's regiments arrived that night, they were unable to proceed more than a few yards from the river's edge. "It rained all the way up and we got off the boat in a drenching rain and mud over shoe top deep," wrote Orderly Sergeant C. C. Briant of the 6th Indiana. "My clothes were wet to the skin, my feet and ankles were blistered, and my legs pained me so badly that to sleep would have been impossible. . . ."

Briant finally became so miserable that in desperation he wandered off, he knew not where, nor did he care. "I followed the road leading back from the river, and had gone only about a hundred yards when my attention was attracted by a large fire off to my right some two or three hundred yards. I determined to go to it at once and struck out through the woods, bumping against men and trees in the midnight darkness. . . . I kept on my course and sometimes would [step on] . . . sleeping men, lying along like poles on a corduroy road but I never halted to apologize."

Briant finally approached the fire. "Such a sight I never saw before. The boys had built a large log fire which was burning fifteen feet high, and around this not less than 300 men were crowded, forming a solid wall of men. . . . Forty feet was as close as I could get to the fire. . . . I walked twice around the ring in mud, walked up until it was ankle deep, watching [for] a chance to get in. It was simply impossible. I could not do it."

As the night dragged on the weather became so demoralizing that countless acts of desperation occurred. "[The events of that night] reminded us . . . that we were not engaged in a holiday excursion," wrote one of the military innocents of Prentiss's division.

Driven to cover by the heavy rainstorm, an exhausted Confederate crawled under a blanket with another man. With a shudder he awoke the following morning to discover that "he had slept with a dead Yankee." In another tent three young soldiers, two of them Confederates, had crawled inside for shelter. Each was desperately wounded. Throughout the long night they talked to one another for encouragement. By morning only one was alive—and he knew that unless help came soon, he too would die.

For those too seriously wounded to move the night was one of indescribable horror. Colonel Julius Raith lay against a tree, his right leg shattered by a musket ball, and endured the rain in silence. Aboard the steamers the wounded lay exposed on the open decks and were compelled to lie in pools of water as the rain flooded their resting-places. Even to those who had managed to find shelter before the rains came, the night was a frightening experience. One young Confederate, rudely introduced to the realities of warfare that Sunday, was unable to sleep. "I attempted it," he wrote, "but the balls would whistle and the musketry would roar [in] my ears."

By 3 A.M. the rain had abated, but the misery continued. One of Buell's men, coming ashore in the middle of the night, was later able to recall, "I think I give the experience of every member of [my regiment] . . . when I say that the night of the 6th of April, 1862 was the worst night of our entire three years service."

The arrival of Buell's fresh troops was a godsend to Grant's hard-pressed army. Beginning with the arrival of Ammen's brigade of Nelson's division before the end of hostilities on the sixth and continuing throughout the night, about seventy-five hundred of Buell's troops trudged ashore before daybreak. Nelson's division was completely across by 9 P.M., ferried from the opposite shore by the small river steamers. Often only three companies could be crowded aboard at one time because of the profusion of wounded present.

From the west shore their arrival was heralded by loud cheering and by a band playing "Hail Columbia" aboard a steamer coming from Savannah. Ironically the Confederate brigade of Preston Pond was near enough to hear this music and cheering. Thinking it was the enemy retreating from the Landing, they sent up lusty cheers in reply.

Having debarked as rapidly as possible, Ammen's brigade, followed by Bruce's and Hazen's commands, extended Grant's line along the Dill Branch ravine before midnight. Heavy picket detachments were sent forward to the enemy's former position along the opposite ridge, and the division settled down for a short night's rest.

About 9 P.M. Crittenden's division also began arriving aboard steamboats from Savannah. Its debarkation was hurried in order that the boats might return for McCook's division, still waiting at Savannah. Crittenden's men had originally prepared to march overland to Pittsburg Landing, but belated orders to travel by boat were

received just before starting. Delayed by the lack of sufficient transportation, Crittenden approached the battle zone having spent most
of Sunday in costly inactivity. The thousands of demoralized soldiers
milling about the landing area shocked Crittenden, who foresaw the
difficulty of landing his troops. "I was so disgusted," Crittenden
wrote, "that I asked General Buell to permit me to land a regiment
and drive them away.—I did not wish my troops to come in contact
with them."

Forcing his way through the mob, Crittenden put William S.
Smith's brigade, followed by Boyle's troops, in position extending
Nelson's line to the west. It was raining hard before the men were
in place, and they were forced to sleep where they stood, without
blankets or overcoats.

Despite their cold and uncomfortable bivouac, the presence of
Buell's troops on the battlefield that night was of great importance.
Where there had been chaos and gloom, there now was a measure
of stability and hope. One of Grant's surgeons, demoralized by the
carnage about him, wrote: "I must confess we were nearly whipped
and feared the morrow. . . . [The advance of Buell's army] was
the most pleasant sight . . . I ever saw. . . . Never were friends
more welcome."

The surgeon was right. A few hours later Buell's men and other
reinforcements would provide the means for what glory the Union
army would reap at Shiloh.

Blithely ignorant of the events occurring within the enemy lines,
Bragg and Beauregard had gone to bed in Sherman's tent that night,
convinced they would have little difficulty with Grant's army on the
morrow. Lieutenant Colonel Gilmer, Beauregard's chief engineer,
had brought word about 9 P.M. that the battle was over and the
enemy gone. Gilmer felt that the victory was as complete as possible.
He predicted no enemy attack and felt that only the presence of
the Federal gunboats would prevent occupation of Pittsburg Landing. Thereafter Beauregard discharged many of the headquarters
staff officers to take Sidney Johnston's body to Corinth.

Before retiring that evening Beauregard had conferred with nearly
all of the high-ranking Confederate generals at his headquarters tent.
According to a staff officer all were elated over the events of the
day. It was admitted by some that the victory was not yet complete,
but even they considered the Confederates to be masters of the field.
Beauregard considered Grant's "shattered fugitive force" likely to be
captured or destroyed the following day.

Although then regarded as so much idle gossip, Benjamin Prentiss's boast provided the first inkling that matters were not as favorable as supposed by Confederate headquarters that night. Prentiss,

who had been interrogated by Beauregard following the collapse of the Hornets' Nest, seemed "communicative and not unwilling to answer every question," thought a staff officer. Beauregard learned that C. F. Smith was sick at Savannah and that Grant had belatedly arrived on the field following the initial attack. When asked where the head of Buell's army lay, Prentiss replied that a junction would be effected that night with Grant's troops at the Landing. Later, when he was sandwiched between Confederate staff officers who were taking him to sleep at a captured Ohio camp, Prentiss continued to torment his captors with news of Buell's coming. With a laugh Prentiss remarked, "You gentlemen have had your way today, but it will be very different tomorrow. You'll see! Buell will effect a junction with Grant tonight, and we'll turn the tables on you in the morning." The staff officers guffawed at Prentiss's bantering, and Adjutant General Jordan even displayed the telegram from Colonel Helm, reporting Buell moving in the direction of Decatur, Alabama.

Ironically, news of heavy enemy reinforcements arriving at Pittsburg Landing was already in Confederate hands, according to one source. However, as a result of an incredible breakdown in communications and the apparent carelessness of several ranking officers this important information allegedly failed to reach Confederate headquarters.

Nathan Bedford Forrest, displaying some of the military sagacity he was later noted for, sent a detachment of scouts under Lieutenant Sheridan to reconnoiter the Federal lines that night. Dressed in Federal overcoats, Sheridan's squad set out and soon discovered Buell's troops rapidly debarking from transports at the landing.

About an hour following his departure Sheridan returned and reported to Forrest what he had observed, remarking that such was the disorder within the Federal lines that he believed an attack in full force would succeed in driving the enemy into the river, provided it was launched that night.

Forrest, aware of the importance of this intelligence, mounted his horse and promptly rode to the rear, looking for the nearest corps commander. Meeting Hardee and Breckenridge nearby, he related the news of Federal reinforcements and suggested that the Confederates should either immediately attack or abandon the battlefield to avoid an encounter with overwhelming numbers of enemy troops.

Hardee told Forrest to take this information directly to Beauregard. Unfortunately for the Confederacy Forrest was unable to find Beauregard. Beauregard had evidently retired for the night in Sherman's captured tent without establishing a central headquarters. Shiloh Church, which Beauregard had used temporarily that evening, was now a hospital.

Forrest returned to his cavalry outposts and again sent his scouts forth. About 2 A.M. they reported the continued arrival of enemy troops. Returning to see Hardee, Forrest was merely instructed to go back to his regiment and maintain a vigilant watch, reporting all hostile movements. Thus was the vital news all but lost.

Several miles across the battlefield the Union generals, like their men, were spending a miserable night. Grant had left the log cabin near the Landing, which was being used as a hospital, to attempt to sleep under a towering oak. Yet his injured ankle was swollen and pained him so severely that he could get no rest. The rain was falling in torrents, and Grant hobbled back to the log cabin, exhausted. Soon thereafter a staff officer found him slumped in a broken split-bottom chair, his arm looped around the back, upon which his head heavily rested.

Unable to sleep here because of the grisly amputations carried on throughout the night, Grant again went outside. "The sight was more unendurable than encountering the enemy's fire," he later wrote, "and I returned to my tree in the rain."

Already fermenting in his mind were bold plans for the morrow. Throughout the long and bloody day Grant had expressed much optimism, his imperturbability being the marvel of staff officers. At one point during the evening McPherson of his staff had ridden up with a report that much of the army was "hors de combat." When asked what he proposed to do under these circumstances—retreat?, Grant fiercely replied, "No! I propose to attack at daylight and whip them."

Indeed, Grant considered his present situation similar to that of the Fort Donelson fight—that either side was ready to give way if the other showed a bold front. Grant reasoned that "a great moral advantage would be gained by becoming the attacking party," and he planned accordingly.

Grant visited Sherman that evening and told him to prepare to assume the offensive in the morning. Grant related the Fort Donelson incident and said the same tactics would win at Shiloh, relying on the arrival of reinforcements under Buell and Lew Wallace.

Despite the considerable controversy that arose over this matter following the war, it appears from contemporary evidence that although Grant planned to attack in the morning, he issued no specific orders that night. Evidently uncertainty as to the condition of his army, the location of Lew Wallace, and the extent of reinforcements brought by Buell was the reason for this.

Buell, however, had already arrived at a decision to attack at daylight with his own troops, and he spent much of the night arranging for an advance. Buell, almost contemptuous of Grant for what he regarded as the disgraceful rout of his army, had no consultation with him that night and "knew nothing of his purpose." Moreover Buell considered his army independent, wholly subject to his own orders. "I did not look upon him [Grant] as my commander," wrote Buell some years later, and he merely "presumed" that Grant would be in accord with his own plans.

At a chance meeting between Buell and Sherman early that night Buell sought information to facilitate his plans. Sherman was found to be a "frank, brave soldier, rather subdued, realizing the critical situation in which . . . his own fault . . . had placed him, but ready . . . to do anything that duty required of him."

When Sherman asked Buell what his plans were, he replied that by daylight he would have eighteen thousand men ashore and planned to attack. Since Buell had no knowledge of the terrain, Sherman gave him a map that he had drawn of the Pittsburg Landing campgrounds to use as a guide.

Thereafter Buell returned to Nelson's and Crittenden's divisions and gave instructions for their deployment in the morning. Having made a personal reconnaissance of Grant's last position, Buell knew where this line lay, and he told his troops to form in its front and advance at daylight.

By 10:30 P.M. a portion of this battle line already had formed about three hundred yards in advance of Grant's line. "[It was] too dark to see," wrote one of Buell's brigade commanders, "[and] we prolonged our line by touch." At 3 A.M. Nelson passed among his officers with instructions to move "as soon as you can see . . . find the enemy and whip him." An hour later he caused his men to be roused and a line of battle formed. With sixty rounds in their cartridge boxes, Nelson's men soon began to advance slowly through the forests, pausing frequently to adjust their alignment. The rain had ceased, yet the undergrowth was dripping wet. Already daylight was beginning to appear.

Across the battlefield to the northwest the sound of cannon fire echoed through the forests. Ironically these first shots at daylight on the seventh were fired nearly a day late, according to U. S. Grant.

News of the belated arrival of Lew Wallace's division from the vicinity of Crump's Landing had been brought to Grant after nightfall on the sixth. Wallace's absence during Sunday was a source of embarrassment to Grant, who later used the matter to avert some of the blame for the heavy casualties at Shiloh. Although Grant apparently did not meet with Wallace that night, some difficulty being encountered in locating Wallace's headquarters, he was relieved to have word of his presence.

The head of Wallace's column had begun to cross the Snake Creek bridge about 7:15 P.M., having marched for more than seven hours over a distance of about fourteen miles. According to Wallace he had no knowledge of the relative positions of the two armies upon his arrival. Consequently, when he had sufficient ground to accommodate his division south of the creek, he ordered a halt. Pickets were promptly sent west of the road, and Wallace began riding about, seeking information. In the dark he nearly ran over a cavalry sergeant from one of W. H. L. Wallace's units. The man soon provided him with what little knowledge he was able to obtain that night —information that the enemy held the ridge across Tilghman Creek hollow with infantry and artillery.

Returning to his division, Wallace spent much of the night deploying his regiments as they arrived along the Hamburg–Savannah Road. By 1 A.M. his infantry and artillery were in place, and Wallace attempted to sleep under a sprawling tree.

At daylight one of his battery commanders, Captain Noah S. Thompson of the 9th Indiana Battery, discovered Ketchum's Alabama Battery in park amid some of McClernand's camps in Jones field. The range was about four hundred yards, and Thompson suddenly opened fire, catching the Alabamans unaware. Yet Ketchum's gunners jumped up to man their pieces, and for a half-hour the reverberations of cannon fire filled the air.

Wallace was alert to the opportunities afforded by the topography

MAJOR GENERAL DON CARLOS BUELL. Austere, independent, and a friend of the influential McClellan, Buell commanded the Army of the Ohio. Inwardly critical of Grant for having allowed his army to be surprised and routed, Buell acted on his own to save the Federal fortunes at Shiloh. His offensive, launched before dawn on April 7, caught the Confederates by surprise and averted what otherwise would have been a major disaster. (U. S. SIGNAL CORPS PHOTO [BRADY COLLECTION], NATIONAL ARCHIVES)

and brought up Thurber's Missouri Battery toward his right. Added to the rain of shells falling on the Confederates, Thurber's fire placed their guns at a further disadvantage.

Grant, who was attracted by this firing, soon appeared to find Wallace at long last. Although Wallace had feared to advance his infantry under bombardment of the Confederate guns, Grant promptly ordered an attack.

By now Ketchum's gunners were beginning to reel under the heavy shelling. Their guns were exposed to a cross fire, and some of their best horses had been killed. Limbering up his cannon, Ketchum retired about one hundred yards to a position affording better cover.

Having witnessed the departure of the enemy artillery from the bluff, Wallace quickly sent his five thousand troops forward. Soon his brigades emerged in echelon, with a long line of skirmishers covering their front.

By now Preston Pond had discovered that the main Confederate line had fallen back the previous evening, leaving his brigade entirely unsupported. Regarding his situation as "perilous," Pond ordered his infantry withdrawn. Only Ketchum's battery and their supports, Wharton's Texas Rangers, remained to cover their withdrawal.

It was already apparent to many of the Confederates that April 7 augured ill fortune. Indeed, in the span of twenty-four hours circumstances seemed to have been completely reversed.

CHAPTER XX

A Day of Reckoning

William "Bull" Nelson's advance had begun rather inauspiciously that morning. His troops had not gone far when a halt was ordered to case the colors; the flags were being caught and torn by the trees and heavy underbrush.

Although there was no enemy opposition, his three brigades had so much difficulty in traversing the broken terrain south of the Landing that frequent halts had to be ordered to correct alignment. The mud was found to be so deep in some of the ravines that the men sank above their shoetops. For nearly a half-mile Nelson's troops stumbled forward in semidarkness, expecting at any moment to meet the enemy. "[Our advance] was made slowly and with caution, the skirmishers examining the ground with great care. . . ." observed one of Nelson's colonels.

About 5:20 A.M. Hazen's brigade, marching on Nelson's right flank, approached Hurlbut's headquarters, "beautifully situated in a little level clearing." Confederate skirmishers were sighted here, and firing broke out in front of the 6th Kentucky and 9th Indiana regiments. Yet little more than token opposition was offered by these Confederates, mostly Forrest's cavalry, and Hazen's men marched steadily on.

By now Nelson's troops were crossing a portion of the battlefield that had been hotly contested on Sunday, and the ground was strewn with dead and wounded. "Many of the wounded were in their last agonies as we passed," wrote a youthful Ohio private who found the sight sickening. "One poor fellow begged most piteously to be put out of his misery, and another kept repeating, 'O God, have mercy! O God, O God!' until we passed out of hearing." Shaken by the "gory corpses lying all about," Nelson's troops pressed grimly ahead.

At a point less than a half-mile beyond Hurlbut's headquarters the skirmishers of the 9th Indiana and 1st Kentucky came to a small clearing, Wicker field, north of the Bloody Pond. Across the field they observed three guns of a Confederate battery posted on a knoll at the edge of the woods, apparently unsupported by infantry. Boldly the Indiana and Kentucky skirmishers struck out across the clearing toward the cannon.

Although not positively identified, this Confederate artillery probably was Robertson's Alabama Battery, covering the retreat of Chalmers's infantry from their bivouac area near Hurlbut's encampments. Chalmers, unaware of Nelson's advance, previously had been advised by his division commander that the enemy was advancing on the far Confederate left. Accordingly, Chalmers had begun to fall back to a position about a half-mile in rear, near the location of Jackson's brigade. From this point the two commands would march to the left, "where it was supposed the fight would be."

Having marched in the direction of the peach orchard for the required distance, Chalmers halted along the edge of Wicker field to await the juncture of Jackson's troops. Yet from this point they suddenly observed Hazen's and Bruce's skirmishers chasing Robertson's battery.

Although the skirmishers apparently overran a portion of this battery, compelling the gunners to abandon one of their cannon, they were soon fired into by Chalmers's men. "We waited quietly until the enemy advanced within easy range, when we opened fire upon him . . ." said Chalmers. The Federal skirmishers promptly fled, abandoning their captured cannon as they recrossed Wicker field.

Then, when Chalmers again prepared to move to the left to join Jackson, a portion of Hazen's brigade, led by the 9th Indiana, rapidly came up to the fence bordering the open field. During the skirmish that followed, both Hazen and Chalmers were uncertain of what to do. For an hour and a half Hazen's and Chalmers's men maintained a desultory fire across the narrow field, effecting little damage.

Nelson, meanwhile, had been instructed to halt and await the arrival of Crittenden's division on his right. "I was halted by commands from General Buell, I having gone farther forward than I should have done, my right flank being exposed," said Nelson. Ammen's, Bruce's, and Hazen's men were told to rest where they stood, and only the 9th Indiana continued to snipe at the enemy in Wicker field.

During this extended lull Mendenhall's battery, 4th U. S. Artillery, came up at a trot from the Landing. Sent by Crittenden to support his own division, Mendenhall was diverted by Buell to Nelson's support, that division being without artillery.

Mendenhall found brisk firing occurring between the Indiana regiment and the enemy, whose artillery was so concealed by the foliage that their position could only be estimated by the dense clouds of gunsmoke. Going into action with a section of Rodman rifled guns, Mendenhall fired case shot at a range of about two hundred yards, shattering the trees about the Confederate cannon.

By the time Crittenden's men came up to join with Nelson it was after seven o'clock. Crittenden had delayed starting his brigades until after daylight, just as firing was heard in front of Nelson. William Sooy Smith, commanding one of Crittenden's brigades, reported it was 6 A.M. before his men were in motion.

Following Crittenden over the rough ground south of the landing was a portion of another fresh division, Alexander McCook's, just off the boats from Savannah. McCook had hastened his men on the overland march to Savannah on the sixth, detouring through fields adjacent to the road when wagons and artillery blocked the way. Arriving after dark on the sixth, McCook found that no preparations had been made to transport his division to the battlefield. "I ordered my staff aboard boats at the Landing, compelling the captains to get out of their beds and prepare their boats for my use," wrote the indignant McCook.

Throughout the night Rousseau's brigade was debarked, followed by Kirk's toward morning. At daylight the last of Rousseau's men hurried from the steamboats and were put into line on Crittenden's right. Receiving Buell's instructions to deploy in line of battle immediately, Rousseau's brigade hastened to the front about 6:30 A.M.

By eight Buell had nearly fifteen thousand men on the field, arrayed in a line nearly a mile long. Nelson's front extended from high ground east of the Hamburg–Savannah Road west along the fringe of Wicker field through the dense Hornets' Nest terrain nearly to Duncan field. Here Crittenden's and McCook's troops prolonged Buell's line along the border of the field to a point west of the main Corinth Road, McCook's flank resting in the timber and thick undergrowth where Sweeny had fought on Sunday.

The unexpected appearance of so many Federals was astounding to most of the Confederates, particularly among the ranks. ". . . At daybreak our pickets came rushing in under a murderous fire and the first thing we knew we were almost surrounded by six or seven regiments of Yankees," wrote a startled Confederate private. "Our men were compelled to throw away their haversacks, blankets, and everything that would retard their flight for it was death to him who lagged behind. I had my Yankee knapsack buckled so tightly that I could not get rid of it. . . . In trying to get it off I fell into a creek, and my trinkets . . . went a flying. I thank God that I got off with my life."

Another Confederate infantryman was dismayed when his booty-laden company was ordered to fall in that morning: "We were all hoping it was to march back to our camp at Monterey, but the booming of cannon and whistle of shells told us that we had bloody work to perform."

Indeed, as Adjutant General Jordan later remembered, "The sound of so much musketry at the front by this time had announced, plainly enough, the advent . . . of Buell's army. . . ."

Beauregard, realizing that the enemy had been heavily reinforced, now found that this army was "not in condition" to fight fresh troops. Bragg, who had spent the night with Beauregard in Sherman's tent, was astounded at the deplorable fighting condition of his men. "Our force was disorganized, demoralized, and exhausted," he wrote. "[They were] mostly out of ammunition, and though millions of cartridges were around them, not one officer in ten [had] supplied his men, relying on the enemy's retreat."

Disorganization was so widespread that many of the subordinate commanders were unable to obtain orders where to form that morning. Robert Trabue of Breckenridge's corps had ridden until 11 P.M. the previous evening, unsuccessfully looking for a general from whom to obtain orders. When Trabue gave up, he sent an aide with a mounted escort to continue the search. "[They] rode all night without success," he reported.

Early the following morning Trabue had an officer go to the front, again seeking orders, while his men discharged and cleaned their wet guns. Firing was heard to the right, and the officer returned bringing Beauregard's vague instructions "to move forward to whatever point the firing seemed heaviest."

Despite the widespread lack of preparations to renew the fight the lengthy halt of Buell's troops allowed the Confederates sufficient time to form several battle lines.

Chalmers, who by 8 A.M. had been sniping at the enemy for an hour and a half, was nearly out of ammunition. Since his ammunition wagons were nowhere to be found, he ordered a retreat across the Sarah Bell farm to the camps of Stuart's brigade.

One of Chalmers's staff officers already had been sent to General Withers for help, and as Chalmers replenished his cartridges from the captured enemy camps, Withers appeared with a column of reinforcements. Withers had been in the vicinity of Stuart's camp earlier that morning, forming a makeshift command from the regiments and stragglers that had spent the night in Stuart's and Prentiss's camps. Marching these troops to the vicinity of Barnes field, Withers had halted according to instructions from Bragg when he learned from Chalmers's staff officer that Chalmers "already had one fierce engagement with the enemy and was then in the second."

Turning his troops about, Withers immediately returned to the vicinity of Stuart's camps, forming a line of battle along the Ham-

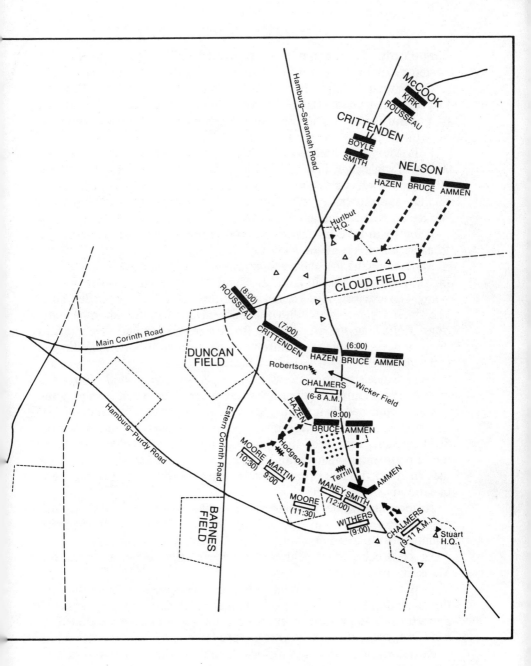

MAP 15
Buell's Offensive (Nelson's Front)
4:30 A.M.–1 P.M., April 7 (Chapter 20)

burg–Purdy Road about 9 A.M. Robertson's battery was quickly posted to sweep the open field, and Withers prepared to advance.

On Withers's left other Confederate troops, including Bowen's brigade under Colonel John Martin, were already shooting at the line of Federal troops across the old cottonfield near the peach orchard.

Following the withdrawal of Chalmers from the vicinity of Wicker field, Nelson's men had cautiously advanced to the peach orchard. Bruce's brigade occupied the low ridge attacked by Johnston on Sunday and on Bruce's left Ammen's brigade swept forward toward the Sarah Bell cabins along the Hamburg and Savannah Road.

Prior to this Federal advance Irving Hodgson's company of the Washington Artillery of New Orleans had appeared in the vicinity of Martin, having lost their way en route to join Anderson. Unlimbering in wooded terrain in front of Mendenhall's battery and their supports, Hazen's brigade, Hodgson's bronze 6- and 12-pounder guns had dueled indecisively with the Federal artillery for about a half-hour. Following the advance of Bruce's troops beyond Wicker field about 9 A.M., Hodgson withdrew to the northwest corner of the old cottonfield.

Here Bruce's troops emerged onto open ground to find Hodgson's guns perpendicular to their exposed flank. The Confederate guns severely punished Bruce's troops, causing momentary confusion in the Federal ranks. Hodgson's support, elements of Martin's and Statham's brigades, fired unexpectedly into Bruce's 1st and 2d Kentucky regiments, intensifying the disorder. Bruce could not hold his men in check, and he ordered a retreat to the edge of the woods near the Bloody Pond.

Hazen, meanwhile, had been ordered to protect Nelson's exposed flank by changing front obliquely to the west. Only the 9th Indiana remained in line facing south, this regiment having advanced in the wake of Bruce's movement to the edge of the cottonfield near the Manse George cabin.

Diagonally across the field Hodgson's Washington Artillery continued to harass Bruce's troops. General Hardee was nearby—"he seemed to be the master spirit, giving all orders and seeing that they were properly executed," wrote an eyewitness. When an order came from Beauregard about ten o'clock "to charge the enemy in conjunction with General Breckenridge," Hardee ordered the Confederate infantry in the vicinity of Hodgson to attack.

Spearheading the assault were Martin's men, led by the 2d Confederate Regiment. Hardee, too, was in their midst, riding his magnificent black and urging his men on. With a wild yell Martin's troops burst from the underbrush and crossed a corner of the open field before reentering the thicket west of the war cabin.

In their front Mendenhall's battery switched from case shot to canister. Several companies of the 6th Kentucky, acting as supports to the guns, fired repeatedly into the oncoming gray ranks. Still they came on, shouting taunts of "Bull Run! Bull Run!"

Although most of Hazen's brigade was out of sight, they could hear the enemy's shrill yells coming toward them. Buell, who was with Nelson just in the rear of Hazen's line, ordered an immediate counterattack.

Hazen, an energetic young Regular officer, had been riding back and forth behind his men all morning, gesturing with his rattan. His men were nervous, and an officer later confided, "It was my first engagement, and I didn't feel any too solid. . . . I remember distinctly that the sight of that switch steadied me."

Shouting for his brigade to advance, Hazen was disgusted to find that a part of the 6th Kentucky refused to comply, became confused, and broke ranks. Aided by an officer of Nelson's staff, Hazen spurred his horse among the Kentuckians and yelled for them to stop.

On Hazen's left flank Bruce's troops had rallied and changed front to meet the enemy threat. The Confederates continued to close rapidly and Bruce's men were soon fighting hand to hand in the underbrush.

By now Hazen's counterattack had begun to gain momentum, with the 41st Ohio leading the way. Loading and firing as they went forward, Hazen's men fell upon the outnumbered Confederate attackers and swept the Southerners before them. "They run!" shouted some of Bruce's Kentuckians, and the cry was taken up along the line.

"It was a wild pursuit, for a long distance, over a rough country," remembered one of Hazen's infantrymen. "It was my first battle, and I can now recall the wild exultation of the moment, when it seemed to me that the whole Southern Confederacy was racing through the thicket before us."

A Louisiana captain who fell, slightly wounded, in front of Hazen desperately sought to fight off his attackers. Hazen saved the man's life by shoving aside one of his men who was about to run the captain through with his bayonet. Other prisoners were captured but left behind. "We . . . kept on, stopping for nothing. . . ." wrote Hazen, and a portion of his men passed on into the open cottonfield in front of the Washington artillery.

Here the Confederate gunners were suddenly confronted by several onrushing Federal regiments. The gunners stood their posts, but Hodgson recognized the imminent danger and ordered his cannon to retire. Yet the Federals came on so rapidly that the guns could not be limbered in time to escape. Within ten minutes of their hand-to-hand encounter in the thicket the 2d Kentucky dashed among three of Hodgson's guns, overrunning the battery. Among the other Federal regiments present were the 6th Kentucky of Hazen's brigade and the 13th Ohio of Crittenden's command. All claimed capture of the three guns on the right of Hodgson's position—two 6-pounder guns and a 12-pounder howitzer.

Yet the rough terrain and heavy Confederate fire had taken a heavy toll among the attackers. Their ranks were broken and scattered as they crossed the open field. One of Hazen's men remembered seeing the fugitive enemy rallying behind a new line of battle, where "officers were riding up and down the line, waving swords and shouting. . . . I turned and looked about me—and found myself almost alone," stammered the man. "The onward movement had spent its force."

Indeed, the Confederates were hastily regrouping. Colonel B. L. Hodge of Louisiana, having taken charge of a reserve detachment, the Crescent (Louisiana) Infantry, observed that Hodgson's guns were in trouble, and boldly led his Louisianans forward in a swift counterattack. Although Hodge was thrown from his horse and knocked senseless, the Crescent regiment dashed into a heavy fire and made for the enemy-held cannon.

To the scattered remnant of Hazen's, Bruce's, and Crittenden's infantry it must have seemed as if everything was going wrong. Some of William Sooy Smith's troops that had crossed in the rear of Hazen's men mistakenly fired into their ranks, causing "great consternation." From the southern edge of the field another Confederate battery was

OFFICERS OF THE CRACK WASHINGTON ARTILLERY. Dapper, well-equipped, and almost over-confident, these young bluebloods of New Orleans were photographed shortly before their severe baptism of fire at Shiloh. Under Captain W. Irving Hodgson they fought in several desperate encounters, losing a portion of their battery on Monday before it was recaptured. (PHOTOGRAPHIC HISTORY OF THE CIVIL WAR)

playing on Hazen's troops, enfilading their line. Before the Louisiana infantry could close with the Federal troops, Hazen observed that what remained of his command "went back as fast as it could go."

A few men paused to ram mud down Hodgson's guns, there being no other means to spike the cannon; then all went back in utter disorder. Hazen ineffectively attempted to rally some of his men, lost his way in skirting the cottonfield, and was out of the battle for the remainder of the day, as were most of his men.

The 2d Kentucky went to the left to escape the pursuing Louisianans. As they ran into another Confederate force opposite the peach orchard, a deadly fire swept through their ranks. Only a third of the regiment was counted present following this encounter.

Hardee, meanwhile, had gone to the right to organize a massive counterattack against the exposed Federal flank. During the fighting in front of Hodgson's guns Hardee had several narrow escapes. His magnificent black had been shot in the shoulder, and several rifle balls had ripped his coat. Hardee was excited and in a hurry. Coming upon a small, temporary brigade made up of Texas and two Alabama regiments, he ordered them to attack, cautioning the men that some of Breckenridge's (Martin's) troops were fighting in front.

John C. Moore of the 2d Texas commanded this brigade, but Hardee soon became angered by the slowness of the Texas troops in forming and led the attack in person. As the 2d Texas marched across the cottonfield toward the peach orchard, the men were again cautioned not to fire at friendly troops.

Ahead, a large force was observed in a thick woods bordering the field, and some thought they were Confederates. Moore's men marched on, only to be staggered by a short-range volley from the edge of the woods. "So sudden was the shock and so unexpected . . . of our supposed friends, that the whole line soon gave way . . . in utter confusion," wrote the dazed Moore.

Hardee had difficulty restraining his anger as the Texans fled the field, only a small portion of the regiment having paused to fire their muskets. "Stop those men—the cowards!" shouted Hardee. Although a staff officer galloped among the fleeing men and ordered them to stop, he was unable to rally the regiment. One officer, found cowering behind a tree with some of his men, was told that Hardee regarded them "a pack of cowards." He promptly replied that he didn't give a damn what Hardee might call them, and they refused to reform.

On Moore's flank, a quarter of a mile east, James Chalmers had reorganized his brigade for further service. Additional regiments had been brought forward by Withers to reinforce the extreme Confederate right, and Chalmers put them in line ahead of his own troops.

When Hardee's urgent orders came to attack, Chalmers relinquished command of his own brigade and led the 5th Tennessee and 26th Alabama forward from the vicinity of Stuart's camps. In their front lay Ammen's brigade, the extreme left flank of Buell's line. Although Ammen's men seemed nervous while awaiting orders to resume their suspended advance, "Old Jakey" Ammen, as his men called him, sat husking corn for his horse, unmindful of the stray bullets zipping about.

About eleven o'clock Ammen's brigade was sent forward to the peach orchard. Several regiments went to the right of the Hamburg–Savannah road, while the 36th Indiana advanced to a fencerow fronting the little clearing east of the orchard.

Passing several downed fencerows, Ammen's men came under bombardment by Robertson's and Harper's batteries from the south and west end of the large open field.

Running from fence to fence, the 36th Indiana approached the Sarah Bell cabins across the road. Here they saw Chalmers's men coming from the south, evidently attempting to gain the same two log cabins. An Ohio unit was close by, lying behind a downed fence near the orchard. When the 36th's colonel, William Grose, asked a fat captain who seemed to be in command why his men were not firing at the enemy, he was told the Ohioans' muskets would not reach the Rebels. "We found the range too great for our muskets, many of the balls striking the ground in front of the enemy, while theirs, fired from the best rifles, flew past us like hail," claimed an officer of the 24th Ohio.

Grose angrily turned to his men and led a portion of his regiment forward to the cabins. Following a fight of about twenty minutes, during which Grose saw the attacking Confederates "drop faster than I could count them," Chalmers's troops were driven back.

Some of the Confederates going into this fight found their guns to be useless, the rain during the night having wet the loads. "I had not a ball screw in the regiment," complained an Alabama officer, "and could not extract them [wet loads]. Owing to these circumstances my men were exceedingly dispirited. . . ." The 26th Alabama had advanced with only one hundred fifty men present, less than half their original strength on the sixth. Chalmers soon found his makeshift brigade so unreliable that he had to order up his own brigade in order to preserve the line.

Still the Confederates were compelled to fall back. Ammen, advancing slowly, followed Chalmers to the Purdy Road ridge. Terrill's Battery H, 5th U. S. Artillery, having arrived during the heavy skirmishing in front of the Bell cabins, poured shot and shell into the retreating ranks from a forward ridge. This added fire was particularly effective, observed one of Ammen's men, and seemed to change

MAJOR GENERAL WILLIAM J. HARDEE. Commander of Johnston's first line of attack at Shiloh, author of *Hardee's Rifle and Light Infantry Tactics,* and an experienced veteran of Indian-fighting and Mexican War campaigns, Hardee was regarded as one of the foremost soldiers in the Confederacy. His role at Shiloh was influenced by the intermingled battle lines. Commanding first on the right, then toward the left on Sunday, and again on the right on Monday, Hardee was somewhat ineffectual in mounting a sustained attack. (LIBRARY OF CONGRESS)

the tide of battle. Their opponents, Robertson's battery, lost a caisson and were soon out of action.

About noon an anxious Confederate general observed that Chalmers's troops were in desperate need of help, it being feared that the enemy would soon envelop this exposed flank. Chalmers complained that he was overwhelmed by large numbers of Federals and that his men were so overcome by exhaustion that they were unresponsive to orders.

Withers already had begun frantically seeking reinforcements. Meeting Colonel Preston Smith with a regiment of Tennesseans, he ordered that officer to hurry to Chalmers's support. Colonel George Maney, with fragments of his own brigade, fell in beside Smith for a short sprint along the Hamburg–Purdy Road.

With Chalmers personally guiding Smith and Maney into line, these Confederates burst from the woods near the Sarah Bell cabins and fell on Ammen's men.

". . . The storm of musket ball, canister shot, and shell . . . was truly awful," wrote a Federal officer. With the Confederates yelling exultantly, Ammen's men were taken by surprise and withdrew to the cover of the woods. This maneuver suddenly exposed Terrill's guns along the orchard ridge, and they suffered severely. Withdrawing by sections, Terrill got his 12-pounder Napoleons and 10-pounder Parrott rifles back to the woods with the loss of one caisson. Yet so many of his gunners had been shot that Terrill served a gun himself, firing canister at point-blank range.

Nelson, who thought these guns about to be captured, dashed up to the 6th Ohio, in reserve, and shouted that the battery was the best in the service—"It must not be taken!"

A detail from the 6th Ohio rushed forward to man the guns, joining several infantrymen from another regiment. Yet Terrill stood his ground, firing deliberately into Smith's and Maney's troops. His gallantry turned the tide.

The advance was soon slowed, and the Confederate troops began to seek cover.

Chalmers, meanwhile, had been attempting to lead his own brigade to Smith's and Maney's support. "I called upon my brigade to make one more effort," he said, "but they seemed too much exhausted to make the attempt and no appeal seemed to arouse them."

As a last resort Chalmers seized the 9th Mississippi's colors and waved it in their front. At last the men moved forward, joining in the protracted fighting in the vicinity of the peach orchard.

On Ammen's right flank, west of the Hamburg–Savannah road, the confusion following Hazen's unsuccessful attack on the Washington artillery had contributed to the stalemate developing in Nelson's front. Here a portion of Bruce's brigade that had joined in the attack came streaming back through the heavy battle smoke in front of Ammen. The 24th Ohio mistook these running soldiers for the enemy and was about to open fire when one of Nelson's aides recognized the cased colors and the dapple gray horse of an officer. He galloped rapidly in front of the Ohioans, and as he reached the oncoming line, he shooks hands with one of Bruce's officers, thus averting a deadly mishap.

Because of the heavy pressure against Ammen, Mendenhall had changed position to the left and was firing into Confederate infantry across the peach orchard. Yet when a line of Federal troops marched in front and intervened, Mendenhall was prevented from firing south. Again the battery changed front, selecting a more remote target west of the orchard.

Other costly mistakes, including the opening of a sizable gap in the Federal battle line following Hazen's repulse, prevented effective Federal action along Nelson's right. Gradually an artillery duel developed, allowing many of the fatigued soldiers on both sides to lie down and rest. Here at least one Federal private snuggled beneath a sapling and fell sound asleep.

Crittenden, operating on Nelson's right flank, had been generally inactive before Hardee's attack against Hazen and Bruce about midmorning. At that time Crittenden was posted along the Sunken Road perimeter near Duncan field, with most of his strength east of the eastern Corinth road. William Sooy Smith's brigade, on the left, and had borne the brunt of an attack led by Robert Trabue of Breckenridge's corps.

Trabue had been ordered by Bragg to support Hardee's advance by inclining to the left, against Crittenden. Coming upon W. S. Smith's men in heavy timber near the Hornets' Nest, Trabue found to his dismay that only a portion of his brigade was intact: at the last minute Bragg had ordered several units out of line to make a separate attack north through Duncan field.

Trabue was easily beaten back by the counterattack generated by Hazen to the east. Barrett's battery, firing from an angle on the right of Smith's line, sprayed the Confederates with a crossfire of canister. So many of Trabue's men fell under this fire that fifty-five bodies later were counted in a space about thirty yards square.

Only the 14th Wisconsin, on Smith's extreme right, had been thrown into disorder by Trabue's attack. Momentarily regaining their alignment, the 14th soon advanced with Smith's troops in a slow but steady pursuit.

Byrne's Kentucky Battery had been shelling the Federal lines from a thicket about two hundred yards across Duncan field. The battery had been in action for several hours and was so depleted in men and munitions that volunteers from the 6th Kentucky had to man the guns.

Guiding on Byrne's battery, Smith's infantry pressed forward. Although the Confederates continued to contest "every inch of the ground," said a Federal officer, Byrne limbered up and followed Trabue to the right.

Fortunately for the Confederate army the direction of Trabue's retreat was nearly south, pulling the pursuing brigades of W. S. Smith and Boyle into the heavy timber adjacent to the eastern Corinth road. Here several of Boyle's regiments were thrown into confusion when fired into at short range in the thick underbrush. A Federal colonel thought the thicket a "jungle" and had difficulty controlling his men when they were accidentally fired upon by Mendenhall's battery. Although the Federals eventually pursued Trabue beyond the wheatfield, their battle lines were so jumbled that when Confederate cavalry and Hodgson's battered Washington Artillery were observed in front, Crittenden's scattered regiments withdrew to Duncan field.

The considerable loss of time that resulted allowed Braxton Bragg to shore up the dangerously thin Confederate line remaining in the vicinity of McClernand's camps near Duncan field. While Trabue with several regiments of his brigade passed to the right, Bragg with the remainder of Trabue's command and R. M. Russell's brigade, which had wandered aimlessly about until led by a staff officer to Bragg, had confronted McCook's division, posted just north of the main Corinth road, near the Duncan farm buildings.

Bragg boldly sent these troops—only four regiments and a battalion strong—in to attack Rousseau's brigade of McCook's division at the north end of the field.

Rousseau reported a "severe contest" lasting twenty minutes, and the Confederates were beaten off with heavy losses. Again Bragg rallied the survivors to another attack, promising support from Anderson's brigade on the left. The second assault was broken up after another sharp fight.

By now Bragg began to understand how serious the situation was in this sector. When Rousseau's brigade attempted a cautious advance, Bragg had only fragments of Trabue's and Russell's infantry and a single battery of artillery, Cobb's, with which to hold the enemy back.

Urgently Bragg sought help. Patton Anderson's brigade, fighting north of the main Corinth road, was ordered to hasten to Trabue's support. Yet Anderson was about a quarter-mile distant and had to march in a circuitous route, coming up through McClernand's camps about an hour later.

Only the cautious, uncoordinated advance by McCook and later Crittenden spared Bragg serious embarrassment. McCook had three full brigades present, but only one, Rousseau's, was in the front line. Like Crittenden, McCook had been inactive much of the morning, merely awaiting orders until Bragg had attacked.

According to Rousseau several messages were received warning that the Federal left flank was giving way—this decreed caution. Moreover the Federals had no artillery, Terrill's battery having gone to Nelson's support and Bartlett's battery having withdrawn for ammunition. Rousseau was so delayed in advancing along the main Corinth Road that some of Crittenden's men, returning from the abortive pursuit of Trabue, were first to press the attack against Bragg.

Along a timbered edge of Sherman's Review field, Cobb's Kentucky Battery had unlimbered to sweep the open ground. Approaching through the timber from the east, a portion of Boyle's and W. S. Smith's infantry suddenly came upon Cobb's guns. There was a general rush toward the cannon, and several regiments claimed the capture of a single section.

Cobb had apparently attempted to extricate his guns, but finding that too many horses had been killed, he had abandoned two field guns where they stood. The 14th Wisconsin, 13th Ohio, and 9th Kentucky were among the first to pass through these guns. A lieu-

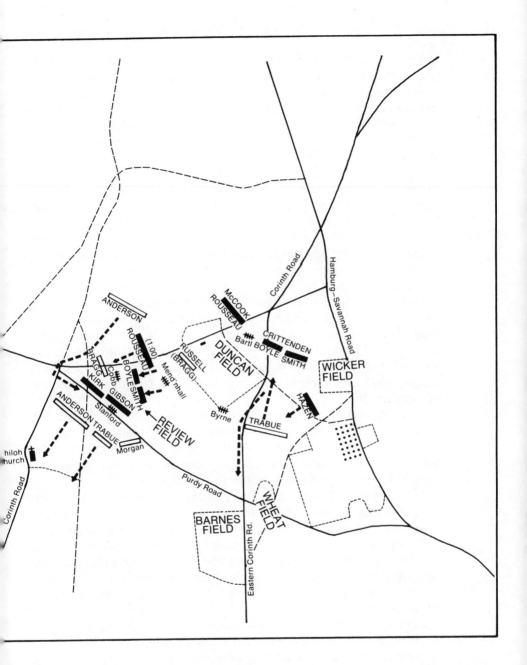

MAP 16
Buell's Offensive (Crittenden's Front)
11 A.M.–3 P.M., April 7 (Chapter 20)

tenant and a private of the 14th Wisconsin spiked the cannon to prevent their further use, and the Federals pressed on. Ahead, Cobb's disabled battery faltered and came to a halt. Bragg's thin line was on the verge of breaking up. Only Captain T. J. Stanford's Mississippi Battery, which had recently come up under Beauregard's orders, was throwing a few shells in the direction of Crittenden's attack from the vicinity of McClernand's camps.

Yet there also was much disorder among the Federal troops. Many of the advanced regiments were scattered, having in the excitement rushed blindly forward without pausing to regroup. Ahead, some of Bragg's infantry had rallied and begun to fire into the onrushing ranks. Stanford's cannon fire was particularly effective, causing the 14th Wisconsin to waver and fall back. When Bragg ordered a counterattack, the entire Federal column was thrown into confusion and went back.

Here a wounded soldier of the 14th Wisconsin staggered to his feet and saw the Confederates rushing forward along the Corinth road. "I looked behind me to see what the rest were doing," said the private. "I saw the colors going [back] out of sight over the hill and only two of our men in sight. As I started to run I heard several shouts, 'Halt!' but I knew it was the Rebs, and I hadn't any thought of obeying them.

"The ground looked queer as though it were boiling but I didn't think what the cause was until afterwards [wounded in the left arm]. . . . At that instant the bullet cut across my right shoulder and it burned like a red hot iron. My first thought was my clothes were afire, and I grabbed it with my left hand. . . ."

"I was going all this time, and I began to realize that the Rebs were shooting at me. I didn't see anything more until I got to the top of the hill. There I saw the regiment forming in line, the officers hollering, 'Fall in! Fall in!' I took my place in the front rank and my left arm began to come to its feeling. It hurt me quite bad and I was trying to raise it up, but couldn't raise it to my head. I thought, 'What will I do if we get to fighting with the bayonet,' as I supposed we were about to do."

Behind W. S. Smith's retiring troops stood a long line of Federal infantry. Firing from the middle of the Corinth Road, Rousseau's brigade halted the advancing Confederates with several short-range volleys. Here the Confederate 4th Kentucky suffered severely, particularly in officers. Major Thomas B. Monroe, Jr., was mortally wounded, and his brother, Benjamin, shot. When a lanky Kentucky captain was struck by a musket ball in the ankle, the ball lodged between the bones, and he was carried from the field screaming with pain. All but lost in the din was the "Kentucky Battle Song," sung by the embattled 4th during the fighting.

When at last these Kentuckians gave way and fell back across the field, another prominent Confederate leader lay in a pool of blood. Kentucky's provisional governor, George W. Johnson, who had lost his horse (he had formally enlisted as a private in Company E, 4th Kentucky) had been shot twice in the melee. With wounds in the right thigh and abdomen Johnson lay helpless on the battlefield, not to be discovered for nearly twenty-four hours.

Despite the obvious carnage in front, Rousseau was hesitant to advance his Federal infantry. "I was fully impressed . . . by your words to me . . ." wrote Rousseau of an earlier conversation with McCook, "that my position was in the center, and must be held at every hazard, and that you would [soon] support me with the balance of your division. . . ."

For forty minutes the fighting continued. Rousseau awaited reinforcements, while other nearby Federal troops merely skirmished in a desultory manner with Bragg's infantry. Of particular annoyance to the Federals during this lull was the fire from Stanford's battery in Review field. Not having artillery with which to counter Stanford's fire, Buell about 1 P.M. ordered Mendenhall's battery to move promptly to Crittenden's and McCook's support.

Mendenhall soon came up to unlimber along a prominent knoll within a half-mile of Stanford's guns. Following a delay while the Federal infantry cleared a forward zone, Mendenhall opened against the Confederate battery.

Emboldened by this artillery support, some of Rousseau's and W. S. Smith's troops that had rested within three hundred yards of the Confederate guns began to creep forward. Although Anderson's and a portion of Trabue's brigade by now had reinforced Bragg, the Confederates couldn't agree on the proper course of action. Anderson wanted to charge, but when Trabue pleaded that his own troops were needed to support Stanford if hard-pressed, the initiative was lost.

Anderson finally took his men back under cover of a hill a short distance south, in order to escape the accurate shelling of Mendenhall's guns. Trabue, who was to support Stanford, was forced back by the advancing Federal infantry. Russell also was caught in a cross fire and went back, leaving only the artillery to contest the ground.

Stanford was angry. Noting that the Federal lines wavered under the repeated discharges of his cannon, he attempted to hold his ground, being determined to sacrifice the battery if necessary. ". . . A little better support from [our] infantry, which was not given us," complained Stanford, "would have sufficed to have routed them completely." Instead his battery was nearly engulfed by the enemy. "Large gaps were made by every gun at each discharge," said Stanford. "Three regimental flags being in full view, I gave orders to point at them, and soon had the satisfaction of seeing two of them fall to the ground, both being raised again [however]. One was again cut down. Being hard pressed, and almost surrounded by their large force, I determined to withdraw my command. . . . My horses being nearly all killed, I could only bring away two pieces, leaving four upon the field."

As some of the 15th U.S. Infantry of Rousseau's brigade dashed among the guns, a wounded Confederate was heard to curse his captors, saying they had slaughtered the gunners like cattle and that they could take the battery and be damned.

Nearby, Cobb's abandoned guns were overrun for the second time by W. S. Smith's and Boyle's troops. When they were found to be spiked, the Federals passed on, only to encounter Anderson's troops behind the brow of the next hill. Anderson had been joined by Russell and some of Cheatham's troops falling back from the vicinity of McClernand's camps. Aided by several batteries of artillery, he was finally able to check the Federal advance.

Smith's and Boyle's troops again were scattered, and Rousseau's were out of ammunition. At least one Federal regimental commander asked for artillery support to move up, but then fell back before it arrived. Mendenhall, who came up at a gallop, was soon throwing canister into the woods from a site near the captured guns. Although the 6th Indiana of Rousseau's brigade was detailed to support these guns, Rousseau withdrew the remainder of his brigade to replenish ammunition.

Kirk, who moved up in Rousseau's place, was joined by Gibson's brigade on the left. They were just in time to meet Anderson's, Cheatham's, Russell's, and other scattered Confederate troops who had moved up into the void created by Rousseau's withdrawal. The pressure was particularly heavy on the Federal left, along the southern edge of Review field.

Here the 6th Indiana fought to drive off the attacking Confederates attempting to get to Mendenhall's guns. "This battery opened on the Rebels and fired with great rapidity," wrote the 6th's colonel, "but fearing the capture of [its] pieces soon left the field. . . ." Face to face with the wildly yelling enemy, the 6th stood its ground and poured volley after volley of musketry into the gray ranks. "They were coming like devils through a thick underbrush, with their stars and bars fluttering high in the air," wrote an eyewitness. The 6th's musketry was so effective that a few minutes later the man observed that only dead and wounded Rebels remained in their front, the rest having fled.

Yet the pressure remained great on Gibson's left, where the Confederates were attempting to outflank the main battle line. The 77th

Pennsylvania of Kirk's brigade was rushed over to help out. Among the troops they encountered were Morgan's Kentucky Cavalry. Here a Confederate infantryman watched anxiously as Morgan's squadron advanced in the direction of Mendenhall's guns. ". . . When within 30 yards of them [they] found a fence between them and the battery and therefore they could not capture it, and were forced to wheel to the left and retreat. As they came back to us many an empty saddle was seen," the man sadly remembered.

Brought to a halt by the large numbers of Federal troops, the Confederates gradually began to give way in front of Gibson's brigade. Retreating from the open field, several regiments became scattered and had to be rallied by officers, including Cheatham. Although a few regiments were urged to counterattack in order to gain time to re-form the line, the appeal fell on deaf ears. Cheatham personally served one of Melancthon Smith's guns, and a staff officer had to risk his life unduly by seizing a battle flag and carrying it forward under a shower of musketry to steady some troops.

By this time the main Confederate line had withdrawn a quarter-mile south to the vicinity of Sherman's former headquarters. "Large numbers of stragglers could now be seen in all directions making their way to the rear," wrote Patton Anderson. A further problem was that many of the Confederates were out of ammunition. Anderson sent an entire battalion to rummage through Sherman's abandoned camps, but they came back with only a few boxes. When Anderson encountered a section of artillery standing idly by, he asked an officer to open fire. He was told the guns were out of ammunition, there were no horses to draw off the guns, and that orders had just been received to spike the cannon and abandon them.

Although the enemy lines had halted momentarily, Anderson's infantry was ordered by Colonel Thomas Jordan to withdraw farther to the main Corinth road near Shiloh Church, an area now overflowing with many Confederate wounded.

Having set fire to some log buildings in the vicinity of McClernand's camps, the Confederates streamed to the rear. "I was completely exhausted . . ." wrote a Mississippi rifleman, who now realized that the enemy was too strong and that they must soon abandon the battlefield.

CHAPTER XXI

A Profitless Combat

P. G. T. Beauregard apparently was among the more surprised Confederate officers on the morning of April 7. According to several staff officers the firing of musketry and field artillery roused the slumbering headquarters staff shortly after daylight. When word soon came that the Federals were in strong force on the left, Beauregard ordered reinforcements to that sector. Yet this was followed by the sound of heavy musketry far to the right. Although there is no evidence that at this point he knew of Buell's presence, Beauregard understood that his army was being attacked, evidently by large numbers of Federal troops. Instead of resuming the offensive as anticipated, Beauregard suddenly was required to conduct an uncertain defensive.

His army was scattered, disorganized, and in poor condition to fight a strong adversary. Nonetheless Beauregard plunged into the task of organizing for a fight with considerable energy.

From his headquarters near Shiloh Church Beauregard sent Captain B. B. Waddell of his staff to find and bring up Leonidas Polk, who had retired to his Saturday-night bivouac area. Thomas Jordan was told to get off a dispatch to Corinth ordering the post commandant to organize all stragglers and unemployed troops and "send them forward to Shiloh [the battlefield] by the Ridge road." "Let them be sent whether armed or not," urged Beauregard.

During the morning the difficult task of organizing the scattered troops roaming the battlefield and fashioning a line of battle occupied much of Beauregard's time. One improvised unit, dubbed the "Beauregard Regiment," was formed of a half-dozen fragments of former regiments. Since no field officers were present, Beauregard put Bragg's engineer, Captain Lockett, in command as acting colonel.

Although the fighting grew more desperate about midday, Beauregard was quite willing to pursue the contest. To a regiment of

Louisianans coming up to join in the fighting he appeared almost eager. "General Beauregard rode up to us with a smile on his face, looking as cool and collected amid the hail storm of minie balls as if he had been in a drawing room. Taking off his hat to us as he passed, he said: 'Men, the day is ours, you are fighting a whipped army, fire low and be deliberate.' With three cheers we rushed into the bloody fray."

Yet as the day wore on Beauregard's mood began to change. Already apparent was the widespread exhaustion of the Confederate troops. "The fire and animation had left our troops," noticed a staff officer. To some it seemed that the army was fighting simply because of shouted orders.

Many of the men were disconsolate and refused to respond to further urging. Terrified by "the most terrific fire of musketry I was ever under," said a Tennessean, his regiment lay flat as a storm of fire swept overhead. Gone was the elation so prevalent that morning: following the ransacking of a captured camp one gleeful sergeant had shown up for roll call with "a big round western reserve cheese" stuck on his bayonet. Most of the men had long since thrown away much of the plunder taken from the enemy tents, and by now they were concerned simply with staying alive.

By early afternoon Beauregard recognized the crucial morale problem threatening his army. Following the collapse of the Confederate line in the vicinity of McClernand's camps Beauregard attempted to rally the troops in person. Yet it became evident that many of the troops were beyond further effort. It was known that the enemy had been heavily reinforced and had continued to receive fresh troops as the fight progressed. Moreover, since large segments of the Confederate army had been dispatched to bolster the right during the morning, it seemed that the weakened left flank must soon be overwhelmed. Accordingly, at 1 P.M. Beauregard instructed one of his staff officers to "have the muskets and arms about the camps in rear loaded into wagons and taken to the rear."

With preparations underway to withdraw the army should further efforts fail to drive back the Federals, Beauregard continued to reorganize the Confederate battle line for one last attempt to gain a decisive victory. But the line was facing in two directions at one time.

Much of the Federal pressure since morning had been exerted against the Confederate left. Here a mixed gathering of Confederate troops under Ruggles and S. A. M. Wood had attempted to halt an enemy advance initially spearheaded by Lew Wallace's division.

Wallace, who began his attack against Preston Pond's brigade west of Tilghman Creek at 6:30 A.M., by midafternoon was poised opposite and beyond the extreme Confederate left flank west of

Shiloh Church. Wallace had thus gained considerably more ground than Buell, but this was largely the result of faulty Confederate troop dispositions.

Preston Pond's brigade had confronted Wallace at daylight and had been forced to withdraw to Marsh's camp at the south end of Jones field. Soon sent by Ruggles to protect the extreme Confederate left near Owl Creek, Pond was re-routed to the support of Hardee following Buell's advance. Pond thus marched to the extreme right and deployed, but was again redeployed by Beauregard. Shortly thereafter he met Polk, who ordered him to support his line. While en route to join Polk's forces, however, Pond was again ordered by Beauregard to move to the extreme left to fight in the vicinity of Shiloh Church. This constant marching and countermarching kept Pond out of the fighting until midafternoon, tired his men, and deprived the Confederate left flank of sorely needed support.

In Pond's absence Ruggles and S. A. M. Wood bore the brunt of the initial fight against an overcautious Wallace.

For a while it appeared there would be little fighting at all. Having advanced to the bluff overlooking Tilghman Creek, Lew Wallace ordered his men to halt until Sherman's division advanced to their support. Sherman, who also moved up cautiously after hastily reorganizing his shattered command, had halted east of Jones field when he came under bombardment from Ketchum's battery, posted in the opposite timber. "Here I remained, patiently waiting for the sound of General Buell's advance upon the main Corinth road," said Sherman. More than two hours after Wallace's troops had occupied the northern fringe of Jones field, Sherman, about 10 A.M., was satisfied from the sound of gunfire that Buell was making progress, and he ordered his troops to resume their advance.

Wallace had become somewhat impatient during the lengthy delay, however, and had ordered a reconnaissance. Noting that the "swampy low grounds" of Snake Creek offered protection to his right and that the Confederate left flank was exposed by Pond's withdrawal, Wallace determined to turn the enemy's flank by "a left half wheel of the whole division." This involved a shift to the right by Thayer's brigade from a line fronting nearly west to a line facing south.

While this movement was in progress, the Confederates had sufficiently recovered to organize a thrust at Wallace's and Sherman's idle troops, lying along the eastern fringe of Jones field. When Pond asked for support upon falling back in the direction of McClernand's camps, Ruggles had responded. Leading Gibson's brigade in the direction of Jones field, Ruggles appeared about 9 A.M. and began

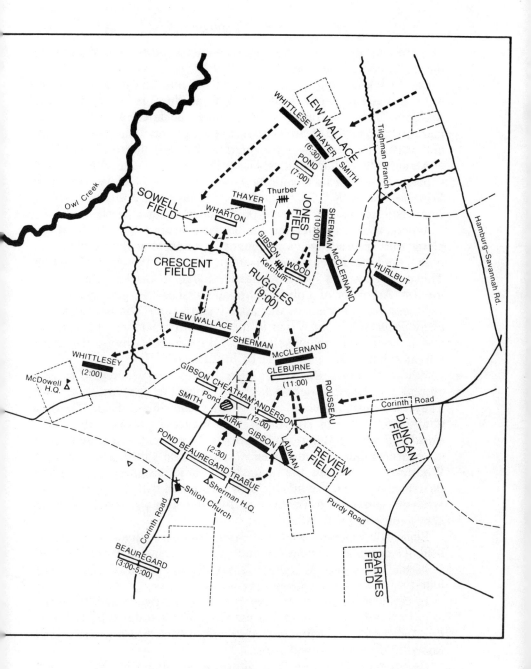

MAP 17
Advance of the Federal Right
6:30 A.M.–5:00 P.M., April 7 (Chapter 21)

preparations to attack Thompson's battery, posted by Wallace at the north end of the field.

On Ruggles's right S. A. M. Wood fell into line by Beauregard's order just as Ruggles ordered Gibson to advance. Emerging from the southern fringe of timber skirting Jones field, Gibson and Wood marched across the cleared ground at an oblique angle to the Federal guns unlimbered nearly a quarter of a mile distant.

Meanwhile Wallace had replaced Thompson's battery, which had expended much of its ammunition, with Thurber's battery. Although firing at first on Ketchum's guns near Pond's last position, Thurber soon changed targets, bringing the infantry under a heavy fire.

Wood, who was directing his advance against Sherman's troops along the eastern edge, was caught in midfield with his flank exposed, and he retreated in disorder. Gibson attempted to get at Thurber's guns and had his brigade charge to the left. Apparently the 1st Arkansas of Gibson's brigade rushed the guns with such swiftness that one cannon was abandoned before Thurber could get away. Wallace's infantry was in the strip of timber nearby, however, and poured such an effective fire into Gibson's troops that they retreated before the gun could be brought off.

Wharton's Texas Ranger Cavalry, ordered by Beauregard to ride around the Federal right flank and attack in the rear, had met Thayer's brigade circling to the right near Sowell field. Thayer's infantry fired five or six volleys into Wharton's ranks with "disastrous" effect, said Wharton. Wharton's horse went down, and "with no prospect but that the men would all be killed . . ." related Wharton, "I withdrew the command a short distance, dismounting the entire regiment." While his men skirmished with Thayer's troops, Wharton sent word to Beauregard that the enemy's reserves were in heavy force in his front.

Beauregard already was convinced the present line could not be held. The remnant of McClernand's and a portion of Hurlbut's divisions had moved up on Sherman's left, and a section of McAllister's battery was firing on Gibson's men from the east.

In front of Ketchum's battery Whittlesey's brigade had advanced to join with Thayer's troops for the flank attack ordered by Wallace. Pushing steadily ahead, they approached Ketchum's position and forced that battery to withdraw.

Beauregard, observing that Gibson was outflanked, ordered him back in the direction of Shiloh Church, along with S. A. M. Wood and Wharton.

Yet the most serious threat was developing farther east, in the vicinity of the main Corinth road. Here the sound of gunfire from Rousseau's brigade of McCook's division encouraged Sherman as it came up the road about 11 A.M. Sherman, advancing south to correspond with McClernand's and Hurlbut's troops, later met Rousseau's men near McClernand's headquarters. They were the same troops he had once commanded while in Kentucky, and Sherman observed: "They all recognized me and such shouting you never heard. I asked to pass their ranks and they gave me the lead."

Bragg, striving to hurl back the heavy Federal columns gathering opposite the Confederate center, hastily sent what troops he could organize to attack this enemy concentration. Pat Cleburne, the battling Irishman who had seen his twenty-seven-hundred-man brigade reduced to eight hundred present following Sunday's fight, was lying nearby, together with some of Breckenridge's troops. When an order came to attack the dense enemy columns immediately, Cleburne balked at what were obviously foolish tactics. "I sent back word that I was completely without support and outflanked on the left [by Wallace], and would be destroyed if I advanced," said Cleburne. Yet Bragg seemed to have learned little from yesterday's bloody repulses at the Hornets' Nest. Cleburne was notified "that the order was from General Bragg, that it was positive, and I must immediately advance."

Cleburne's isolated attack was hardly under way when an abrupt halt was ordered because Confederate artillery was firing diagonally across his path. When Federal rifled cannon responded, Cleburne crept forward to a ravine and lay for a half-hour watching "the fiercest [artillery fight] I saw during the day." Finally the Confederate guns were driven away, and Cleburne attempted to execute Bragg's order. Charging into a thick undergrowth of young trees where he was unable to see right or left, he saw his men "dropping all around before the fire of an unseen foe."

"My brigade was repulsed and almost completely routed in this unfortunate attack," wrote the angered Cleburne. Only one of his four original regiments could be rallied, the rest having scattered to fight with other units or having fled the field.

Among the troops Cleburne had encountered was a large portion of Grant's Pittsburg Landing army. Battered and disorganized by Sunday's fighting, Grant's effectives now numbered less than seven thousand by Buell's estimate.* Those units still operational and serving with their original commands were mostly from McClernand's, Hurlbut's, and Sherman's divisions. Because of their limited numbers Grant's troops occupied only a quarter-mile front between Rousseau on the left and Wallace on the right.

Following the disaster of Sunday many of Grant's soldiers were shaken, particularly Sherman's. As they approached McClernand's Second Brigade camps just before Cleburne's attack, the men of the 53d Ohio took a scattered volley. Confederate skirmishers were firing

* Excluding Lew Wallace's fresh division, not in Sunday's fight.

from behind rude breastworks fashioned of cut timber that had originally been felled by McClernand's men to clear a parade ground.
Immediately the 53d bolted to the rear, breaking through McClernand's ranks on the way. Colonel Marsh attempted to rally them and
was infuriated when they refused to halt. "Despite all my efforts
and those of General McClernand and staff, they crossed the field
and sought protection in rear of the timber. Their officers, instead of
seconding the efforts made to rally the soldiers, set them an example
of speed in flying from the enemy that even [Confederate Brigadier
General John B.] Floyd might envy. So disgusted was I with their
conduct that I asked General McClernand to order them off the field,
which he did."

Pushing rapidly ahead with his own troops, Marsh easily reoccupied his brigade camps. Yet McClernand was soon informed that the
Confederates were advancing and about to turn his left flank. To
prevent this McClernand ordered his infantry to march to the east.
They soon came directly into the path of Cleburne's attack.

"Here one of the severest conflicts ensued that occurred during the
two days," wrote McClernand. Despite Cleburne's inability to see
what was in front, his riflemen caused a portion of McClernand's line
to fall back "in great confusion" to a nearby ravine. These troops
were soon rallied, however, and were led back to their former position. When Cleburne retreated under heavy pressure toward Review
field, McClernand's infantry doggedly followed.

Yet the Confederates were reinforced at the crucial moment by
troops brought from their rear bivouac area by Benjamin F. Cheatham. "My engagement here commenced almost the instant I had
formed," wrote Cheatham, who thought the fighting was "the most
hotly contested I have ever witnessed."

Although many of Cheatham's men were of Bushrod Johnson's
brigade, the Confederate battle line here was decidedly mixed. Randall Gibson's brigade, sent from the extreme left to aid the hard-
pressed Bragg, quickly came up and joined in the fight. Several units
from other commands also were present, including Girardey's battery
of artillery, which had supported Cleburne before his attack. Farther
to the right a portion of Patton Anderson's brigade moved into line
to support Cheatham. As a result of this large influx of Confederate
reinforcements the tide of battle soon swung in favor of the South.
". . . Summoning everything . . ." wrote a Confederate general,
"we led the columns up with a volley and a shout from the whole
line, which proved irresistible and sent [the enemy] flying back to his
second line. . . ."

Dashing forward with a small unit of infantry, Major John H.
Kelly of S. A. M. Wood's brigade led his men through a waist-deep

pond and forward into McClernand's much fought over Second
Brigade camps.

The fighting at this point, near Water Oaks Pond, soon became
so desperate that an awed William Tecumseh Sherman said it was
"the severest musketry fire I ever heard." By now the Federal battle
lines were in considerable disorder. Instead of retreating slowly, at
least one Federal regiment was thrown into confusion when "by bad
management" friendly regiments fired into the more advanced troops.

McClernand regarded his position "most critical" and considered
that a general retreat was inevitable. In order to slow the onrushing
enemy a single regiment of Indiana infantry, the 32d under Colonel
August Willich, was told to make a bayonet charge. An admiring
Sherman watched Willich's men enter the Water Oaks thicket "in
beautiful style," only to be hurled back after a fight of about twenty
minutes.

Then, marching up the smoke-shrouded main Corinth road, Rousseau's brigade appeared. Both Sherman and McClernand agreed that
Rousseau's men saved the vulnerable Federal line from further retreat. ". . . Fortunately the Louisville Legion [5th Kentucky], forming a part of General Rousseau's brigade, came up and succored me,"
wrote the relieved McClernand.

Pouring "one of the most terrible fires" McClernand had ever witnessed into the Confederate ranks, Rousseau's troops pressed forward
toward the "green point of timber." For forty minutes the fight continued in great fury. Sherman, attempting to do everything possible
to win the day, personally directed the fire of two 24-pounder howitzers of McAllister's battery, which he said "by almost Providential
decree" happened to be present.

The fire of the heavy howitzers, aided by several other Federal
batteries with McClernand's and Hurlbut's troops, helped diminish
the volume of fire coming from Girardey's and Robertson's batteries.
Finally Rousseau's heavy pressure on the Confederates east of Water
Oaks Pond forced the gray battle line to fall back.

Observing that "large masses" of enemy were moving against
him, S. A. M. Wood found that he could not hold his ground. "The
regiment next to my brigade on the left broke and fell back two or
three times," said Wood. "I went to it for the purpose of trying to
steady the men. One of the colonels informed me his men were worn
out and could not be rallied. He was alone. The men were scattered
in the bushes. . . ." Cheatham, who also was carried back, complained of the want of artillery, his own batteries being scattered
on other parts of the field. Anderson had been withdrawn to help
Trabue's infantry farther to the south. Gibson's men admittedly were
disorganized and "sinking with fatigue," and they followed the gen-

eral rearward movement that carried past Water Oaks Pond to the vicinity of Shiloh Church.

Lew Wallace, who had long since suspended the flank attack ordered of Thayer's and Whittlesey's brigades, now sent orders to pursue the Confederates. Wallace had been alarmed by the noon attack led by Cheatham, Gibson, and Wood "as isolation from the rest of the army seemed imminent." Utilizing his reserves and the 15th Michigan Infantry, temporarily serving with his division, Wallace had anxiously maneuvered his troops to protect his left flank, which had been made vulnerable by the disorder in Sherman's lines. Whittlesey's brigade had been recalled from the far right to support one of Sherman's brigades, and Thurber's battery had been unlimbered to cover a retreat. Thayer's brigade had been pinned down by bursting Confederate shells that fell with great accuracy among the infantry.

Only when Willich's bayonet charge, followed by Rousseau's counterattack, checked the Confederate advance along the Corinth road did Wallace regain his confidence. Yet most of Thayer's brigade by now had expended its ammunition, causing a delay in the pursuit of the enemy while a fresh supply was found.

When Wallace heard firing toward the west, he transferred most of Whittlesey's brigade back to the extreme Federal right. Eventually they came upon a single Confederate battery and sharpshooters, posted near McDowell's ransacked camps, and easily drove them off. Having thus delayed in following up the Confederate withdrawal from Water Oaks Pond, Wallace unwittingly relieved much of the pressure on Beauregard, who about 2 P.M. was attempting to re-form his shattered left flank in the vicinity of Shiloh Church.

Beauregard had been further apprised of the mounting crisis on the left by Bragg, who was hard-pressed by Crittenden and McCook. Riding among the exhausted Confederate infantry streaming to the rear past Shiloh Church, Beauregard could not rally the men. Governor Harris of Tennessee was with him, making speeches to those who would listen. When Beauregard found that his appeals to re-form were mostly unheeded, he seized a passing battle flag and led a handful of men up to their alignment.

Beauregard had one unplayed card in his hand—he held in reserve a large portion of Preston Pond's brigade, which had been marched and countermarched most of the day. Fifteen minutes following their arrival at Shiloh Church, Governor Harris was dispatched with orders for the brigade to charge and drive back the advancing enemy. Since only two regiments were present with Pond, Beauregard hastened to support the attack with all available troops.

Colonel Thomas H. Hunt of the 5th Kentucky was found nearby with some of Trabue's men. Beauregard, now grim and taciturn, spoke but few words. Without addressing Hunt, Beauregard turned to his regiment and said, "Forward." Bullets and shells were shrieking through the air, and Hunt asked for directions. "Put them in right here," came the reply. In this manner about six regiments were finally brought into line near Sherman's headquarters, though with no enthusiasm on the part of the men.

Beauregard, loath to give up hope of victory, personally had to lead at least one of these regiments into the fight. Grasping a battle flag, he carried the banner forward to induce the men to attack. Although his staff officers remonstrated with him against exposing himself, Beauregard, together with Braxton Bragg, went among the ranks as the command, "Fix bayonets!—charge," rang out.

Despite the feeble effort of some of the Confederate troops, enough of Pond's and Trabue's men ran forward to achieve a limited success.

Having paused to regroup and replenish ammunition following the rout of the Confederates from the vicinity of Water Oaks Pond, the Federal troops near McClernand's forward camp about 2:30 P.M. were suddenly struck and pushed back by Beauregard's attack.

William H. Gibson, whose brigade had helped replace Rousseau's in the front line, found that the Confederates were flanking him on his left under cover of a ravine. Hurriedly Gibson sought to change front under a heavy fire.

Colonel E. N. Kirk's brigade, fighting on the right of Gibson, was already in trouble. Several field officers had been shot from their horses, and an Illinois regiment was wavering under the terrific fire. Kirk, seeing the confusion, rode among his soldiers, seized a flag, and rushed forward. He was struck in the shoulder and nearly killed. One of Kirk's colonels, Sion S. Bass of the 30th Indiana, already had taken one wound, but refused to quit the fight. His regiment was in disorder when Bass was again shot.

Division commander McCook anxiously observed that "the fires from the contending ranks were two continuous sheets of flame." Lew Wallace, whose First Brigade was also in danger of being outflanked, thought the firing was "grand and terrible." When one of his colonels asked for assistance, Wallace sent word to fall back "if it got too hot."

". . . [This was] the most trying moment to us of the day," remembered an Indiana officer who thought the reputation of his regiment at stake. Yet the Confederates were suffering equally severe losses. Colonel Alfred Mouton of Pond's brigade was shot in the head, and Looney's regiment, the 38th Tennessee, which attacked in the face of a "galling" fire, was badly cut up. Moreover Federal cannon were raking the nearly exhausted Confederate troops at close range.

One of Trabue's men, Johnny Green of the 5th Kentucky, was just raising his gun to fire when a Minie ball knocked him down: ". . . Just as I had loaded and was raising my gun to fire I fell from a bullet which struck me just over the heart. I felt sure it had gone clear through me and it flashed through my mind that I would live until the arterial blood started back to my heart, when I would drop dead, as I had once seen a deer do which my father shot through the heart. I rose to my knees, took a hurried aim and fired at a clump of the enemy. By this time I was surprised to find that I was still alive. I felt my breast to learn the extent of my wound . . . I found one piece of the bullet laying against my skin inside my clothes just over my heart. The ball had passed through the stock of my gun, split on the iron ramrod . . . and the other piece had passed through my jacket and buried itself in a little testament in my jacket pocket. The force of the blow knocked me down, but nothing more serious had befallen me."

At a point near McClernand's camps the momentum of the Confederate charge was spent. McCook had been asked by McClernand for reinforcements, and he sent Lauman's brigade of Hurlbut's division to attack toward the right. ". . . We arrived at a very opportune moment," wrote Colonel Hugh Reed of the 44th Indiana. "We found the enemy charging upon and driving our forces to the left and front over cleared ground used as a drill ground by our troops. I immediately brought my regiment into line and opened fire on the enemy. Our charge took them by surprise. They immediately retreated to their right and rear."

In addition to Hurlbut's troops, previously held in reserve, Rousseau's brigade was marched back to the front with replenished cartridge boxes. Present also was Willich's 32d Indiana regiment, having regrouped following their bayonet charge at Water Oaks Pond.

The appearance of a large column of Federal infantry moving to the attack was the final blow to Beauregard's small contingent. About 3:30 P.M. the utterly exhausted Confederate troops broke to the rear, taking a heavy bombardment from several batteries of artillery that had just come up, including Bouton's battery of the Chicago Light Artillery. ". . . As we were ordered to retreat across an open field in full view of that battery we ran at full speed," wrote one of Trabue's privates. When Breckenridge saw his Kentuckians fleeing, however, he dashed among them and chided them for running away.

Nearby, a Louisiana officer observed that his men "were completely exhausted from inanition and physical fatigue, many dropping in the attempt to move onward." Another officer, one of Anderson's men, said he experienced "the most terrific fire of musketry I was ever under." "We had been double quicked until I was exhausted," wrote the officer. "We lay flat down and the fire swept over us. The regiment retreated. I was the last to leave. Every person appeared to be ahead of me. Getting up and retreating under that fire appeared to be almost certain death. To lay still seemed certain capture, and I told the boys to get away. I had no sooner got up and started than my foot struck a vine and I pitched head foremost to the ground. Again I got up, and again I pitched headlong. [I got] up again and crept away, [but] I could not run. I told the boys who were with me, if they could fight any more to do so, that I could not. I never was exhausted so completely in my life."

Beauregard had by now accepted what was obvious. Adjutant General Jordan, speaking with Governor Harris, agreed that the day was lost and thought it best to withdraw. Riding up to Beauregard's side, Jordan spoke candidly: "General, do you not think our troops are very much in the condition of a lump of sugar thoroughly soaked with water, but yet preserving its original shape, though ready to dissolve? Would it not be judicious to get away with what we have?"

Beauregard's reply was hushed. "I intend to withdraw in a few moments," he said.

Summoning his staff, Beauregard gave the necessary orders—to post a covering force and withdraw the troops. While the aides dashed away on their errands, Beauregard rode south toward Shiloh Church, where he found some idle troops milling about. Placing them in position to face the enemy, Beauregard continued to the rear, organizing a mixed command of S. A. M. Wood's and Trabue's infantry along the ridge overlooking Shiloh Church. Ketchum's battery, joined by a single gun from a shattered battery, was posted along the left of this line. Farther to the rear, in front of Wood's house along the main Corinth road, Beauregard soon placed another battery.

By 3:30 P.M. the retreat had begun.

On the far Confederate right desultory firing had continued from midday throughout the long and weary afternoon. Many of the Southern units had utilized the impasse to replenish ammunition. Unfortunately the whereabouts of the munitions wagons was generally unknown, and a sufficient supply had to be scavenged from the captured Federal camps. Having marched to the rear with empty guns, Preston Smith's regiment and Martin's brigade were absent from Withers's battle line for a considerable length of time. A. P. Stewart's brigade was so destitute of ammunition that he withdrew his men and went himself in search of cartridges.

Although Terrill's battery of U. S. regulars continued to shell the Confederate lines, Colonel George Maney finally became so impatient at the enemy's lack of aggressiveness that he sent several regiments and detachments of stragglers to aid Cheatham on the left.

By early afternoon Withers had been seriously weakened by the continuous straggling and withdrawal of combat units to search for ammunition. ". . . Finding that the enemy were content to hold their position and not advance on us," said Withers, "our line of the morning was resumed."

Withers's withdrawal route led west along the Purdy road, past the peach orchard and the old cottonfield, to a point south along the eastern Corinth road near Prentiss's old camps.

While this movement was in progress, Buell ordered Nelson's division to advance against the retreating enemy. With arms trailed and at double-quick, Nelson's men passed over a forward knoll just in time to see Withers's troops disappear from sight along the eastern Corinth road.

Only toward the west, where Harper's Jefferson (Mississippi) Battery had been dueling with Terrill's Federal battery, was there spirited action. Here the 2d Kentucky Infantry of Bruce's brigade had been resting quietly, supporting Terrill's battery, when one of Buell's staff officers rode up to order an attack. Joined by a portion of the 9th Indiana that had been separated in the earlier fighting, the 2d Kentucky boldly charged with fixed bayonets.

Ahead, Harper's battery had been reduced to a near shambles by the protracted fighting. Its guns were undermanned, horses and equipment were missing, gunners were dropping at their posts from exhaustion, and worse still, they were out of canister.

When Harper's infantry supports fell back, the battery was forced to limber up under a heavy fire. Before the guns could get away, the 2d Kentucky closed to about fifty yards and fired into the battery, felling five horses hitched to one of the pieces. The cannon was promptly abandoned, and the 2d Kentucky dashed on, overrunning another of Harper's guns that was held fast by dead horses.

Yet Confederate reinforcements were nearby. Martin's brigade, returning from ransacking Prentiss's encampments for ammunition, saw the panic and confusion in the Southern battle line. Martin led his brigade in a brisk countercharge and easily routed the lone Federal regiment in a brief encounter.

A Federal captain who moments before had watched his men overrun Harper's guns was shot and left behind in the chaos. "The shock of a musket ball striking one in the hip has about the same feeling as if a person is struck with a blunt instrument or club, and produces a paralyzing sensation," the captain recalled. "When struck

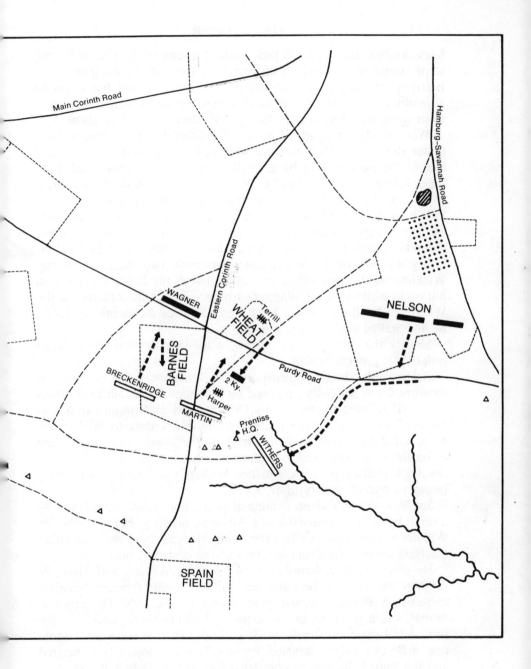

Main Corinth Road

Hamburg-Savannah Road

Eastern Corinth Road

WAGNER

WHEAT FIELD

Terrill

NELSON

BARNES FIELD

BRECKENRIDGE

2 Ky.

Harper

Purdy Road

MARTIN

Prentiss H.Q.

WITHERS

SPAIN FIELD

MAP 18
Final Action on the Federal Left
1 P.M.–3 P.M., April 7 (Chapter 21)

I fell doubled like a closed jack knife. I attempted to rise, believing some friend or foe had struck me with the butt of his gun . . ." Bleeding profusely, the crippled Federal officer could but crawl to a nearby log for shelter and watch helplessly as his men disappeared from sight, wheeling one of the spiked cannon ahead of them.

West of Martin's path of attack, Confederate troops immediately under Breckenridge's command were ordered to move forward and join in the pursuit. Led by a small brigade of Tennessee and Kentucky infantry under Colonel C. Wickliffe of the 7th Kentucky, these troops quickly moved across a small creek and up the slope of a hill in thick underbrush near the eastern Corinth road. Here they ran into Wagner's brigade of Thomas J. Wood's division, posted along the roadside to await orders. This fresh brigade of Federal infantry was just off the boats from Savannah, two thousand strong. Wickliffe went down with a mortal wound in the head, and his men fell back, while some of Wagner's troops also retreated momentarily. When Martin discovered a large Federal force menacing his flank, he also halted and withdrew to the west.

Shortly thereafter, about 3 P.M., a message arrived from Bragg ordering a general retreat.

Bragg, who found the prospect of quitting the fight "sad beyond measure," was allegedly surprised by Beauregard's withdrawal order. ". . . [I] refused to obey until I could send and inquire if it was correct," Bragg wrote the following day. His orders to Withers on the Confederate right were to withdraw the troops and form a line of battle on a prominent hill along the Bark road. With Clanton's cavalry screening their movements, Withers's and Hardee's infantry began to retreat shortly after 3 P.M.

Joe Wheeler was given command of the rear-guard detachment— a small brigade of Louisiana and Alabama infantry. Behind Wheeler Withers posted Martin's brigade, with Moore's 2d Texas watching the Bark road beyond the junction of the eastern Corinth road.

By early evening, between 5 and 6 P.M., Withers and Hardee's infantry had cleared the battlefield. Soon thereafter orders were received from Bragg to continue the march to Mickey's. The order to retreat was a godsend to the exhausted Confederate soldiers. "We turned and marched slowly away, gathering men as we went," wrote one of Breckenridge's wearied privates. "I was completely exhausted and felt that if the march continued forward, I could not last long. We halted about two miles from the scene of action. Our company was counted off—only ten present out of 48 that came into action. Our regiment [15th Mississippi] numbered barely 57. Some companies were not represented."

Elsewhere the scene was much the same. The jaded Confederate troops that had fought near Shiloh Church slowly plodded south along the main Corinth road. "We were greatly exhausted and suffering for water (biting off the end of your cartridge will get some powder in your mouth and this increases your thirst)," advised one of Trabue's men.

As the men stumbled onward they viewed gruesome sights. "The field presents an awful scene," thought one of Bragg's soldiers, "the mangled bodies of the dead are lying in all directions."

Adding to the dismal surroundings, the abandoned Federal camps had been set afire, creating a nauseating pall of smoke. Although some difficulty was encountered in torching many of the tents soaked by the rain of the previous night, orders were hastily given to burn everything before withdrawing from the battlefield.

While the flames licked at the tents and stores in Sherman's and Prentiss's much fought-over encampments, Confederate detachments hastened to load captured small arms into wagons for removal to Corinth.

Across the battlefield Sam Grant, having spent much of the day in the rear dispatching ammunition and reinforcements to the front, sat with his staff officers and observed that the enemy was retiring. Although he considered his own troops "too much fatigued from two days' hard fighting and exposure . . . to pursue immediately," he ordered an attack by some of Buell's and Hurlbut's troops that were nearby in reserve. Colonel James C. Veatch led the charge, aided by the 1st Ohio of Rousseau's brigade.

Barely two regiments strong, this small command double-quicked across open ground toward the Confederate lines only to be met and halted by Rousseau, who had no knowledge of the movement. Informed by the 1st Ohio of Grant's order, Rousseau allowed the attack to continue, yet it soon sputtered to a halt near Sherman's camp when the Federals were fired on by Beauregard's rear guard.

It was already after 5 P.M. Grant, his injured leg so swollen that he had to be lifted into and out of the saddle, was content to allow the Confederates to depart without further molestation.

Once Lew Wallace had replenished his ammunition supply, however, he independently ordered his division to make a limited pursuit. Wallace's rather cautious and deliberate march continued for nearly a mile along the main Corinth road to Wood's house. Here "a hospital filled with wounded Rebels, attended by five Rebel surgeons" was found, and the advance was recalled. Wallace soon issued orders for his troops to fall back within the Federal lines for the night.

With darkness rapidly approaching, Buell, like Grant, made no effort to pursue the Confederates. "I was without cavalry, and the different corps had become a good deal scattered in a pursuit over a country which screened the movements of the enemy, and the roads of which I knew practically nothing," he wrote.

Buell mistakenly believed that a large portion of the Confederates had retreated along the Hamburg–Savannah road, and he directed Nelson's division to proceed toward Lick Creek. Stuart's camps were reoccupied, and Buell soon arrived to take charge of preparations "for tomorrow's fight." Long after dark Buell was examining the ground, realigning his divisions, and laying out a line of battle.

Although many of the Federal commanders, including Grant, remained apprehensive that there would be another fight on the morrow, it seemed a great relief to most of the men that the fighting at long last had ended. When some of Wallace's soldiers learned that the enemy was withdrawing, they sent up three lusty cheers. Other Federal troops were too exhausted to do little more than fling themselves on the ground and sleep.

Only James A. Garfield's brigade of Wood's division, arriving on the battlefield just as the last volleys were fired, pressed on for a short distance in belated pursuit. "We did some heavy shouting and yelling with the rest," wrote a sergeant, "for we felt that we at least earned the right to do that." One of Garfield's regiments encountered a wounded Confederate sitting against a stump, his leg shattered by a rifle ball. "We took all the tricks yesterday, but I reckon you Yanks hold too many bowers for us today," shouted the man as the Ohioans ran past.

When Garfield's men were soon recalled, there was "genuine disappointment" that despite the forced marches, they had only arrived in time to "see the enemy's heels."

As darkness descended, many of Grant's troops returned to their ransacked camps, only to be stunned by the horrid sights they beheld. Most of the camps were strewn with debris and mangled bodies. Many of the tents had been burned, especially in Prentiss's encampment. "Our knapsacks had all been broken into," observed an Iowa soldier. "Our blankets were all taken. From my knapsack they had pilfered a pair of sky blue pantaloons which were my especial pride and joy. . . . I fared no worse than my neighbors, however. Each man lost something, and the Texas Rangers, who are generally supposed to have perpetrated the theft, are in consequence by no means popular."

Another soldier, one of McClernand's men, counted thirty-one bullet holes in his Fremont tent. A barrel of hardtack standing inside was riddled with lead fragments. "We had a sheet iron cook stove outside . . . bored full of holes," said the man, who sealed the holes with mud so he could cook that night.

Even Sherman was dismayed by the sight of his former headquarters. ". . . The tents were still standing, though riddled with bullets," he wrote. "At the picket rope in front lay two of my horses, dead. Dead bodies of men in blue and gray lay around thick, side by side, and scraps of paper showed . . . that Beauregard, Breckenridge and Bragg—old personal friends—had slept the night before in my camp, and had carried away my scanty bedding."

The most disheartening aspect of the battlefield, however, was the hundreds of maimed soldiers who lay helpless, suffering in great misery. "The battlefield was one of the most heart-rending sights it was ever my lot to witness," wrote one of W. H. L. Wallace's men. "For miles the ground was strewn with the mangled remains of the dead and the dying. . . ."

Entering his battered tent in Prentiss's encampment, a Union officer found a Confederate corpse together with a desperately wounded Federal youth: "As I raised his head and placed my canteen to his parched and bloodless lips, the last faint rays of the setting sun came struggling through the pines and illuminated, as with a halo, the face of that dying lad. With silence unbroken, save by the cries and groans of the wounded, came fainter and fainter the labored breath, and more feeble the clasp of that little hand. Suddenly arousing himself, in [a] whispered [voice] he said: 'Tell mother where you found me, on the front line.'"

Another officer, one of McClernand's command, found a wounded Rebel lying on a mattress near his tent. "He followed us with his eyes thinking perhaps we would kill him," he wrote. "I got a canteen of water for him [and] we left him there [to be cared for]."

When a Michigan private encountered several badly wounded Confederates near his camp, he was touched by the pathetic scene. "One [of the wounded] was a beardless boy, not more than fourteen or fifteen years old," remembered the private. ". . . As I approached him he called out in a clear voice, 'Well, if you are going to kill me—kill me!'" When asked why he thought he was to be killed, the Confederate replied, "Our folks say that you kill all the prisoners." Informed that his captors were not savages, the youth blurted out, "But what are you going to do with me?" "Why," said the Federal private, "the ambulances are out picking up all the wounded and they will come for you too." When an ambulance soon came by, the Confederate was loaded aboard. Mystified by this humane treatment, the wounded youth could but ask as he was being hauled away, "What you'se came down to fight we uns for? If you want the niggers I wisht you had all of them. I haven't got any."

Elsewhere there were scenes of far less compassion. An exhausted Illinois artilleryman entered his old tent and discovered an enemy soldier who had crawled inside to die. Coolly rolling the body off his blanket, he lay down and slept alongside the corpse.

When a half-dead Iowa infantrymen crawled to the rear with a gaping wound in the chest, he came upon an ambulance whose driver steadfastly refused to haul him away. ". . . He did not know me and he was only hauling for his own regiment," the wounded soldier bitterly remembered.

The problem of gathering and caring for the thousands of wounded, many of whom had been unattended for a full day, was enormous. Not only were medical supplies scanty, but many of the instruments had been lost in the captured camps. Most of the wounded were brought to the vicinity of the Landing, overcrowding the little log hospital atop the bluff. A lone Federal surgeon with three assistants was present to perform operations. ". . . Every part of the old [cabin] was occupied with prostrate forms, and yet the door was surrounded with ambulances loaded with wounded men. To make room for these I removed the bodies of such as had already died, and laid them in tiers outside the building," wrote the surgeon. Later a few tents were erected to shelter some of the more critical cases, while others were crammed aboard transports for a rough and hasty trip to Savannah.

"The agonies of the wounded are beyond all description," observed an overworked Federal surgeon. "You may imagine the scene of from two to three thousand wounded men at one point calling to have their wounds dressed," wrote another. "We worked to the best advantage we could, but the crowded state of everything, and the absence of extensive preparations for such an event, caused a great deal of suffering that might have been prevented."

In a valiant effort to accommodate the profusion of wounded Assistant Surgeon Bernard J. D. Irwin, William Nelson's medical inspector, improvised a tent field hospital on the Noah Cantrell farm near Stuart's encampment. Tents were removed from Stuart's camp and pitched on level ground around the white frame Cantrell house, which was then utilized as an operating room, dispensary, office, kitchen, and officers' dining room. Irwin was so successful in his venture that three hundred patients were ultimately accommodated, earning Irwin special commendation from Nelson.

Throughout the night of the seventh the grisly work of the surgeons continued. Several Ohio boys walked in the direction of Irwin's hospital and heard "groans and cries [that] would have melted a heart of stone."

By nightfall many of the prominent officers who had been reported missing during the fight of the sixth had been found and removed from the battlefield. Colonel Julius Raith of Illinois was found still alive in a recaptured camp, his pockets rifled and his shattered right leg caked with blood. They carried him to the Landing, where the following morning he was put aboard the steamer *Hannibal*. Although his leg was amputated above the knee, Raith's condition continued to worsen. Debilitated by loss of blood, shock, and perhaps shoddy medical treatment, Raith died on Friday, April 11.

Another important Federal officer, Everett Peabody, was discovered dead where he had fallen. All of the buttons and shoulder straps had been cut from his uniform, and his sword and pistols were gone. His officers buried him in a gun box that night, marking the spot with a single board upon which they scrawled: "A braver man ne'er died upon the field."

Perhaps the most poignant incident of all, however, involved the recovery of W. H. L. Wallace from the field. At 11 A.M. during Monday's fight his aide and brother-in-law, Cyrus Dickey, discovered what he felt sure was Wallace's body near the place they had left him on the sixth. To Dickey's great surprise Wallace was still breathing despite his horrible head wound. Passing Confederates had wrapped him in a blanket, but he still was wet and cold from Sunday night's rainstorm. Rapidly carrying Wallace to the Landing, they placed him aboard a transport, and Cyrus hastened to find his sister, Ann Wallace.

Ann was still aboard the *Minnehaha*, talking with a wounded soldier when Cyrus approached. Learning that her husband was alive and aboard an adjoining transport, Ann was overjoyed. "I almost flew to where he was," she bubbled. "He lay on a narrow mattress on the floor in the middle of the cabin, his face flushed, but breathing naturally—so like himself, except the fearful wound in the temple . . . that made it seem like a miracle for him to be yet alive. . . . Will recognized my voice right off and clasped my hand. I noticed it and exclaimed, 'He knows me!' Those around me said, 'It could not be.' Will's lips moved and with difficulty said 'Yes.' Words cannot tell how sweet it was! I had believed him dead! And he was alive! And he knows me! Father I thank Thee!"

Later that afternoon the transport departed for Savannah, where Wallace was carried to Grant's headquarters, the Cherry mansion. A bed was prepared in the library, which was also occupied by the post commandant, Colonel Walter Q. Gresham. A curtain was thrown up to divide the room, and Wallace lay calm, seemingly without pain, lapsing from occasional consciousness to periods of stupor. ". . . His pulse was strong and healthy," wrote Ann Wallace, "[and] we could not but hope that he would recover."

A few miles away darkness had enshrouded the battlefield. It began to rain, not in torrents, like the night before, but a steady, cold downpour that fell throughout most of the night. Pittsburg Landing was again laden with the debris of war. ". . . Every inch of shelter afforded by tents, houses, or wagons were occupied and used as hospitals," commented a bewildered youth who had just come ashore.

Farther afield many of Buell's troops huddled miserably without tents or shelter, their equipment having been left behind in the rapid march to Pittsburg Landing. "Every thread of our clothing was saturated, and we were chilled to the very marrow," wrote one of Garfield's men. "Our teeth chattered, and every muscle quivered as with . . . ague. Blankets and overcoats . . . were gathered from the field. They were stripped from the dead . . . to cover and warm the living. Three or four [men] would stand together . . . throw a blanket soaked with water over their heads, and thus by close contact seek to infuse into each other a little warmth."

Nearby, a sergeant witnessed two dripping Federal soldiers standign over a mortally wounded Confederate who was covered with an Army blanket. They were waiting for him to die in order to get the blanket, thought the sergeant with a shudder.

For the Confederates, plodding wearily through the mud toward Corinth, the night of the seventh was dire misery.

One of Bragg's infantrymen thought that he had marched about seven miles from the battlefield before his strength gave out. "It soon commenced to rain hard," complained the man. "I stood under a tree for shelter but was so exhausted that I actually fell asleep in that position. All I could do, I could not keep awake; but I would surely fall, so I lay down and spread my overcoat over me and slept for three or four hours. When I awoke I was lying in water; the rain pouring down. I started once more, but I was not alone, for the roadside for miles was strewn with broken down soldiers. One poor fellow lay down and died in a few minutes from exhaustion."

Another rifleman of Breckenridge's command became so miserable in the cold rain that he attempted to crawl into the tent of his lieutenant, who brutally sought to evict all unwanted guests. "[As] the tent was already crowded . . . I concluded that I had as good a right as any of them, and accordingly [stayed]. . . . I scarcely had space to stand but after stomping around for sometime, I found room to sit down and finally got a place to lay my head. It was in a puddle of water but I slept finely."

Everywhere the scene was much the same. Never was the havoc of war more evident. Throughout the long night a wretched mass of humanity sat in the pelting rain and endured in silence. To some it would be remembered as the most miserable night of the entire war.

CHAPTER XXII

War Is Horrible

Ironically, the Battle of Shiloh ended much as it had begun, with a sudden rout of Federal troops commanded by William Tecumseh Sherman.

On Tuesday, April 8, Grant, although making allowance for a renewal of the fight, presumed Beauregard's army to be retiring and organized a limited pursuit. His telegram to Halleck on the night of the seventh revealed his considerable caution: "I shall follow tomorrow far enough to see that no immediate renewal of an attack is contemplated." Similarly Grant wrote to Buell that evening, "My . . . plan will be to feel on in the morning with all the troops on the outer lines until our cavalry force can be organized. . . . Under instructions which I have previously received, and a dispatch also of today from Major General Halleck, it will not then do to advance beyond Pea Ridge, or some point which we can reach and return in a day. . . . Instructions have been sent to the different division commanders . . . either to find if an enemy was in front or to advance."

Although McClernand's and Sherman's infantry were first designated as supports for Taylor's cavalry, the reconnaissance was actually made by two brigades each of Thomas Wood's and Sherman's divisions, aided by Colonel Dickey's 4th Illinois Cavalry.

Ominously, the expedition was delayed until midmorning by a false alarm that occurred in Wood's division and spread through much of the front line.

Having risen to a dreary, bleak day, the men of Wood's division already were exhausted, many having spent a sleepless night in line of battle. "We seemed more dead than alive that morning," remembered a bedraggled sergeant. "No fires had . . . been allowed during the night. . . . Stiff and sore, chilled through and wet to the skin for thirty-six hours, we were scarcely able to move hand or foot." Having just brewed several kettles of coffee from rainwater gathered on the battlefield, Wood's men were called into line.

Garfield's brigade was promptly ordered to draw the wet loads from their muskets, but instead of removing the cartridges with a ball screw, several soldiers emptied their guns by firing—apparently to see if they would "go off."

Spontaneously, other men along the line began firing, many believing they were under attack. As the firing spread, regiments began shooting at an imaginary foe in the woods ahead. "In vain the officers tried to stop the senseless fusillade," wrote a sergeant of the 65th Ohio. "This was the only time we ever heard Colonel [Charles G.] Harker swear. . . . At the first discharge he mounted his horse and dashed along the line, ordering his men to 'cease firing,' and as the racket increased he launched profane expletives at the top of his voice."

In Sherman's nearby camps the firing caused "a small stampede," according to a private, before the men were brought under control by several energetic officers.

For about fifteen minutes the firing continued in Wood's command before its officers could make themselves understood. Later it was discovered that more than half the men had participated in the firing, many having expended from six to ten rounds each.

By the time the firing ended drum rolls and bugle calls were sounding throughout the front-line camps. "The unexpected alarm came near throwing the army into a panic," wrote an observer. "Generals and staff officers came riding out at a mad gallop to see what it was all about. . . . When the ridiculous truth was known, our regiments were the target for such a volley of profanity as the ear of man has seldom heard."

Because of the delay it was about ten o'clock when the march began. Sherman followed the main Corinth road to its junction with the Bark road, where he met the head of Wood's column. Following a reconnaissance by the cavalry, Sherman was asked for assistance by Dickey, who after noon encountered Confederate cavalry along the Bark road to Mickey's. Sending Wood south along the main road to Monterey, Sherman advanced nearly a half-mile with his two brigades in the direction taken earlier by Dickey.

Approaching a muddy, open field through which the Bark road passed, Sherman observed an adjacent belt of fallen timber, beyond which was a Confederate camp and field hospital. Rebel cavalry were observed riding in front.

Although only about three hundred fifty strong, the Confederate force at this point was well led, some of the South's most daring cavalrymen being present. Bedford Forrest was the senior ranking officer, his detachment consisting of a company of Wirt Adams's cavalry, a battalion of Texas Rangers, perhaps some of John Hunt Morgan's Kentuckians, and about forty of Forrest's own men.

Sherman was cautious. Sending several companies of the 77th Ohio Infantry ahead as skirmishers, he ordered the remainder of the regiment to follow at an interval of one hundred yards and to clear out the woods. Like Sherman's other regiments, the 77th Ohio had been sadly depleted by casualties of the past two days. Only about two hundred and forty men were present, many of whom were on the verge of exhaustion.

As the Federal infantry entered the belt of standing timber, Forrest noticed momentary confusion in their ranks and ordered an immediate charge. With bugles sounding, Forrest's cavalrymen suddenly dashed over the crest of a ridge and fell on the startled skirmishers. The 77th's two advance companies fled in terror, and the remainder of the regiment paused only to fire a hurried volley. Firing their double-barreled shotguns at short range, Forrest's men charged boldly ahead, dashing among the fallen timber to fight with pistols and sabers.

Not having time to reload, some of the Federal infantrymen attempted to fix bayonets on their unwieldy muskets. Forrest's men rode right over them, shooting down men by the score. Dickey's cavalry battalion was a short distance behind, and as the infantry broke, they too fell into disorder and began firing their carbines wildly. Here the Texas Rangers fought hand to hand with troopers of the 4th Illinois, quickly routing the blue cavalrymen and capturing many prisoners. "The slaughter was great," observed a Confederate officer. ". . . There was . . . a [mixture] of cavalry and infantry, running in every direction, officers shouting and cursing and the hurt groaning."

Sherman, who had ridden forward close to the 77th Ohio with his staff, was caught in the tumult and nearly killed. "My aide-de-camp, [James C.] McCoy, was knocked down, horse and rider, into the mud, but I and the rest of my staff ingloriously fled pell mell through the mud, closely followed by Forrest and his men . . ." wrote Sherman following the war.

Forrest was well in advance of his men, pursuing with reckless abandon, his revolver blazing. "I am sure that had he not emptied his pistols as he passed the skirmish line, my career would have ended right there," thought Sherman many years later.

Ahead, Sherman found Hildebrand's brigade hastily forming in the open cottonfield, presenting a solid front to the charging Confederates. "We sought safety behind the brigade," recalled Sherman, ". . . and Forrest and his followers were in turn 'surprised' by a fire of the brigade which emptied many a saddle. . . ."

Forrest, unaware that his men had already turned back, galloped to within fifty yards of the brigade line before halting. Looking about him, he saw that he was virtually alone. Desperately, Forrest wheeled his horse about and sought to escape. Shouts of "Kill him! Kill him and his horse!" rose along the Federal line. Hundreds of shots were fired as Forrest dashed for the woods south of the road.

One Austrian rifle ball struck Forrest in the left side, just above the hip, penetrating nearly to the spine. The stunning blow left his leg dangling useless in the stirrup, but Forrest still clung to the saddle. His horse was shot twice and fatally wounded, yet galloped on. At last Forrest passed into the woods and rejoined his command, soon going to the rear for medical aid.*

The ugly wound that Forrest took was of significance. Strangely, Forrest had become the last casualty of the Battle of Shiloh. Yet the brief fight at Fallen Timbers had been more costly to the Federals— about nineteen killed, thirty wounded, and more than forty prisoners. Although the total Confederate loss was not recorded, the Texas Rangers reported two killed, seven wounded, and one missing.

Breckenridge, who had heard the sharp firing about three miles west at Mickey's, sent orders for Forrest's command to withdraw. When Sherman re-formed his lines and advanced through the fallen timber, he found a Confederate camp and field hospital in charge of Surgeon William D. Lyles of Polk's corps. About three hundred fifty wounded, both Union and Confederate, were lying about the hospital, presenting an appalling sight. "Wagons [were] hauling in dead men and dumping them on the ground, as cordwood, for burial in long trenches, like sardines in a box," wrote a distressed Sherman. "Wounded men with mangled legs and arms, and heads half shot away [were there], horrible to behold, [with] still more of the wounded appealing for water, and for help in any form."

After burying the dead on the battleground and sending for wagons to carry some of the wounded back to camp, Sherman destroyed the large camp and paroled the Confederate surgeons. Nightfall came before the work was completed, and Sherman ordered a return to Shiloh Church, "our troops being fagged out by three days hard fighting, exposure, and privation . . ."

Several miles distant, at Mickey's House, Breckenridge, commanding a portion of the Confederate rear guard, pondered the miserable condition of his men as the last of Beauregard's army withdrew toward Corinth. "My troops are worn out, and I don't think can be relied on after the first volley," he warned. Braxton Bragg observed the retreat of his soldiers through nearby Monterey and was even more dismayed. "Our condition is horrible. Troops utterly disorga-

---

* Forrest was seriously wounded and returned to Corinth in great pain. Granted a sixty-day leave, he nonetheless returned to the field on April 29, following a brief convalescence at Memphis. His horse that carried him from the field on the eighth died the following day.

nized and demoralized. Road almost impassable. No provisions and no forage; consequently everything is feeble," complained Bragg. "It is most lamentable to see the state of affairs, but I am powerless and almost exhausted. Our artillery is being left all along the road by its officers; indeed I find but few officers with their men."

The roads by now had been kneaded into a thick muck by the intermittent rain, which had fallen in a heavy downpour much of the day. The distance from Monterey to Corinth was about twelve miles. "Those were twelve of the longest miles I ever travelled," wrote one of Bragg's exhausted soldiers. "I am not exaggerating when I inform you that all the way the mud was knee deep, and we were obliged to wade several streams which were waist deep." Another rifleman thought that the army "looked like a pack of fox hounds after a hard chase" as it stumbled back to Corinth. Everywhere along the route was strewn the debris of war—abandoned wagons, limber chests, and mired cannon. "Every house between here [Corinth] and the battlefield is a hospital, and the whole road is lined with wagons freighted with dead and wounded," sadly noted a Tennessee soldier.

At Corinth the scene was disordered beyond description. It was nightfall before most of the troops arrived, without rations, many of them having lost or thrown away all but the clothes they wore. "On arriving the boys had some strong coffee and good bread—and that was a feast indeed," said one of Bragg's men. Others, however, were able to find only a few crackers to eat. ". . . For water, all we had to do was dig a foot or two anywhere and we could get it," said a dysentery-ridden soldier. "The water would soon come, a milky, cloudy liquid, tasting of the swamp and decaying leaves."

On the ninth the rains continued, intensifying the wretched conditions in the overcrowded city. Hospitals were overflowing, and many private residences were used to shelter the wounded. Meat was in short supply, and what was available was often spoiled or maggot-infested. A surgeon who wandered through much of the city seeking to obtain brandy to alleviate the suffering of the wounded was "unable to obtain a drop of liquor of any kind. . . . A change of locality from this horrible graveyard, and the thought of going home may prevent the result, which would certainly prove fatal at this place," thought the doctor, who prescribed furloughs as a means of saving his patients.

By strange contrast many of the Federal prisoners taken on the first day of battle already had been removed from the pitiful conditions at Corinth and were being feted by their captors in Memphis. After a torturous march from their bivouac to Corinth on the seventh, the Federal captives were herded into the townsquare and loaded onto "cattle cars" that night. Following a much-interrupted train ride on the eighth to Memphis, during which the captives were exhibited to the populace at nearly every station, the Union prisoners were made to march for the large gathering that had turned out. Somewhat as quasi-celebrities, the Federal soldiers were marched to City Hall, with Prentiss and other ranking officers riding in a carriage. At City Hall, their temporary prison, the captives were "very kindly treated to a bountiful supper of ham, sardines, [and] champagne. . . ." Prentiss, saucy and full of life, was quite willing to discuss the war and agreed to the proposal of an exchange for Confederate General S. B. Buckner, captured at Fort Donelson.

At Corinth, meanwhile, the soldiers who had fought at Shiloh were dispirited and sick of the war. "Oh, how I long for Home!" wrote a discouraged Louisiana private, made to live "like a vagrant" after the battle. Another soldier admitted in a letter to his wife that he had made a terrible mistake in joining the army: ". . . I long to be at home with you [and] I would [forfeit] all that I have in this world if I were loose from this. . . ." Even many of the officers had become disaffected. "Bless me, hon, how tired I am getting of the war!" wrote a physician. "How I long for it to be over so that I may go quietly to my profession—and make a living . . . by curing, not by killing people."

Yet, because another battle with Grant and Buell was expected within a few weeks, preparations already were under way to fight again. As a matter of first importance the Confederate high command hastily sought to reinforce the bedraggled Army of the Mississippi, whose strength had now dwindled to about thirty-five thousand effectives. Beauregard called for reinforcements from East Tennessee and the Deep South, temporarily stripping several locations of adequate garrisons. "If defeated here [Corinth] we lose the Mississippi Valley and probably our cause," warned Beauregard, "whereas we could even afford to lose for a while Charleston and Savannah for the purpose of defeating Buell's army. . . ."

It was not until the arrival of Van Dorn's troops from the trans-Mississippi region in mid-April that Beauregard was able to feel some reassurance.

As the task of revitalizing and replenishing the Confederate army continued at Corinth, the gruesome task of cleaning up the battlefield began at Pittsburg Landing. Dawn on April 8 revealed a battlefield such as had never been seen before on the North American continent. "As far as the eye could reach, in every direction, lay the silent forms of those who went down before the storm of battle," wrote one of Buell's men. Another participant found the battlefield a "heart sickening sight. . . . The bodies of dead horses and wrecks of wagons, caissons, guns and all kinds of war implements, were strewn over the battlefield. The dead were lying in every conceivable shape.

Some had fallen with guns fast in their hands, others had . . . sought the shelter of logs and trees, and laid down to die," he wrote.

". . . [It was] a horrible sight," observed another soldier. "In places dead men lay so closely that a person could walk over two acres of ground and not step off the bodies." At the Hornets' Nest one of W. H. L. Wallace's men saw the terrible toll that the fight of the sixth had taken in enemy lives. "I could have walked across that field on dead Rebels, they were so thick," he said, "and all were as black as could be—a most sickening sight."

In the warm weather many of the corpses already had bloated and turned black, causing at least one young Federal to believe that the Confederates had consumed liquor. "The Rebels was all drunk," he advised, "for their dead has turned black and ours did not."

Throughout the budding woods, hidden in the sheltered ravines, the search parties discovered many pathetic sights as the grim work of removing the dead and wounded began in earnest.

Some of David Stuart's men found a bugler of the 55th Illinois lying in a ravine. The man was "leaning against a tree and holding in his extended hand an open letter, which he was apparently reading. His form was rigid in death, and his last moment came while reading the last letter received from his wife. . . . His bugle had been cut from his person, leaving [only] the cord around his neck." At another point a detail found a pile of unhusked corn, estimated at several hundred bushels, upon which wounded soldiers had crawled for comfort. During a fire that had swept through a nearby camp during the battle the men had been unable to crawl away. Their charred corpses were found where they had lain.

Yet among the profusion of slain were found many men still alive. Some, too weak to move, were carried away to an uncertain fate at the hands of the overworked and often unskilled surgeons.

At Pittsburg Landing the chaos of the night of the sixth continued through the seventh and eighth. "Here all was hurry and confusion," found an Iowa soldier, "wagons were hurrying off to the battlefield after wounded, soldiers were running around hunting comrades to learn the whereabouts of their regiments, details were coming in for provisions . . . [and] squads of 'Secesh' prisoners were scattered over the shore, guarded. . . . I went up the hill to a lot of tents and a log house, but all were full of the wounded; . . . every inch of shelter afforded by tents, houses, or wagons was occupied and used as [a] hospital."

By now the suffering was extreme among the thousands of wounded, many of whom were still waiting to have their wounds dressed. ". . . The agonies of the wounded were beyond all description," wrote one of Grant's surgeons, laboring without adequate supplies of medicines and surgical instruments. As rapidly as an empty transport would return to Pittsburg Landing, the wounded were crammed aboard for the trip to Savannah. "The scene upon the boat was heart rending," wrote an injured Iowa corporal, "men wounded and mangled in every conceivable way— . . . some with arms, legs, and even their jaws shot off, bleeding to death, and . . . no surgeons to attend us." On one steamer a Federal officer searching for a friend found the seriously wounded Colonel S. S. Bass of the 30th Indiana, lying on the cabin floor among other critical cases. Bass informed the officer that his wound had not as yet been examined by a surgeon. Although the officer searched the boat for help, he was told by the crew: "The staterooms are all filled; there is no room for more, we are doing all we can."

Downriver at Savannah, nearly every house had been filled with wounded by Tuesday. The post commandant, attempting to find room for the boatloads of wounded descending upon the town, was overwhelmed by the human misery he saw. "You can have no conception of the amount of suffering here," he advised in a letter to his wife. "Men lay out in stables and die without having their wounds dressed." Horrified by the inefficiency and incompetence of many surgeons, he regarded the Army physicians with disdain. "They all seem to have a mania for cutting off arms and legs . . ." he complained.

Throughout the week the work of the surgeons continued night and day. At the log hut near Pittsburg Landing the pile of severed limbs just outside the door reached three feet in height. By Friday most of the operations had been performed, however, and the exhausted medical staff could pause to consider their ordeal. Of approximately 111,000 men who had participated in the battle nearly 24,000 were casualties. Of these more than 16,000 wounded had sought aid, many of whom were processed through Pittsburg Landing. It was with considerable candor that Surgeon J. H. Brinton later reported that the labors of the medical officers at Shiloh were "most arduous" and had been done "under every disadvantage."

Once the wounded had been removed from the battlefield, the grisly task remained of burying the dead.

Although it had been raining at frequent intervals, the weather was warm immediately following the battle. Beauregard, who sought to help inter the dead, sent an officer under a flag of truce to Grant on April 9. Grant's curt reply was forwarded that afternoon. "Owing to the warmth of the weather I deemed it advisable to have all the dead of both parties buried immediately. Heavy details were made for this purpose, and it is now accomplished."

Burial details had been sent out from nearly every regiment beginning on the eighth, when it was learned that the Confederates had withdrawn. Long trenches, some more than fifty feet long, six feet wide, and four feet deep, were dug to receive the dead. On Nelson's front the Confederates were generally buried first in order to allow as much time as possible for the Federal dead to be identified. The bodies were laid side by side upon their backs at the bottom of the trench and covered with a few shovels of yellow clay. "Our own dead were buried with more care," observed one of Nelson's men. ". . . [We] fasten[ed] the arms across the breast with the cross belt from the man's own equipment, and the knees close together with his cartridge box belt. Many men were buried singly, and all those who could be identified had rough head boards placed over them. [These were] made from the sides of cracker boxes, barrel staves, and the like. In other cases, a pen of rails was built around the grave."

Elsewhere on the battlefield burial details interred the bodies two or three deep, Federal and Confederate in separate trenches, the Union grave sites generally being on high ground and in front where possible. In one large burial trench near McClernand's camps an estimated 571 Confederate dead were stacked in layers seven deep.

Among the dead found in the vicinity of McClernand's headquarters was a body believed to be that of Sidney Johnston, the Confederate commander. Both McClernand and Lew Wallace proclaimed this fact soon after the battle, news of Johnston's death having been learned from prisoners taken during the seventh. Kentucky Governor George W. Johnson, critically wounded and himself a prisoner, identified the corpse as that of Johnston. When taken to "Bull" Nelson's headquarters, an orderly who had served with Johnston in Utah confirmed the identity. Nelson provided one of his own shirts for burial, as the body had been stripped to the underclothes when found. The corpse was cleaned and shaved before being buried in a blanket, and the grave fenced.

Several days later the truth became known. Captain Thomas W. Preston, A. P. Stewart's adjutant general, who had a close resemblance to Johnston, had been mistaken for the Confederate commander.

Amid the confusion following what was then the bloodiest battle in the nation's history, the work of the burial details continued for several days. The dead were so numerous and scattered over such a large area that big Army wagons drawn with six-mule teams were used to gather the slain. On into the ninth the burial parties worked with a sense of urgency. By now the stench of decaying flesh had begun to pervade the air. Particularly obnoxious was the odor from dead horses, many of which were scattered across the battlefield. To

Colonel T. Kilby Smith of Sherman's division the effluvia "mingled painfully" with the sweet smell of the azalea and wild honeysuckle that carpeted the woods.

Fortunately the weather turned damp and cool during the ninth, slowing the rapid decomposition of the remains. By Thursday noon the last of the dead had been buried, although scattered corpses continued to be found more than a week later. Following a series of heavy rainstorms during mid-April, some of the earth washed away, exposing many of the hastily buried corpses in the burial trenches. When hot weather set in toward the end of the month, the pungent odor of rotting flesh again tainted the air.

To an unsuspecting nation the news of Shiloh was like a thunderbolt. Although only about a half-dozen newspaper correspondents were with Grant's army at the time of the battle, an enterprising if unscrupulous correspondent of the New York *Herald,* Frank Chapman, obtained the use of the Army telegraph at Fort Henry on a pretext and sent an exaggerated account of fighting to his paper. On Wednesday morning, April 9, the United States Senate suspended its order of business to hear Chapman's dispatch, the first of what was soon to be a plethora of news of the battle.

Whitelaw Reid of the Cincinnati *Gazette,* who had clambered aboard the *Tigress* at Crump's Landing to reach the battlefield with Grant; Henry Bentley of the Philadelphia *Inquirer,* who had been captured but escaped from the Confederates on the seventh; and Henry Villard of the New York *Herald* followed with eyewitness descriptions.

By Thursday the tenth newspapers throughout the North were publishing accounts of "the great battle of the war—the Waterloo of America." As sensational and overwrought accounts of desperate hand-to-hand fighting were published, including news of Sherman's men being surprised and bayoneted in their tents, a wave of indignation swept the nation. Many correspondents who were not present contributed to the furor by drafting imaginary accounts based on camp rumors. A stigma of incompetence was cast upon the army's high command, particularly on Grant and Sherman. Troops from Ohio, said to have disgraced themselves during the battle, were held in contempt in the Chicago papers. Secretary of War Stanton was appalled by the heavy casualties and demanded an explanation.

Halleck was shocked by a belated dispatch from Grant that he received at his St. Louis headquarters during the night of the eighth, telling of a fight at Pittsburg Landing. "I leave immediately to join you with considerable reinforcements," advised Halleck in a return telegram. "Avoid another battle, if you can, till all arrive. We then shall be able to beat them without fail."

Halleck's arrival at Pittsburg Landing on the twelfth was heralded by a fifteen-gun salute. After tendering his thanks to Grant and Buell for having "defeated and routed the entire Rebel army," Halleck plunged into the task at hand. One of his first moves was to order John Pope's Army of the Mississippi, fresh from its victory at Island No. 10, to Pittsburg Landing. Grant, meanwhile, had learned from a spy in Corinth and "through Southern newspapers" that the Confederates were concentrating at Corinth all available forces, "leaving many points heretofore guarded entirely without troops."

Halleck immediately ordered a small force to sail upriver and cut the Memphis & Charleston Railroad at Bear Creek. The resulting expedition under Sherman succeeded in destroying this important railroad bridge, easily accomplishing what the entire Tennessee expedition had set out to do a month earlier.

Sherman, who was on friendly terms with Halleck, was lauded by the department commander for his part in the recent battle. "It is the unanimous opinion here that Brigadier General W. T. Sherman saved the fortune of the day on the 6th instant, and contributed to the glorious victory on the 7th," wrote Halleck the day following his arrival. "He was in the thickest of the fight on both days, having three horses killed under him and being wounded twice. I respectfully request that he be made a major general of volunteers, to date from the 6th instant."

Sherman was greatly pleased that his reputation had been restored. ". . . They say I accomplished some important results, and General Grant makes special mention of me in his report . . ." boasted Sherman. "I have worked hard to keep down, but somehow I am forced into prominence and might as well submit." His commission as major general of volunteers was received in mid-May.

Grant, however, continued to be regarded with distrust by Halleck. Although seemingly complimenting Grant for "bravery and endurance" during the battle, Halleck blistered Grant shortly after his arrival at Pittsburg Landing. "Immediate and active measures must be taken to put your command in condition to resist another attack by the enemy," warned Halleck. "Your army is not now in condition to resist an attack."

When Secretary of War Stanton demanded to know if "any neglect or misconduct of General Grant or any other officer contributed to the sad casualties . . ." Halleck demurred, saying only, "I prefer to express no opinion in regard to the misconduct of individuals till I receive the reports of commanders of divisions."

In effect, however, Grant was stripped of active command. When the army was reorganized during the ensuing siege of Corinth, Grant was designated as second-in-command, a meaningless assignment, with little direct operational responsibility. ". . . I was little more than an observer," commented Grant with some rancor. "Orders were sent direct to the right wing or reserve, ignoring me, and advances were made . . . without notifying me. My position was so embarrassing, in fact, that I made several applications during the siege to be relieved."

One evening Sherman found Grant, visibly shaken, packing his belongings to leave the army. "There is nothing here for me," moaned Grant, tears swelling in his eyes. "I am not allowed to do anything here. I am going to Saint Louis." It was with difficulty that Sherman persuaded him to stay. Finally, following Halleck's mid-July departure to Washington as commanding general of all the armies, Grant belatedly resumed active department command.

Although Grant and Sherman steadfastly insisted that they were unjustly blamed for the near disaster at Shiloh, their own troops were among the most active critics of the army's high command. "The conduct and merits of the battle were almost the exclusive topic of discussion for weeks," wrote the colonel of one of Grant's Indiana regiments. "In the 44th there was but one opinion . . . that the surprise [of the sixth] was the result of gross carelessness and an insufficient system of picketing."

More pointedly, one of Hurlbut's men leveled strong accusations at Grant in his personal journal: "For the great loss of life in this battle, General Grant is in a great degree responsible, as it cannot be denied that we were completely surprised, for which there was, nor is, the least explanation or excuse." Another soldier, a sergeant of one of McClernand's regiments, wrote to a friend that Grant must be regarded "an imbecile character" for his blundering generalship. When a justice from Iowa, visiting state troops following the battle, heard many accounts of the bloody surprise, he wrote a blistering attack on Grant and sent it home for publication: "The criminal carelessness, or something worse, on the part of General Grant, whereby so many brave soldiers were slaughtered, admits of no . . . excuse. Newspaper correspondents may write as they please, but the united voice of every soldier in Grant's army condemns him. . . ."

Although a few individuals, notably his staff officers, were quick to defend Grant, even staunch supporters found some cause for criticism. "[Grant] made the great mistake of his military life at Shiloh," said an Illinois veteran after the war. A staff officer, having gone to Ohio for a brief visit following the battle, returned and told his general that if anyone in Ohio openly expressed confidence in Grant, he would need a bodyguard for protection due to the strong feeling against him. Grant's laconic reply was characteristic of his indomitable will: "I have tried to do my duty, and I believe that history will do me justice."

The storm of controversy that arose over Grant's generalship at

Shiloh eventually carried all the way to the President, where the matter was decided. When a fellow Republican, A. K. McClure of Pennsylvania, called on the President to demand Grant's removal, Lincoln considered the matter in front of the fireplace in the old cabinet room. Finally gathering himself up in his chair, he spoke in an earnest voice, "I can't spare this man; he fights."

For Sherman the criticism, although perhaps less vociferous, was no less vicious and caused "Cump" considerable difficulty. Benjamin Stanton, the Lieutenant Governor of Ohio, condemned Grant and Sherman for "blundering stupidly." Moreover newspapers were filled with accounts of bad management by the Union generals. Men were allegedly bayoneted in their tents, officers had not had breakfast, and the army was said to have been totally unprepared. Sherman was greatly provoked and lashed out at his critics in both public and private correspondence. "All but the worthless cowards had had breakfast," protested Sherman, "[and] not a man was bayoneted in or near his tent." When the furor continued to mount over the extent of surprise, Sherman became more irate. Terming the men who broke and failed to recover "scamps," he wrote to his brother: "For two days they hung about the river bank filling the ears of newspaper reporters with their tales of horrid surprise . . . and to our utter amazement we find it settling down as history. . . . It is outrageous for the cowardly newsmongers . . . to defame men whose lives are exposed. The real truth is, the private soldiers in battle leave their ranks, run away and then raise these false issues."

By far the severest critic of Sherman was one of his own regimental commanders, Colonel Thomas Worthington. Worthington had allowed to be published extracts from his personal diary that were highly derogatory of his commander. Sherman ultimately court-martialed him, and although unable to prove that he was not surprised at Shiloh, Sherman succeeded in having Worthington dismissed from the service.

Even in postwar years, when the controversy was less emotional, many of Sherman's close friends and supporters continued to blame their former commander for the surprise at Shiloh. Major E. G. Ricker of the 5th Ohio Cavalry remarked that although he was a friend of Sherman who considered him to be "one of our ablest officers," he did not believe "in decreasing the general's carelessness on that terrible occasion . . ." Another former Federal soldier concluded that there was but "one cloud on [Sherman's] horizon; one blot on his escutcheon—he was surprised at Shiloh."

In the South the controversy over the battle was diminished by a succession of unfavorable events, beginning with news of the fall of Island No. 10 and continuing with the surrender of Fort Pulaski.

The death of Albert Sidney Johnston, however, produced a lingering despair. Thomas Bragg, the former Confederate Attorney General, was stung by the sad news. "Thus has fallen one of our best, if not the very best officer in the service.—A man who was worth all the worthless demagogues and maligners in the Confederacy. The reaction has already commenced . . . but it comes too late. Poor Johnston, proud and sensitive, and stung by the unjust attacks, probably exposed himself more than he ought to have done and thus met his fate. This leaves Beauregard in command—Will he be equal to it? . . . Those who know him well doubt his capacity. The President, I think, does not entertain a high opinion of him."

Jefferson Davis, who was grief-stricken by the loss of his close friend, thought ". . . Our loss is irreparable." Aside from Franklin Pierce and his own brother Joseph, there was probably no other man whom Davis more admired or loved than Sidney Johnston. In later years Davis often remarked, "When Sidney Johnston fell, it was the turning point of our fate; for we had no other hand to take up his work in the West."

Johnston's death was formally announced to the Confederate Army on April 10, although most had known of it on April 7. In the rush of defensive preparations that followed there was little opportunity for mourning, however. Another battle was anticipated momentarily, and the Army of the Mississippi began to gird for a second desperate conflict.

Yet, as the days slipped into weeks, the Union armies languished at Pittsburg Landing and vicinity. The addition of John Pope's Army of the Mississippi and the remaining units of Buell's Army of the Ohio had swelled Halleck's ranks to more than 120,000 men. As the cautious and methodical Halleck continued to organize for his grand offensive on Corinth, dysentery and foul weather plagued the Federal troops, who were still encamped on the battlefield.

"This is the meanest place I ever saw after a rain," complained one of Sherman's soldiers, "the soil is red clay and has no bottom. . . . We are in hopes that we will get off this graveyard before the weather becomes very warm. Then again we know we cannot, for the roads must dry first."

Contributing to the dreary environment were a vast number of sightseers and volunteer aid societies that hurried to the battlefield, ostensibly to relieve the suffering. Lew Wallace observed that "since the battle the rush of visitors has been tremendous. Every body and every place seems to have been represented. Actually, I now believe the country has more Sanitary Commissions than regiments."

Many of these volunteer aid groups soon proved obnoxious to the soldiers. Frequently scorning to aid soldiers other than those of their local area, they were often found "roaming over the battlefield like so many hyenas, gathering up relics, old swords and guns that a soldier would scorn to touch, selfishly anxious to secure trophies, [and] utterly neglectful of their trust. . . ." Lew Wallace was so disgusted with the behavior of the sanitary commissioners he confided to his wife: "I have seen them cut down trees to secure pieces of shells, cut off horse tails, pick up the shoes of the dead soldiers. Each one is a museum collector with the talent and industry of Barnum. One citizen has a horse loaded down with every sort of shot and shell—from the small grape to the elongated thirty-two pound rifle shell—he intended taking them home to sell. . . . Those shot which had killed a horse, so much the more valuable; those which had killed a man, precious as gold. After all, there is some justification for the intense hatred the Butternuts seem to have against the trading Yankees."

When other contingents of Northern citizens arrived to claim the dead, there were more revolting incidents. ". . . They are digging up the dead and taking them home," observed a disgusted Illinois sergeant. "I think they had better let them remain where they are, for they look so bad they are not fit to be seen . . . after being buried two weeks. . . . When they take them out now they look

FEDERAL TRANSPORTS AT PITTSBURG LANDING. This photograph, taken shortly after the battle, reveals a group of transports at the landing ready to discharge supplies. Among the rush of visitors to the battlefield were the often corrupt Sanitary Commissioners, in whose service the transport at the right has been outfitted. (PHOTOGRAPHIC HISTORY OF THE CIVIL WAR)

like a lot of mud. Most of them are laying in water, and plenty are scarcely under the surface, some with their hands sticking out, the rains having washed the dirt off."

Ill equipped with "worthless" tents, lacking stoves, bedding, and proper sanitation, and surrounded by a demolished campground that bore the scars of a cannon shot or musket ball on nearly every tree, the Federal troops could but endure in discomfort. It was April 29 before the general advance on Corinth of Halleck's combined forces began. Following a month of sparring the Confederates evacuated the town, allowing the strategic objective that had cost so many American lives to fall into Federal hands. In the months ahead the opposing Western armies would travel the bloody path that led to Stone's River, Vicksburg, Chickamauga, Atlanta, and ultimate defeat for the South in the Carolinas.

Although the bloody season had only begun at Shiloh, the battle was to prove of lasting significance. It has been said that the South never smiled after Shiloh. As contemporary historian Bruce Catton has noted, it was a battle the Confederacy simply had to win. The strategic objective had been to restore the lost balance of power in the West, to reestablish the Confederate frontier in Kentucky, and above all to save the vital Mississippi Valley. Beyond this, the battle saw the Confederacy presented with perhaps its greatest opportunity of the war to annihilate a major Federal army, and a chance to ruin the careers of two of its principal antagonists. ". . . We were so near accomplishing [the complete overthrow of the enemy], which would have changed the entire complexion of the war," lamented Bragg shortly after the battle.

The fact that the Confederacy had come close to succeeding did not compensate for the utter failure to achieve these results. Thereafter the South was further ensnarled in what one early student of the battle termed "the wasting war of defense." For these reasons Shiloh must be regarded as one of the most decisive battles of the Civil War, and of history.

Grant had learned much at Shiloh, and he long remembered its significance. "In numbers engaged, no such contest ever took place on this continent," he wrote shortly after the battle; "in importance of results, but few such have taken place in the history of the world." Following the war Grant said that "Shiloh was the severest battle fought at the West during the war, and but few in the East equalled it for hard, determined fighting." Sherman thought Shiloh "one of the most fiercely contested [battles] of the war." ". . . That victory was one of the most important which has ever occurred on this continent," lectured Sherman in a postwar address to the veterans of the Army of the Tennessee. "I have always estimated the victories . . . at

Fort Donelson and Shiloh the most valuable of all, because of their moral effect. They gave our men confidence in themselves. . . ."

Yet through the years the importance of Shiloh has been over-shadowed by the intense controversy that developed between partici-pants on both sides. One of the battle's most serious students, Otto Eisenschiml, has observed, "Perhaps no other battle of the Civil War has been so often and so bitterly refought in later years." In-deed, the controversy began almost from the moment the last shot was fired.

Beauregard, mindful of the military spoils from the battle, was quick to claim "a complete victory" on the sixth, saying that only "untoward events [had] saved the enemy from annihilation." As hard evidence of his victory Beauregard cited the capture of more than twenty-five Federal flags and standards, several batteries of artillery, and over three thousand prisoners.

Halleck, Grant, Buell, and others of the Union Army, meanwhile, were heralding the success of the Federal arms. Halleck telegraphed to the War Department of a "glorious victory." Grant announced the rout of a "numerically superior force of the enemy, composed of the flower of the Southern Army, commanded by their ablest generals. . . ." Buell congratulated his army for the triumph that had earned them "a brilliant page in history." Even Secretary of War Stanton ordered that a prayer be offered at the head of every regiment at noon on Sunday, April 13, in thanks for the recent Federal victories; in addition, a one hundred-gun salute was fired at the Washington Arsenal.

These flattering remarks and events notwithstanding, both armies, North and South, already were racked with dissension created or exacerbated by the many mistakes that had occurred at Shiloh. Mc-Clernand, the Federal Army's quidnunc, was among the first to cast the blame on his fellow generals for the near disaster. In his official report McClernand wrote: "Considering . . . that a por-tion of our forces were in a manner surprised and driven back in confusion, it is marvelous, may I not say providential, that we were not captured or destroyed. . . ." Grant icily remarked that Mc-Clernand's report was faulty in several particulars, including "report-ing too much of other divisions," since generally conflicting state-ments had been received from these sources.

Of more serious consequence was the controversy, just emerging, between Grant and Lew Wallace. Grant appended an endorsement to Wallace's report implying Wallace had been dilatory in marching from the vicinity of Crump's Landing to the battlefield. Wallace's military career was gravely damaged, and the ensuing squabble carried over into the postwar years. The matter finally became such an obsession to Wallace that he spent much effort during the remainder of his lifetime attempting to clear his name, with but limited success.

Other rifts in Grant's army were many, including the considerable animosity between Sherman and some of his troops. At one point, shortly after the battle, Sherman drew up the 53d Ohio Infantry and told the regiment they "were a pack of cowards." If the regiment was attacked and routed again, Sherman declared, he would take as much pleasure in pouring shot and shell into them as into the Rebels.

In the Confederate army there were equally bitter confrontations. Hardee, quick to condemn Moore's 2d Texas Infantry for having "broke and fled disgracefully from the field" during the seventh, had charges preferred against him by Congressman Louis T. Wigfall of Texas. The irascible Bragg, always spoiling for a fight, found cause to condemn Randall Gibson's leadership, this prompting a request for a formal court of inquiry from Gibson. Other flareups resulted in the outright dismissal or resignation of several officers at the regimental level. In postwar years controversy began anew over battle plans and command decisions, involving Beauregard, Bragg, and Jordan as principals in a spirited dispute.

On through the years the many facets of Shiloh were argued with heated emotion by the aging participants. Charges and countercharges led to distorted and exaggerated accounts of what had occurred, contributing to the general confusion about the battle. Grant, in his memoirs, noted that: "The battle of Shiloh . . . has been perhaps less understood, or to state the case more accurately, more persistently misunderstood than any other engagement between National and Confederate troops during the entire rebellion." For more than a hundred years that confusion has been perpetuated, detracting from the true significance of the battle.

Once the armies had cleared the battlefield, a stark and desolate plot of ground remained. Where there had once been budding oaks, a pleasant carpet of wildflowers, and tiny pink blossoms that fluttered in the breeze, there remained only the shattered wilderness and a lingering effluvia of death. "Scarcely a tree or brush had escaped the musket balls," wrote an awed observer, "bushes were cut off, while trees had been hit on every side . . . from the ground to the limbs. Cannon balls had ploughed through tree tops, and in many cases left them without a branch. Trees had been shivered into splinters, while the ground was covered with brush and downed timber. In many places could be seen where the huge shells from the gunboats had ploughed great pits in the ground. . . ."

"The desolation is complete," was the way another onlooker put it.

Eventually the influence of time and a bountiful nature combined to restore the dense wilderness and mask the many scars of battle. What could not be effaced, however, were the countless personal tragedies that had occurred, nor the anguish that touched the very essence of human consciousness.

In an improvised sick room at the Cherry mansion, the hideously wounded W. H. L. Wallace languished through the dreary days following the battle. Ann was constantly at his side. "He seemed so happy and satisfied to have me near him," she later wrote. "Although he could talk, we did not encourage it. And so the days went by—hope growing stronger until Thursday, the 10th, when inflammation and fever . . . came. He suffered so much, so much, for two or three hours and was delirious. Then consciousness returned, his pulse began to fail and we knew his moments on earth were few. . . . My darling knew that he was going! [He] pressed my head to his breast long and fondly, then waved me away and said, 'We meet in Heaven.' Heaven was the last word on those loved lips. He faded away like a fire going out. . . . After he could not see, he had run his fingers over every hand that he touched to assure himself, by touching the ring I wore, that he held my hand. In his restlessness, he would soon drop the hand, and then in a moment would reach for it again—always placing his fingers on the ring. If he took my right, that had no ring on it, he would drop it and reach for the other, so as to be sure all the time that it was my hand he held. He seemed conscious of my presence to the very last."

In an upstairs bedroom Charles F. Smith, the man who had begun it all by leading his Tennessee expedition to Savannah and Pittsburg Landing, lay dying of a tetanus infection. Although named commander of the post of Savannah on the ninth, General Smith began to worsen in mid-April, weakened by dysentery. On the afternoon of April 25 Smith quietly passed away, the last of the notable casualties of the Shiloh campaign.

In the short span of less than a month events that served to shape the destiny of the nation had occurred with terrible impact. The complexion of the war had somehow changed, as had the perspective of the soldiers. Men who had known the agony of Shiloh had well learned the common lesson of war. "War is horrible," wrote an enlightened Union infantryman, "and you can have no idea of it until you have been in battle." Another participant, an Illinois lieutenant colonel, remembered Shiloh's scenes of slaughter and wrote what could be a permanent indictment of warfare. "What a pity it is that men do not use reason instead of rifles, and common sense instead of cannon."

His words well reflect the sorrow of a young Confederate soldier who, before his regiment left the battlefield on the seventh, observed the vast toll in human life and later wrote: "I shall never forget the face of a young lieutenant from Louisiana with [a] smooth face and the bluest-blue eyes. . . . He lay with his revolver in his right hand, a most peaceful smile on his face, and a great big Yankee laying across him cold in death, with his musket still firmly grasped in his hand. The Yankee's gun was empty, and the lieutenant's pistol had two empty chambers. The lieutenant had a death wound made by a musket ball, and the other man had two pistol ball holes clear through him; neither face had any expression of pain or anger. . . . I don't know but what we should have put them both to sleep in the same grave, but we did not."

APPENDIX A

THE DEATH OF ALBERT SIDNEY JOHNSTON

Probably no one event of the many of importance that occurred at Shiloh was more mourned than the death of the Confederate commanding general. If for no other reason than that the successors who commanded the Army of the Mississippi (later the Army of the Tennessee) in Johnston's place proved lacking, it was a staggering blow to the Confederacy.

Although some of Johnston's decisions on the battlefield at Shiloh were erroneous—for instance, his order pulling Chalmers's and Jackson's brigades out of the front line following the receipt of sketchy intelligence—he had accomplished much of importance.

Shiloh was more than one of the most complete surprise attacks in the annals of warfare, for here the Confederates were presented with perhaps their best opportunity of the entire war to destroy a large enemy army.

Johnston had achieved this outstanding strategical coup in his first battle as an army commander. He had further evidenced the very qualities that Grant later applied to achieve final victory for the Federal government— strong determination and a driving will to win.

Certainly, in contrast, Johnston's performance at Shiloh must be considered to be far superior to that of Grant and Sherman. As his modern biographer, Charles P. Roland, has suggested, Johnston had the ability to learn from his mistakes. He was denied this opportunity by one of war's chance mishaps.

The circumstances involving Johnston's fall, although documented in some detail, have yet to be fully examined.

At the time of his death Johnston was fifty-nine years of age, a robust two hundred pounds in weight, and in good general health. Some felt an old dueling wound in the hip, inflicted by the pistol of Felix Huston twenty-five years earlier, had impaired Johnston's awareness of the fatal wound. In the light of modern medical knowledge this might be generally discounted; other evidence provides a more positive explanation.

For many years following the battle it was believed that Johnston had been shot "on the ridge by one of the last volleys fired by the enemy." *Battles and Leaders of the Civil War* published several engravings made from photographs taken in the 1880's, showing the death spot to be in the clearing to the east of the peach orchard, near the position of Willard's battery.

In April, 1896, Governor Isham G. Harris returned to the battlefield and selected a site under a large oak tree near the intersection of the Hamburg–Savannah and Hamburg–Purdy roads as the place where he saw Johnston reeling in the saddle.

Under the scrutiny of contemporary evidence Harris's location, although plausible, becomes highly suspect. Colonel Preston, writing two weeks after Johnston's death, said the ravine where Johnston lay was "about 100 yards"

443

north of the two cabins (Sarah Bell's) where Preston happened to be at the time. Writing on the very eve of Johnston's death, Harris said the enemy line fell back "between a fourth and one-half mile" following the charge led by Johnston, at which time he referred to "our advanced position."

During the 1870's Harris wrote that Statham's position was "only about 200 yards distant" from Johnston's location, "a few feet in rear" of his battle line. In April, 1896, Harris was seventy-eight years old. He had not visited the battlefield since the event itself, thirty-four years earlier. Moreover, during his visit Harris seems to have contradicted the deposition he made at the time of the battle, saying "the story that he [Johnston] was leading a charge is a fallacy."

It would appear that Harris, though sincere and well meaning, may have mislocated the death site several hundred yards south of the actual point.

Although not of major significance this site is of some importance in reconstructing the circumstances of Johnston's wound. The fatal missile was identified as a "Minie ball," the type of bullet generally fired from a rifled weapon. Many of the troops at Shiloh were armed with foreign muskets firing a large round ball, or "buck and ball" cartridges.

Yet many units of Statham's brigade were armed with Enfield rifles, including the 20th Tennessee, known to be across the Hamburg–Savannah road on Johnston's right during the fateful charge. Moreover the left of Bowen's brigade simultaneously attacked Willard's battery from an oblique angle, just to the east of the peach orchard. The result was a "terrible" cross fire, as reported by one of Willard's gunners.

Johnston, in the forefront of Statham's brigade, was struck from the rear, the fatal Minie ball having been fired from about a forty-five degree angle to his right.

Certainly the movements of a general on horseback are not precisely definable, and it is impossible to say with certainty where Johnston was positioned when he was struck. From the direction of the charge, the weapons carried, and the position of Statham's and Bowen's troops at the time, however, it seems probable that a stray ball fired by one of his own men during the attack inflicted the fatal wound.

That he was in the forefront of the charge is evidenced by the autopsy made the night following his death. Four missile marks were found on his body. Colonel Munford of his staff reported the following: "Besides the wound which killed him, he was hit three other times; once by a spent ball on the outside and about midway of the right thigh; once by a fragment of a shell just above and to the rear of the right hip; and once by a Minie ball cutting the left boot sole entirely in two. . . ."

In the light of current medical knowledge it might be reasonably estimated that Johnston lived nearly an hour following his fatal wound.

Dr. D. Emerick Szilagyi, Chief, Department of Surgery, Henry Ford Hospital, Detroit, Michigan, has kindly provided the following:

"The popliteal artery that was lacerated in the case of General Johnston carries about 210 milliliters of blood per minute, with the body at rest. [Thirty milliliters equal one ounce.] The total amount of circulating blood is about 5,500 ml. [or 5.5 quarts]. The sudden loss, say in [the] course of 5 to 10 minutes, of 1,000 ml. of blood will cause generalized weakness but probably no serious clouding of consciousness. Recovery in an otherwise vigorous person is possible even after this point, but further loss of another 1,000 ml. would almost invariably lead to irreversible hemorrhagic shock and death. . . .

"[General Johnston's loss of blood] would be rapid during the first four to five minutes, but as his blood pressure dropped, the rate of blood loss would decline and he would lose considerably less blood during the second period of five or ten minutes after the occurrence of injury. . . .

"In taking account of this circumstance, I believe it safe to say that he probably remained conscious for about 30 minutes, and continued to be biologically alive for 25 to 30 minutes more. . . .

"It is factual detail that appears to be rather insignificant but is of the greatest importance that the popliteal artery was not completely severed but only torn. . . . When the artery is completely parted, the ends tend to retract and the blood in the retracted ends is prone to clot. When the artery is only lacerated, the wound in the wall of the artery will continue to gape, which will allow the bleeding to continue.

"Under the stressful conditions of battle . . . it seems to me quite easy to understand that he did not notice when he was struck by a bullet in the bend of the knee. This would not be a particularly painful wound. The blood escaping from his wound very likely would have run into his high boot . . . and it may not have left much of a mark on his clothing. The events after he had been wounded followed a pattern which conspired to conceal the seriousness of the situation. . . . The only opportunity of saving his life by placing a tourniquet above the site of the wound the moment he began to faint was lost."

Under these circumstances it is easy to perceive that Johnston probably was shot at least ten minutes before he told Harris to order Statham to charge the enemy battery. Harris said that he was gone on this mission only a short while. "I galloped to Colonel Statham, only about 200 yards distant, gave the order, galloped back to the general where a moment before I had left him . . ." Harris wrote.

Immediately thereafter Johnston collapsed in the saddle, indicating, as Dr. Szilagyi has written, that he had lost about two-fifths of his circulating blood supply, a circumstance requiring about thirty minutes, from the nature of the injury.

The prospect of Johnston concealing his leg wound was immediately discussed by his staff following his death. Johnston was known for his great pride, strong will, and iron discipline. Both Preston and Munford believed he had concealed the fact that he was wounded from those about him.

During the subsequent autopsy, both Dr. Yandell, Johnston's physician, and Dr. Choppin, Beauregard's surgeon, examined the body. Choppin said that the best means of preventing rapid decomposition was to inject whiskey into the blood vessels, and he performed the operation that night.

At 6 A.M. the following morning, April 7, under Beauregard's advice an escort contingent comprised of Johnston's staff officers began the return journey to Corinth. Wrapped in a muddy Army blanket, Johnston's body was taken to his former headquarters at Corinth, the Inge Rose Cottage home. Mrs. Inge, assisted by a neighbor, Ellen Polk, prepared the body for interment. In the general's pocket Mrs. Inge found half of a sandwich and a small piece of cake, remnants of the food she had secreted in Johnston's coat.

After carefully cleaning his face and uniform, the two women draped a Confederate flag about Johnston's body and readied it for the trip South.

From Corinth the remains were swiftly transported to New Orleans and interred in St. Louis Cemetery. Yet Johnston had once remarked to his staff that "he desired of his country six feet of Texas soil." Following the war his body was exhumed and sent on to Austin, Texas—Johnston's beloved, adopted state.

In the grief and shock that followed the news of his fall perhaps his old friend Jefferson Davis best summarized what had occurred: "Bent on obtaining the victory which he deemed essential . . . he rode on . . . forgetful of self, while his very lifeblood was ebbing away. . . ."

Like Johnston's lifeblood, the Southern Confederacy's hopes also began to ebb rapidly following the momentous events of Shiloh.

APPENDIX B

ORDER OF BATTLE
BATTLE OF SHILOH
April 6–7, 1862

UNION ARMY OF THE TENNESSEE
Maj. Gen. U. S. Grant, Commanding

First Division

Maj. Gen. John A. McClernand

First Brigade

Col. Abraham M. Hare, 11th Iowa (w)
Col. Marcellus M. Crocker, 13th Iowa
8th Illinois:
  Capt. James M. Ashmore (w)
  Capt. William H. Harvey (k)
  Capt. Robert H. Sturgess
18th Illinois:
  Maj. Samuel Eaton (w)
  Capt. Daniel H. Brush (w)
  Capt. William J. Dillon (k)
  Capt. Jabez J. Anderson
11th Iowa, Lieut. Col. William Hall (w)
13th Iowa, Col. Marcellus M. Crocker

Second Brigade

Col. C. Carroll Marsh, 20th Illinois
11th Illinois:
  Lieut. Col. Thomas E. G. Ransom (w)
  Maj. Garrett Nevins (w)
  Capt. Lloyd D. Waddel
20th Illinois:
  Lieut. Col. Evan Richards (w)
  Capt. Orton Frisbie
45th Illinois, Col. John E. Smith
48th Illinois:
  Col. Isham N. Haynie
  Maj. Manning Mayfield

Third Brigade

Col. Julius Raith, 43d Illinois (k)
Lieut. Col. Enos P. Wood, 17th Illinois
17th Illinois:
  Lieut. Col. Enos P. Wood
  Maj. Francis M. Smith

(c) captured
(k) killed
(w) wounded

447

29th Illinois, Lieut. Col. Charles M. Ferrell
43d Illinois, Lieut. Col. Adolph Engelmann
49th Illinois, Lieut. Col. Phineas Pease (w)

Unattached

Dresser's Battery (D), 2d Illinois Light Artillery, Capt. James P. Timony
McAllister's Battery (D), 1st Illinois Light Artillery, Capt. Edward McAllister (w)
Schwartz's Battery (E), 2d Illinois Light Artillery, Lieut. George L. Nispel
Burrows's Battery, 14th Ohio Light Artillery, Capt. Jerome B. Burrows (w)
1st Battalion, 4th Illinois Cavalry, Lieut. Col. William McCullough
Carmichael's Company, Illinois Cavalry, Capt. Eagleton Carmichael
Stewart's Company, Illinois Cavalry, Lieut. Ezra King

Second Division

Brig. Gen. William H. L. Wallace (k)
Col. James M. Tuttle, 2d Iowa

First Brigade

Col. James M. Tuttle
2d Iowa, Lt. Col. James Baker
7th Iowa, Lt. Col. James C. Parrott
12th Iowa:
    Col. Joseph J. Woods (w+c)
    Capt. Samuel R. Edgington (c)
14th Iowa, Col. William T. Shaw (c)

Second Brigade

Brig. Gen. John McArthur (w)
Col. Thomas Morton, 81st Ohio
9th Illinois, Col. August Mersy
12th Illinois:
    Lieut. Col. Augustus L. Chetlain
    Capt. James R. Hugunin
13th Missouri, Col. Crafts J. Wright
14th Missouri, Col. B. S. Compton
81st Ohio, Col. Thomas Morton

Third Brigade

Col. Thomas W. Sweeny, 52d Illinois (w)
Col. Silas D. Baldwin, 57th Illinois
8th Iowa, Col. James L. Geddes (w+c)
7th Illinois, Maj. Richard Rowett
50th Illinois, Col. Moses M. Bane (w)
52d Illinois
    Maj. Henry Stark
    Capt. Edwin A. Bowen
57th Illinois:
    Col. Silas D. Baldwin
    Capt. Gustav A. Busse
58th Illinois, Col. William F. Lynch (c)

Artillery

Willard's Battery (A), 1st Illinois Light Artillery, Lieut. Peter P. Wood
Maj. J. S. Cavender's Battalion Missouri Artillery:
  Richardson's Battery (D), 1st Missouri Light Artillery, Capt. Henry Richardson
  Welker's Battery (H), 1st Missouri Light Artillery, Capt. Frederick Welker
  Stone's Battery (K), 1st Missouri Light Artillery, Capt. George H. Stone

Cavalry

Company A, 2d Illinois Cavalry, Capt. John R. Hotaling
Company B, 2d Illinois Cavalry, Capt. Thomas J. Larison
Company C, 2d United States Cavalry, ⎫
Company I, 4th United States Cavalry, ⎬ Lieut. James Powell

Third Division

Maj. Gen. Lew Wallace

First Brigade

Col. Morgan L. Smith, 8th Missouri
11th Indiana, Col. George F. McGinnis
24th Indiana, Col. Alvin P. Hovey
8th Missouri, Lieut. Col. James Peckham

Second Brigade

Col. John M. Thayer, 1st Nebraska
23d Indiana, Col. William L. Sanderson
1st Nebraska, Lieut. Col. William D. McCord
58th Ohio, Col. Valentine Bausenwein
68th Ohio, Col. Samuel H. Steadman

Third Brigade

Col. Charles Whittlesey, 20th Ohio
20th Ohio, Lieut. Col. Manning F. Force
56th Ohio, Col. Peter Kinney
76th Ohio, Col. Charles R. Woods
78th Ohio, Col. Mortimer D. Leggett

Artillery

Thompson's Battery, 9th Indiana Light Artillery, Lieut. George R. Brown
Buel's Battery (I), 1st Missouri Light Artillery, Lieut. Charles H. Thurber

Cavalry

3d Battalion, 11th Illinois, Maj. James F. Johnson
3d Battalion, 5th Ohio Cavalry, Maj. Charles S. Hayes

Fourth Division

Brig. Gen. Stephen A. Hurlbut

First Brigade

Col. Nelson G. Williams, 3d Iowa (w)
Col. Isaac C. Pugh, 41st Illinois

28th Illinois, Col. Amory K. Johnson
32d Illinois, Col. John Logan (w)
41st Illinois:
        Col. Isaac C. Pugh
        Lieut. Col. Ansel Tupper (k)
        Maj. John Warner
        Capt. John H. Nale
3d Iowa:
        Maj. William M. Stone (c)
        Lieut. George W. Crosley

Second Brigade

        Col. James C. Veatch, 25th Indiana
14th Illinois, Col. Cyrus Hall
15th Illinois:
        Lieut. Col. Edward F. W. Ellis (k)
        Capt. Louis D. Kelley
        Lieut. Col. William Camm, 14th Illinois
46th Illinois:
        Col. John A. Davis (w)
        Lieut. Col. John J. Jones
25th Indiana:
        Lieut. Col. William H. Morgan (w)
        Maj. John W. Foster

Third Brigade

        Brig. Gen. Jacob G. Lauman
31st Indiana:
        Col. Charles Cruft (w)
        Lieut. Col. John Osborn
44th Indiana, Col. Hugh B. Reed
17th Kentucky, Col. John H. McHenry, Jr.
25th Kentucky:
        Lieut. Col. Benjamin H. Bristow
        Maj. William B. Wall (w)
        Capt. B. T. Underwood
        Col. John H. McHenry, Jr., 17th
        Kentucky

Artillery

Ross's Battery, 2d Michigan Light Artillery, Lieut. Cuthbert W. Laing
Mann's Battery (C), 1st Missouri Light Artillery, Lieut. Edward Brotzmann
Myers's Battery, 13th Ohio Light Artillery, Capt. John B. Myers

Cavalry

1st and 2d Battalions, 5th Ohio Cavalry, Col. William H. H. Taylor

Fifth Division

Brig. Gen. William T. Sherman   (w)

First Brigade

Col. John A. McDowell, 6th Iowa

40th Illinois
        Col. Stephen G. Hicks (w)
        Lieut. Col. James W. Boothe
   6th Iowa:
        Capt. John Williams (w)
        Capt. Madison M. Walden
46th Ohio, Col. Thomas Worthington

Second Brigade

Col. David Stuart, 55th Illinois (w)
Lieut. Col. Oscar Malmborg, 55th Illinois
Col. T. Kilby Smith, 54th Ohio
55th Illinois, Lieut. Col. Oscar Malmborg
54th Ohio:
        Col. T. Kilby Smith
        Lieut. Col. James A. Farden
71st Ohio, Col. Rodney Mason

Third Brigade

Col. Jesse Hildebrand, 77th Ohio
53d Ohio:
        Col. Jesse Appler
        Lieut. Col. Robert A. Fulton
57th Ohio, Lieut. Col. Americus V. Rice
77th Ohio:
        Lieut. Col. Wills De Hass
        Maj. Benjamin D. Fearing

Fourth Brigade

Col. Ralph P. Buckland, 72d Ohio
48th Ohio:
        Col. Peter J. Sullivan (w)
        Lieut. Col. Job R. Parker
70th Ohio, Col. Joseph R. Cockerill
72d Ohio:
        Lieut. Col. Herman Canfield (k)
        Col. Ralph P. Buckland

Artillery

Maj. Ezra Taylor, Chief of Artillery
Taylor's Battery (B), 1st Illinois Light Artillery, Capt. Samuel E. Barrett
Waterhouse's Battery (E), 1st Illinois Light Artillery:
        Capt. Allen C. Waterhouse (w)
        Lieut. Abial R. Abbott (w)
        Lieut. John A. Firch
Morton Battery, 6th Indiana Light Artillery, Capt. Frederick Behr (k)

Cavalry

2d and 3d Battalions, 4th Illinois Cavalry, Col. T. Lyle Dickey
Thielemann's two companies, Illinois Cavalry, Capt. Christian Thielemann

Sixth Division

Brig. Gen. Benjamin M. Prentiss (c)

First Brigade

Col. Everett Peabody, 25th Missouri (k)
12th Michigan, Col. Francis Quinn
21st Missouri:
    Col. David Moore (w)
    Lieut. Col. H. M. Woodyard
25th Missouri, Lieut. Col. Robert T. Van Horn
16th Wisconsin, Col. Benjamin Allen (w)

Second Brigade

Col. Madison Miller, 18th Missouri (c)
61st Illinois, Col. Jacob Fry
18th Missouri, Lieut. Col. Isaac V. Pratt (c)
18th Wisconsin, Col. James S. Alban (k)

Not Brigaded

16th Iowa:
    Col. Alexander Chambers (w)
    Lieut. Col. Addison H. Sanders
15th Iowa, Col. Hugh T. Reid (w)
23d Missouri:
    Col. Jacob T. Tindall (k)
    Lieut. Col. Quin Morton (c)

Artillery

Hickenlooper's Battery, 5th Ohio Light Artillery, Capt. Andrew Hickenlooper
Munch's Battery, 1st Minnesota Light Artillery:
    Capt. Emil Munch (w)
    Lieut. William Pfaender

Cavalry

1st and 2d Battalions, 11th Illinois Cavalry, Col. Robert G. Ingersoll

Unassigned Troops

15th Michigan, Col. John M. Oliver
14th Wisconsin, Col. David E. Wood
Battery H, 1st Illinois Light Artillery, Capt. Axel Silfversparre
Battery I, 1st Illinois Light Artillery, Capt. Edward Bouton
Battery B, 2d Illinois Artillery, siege guns, Capt. Relly Madison
Battery F, 2d Illinois Light Artillery, Capt. John W. Powell (w)
8th Battery, Ohio Light Artillery, Capt. Louis Markgraf

UNION ARMY OF THE OHIO

Maj. Gen. Don Carlos Buell, Commanding

Second Division

Brig. Gen. Alexander McD. McCook

Fourth Brigade

Brig. Gen. Lovell H. Rousseau

6th Indiana, Col. Thomas H. Crittenden
5th Kentucky, Col. Harvey M. Buckley
1st Ohio, Col. Benjamin F. Smith
1st Battalion, 15th U. S., Capt. Peter T. Swain ⎫
1st Battalion, 16th U. S., Capt. Edwin F. Townsend ⎬ Major John H. King
1st Battalion, 19th U. S., Maj. Stephen D. Carpenter ⎭

Fifth Brigade

Col. Edward N. Kirk, 34th Illinois (w)
34th Illinois:
      Maj. Charles N. Levanway (k)
      Capt. Hiram W. Bristol
29th Indiana, Lieut. Col. David M. Dunn
30th Indiana:
      Col. Sion S. Bass (k)
      Lieut. Col. Joseph B. Dodge
77th Pennsylvania, Col. Frederick S. Stumbaugh

Sixth Brigade

Col. William H. Gibson, 49th Ohio
32d Indiana, Col. August Willich
39th Indiana, Col. Thomas J. Harrison
15th Ohio, Maj. William Wallace
49th Ohio, Lieut. Col. Albert M. Blackman

Artillery

Terrill's Battery (H), 5th United States Artillery, Capt. William R. Terrill

Fourth Division

Brig. Gen. William Nelson

Tenth Brigade

Col. Jacob Ammen, 24th Ohio
36th Indiana, Col. William Grose
6th Ohio, Lieut. Col. Nicholas L. Anderson
25th Ohio, Lieut. Col. Frederick C. Jones

Nineteenth Brigade

Col. William B. Hazen, 41st Ohio
9th Indiana, Col. Gideon C. Moody
6th Kentucky, Col. Walter C. Whitaker
41st Ohio, Lieut. Col. George S. Mygatt

Twenty-second Brigade

Col. Sanders D. Bruce, 20th Kentucky
1st Kentucky, Col. David A. Enyart
2d Kentucky, Col. Thomas D. Sedgewick
20th Kentucky, Lieut. Col. Charles S. Hanson

First Division

Brig. Gen. Thomas L. Crittenden

Fourteenth Brigade

Brig. Gen. Jeremiah T. Boyle
9th Kentucky, Col. Benjamin C. Grider
13th Kentucky, Col. Edward H. Hobson
19th Ohio, Col. Samuel Beatty
59th Ohio, Col. James P. Fyffe

Eleventh Brigade

Col. William Sooy Smith, 13th Ohio
11th Kentucky, Col. Pierce B. Hawkins
26th Kentucky, Lieut. Col. Cicero Maxwell
13th Ohio, Lieut. Col. Joseph G. Hawkins

Artillery

Bartlett's Battery (G), 1st Ohio Light Artillery, Capt. Joseph Bartlett
Mendenhall's batteries (H and M), 4th United States Artillery, Capt. John
Mendenhall

Sixth Division

Brig. Gen. Thomas J. Wood

Twentieth Brigade

Brig. Gen. James A. Garfield
13th Michigan, Col. Michael Shoemaker
64th Ohio, Col. John Ferguson
65th Ohio, Col. Charles G. Harker

Twenty-first Brigade

Col. George D. Wagner, 15th Indiana
15th Indiana, Lieut. Col. Gustavus A. Wood
50th Indiana, Col. John W. Blake
57th Indiana, Col. Cyrus C. Hines
24th Kentucky, Col. Lewis B. Grigsby

CONFEDERATE ARMY OF THE MISSISSIPPI

Gen. Albert Sidney Johnston (k)
Gen. G. T. Beauregard

FIRST ARMY CORPS
Maj. Gen. Leonidas Polk

First Division

Brig. Gen. Charles Clark (w)
Brig. Gen. Alexander P. Stewart

First Brigade

Col. Robert M. Russell, 12th Tennessee
11th Louisiana:
Col. Samuel F. Marks (w)
Lieut. Col. Robert H. Barrow

12th Tennessee:
    Lieut. Col. Tyree H. Bell
    Maj. Robert P. Caldwell
13th Tennessee, Col. Alfred J. Vaughan, Jr.
22d Tennessee, Col. Thomas J. Freeman (w)
Tennessee Battery, Capt. Smith P. Bankhead

Second Brigade

Brig. Gen. Alexander P. Stewart
13th Arkansas
    Lieut. Col. A. D. Grayson (k)
    Maj. James A. McNeely (w)
    Col. James C. Tappan
 4th Tennessee:
    Col. Rufus P. Neely
    Lieut. Col. Otho F. Strahl
 5th Tennessee, Lieut. Col. Calvin D. Venable
33d Tennessee, Col. Alexander W. Campbell (w)
Mississippi Battery, Capt. Thomas J. Stanford

Second Division

Maj. Gen. Benjamin F. Cheatham (w)

First Brigade

Brig. Gen. Bushrod R. Johnson (w)
Col. Preston Smith, 154th Tennessee (w)
Blythe's Mississippi:
    Col. A. K. Blythe (k)
    Lieut. Col. David L. Herron (k)
    Maj. James Moore
 2d Tennessee, Col. J. Knox Walker
15th Tennessee:
    Lieut. Col. Robert C. Tyler (w)
    Maj. John F. Hearn
154th Tennessee (senior):
    Col. Preston Smith
    Lieut. Col. Marcus J. Wright (w)
Tennessee Battery, Capt. Marshall T. Polk (w)

Second Brigade

Col. William H. Stephens, 6th Tennessee
    Col. George Maney, 1st Tennessee
7th Kentucky:
    Col. Charles Wickliffe (k)
    Lieut. Col. William D. Lannom
1st Tennessee (Battalion):
    Col. George Maney
    Maj. Hume R. Feild
6th Tennessee, Lieut. Col. Timothy P. Jones
9th Tennessee, Col. Henry L. Douglass
Mississippi Battery, Capt. Melancthon Smith

Cavalry

1st Mississippi, Col. Andrew J. Lindsay
Mississippi and Alabama Battalion, Lieut. Col. Richard H. Brewer

Unattached

47th Tennessee, Col. Munson R. Hill

SECOND ARMY CORPS
Maj. Gen. Braxton Bragg

Escort

Company Alabama Cavalry, Capt. Robert W. Smith

First Division

Brig. Gen. Daniel Ruggles

First Brigade

Col. Randall L. Gibson, 13th Louisiana
1st Arkansas, Col. James F. Fagan
4th Louisiana:
      Col. Henry W. Allen (w)
      Lieut. Col. Samuel E. Hunter
13th Louisiana:
      Maj. Anatole P. Avegno (k)
      Capt. Stephen O'Leary (w)
      Capt. Edgar M. Dubroca
19th Louisiana:
      Col. Benjamin L. Hodge
      Lieut. Col. James M. Hollingsworth
Vaiden, or Bain's, Mississippi Battery, Capt. S. C. Bain

Second Brigade

Brig. Gen. Patton Anderson
1st Florida Battalion:
      Maj. Thaddeus A. McDonell (w)
      Capt. W. G. Poole
      Capt. W. Capers Bird
17th Louisiana, Lieut. Col. Charles Jones (w)
20th Louisiana, Col. August Reichard
Confederate Guards Response Battalion, Major F. H.
  Clack
9th Texas, Col. Wright A. Stanley
Washington (Louisiana) Artillery, Fifth Company,
  Capt. W. Irving Hodgson

Third Brigade

Col. Preston Pond, Jr., 16th Louisiana
16th Louisiana, Maj. Daniel Gober
18th Louisiana:
      Col. Alfred Mouton (w)
      Lieut. Col. Alfred Roman
Crescent (Louisiana) Regiment, Col. Marshall J. Smith
Orleans Guard (Louisiana) Battalion, Maj. Leon
  Querouze (w)

38th Tennessee, Col. Robert F. Looney
Ketchum's Alabama Battery, Capt. William H.
Ketchum

Cavalry

Alabama Battalion (5 companies—Jenkins, Cox, Robins, Tomlinson, and Smith), Capt. Thomas F. Jenkins

Second Division

Brig. Gen. Jones M. Withers

First Brigade

Brig. Gen. Adley H. Gladden (k)
Col. Daniel W. Adams (w), 1st Louisiana
Col. Zach C. Deas (w), 22d Alabama
21st Alabama:
      Lieut. Col. Stewart W. Cayce
      Maj. Frederick Stewart
22d Alabama:
      Col. Zach C. Deas
      Lieut. Col. John C. Marrast
25th Alabama:
      Col. John Q. Loomis (w)
      Maj. George D. Johnston
26th Alabama:
      Lieut. Col. John G. Coltart (w)
      Lieut. Col. William D. Chadick
1st Louisiana:
      Col. Daniel W. Adams
      Maj. Fred H. Farrar, Jr.
Robertson's Alabama Battery, Capt. Felix H. Robertson

Second Brigade

Brig. Gen. James R. Chalmers
5th Mississippi, Col. Albert E. Fant
7th Mississippi, Lieut. Col. Hamilton Mayson
9th Mississippi, Lieut. Col. William A. Rankin (k)
10th Mississippi, Col. Robert A. Smith
52d Tennessee, Col. Benjamin J. Lea
Gage's Alabama Battery, Capt. Charles P. Gage

Third Brigade

Brig. Gen. John K. Jackson
17th Alabama, Lieut. Col. Robert C. Fariss
18th Alabama, Col. Eli S. Shorter
19th Alabama, Col. Joseph Wheeler
2d Texas:
      Col. John C. Moore
      Lieut. Col. William P. Rogers
      Maj. Hal. G. Runnels
Girardey's Georgia Battery, Capt. Isadore P. Girardey

Cavalry

Clanton's Alabama Regiment, Col. James H. Clanton (w)

THIRD ARMY CORPS
Maj. Gen. William J. Hardee (w)

First Brigade

Brig. Gen. Thomas C. Hindman (w)
Col. R. G. Shaver, 7th Arkansas (w)
2d Arkansas:
    Col. Daniel C. Govan
    Maj. Reuben F. Harvey
6th Arkansas, Col. Alexander T. Hawthorn
7th Arkansas:
    Lieut. Col. John M. Dean (k)
    Maj. James T. Martin
3d Confederate, Col. John S. Marmaduke
Warren Light Artillery, or Swett's Mississippi Battery,
    Capt. Charles Swett
Pillow's Flying Artillery, or Miller's Tennessee Bat-
    tery, Capt. Miller

Second Brigade

Brig. Gen. Patrick R. Cleburne
15th Arkansas, Lieut. Col. Archibald K. Patton (k)
6th Mississippi:
    Col. John J. Thornton (w)
    Capt. W. A. Harper
2d Tennessee:
    Col. William B. Bate (w)
    Lieut. Col. David L. Goodall
5th (35th) Tennessee), Col. Benjamin J. Hill
23d Tennessee:
    Lieut. Col. James F. Neill (w)
    Maj. Robert Cantrell
24th Tennessee, Lieut. Col. Thomas H. Peebles

(Shoup's Battalion)

Trigg's (Austin) Arkansas Battery, Capt. John T. Trigg
Calvert's (Helena) Arkansas Battery, Capt. J. H. Calvert
Hubbard's Arkansas Battery, Capt. George T. Hubbard

Third Brigade

Brig. Gen. Sterling A. M. Wood (w)
Col. William K. Patterson, 8th Arkansas, temporarily
15th Alabama, Lieut. Col. John W. Harris
8th Arkansas, Col. William K. Patterson
9th (14th) Arkansas (battalion), Maj. John H. Kelly
3d Mississippi Battalion, Maj. Aaron B. Hardcastle
27th Tennessee:
    Col. Christopher H. Williams (k)
    Maj. Samuel T. Love (k)
44th Tennessee, Col. Coleman A. McDaniel
55th Tennessee, Col. James L. McKoin
Harper's (Jefferson Mississippi) Battery:
    Capt. William L. Harper (w)

Lieut. Put Darden
Georgia Dragoons, Capt. Isaac W. Avery

RESERVE CORPS
Brig. Gen. John C. Breckenridge

First Brigade

Col. Robert P. Trabue, 4th Kentucky
(Clifton's) 4th Alabama Battalion, Maj. James M.
  Clifton
31st Alabama, Lieut. Col. Montgomery Gilbreath
3d Kentucky, Lieut. Col. Benjamin Anderson (w)
4th Kentucky, Lieut. Col. Andrew R. Hynes (w)
5th Kentucky, Col. Thomas H. Hunt
6th Kentucky, Col. Joseph H. Lewis
Crew's Tennessee Battalion, Lieut. Col. James M.
  Crews
Lyon's (Cobb's) Kentucky Battery, Capt. Robert Cobb
Byrne's Mississippi Battery, Capt. Edward P. Byrne
Morgan's Squadron, Kentucky's Cavalry, Capt. John
  H. Morgan

Second Brigade

Brig. Gen. John S. Bowen (w)
Col. John D. Martin
9th Arkansas, Col. Isaac L. Dunlop
10th Arkansas, Col. Thomas D. Merrick
2d Confederate:
  Col. John D. Martin
  Maj. Thomas H. Mangum
1st Missouri, Col. Lucius L. Rich
Pettus Flying Artillery, or Hudson's Mississippi Battery, Capt. Alfred Hudson
Watson's Louisiana Battery, Capt. Daniel Beltzhoover
Thompson's Company, Kentucky Cavalry, Capt. Phil B. Thompson

Third Brigade

Col. Winfield S. Statham, 15th Mississippi
15th Mississippi, unknown
22d Mississippi, unknown
19th Tennessee, Col. David H. Cummings
20th Tennessee, Col. Joel A. Battle (c)
28th Tennessee, unknown
45th Tennessee, Lieut. Col. Ephraim F. Lytle
Rutledge's Tennessee Battery, Capt. Arthur M. Rutledge
Forrest's Regiment Tennessee Cavalry, Col. Nathan B.
  Forrest (w)

Unattached

Wharton's Texas Regiment Cavalry, Col. John A. Wharton (w)
Wirt Adams's Mississippi Regiment, Cavalry, Col. Wirt Adams
McClung's Tennessee, Battery, Capt. Hugh L. W. McClung
Roberts Arkansas Battery, unknown

APPENDIX C

NUMBERS AND LOSSES
BATTLE OF SHILOH

April 6–7, 1862

	Present For Duty			Casualties			
	Officers	Men	Total	Killed	Wounded	Missing	Total
UNION ARMY OF THE TENNESSEE							
1st Division (McClernand)	347	6,594	6,941	285	1,372	85	1,742
2d Division (W. H. L. Wallace)	401	8,007	8,408	270	1,173	1,306	2,749
3d Division (Lew Wallace)	314	7,250	7,564	41	251	4	296
4th Division (Hurlbut)	329	7,496	7,825	317	1,441	111	1,869
5th Division (Sherman)	367	8,213	8,580	325	1,277	299	1,901
6th Division (Prentiss)	347	7,198	7,545	236	928	1,008	2,172
Unassigned	79	1,952	2,031	39	159	17	215
Total	2,184	46,710	48,894	1,513	6,601	2,830	10,944
UNION ARMY OF THE OHIO							
2d Division (McCook)	–0–	–0–	7,552	88	823	7	918
4th Division (Nelson)	–0–	–0–	4,541	93	603	20	716
5th Division (Crittenden)	–0–	–0–	3,825	60	377	28	465
6th Division (Wood)	–0–	–0–	2,000	–0–	4	–0–	4
Total	–0–	–0–	17,918	241	1,807	55	2,103

460

CONFEDERATE ARMY OF THE MISSISSIPPI

1st Army Corps (Polk)	581	8,823	9,404	385	1,953	19	2,357
47 Tenn. (Apr. 7)	-0-	-0-	731	-0-	-0-	-0-	-0-
2d Army Corps (Bragg)	1,028	15,251	16,279	353	2,441	634	3,628
3d Army Corps (Hardee)	438	6,320	6,758	404	1,936	141	2,481
Reserve (Breckenridge)	498	6,713	7,211	386	1,682	165	2,233
Cavalry (miscellaneous)	201	4,115	4,316	-0-	-0-	-0-	-0-
Total	2,746	41,222	44,699	1,728	8,012	959	10,699
Grand Total			111,511	3,482	16,420	3,844	23,746

COMPARISON

Confederates, April 6	43,968
Federals, April 6	39,830
Confederate Excess, April 6	4,138
Federals, April 7	54,592
Confederates, April 7	34,000
Federal Excess, April 7	20,592
Aggregate in the Field, April 6 & 7	
Federal	66,812
Confederate	44,699

Bibliography

Unit Histories

Ambrose, D. Lieb, *History of the 7th Regiment Illinois Volunteer Infantry.* Springfield, Illinois, 1868.

Anders, Leslie, *The 18th Missouri.* Indianapolis, Indiana, 1968.

Bell, John T., *Tramps and Triumphs of the 2d Iowa Infantry.* Omaha, Nebraska, 1886.

Bering, John A., and Montgomery, Thomas. *History of the 48th Ohio Volunteer Infantry.* Hillsboro, Ohio, 1880.

Briant, C. C., *History of the 6th Regiment Indiana Volunteer Infantry.* Indianapolis, Indiana, 1891.

Connelly, T. W., *History of the Seventieth Ohio Regiment.* Cincinnati, Ohio, 1902.

Crooker, Lucien B., and committee, *The Story of the 55th Regiment Illinois Volunteer Infantry in the Civil War 1861–1865.* Clinton, Massachusetts, 1887.

Duke, Basil W., *A History of Morgan's Cavalry.* Bloomington, Indiana, 1960.

Duke, John K., *History of the 53rd Regiment Ohio Volunteer Infantry During the War of Rebellion.* Portsmouth, Ohio, 1900.

George, Henry, *History of the 3d, 7th, 8th, and 12th Kentucky C. S. A.* Louisville, Kentucky, 1911 (1970 reprint).

Grose, William, *The Story of the Marches, Battles, and Incidents of the 36th Regiment Indiana Volunteer Infantry.* New Castle, Indiana, 1891.

Hannaford, E., *The Story of a Regiment* (6th Regiment Ohio Volunteer Infantry). Cincinnati, Ohio, 1868.

Hart, E. F., *History of the Fortieth Illinois Infantry.* Cincinnati, Ohio, 1864.

Hartpence, William R., *History of the 51st Indiana Veteran Volunteer Infantry from 1861–1866.* Harrison, Ohio, 1894.

Hinman, Wilbur F., *The Story of the Sherman Brigade.* Privately published, 1897.

McMurray, W. J., *History of the Twentieth Tennessee Regiment Volunteer Infantry, C. S. A.* Nashville, Tennessee, 1904.

Michigan at Shiloh, *Report of the Michigan Shiloh Soldier's Monument Commission Bulletin No. 13.* Lansing, Michigan, 1920.

Morrison, Marian, *A History of the Ninth Regiment Illinois Volunteer Infantry.* Monmouth, Illinois, 1864.

Neal, W. A., *An Illustrated History of the Missouri Engineer and the 25th Infantry Regiments.* Chicago, Illinois, 1889.

Obreiter, John, *History of the Seventy-seventh Pennsylvania Volunteers.* Harrisburg, Pennsylvania, 1908.

Rerick, John H., *The Forty-fourth Indiana Volunteer Infantry.* LaGrange, Indiana, 1880.

Robertson, John, *Michigan in the War.* Lansing, Michigan, 1882.

Rood, H. H., *History of Co. A Thirteenth Iowa Veteran Infantry.* Cedar Rapids, Iowa, 1889.

Thompson, E. Porter, *History of the First Kentucky Brigade (C. S. A.).* Cincinnati, Ohio, 1868.

Thompson, S. D., *Recollections with the 3rd Iowa Regiment.* Cincinnati, Ohio, 1864.

Worthington, Thomas, *Brief History of the 46th Ohio Volunteers.* Washington, D. C., 1880.

Wright, Henry H., *A History of the 6th Iowa Infantry.* State Historical Society of Iowa, 1923.

General Sources

Ambrose, Stephen E., *Halleck: Lincoln's Chief of Staff.* L. S. U., Baton Rouge, La., 1962.

Andreas, Alfred T., "The 'Ifs and Buts' of Shiloh." *Military Essays and Recollections.* Military Order of the Loyal Legions of the United States, Illinois Commandery, Vol. 1–1891, pp. 118-123.

Andrews, J. Cutler, *The North Reports the Civil War.* Pittsburgh, Pennsylvania, 1955.

Boatner, Mark Mayo III, *The Civil War Dictionary.* New York, New York, 1959.

Boynton, H. V., *Sherman's Historical Raid.* Cincinnati, Ohio, 1875.

Brazelton, B. G., *A History of Hardin County, Tennessee.* Nashville, Tennessee, 1885.

Catton, Bruce, *This Hallowed Ground.* Garden City, New York, 1956.

————, The Coming Fury. Garden City, New York, 1961.

————, Terrible Swift Sword. Garden City, New York, 1963.

Davidson, Donald, *The Tennessee,* Volume 1 "The Old River" Frontier to Secession, New York. New York, 1946.

Deaderick, J. B., *The Truth About Shiloh.* Memphis, Tennessee, 1942.

Dufour, Charles L., *Nine Men in Gray.* New York, New York, 1963.

Dyer, Frederick, H., *A Compendium of the War of the Rebellion.* 3 volumes, New York, New York, 1959.

Eddy, T. M., *The Patriotism of Illinois.* 2 volumes, Chicago, Illinois, 1865.

Eisenschiml, Otto, *The Story of Shiloh.* Chicago, Illinois, 1946.

————, "Shiloh—The Blunders and the Blame." *Civil War Times Illustrated,* Vol. 2, No. 1 (April 1963), p. 6.

————, and Newman, Ralph, *The American Iliad.* New York, New York, 1947.

Fuller, Claud E., and Steuart, Richard D., *Firearms of the Confederacy.* Huntington, West Virginia, 1944.

Fuller, J. F. C., *The Generalship of Ulysses S. Grant.* New York, 1929.

Hancock, Mrs. A. R., *Reminiscences of Winfield Scott Hancock.* New York, New York, 1887.

Hardee, W. J., *Rifle and Light Infantry Tactics,* Vol. 1. Philadelphia, Pennsylvania, 1860.

Hartje, Robert G., *Van Dorn: The Life and Times of a Confederate General.* Nashville, Tennessee, 1967.

Harvard Memorial Biographies, Vol. 1. Cambridge, Massachusetts, 1867.

Harwell, Richard B., editor, *The Union Reader.* New York, New York, 1958.

Henry, Robert Selph, editor, *As They Saw Forrest.* Jackson, Tennessee, 1956.

Hicken, Victor, *Illinois in the Civil War.* University of Illinois Press, 1966.

Horn, Stanley F., *The Army of the Tennessee.* New York, New York, 1941.

Hughes, Nathaniel Cheairs Jr., *General William J. Hardee, Old Reliable.* Baton Rouge, Louisiana, 1965.

Johnston, William Preston, *The Life of General Albert Sidney Johnston.* New York, New York, 1878.

Jordan, Thomas, and Pryor, R. P., *The Campaigns of Lieutenant General N. B. Forrest and of Forrest's Cavalry.* New York, New York, 1868.

Lewis, Lloyd, *Sherman: Fighting Prophet.* New York, New York, 1932.

McClure, A. K., *Abraham Lincoln and Men of War-Times.* Philadelphia, Pennsylvania, 1892.

McWhitney, Grady, *Braxton Bragg and Confederate Defeat,* Vol. 1. New York, New York, 1969.

Mason, George, "Shiloh." *Military Essays and Recollections.* Military Order of the Loyal Legion of the United States, Illinois Commandery, Vol. 1–1891, pp. 98-101.

Merrill, James M., *William Tecumseh Sherman.* Chicago, Illinois, 1971.

Miller, Francis Trevelyan, editor, *The Photographic History of the Civil War,* 10 volumes. New York, New York, 1912.

Montross, Lynn, *War Through the Ages.* New York, New York, 1946.

New York *Weekly Tribune,* July 26, 1862.

Polk, William M., *Leonidas Polk: Bishop and General,* 2 volumes. New York, New York, 1915.

Randall, J. G., *The Civil War and Reconstruction.* Boston, Massachusetts, 1953.

Reed, D. W., *The Battle of Shiloh and the Organizations Engaged.* Washington, D. C., 1913.

Rich, Joseph W., "The Death of General Johnston." *Iowa Journal of History and Politics,* Vol. 16, No. 1 (April, 1918), pp. 276-284.

———, "General Lew Wallace at Shiloh: How He was Convinced of an Error after 45 Years." *Iowa Journal of History and Politics,* Vol. 18, No. 2 (April, 1920), pp. 302-308.

———, *The Battle of Shiloh.* Iowa City, Iowa, 1911.

Richardson, Albert D., *The Secret Service, The Field, The Dungeon, and The Escape.* Chicago, Illinois, 1865.

Ripley, Warren, *Artillery and Ammunition of the Civil War.* New York, New York, 1970.

Roland, Charles P., *Albert Sidney Johnston: Soldier of Three Republics.* Austin, Texas, 1964.

Roman, Alfred, *The Military Operations of General Beauregard in the War Between the States 1861–1865,* 2 volumes. New York, New York, 1884.

Saginaw *Enterprise* Newspaper, April 10, 1862. April 17, 1862. Saginaw Public Library, Saginaw, Michigan.

Shea, John Gilmory, *The American Nation.* New York, New York, 1862.

Soldiers and Citizens' Album of Biographical Records, Vol. 1–Wisconsin. Chicago, Illinois, 1888.

Strode, Hudson, editor, *Jefferson Davis: Private Letters 1823–1889.* New York, New York, 1966.

Stuart, A. A., *Iowa Colonels and Regiments*. Des Moines, Iowa, 1865.

Sword, Wiley, "How It Felt to be Shot at in the Civil War." *American History Illustrated*, Vol. II, No. 6 (October, 1967), p. 26.

U. S. War Department, *The War of the Rebellion: A Compilation of the Official Records of the Union and Confederate Armies*, 127 volumes and index. Washington, D. C., 1880–1901.

———, *The Medical and Surgical History of the War of the Rebellion 1861–1865*, Part 1, Vol. 1. Washington, D. C., 1870

———, *Official Records of Union and Confederate Navies in the War of the Rebellion*, Series I, Vol. 22. Washington, D. C.

Van Horne, Thomas Budd, *History of the Army of the Cumberland*, 2 volumes. Cincinnati, Ohio 1875.

Warner, Ezra J., *Generals in Blue. Lives of the Union Commanders*. Louisiana State University Press, 1964.

———, *Generals in Gray. Lives of the Confederate Commanders*. Baton Rouge, Louisiana, 1959.

Williams, Harry T., *P. G. T. Beauregard: Napoleon in Gray*. Baton Rouge, Louisiana, 1954.

Worthington, Thomas, *Shiloh; or, The Tennessee Campaign of 1862*. Washington, D. C., 1872.

Wyeth, John A., *That Devil Forrest: Life of General Nathan Bedford Forrest*. New York, New York, 1959.

Personal Accounts (Published)

Abernethy, Byron R., editor, *Private Elisha Stockwell, Jr., Sees the Civil War*. University of Oklahoma Press, 1958.

Arndt, A. F. R., "Reminiscences of an Artillery Officer." *War Paper—Michigan Commandery Military Order of the Loyal Legion of the United States*, Vol. 1, No. 13, pp. 4-5.

Biel, John G., editor, "Notes and Documents: The Battle of Shiloh: From the Letters and Diary of Joseph Demmet Thompson." *Tennessee Historical Quarterly*, Vol. 27-3, pp. 250-274.

Boos, J. E., contributor, "Civil War Diary of Patrick H. White." *Journal of the Illinois Historical Society*, Vol. 15 (1923), pp. 640-663.

Buckland, Ralph P.; Miller, Madison; Shaw, William T.; Sherman, W. T., contributors, *Report of the Proceedings of the Society of the Army of the Tennessee at the Fourteenth Annual Meeting*. Cincinnati, Ohio 1881.

Camm, William, "Diary of Colonel William Camm, 1861 to 1865." *Journal of the Illinois State Historical Society*, Vol. 18, Part 2, pp. 793-861.

Capron, Thaddeus H., "War Diary of Thaddeus H. Capron 1861–1865." *Journal of the Illinois State Historical Society*, Vol. 12 (1919), p. 343.

Chetlain, Augustus L., *Recollections of Seventy Years*. Galena, Illinois, 1899.

Cleveland, Charlotte, and Daniel, Robert, editors, "The Diary of a Confederate Quartermaster" (Frank M. Gailor). *Tennessee Historical Society*, Vol. 11 (1952), p. 78.

Crummer, Wilbur F., *With Grant at Donelson, Shiloh and Vicksburg*. Oak Park, Illinois, 1915.

Deupree, J. G., "Reminiscences of Service with the First Mississippi Cavalry." *Publications of the Mississippi Historical Society*, Vol. 7 (1903), pp. 88-99.

Fearing, B. D., "The 77th Ohio Volunteer Regiment at Shiloh." *The College Olio*, Marietta College, Marietta, Ohio, Vol. 13, No. 5, February 7, 1885.

Fisher, Horace Cecil, *A Staff Officer's Story: The Personal Experiences of*

Colonel Horace Newton Fisher in the Civil War. Boston, Massachusetts, 1960.

Flemming, Robert H., "The Battle of Shiloh as a Private Saw It." Military Order of the Loyal Legion of the United States, Ohio Commandery, Vol. 6, pp. 132-146.

Grant, Ulysses S., *Personal Memoirs of U. S. Grant,* 2 volumes. New York, New York, 1885.

Hazen, W. B., *A Narrative of Military Service.* Boston, Massachusetts, 1885.

Hickenlooper, Andrew, "The Battle of Shiloh." *Sketches of War History 1861–1865.* Military Order of the Loyal Legion of the United States, Ohio Commandery, Vol. 5 (1903), pp. 408-437.

Howe, M. A. DeWolfe, editor, *Home Letters of General Sherman.* New York, New York, 1909.

Hurter, Henry S., "Narrative of the First Battery of Light Artillery." *Minnesota in the Civil and Indian Wars 1861-1865,* Vol. 1, pp. 640-644, Vol. 2, pp. 91-96.

Johnston, R. U., and Buel, C. C., editors, *Battles and Leaders of the Civil War,* 4 volumes, New York, 1884–1888.

Jones, D. Lloyd, "The Battle of Shiloh, Reminiscences by D. Lloyd Jones." Military Order of the Loyal Legion of the United States, Wisconsin Commandery, Vol. 4, pp. 51-60.

Jordan, Philip D., and Thomas, Charles M., "Reminiscences of an Ohio Volunteer" (Edwin W. Brown). *The Ohio State Archaeological and Historical Quarterly,* Vol. 48 (1939), pp. 310-313.

Jordan, Thomas, "The Battle of Shiloh." *Southern Historical Society Papers,* Vol. 35, 1907.

Kirwan, A. D., editor, *Johnny Green of the Orphan Brigade. The Journal of a Confederate Soldier.* University of Kentucky Press, 1956.

McBride, George W., "My Recollections of Shiloh." *Blue and Gray, the Patriotic American Magazine,* Vol. 3, No. 1 (January, 1894), pp. 8-12.

McCormick, Andrew W., "Sixteen Months a Prisoner of War." *Sketches of War History 1861-1865.* Military Order of the Loyal Legion of the United States, Ohio Commandery, Vol. 5 (1903), pp. 69-87.

McGinnis, George F., "Shiloh." War Papers Read Before the Indiana Commandery, Military Order of the Loyal Legion of the United States, 1898, pp. 1-41.

Morton, Charles A., "A Boy at Shiloh." Military Order of the Loyal Legion of the United States, New York Commandery, 3d Series, New York, New York, 1907.

Palmer, David, "Recollections of War Times." *Annals of Iowa,* 3d Series, Vol. 9, No. 2 (April 1909–January 1911), pp. 134-141.

Putnam, Douglas, Jr., "Reminiscences of the Battle of Shiloh." *Sketches of War History 1861-1865.* Military Order of the Loyal Legion of the United States, Ohio Commandery, Vol. 3, pp. 197-211.

Ruff, Joseph, "Civil War Experiences of a German Emigrant." *Michigan History Magazine,* Vol. 27 (Spring, 1943), pp. 271-301.

Searle, Charles P., "Personal Reminiscences of Shiloh." War Papers Read Before the Iowa Commandery, Military Order of the Loyal Legion of the United States, Vol. 1 (1893), pp. 326-339.

Shaw, William T., "That Battle of Shiloh." War Papers Read Before the Iowa Commandery, Military Order of the Loyal Legion of the United States, Vol. 1, pp. 183-207.

Sherman, William Tecumseh, *Personal Memoirs of General W. T. Sherman,* 2 volumes, New York, New York, 1891.

Smith, Jacob H., "Personal Reminiscences—Battle of Shiloh." War Papers,

Michigan Commandery, Military Order of the Loyal Legion of the United States (1894), pp. 8-15.

Stanley, Dorothy, editor, *The Autobiography of Sir Henry Morton Stanley*. Boston, Massachusetts, 1909.

Stillwell, Leander, "In the Ranks at Shiloh." *Journal of the Illinois Historical Society,* Vol. 15 (1922), pp. 460-476.

———, *The Story of a Common Soldier of Army Life in the Civil War.* Erie, Kansas, 1920.

Strobridge, Truman R., "The Letters of D. C. Donnohue, Special Agent for the Procuring of Cotton Seed." *Tennessee Historical Quarterly,* Vol. 21, No. 4, (December 1962) pp. 379–386.

Taylor, F. Jay, editor, *Reluctant Rebel: The Secret Diary of Robert Patrick 1861–1865.* Baton Rouge, Louisiana, 1959.

Taylor, John T., "Reminiscences of Services as an Aide-de-Camp with General William Tecumseh Sherman." War Papers, Kansas Commandery, Military Order of the Loyal Legion of the United States, 1892.

Thomas, B. F., *Soldier Life.* Privately published, 1907.

Thorndike, Rachel Sherman, editor, *The Sherman Letters, Correspondence Between General and Senator Sherman from 1837 to 1891.* New York, New York, 1894.

Throne, Mildred, editor, "Civil War Letters of Abner Dunhan, 12th Iowa Infantry." *Iowa Journal of History,* Vol. 53 (1955), pp. 310-311.

———, editor, "Letters from Shiloh." *Iowa Journal of History,* Vol. 52 (1954), pp. 235-280.

Vail, David F., *Company K, of the 16th Wisconsin, at The Battle of Shiloh.* No publisher listed, 1897.

Wallace, Isabel, *Life and Letters of General W. H. L. Wallace.* Chicago, Illinois, 1909.

Wallace, Lewis, *Lew Wallace, An Autobiography.* New York, New York, 1906.

Watkins, Sam R., *Co. Aytch—Maury's Grays First Tennessee Regiment or a Side Show of the Big Show.* Jackson, Tennessee, 1952.

Wheeler, Joseph, "The Battle of Shiloh." *Southern Historical Society Papers,* Vol. 24, 1895.

Manuscripts and Unpublished Materials

Bailey, Franklin H., Letters March 7, 10, 18, 21, 27, April 8, 1862, Michigan Historical Collections, University of Michigan, Ann Arbor, Michigan.

Bearss, Edwin C., "Captain Irwin's Field Hospital." Shiloh National Military Park Library, Shiloh, Tennessee.

———, "Artillery Study." Shiloh National Military Park Library, Shiloh, Tennessee.

Beatty, Taylor, Diary 1862. Southern Historical Collection, University of North Carolina Library, Chapel Hill, North Carolina.

Bragg, Braxton, Papers, William P. Palmer Collection, Western Reserve Historical Society, Cleveland, Ohio.

———, Papers, Letters to his wife, March 25, April 8, 1862. Missouri Historical Society, St. Louis, Missouri.

———, "General Albert Sidney Johnston and the Battle of Shiloh." Mrs. Mason Barrett Collection, Manuscripts Division, Howard Tilton Memorial Library, Tulane University, New Orleans, Louisiana.

Bragg, Thomas, Diary 1862. Southern Historical Collection University of North Carolina Library, Chapel Hill, North Carolina.

Buckner, John A., Letter April 21, 1862. Henry E. Huntington Library, San Marino, California.

Carpenter, Arthur, Letter April 9, 1862. Yale University Library, New Haven, Connecticut.

Carrington, George, Diary 1862. Chicago Historical Society, Chicago, Illinois.

Claxton, William C., "Shiloh Reminiscences." Michigan Historical Collection, University of Michigan Library, Ann Arbor, Michigan.

Colby, Francelia, "Our Family" (manuscript) containing the letters of Enoch Colby, Jr., April 4, 14, 26, May 14, 28, 1862. Chicago Historical Society, Chicago Illinois.

Dickey, Cyrus, Letter, April 10, 1862. Illinois State Historical Library, Springfield, Illinois.

Ellis, E. John and Family, Papers, Letters of Stephen Ellis, April 11, 1862. Louisiana State University Library, Baton Rouge, Louisiana.

Embree, Joseph, Papers, Letters, Bennie D. Wall to P. B. Wall, April 3, 1862. Dept. of Archives and Manuscripts, Louisiana State University, Baton Rouge, Louisiana.

Engelmann, Adolph, Letters, April 8, 9, 12, 13, 17, 19, 20, 21, 1862. Illinois State Historical Library, Springfield, Illinois.

Floyd, C. H. Letter, July 6, 1862. Illinois State Historical Library, Springfield, Illinois.

Greshman, Walter Quintin, Papers, April 8, 12, 1862. Library of Congress, Washington, D. C.

Hardee, William J., Papers, Letters to Mrs. Felicia Shover February 25, March 22, April 3, 9, 1862. Manuscripts Division, Library of Congress, Washington, D. C.

Harmon, Francis M., Letters (copy) April 11, 1862. William Henry Smith Memorial Library, Indiana Historical Society, Indianapolis, Indiana.

Howard, W. A., Letter April 10, 1862. Miscellaneous Manuscripts Collection, Shiloh National Military Park Library, Shiloh, Tennessee.

Johnson, Charles James, Letters April 4, 9, 11, 15, 20, 1862. Louisiana State University Library, Baton Rouge, Louisiana.

Johnston, Albert Sidney, "Headquarters Book Albert Sidney Johnston." Louisiana Historical Association Collection, Manuscripts Division, Howard Tilton Memorial Library, Tulane University, New Orleans, Louisiana.

————, and Johnston, William Preston, Papers. Mrs. Mason Baret Collection, Manuscripts Division, Howard Tilton Memorial Library, Tulane University, New Orleans, Louisiana.

Kennedy, W. P., Letters March 24, 29, April 12, 17, 22, 27, May 1, 2, 1862. Illinois State Historical Library, Springfield, Illinois.

Latta, S. R., Letters April 10, 13, 18, 1862. Department of Archives and Manuscripts, Louisiana State University, Baton Rouge, Louisiana.

Lauman, Jacob G., Letters March 19, 24, 26, April 2, 4, 13, 19, 1862. Chicago Historical Society, Chicago, Illinois.

Lyman, Joseph B., Letters April 1, 3, 11, 1862. Yale University Library, New Haven, Connecticut.

Martin, S. F., Letters April 11, 14, 1862. Missouri Historical Society, St. Louis, Missouri.

Mecklin, A. H., Diary 1862. Mississippi Department of Archives and History, Jackson, Mississippi.

Miller, Madison, Diary 1862. Missouri Historical Society, St. Louis, Missouri.

Munford, Edward W., "Albert Sidney Johnston." No date. Albert Sidney Johnston Papers, Mrs. Mason Barret Collection, Manuscripts Division, Howard Tilton Memorial Library, Tulane University, New Orleans, Louisiana.

Peabody, Everett; Powell, James E.; Prentiss, Benjamin M.; Scott, John S., Personal Military Service Records. General Services Administration, National Archives and Records Service, Washington, D. C.

Preston, William, "Memoranda of A. S. Johnston's Death." A. S. Johnston Papers, Mrs. Mason Barret Collection, Howard Tilton Memorial Library, Tulane University, New Orleans, Louisiana.

———, Diary and Papers, 1862. U. S. War Department Collection of Confederate Records, National Archives Record Group 94, Washington, D. C.

Prickett, Thomas, Papers, April 18, 21, 1862. William Henry Smith Memorial Library, Indiana Historical Society, Indianapolis, Indiana.

Pugh, Richard L., Letters, April 8, 11, 13, 1862. Department of Archives and Manuscripts, Louisiana State University, Baton Rouge, Louisiana.

Rennolds, Edwin Hansford, An Autobiography (copy). In possession of Shiloh Military Trail Committee, Memphis, Tennessee.

Robertson, Thomas Chinn, Letter, April 9, 1862. Department of Archives and Manuscripts, Louisiana State University, Baton Rouge, Louisiana.

Rockwell, Almon Ferdinand, Papers, Journal, April 3-10, 1862. Library of Congress, Washington, D. C.

Shumway, Payson, Diary and Letters, April 8, 13, 1862. Illinois State Historical Library, Springfield, Illinois.

Smith, Clifton H., Letter to General G. T. Beauregard, August 5, 1880. Chicago Historical Society, Chicago, Illinois.

Smith, T. Kilby, Papers, April 11, 13, 15, 17, 1862. Henry E. Huntington Library, San Marino, California.

Stevenson, P. D. Memoirs. Department of Archives and Manuscripts, Louisiana State University, Baton Rouge, Louisiana.

Wallace, Lew, Letters, March 12, 15, 21, April 9, 17, 1862. William Henry Smith Memorial Library, Indiana Historical Society, Indianapolis, Indiana.

Wallace, Mrs. W. H. L., Letter, n/d. Shiloh National Military Park, Shiloh, Tennessee.

Washburne, Elihu B., Papers, Letter of W. R. Rowley, April 19, 1862. Library of Congress, Washington, D. C.

Whittlesey, Charles, Letter, March 18, 1873. Lew Wallace Papers, William Henry Smith Memorial Library, Indiana Historical Society, Indianapolis, Indiana.

Wilcox, E. S., Letters, April 9, 25, 1862. Illinois State Historical Library, Springfield, Illinois.

Wilkinson, B. F., Letter, April 16, 1862. Department of Archives and Manuscripts, Louisiana State University, Baton Rouge, Louisiana.

Worthington, Thomas, Court Martial Proceedings, August, 1862. General Services Administration, National Archives and Records Service, Washington, D. C.

Yandell, D. W., Letter to William Preston Johnston, November 11, 1877. Albert Sidney Johnston Papers, Mrs. Mason Barret Collection, Manuscripts Division, Howard Tilton Memorial Library, Tulane University, New Orleans, Louisiana.

Yerger, William, Papers, March 10, 1862–November 6, 1910. Mississippi Department of Archives and History Jackson, Mississippi.

Zearing, James Robert, Letters, March 21, April 8, 27, 30, 1862. Chicago Historical Society, Chicago, Illinois.

Reference Notes

CHAPTER I—THE RIVER HAS RISEN

Page **1-3** Davidson; **3-4** Ambrose; **4** "Now where . . ." Sherman *Memoirs* I 248; **5** "Fort Henry . . ." *War of Rebellion* I-7-124; **5** "It is . . ." *W of R* I-7-599; **5** "We have . . ." *W of R* I-7-625; **5** "brilliant results . . ." *W of R* I-7-648; **5** "Give me . . ." *W of R* I-7-628-29; **6** "split secession . . ." *W of R* I-7-636; **6** "Avoid any . . ." *W of R* I-7-674; **6** "The weather . . ." Worthington, *Shiloh* 73; **7** Smith-Wallace conference, L. Wallace autob., I-443-444; **7** "gout in . . ." L. Wallace, ltr 3-15-62; **7** "Still they . . ." L. Wallace 3-12-62; **8** Wallace's operations, *W of R* I-10-1-9, 13; **8** "Nothing saved . . ." L. Wallace 3-15-62; **8** "preclude the . . ." *W of R* I-10-1-10; **9** March 1 fight, *W of R* I-7-435; **9** Sherman's caution, *W of R* I-10-1-22, Sherman *Memoirs* I 256; **10-11** Sherman's operations March 14, *W of R* I-10-1-22, 28; **11** "No human . . ." *W of R* I-10-1-23; **11** "encroaching river" Flemming 133; **11** "They think . . ." L. Wallace 3-15-62; **11** "no alternative," *W of R* I-10-1-23.

CHAPTER II—TO WAGE AN OFFENSIVE

12 "The purpose . . ." *W of R* I-7-102; **12** "Delay is . . ." *W of R* I-7-535; **12** "Savannah is . . ." *W of R* I-7-942; **12** "I shall . . ." *W of R* I-10-2-25; **12** "A golden . . ." *W of R* I-7-655; **12** "we had . . ." J. T. Taylor 6; **13** "Fort Donelson will . . ." *W of R* I-7-629; **13** "Grander sight . . ." Camm 839; **13** "we tied . . ." Camm 840; **13** "The river . . ." Camm 840; **13** "the most . . ." L. Wallace 3-12-62; **14** "We have . . ." Camm 840; **14** "an epidemic . . ." *Med. & Surg. Hist.* 1-1-29; **14** "a boatload . . ." L. Wallace 3-21-62; **14** "one division . . ." *W of R* I-10-1-22; **14** "By seemingly . . ." *W of R* I-10-1-24; **14** "saw in . . ." Sherman *Memoirs* I-256; **14** "to occupy . . ." *W of R* I-10-1-25; **14-15** "a strong . . ." *W of R* I-10-1-24; **15** "slowly and . . ." *W of R* I-10-1-26; **15** "Don't hesitate . . ." *W of R* I-10-1-26; **15** "I saw . . ." *W of R* I-10-1-25; **15** "in utter . . ." *W of R* I-10-1-27; **15** "I have . . ." *W of R* I-10-1-26; **16** "I am . . ." *W of R* I-10-1-27; **16** "I have . . ." *W of R* I-10-2-679, 680; **16** "The future . . ." *W of R* I-10-2-680; **16** "If so . . ." *W of R* I-7-682; **16-17** Grant's removal, Grant's *Memoirs* I-326, *W of R* I-10-2-15, 10-1-15, 29, 43; **17** Lincoln's involvement *W of R* I-7-683; **17** "acted from . . ." *W of R* I-7-683; **17** "Instead of . . ." *W of R* I-10-2-32; **17-18** Grant's background, Grant's *Memoirs;* **19** "Sam" Grant, *Photo Hist. of Civil War* 10-36; **19** "why I . . ." *W of R* I-10-2-36; **19** "We must . . ." *W of R* I-10-2-16; **19** "As Savannah . . ." *W of R* I-10-2-21; **20** Grant transfers army, *W of R* I-10-1-43, 45; **20** "I have . . ." *W of R* I-7-632; **20** "Tell me . . ." *W of R* I-7-639; **20** "I must . . ." *W of R* I-7-641, 655; **21** "If it . . ." *W of R* I-7-660; **21** "If Johnston . . ." *W of R* I-7-682; **21** "Their plan . . ." *W of R* I-7-945; **21** "What a . . ." *W of R* I-10-2-10; **21** "The point . . ." *W of R* I-10-2-22, 23; **21** "I am . . ." *W of R* I-10-2-24; **22** "The new . . ." *W of R* I-10-2-33; **22** "I am . . ." *W of R* I-10-2-38, 39; **22** "Move your . . ." *W of R* I-10-2-42; **22** Buell's strength *W of R* I-10-2-37.

CHAPTER III—A CAMPSITE IN THE WILDERNESS

23 "Pittsburg Landing . . ." Crooker 66; **23** description of Landing, Stilwell "Ranks" 463, Connelly 17; **23** "an uninteresting . . ." Crooker 67; **24** "to take . . ." Sherman *Memoirs* I-256: **24-26** Sherman's background, Lewis, Sherman *Memoirs;* **26** "Cumps all right . . ." Putnam 198; **26** "to report . . ." *W of R* I-10-2-43; **27** description of land Battles and Leaders I 495; **27** "an admirable . . ." *W of R* I-10-1-27; **27** "easy defense . . ." Worthington, court-martial; **27** "I acted . . ." Sherman *Memoirs* I-257; **28** "didn't expect . . ." Bailey 3-27-62; **28** "a sort of . . ." Crooker 68; **28** "each brigade . . ." *W of R* I-10-2-50; **29** description of camps, Bailey 3-27-62, Claxton, Connelly, Crooker; **29** "occupied with . . ." Lauman 3-19-62; **29** McArthur's road, Sherman *Memoirs* I-260; **30** Shiloh Church, Connelly 48; **30** Smith sick, *W of R* I-10-2-53; **30** "the only . . ." *W of R* I-10-2-48; **32** "to strike . . ." *W of R* I-10-2-44; **32** "General Smith . . ." *W of R* I-10-2-46; **32** "immediate preparations" *W of R* I-10-2-51; **32** "that thirteen . . ." *W of R* I-10-2-55; **32** "Corinth will . . ." *W of R* I-10-2-55; **32** "Don't let . . ." *W of R* I-10-2-50, 51; **33** "no movement . . ." *W of R* I-10-2-57; **33** "I am . . ." *W of R* I-10-2-67; **33** "make desperate . . ." *W of R* I-10-2-53; **33** Sherman's reconnaissance, *W of R* I-10-2-57, 61, Crooker 71; **34** Sherman's racehorse, Sherman (Soc. Army of Tenn 1881).

CHAPTER IV—GATHERING OF THE HOST

35 "Men were . . ." McBride 8; **35** "march for . . ." Lauman 4-2-62; **35** sutlers, Connelly 17, Crooker 71; **35** strength, *W of R* I-10-2-84; **36** McClernand, Warner (Blue); **37** discipline, *W of R* I-10-2-74; **37** "There seems . . ." *W of R* I-10-2-63; **37** "arrest all . . ." *W of R* I-10-2-73; **37** "gross irregularities . . ." *W of R* I-10-2-63; **37** "alternate days . . ." *W of R* I-10-2-57; **37** sickness on *Fairchild,* Ambrose 46; **37** "When I . . ." Bailey 3-27-62; **37** general sickness, Zearing 3-21-62, Rerick 43, 44; **38** "we shall . . ." Colby 4-4-62; **38** "for 10,000 . . ." *W of R* I-10-2-57; **38** "By whose . . ." *W of R* I-10-2-63; **38** "This army . . ." *W of R* I-10-2-73; **38** sickness in army, Rerick 44, L. Wallace 3-21-62, *Med. & Surg. Hist.* I-1-29; **38** "I rank . . ." Hicken 51; **38** "while entertaining . . ." Hicken 51; **39** "without the . . ." *W of R* I-10-2-70; **39** "we have . . ." Kennedy 3-24-62; **40** Lauman's fare, Lauman 3-24-62, 3-26-62; **40** "Bacon" expedition, *W of R* I-10-2-63, 64, 70; **40** cotton prices, NY Weekly *Tribune* 7-26-62; **40** "I think . . ." *W of R* I-10-2-53; **40** "could not . . ." *W of R* I-10-2-80; **41** "proposed to . . ." *W of R* I-10-2-57; **41** "surplus mules" *W of R* I-10-2-66; **41** army returns, *W of R* I-10-2-84; **41-42** Wallace's dispositions, L. Wallace autob. I-448-453; **42** March 31 skirmish, *W of R* I-10-2-78, 79; **42-43** Grant—Naval operations, *W of R* I-10-2-82, 52-2-291; **43** Sherman's April 1 expedition, *W of R* I-10-2-82, 83; **43** "cannon balls . . ." Flemming 134; **43** "is the . . ." *W of R* I-10-1-83; **43** Sherman's report, *W of R* I-10-1-84; **44** Webster's reconnaissance, *W of R* I-10-1-84, 85, 10-2-50; **44-45** Buell's march from Nashville, Hannaford, 227, 228, 10-2-48, 613; **44** "three divisions . . ." *W of R* I-10-2-48; **44-45** Buell at Nashville, *W of R* I-10-2-37, 54, 58, 60, 84; **45** Halleck prods Buell, *W of R* I-10-2-43, 51, 64, 65, 71; **45** "much slower . . ." *W of R* I-10-2-70, 71; **45** Buell's knowledge of Grant's dispositions, *W of R* I-10-2-44, 47, 59; **46** Nelson, Hannaford 182, 231, Boatner, 586, Warner 343, 344; **46** Nelson asks to cross Duck River, Hannaford 231, 232; **46** "we must . . ." *W of R* I-10-2-77; **46** "the river . . ." *W of R* I-10-1-329, 330; **46** "on reaching . . ." Hannaford 232; **46** Nelson crosses river, Hannaford 232-234, *W of R* I-10-1-330; **47** "The people . . ." Hinman 134; **47** Buell's march, Hannaford 234, *W of R* I-10-1-330, 10-2-60; **47** "The road . . ." Hannaford 235, 558; **47** "kept the . . ." *W of R* I-10-2-75; **47** Buell's plans, *W of R* I-10-2-42; **47** Buell's plans, *W of R* I-10-2-42, 46, 94, 95; **48** "You are . . ." *W of R* I-10-2-94; **48** "exercise his . . ." *W of R* I-10-2-94; **48** Nelson at Savannah, *W of R* I-10-1-330; **48** delayed communications, *W of R* I-10-2-51, 64, 82, 83, Rockwell, 4-3, 4-62; **48** "I have . . ." *W of R* I-10-2-83; **48** Nelson's arrival, Hannaford 234, 237; **48** Grant's correspondence, *W of R* I-10-2-82, Hannaford 236, 559, *Battles and Leaders* I-491, Roman I-334, W. P. Johnston 536, Van Horn 1-102.

CHAPTER V—STORM SIGNALS IN THE WEST

49 Clamor against Johnston, W. P. Johnston 511; **49-50** Johnston's background, W. P. Johnston, Roland; **51** Johnston joins South, Roland 252-261; **51** most formidable opponent, Grant *Memoirs* I-187; **51** Kentucky's situation, W. P. Johnston 300, 305, *W of R* I-4-179; **51** Johnston at Nashville, W. P. Johnston 306; **52** defense of rivers, W. P. Johnston 407; **52** Fort Henry, *Battles and Leaders* I-369, *W of R* I-7-120, W. P. Johnston 422, 423; **52** Johnston's dispositions, *W of R* I-7-844, 849, W. P. Johnston 408, 417, 425; **52-53** Tilghman, *W of R* I-4-560, 7-817; **53** Gilmer's investigation, *W of R* I-7-137, 138, Munford 29; **53** "extremely bad . . ." *W of R* I-7-138; **53** "glorious chance . . ." *W of R* I-7-858; **53** action at Fort Henry, *W of R* I-7-141, 142, W. P. Johnston 428-432; **54** Johnston attempts to hold Donelson, W. P. Johnston 437, 443, 444, 486, 496; **54** Johnston's misgivings, *W of R* I-7-863, 864; **54** controversy over defending Donelson, W. P. Johnston, 435-438, *W of R* I-7-865; **54** "I do not . . ." W. P. Johnston 438; **54-55** Floyd and Pillow, Boatner, Warner, *W & L* I-401; **55** Buckner, Boatner, Warner, W. P. Johnston 309; **55** Buckner, Pillow disagree, W. P. Johnston 437; *W of R* I-7-328; **55** Johnston's instructions, W. P. Johnston 438; **55** "all is . . ." *W of R* I-7-609, 613; **55** Pillow's instructions, *W of R* I-7-329; **56** cold weather, *W of R* I-7-613; **56** Foote's attack, *W of R* 1-7-166, 167, W. P. Johnston 451-452; **56** proposed retreat, W. P. Johnston, 454-456; **56** attack of the 15th, W. P. Johnston 459; **56** Pillow-Buckner disagree, *W of R* I-7-269, 333, W. P. Johnston 464; **57**

Grant's actions, Grant *Memoirs* I-90, 91, *W of R* I-7-159; **57** Buckner attacked, *W of R* I-7-333, W. P. Johnston 466, 467; **57** C. S. generals confer on army's fate, W. P. Johnston 469, 470, *W of R* I-7-293, 299, 300, 334, 386, *B & L* I-401; **58** Forrest's escape, *W of R* I-7-386, W. P. Johnston 473, 474; **58** Floyd's escape, *W of R* I-7-274, 275, 381, 382; **58** surrender, *W of R* I-7-335, 364; **59** Johnston's reaction, W. P. Johnston 495, *W of R* I-7-255, 256; **59** Reaction in South, W. P. Johnston 495-496, 517, 518; **59** opinion of Floyd and Pillow, *W of R* I-7-256, 258; **60** Logan's Cross Roads, W. P. Johnston, 394-404; **61** Johnston's retreat, W. P. Johnston 493, 500, Johnston HQ Book; **61** prospect of reinforcement, *W of R* I-7-862, 863; **61** army strength, W. P. Johnston 508, 509, *W of R* I-7-905; **61** despair in army, W. P. Johnston, 509-512; **62** "errors of . . ." *W of R* I-7-314; **62** evacuation of Nashville, *W of R* I-7-314, 425-430, 890, W. P. Johnston 498, 499, 504; **63** reorganization of army, *W of R* I-7-904; **62-63** Morgan's raids, B. Duke 122-126, *W of R* I-10-1-31-33; **63** "a hazardous . . ." A. S. Johnston 3-18-62, W. P. Johnston 521; **63** Beauregard, Roman; **64** Beauregard meets Johnston, *B & L* I-570-573, Roman 210-215; **64** Covington house meeting, *B & L* I-571, Roman 220, *W of R* I-861, 895, 896; **64** Beauregard's role, Roman 221-223, *W of R* I-7-861, 897; **64** Beauregard's departure, Roman 224, 232; **65** situation in west, Roman 233, 247, *W of R* I-7-880, 886; **65** troop dispositions, Roman 235, 247, *W of R* I-7-899; **65** Pope's expedition, Roman 246, 247; **65** "I am . . ." *W of R* I-7-880; **65** Beauregard's strategy, *W of R* I-7-896; **66** reinforcements, *W of R* I-7-896, Roman 237; **66** Ruggles, *W of R* I-7-863, 878, 891; **66** Chalmers, *W of R* I-7-300, Roman 520; **66** strength, *W of R* I-7-899; **66** "seize and . . ." *W of R* I-7-900; **66** "from 5,000 . . ." *W of R* I-7-900; **66** Shorter, *W of R* I-7-914; **66** "Let the . . ." *Roman* 504; **66** Harris, Roman 498, 499; **66** Levies approved, *W of R* I-7-917, 918, Roman 502; **67** Bragg's reinforcement, Roman 243; **67** "serve under . . ." *W of R* I-7-912; **67** Chisolm, *W of R* I-7-823, 824, 862, 913; **67** Bragg's forwarding of reinforcements, *W of R* I-7-419, 420, 872, 888, 907, 6-826, 827, McWhitney I-200, Roland 302; **67** "We are . . ." McWhitney 200; **67** Bragg goes to Corinth, *W of R* I-7-894, 913; **67** Bragg's troops arrive, Roman 250, *W of R* I-10-1-12; **67** Furgeson, Roman 237, 243, 567; **68** Beauregard to Johnston, Roman, 243, 506, 507; **68** "This army . . ." *W of R* I-7-905; **68** "I am . . ." W. P. Johnston 504; **68** opposition to plan, W. P. Johnston 505, Roland 300, 303; **68** "If I . . ." W. P. Johnston 521; **68** evacuation of Murfreesboro, *W of R* I-7-904, 905; **68** "in good . . ." *W of R* I-7-905; **69** reinforcements, W. P. Johnston 504, 508, *W of R* I-7-907, 10-2-308; **69** "under the . . ." W. P. Johnston 506; **69** problems of retreat, W. P. Johnston 507, 508; **69** disguises direction of retreat, A. S. Johnston HQ Book 186, *W of R* I-7-911; **69** ruse successful, *W of R* I-7-666, 667, 670, 671, 10-2-11; **69** incidents of retreat, *W of R* I-7-911, 912, 917, Johnston HQ Book 190-196; **70** news of enemy, Roman 513, 514; **70** Johnston to come on, Johnston HQ Book 188, *W of R* I-10-2-302; **70** delays enroute, *W of R*, I-7-917, 10-2-297, 302; **70** Decatur, *W of R* I-10-2-310, 327; **70** "in good . . ." *W of R* I-10-2-310; **70** dissatisfaction with Johnston, Duke 118, W. P. Johnston 511, Roland 303*n;* **71** "no general," W. P. Johnston 496; **71** pressure for explanation, W. P. Johnston 517, Johnston HQ Book 245-247; **71** Johnston's reaction, W. P. Johnston 514-520, Johnston HQ Book 200-206; **71** improvements, Johnston HQ Book 192-199; **71** storm in camp, E. P. Thompson 83; **71** Johnston sends troops to Corinth, *W of R* I-10-2-316, 327, 339, 341, Johnston HQ Book 192; **72** rail cars, Roman 522; **72** delays on RR, *W of R* I-10-2-349; **72** RR inefficient, *W of R* I-10-2-340; **72** "palpable dereliction . . ." *W of R* I-10-2-304; **72** Johnston's movements, Johnston HQ Book 203, *W of R* I-10-2-354, 361, B. Bragg 3-25-62; **72** "saved me . . ." B. Bragg 3-25-62; **72** "The test . . ." Johnston HQ Book 206.

CHAPTER VI—A MOST DIFFICULT TASK

73 lack of troops, *W of R* I-7-135, 156, 157, Roman 520, **73** gunboat raid Feb. 7-8, *W of R* I-7-153-156; **74** Walker, Warner 320-321; **74** "the vertebrae . . ." *W of R* I-7-887, 888; **74** Ruggles, *W of R* I-7-891, 894, 10-2-304; **74** *Tyler's* raid, *W of R* I-7-421, 619, 894, 895; **75** "the utmost . . ." *W of R* I-7-906; **75** River under surveillance, *W of R* I-7-907, 909, Roman 520; **75** "to attack . . ." *W of R* I-7-909; **75** heavier river patrols, *W of R* I-7-665; **75** *Tyler* refitted, *B & L* I-620; **75** March 1 fight, *W of R* I-7-435, *Off. Rec. Nav.* I-22-643, Roman 520; **75** losses, *W of R* I-7-435, 10-2-8; **75** "under the . . ." *W of R* I-10-2-317; **75** camp withdrawn, *W of R* I-10-2-8; **75** "nervous affection . . ." *W of R* I-7-912; **76** Bragg in command, *W of R* I-7-915, 10-2-297; **76** stern discipline, *W of R* I-10-2-297, 298, Roland 314, 315; **76** Bragg anticipates enemy, *W of R* I-10-2-300; **76** News of enemy on river, *W of R* I-10-2-302, 312; **76** Entrench at Corinth, *W of R* I-10-2-305, 306; **76** Savannah occupied, *W of R* I-10-2-310; **76** point of attack unknown, *W of R* I-10-2-316, 317, 319; **76** Chalmers's defenses, Roman 520; *Off. Rec. Nav.* I-22-667, **77** exchange of fire, *Off. Rec. Nav.* I-22-666-668, *W of R* I-10-2-319; **77** river's influence, *W of R* I-10-2-312, 316, 319; **77** Beauregard in command, *W of R* I-10-2-297; **77** "Our cause . . ." *W of R* I-10-2-297; **77** News of landing, *W of R* I-10-2-316, 317, 319; **77** Gladden's anxiety, *W of R* I-10-2-317; **77** News of landing, *W of R* I-10-2-319, 327, 10-1-13; **77** crisis at hand, *W of R* I-10-2-319, 320, 328, 331; **78** "in readiness . . ." *W of R* I-10-2-327; **78** "Don't change . . ." *W of R* I-10-2-328; **78** Chalmers's movements, *W of R* I-10-2-327, 328; **78** Sherman's raid, *W of R* I-10-1-22; **78** "seeming abandonment," *W of R* I-10-2-327; **78** Beauregard overreacts, *W of R* I-10-2-318, 327, 329, 7-915; **78** shoot at feet, *W of R* I-10-2-325; **78** Bragg at Bethel, *W of R* I-10-2-328; **79** broken communications, *W of R* I-10-2-329, 330; **79** Bragg calls off alert, *W of R* I-10-1-11, 10-2-328; **79** proposes New Madrid attack, *W of R* I-10-1-12, 10-2-329; **79** Polk's orders, *W of R* I-10-2-331; **79** Polk, Horn 49, Boatner 657, W. P. Johnston 320, 321; **79** Polk objects to Columbus evacuation, Roman 234, *W of R* I-7-438, 10-2-311; **80** Polk withdraws, *W of R* I-7-436, 438, 10-2-311; **80** Polk at Humboldt, *W of R* I-10-2-303, 311, 382; **80** King at Paris, *W of R* I-10-1-16-19, 10-2-302; **80** "entirely in . . ." *W of R* I-10-1-12; **80** "the most . . ." *W of R* I-10-1-11, 12; **80** another beachhead, *W of R* I-10-2-329, 332, 10-1-12; **80** "the country . . ." *W of R* I-10-1-12; **80** Ruggles telegram, *W of R* I-10-1-29; **81** "in any . . ." *W of R* I-10-2-332; **81** Ruggles confirms landing, *W of R* I-10-1-29; **81** Bragg learns news himself, *W of R* I-10-2-328, 332, 340; **81** "anxious to . . ." *W of R* I-10-2-332; **81** Polk comes to Bethel, *W of R* I-10-1-11, 10-2-332, W. P. Johnston 542; **81** "The troops . . ." *W of R* I-10-2-341; 81 "radical defects . . ." *W of R* I-10-2-340; **81** Beauregard's plans, W. P. Johnston 542; **82** reconnaissance to Pittsburg Landing, *W of R* I-10-2-341, 342, 10-1-25; **82** Beauregard's orders, *W of R* I-10-2-335, 336; **82** Bragg's orders, *W of R* I-10-2-338; **82** 149 look to Johnston, *W of R* I-10-2-332, 339, 341, 342; **82** Bragg in formal command, *W of R* I-10-2-342, 343; **82** Johnston arrives, *W of R* I-10-2-349, 354, 361; **83** Beauregard meets Johnston, Bragg 3-25-62; **83** "They might . . ." W. P. Johnston 542; **83** Corinth conference, *W of R* I-10-2-362; **83** Johnston's strength, *W of R* I-10-2-377; **83** Van Dorn, Warner 314; **83** plans to attack St. Louis, *W of R* I-8-749, 750; **83** Campaign in Arkansas, *B & L* I-276, 319 ff.; **83** Beauregard's letter, *W of R* I-7-900, 8-755, Roman 242; **84** Pea Ridge fight, *B & L* I-321, 325, 337; **84** Beauregard's appeal, *W of R* I-8-789, 791, Roman 523; **84** Van Dorn ordered to Corinth, *W of R* I-10-2-354; **84** Van Dorn's movements, *W of R* I-10-2-354, Roman 523, *B & L* III-441, 443, Hartje 166; **84** arrives at Memphis, *B & L* III-443, *W of R* I-10-2-414; **84** reorganization, *W of R* I-10-2-370, 371, Roman 266, *B & L* I-550; **85** Beauregard's role, Roman 266-268; **85** Bragg's role and background, Roman 268, Roland 314, Warner (*g*) 30, W. P. Johnston 547, Boatner 78; **85** summary punishment, *W of R* I-10-2-338; **85** "Stern, dictatorial . . ." Bragg 3-25-62; **86** Bragg and Crittenden, *W of R* I-10-2-371, 379, 10-1-394, W. P. Johnston 547; **86** shortage of generals, Roman 509-515, *W of R* I-10-1-382, 384; **86** "What in . . ." Roman 512, 513; **86** lack of arms, Roman 254, 260, 517, *W of R* I-10-2-334, 10-1-575, E. P. Thompson 58; **87** importation of Enfields, Fuller & Stuart 218, E. P. Thompson 87, *W of R* I-7-863, 872, 883, 886; **87** church bells to cannon, *W of R* I-10-2-350, 362, 10-1-382-384, 414, Roman 518; **87** gunboat patrols, *W of R* I-10-2-351, 358; **88** B. R. Johnson's report, *W of R* I-10-2-359, 360; **88** Sherman to Monterey, *W of R* I-10-2-65, 361, 363, 52-2-290; **88** C. S. estimate of enemy's moves, *W of R* I-52-2-290, 291, W. P. Johnston 538; **88** evacuation of Eastport, *W of R* I-10-2-291; **88** Bethel Station's importance, *W of R* I-10-2-366-368; **88** advance by enemy anticipated, *W of R* I-10-2-368, 373; **89** Sherman threatens Iuka, *W of R* I-52-2-293, 296, Johnston HQ Book 233; **89** Johnston's situation, Johnston HQ Book 231, *W of R* I-52-2-293, W. P. Johnston 514, 515.

CHAPTER VII—A RENDEZVOUS WITH DESTINY

90 dissension in 1st La. Cav., *W of R* I-10-2-507, 543, 544; **90** assignment on left flank, *W of R* I-10-2-310, 7-911; **90** Capt. Scott detached, *W of R* I-10-1-7, 8; **90** Capt. Scott's operations, *W of R* I-10-2-310, 10-1-7, 8, 7-261; **90** Col. Scott's operations, *W of R* I-10-2-342, Johnston HQ Book 205; **91** importance of Scott, Johnston HQ Book 207, 208, 211, *W of R* I-10-1-330, 10-2-349, 362, 387; **91** Davis-Johnston correspondence, W. P. Johnston 521, 522, 551, *W of R* I-10-2-365; **92** Early defensive preparations *W of R* I-10-2-312-314; **92** reconnaissance ordered, *W of R* I-10-2-375, 376; **92** "Corps of . . ." Johnston HQ Book 231; **92** "placed in readiness . . ." *W of R* I-10-2-381; **92** Bragg to remain, *W of R* I-52-2-293; **92** "it would not . . ." *W of R* I-10-2-378; **92** prospect of Van Dorn, *B & L* I-550; **94** troops at Bethel Station, *W of R* I-10-2-360, 366, 374; **94** skirmish of March 31, *W of R* I-10-2-374, 375, 10-1-78, 79; **94** Cheatham's instructions, *W of R* I-10-2-367, 368; **95** "as close . . ." *W of R* I-10-2-378; **95** Cheatham's reconnaissance, *W of R* I-10-2-90; **95** observed by Federals, L. Wallace autob. I-450-454, McGinnis 6; **95**

alarm of Federals, *W of R* I-10-1-79, L. Wallace 454, McGinnis 6; **95** Confederates fear attack, *B & L* I-594, *W of R* I-10-1-400; **95** Beauregard's extent of knowledge, *W of R* I-10-1-385, 10-2-372, 387; **95** "the junction . . ." *W of R* I-10-1-385; **95** "Now is . . ." *B & L* I-579; **95** "Colonel Jordan . . ." *B & L* I-594; **96** Jordan, *W of R* I-10-2-373; Warner (*g*) 167, 168; **96** Mackall transferred, Roman 212, 358, 359, 466, 563; **96** discussion of Cheatham's dispatch, *B & L* I-594, Roman 270, 271; **97** Johnston's nature, W. P. Johnston 544, 719, 726, 731; **97** Bragg's criticism of army, Bragg 3-25-62, 4-8-62, *W of R* I-10-2-340; **97** controversy over attack; Jordan and Pryor 108, 109; **97** Beauregard's estimate of urgency, *B & L* I-594, Roman 270-271; **97** Johnston's telegram, *W of R* I-10-1-385; **97** Buell via Clifton, *W of R* I-10-2-387; **98** News of Purdy threatened, *W of R* I-10-400; **98** location of Buell, *W of R* I-10-330; **98** Johnston orders attack, *W of R* I-10-2-383, *B & L* I-595, Roman 271; **98** instructions sent, *B & L* I-595, *W of R* I-10-2-383; **98** Jordan sees Chisolm, *B & L* I-606, Roman 271; **98** Beauregard's notes, Roman 271, *B & L* I-595; **98** Morning conference, *B & L* I-581, 595, Roman 271, 272; **98** "strike a . . ." *W of R* I-10-1-385; **99** "(as) it was . . ." *W of R* I-10-1-385, 10-2-405, Pugh 4-8-62; **99** Jordan's affidavit, Roman 274; **99** Beauregard in charge of orders, *B & L* I-579, 580; **99** sketch on tabletop, Roman 271; **99** verbal orders, *B & L* I-596, Roman 272; **99** Special orders #8, *W of R* I-10-1-392-395; **99** march delayed, *B & L* I-581, 586, 596, *W of R* I-10-1-596, 607; **99** "as soon . . ." *W of R* I-10-2-387; **100** Waddell, Roman 529, 530; **100** Polk camped in city, W. Polk 93; **100** clog streets, *B & L* I-596; **100** hours of march, *W of R* I-10-1-596, 585, 607; **100** lengthy march, *W of R* I-10-1-393, 403, 607; **100** march along blind road, Roman 530; **100** Road blocked, Roman 530, *W of R* I-10-1-414; **101** Bragg's planned march, *W of R* I-10-1-393, W. P. Johnston 565; **101** bad start, *W of R* I-10-2-388, 389; **101** Bragg's march begins, *W of R* I-10-2-391, 10-1-464, 545; **101** change of route, *W of R* I-10-2-390, 391; **101** Polk delayed, *W of R* I-10-1-414; **102** Ruggles delayed, *W of R* I-10-1-464, 527, 614; **102** troops night of 4th, *W of R* I-10-1-607, 614, W. P. Johnston 559, 560; **102** "Buell is . . ." *W of R* I-10-2-387; **102** "with the . . ." *W of R* I-10-1-396; **102** Beauregard leaves Corinth, *W of R* I-10-1-400; **102** Johnston's departure, Eisenshiml 59, *W of R* I-10-2-390; **103** Johnston at Monterey, *W of R* I-10-2-390; W. P. Johnston 562, *B & L* I-596, 597; **103** April 4 conference, W. P. Johnston 559, 562, 563, *W of R* I-10-2-391, 392; **103** rain at 2 A.M., *W of R* I-10-1-461, W. P. Johnston 561; **103** troops in line at 3 A.M., *W of R* I-10-1-414, 464; **103** troop movements in A.M., *W of R* I-10-1-393, 406, 414, 464, 495, 567, 585, 591, W. P. Johnston 562; **104** Bragg detaches Gladden, *W of R* I-10-1-393, 494, 532, 547; **104** line forms late A.M., W. P. Johnston 563, *W of R* I-10-1-547, 553; **104** Johnston impatient, W. P. Johnston, 563; **104** general's movements, *W of R* I-10-1-400, 464, Biel 256; **104** Munford sent to find troops, *W of R* I-10-1-470; **105** "This is . . ." W. P. Johnston 563; **105** Ruggles, Warner (*g*) 265, 266; **105** Ruggles way blocked, W. P. Johnston 563, Biel 256; **105** "move promptly . . ." *W of R* I-10-1-406; **105** gap between Jackson and Ruggles, *W of R* I-10-1-527; **105** Ruggles in line 4 P.M., *W of R* I-10-1-480, 495, 516; **106** Polk's movements, *W of R* I-10-1-296, 297, 395, 414, 427, 444, 461; **106** Breckenridge's march, *W of R* I-10-1-614, W. P. Johnston 559, 560, E. P. Thompson 87; **106** Beauregard on 5th, Roman 345, 530, 553, *W of R* I-10-1-400; **107** Bragg-Beauregard-Polk controversy, *W of R* I-10-1-400, 407, 495, W. P. Johnston 571, Roland 323, Roman 530, Preston diary 4-5-62; **107** Johnston joins conference, *W of R* I-10-1-407, W P. Johnston 566, 569, 570; **107** "entrenched to . . ." Roman 278; **107** rations gone, *W of R* I-10-1-407, 464, W. P. Johnston 569; **108** "gentlemen, we . . ." W. P. Johnston 568; **108** "I would . . ." W. P. Johnston 569; **108** Johnston aroused, W. P. Johnston 570; **108** Beauregard's role designated, *B & L* I-599, Roland 327; 108 Yandell's comments, Yandell letter (1877) p. 9, W. P. Johnston papers; **108** "iron dice . . ." Jordan & Pryor 108, 109; **108** "I have . . ." W. P. Johnston 571; **108** Johnston anxious to attack, W. P. Johnston 569; **109** "I have a . . ." Gailer 78, 79; **109** "If we . . ." Biel 256; **109** new flags, Roman 521; **109** food, Biel 256, 262, Kirwan 19; **109** lack of provisions, *W of R* I-10-1-464; **109** knowledge of enemy camps, W. P. Johnston 569, *B & L* I-597, 604, *W of R* I-10-1-375, 376, 392, 393; **109** Chalmers's early reconnaissance, *W of R* I-10-2-375, 376, 384; **110** Chalmers April 3, *W of R* I-10-1-87, 90, 10-2-384, 387; **110** Sherman's foray, *W of R* I-10-2-86, 87, 90, 388; **110** "gallant to . . ." *W of R* I-10-2-299; **111-112** Skirmish of 4th, *W of R* I-10-1-90-93, 567 Worthington (*Shiloh*) 140, *B & L* I-596, 597; **112** "This means . . ." *B & L* I-596, 597; **112** Jordan interrogates Crockett, Preston diary 1, 2; **112** Avery's Georgia dragoons, *W of R* I-10-1-612; **112** "to see if . . ." W. P. Johnston 561; **112** widespread carelessness, Worthington (*Shiloh*) 137, 140, 143, Roman 282; **113** ass't. surgeon captured, Roman 282; **113** conference of generals, *B & L* I-604, W. P. Johnston 554, 568; **113** "Polk, left . . ." *W of R* I-10-2-387; **113** Jordan's use of Napoleon's order, *B & L* I-595; **113** "no force . . ." Munford-W. P. Johnston papers, 7; **113** army committed per plan, *B & L* I-599; **113** Confederate plan, W. P. Johnston 557, *B & L* I-604; *W of R* I-10-1-397; **114** troops' enthusiasm, *B & L* I-604, Robertson 325, *W of R* I-10-1-400, W. P. Johnston 566; **114** Beauregard's general orders #3, *W of R* I-10-2-325, 326; **114** Jordan chats with Johnston, *B & L* I-598, 599, *W of R* I-10-1-400, Hancock 69.

CHAPTER VIII—THE UNSUSPECTING SHERMAN

115-116 Brazelton 10-15, 23, 24, 35, 56, 67, 87, 98, 99; **116** Hardin Co. pro Union, *W of R* I-10-2-8; **116** Savannah's Union sentiment, Worthington (*Shiloh*) 70, 72, *W of R* I-10-2-80; **116** drafting at Savannah, Worthington (*Shiloh*) 69-71, Brazelton 62; **116** "A grand . . ." Brazelton, 61, 62; **117** farmers' source of information, *W of R* I-10-2-359, 368; **117** "the enemy . . ." *W of R* I-10-2-384; **117** Dr. Parker's warning, *W of R* I-10-2-90; **117** "to the . . ." Strobridge 383, see also Camm 841; **117-118** Wallace and scouts, L. Wallace autob. I, 450-458; **118** McClernand-Grant animosity, L. Wallace autob. I 376, 377; **118** Grant's note of April 5 implied, *W of R* I-10-2-93; **118** C. F. Smith at Savannah, *W of R* I-10-1-331; **118** "give me . . ." *W of R* I-10-2-82; **119** information from deserters, *W of R* I-10-1-84; **119** purpose of Sherman's patrol, *W of R* I-10-2-87; **119** Lammon prisoner, *W of R* I-10-2-90; **119** "large and . . ." *W of R* I-10-1-89; **119** Grant reviews army, *W of R* I-10-1-84, 88, 89; **119** "sick boys . . ." Isabel Wallace, 181; **119** "we go . . ." Colby 4-4-62; **119** "but the . . ." I. Wallace 181; **119** "nothing to . . ." Kennedy 3-29-62; **119** "three times . . ." I. Wallace 181; **119** daily drill, Bering 18; **119** "drill and . . ." *W of R* I-10-2-90; **120** "a kind of . . ." Connelly 19; **120** "Halt! Who . . ." Connelly 19, 20; **120** reorganization of art. and cav., *W of R* I-10-87, 88; **120** Ricker's knowledge, Ricker, 3, 5; **120** reorganization of artillery, *W of R* I-10-2-87-92; **121** L. Wallace's request, *W of R* I-10-2-91, L. Wallace autob. I 454; **121** "it may . . ." *W of R* I-10-2-91; **121** "My apprehension . . ." Grant *Memoirs* I, 334, 336; **121** transfers, *W of R* I-10-2-88; **121** Lauman's disappointment, Lauman 4-4-62; **121** "that he . . ." I. Wallace 176; **121** "to fill . . ." I Wallace 180; **121** confusion in camp, Worthington (*Shiloh*) 121; **122** Sherman's testimony, Worthington court-martial 8; **122** "as much . . ." Thorndike 149; **122** Eagler's discovery, Flemming 137; **122** outpost captured, *W of R* I-10-1-90; **123** Buckland-Crockett, Soc. Army of Tenn. (1881) 76, *W of R* I-10-90, 91; **123** Ricker investigates, Ricker 3, *W of R* I-10-1-92, Soc. Army of Tenn. (1881) 76; **123** Encountered advance of C. S. Army, *W of R* I-10-1-567; **124** "prudent to . . ." Soc. Army of Tenn. (1881) 77; **124** prisoners, trophies, *W of R* I-10-1-92, 93; **124** Sherman waiting, *W of R* I-10-1-90, Soc. Army of Tenn. (1881) 77, Worthington court-martial 10; **124** "irregular proceedings . . ." Soc. Army of Tenn. (1881) 77; **124** "at least . . ." *W of R* I-10-1-92; **124** "Oh! tut . . ." B. Ricker 7-7-1901; **124** Reconnaissance in force, Ricker 5; **124** "in some . . ." *W of R* I-10-1-90; **124** alarm in camps, I. Wallace 181; **124** Grant advised, *W of R* I-10-1-89, Worthington court-martial 4-4-62; **125** Grant to Pittsburg Landing, Grant *Memoirs* I-172; **125** "everything quiet . . ." I. Wallace 181; **125** critique, *W of R* 1-10-2-92; **125** "afraid of . . ." Howe 224; **125** "I will . . ." Thorndike 148, 149; **126** Worthington, Sherman *Memoirs* I-54; **126** men billeted in homes, Worthington (*Shiloh*) 76; **126** axes denied, Worthington (*Shiloh*) 122, 140; **127** Worthington gathers ammo, Worthington (*Shiloh*) 120; **127** threatened with arrest, Worthington court-martial 21; **127** paid no attention, Worthington (*Shiloh*) 123; **127** Appler, J. Duke 39; **127** "What appeared . . ." J. Duke 41; **127** "Colonel Appler . . ." J. Duke 41; **127** Hildebrand, J. Duke 40; **127-128** McDowell, Stuart 150; **128** "I have . . ." Thorndike 148; **128** rumors, J. Duke 41; **128** prisoner's warnings, *W of R* I-10-2-93, Worthington (*Shiloh*) 118, J. Duke 41; **128** "Graybacks to . . ." Hickenlooper 411; **128** pickets strengthened, Crooker 73; **128** pickets driven in, Worthington (*Shiloh*) 102, 121, 137, 139, 140, Worthington court-martial 11; **128** Grant's query, *W of R* I-10-2-93; **128** "I have . . ." *W of R* I-10-2-94; **129** "all is . . ." *W of R* I-10-2-93; **129** transfer of cavalry, Thorndike 144, Worthington (*Shiloh*) 102; **129** reason for lack of vigilance, Thorndike 144, 146; **129** artillery in woods, Worthington (*Shiloh*) 139, Worthington court-martial; **129** "I looked . . ." Worthington court-martial 53; **129** Sharp discovers cannon, Worthington court-martial 53; **129** driven from Seay's house, Worthington court-martial 60; **129** two officers see Sherman, I. Wallace 191; **130** "to bring . . ." I. Wallace 191; **130** "drive away . . ." J. Duke 41, 42; **130** White's chat with Stuart, Boos 652; **130** no alarm in camp, Crooker 73, 78; **130** Confederates watch drill, Connelly 20; **130** weather, I. Wallace 182; **130** wildflowers, etc., Stillwell (*Ranks*) 463, 464; **130** "not yet . . ." I. Wallace 182; **130-131** letters mailed, Kennedy 4-29-62, **131** boredom, Crooker 73, Connelly 20; **131** "Nothing of . . ." I. Wallace 181; **131** "dull and . . ." Capron 343; **131** Buell's note to Grant,

W of R I-10-2-91; **131** Grant's note to Buell, *W of R* I-10-2-91, 93; **131** Nelson's arrival, Fisher 10; **131** "They're all . . ." Fisher 10; **131** Grant sees Ammen, *W of R* I-10-1-330; **131** "You cannot . . ." *W of R* I-10-1-330-331; **132** Buell sleeps in Nelson's tent, Rockwell April 5.

CHAPTER IX—SOME QUEER GENERALS

133 "to examine . . ." *W of R* I-10-1-89; **133** McPherson, Grant's *Memoirs* I-333; **133** scout of April 5, *W of R* I-10-1-257, Boos 652; **133** prisoners aboard *Tigress,* Worthington (*Shiloh*) 118; **133** Grant up after 12 P.M. I. Wallace 186; **133** "The main . . ." *W of R* I-10-2-94; **133** "I have . . ." *W of R* I-10-1-89; **134** L. Wallace to W. H. L. Wallace, I. Wallace, photograph opposite 189; **134** Camm fears attack, Camm 841, 842; **134** Prentiss, Warner (*Blue*) 385, 386; **134** Prentiss takes command, *W of R* I-10-2-67; **134** Prentiss-Grant disputes, Grant *Memoirs* I-257-263; **135** "kind of . . ." Stillwell (*Ranks*) 464; **136** Graves, Robertson 838; **136** Chambers, Warner (*Blue*) 78; **136** Miller, Boatner 551; **136** officers of 15th Michigan, Robertson 354, 883, 900; **136** 25th Missouri, Neal, Harvard 159-163; **136** "a very . . ." Harvard 163; **136** encampment of the 6th division, Worthington (*Shiloh*) 10; **136** Prentiss's pickets, Robertson 325; **136** concern of officers, I. Wallace 191; **136** Review postponed, *W of R* I-52-232; **137** Powell sees butternuts, Robertson 325; **137** "After my . . ." Robertson 325; **137** Moore's reconnaissance, *W of R* I-10-1-282, Robertson 325, Neal 130; **137** "a thorough . . ." *W of R* I-10-1-282; **137** "an old . . ." Neal 130; **137** Moore reports 7 P.M., *W of R* I-10-1-282; **137** "he could . . ." Robertson 325; **137** "He [Prentiss] remarked . . ." Robertson 325; **137** "all right . . ." Robertson 325; **138** Peabody, *Harv. Mem. Bio.* 150-163; **138** "exciting mutiny . . ." E. Peabody Pers. Mil. Service Records; **138** "I have . . ." *Harv. Mem. Bio.* 159; **139** Peabody alarmed, Robertson 325; **139** sees Prentiss, Neal 126; **139** "as there . . ." Neal 126; **139** Peabody orders patrol, Neal 125-127; **139** "drive in . . ." Neal 127; **139** two companies of 12th Michigan included, Robertson 325, Bailey 4-9-62; **140** Peabody shakes hands, Neal 127.

CHAPTER X—THE SUN OF AUSTERLITZ

141 "open spot . . ." Ruff 295; **141** Fraley field occupied 5th, *W of R* I-10-1-607; **141** Hardcastle's battalion, *W of R* 7-689; **141** deploys at nightfall, *W of R* I-10-1-602; **142** "singular beats . . ." *W of R* I-10-1-603; **142** "crowing of . . ." Ruff 294; **142** near disaster, Ruff 294; **142** time, Roman I, 527, 529; **142** first fire, *W of R* I-10-1-602, 603; **143** confrontation, *W of R* I-10-1-603, Ruff 295, Neal 127-131; **143** "most of . . ." *W of R* I-10-1-603; **143** Klinger first casualty, Neal 131; **143** cover in Fraley field, Ruff 295; **143** bullets strike tree, Ruff 295; **143** Bailey's experience, Bailey 4-8-62; **144** Johnston hears firing, Munford, 12; **144** Wood sends instructions, *W of R* I-10-1-591; **144** skirmish continues, *W of R* I-10-1-603; **144** cloudless sky, Stillwell (*Ranks*) 464; **144** wounded come in, *W of R* I-10-1-280, 282; **144** Peabody orders Moore out, *W of R* I-10-1-282; **144** expects no enemy, Neal 125; **144** time (6:15), *W of R* I-10-1-282, 603; **144** Confederates withdraw, *W of R* I-10-1-598; **144** cavalry turns flank, Ruff 295; **146** Wood advances, *W of R* I-10-1-603; **146** skirmishing continues, *W of R* I-10-1-600; **146** "like an . . ."

W of R I-10-1-386; **146** C. S. deployment, *W of R* I-10-1-383, 386, W. P. Johnston 572; **146** Arkansans, Stanley; **146-147** Hardee, Warner (*Gray*) 124, W. P. Johnston 353, 584; **147** Cleburne, Warner (*Gray*) 53; **147** S. A. M. Wood, Warner (*Gray*) 344; **147** called into line, *W of R* I-10-1-576; **147** hour delay, Stanley 187; **147** Shaver's brigade advances, *W of R* I-10-1-573; **147** white mist, T. Jordan (*SHSP*) 205; **147** Johnston rides to Y in road, W. Preston 4-18-62 A. S. Johnston papers; **147** Beauregard arrives, Roman I 349; **147** Johnston fond of coffee, Yandell 11-11-77; **148** plan of operations, Roman I-349; **148** meeting around campfire, Bragg (*ASJ*) 4, *W of R* I-10-1-386; **148** "The battle . . ." Bragg (*ASJ*) 4; **148** Fire-eater, Munford 22, W. P. Johnston 612, 719; **148** "the ideal . . ." Roland 346; **148** "Tonight we . . ." W. P. Johnston 582; **148** time (6:40), Roman I, 527; **148** "sun of Austerlitz," W. P. Johnston 582; **148** Powell meets Moore, Neal 125, *W of R* I-10-1-283; **148** "Together they . . ." Neal 125, also Ruff 196; **148** Moore sends for all of regt., *W of R* I-10-1-282, 283; **149** Prentiss angry, *Harv. Mem. Bio.* 164, Morton; **149** advance resumed, *W of R* I-10-1-283; **149** meet company of 16th Wisc., D. L. Jones, 56, 57; **149** "Boys, we . . ." D. L. Jones 57; **149** Saxe and Williams killed, D. L. Jones 56; **149** Moore deploys, Neal 125; **149** Arkansas skirmishers, *W of R* I-10-1-576; **150** Moore shot, *W of R* I-10-1-282, 283; **150** Powell withdraws, Neal 126; **150** Saxe's men return to camp, D. L. Jones 56; **150** Woodyard's movements, *W of R* I-10-1-283; **150** joined by 3 co's of 16th Wisconsin, D. L. Jones 54, *W of R* I-10-1-283, 285; **151** Shaver's caution, *W of R* I-10-1-577; **151** Federals retreat, D. L. Jones 55, *W of R* I-10-1-283, 557; **151** Peabody at breakfast, Shea 356; **151** Peabody orders "long roll," Morton, Claxton 2; **151** Wisc. regt. not summoned, *W of R* I-10-1-285; **151** most of 25th Mo. formed, Morton; **151** Prentiss angry with Peabody, Morton, Claxton, Shea 356, *W of R* I-10-1-278; **152** Peabody's 1,100 men, W. P. Johnston 683; **152** Peabody meets Powell, Neal 126; **152** Woodyard's flight, *W of R* I-10-1-283; **152** Peabody's deployment, Morton, *W of R* I-10-1-283; **152** "grandest scene . . ." Claxton 6; **152** hilltops covered, *W of R* I-10-1-280; **152** "Attention, battalion . . ." Morton; **152-153** Stanley, Stanley 187-204; **153** Shaver's fire fight, *W of R* I-10-1-577, Stanley 190; **153** Wood finds gap, *W of R* I-10-1-591; **153** 55th Tennessee, *W of R* I-10-1-591; **153** "Do not . . ." McWhitney 217; **154** Hardcastle separated, *W of R* I-10-1-603; **154** "retreat, retreat," *W of R* I-10-1-577; **154** 55th Tennessee disrupts Martin, W. P. Johnston 676, *W of R* I-10-1-403, 577, 591; **154** Swett's plight, *W of R* I-10-1-574, Morton; **154** "Fix bayonets! . . ." Stanley 190; **154** "In a few . . ." Claxton 5; **154** "we will . . ." Morton; **155** Woodyard encounters crossfire, *W of R* I-10-1-283; **155** "a mad . . ." D. L. Jones 55; **155** flight thru camp, *W of R* I-10-1-283; **155** Peabody looks for Prentiss, Anders 52; **155** Prentiss receives Moore's dispatch, *W of R* I-10-1-282; **155** Miller at breakfast, Miller diary, Anders 49; **155** camp of 61st Illinois alarmed, Stillwell (*Ranks*) 465; **155** Prentiss orders 16th Wisc. out, *W of R* I-10-1-285; **156** breakfast in progress, D. L. Jones 56, Vail 1, 2; **156** Wisc. regt's. deployment, *W of R* I-10-1-285; Vail 1; **156** 18th Wisconsin unprepared, *Soldiers & C.* 479, Anders 49, 51; **156** "going to . . ." *Soldiers & C.* 745; **156** Miller redeployed, Anders 49, *W of R* I-10-1-278; Stillwell (*Ranks*) 467; **157** Hickenlooper's battery, Hickenlooper 407, 413, *W of R* I-10-2-33; **157** "Everything seemed . . ." Anders 50; **157** Gladden's left wheel, *W of R*

I-10-1-532; **157** Chalmers advances on right, *W of R* I-10-1-532, 547, 548; **158** 1st Louisiana rushes ahead, *W of R* I-10-1-545; **158** "blue rings . . ." Stillwell (*Ranks*) 467; **158** "sweep of . . ." Stillwell (*Ranks*) 467, 468; **158** seeing elephant, Sword 27; **158** "From one . . ." Stillwell, 468; **158** "fairly wild . . ." Stillwell (*Common Soldier*) 54; **159** Gladden's slower regts., *W of R* I-10-1-548; **159** retreat thru Spain field, Stillwell (*Ranks*) 468; **159** "change front . . ." *W of R* I-10-1-285, Hickenlooper 414; **159** orders to 16th Wisc., *W of R* I-10-1-285, D. L. Jones 57; **159** Miller's brigade retires, Stillwell (*Ranks*) 468; **159** 15th Mich. goes to front, McBride 8, 9, Miller diary; **160** 18th Wisc. falls back, *Soldiers & Citizens,* 745, 746; **160** voice trembles and cracks, Anders 51; **160** men aroused, Anders 51; **160** 16th Wisc. separated, *W of R* I-10-1-285; **161** Munch & Hickenlooper engaged, Hickenlooper 414; **161** Gladden, Warner (*Gray*) 107, W. P. Johnston 589; **161** "Tell General . . ." Watkins 41; **161** Gladden shot, *W of R* I-10-1-536, 538; **161** Gladden's death, Warner (*Gray*) 107; **162** Daniel Adams, Boatner 3, 4, *W of R* I-10-1-612; **162** Adams's attack, *W of R* I-10-1-536; **162** canister, Ripley 379; **162** time of fire, Ripley 66; **162** double charges, Hickenlooper 414; **162** "The fire . . ." *W of R* I-10-1-536; **162** Adams seizes flag, *W of R* I-10-1-257, 537; **162** quartermaster evacuates camp, Anders 52; **162** "cut his . . ." Anders, 53; **162** Prentiss sends couriers, *W of R* I-10-1-278; **163** Peabody looks for Prentiss, Anders 52; **163** confused fighting in camp, *W of R* I-10-1-283; **163** Peabody alone, *Harv. Mem. Bio.* 165; **163** firing from behind hay, logs, D. L. Jones 55, *W of R* I-10-1-280; **163** Dutch ovens, Claxton 2, 5; **163** "stand to . . ." Shea 357; **163** Peabody killed, *Harv. Mem. Bio.* 165; **163** body rests on log, Ruff 298-300; **163** horse bolts away, Morton; **163** Ruff's experience, Ruff 296; **164** private runs, Claxton 5; **164** Quinn rallies men, Bailey 4-8-62; **164** "The more . . ." Bailey 4-8-62; **164** 21st Missouri scattered, *W of R* I-10-1-283; **164** 16th Wisc. in "desperate conflict," *W of R* I-10-1-285; **165** blankets in brush, Vail 2; **165** Regt. outflanked, *W of R* I-10-1-286; **165** Vail, Vail 2; **165** Graves, D. L. Jones 56; **166** Prentiss's orders to fall back, *W of R* I-10-1-286; **166** couriers again sent, *W of R* I-10-1-278; **166** "had to . . ." Anders 55; **166** 297 supports give way, Hickenlooper, 415; **166** Adams leads attack, *W of R* I-10-1-537; **166** "[It] caused . . ." Hickenlooper, 414; **166** loss of Armistead, *W of R* I-10-1-540-42; **166** Robertson present, *W of R* I-10-1-541; **166-167** Hickenlooper's retreat, Hickenlooper 415, 436, *W of R* I-10-1-541; **167** Munch's ordeal, Hurster I-612, 640-642, II 95; **168** "I saw . . ." Stillwell (*Ranks*) 468; **168** Hudson captured, Miller diary 2; **168** men lost all control, Anders 56; **168** wounded youth with intestine, Anders 54; **168** Chalmers attacks 18th Wisc., *W of R* I-10-1-547-553; **169** Baldock, *Soldiers & Citizens* 746; **169** Prentiss's division wrecked, *W of R* I-10-1-283; **169** Seven colors captured, *W of R* I-10-1-537; **169** camp afire, Bailey 4-8-62; **169** time of rout, *W of R* I-10-1-278; **170** thinks now about noon, Bailey 4-8-62; **170** Gray Eagle returns, Hickenlooper 417; **170** out of ammunition, Miller diary 2; **170** "what will they . . ." Stillwell (*Ranks*) 469.

CHAPTER XI—SHERMAN WILL BE SHOT

171 reveille and camp routine, Howe 224; **171** Sherman's breakfast, Sherman *Memoirs* I-258; **171** Sunday inspection, Boos 652; **171** situation in 53d Ohio,

J. Duke 40-43; **171-172** Appler and Dawes, J. Duke 42; **172-173** 53d Ohio discovers enemy, J. Duke 40-44; **173** Waterhouse's guns limbered 7 A.M., *W of R* I-10-1-276, Boos 652; **173** Taylor about to survey ground, *W of R* I-52-1-23; **173** deployment of battery, *W of R* I-10-1-264, 276, J. Duke 44; **174** sorrel race mare, Howe 220; **174** Holliday, Howe 220, *W of R* I-10-1-249; **174** Sherman's location, J. Duke 44; **176** Sherman shot at, J. Duke 44; **176** "The shot . . ." Howe 221; **176** enemy armed with smoothbore muskets, *Med. & Surg. Hist.* I-1-31; **176** wound in right hand, Thorndike 141; **176** "Appler, hold . . ." J. Duke 44; **176** "never to . . ." J. Duke 44; **176** Cleburne muddied, *W of R* I-10-1-581; **177** Cleburne, Warner (*Gray*) 53, 54, Doufour 76, 77; **177** "An almost . . ." *W of R* I-10-1-581; **177** gap in brigade, *W of R* I-10-1-581; **177** Federal section withdraws, *W of R* I-10-1-273; **177** Trigg's fire, J. Duke 45, Flemming 140; **177** "He (the enemy) was . . ." *W of R* I-10-1-581; **177** Austrian muskets in 53d Ohio, J. Duke 6; **178** "There was . . ." J. Duke 45; **178** "musketry and . . ." *W of R* I-10-1-581; **178** Cleburne repulsed, *W of R* I-10-1-264, 581, 582; **178** extent of 6th Miss. loss, F. Miller 10-158; **179** Appler's panic, J. Duke 45, *W of R* I-10-1-262, 264; **179** position of brigade, *W of R* I-10-1-262, Flemming 138; **179** Waterhouse's guns silent, *W of R* I-10-1-262, 273; **180** Wood shelled, *W of R* I-10-1-596, 605; **180** Wood prepares to charge, *W of R* I-10-1-597, 605; **180** "only see . . ." *W of R* I-10-1-581; **180** situation at 8 A.M., *W of R* I-10-1-581; **180** Buckland investigates firing, *W of R* I-10-1-266, Soc. Army of Tenn. (1881) 74, 78, 79; **181** Sullivan, Boatner 818; **181** Sullivan advances, Bering 19 ff; **181** orders countermarch, Soc. Army of Tenn. (1881) 79; **181** "They came . . ." *W of R* I-10-1-270; **181** Jones deserts, Bering 20; **182** strength of combatants, *W of R* I-10-1-112, W. P. Johnston 676; **182** Confederate left overlapped, *W of R* I-10-1-266, 267, 585; **182** "A murderous . . ." *W of R* I-10-1-581; **182** "The fire . . ." W. P. Johnston 594; **182** Jesse Nelson, Bering 28; **182** band in fight, Bering 39; **182** mounted officers shot, *W of R* I-10-1-268, 272, Bering 20; **183** Buckland takes command, *W of R* I-10-1-267; **183** fight in front of 70th Ohio, *W of R* I-10-270, 273, 276; **183** "Both the . . ." *W of R* I-10-1-273; **183** extremes in behavior, *W of R* I-10-1-589; **184** Hardee's line stalled 8:30, *W of R* I-10-1-267; **184** "A battery . . ." *W of R* I-10-1-496; **184** sight never forgotten, J. Duke 44; **184** "saw the . . ." *W of R* I-10-1-249; **184** "It was . . ." Thorndike 144; **184** more than foray, *W of R* I-10-1-249; **184** "far superior . . ." Bragg (*Mo.*) 3-25-62; **185** "faulty arrangement . . ." Bragg 12-16-74 in W. P. Johnston papers; **185** advance and alignment, *W of R* I-10-1-393, 471, 480, 492, 495, Roman I-529; **185** "simply execrable . . ." Bragg 12-16-74 in W. P. Johnston papers; **185** Anderson awaits help, *W of R* I-10-1-496, 505; **185** Hodgson opens fire, *W of R* 1-10-1-513; **186** joined by Shoup, *W of R* I-10-1-513; **186** Russell appears, *W of R* I-10-1-415, 420; **187** "charge through . . ." *W of R* I-10-1-416, 420; **187** infantry attacks, *W of R* I-10-1-471; **187** advance of Anderson, *W of R* I-10-1-496, 508; **187** "a dense . . ." *W of R* I-10-1-507; **187** 20th La. separated, *W of R* I-10-1-537; **187** 2d Tenn. re-forms, *W of R* I-10-1-585; **187** "Some wept . . ." W. P. Johnston 594; **187** fighting slackened, *W of R* I-10-1-497; **187** "I [now] feared . . ." Soc. Army of Tenn. (1881) 79; **187** McDowell not yet engaged, *W of R* I-10-1-254, 255; **187** "advancing past . . ." Worthington 121; **188** McDowell's brigade, *W of R* I-10-1-254, 256; **188**

McDowell confused, Worthington court-martial; **188** detachments, *W of R* I-10-1-254, 255; **188** 40th Illinois detached, Soc. Army of Tenn. (1881) 79, 80, *W of R* I-10-1-267; **188** "Sunday [was a day] we . . ." Howe, 221; **188** Sherman rides to front, Soc. Army of Tenn. (1881) 53, Howe 220; **188** warnings of attack, Fearing 49; **188** sends staff officers, *W of R* I-10-1-248, Sherman *Memoirs* I-258; **189** "I confess . . ." Thorndike 146; **189** "glistening bayonets . . ." *W of R* I-10-1-249; **189** Taylor's conversation, Taylor 6; **189** Sherman's appearance, Lewis; **189** "Many wondered . . ." Howe 224; **189-190** 77th Ohio's movements, *W of R* I-10-1-263, Fearing 50, J. Duke 42, Flemming 138, 139.

CHAPTER XII—SEEING THE ELEPHANT

191 Anderson's attack, *W of R* I-10-1-416, 510; **191** "Instead of . . ." *W of R* I-10-1-416; **191** Russell's attack, *W of R* I-10-1-415, 420; **191** "We saw a . . ." Boos 653; **192** effect in Confederate ranks, *W of R* I-10-1-416; **192** "The enemy . . ." *W of R* I-10-1-421; **192** chaos spreads, *W of R* I-10-1-416, 417, 510; **192** 17th La. retreats, *W of R* I-10-1-505; **192** "Owing to . . ." *W of R* I-10-1-421; **192** Bragg observes fight, Bragg (*Mo.*) 4-8-62; **192** Clark fills void, *W of R* I-10-1-415, 465; **194** Bushrod Johnson appears, *W of R* I-10-1-444; **194** Preston Smith's attack, *W of R* I-10-1-446; **194** Clark and Russell's mixed attack, *W of R* I-10-1-421; **194** fighting in front of 57th Ohio, J. Duke 46; **194** "teams were . . ." Martin 4-11-62; **194-195** Break up of 57th Ohio, *W of R* I-10-1-265, J. Duke 46; **195** "I saw . . ." ff, J. Duke 46, 47, *W of R* I-10-1-265; **195** Waterhouse's guns, J. Duke 46; **195** "all the . . ." Flemming 140; **195** Polk's cannon, *W of R* I-10-1-408, 446; **195** "The order . . ." *W of R* I-10-1-451; **195** Waterhouse shot, *W of R* I-10-1-277; **196** "not having . . ." *W of R* I-52-1-24; **196** cannon abandoned, *W of R* I-10-1-277; **196** "I ordered . . ." *W of R* I-10-1-273; **196** guns turned about, *W of R* I-10-1-273, 277, J. Duke 47; **196** Vaughan, Warner (*Gray*) 315; **196** Vaughan's movements, *W of R* I-10-1-425; **197** Williams leads attack, *W of R* I-10-1-415, 417; **197** battery retreats again, *W of R* I-10-1-276, 277; **197** Vaughan takes guns, *W of R* I-10-1-425, Latta 4-10-62; **197** "They swarmed . . ." J. Duke 48; **197** "the colors . . ." *W of R* I-10-1-141; **197** 13th Tenn. out of ammo., *W of R* I-10-1-425; **197** pointer dog, Latta 4-10-62, Obreiter 97; **198** Attack on 77th Ohio, Flemming 141; **198** "The men in . . ." Flemming 142; **198** Flemming's experience, Flemming 134, 138, 142; **198** Hildebrand's disregard of danger, Flemming 139, Putnam 200, J. Duke 49; **199** ordered back to road, J. Duke 47; **199** Sherman's presence, Fearing 51, J. Duke 49; **199** race mare killed, Howe 220; **199** "The firing . . ." Howe 220; **199** "well, my . . ." Taylor 7; **199** advance of Ross's brigade, Shea 330; **199** command passes to Raith, Shea 329, *W of R* I-10-1-115, 141, 143; **199-200** Englemann turns out 49th Illinois, *W of R* I-10-1-143; **200** movements of Raith, *W of R* I-10-1-141, 143; **200** Dawes asks for help, J. Duke 48; **200** "telling the . . ." J. Duke 48, 49; **201** Confederates pause in front of Raith, *W of R* I-10-1-415; **201** advance of C. S. reinforcements, *W of R* I-10-1-427, 591; **201** Stewart's advance, *W of R* I-10-1-427; **201** led by Johnston, *W of R* I-10-1-415, 427; **201** 33d Tenn. detached, *W of R* I-10-1-423, 427, 434; **201**

fight between Tenn. regts., *W of R* I-10-1-423, 433, 435; **202** Woods's difficulties, *W of R* I-10-1-591, 592, 598, 605, 608; **202** "came up . . ." Rennolds 13, 14; **202** "The whole . . ." *W of R* I-10-1-608; **203** "[It] was recognized . . ." Rennolds 14; **203** "before making . . ." *W of R* I-10-1-574; **203** McClernand's brigades form, *W of R* I-10-1-115, 126, 130, 133; **203** Ryan sees McClernand, *W of R* I-10-1-139, 143; **204** "passing beyond . . ." *W of R* I-10-1-144; **204** pillaging of tents, Rennolds 14; **204** Polk's gun advanced, *W of R* I-10-1-144, 447; **204** "There was . . ." J. Duke 49; **204** "Cap, give . . ." J. Duke 49; **204** "pouring a . . ." *W of R* I-10-1-141; **204** Hildebrand despondent, J. Duke 49; **204** "some change . . ." Thorndike 143; **205** Sherman's situation, *W of R* I-10-1-249; **205** "This . . . convinced . . ." Buckland, Soc. of Army of Tenn. (1881) 80; **205** 72d Ohio withdraws for ammo., Soc. Army of Tenn. (1881) 80, 81; **205** Barrett's battery, Boos 652, 653, *W of R* I-10-1-276; **205** Bragg's combined assault, *W of R* I-10-1-445, 504, 505, 508; **205** "After our . . ." Boos 652, 653; **206** "They ran . . ." Boos 653; **206** "almost impossible . . ." *W of R* I-10-1-508; **206** B. R. Johnson's attack, *W of R* I-10-1-445; **206** "More than . . ." *W of R* I-10-1-445; **206** Johnson shot, *W of R* I-10-1-408, 445; **206** "Their object . . ." Boos 653; **206** fire went high, Boos 653; **206** Bates's charge, *W of R* I-10-1-581, 585, 586; **207** "I was . . ." *W of R* I-10-1-445; **207** left flank turned, Boos 653, *W of R* I-10-1-270; **207** Sherman orders retreat, *W of R* I-10-1-250; **207** "I knew . . ." Boos 653; **207** two caissons abandoned, *W of R* I-10-1-274, 587, Boos 653; **207** 70th Ohio retreats, *W of R* I-10-1-270; **207** staff officers carry orders to fall back, Worthington court-martial 24; **207** Hammond delivers orders, *W of R* I-10-1-270, Bering 20, 21; **207** "We about . . ." Bering 21; **207** 70th Ohio shelled from camp, *W of R* I-10-1-270, 587; **208** "The rebels . . ." Connelly 22; **208** taunts of "Bull Run," Connelly 22; **208** McDowell's movements, Wright 79, *W of R* I-10-1-255; **208** lieut. col. drunk, Wright 80; **209** Behr's battery scatters infantry, Worthington court-martial 41, *W of R* I-10-1-255, 267; **209** "We were . . ." Soc. Army of Tenn. (1881) 81; **209** "a mass of . . ." *W of R* I-10-1-267; **209** "The fleeing . . ." *W of R* I-10-1-267; **209** "I . . . met . . ." *W of R* I-10-1-250; **209** gunners flee, Connelly 22; **209** "Riding over . . ." Taylor 7; **209** Sherman's appearance, Putnam 200; **209** "the coolest . . ." Boos 654; **210** "Here was . . ." J. Duke 49; **210** guns stuck between trees, J. Duke 50; **210** "substantially disappeared . . ." *W of R* I-10-1-250; **210** "We made . . ." *W of R* I-10-1-267; **210** Pond's movements, *W of R* I-10-1-516, 527; **210** "where it . . ." *W of R* I-10-1-527; **210** advance of Pond, *W of R* I-10-1-516, 517, 521, 527; **210** Clark advances, is shot, *W of R* I-10-1-415, 419; **211** "we found . . ." Rennolds 14; **211** Beauregard sends escort, Roman I-527, 534; **211** "superior and staff . . ." *W of R* I-10-1-469; **211** "due entirely . . ." Bragg 4-8-62; **211** "at least half . . ." Howe 222; **211** "struggling to . . ." *W of R* I-10-1-250.

CHAPTER XIII—ROOTS OF DESPAIR

212 "is a quiet . . ." I. Wallace 175; **212** camp of Nelson, Hannaford 559; **212** congestion, Gresham 4-12-62; **212** "beautifully clear . . ." Hannaford 560; **212** inspection ordered, *W of R* I-10-1-331; **212** Fisher hears fire, Fisher

10; **212** "all the . . ." Fisher 10; **212** Ammen's men, Hannaford 561, *W of R* I-10-1-331; **213** "not an . . ." *W of R* I-10-1-331; **213** men get ready, Hannaford 561; **213** "Nelson . . . chafed . . ." Hannaford 241, 242; **213** Ammen sees Nelson, *W of R* I-10-1-331; **213** Grant A.M. of 6th, *W of R* I-10-1-184, Grant *Memoirs* I-336 (time of firing, Roman I-524), *W of R* I-10-1-331, Putnam 198; **213** "an attack . . ." *W of R* I-10-295; **213** "Heavy firing . . ." *W of R* I-52-1-232; **214** Nelson at HQ, Fisher 11; **214** "All knew . . ." Hannaford 246; **214** Kendrick scouts roads, Fisher 11, Hannaford 249; **214** Nelson awaits boats, Hannaford 247; **214** Ammen ready to move, Hannaford 562, *W of R* I-10-1-331; **214** "The boats . . ." *W of R* I-10-1-331; **214** Ammen sees C. F. Smith, *W of R* I-10-1-331; **214** Kendrick returns, Hannaford 249, Fisher 11, *W of R* I-10-1-331; **215** steamer appropriated by Buell, *W of R* I-10-1-331; **215** "ready to . . ." *W of R* I-10-1-331; **215** orders arrive, march begins, *W of R* I-10-1-323, 331, 332; **215** "Now, gentlemen . . ." Hannaford 652; **215** *Tigress* at Crump's Landing, Whittlesey 3-18-73; **215** "Up to that . . ." Grant *Memoirs* I-336; **215** Grant fears attack on Crump's Landing, Whittlesey 3-18-73, Grant *Memoirs, W of R* I-10-1-85; **215-216** Grant talks with Wallace, L. Wallace autob. I-461, Putnam 199; **216** "to hold . . ." *W of R* I-10-1-109; **216** Wallace fears attack on self, Whittlesey 3-18-73, L. Wallace autob. I-461; **216** "hear guns . . ." L. Wallace autob. I-459; **216** Wallace concentrates at Stoney Lonesome, *W of R* I-10-1-170; **216** aide carries orders, L. Wallace autob. I-459, 460; **216** Wallace goes to Stoney Lonesome, Whittlesey 3-18-73, L. Wallace autob. I-462; **216** "diminished the . . ." Whittlesey 3-18-73, *W of R* I-10-1-185; **217** "The men stood . . ." L. Wallace autob. I-462; **217** long wait, L. Wallace 4-17-62, *W of R* I-10-1-112; **217** "Still the . . ." L. Wallace autob. I-462, 463; **217** Grant arrives at Pittsburg, *W of R* I-10-1-175, 178, 185; **218** "the particulars . . ." *W of R* I-10-1-185; **218** Grant sends Baxter to Wallace, *W of R* I-10-1-109, 185; **218** extent of Grant's instructions, *B & L* I-468, Putnam 199; **218** "I . . . do not . . ."*B & L* I-468; **218** Baxter writes orders, *W of R* I-10-1-185; **218** context of orders, L. Wallace autob. I-463, *B & L* I-607, *W of R* I-10-1-170; **218-219** Baxter sees Wallace, L. Wallace autob. I-463, *W of R* I-10-1-170, 175, *B & L* I-607; **219** Knefler loses note, L. Wallace autob. I-464, *B & L* I-607; **219** Wallace delays for dinner, L. Wallace autob. I-465, *W of R* I-10-1-193; **219** march begins, *W of R* I-10-1-170, 193, L. Wallace autob. I-465; **219** "swift and . . ." L. Wallace autob. I-465; **219** "The cannonading . . ." *W of R* I-10-1-170, also L. Wallace 4-17-62; **219** chooses wrong road, Rich (*Wallace at Shiloh*) 302; **219** "Every step . . ." L. Wallace 4-17-62, also L. Wallace autob. I-465; **219** "We'll find . . ." Putnam 199; **220** Putnam sees Grant, Putnam 198-200; **220** Grant sends 2d courier to L. Wallace, *W of R* I-10-1-185; **220** 2d courier sees Wallace, *W of R* I-10-1-179, 186; **220** "I will . . ." L. Wallace autob. I-466; **220** Grant mistakes troops, Putnam 201; **220** Grant's orders to hold, *W of R* I-10-1-279; **221** "Commanding officer . . ." *W of R* I-10-2-95; **221** message put on steamer, *B & L* I-492; **221** "would have been . . ." *B & L* I-474; **221** tents overflowing with wounded, Zearing 4-8-62; **221** no room on deck, Flemming 143; **221** poor sanitary conditions, *Harv. Mem. Bio.* I-389; **221** "army [was] verging . . ." Fisher 13; **221** "coolness, confidence . . ." Bragg (*Shiloh*) 5; **221** Johnston rides to front, Roman I-527; **221** "Randall, I . . ." W. P. Johnston 583; **221** Johnston at Seay field, Preston (*Memor.*) 3, *W of R* I-10-1-576; **222** "Men of . . ." W. P. Johnston 584; **222** "My son . . ." W. P. Johnston 584; **222** Johnston's movements, Preston (*Memor.*) 3, Munford 14; **222** Stewart led to right, *W of R* I-10-1-415, 427, Munford 14, Preston (*Memor.*) 3; **222** "breakfast . . . on the . . ." *W of R* I-10-1-403; **222** in camp of 18th Wisc., *W of R* I-10-1-404, Preston 4-18-62; **222** "None of that . . ." W. P. Johnston 612; **223** "why men . . ." Yandell 11-11-77; **223** "Doctor, send . . ." Yandell 12, 13; **223** Johnston meets Hardee, Preston 4-18-62, *W of R* I-10-1-404; **223** Willard fires on Johnston, *W of R* I-10-1-233, 404, Preston 4-18-62; **223** Lockett's dispatch, Preston (*Memor.*) 3, Preston 4-18-62; **223** Lockett's activities, *B & L* I-604, *W of R* I-10-1-391; **224** "The whole . . ." *B & L* I-604; **224** Stuart's brigade present, Crooker 95, 96; **224** Johnston ponders decision, Preston (*Memor.*) 3, Preston 4-18-62; **224** Johnston orders Breckenridge up, *W of R* I-10-1-404, 548; **224** Stuart, Crooker 18-22, 69, 224; **224** Stuart's strength, *W of R* I-10-1-92, 112; **225** "that the . . ." *W of R* I-10-1-257; **225** Stuart's deployment, *W of R* I-10-1-258, Crooker 105, 106, 125, 126; **225** "that the Rebels . . ." Crooker 126; **225** skirmishers see cavalry, Crooker 126, 127, *W of R* I-10-1-257; **225** Chalmers, Warner (*Gray*) 46; **225** Chalmers falls back, *W of R* I-10-1-548; **225** Chalmers goes to right, *W of R* I-10-1-548, 552, Crooker 109; **225** "until the cavalry . . ." *W of R* I-10-1-532; **225** Clanton rides ahead, *W of R* I-10-1-549, Crooker 127; **226** skirmish fire, Crooker 127; **226** "broke and fled . . ." *W of R* I-10-1-549; **226** advance resumed, *W of R* I-10-1-532, 553; **226** movements of 55th Illinois, Crooker 106; **226** "The companies . . ." Crooker 106; **226** Stuart rallies men, *W of R* I-10-1-258, Crooker 106; **226** C. S. cannon firing, Crooker 96, *W of R* I-10-1-258, 549; **228** 71st Ohio wavers, Crooker 86, *W of R* I-10-1-261; **228** "I regret . . ." *W of R* I-10-1-261; **228** "could not . . ." *W of R* I-10-1-258; **228** Mason labeled coward, Grant *Memoirs* I-398, 399; **228** movements of the 54th Ohio, *W of R* I-10-1-549, T. K. Smith 4-11-62, 4-15-62; **229** path cleared at 11 A.M., Crooker 113; **229** Stuart seeks support, *W of R* I-10-1-258; **229** 55th Illinois formed in squares, Crooker 96; **229** "to harass . . ." *W of R* I-10-1-258; **229** "Fortunately . . . no aggressive . . ." Crooker 108; **229** Chalmers out of ammo., *W of R* I-10-1-549; **229** Jackson's movements, *W of R* I-10-1-554, 560, 561, 564, 565; **229** Johnston orders charge, *W of R* I-10-1-558, 565; **229** Bown in log house, *W of R* I-10-1-261, 554, Crooker 86; **230** Moore's attack, *W of R* I-10-1-262, 554, 560, 561; **230** Kyle's stand, Crooker 86, *W of R* I-10-1-554; **230** "advancing in . . ." *W of R* I-10-1-257; **230** McArthur's advance, *W of R* I-10-1-155, 156, 271; **230** Willard's losses, Colby 5-28-62; **231** confusion in identity, *W of R* I-10-1-155, 156; **231** McArthur reinforced—enemy halts, *W of R* I-10-1-558, 561; **231** Chalmers attacks at noon, *W of R* I-10-1-549, Crooker 100; **231** Stuart's position, Crooker 97; **231** Chalmers deploys deliberately, *W of R* I-10-1-258; **231** promise of reinforcement, *W of R* I-10-1-258; **231** terrain, *W of R* I-10-1-554; **231** lieut. shot in head, Crooker 121; **232** great bloodshed, Crooker 124; **232** chaplain and litter-bearer, Crooker 444, 445; **232** chaplain blacks boots, Crooker 444; **232** Weller killed, *W of R* I-10-1-549; **232** "We fought . . ." Wilkinson 4-16-62; **233** Chalmers's loss heavy, *W of R* I-10-1-549, 553; **233** "It was . . ." *W of R* I-10-1-550; **233** two hours elapsed, *W of R* I-10-1-258; **233** "in a commanding . . ." *W of R* I-10-1-259; **233** Stuart apprehensive, *W of R* I-10-1-259.

CHAPTER XIV—A SWARM OF HORNETS

234 "by reason of . . ." *W of R* I-10-1-278; **234** postmaster finds chaos, Crooker 122; **234** "Prentiss's regiments . . ." Rerick 230; **234** Hurlbut, Warner (*Blue*) 245; **235** "It was a . . ." Camm 843; **235** "The balmy . . ." Rerick 45; **235** "As we . . ." Camm 843; **235** orders anticipated, *W of R* I-10-1-220, 235; **235** "he was attacked . . ." *W of R* I-10-1-203; **235** "In ten . . ." *W of R* I-10-1-203; **235** formed near camp, *W of R* I-10-1-235, 242; **235** Prentiss's request, *W of R* I-10-1-203, 233; **235** Lauman advances, *W of R* I-10-1-233; **235** encounter Prentiss's fugitives, Rerick 133, 231; **236** Hurlbut deploys, *W of R* I-10-1-203, 206; **236** "could be seen . . ." *W of R* I-10-1-245; **236** C. S. batteries fire, *W of R* I-10-1-238, 537, 554; **236** Williams injured, *W of R* I-10-1-206, 211, Throne (*Letters*) 260; **236** Meyers' caisson explodes, *W of R* I-10-1-245; **236** Meyers breaks, *W of R* I-10-1-208, 209; **236** "All then . . ." *W of R* I-10-1-245; **238** guns spiked, *W of R* I-10-1-203, 245; **238** battery disbanded, *W of R* I-10-1-210; **238** Federals lie down, *W of R* I-10-1-214; **238** firing begins, *W of R* I-10-1-241, 243; **238** Logan's regt. fires, *W of R* I-10-1-214; **238** Pugh retires, *W of R* I-10-1-214, 217, 548; **238-239** Hurlbut withdraws, *W of R* I-10-1-211, 214; **239** two small regiments, *W of R* I-10-1-537; **239** Adams forms square, *W of R* I-10-1-537, 554; **239** Hardee orders reconnaissance, *W of R* I-10-1-537; **239** "was being . . ." *W of R* I-10-1-537; **240** "We were . . ." *W of R* I-10-1-548; **240** Jackson's withdrawal, *W of R* I-10-1-554; **240** Breckenridge two hours' distant, *W of R* I-10-1-291, 404; **240** Johnston along bluff, Rich (*Johnston*) 278; **240** Johnston meets Lockett, *B & L* I-604; **240** "Tell him . . ." *B & L* I-604; **240** Hurlbut replenishes line, *W of R* I-10-1-204, 214; **241** "General Prentiss . . ." *W of R* I-10-1-204; **241** Prentiss re-forms, M. Miller 3, Soc. Army of Tenn. (1881) 64, *W of R* I-10-1-286; **241** "acted like . . ." Rerick 231; **241** "clamoring for . . ." Rerick 132; **241** fight way back, *W of R* I-10-1-280; **241** arrival of 23d Mo., *W of R* I-10-1-290, 291, McBride 9, M. Miller; **242** deployment of artillery, Hurter 641, Hickenlooper 418; **242** sunken road, Hurter 643; **242** W. H. L. Wallace, Warner (*Blue*) 536, I. Wallace 175, 192; **242** W. Wallace's dispositions, *W of R* I-10-1-150, 165, I. Wallace 192; **243** "They were . . ." Throne (*Letters*) 266; **243** "We were met . . ." Throne (*Letters*) 273; **243** prisoners chide Federals, Throne (*Letters*) 259; **243** troops deploy, *W of R* I-10-1-153, Throne (*Letters*) 252, 268; **243** sunken-road perimeter, *W of R* I-10-1-112; **244** Beauregard's maxims, *W of R* I-10-1-438, H. T. Williams 93; **244** Cheatham sends B. R. Johnson, *W of R* I-10-1-440; **244** Cheatham ordered right, *W of R* I-10-1-438; **244** Augustin reports, Roman I-526, 529; **244** "to ascertain . . ." *W of R* I-10-1-438; **244** Cheatham advances, *W of R* I-10-1-438, 453; **244** artillery exchange, *W of R* I-10-1-233, 438, Throne (*Letters*) 268, Roman I-529; **245** foot mangled, Bell 8; **245** "I am . . ." Bell 8; **245** Jordan on field, *W of R* I-10-1-438, *B & L* I-599, 600; **245** Cheatham attacks, *W of R* I-10-1-438, 453, 483, 487-489, Lauman 4-13-62; **246** Shaw adjusts line,

W of R I-10-1-153, 438; **246** "[We then] opened . . ." *W of R* I-10-1-153; **246** Cheatham staggered, *W of R* I-10-1-127, 153, 438; **246** 8th Ill. opens on flank, *W of R* I-10-1-127; **246** Lauman fights in woods, *W of R* I-10-1-233; **246** "Soon the . . ." Throne (*Letters*) 273; **246** fight at close range, Rerick 232; **246** "the slaughter . . ." *W of R* I-10-1-235; **246** Half-hour—30 rounds, *W of R* I-10-1-203, 235; **246** Lauman sickened, Lauman 4-13-62, *W of R* I-10-1-233; **247** Stephens thrown, *W of R* I-10-1-453; **247** Shaw counterattacks, *W of R* I-10-1-153, 488, 492; **247** Bragg's arrangement, *W of R* I-10-1-408; **247** "The want . . ." *W of R* I-10-1-469; **247** Bragg's horse shot, Bragg (*Mo.*) 4-8-62; **248** "was in . . ." *W of R* I-10-1-466; **248** "I had not . . ." Bragg (*Mo.*) 4-8-62; 248 Gibson "commanded," *W of R* I-10-1-480; **248** Gibson, Warner (*Gray*) 104; **248** "I had . . ." *W of R* I-10-1-483; **248** Gibson's movements, *W of R* I-10-1-483, 487, 488, 492; **248** Allen fired into, *W of R* I-10-1-438, 483, 489; **248** "Young Vertner . . ." Robertson 4-9-62; **248** "This was . . ." *W of R* I-10-1-489; **248** Gibson advances, *W of R* I-10-1-488, 492; **249** "[The ground] was . . ." Robertson 4-9-62; **249** "It was almost . . ." *W of R* I-10-1-488; **249** adjustments in Federal line, *W of R* I-10-1-153, 278, 279, 291, Searle 332; **249** "We were first . . ." *W of R* I-10-1-491, 492; **249** "[It was] a perfect . . ." *W of R* 1-10-1-488; **249** artillery fire, *W of R* I-10-1-153, 168, 483; **249** "For God's . . ." *W of R* I-10-1-489; **249** "From the . . ." *W of R* I-10-1-492-493; **250** Hodge's charge, *W of R* I-10-1-493; **250** Bragg attempts to rally, *W of R* I-10-1-466, 483, 489; **250** valley of death, *W of R* I-10-1-488; **250** heavy losses, *W of R* I-10-1-483, 484, 489, Robertson 4-9-62; **250** ordeal of 8th Iowa, *W of R* I-10-1-154, 166, Soc. Army of Tenn. (1881) 64; **250** Grant sees Prentiss, *W of R* I-10-1-278, Hickenlooper 431, Soc. Army of Tenn. (1881) 65; **250** guns moved up, Searle 332, M. Miller, *W of R* I-10-1-166; **251** Hickenlooper sees father, Hickenlooper 432; **251** smoke clears, Hickenlooper 419, *W of R* I-10-1-166; **251** Bragg, McWhitney; **251** Bragg "talks" to men, Bragg (*Mo.*) 4-8-62; **252** Gibson's plight, *W of R* I-10-1-394, 483, 486; **252** "The request . . ." *W of R* I-10-1-483; **252** "I thought it . . ." *W of R* I-10-1-493; **252** "on came . . ." *W of R* I-10-1-281; **252** Hickenlooper's guns in action, Hickenlooper 420; **252** fight at 20 yards, Robertson 4-9-62, Hickenlooper 420; **252** "[They] mow[ed] us . . ." Robertson 4-9-62; **252** desperate fighting, *W of R* I-10-1-166; **252** "our men . . ." *W of R* I-10-1-281; **252** "almost every . . ." Searle 333; **252** "The crisis . . ." Searle 332, 333; **253** Geddes shot, *W of R* I-10-1-166, 235; **253** Allen shot, *B & L* I-605, Robertson 4-9-62; **253** "Our men . . ." Robertson 4-9-62; **253** dead in piles, *W of R* I-10-1-233, 235; **253** "It somewhat . . ." Rerick 233; **253** "It was . . ." Hickenlooper 433, 434; **253** "Hornet's Nest" Shiloh Nat'l. Mil. Park Handbook; **253** woods afire, *W of R* I-10-1-233; **253** guns hauled to rear, *W of R* I-10-1-166, 281, Searle 333, D. Palmer 135, M. Miller (*Mo.*) 2; **253** "[They] moved to . . ." *W of R* I-10-1-466; **253** resentment among officers, *W of R* I-10-1-484, 486; **254** "The flag . . ." ff., *B & L,* I-605; **255** "Serve them as . . ." *W of R* I-10-1-486; **255** Gibson again leads, *W of R* I-10-1-483; **255** "Here we . . ." *W of R* I-10-1-493; **255** Fagan gets close, *W of R* I-10-1-488; **255** Prentiss's line adjusted, *W of R* I-10-1-154, 166; **255** Powell shot, *W of R* I-10-1-284; **255** "In justice . . ." *W of R* I-10-1-493; **256** "was not . . ." Hurter 643; **256** "The result . . ." *W of R* I-10-1-486; **256** "The brigade . . ." *W of R* I-10-1-486; **256** Gibson's losses, *W* *of R* I-10-1-483, 490; **256** "were demoralized . . ." Bragg (*Mo.*) 4-8-62; **256** "Finding I . . ." Bragg (*Mo.*) 4-8-62; **256** nearly 3 P.M., *W of R* I-10-1-284.

CHAPTER XV—INTO THE MOUTH OF HELL

257 Breckenridge, Warner (*Gray*) 34, Randall 180, 182, 364; **257** "The Constitution . . ." Randall 180; **257** "a well-fitting . . ." *B & L* I 601; **257** strength, *W of R* I-10-1-396, 398; **257** advance 7:30 A.M., Roman I 527; **257** troops wait, Mecklin 47, 48; **258** reserve to advance, Roman I 533, 534, W. P. Johnston 598; **258** "Under this . . ." Roman I 533; **258** "not strong" Roman I 534; **258** Augustin, Roman I 529; **258** countermarch at 9:00 A.M., *W of R* I-10-1-401, 614, 616, Roman I 529; **258** Johnston orders reserve up, Preston (*Memor.*), Preston 4-18-62, *W of R* I-10-1-404; **258** Bowen met, Preston (memoranda) 3; **258** Breckenridge's arrival, *W of R* I-10-1-396, 404, 553; **259** "Some [were] torn . . ." Mecklin 49; **259** "On all . . ." Mecklin 49; **259** cheers for officer, Mecklin 50, 51; **259** Breckenridge advances, Preston (*Memor.*) 4, *W of R* I-10-1-404; **259** "our movements . . ." Mecklin 48; **259** footnote, Roman I 551, *B & L* 601, Preston diary 4; **259** mishaps, Mecklin 48-50; **260** Bowen, Boatner 75; **260** Bowen's advance, *W of R* I-10-1-621; **260** "A few . . ." *W of R* I-10-1-621; **260** Withers meets McArthur, *W of R* I-10-1-561; **260** advance of 20th Tenn., McMurray, 125, 208; **260** "After the . . ." McMurray 125; **261** herd of goats, McMurray 126; **261** attack stopped, McMurray 209; **261** Johnston's energy on field, W. P. Johnston 598, 658, 716-730; **261** "General Johnston . . ." W. P. Johnston 598; **261** ". . . his countenance . . ." W. P. Johnston 717; **261** "that checkmates . . ." Munford 15; **261** Johnston with Bowen, *W of R* I-10-1-621, 622; **262** Johnston and Harris go to Statham, *W of R* 10-1-611, Munford 15, 16; **262** "mule lot . . ." McMurray 125; **262** "I saw our . . ." Munford 16; **262** Breckenridge's presence, W. P. Johnston 611, *W of R* I-10-1-544, 622; **262** "General, I have . . ." W. P. Johnston 611; **262** 45th Tenn. won't fight, W. P. Johnston 610, *W of R* I-52-1-29; **262** position of 45th Tenn., McMurray 208, 209; **262** "poured a very . . ." McMurray 208, 209; **262** "delivered its fire . . ." W. P. Johnston 610; **263** Harris goes to 45th Tenn., W. P. Johnston 610; **263** Breckenridge appeals to Johnston, W. P. Johnston 610; **263-264** Johnston inspires men, W. P. Johnston 611, 612; **264** Breckenridge appeals to men, McMurray 85, 209; **264** ". . . charge and they . . ." McMurray 85; **264** before charge, George 24, W. P. Johnston 612; **264** "which rose . . ." McMurray 85; **264** enemy attacks, Throne (*Letters*) 260; **264-266** Hurlbut's position, *W of R* I-10-1-203-248; **266** position of 3d Iowa, *W of R* I-10-1-219; **266** Stephens aids Statham, *W of R* I-10-1-404, 439; **266** 41st Illinois out of ammo, *W of R* I-10-1-218; **266** Bowen's attack, *W of R* I-10-1-157, 215, 557, Floyd 7-6-62; **266** "The Rebels came . . ." Floyd 7-6-62; **267** close-range fight, Floyd 7-6-62, *W of R* I-10-1-557; **267** Martin's losses, *W of R* I-10-1-622; **267** 12th Ill. withdraws, *W of R* I-10-1-155; **267** "A most . . ." *W of R* I-10-1-155; **267** plight of 9th Ill., Mason 99, *W of R* I-10-1-158, Reed (*Shiloh*) 91, McMurray 209; **267** "[We] drove them . . ." McMurray 209; **268** Mann changes front, *W of R* I-10-1-247; **268** "On they . . ." Rerick 235; **268** "[We made] our Bull Dogs . . ." Colby 4-14-62; **268** "his front . . ." *W of R* I-10-1-238; **268** 41st Ill. breaks, *W of R* I-10-1-218, Colby 4-14-62; **268**

"what did you . . ." Colby 7; **268** "within a . . ." Colby 5; **269** cannon-horse incident, Colby 5, 7; **269** general retreat, *W of R* I-10-1-213, 247; **269** extent of resistance, W. P. Johnston 613, Mecklin 52; **269** ground littered with dead, Crooker 133; **269** "so covered . . ." Grant *Memoirs* I 356; **269** "Never was . . ." Mecklin 52; **270** Johnston observed after charge, W. P. Johnston 614, 615, 718, I. G. Harris 4-6-62 Preston diary, Munford 19; **270** Welker's presence, *W of R* I-10-1-204; **270** "order Colonel . . ." W. P. Johnston 614; **270** only Wickham present, *B & L* I 564, W. P. Johnston 717; **270** Johnston wounded, *W of R* I-10-1-404, W. P. Johnston 615, Preston 4-18-62; **270** "the outer and . . ." Munford 22; **270** "torn without . . ." Yandell 11-11-77; **271** tourniquet in pocket, Yandell 11-11-77; **271** Harris leads Johnston away, Harris 4-6-62 Preston diary, W. P. Johnston 614, Munford 20; **271** site later identified, Rich (*Death of Gen. Johnston*) 276-284; **271** Harris with Johnston, in ravine, Harris 4-6-62, Preston diary, W. P. Johnston 614, Rich (*Death of Gen. Johnston*) 279, *W of R* I-10-1-404; **272** Preston sees Johnston, Preston (*Memor.*) 4, Preston 4-18-62, *W of R* I-10-1-404, Roland 338, Munford 22, W. P. Johnston 614, 615; **272** time of death, Preston (*Memor.*) 4, Harris 4-6-62; **272** actions of officers, W. P. Johnston 614, 615, Preston (*Memor.*) 4, Munford, 22; **273** Hodge sees Munford, Munford 17, 18; **273** Stuart's plight, *W of R* I-10-1-258, 259, Crooker 100, 110; **273** "They were . . ." Kennedy 4-12-62; **273** Stuart retreats, *W of R* I-10-1-259, Crooker 109, 110; **273** "It was . . ." Crooker 110; **273** "The merciless . . ." Crooker 102; **273-275** Crooker and Bagley, Crooker 123; **275** losses of 55th Ill., Crooker 97, 98; **275** Stuart unable to rally brigade, *W of R* I-10-1-259; **276** Stuart goes to landing, *W of R* I-10-1-259, Crooker 111.

CHAPTER XVI—SURRENDER IN THE THICKETS

277 "leading back . . ." Bragg 4-8-62; **277** "a strong . . ." *W of R* I-10-1-466; **277** "holding back . . ." Bragg 4-8-62; **277** "No one . . ." *W of R* I-10-1-469; **277** "leaped the fence . . ." S. D. Thompson 219; **277** "boys, lay . . ." Throne (*Letters*) 260; **277** Stephen's attack, *W of R* I-10-1-454, Throne (*Letters*) 260, S. D. Thomson 214; **278** "gave them . . ." *W of R* I-10-1-215; **278** Federals on flank, *W of R* I-10-1-238, **278** Stephen's breaks, Throne (*Letters*) 260; **278** "lay so . . ." S. D. Thompson 220; **278** Ross retires, *W of R* I-10-1-245; **278** flag riddled, Throne (*Letters*) 260; **278** 15th Miss. attacks, W. P. Johnston 614; **278** "on they came . . ." Throne (*Letters*) 260; **278** Hurlbut's exposed flank, *W of R* I-10-1-213, 215; **278** messenger from Stuart, *W of R* I-10-1-204; **278** Hurlbut under fire, Eddy 277; **279** Lauman ordered to left, *W of R* I-10-1-204, 235; **279** Logan goes to left, *W of R* I-10-1-215; 279 Breckenridge asks for help, *W of R* I-10-1-554, 622; **279** Jackson already moving, *W of R* I-10-1-554; **279** Withers wheels to left, *W of R* I-10-1-553, 558; Wheeler 122; **280** lack of attack coordination, Rerick 237, *W of R* I-10-1-212; **280** 20th Tenn. movements, McMurray 126; **280** "Our line . . ." McMurray 126; **280** Logan's maneuvering, *W of R* I-10-1-215; **280** "I then . . ." *W of R* I-10-1-215; **280** 32d Ill. retreats, *W of R* I-10-1-216, 217; **280** Hurlbut's line in Wicker field, *W of R* I-10-1-238, Rerick 236; **282** Lauman present, *W of R* I-10-1-234, Lauman 4-13-62; **282** Willard nearby, *W of R* I-10-1-235; **282** Hurlbut shot at, Rerick 236, 239; **282**

"While we . . ." Rerick 237; **282** Statham's men drink at pond, Mecklin 52; **282** "If the water . . ." Mecklin 52; **282** Bowen strikes Lauman, *W of R* I-10-1-622; **282** "I had no . . ." Colby 5-26-62; **282** "At this point . . ." *W of R* I-10-1-622; **283** Column delayed by burning wood, *W of R* I-10-1-157, 558; **283** Chalmers in front of Jackson, *W of R* I-10-1-558; 561; **283** Chalmers goes toward center, *W of R* I-10-1-550; **283** Tyler opens fire, *Off. Rec. Nav.* I-22-762, 763, Ripley 379; **284** din adds to confusion, Mecklin 53; **284** "the most hotly . . ." *W of R* I-10-1-238; **284** "our flag . . ." Rerick 237; **284** 44th Ind. out of ammo, *W of R* I-10-1-239; **284** "Regiment after . . ." *W of R* I-10-1-235; **284** Hurlbut advances left, *W of R* I-10-1-235, 236, Reed (*Shiloh*) 50, Zearing 4-8-62; **285** "It was soon . . ."*W of R* I-10-1-235; **285** Chalmers rests brigade, *W of R* I-10-1-550; **285** "worn out . . ." *W of R* I-10-1-558; **285** "I was impressed . . ." Wheeler 122; **285** "Both lines . . ." Wheeler 123; **285** Jackson encounters difficulty, *W of R* I-10-1-204, 555, 561; **286** Chalmers's men renew attack, *W of R* I-10-1-550; **286** Hurlbut orders retreat, *W of R* I-10-1-204, 233, 236, 239; **286** Lauman retreats 4 P.M., *W of R* I-10-1-233; **286** Hurlbut unable to make stand, *W of R* I-10-1-204; **286** rear guard of 44th Ind., *W of R* I-10-1-239, Rerick 241; **286** "[This] was done . . ." Rerick 241; **286** regt. leaves line, *W of R* I-10-1-555; **286** "it was their . . ." *W of R* I-10-1-562; **286** "Boys, for . . ." *W of R* I-10-1-562; **287** regt. near cottonfield, S. D. Thompson 224; **287** "lying down . . ." B. Bragg 4-8-62; **287** Deas advances, *W of R* I-10-1-538; **287** 3d Iowa in front, S. D. Thompson 224, 225; **287** "Looking forward . . ." S. D. Thompson 224; **287** Deas attack—3d Iowa retreats, *W of R* I-10-1-538, S. D. Thompson 224-226; **288** Prentiss's position, Searle 333, Claxton, Shaw 203, *W of R* I-10-1-154, 279, 291; **288** Prentiss lights cigar, Richardson 237; **288** Prentiss confers with W. Wallace, *W of R* I-10-1-279, I. Wallace 214, 215; **288** tells colonel to hold ground, Miller-Soc. Army of Tenn. (1881) 65; **289** extent of Grant's information, *W of R* I-10-1-279; **289** "had fallen . . ." *W of R* I-10-1-279; **289** McMichael's account, I. Wallace 214, 215; **289** "I must not . . ." I. Wallace 183; **289** wife's trip to Tenn., I. Wallace 182-185; **290** ". . . my husband . . ." I. Wallace 185-187; **290** "That long . . ." I. Wallace 187; **290** "The roar of . . ." Mrs. W. H. L. Wallace; **290** "half a mile to . . ." I. Wallace 193; **290** Sweeny, Boatner 823; **291** Sweeny's participation, Throne (*Letters*) 268; Reed (*Shiloh*) 50; **291** reconnaissance ordered, *W of R* I-10-1-162; **291** "ascertained that . . ." *W of R* I-10-1-162, 163; **291** Sweeny advances, *W of R* I-10-1-164; **291** accurate artillery fire, *W of R* I-10-1-472, 479, Throne (*Letters*) 268; **291** "played over . . ." Throne (*Letters*) 268; **291** "solid shot . . ." Bell 8; **291** largest artillery concentration, Shiloh Nat'l. Park Handbook; **291** "to go where . . ." *W of R* I-10-1-513; **291** Hubbard's battery opens, *W of R* I-10-1-479; **291** "It [was] a . . ." *W of R* I-10-1-479; **292** more than infy. needed, *W of R* I-10-1-476; **292** "bring forward . . ." *W of R* I-10-1-472; **292** concentration of artillery, *W of R* I-10-1-472, 475, 476, 479; **292** "it seemed . . ." Throne (*Letters*) 265; **292** "galling fire . . ." *W of R* I-10-1-150; **292** "the shells . . ." Throne (*Letters*) 269; **292** Anderson comes up, *W of R* I-10-1-496, 497; **293** Anderson highly regarded, McWhitney 277; **293** Smith-Anderson coordinate attacks, *W of R* I-10-1-498, 523; **293** mistake in identity, Throne (*Letters*) 269; **294** Shaver's forlorn attack, *W of R* I-10-1-154, 574, 578, Shaw 201, Hurter 643;

294 footnote, *W of R* I-10-1-488, 574, 576, B. Bragg 4-8-62; **294** "We lay in . . ." Throne (*Letters*) 269; **294** Anderson's bloody fight, *W of R* I-10-1-498, 507; **295** Smith's assault, *W of R* I-10-1-498; **295** "Go on my . . ." Biel 264; **295** Sweeny's defense, *W of R* I-10-1-163, 164; **295** "the field . . ." Biel 264; **295** "To avoid . . ." *W of R* I-10-1-164; **295** Confederates turn flank, *W of R* I-10-1-523; **296** Polk directs attack, *W of R* I-10-1-526; **296** Sweeny's brigade breaks up, *W of R* I-10-1-163, 164, 435; **296** "Almost fainting . . ." A. D. Richardson 239; **296** Sweeny seeks W. Wallace, I. Wallace 193; **296** "General Wallace . . ." I. Wallace 193; **296** Wallace's situation, *W of R* I-10-1-149; **296** retreat ordered, *W of R* I-10-1-149; **296** orders garbled, *W of R* I-10-1-151; **297** "We fought on . . ." Throne (*Letters*) 266; **297** Wallace orders section back, Hurter 92, 641, 643, Shaw 201; **297** W. Wallace shot, Throne (*Letters*) 270, I. Wallace 198, 213, Mrs. W. H. L. Wallace letter 5, *W of R* I-10-1-409, Dickey 4-10-62; **297** "gain greater . . ." Biel 9; **298** Woods surrounded, *W of R* I-10-1-151; **298** Anderson blocks way, *W of R* I-10-1-152, 434, 435, 498; **298** staff officers send C. S. reinforcements, *W of R* I-10-1-434, 435; **299** "We gave . . ." Biel 265; **299** 12th Iowa surrenders, *W of R* I-10-1-152; **299** surrender of 58th Ill., *W of R* I-10-1-164, 165, 417, 428, 550, 614; **299** Prentiss adjusts line, *W of R* I-10-1-166; 279, 291, Soc. Army of Tenn. (1881) 68, 69; **299** requests more help from Wallace, I. Wallace 215, Miller diary, *W of R* I-10-1-279; **299** Shaw goes to aid Prentiss, *W of R* I-10-1-154, 166, 279, Soc. Army of Tenn. (1881) 68; **300** Forrest's assignment, *W of R* I-10-1-454; **300** "Boys . . . do you . . ." Henry 59; **300** Forrest's arrival on field, Henry 59, 60, *W of R* I-10-1-438, 546; **301** Forrest's attack, Henry 60, 61, Soc. Army of Tenn. (1881) 68; **301** ". . . The bugle . . ." Henry 61; **301** "We were . . ." Henry 61; **301** Prentiss realizes predicament, *W of R* I-10-1-279; **301** Prentiss's command and terrain, Shaw 203, *W of R* I-10-1-166, 168; **302** "We were . . ." Searle 233; **302** "I found . . ." *W of R* I-10-1-279; **302** Deas beaten back, *W of R* I-10-1-546; **302** Many attacks, *W of R* I-10-1-439, 455; **302** "I was so . . ." *W of R* I-10-1-455; **302** "flicker! flicker! . . ." Watkins 65; **302** "I . . . ordered . . ." *W of R* I-10-1-455; **303** "considered it my . . ." *W of R* I-10-1-166; **303** "frightful assault . . ." Searle 333; **303** "We started back . . ." Searle 333; **303** "At the same . . ." Searle 333; **303** "fine gray mare . . ." Watkins 67; **303** "W. H. . . . rushed . . ." Watkins 67; **303** Tindall's regt. breaks, *W of R* I-10-1-291; **304** Polk's battery engaged, Henry 61; 534 Hickenlooper told to escape, Hickenlooper 422; **304** Prentiss's men rallied, *W of R* I-10-1-281; **304** "Without waiting . . ." Soc. Army of Tenn. (1881) 65; **304** Prentiss holds white flag, Searle 334; **304** Simms captures Prentiss, *W of R* I-10-1-417, 418, 523; **304** Crescent regt. captures Federals, *W of R* I-10-1-523; **304** Miller surrenders, Miller diary, Soc. Army of Tenn. (1881) 65; **305** Shaw captured, Soc. Army of Tenn. (1881) 68, 69, *W of R* I-10-1-550; **305** "Colonel . . . I think . . ." Soc. Army of Tenn. (1881) 69; **305** 18th Mo. & 58th Ill. surrender, *W of R* I-10-1-550; **305** 3d Iowa captured, S. D. Thompson 227, 228; **305** Iowans smash rifles, Thomas, Throne (*Letters*) 276, Searle 334; **306** tears in eyes, Soc. Army of Tenn. (1881) 65; **306** "You damned . . ." Searle 335; **306** "They rode . . ." Thomas; **306** acts of magnanimity, Miller diary, Soc. Army of Tenn. (1881) 65; **306** Federal losses, *W of R* I-10-1-165, 212, 279, 409, Shaw 203; **306** Confederate impressions of prisoners, Biel 260, Henry 61, **307** "delayed the enemy . . ." S. D. Thompson 228, 229; **307** "where . . . were the . . ." Throne (*Letters*) 276; **307** "It is time . . ." Throne (*Letters*) 272.

CHAPTER XVII—AT A HEAVY COST IN LIFE

308 preparations for inspection, Carrington 48, Throne (*Letters*) 253; **308** "It is good . . ." Throne (*Letters*) 252; **308** visitors in camp, Throne (*Letters*) 250, Carrington 49; **308** fight begins, Carrington 48; **308** impending disaster, Throne (*Letters*) 252; **308** McClernand's reaction, *W of R* I-10-1-115; **308** Raith's movements, *W of R* I-10-1-141, 126; **308** other brigades ordered up, *W of R* I-10-1-123, 133; **309** Marsh's movements, *W of R* I-10-1-124, 128, 137; **310** Raith's aide sees McClernand, *W of R* I-10-1-139; **310** Raith driven back, *W of R* I-10-1-139, 141, 143, 415, Shea 330; **310** McClernand engaged, *W of R* I-10-1-115, 126, 128, 132; **310** artillery positions, *W of R* I-10-1-115, 116, 124, 130, 132, 133, Bearss (*Artillery*); **312** "The enemy were . . ." *W of R* I-10-1-133; **312** Wood's advance, *W of R* I-10-1-592; **312** avoid fire from friendly troops, *W of R* I-10-1-598; **312** advance of C. S. right flank, *W of R* I-10-1-423, 440, 447, 592, 608; **312** "I turned . . ." *W of R* I-10-1-427; **312** loss of 4th Tenn., *W of R* I-10-1-432; **312** "If you ever . . ." Martin 4-11-62; **312** "We were . . ." *W of R* I-10-1-432; **312** 48th & 45th Ill. in front, *W of R* I-10-1-133; **313** "What does . . ." Crummer 57; **313** flag mistaken, Crummer 57; **313** "Our men fell . . ." Crummer 57; **313** "During the . . ." *W of R* I-10-1-133; **313** 48th Ill. breaks, *W of R* I-10-1-133; **313** other Confederates advance, *W of R* I-10-1-133, 592; **313** McAllister retreats, *W of R* I-10-1-116; **313** "who did not . . ." *W of R* I-10-1-432; **313** Burrows captured, *W of R* I-10-1-116, 432, 592; **314** "[They] fell back . . ." *W of R* I-10-1-137; **314** Timony attacked, *W of R* I-10-1-130, 446, Throne (*Letters*) 253; **314** "The regiment . . ." Throne (*Letters*) 253; **314** artillery fight begins, *W of R* I-52-1-23; **314** "[The fire here was] the most . . ." *W of R* I-10-1-275; **314** Timony's guns overrun, *W of R* I-10-1-116, 130, 226, 52-1-23; **315** attack on Hare, W. P. Johnston 584, *W of R* I-10-1-423; 574, 578; **315** "We gave them . . ." *W of R* I-10-1-132; **315** Hare's men fall back, *W of R* I-10-1-127, 128, 132; **315** Veatch sent to Sherman's support, *W of R* I-10-1-112, 203, Camm 843; **315** to support of Marsh, *W of R* I-10-1-220, 223, 226, 228; **315** "belching like a . . ." Camm 845; **315** 14th Ill. in disorder, *W of R* I-10-1-223; **315** "I could see . . ." Camm 845; **315** Colonel sees men in blue, *W of R* I-10-1-223; **316** "What [horrors] . . ." Camm 845; **316** "The enemy . . ." Camm 845; **316** 15th Illinois driven back, *W of R* I-10-1-220, 226, 227; **316** "Everything was . . ." *W of R* I-10-1-226; **316** 46th Illinois mauled, *W of R* I-10-1-228; **316** Veatch fights with two regts., *W of R* I-10-1-220, 230, Camm 846; **317** Veatch reforms with McAllister's support, Camm 846, 847, *W of R* I-10-1-223, 578; **317** "What in . . ." Camm 847; **317** Confederates driven off, *W of R* I-10-1-223, 578; **317** "was an awful . . ." Howard 4-11-62; **317** Wood's heavy losses, *W of R* I-10-1-592; 597, 598, 605; **318** Shaver's men disordered, *W of R* I-10-1-574, 576, 578; **318** "They were in . . ." *W of R* I-10-1-578; **318** inactivity following attack, *W of R* I-10-1-598, 606; **318**

"supply my . . ." *W of R* I-10-1-574; **318** Hardee goes to right, *W of R* I-10-1-569; **318** Bragg leaves Polk in charge, *W of R* I-10-1-465, 466; **318** troops scattered, *W of R* I-10-408, 428, 432; **319** Stewart attacks Veatch, *W of R* I-10-1-428; **319** Russell fights Raith, *W of R* I-10-1-416; **319** Englemann loses coat, Englemann 4-12-62, 4-17-62; **319** Raith rallies men, *W of R* I-10-1-144, 249; **319** Raith, Shea 328; **319-320** Schwartz's battery, *W of R* I-10-1-116, 146; **320** Raith's position, Shea 331; **320** Raith connects with Sherman, *W of R* I-10-1-139; **320** Raith attacked, *W of R* I-10-1-144; **320** Blythe killed, *W of R* I-10-1-144, 146, 408; **320** "[This gesture] seemed . . ." *W of R* I-10-1-497; **320-321** Anderson attacks again, *W of R* I-10-1-497, Soc. Army of Tenn. (1881) 81; **321** Schwartz advances infantry, *W of R* I-10-1-139, 141, 146; **321** obstinate resistance, *W of R* I-10-1-417; **321** Raith's troops retreat, *W of R* I-10-1-116, 141, 144, 146; **321** "Our whole . . ." *W of R* I-10-1-146; **321** 43d Ill. last in line, Shea 331; **321** Raith shot, Shea 332, *W of R* I-10-1-144; **322** gun spiked by Nispel, *W of R* I-10-1-144, 146, 147; **322** Raith's brigade scattered, *W of R* I-10-1-139, 144; **322** "[The scene] was . . ." Carrington 4-6-62; **322** disorder in C. S. ranks, *W of R* I-10-1-421; **322** "I had no . . ." Pugh 4-8-62; **322** regts. rest and pillage camps, *W of R* I-10-1-417; **322** "the sight of . . ." C. J. Johnson 4-11-62; **322** "Fearing they were . . ." *W of R* I-10-1-417; **322-323** skirmishing in Woolf field, *W of R* I-10-1-433, 435, 447; **323** Preston Smith's attack, *W of R* I-10-1-228, 274, 447; **323** Polk's gun abandoned, *W of R* I-10-1-417, 447; **323** Russell falls back, *W of R* I-10-1-417; **323** "I wish to . . ." Howard 4-10-62; **323** Anderson moves away, *W of R* I-10-1-494; **323** Sherman amid chaos, Putnam 200, *W of R* I-10-1-250, 267; **323** "to avail themselves . . ." *W of R* I-10-1-250; **324** Ill. regts. withdrawn, *W of R* I-10-1-228; **324** Grant meets Sherman on field, Putnam 200, Boos 654, Howe 223, *W of R* I-10-1-110; Eddy I 257, Sherman *Memoirs* I 273; **324** Sherman's dispositions, *W of R* I-10-1-255, 276; **324** McDowell's movements, *W of R* I-10-1-255, 256, Hart 88; **325** "[It caused] us to . . ." Hart 88; **325** Sherman's line, *W of R* I-10-1-147, 271, 274, 276; **325** mixed command on left, *W of R* I-10-1-144, 159, 160; **325** "We felt sorry . . ." Carrington 49; **325** decision to counterattack, *W of R* I-10-1-250, 271; **325** orders given, *W of R* I-10-1-117, 144, 228, 271; **325** Marsh's attack, *W of R* I-10-1-137, Throne (*Letters*) 254; **325** Confederates abandon guns, *W of R* I-10-1-137; **325** Sherman and McDowell advance, *W of R* I-10-1-256, 271; **326** "We moved . . ." Hart 88; **326** protracted fire fight, *W of R* I-10-1-117, 134, 159, Throne (*Letters*) 254; **326** Trabue, E. P. Thompson 403; **326** Trabue's movements, *W of R* I-10-1-614; **326** "By this . . ." E. P. Thompson 450; **326** Trabue fights 46th Ohio, *W of R* I-10-1-615; **328** "Squat boys! . . ." Worthington (*Hist. of 46th Ohio*) 8; **328** losses in 46th Ohio, *W of R* I-10-1-255, Worthington (*Hist. of 46th Ohio*) 9; **328** "Ignorant of the . . ." *W of R* I-10-1-615; **328** fight of 1¼ hours, *W of R* I-10-1-256, 615; **328** C. S. reinforcements, *W of R* I-10-1-417, 615; **328** Hodgson's arrival, *W of R* I-10-1-513; **328** "Here we . . " Pugh 4-8-62; **328** "White powder . . ." *W of R* I-10-1-513; **328** "[I] saw his . . ." *W of R* I-10-1-503; **328** effect of Hodgson's fire, Hart 88, 89, Worthington (*Shiloh*) 160; **329** Marsh retreats, *W of R* I-10-1-130, 134, 137, 145, 228, Throne (*Letters*) 254; **329** reinforcements for McClernand, *W of R* I-10-1-129, 228, 250; **329** arrival of 15th Iowa, Throne (*Letters*) 244-247, *W of R* I-10-1-288; **329** "This looked . . ." Throne

(*Letters*) 245; **330** 16th Iowa marches to front, Throne (*Letters*) 247; **330** "In front of . . ." Throne (*Letters*) 245; **330** "it promised . . ." Throne (*Letters*) 248; **330** losses of Iowans, *W of R* I-10-1-288, 289; **330** Brayman's attack, *W of R* I-10-1-129, 134, 142, 145, 447, *Soldiers and Citizens* 618; **330** "[My] men gathered . . ." *W of R* I-10-1-145; **330** "One of our . . ." Throne (*Letters*) 254, 255; **331** McClernand retreats, *W of R* I-10-1-142, 289, Throne (*Letters*) 254; **331** Hardee present, *W of R* I-10-1-569; **331** "the enemy in . . ." *W of R* I-10-1-569; **331** "Knowing that I . . ." *W of R* I-10-1-435; **331** McClernand's line gives way, *W of R* I-10-1-434, 569; **331** McDowell driven back, *W of R* I-10-1-255, 256, 417, 615; **331** "They took . . ." Throne (*Letters*) 241; **332** forty men captured, *W of R* I-10-1-103; **332** artillery fire, *W of R* I-10-1-616; **332** "The fight . . ." *W of R* I-10-1-142; **332** Barrett quits fight, *W of R* I-10-1-276; **332** shortage of ammo., *W of R* I-10-1-130, 140, 145, Throne (*Letters*) 254, Eddy 274; **332** "Searching through . . ." *W of R* I-10-1-140; **332** "What regiment . . ." Hart 89; **333** Confederate offensive halts, *W of R* I-10-1-435, 514, 616; **333** advance of Wharton's cavalry, *W of R* I-10-1-569, 626; **333** Morgan's cavalry attack, B. Duke 148, 149, *W of R* I-10-1-118, 250, Hickenlooper 423; **333** "They delivered . . ." B. Duke 150; **334** Sherman protects Hamburg-Savannah road, Soc. Army of Tenn. (1881) 55, *W of R* I-10-1-250; **334** furor expended, Eddy 257; **335** Veatch defends Corinth road, *W of R* I-10-1-224, 231, Camm 848; **335** "our guns . . ." Camm 848; **335** Veatch withdraws to Cavalry field, *W of R* I-10-1-231; **335** Pond's brigade appears, Camm 848, *W of R* I-10-1-516, 518, 521, B. Duke 148, Boatner 572; **335** "to keep my . . ." *W of R* I-10-1-518; **335** blue-uniformed 18th Louisiana, B. Duke 149; **336** Mouton collides with Trabue, *W of R* I-10-1-517, 521, 616; **336** "we fire at . . ." B. Duke 149; **336** staff officer stops firing, *W of R* I-10-1-521, 616; **336** Pond retreats, *W of R* I-10-1-517, 521; **336** Pond stalls, *W of R* I-10-1-517; **336** artillery firing, *W of R* I-10-1-521; **336** Ferguson sent by Beauregard, Roman I 528; **336** "by the left . . ." Roman I 528; **336** Pond-Ferguson controversy, *W of R* I-10-1-517, 527, 593; **337** Pond attacks Veatch, *W of R* I-10-1-125, 517, 521; **337** "[They] dashed up . . ." Camm 849; **337** Veatch directs crossfire, *W of R* I-10-1-224, 521; **337** "The yell . . ." Camm 849; **337** heavy loss in 18th La., *W of R* I-10-1-521; **337** "I was alone . . ." *W of R* I-10-1-522; **337** "The order to . . ." *W of R* I-10-1-521; **338** Veatch plans countercharge, *W of R* I-10-1-127, 224, 231; **338** "I saw nothing . . ." *W of R* I-10-1-231; **338** "Run, Colonel . . ." Camm 850; **338** "I heard a . . ." Camm 851; **338** "[Here I] found a . . ." Camm 851; **338** "No one ran . . ." Carrington 49; **338** "The clouds of . . ." Shumway 4-13-62; **338** battle seems lost, Shumway 4-7-62.

CHAPTER XVIII—BRINK OF DISASTER

339 "As far as . . ." S. D. Thompson 227; **339** miracle to save army, Throne (*Letters*) 274; **339** "Back, bejabers!" McBride 9; **339** "enough Union . . ." Bell 9; **339** "The hair . . ." McBride 9; **340** "To prevent . . ." Hurter 643; **340** "amid a terrible . . ." Hurter 93; **340** 81st Ohio advances, *W of R* I-10-1-161, Boos 654; **340** "Here the . . ." S. D. Thompson 231; **340** "All was on . . ." S. D. Thompson 229; **340** "the space under . . ." Putnam 201; **340**

"The appeal . . ." Putnam 201; **341** "A man on . . ." McBride 10; **341** "At the landing . . ." Throne (*Letters*) 263; **341** "All appeared . . ." Hickenlooper 425; **341** "It was now . . ." Bragg 4-8-62; **341** "[This warned us] to press . . ." *W of R* I-10-1-466; **341** "sweep everything . . ." *W of R* I-10-1-534; **341** "drive the enemy . . ." *W of R* I-10-1-550; **341** "The field was . . ." *W of R* I-10-1-410; **342** "take command of . . ." *W of R* I-10-1-459; **342** Miller leads cavalry, *W of R* I-10-1-459, 460; **342** "Look, Colonel . . ." Deupree 91; **342** Ross's battery escaping, Deupree 98, *W of R* I-10-1-460; **342** "We came upon . . ." Deupree 91; **342** Ross's battery captured, Deupree 91, *W of R* I-10-1-460; **342** "It was a . . ." Bragg 4-8-62; **342** "running through . . ." Henry 61, 62; **342** horses watered in Tenn., *W of R* I-10-1-410, 460; **343** Confederates fire into prisoners, Soc. Army of Tenn. (1881) 69, *W of R* I-10-1-550, B. F. Thomas; **343** "We did so . . ." B. F. Thomas; **343** processing of prisoners, Searle 335, Wheeler 130, *W of R* I-10-1-555; **343** "We all helped . . ." Biel 265; **344** "I took a . . ." Biel 265; **344** "There is nothing . . ." Biel 265; **344** gunboats open fire, *Off. Rec. Nav.*, I-22-763, 764; **344** "taking our hats . . ." P. D. Jordan 311; **344** "expected to see . . ." Rennolds 14; **344** actual danger small, *W of R* I-10-1-410, 466; **344** "The height . . ." *W of R* I-10-1-410; **344** "Drive the . . ." *W of R* I-10-1-550; **344** orders Ruggles and Withers, *W of R* I-10-1-472, 534; **344-345** Confederates begin to advance, *W of R* I-10-1-550, 555, 616; **345** "The sun . . ." *W of R* I-10-1-499; **345** positions of troops, *W of R* I-10-1-616; **345** Chalmers approaches Dill chasm, *W of R* I-10-1-534, 550; **345** Grant's anxiety, *B & L* I 493; **345** "became very anxious . . ." *W of R* I-10-1-181; **345** report of Wallace not marching, *W of R* I-10-1-179; **345** orders to Rowley, *W of R* I-10-1-179, 186; **345** ". . . see that . . ." *W of R* I-10-1-179; **345-346** Rowley's journey to reach Wallace, *W of R* I-10-1-179, L. Wallace autob. 466; **346** "sitting upon . . ." *W of R* I-10-1-179; **346** "[That's] a damned . . ." *W of R* I-10-1-179; **346** only road Wallace knew, *W of R* I-10-1-180; **346** "great God! . . ." L. Wallace autob. 167; **346** "rattled" L. Wallace autob. 167; **346** Wallace questions cavalry, *W of R* I-10-1-180; **346** "in danger of . . ." *W of R* I-10-1-170; **346** Wallace's position, Rich (*L. Wallace*) 302-308, *W of R* I-10-1-200; **348** "My object . . ." L. Wallace autob. 469 *n;* **348** Whittlesey waits for hour, Rich (*L. Wallace*) 307; **348** "appeared intolerably . . ." *W of R* I-10-1-180; **348** "was toilsome . . ." L. Wallace autob. 469; **348** Whittlesey resumes march 4 P.M., *W of R* I-10-1-200; **348** Grant sends two staff officers, *W of R* I-10-1-181, 186; **348** officers meet Thayer, Rich (*L. Wallace*) 303, *W of R* I-10-1-187; **348** "God's sake . . ." *W of R* I-10-1-182; **348** "that the army . . ." *W of R* I-10-1-187; **348** Wallace's uncertainty, *W of R* I-10-1-187, 188; **348** "Dismounting and . . ." L. Wallace autob. 470; **348** "I told . . ." *W of R* I-10-1-182; **349** "which was immediately . . ." *W of R* I-10-1-187; **349** "that the bridge . . ." *W of R* I-10-1-187; **349** "We . . . knew that . . ." *W of R* I-10-1-187; **349** sun goes down, *W of R* I-10-1-182, 188; **349** Grant goes to log cabin, *W of R* I-10-1-179, 186, *W of R* I-10-2-95; **349** Grant with staff officers, Putnam 201, Grant *Memoirs* I 353; **349-350** Melancton Smith's battery, *W of R* I-10-1-438; **350** "The shells . . ." Grant *Memoirs* I 353; **350** "panting as if . . ." Grant *Memoirs* I 353; **350** "struck the metal . . ." Grant *Memoirs* I 354; **350** McPherson takes Putnam's horse, Putnam 201; **350** Grant goes aboard *Tigress*, *W of R*

I-10-1-186, *B & L* 493; **350** Buell sees Grant, *B & L* I-493; **350** "Certainly there was . . ." *B & L* I 493; **350** Grant calm, *W of R* I-10-1-186, Putnam 202; **350** "I have not . . ." *W of R* I-10-1-186; **350** Grant-Buell conference, *B & L* I 493, Grant *Memoirs* I 344, *W of R* I-10-1-292; **350** Buell sees stragglers, *W of R* I-10-1-292; **351** "a stream of . . ." *B & L* I 492; **351** Buell berates stragglers, *B & L* I 493, Putnam 202, Grant *Memoirs* I 344, *W of R* I-10-1-292; **351** "men mounted . . ." *B & L* 494; **351** Grant's behavior, A. D. Richardson 238, *W of R* I-10-1-181; **351** "The enemy has . . ." Chetlain 89; **351** "appeared as cool . . ." Putnam 202; **351** "Reports of the . . ." Putnam 202; **351** "all appeared . . ." Hickenlooper 435; **351** *Rocket* sent out of range, Putnam 203; **351** "the most continuous . . ." *W of R* I-10-1-109; **352** Tuttle's line, *W of R* I-10-1-132, 149, 150; **352** "When we got . . ." Throne (*Letters*) 270; **352** reinforcements for Tuttle's line, *W of R* I-10-1-132, 155; **352** Webster places siege guns, Grant *Memoirs* I 345, Bearss (*Artillery*); **353** other batteries form, *W of R* I-10-1-204; **353** Hurlbut's instructions, *W of R* I-10-1-131, 204, 256; **353** Veatch outflanked, *W of R* I-10-1-134, 221; **353** "A dense mass . . ." *W of R* I-10-1-221; **353** Veatch retreats, *W of R* I-10-1-224, 231; **353** ". . . We were run . . ." *W of R* I-10-1-244; **354** "Cavalry, infantry . . ." *W of R* I-10-1-227; **354** McClernand acts to restore line, *W of R* I-10-1-119, 121, 124, 125, 134; **354** "I . . . gathered . . ." *W of R* I-10-1-134; **354** McClernand's line, *W of R* I-10-1-119, 134; **354** fate of army pending, *W of R* I-10-1-118; **356** "[His] presence was . . ." Throne (*Letters*) 272; **356** Tuttle sees Buell, Throne (*Letters*) 266; **356** "By God . . ." Throne (*Letters*) 266; **356** "I rode up . . ." Rerick 241; **356** *Minnehaha* nearly swamped, Mrs. W. H. L. Wallace letter; **356** men swim river, S. D. Thompson, 232; **357** chaplain goes to landing with wounded, Crooker 446; **357** "This was all . . ." Crooker 446; **357** Buell's army across river, Grose 102, Crooker 446, *W of R* I-10-1-332; **357** "[He consoled] us by . . ." *W of R* I-10-1-332; **357** "Colonel Ammen . . ." *W of R* I-10-1-332; **358** "You have . . ." *W of R* I-10-1-333; **358** "The 36th . . ." *W of R* I-10-1-333; **358** Ammen reaches Tenn. River, *W of R* I-10-1-323, 337; **358** "Signals [flashed] . . ." *W of R* I-10-1-333; **358** Nelson's troops embark, *W of R* I-10-1-333, Fisher 12; **358** "frantic with . . ." *W of R* I-10-1-324; **358** men floating on logs, *W of R* I-10-1-333; **358** "Such looks . . ." *W of R* I-10-1-333; **358** Nelson orders steamer ahead, Fisher 13; **359** "We're whipped . . ." Hannaford 261; **359** "We're cut . . ." *W of R* I-10-1-324; **359** Nelson's appearance, Hannaford 580; **359** "Gentlemen, draw . . ." Fisher 13; **359** time of arrival, Fisher 11, 13; **359** Grant, Nelson, Buell at cabin, Grose 103, Fisher 13, *W of R* I-10-1-333; **360** 36th Ind. comes up, *W of R* I-10-1-323; **360** seemed to be crisis, Putnam 203; **360** panic-stricken men, Grose 103; **360** "insensible to . . ." *W of R* I-10-1-324; **360** "Some wading . . ." Hannaford 568; **360** cheers greet Buell's men, Hannaford 567, 568; **360** "a little drummer . . ." Hannaford 567; **360** "Shout after . . ." Throne (*Letters*) 263; **360** Nelson unconcerned under fire, Grose 103; **360** "I heard . . ." Fisher 13, 17, 18; **360** "Straighten up . . ." Grose 103; **360** Ammen to Stone's support, *W of R* I-10-1-337; **361** 36th Ind. engaged, Grose 104; **361** Webster's siege guns, F. T. Miller Vol. 10; Bearss (*Artillery*), Ripley 366, Camm 853; **361** ground shakes, Hurter 643; **361** "the noise [was] . . ."

Putnam 203; **361** "It was nearing . . ." McBride 10; **361** ". . . The sun looked . . ." Camm 852; **361** last resource is bayonet, Throne (*Letters*) 256; **362** "[There] was every . . ." *W of R* I-10-1-467; **362** Withers active gathering reinforcements, *W of R* I-10-1-534; **362** woods seem alive, McBride 11; **362** Lindsay's cavalry pursuit, Deupree 91, *W of R* I-10-1-247, 460; **363** "They fired at . . ." Deupree 92; **363** lull occurs, McBride 10; **363** "[They] attacked from . . ." Camm 852; **363** Chalmers and Jackson held at bay, *W of R* I-10-1-550, 551, 555; **363** "[The men] could not . . ." *W of R* I-10-1-555; **363** "[I] sent orders . . ." *W of R* I-10-1-534; **363** "one more . . ." *B & L* I 605; **363** one of great mistakes, B. Bragg (*Gen. A. S. Johnston*); **363-364** Beauregard learns news from Harris, *W of R* I-10-1-402, Roman I 531, 537, *B & L* I 590, Munford 21; **364** "expressed the . . ." Munford 21; **364** Munford sees Beauregard, Munford 18; **364** "the responsibility . . ." *W of R* I-10-1-387; **364** Beauregard sends staff officers to front, *B & L* I 590, Roman I 525; **364** officers round up stragglers, Roman I 529, 551; **364** "over one third . . ." Roman I 551; **364** Beauregard rallies stragglers, Lotta 4-10-62; **364** Helm's telegram arrives, *B & L* I 602, T. Jordan 219, *W of R* I-10-2-104; **364** Beauregard at Shiloh Church, Roman I 531, 532; **365** "[The gunboats] opened on . . ." *W of R* I-10-1-387; **365** Prentiss brought to Beauregard, *B & L* I 606; **365** Prentiss taunts captors, T. Jordan 218, *B & L* I 602; **365** "A complete . . ." *W of R* I-10-1-384; **365** Beauregard orders a withdrawal, Putnam 210, Roman I 529; **365** "First, his men . . ." Putnam 210; **366** "to arrest the . . ." Roman I 529, *B & L* I 605; **366** Augustin orders Ruggles back, *W of R* I-10-1-472; **366** "This order was . . ." *W of R* I-10-1-555; **366** "The general directs . . ." *B & L* I 605; **366** "Have you given . . ." *B & L* I 605; **366** "My God . . ." *B & L* I 605; **366** "Looking back . . ." Wheeler 125; **366** firing halts at dark, *W of R* I-10-1-551, Howard 4-10-62; **366** "Shells were . . ." Fisher 14; **367** crisis within artillery units, Grose 104, Crooker 114; **367** "Don't stop to . . ." Hannaford 257; **367** "The belligerent . . ." Crooker 115; **367** Iowa volunteers for 36th Ind., Grose 104; **367** ammo. expended, Hannaford 259; **367** losses, *W of R* I-10-1-334; **367** 6th Ohio not in fight, Hannaford 258; **367** "All feel . . ." Throne (*Letters*) 275; 646 "the most pleasant . . ." Zearing 4-8-62; **367** "All who had . . ." Putnam 204; **368** "I rode forward . . ." Fisher 14.

CHAPTER XIX—NIGHT OF HORRORS

369 Ann Wallace's ordeal, Mrs. W. H. L. Wallace letter, I. Wallace 187; **370** "Nearly every spot . . ." Throne (*Letters*) 263; **371** lack of medicine, etc., *Medical & Surg. Hist.* 1-1-29, 30; **371** pile of severed limbs, Hannaford 287; **371** drummer boy amid corpses, Crooker 125; **371** sutler stores rifled, Hartpence 38, Throne (*Letters*) 256; **372** ghastly light, S. D. Thompson 232; **372** Cheatham withdraws three miles, *W of R* I-10-1-410, 448; **372** Beauregard's intentions, *W of R* I-10-1-387, 467; **372** Pond confronts Sherman, *W of R* I-10-1-518; **372** battle considered over, T. C. Robertson 4-9-62; **372** medical whiskey consumed, Throne (*Letters*) 251, Kirwan 28; **372** drunk on Cincinnati whiskey, C. J. Johnson 4-11-62; **372** "Our boys say . . ." Latta 4-10-62;

372 "fresh beef . . ." T. C. Robertson 4-9-62; **372** "Not expecting . . ." T. C. Robertson 4-9-62; **372** bakery improved, H. H. Wright 103; **373** "too lazy . . ." Bragg 4-8-62; **373** "I would have . . ." Wilkinson 4-16-62; **373** "We were hungry . . ." Searle 336; **373** prisoners sing, Searle 336; **373** "I was thankful . . ." Searle 336; **373** Palmer's experience, Palmer 136, 137; **374** "to keep the . . ." J. H. Smith 11; **374** Nelson orders gunboats to fire, *W of R* I-10-1-324, *Off. Rec. Nav.* 1-22-763; **374** "throw an . . ." *W of R* I-10-1-324; **374** *Tyler* fires at intervals, *Off. Rec. Nav.* 1-22-763; **374** flash of light, Carrington 50; **374** *Lexington* relieves *Tyler*, *Off. Rec. Nav.* 1-22-763, 764; **374** curse "black rascals," T. C. Robertson 4-9-62; **374** dead card players, Abernathy 21, 22; **374** rain begins 10 P.M.—thunderstorm at midnight, P. D. Jordan 311, S. D. Thompson 233; **374** "It seemed like . . ." P. D. Jordan 311; **374** "I never saw . . ." D. L. Jones 59; **374** "I put my . . ." Abernathy 15; **375** "Vivid flashes of . . ." Mecklin; **375** "Oh, what a . . ." Biel 266; **375** "The night was . . ." Camm 854; **375** rain brought on by battle, Rockwell *Journal;* **375** "It rained all . . ." Briant 102-105; **375** "I followed the . . ." Briant 102-105; **375** "[The events of . . .]" D. L. Jones 59; **376** "he had slept . . ." Stevenson 86; **376** three wounded crawl in tent, Bell 11; **376** Raith night of 6th, Shea 332; **376** wounded lie in pools of water, Flemming 143; **376** "I attempted . . ." Mecklin 54; **376** rain abated 3 A.M., *W of R* I-10-1-335; **376** "I think I . . ." Briant 102-105; **376** Buell's reinforcements number about 7,500, *W of R* I-10-1-292, 325, 10-2-148; **376** Nelson's division across, *W of R* I-10-1-334, J. H. Smith 10; **376** Pond hears music, *W of R* I-10-1-518; **376** Nelson's division deploys, *W of R* I-10-1-324; **376** Crittenden's arrival, *W of R* I-10-1-354, 355, 372; **377** "I was so . . ." *W of R* I-10-1-355; **377** Crittenden prolongs Nelson's line, *W of R* I-10-1-355, 359; **377** "I must confess . . ." Zearing 4-8-62; **377** Beauregard night of April 6, *B & L* I 602, Roman I 532, Soc. Army of Tenn. (1881) 54, *W of R* I-10-1-387; **377** Gilmer's intelligence, Preston diary, 4-6-62; **377** Beauregard confers with generals, Roman I 305, 536; **377** "shattered fugitive force" *W of R* I-10-1-387, T. Jordan 219; **378** "Communicative and . . ." C. H. Smith 8-5-80; **378** News learned from Prentiss, C. H. Smith 8-5-80; T. Jordan 218; **378** "You gentlemen have . . ." *B & L* I 602; **378** Forrest's scout of lines, T. Jordan 219, 220, *W of R* I-10-1-387, 402; **379** Grant night of 6th, Grant *Memoirs* I 349, Fisher 15; **379** "The sight was . . ." Grant *Memoirs* I 349; **379** Grant's imperturbability, Fisher 14, 15; **379** "No! I propose to . . ." Putnam 205; **379** situation similar to Donelson, Eddy 258; **379** "a great moral . . ." *W of R* I-10-1-109; **379** Grant sees Sherman, Sherman *Memoirs* I 273, Grant *Memoirs* I 348; **379** appears no orders issued, *B & L* I 524, *W of R* I-10-1-109, 251; **379** Buell night of 6th, *B & L* I 519, *W of R* I-10-1-292, 334; **380** "I did not . . ." *B & L* I 519; **380** Buell-Sherman meeting, *B & L* I 519, Eddy 258, Sherman *Memoirs* I 273; **380** "frank, brave . . ." *B & L* I 519; **380** Buell orders advance at daylight, *B & L* I 518, *W of R* I-10-1-292, Hazen 25; **380** "It was too . . ." *W of R* I-10-1-334; **380** "as soon as . . ." *W of R* I-10-1-335; **380** Nelson begins advance, *W of R* I-10-1-324, 334, 335; **380** news of L. Wallace's arrival, Putnam 206, *W of R* I-10-1-188; **380** Grant averts blame, *W of R* I-10-1-178; **380** Grant did not see Wallace, L. Wallace autob. I 474, Putnam 206; **381** Wallace's arrival & movements, *B & L* I 609, Rich (*L. Wallace*) 301, L. Wallace autob. I 473, 474, *W of R*

I-10-1-170, 173; **381** Thompson opens on Ketchum, *W of R* I-10-1-170, 193, 518, 528; **382** Grant orders attack, *W of R* I-10-1-170; **382** Ketchum withdraws—Wallace attacks, *W of R* I-10-1-170, 518, 528.

CHAPTER XX—A DAY OF RECKONING

383 colors cased, Fisher 15; **383** advance makes slow progress, *W of R* I-10-1-304, Hannaford 572; **383** "[our advance] was made . . ." *W of R* I-10-1-328; **383** skirmishing near Hurlbut's H.Q., Hannaford 572, *W of R* I-10-1-340, 344, T. Jordan 221; **383** "One poor fellow . . ." Hannaford 572, 573; **384** Nelson's skirmishers encounter cannon, *W of R* I-10-1-341, 342, 350, 534, 551; **384** Chalmers discovers Hazen, *W of R* I-10-1-342, 348, 350, 551; **384** "We waited . . ." *W of R* I-10-1-551; **384** cannon abandoned, *W of R* I-10-1-349, 350, 551; **384** desultory fire, *W of R* I-10-1-341, 551; **384** "I was halted . . ." *W of R* I-10-1-324; **384** inactivity during lull, *W of R* I-10-1-341; **384** Mendenhall comes up, *W of R* I-10-1-373, 375; **385** Crittenden comes up, *W of R* I-10-1-359, 361, 365-367; **385** McCook's movements, *W of R* I-10-1-302, 307; **385** "I ordered my . . ." *W of R* I-10-1-302; **385** Rousseau's arrival, Obreiter 79, *W of R* I-10-1-303, 307; **385** Buell's line, Reed (*Shiloh*) 99-102, *W of R* I-10-1-308; **385** "At daybreak . . ." Biel 266; **385** "We were all . . ." Robertson 4-9-62; **386** "The sound of . . ." T. Jordan 221; **386** army not in condition to fight, *W of R* I-10-1-387; **386** "Our force . . ." Bragg 4-8-62; **386** Trabue unable to obtain orders, *W of R* I-10-1-617; **386** Chalmers retreats, *W of R* I-10-1-551; **386** Withers comes up with reinforcements, *W of R* I-10-1-514, 534, 551; **388** Martin's presence, *W of R* I-10-1-534, 622, 625; **388** Nelson's advanced positions, *W of R* I-10-1-339, 350, 351; **388** Hodgson opens on Mendenhall, *W of R* I-10-1-373, 374, 514, 515; **388** Bruce's troops shelled, *W of R* I-10-1-350, 351, 515; **388** Hazen changes front, Hazen 26, 40, 44; **388** "he seemed to . . ." *W of R* I-10-1-514; **388** "to charge the . . ." *W of R* I-10-1-534; **388** Martin's attack led by Hardee, *W of R* I-10-1-622, Hardee 4-9-62; **389** fighting in front of guns, *W of R* I-10-1-343, 373, Hazen 26; **389** taunts of Bull Run, Hazen 46; **389** Hazen's gesturing, Hazen 42; **389** "It was my . . ." Hazen 42; **389** confusion in 6th Ky., Hazen 26; **389** Bruce fights hand to hand, J. H. Smith, 10-1-349; **389** Hazen's counterattack, Hazen 44; **389** "It was a . . ." Hazen 44; **389** Hazen saves La. captain, Hazen 27; **389** "We kept on . . ." Hazen 27; **389** Hazen overruns Hodgson, Hazen 44, *W of R* I-10-1-345, 351, 370, J. H. Smith 18; **390** "officers were riding . . ." Hazen 44; **390** Hodge counterattacks, *W of R* I-10-1-494, 514; **390** Hazen fired into by Smith, Hazen 29; **391** Hazen retreats, Hazen 27, 28; **391** guns spiked with mud, Hazen 37; **391** Hazen loses way, Hazen 28; **391** 2d Ky. decimated, J. H. Smith 13, *W of R* I-10-1-351, 352; **391** Hardee under fire, Hardee 4-9-62; **391** Hardee leads 2d Tex. attack, *W of R* I-10-1-556, 564, 571; **391** "So sudden was . . ." *W of R* I-10-1-556; **391** "Stop those men . . ." *W of R* I-10-1-571, 572; **391** Chalmers advances, *W of R* I-10-1-551; **392** Ammen husking corn, Hannaford 581; **392** Ammen occupys Bell farm, *W of R* I-10-1-338, 339, Grose 109; **392** "We found . . ." *W of R* I-10-1-340; **392** Grose drives Chalmers back, Grose 110, *W of R* I-10-1-340; **392** "I had not . . ." *W of R* I-10-1-546; **392** Chalmers orders up own brigade, *W of R* I-10-1-547, 551; **392** Ammen pursues,

aided by Terrill, *W of R* I-10-1-321, 325, 340, 551, Hannaford 574; **393**
Chalmers's plight, *W of R* I-10-1-442, 456, 551; **393** Maney's and Smith's
reinforcements, *W of R* I-10-1-449, 456; **393** ". . . The storms of . . ."
W of R I-10-1-321; **393** Ammen driven back, *W of R* I-10-1-321, 322; **393**
Terrill's guns in peril, *W of R* I-10-1-294, 322, 325, Hannaford 267; **394** "I
called upon . . ." *W of R* I-10-1-551; **394** Protracted fighting, *W of R* I-10-
1-336, 552; **394** mistake in identity, Fisher 15, 16; **394** Mendenhall's movements, *W of R* I-10-1-374; **394** desultory firing, J. H. Smith 13, Hannaford
574; **394-395** Crittenden's position, *W of R* I-10-1-357, 360, 366; **395** Trabue's attack against Crittenden, *W of R* I-10-1-366, 376, 617, 618; **395** Byrne's
battery withdraws, *W of R* I-10-1-372, 617, 618, E. P. Thompson 95; **395**
Smith's and Boyle's pursuit, *W of R* I-10-1-354, 359, 360, 364; **396** Bragg
attacks McCook, *W of R* I-10-1-308, 418, 424, 467, 617, 618; **396** Bragg
seeks help, *W of R* I-10-1-308, 309, 500; **396** McCook's inactivity, *W of R*
I-10-1-303; **396** reasons for caution, *W of R* I-10-1-308, 321, 360, 373, 376;
396 Cobb's battery captured, *W of R* I-10-1-360, 366, 372, 620, 695; **398**
Stanford's battery in action, *W of R* I-10-1-360, 437, 500; **398** Bragg rallies
and counterattacks, *W of R* I-10-1-366, 373, 418, 437; **398** "I looked . . ."
Abernathy 19-21; **398** Federals halt Bragg's attack, *W of R* I-10-1-295, 308,
618, E. P. Thompson 384, 530; **399** Gov. Johnson mortally wounded, E. P.
Thompson 530; **399** "I was fully . . ." *W of R* I-10-1-308, 309; **399** skirmishing and lull, *W of R,* I-10-1-309, 301, 360, 366, 374, 437; **399** Rousseau's
and Smith's men creep up, *W of R* I-10-1-366, 437; **399** disagreement on action to take, *W of R* I-10-1-419, 424, 500; **399** Confederates retire, *W of R*
I-10-1-418, 424, 501, 618; **399** ". . . A little better . . ." *W of R* I-10-1-437;
400 gunners slaughtered like cattle, Harwell 119; **400** Cobb's guns overrun,
W of R I-10-1-314, 365, 371, 501; **400** Anderson checks Federal advance,
W of R I-10-1-441, 528; **400** ammunition depleted—Federals withdraw, *W of
R* I-10-1-304, 309, 365, 374; **400** Kirk and Gibson meet C. S. advance, *W
of R* I-10-1-315; **400** "This battery . . ." *W of R* I-10-1-311; **400** "They
were coming . . ." Briant 108; **401** 77th Pa. fights Morgan, *W of R* I-10-1-
304, Obreiter 81, 82; **401** ". . . When within 30 . . ." Kirwan 30; **401**
Confederates retreat in disorder, *W of R* I-10-1-441, 501; **401** "Large num-
bers . . ." *W of R* I-10-1-501; **401** Jordan orders further withdrawal, *W of
R* I-10-1-502, Rennolds 14; **401** buildings on fire, *W of R* I-10-1-365; **401**
"I was completely . . ." Mecklin 59, 60.

CHAPTER XXI—A PROFITLESS COMBAT

402 firing rouses H.Q., *B & L* I 603, Roman I 532; **402** Federals strong on
left, *W of R* I-10-1-402; **402** Beauregard understands army attacked, *W of R*
I-10-1-387; **402** army's poor condition, *W of R* I-10-1-387; **402** Beauregard
sends for help, *W of R* I-10-1-390, 411, 10-2-397, Roman I 532; **402** "send
them . . ." *W of R* I-10-2-397; **402** "Beauregard Regiment" *B & L* I 605;
403 "General Beauregard rode . . ." Robertson 4-9-62; **403** "The fire
and . . ." *W of R* I-10-1-402; **403** "the most terrific . . ." Lotta 4-10-62;
403 cheese on bayonet, Kirwan 29; **403** plunder thrown away, Robertson
4-9-62; **403** situation in early afternoon, *W of R* I-10-1-388, 402, 10-2-405,
Roman I 532; **403** "have the muskets . . ." Roman I 532; **403** Wallace's

position P.M., *W of R* I-10-1-190; **404** Pond's marching and countermarching, *W of R* I-10-1-519; **404** Wallace's cautious advance, *W of R* I-10-1-170, 190; **404** "Here I remained . . ." *W of R* I-10-1-251; **404** Sherman advances 10 A.M., *W of R* I-10-1-190, 251; **404** Wallace turns south, *W of R* I-10-1-172; **404-405** Confederates attack on Sherman's front, *W of R* I-10-1-172, 473, 480, 593; **406** attack on Thurber, *W of R* I-10-1-171, 172, 473, 480, 488, 593; **406** Wharton encounters Thayer, *W of R* I-10-1-194, 196, 626, 627; **406** "with no prospect . . ." *W of R* I-10-1-627; **406** Beauregard forced to withdraw, *W of R* I-10-1-119, 135, 171, 194, 251, 480, 488, 594, 627; **406** fighting along Corinth road, *W of R* I-10-1-251; **407** "They all recognized . . ." Howe 222; **407** Cleburne ordered to attack, *W of R* I-10-1-583, 601; **407** "I sent back . . ." *W of R* I-10-1-583; **407** 712 Cleburne advances, is repulsed, *W of R* I-10-1-583; **407** Grant's 7,000 effectives, *B & L* I 522; **407** 53d Ohio routed, *W of R* I-10-1-119, 135; **408** "Despite all my . . ." *W of R* I-10-1-135; **408** McClernand marches east to meet Cleburne, *W of R* I-10-1-119, 120; **408** "Here one of . . ." *W of R* I-10-1-120; **408** McClernand's movements, *W of R* I-10-1-120, 145; **408** "My engagement here . . ." *W of R* I-10-1-410, 411; **408** mixed character of C. S. troops, *W of R* I-10-1-441, 481, 488, 500, 565, 566; **408** "Summoning everything . . ." *W of R* I-10-1-500; **409** fighting at Water Oaks Pond, *W of R* I-10-1-251, 318, 594; **409** "the severest musketry . . ." *W of R* I-10-1-251; **409** fired into by "friendly" troops, *W of R* I-10-1-318; **409** Willich's charge, *W of R* I-10-1-120, 251, 318; **409** Rousseau's brigade saves line, *W of R* I-10-1-120, 251; **409** fighting at "green point of timber," *W of R* I-10-1-120, 251, 308, 566, 594; **409** "The regiment next . . ." *W of R* I-10-1-594; **410** Confederates withdraw to Shiloh Church, *W of R* I-10-1-441, 481, 500, 594; **410** Wallace's movements, *W of R* I-10-1-172, 190, 194, 200; **410** Wallace's delay in pursuit, *W of R* I-10-1-190, 200, 202, 388, 411, 522; **410** Beauregard amid crisis on left, *B & L* I 593, 10-1-390, 402, 526, 594, 619; **410** attack spearheaded by Pond, *W of R* I-10-1-522, 526, 619; **411** "Put them in . . ." Kirwan 31; **411** six regiments in line, *W of R* I-10-1-522, 526, 539; **411** Beauregard grasps flag, *W of R* I-10-1-402, Roman I 532, Robertson 4-9-62; **411** Beauregard among ranks, *W of R* I-10-1-402, 522, Kirwin 31; **411** Beauregard's attack pushes Federals back, *W of R* I-10-1-120, 190, 304, 305, 315, Obreiter 83; **411** Wallace's perspective, *W of R* I-10-1-173, 190; **411** " . . . [This was] the most . . ." *W of R* I-10-1-191; **411** Confederate losses, *W of R* I-10-1-522, Biel 260; **412** ". . . Just as I . . ." Kirwan 31; **412** attack spent, *W of R* I-10-1-237, 239, 304; **412** "We arrived . . ." *W of R* I-10-1-239; **412** appearance of Federal reinforcements, *W of R* I-10-1-191, 304, 318; **412** Confederates retreat in disorder, *W of R* I-10-1-120, 315, 522, Biel 260; **412** ". . . As we were . . ." Kirwan 32; **412** "Were completely . . ." *W of R* I-10-1-522; **413** "We had been . . ." Latta 4-10-62; **413** "General, do you . . ." *B & L* I 603; **413** Beauregard's withdrawal, *W of R* I-10-1-338, 402, 430, 515, 522, 528, 594, 619; **413** Confederates during impasse, *W of R* I-10-1-321, 429, 449, 457, 623; **414** " . . . finding that . . ." *W of R* I-10-1-534; **414** route of withdrawal, *W of R* I-10-1-338; **414** Nelson too late in pursuit, *W of R* I-10-1-325, 338; **414** 2d Kentucky charges Harper's guns, *W of R* I-10-1-349, 352, 611, J. H. Smith 13; **414** Martin's countercharge, *W of R* I-10-1-349, 623, 625; **414** "The shock of . . ." J. H. Smith 13, 14; **416** Wickliffe's attack, *W of R* I-10-1-377,

381, 457-459, 535, 623, 625; **416** ". . . [I] refused to . . ." Bragg 4-8-62; **416** Confederate retreat on right, *W of R* I-10-1-524, 536, 559; **416** "We turned and . . ." Mecklin 60; **417** "We were greatly . . ." Kirwan 32; **417** "The field . . ." Biel 260; **417** camps on fire, Biel 260, Pugh 4-8-62; **417** captured small arms loaded, *W of R* I-10-1-172, 302, Roman I 532; **417** Grant's movements, *W of R* I-10-1-109, 252, 298, 309, 378, 380; **417** "too much fatigued . . ." *W of R* I-10-1-109; **417** 729 Veatch's charge, *W of R* I-10-1-221, 309, 526; **417** Grant allows Confederates to depart, *W of R* I-10-1-109, 194, 524; **417** Lifted into saddle, Putnam 207; **417** Wallace's limited pursuit, *W of R* I-10-1-194, 198, 202; **417** "I was without . . ." *W of R* I-10-1-295; **418** Buell's preparations for another fight, *W of R* I-10-1-295, 336, 10-2-97; **418** mood of troops, *W of R* I-10-1-191, Hannaford 574, Hinman 146; **418** "We did some . . ." Hinman 146; **418** "We took all . . ." Hinman 146; **418** burned tents, Ruff 299; **418** "Our knapsacks had . . ." Throne (*Letters*) 257; **418** "We had a sheet iron . . ." Carrington 4-7-62; **419** "The tents were still . . ." Soc. Army of Tenn. (1881) 54; **419** "The battlefield was . . ." Throne (*Letters*) 275; **419** "As I raised his . . ." Hickenlooper 430, 431; **419** "He followed us . . ." Carrington 50; **419** "One [of the wounded] was . . ." Ruff 299; **419** rolls body off blanket, Boos 654; **420** ". . . He did not know . . ." D. Palmer 140, **420** medical difficulties, *Med. & Surgical Hist* 1-1-30, 31, Hannaford 285; **420** ". . . Every part of . . ." Hannaford 286; **420** "The agonies of . . ." *Med. & Surg. Hist* 1-1-30, 31; **420** "You may imagine . . ." Zearing 4-8-62; **420** Irwin's field hospital, *Med. & Surg. Hist* 1-1-30; *W of R* I-10-1-326, Bearss (*Irwin*) 7, 8; **420** "groans and cries . . ." Hannaford 574; **420** Raith's fate, *W of R* I-10-1-144, Shea 332, 333, Englemann 4-9-62; **421** Peabody's corpse, Ruff 300, *Harv. Mem. Bio.* 166; **421** recovery of W. H. L. Wallace, I. Wallace 217, 218, Dickey 4-10-62; **421** "I almost flew . . ." Mrs. W. H. L. Wallace letter n/d; **421** Wallace at Cherry mansion, I. Wallace 197, Gresham 4-8-62, Dickey 4-8-62; **421** ". . . His pulse was . . ." Mrs. W. H. L. Wallace letter n/d; **421** rain on 7th, Throne (*Letters*) 279, Hinman 147; **421** ". . . Every inch of . . ." Throne (*Letters*) 280; **422** "Every thread of our . . ." Hinman 147; **422** soldiers waiting for blanket, Hinman 148; **422** "It soon commenced . . ." Biel 268; **422** "[as] the tent was . . ." Mecklin 61; **422** most miserable night, Hart 99.

CHAPTER XXII—WAR IS HORRIBLE

423 "I shall follow . . ." *W of R* I-10-1-108; **423** "My . . . plan will be . . ." *W of R* I-10-2-96; **423** infantry supports designated, *W of R* I-10-2-97; **423** reconnaissance made by Wood-Sherman-Dickey, *W of R* I-10-1-378, 639; **423** alarm spreads thru front line, Connelly 25; **423** "We seemed more . . ." Hinman 146; **424** Garfield's men fire off guns, Hinman 150, 151; **424** "In vain the . . ." Hinman 151; **424** "a small stampede," Connelly 25; **424** "The unexpected alarm . . ." Hinman 152; **424** march begins at 10 A.M., *W of R* I-10-1-378; **424** Sherman's movements, *W of R* I-10-1-639, 640, 10-2-400; **424** Confederates present, *W of R* I-10-1-923, Henry 64; **424** Sherman advances 77th Ohio, *W of R* I-10-1-640, McCormick 67, Henry 64; **424-425** Forrest routs skirmishers, Henry 64, *W of R* I-10-1-263, 640, 923, McCormick 70; **425** "The slaughter was . . ." Henry 64; **425** "My aide-de-camp . . ." Soc. Army of Tenn. (1881) 57; **425** "We sought safety . . ." Soc. Army of Tenn. (1881) 56; **425-426** Forrest shot, Henry 64, 65, T. Jordan 147, 148, *W of R* I-10-1-263, 266, 640, Soc. Army of Tenn. (1881) 56; **426** losses at Fallen Timbers, *W of R* I-10-1-263, 640, 923; **426** Breckenridge orders withdrawal, *W of R* I-10-1-924, 10-2-399, 400; **426** Confederate field hospital, *W of R* I-10-1-412, 640; **426** "Wagons [were] hauling . . ." Soc. Army of Tenn. (1881) 57; **426** Sherman returns to camp, *W of R* I-10-1-640; **426** "Our troops being . . ." *W of R* I-10-1-641; **426** "My troops are . . ." *W of R* I-10-1-400; **426** "Our condition is . . ." *W of R* I-10-1-398; **427** intermittent rain, Rockwell 4-8-62; **427** "Those were twelve . . ." Robertson 4-9-62; **427** "looked like a . . ." Wilkinson 4-16-62; **427** abandoned equipment, *W of R* I-10-1-400, 640; **427** "Every house between . . ." Biel 270; **427** arrival at nightfall, Biel 269, Robertson 4-9-62; **427** "On arriving . . ." Biel 269; **427** few crackers to eat, Lyman 4-11-62; **427** ". . . For water, all . . ." P. D. Stephenson; **427** wretched conditions on 9th, C. J. Johnson 4-9-62, Stephenson; **427** "unable to obtain . . ." C. J. Johnson 4-15-62; **427** "A change of locality . . ." C. J. Johnson 4-20-62; **427** fate of Federal prisoners, Eisenshiml (*Shiloh*) 57, Searle 337, M. Miller 4-8-62; **428** "very kindly treated . . ." M. Miller 4-8-62; **428** Prentiss agrees to exchange, Buckner 4-21-62; **428** "oh, how I . . ." Lyman 4-11-62; **428** ". . . I long to be . . ." Howard 4-10-62; **428** "Bless me, hon . . ." C. J. Johnson 4-11-62; **428** battle expected, Lyman 4-11-62; **428** effectives and reinforcements, *W of R* I-10-2-403, 405, 406, 409, 414; **428** "If defeated here . . ." *W of R* I-10-2-403; **428** "As far as the . . ." Hinman 148; **428** "heart sickening . . ." Bering 26, 27; **429** ". . . [It was] a horrible . . ." Biel 10; **429** "I could have walked . . ." Searle 336; **429** "The Rebels was . . ." Harmon 4-11-62; **429** "leaning against a . . ." Crooker 124; **429** dead on pile of corn, Biel 10; **429** "Here all was . . ." Throne (*Letters*) 279, 280; **429** ". . . The agonies of the . . ." *Med & Surg. Hist* 1-1-31; **430** "The scene upon the . . ." Throne (*Letters*) 263; **430** "The staterooms are . . ." Rerick 254; **430** "You can have no . . ." Graham 4-8-62; **430** "Men lay out in . . ." Graham 4-12-62; **430** pile of severed limbs, Hannaford 577; **430** ordeal of medical staff, *Med. & Surg. Hist* 1-1-29-31, Reed (*Shiloh*) 110; **430** warm weather, Englemann 4-21-62; **430** Beauregard's flag of truce, *W of R* I-10-1-111, 10-2-401, 403; **430** "Owing to the . . ." *W of R* I-10-1-111; **430** burial of dead, Hannaford 575; **431** "Our own dead were . . ." Hannaford 576; **431** large burial trenches, Throne (*Letters*) 278, 280, Shiloh Nat'l Park Service Handbook; **431** Johnston's body allegedly found, *W of R* I-10-1-114, 428, L. Wallace 4-9-62, W. P. Johnston 659, Fisher 16; **431** body that of T. W. Preston, *W of R* I-10-1-428; **431** burial parties work thru 9th, Carrington 4-9-62; **431** odor of decaying flesh, Carrington 4-9-62, Throne (*Letters*) 271; **432** smell of dead with azalea, T. K. Smith 4-10-62; **432** weather turns cool, Carrington 4-9-62, Throne (*Letters*) 271; **432** last of dead buried, Hannaford 576; **432** rain exposes bodies, Englemann, Prickett 4-21-62; **432** newspaper correspondents, J. C. Andrews 176, 177, 179, 180, 680; **432** "the great battle . . ." Saginaw *Enterprise* 4-16-62; **432** Stanton demands explanation, *W of R* I-10-1-98, 99; **432** Halleck receives news, *W of R* I-10-1-108; **432** "I leave immediately . . ." *W of R* I-10-2-99; **433** Halleck's arrival, Rockwell 4-12-62, Englemann 4-12-

62, *W of R* I-10-1-105; **433** Pope ordered to Pittsburg Landing, *W of R* I-10-2-107, 108; **433** "through Southern newspapers," *W of R* I-10-2-99; **433** Bear Creek expedition, *W of R* I-10-1-645, 10-2-102; **433** "It is the unanimous opinion . . ." *W of R* I-10-1-98; **433** ". . . They say I accomplished . . ." Howe 220; **433** commission as major general, *W of R* I-10-2-198; **433** Grant distrusted by Halleck, *W of R* I-10-2-105; **433** "any neglect or . . ." *W of R* I-10-1-98, 99; **433** "I prefer to . . ." *W of R* I-10-1-99; **433** Grant snubbed, *W of R* I-10-1-144, 10-2-154, Grant *Memoirs* I 377, 384, 392, 393, Merril 202, 203; **434** Grant-Sherman deny blame, Grant *Memoirs* I, Howe; **434** "The conduct and . . ." Rerick 60; **434** "For the great . . ." Shumway 4-62; **434** "An imbecile character" Throne (*Letters*) 257; **434** "The criminal carelessness . . ." Throne (*Letters*) 258; **434** Grant's defenders, Putnam 208, Washburne papers (Rowley) 4-19-62; **434** "[Grant] made the great . . ." Andreas 123; **434** Ohio against Grant, Putnam 208; **434** "I have tried . . ." Putnam 208; **435** McClure sees Lincoln, McClure; **435** criticism of Sherman, Merril 202, Sherman *Memoirs* I 274, Thorndike 143; **435** "All but the worthless . . ." Thorndike 143; **435** "For two days . . ." Thorndike 146; **435** "It is outrageous . . ." Howe 224; **435** Worthington's criticism, Worthington court-martial; **435** "One of our ablest . . ." Ricker 7-7-1901; **435** "one cloud on . . ." Andreas 123; **435** succession of unfavorable events, T. Bragg diary 4-11-62; **436** "Thus has fallen our . . ." T. Bragg diary 4-7-62; **436** ". . . Our loss is . . ." W. P. Johnston 690; **436** Davis's love for Johnston, Strode 121; **436** formal death announced, *W of R* I-10-1-408, Beatty diary; **436** Halleck's army organizes, *W of R* I-10-1-146, 148, 151, 10-2-177; **436** foul weather, *W of R* I-10-1-672, W. P. Kennedy 4-22-62; **436** "This is the . . ." W. P. Kennedy 4-22-62; **436** civilians on field, Shumway 4-13-62; **436** "Since the battle . . ." L. Wallace 4-17-62; **437** aid only own states, *Med. & Surg. Hist* 1-1-30; **437** "roaming over the . . ." T. K. Smith 4-15-62; **437** "I have seen them . . ." L. Wallace 4-17-62; **437** ". . . They are digging up . . ." W. P. Kennedy 4-22-62; **438** ill equipped, W. P. Kennedy 4-22-62; **438** demolished campground, Throne (*Letters*) 278; **438** advance begins April 29, *W of R* I-10-1-660; **438** Catton's observations, Catton (*Hallowed Ground*); **438** greatest opportunity, J. F. C. Fuller; **438** ". . . We were so near . . ." *W of R* I-10-1-469; **438** "the wasting war of . . ." W. P. Johnston 658; **438** "In numbers engaged . . ." *W of R* I-10-1-111, 112; **438** "Shiloh was the . . ." Grant *Memoirs* I 355; **438** "One of the most . . ." Sherman *Memoirs* I 275; **438** ". . . That victory was one . . ." Soc. Army of Tenn. (1881) 58; **439** "Perhaps no other . . ." Eisenschiml (*C.W.T.*) 34; **439** Beauregard claims victory, *W of R* I-101-384; **439** Union Claims, *W of R* I-10-1-98, 109, 111; **439** "numerically superior force . . ." *W of R* I-10-1-111; **439** Buell's congratulations, *W of R* I-10-1-297; **439** Stanton orders prayer, *W of R* I-10-1-381; **439** "Considering . . . that a portion . . ." *W of R* I-10-1-121; **439** Grant's icy remarks, *W of R* I-10-114; **439** Grant-Wallace controversy, *W of R* I-10-1-174, L. Wallace autob.; **440** Sherman chastises 53d Ohio, Worthington (*Shiloh*) 158, 159; **440** Hardee-Wigfall dispute, *W of R* I-10-1-571, 572; **440** Bragg-Gibson controversy, *W of R* I-10-1-466, 482, B. Bragg 4-8-62; **440** other flare-ups, Yerger 4-10-62; **440** "The battle of Shiloh . . ." Grant *Memoirs* I 369; **440** "Scarcely a tree of . . ." Briant 128; **440** "The desolation is . . ." Throne (*Letters*) 278; **441** "He seemed so happy . . ." Mrs. W. H. L. Wallace letter n/d; **441** C. F. Smith dies, *W of R* I-10-2-100, 130, Warner (*Blue*) 456; **441** "War is horrible," Carpenter 4-9-62; **441** "What a pity it is . . ." Camm 4-8-62; **441** "I shall never forget . . ." Kirwan 33.

APPENDIX A—THE DEATH OF ALBERT SIDNEY JOHNSTON

443 Johnston's physical condition, W. P. Johnston 1, 74, 722; **443** "on the ridge by . . ." Munford 22; **443** death spot near Willard's battery, *B & L* I 561, 563; **443** Harris identifies site in 1896, Rich (*Death of Johnston*) 276; **443** Preston's statement, *W of R* I-10-1-404; **444** Harris's descriptions, Preston (*Memor.*) 7; **444** "only about 200 yards . . ." W. P. Johnston 613, 614; **444** "the story that he . . ." Rich (*Death of Johnston*) 280; **444** missile identified, Munford 22; **444** Statham's brigade armed with Enfields, *W of R* I-10-1-305, McMurray 84, Bragg papers (Palmer Collection); **444** "terrible crossfire" Colby 7; **444** angle of wound, Dr. Charles G. Child III (letter) 11-17-1970; **444** four wounds on body, *W of R* I-10-1-405; **444** "Besides the wound . . ." W. P. Johnston 615; **444-445** Dr. Szilagyi's observations, Dr. D. E. Szilagyi (letters) 4-12-1971, 5-10-71; **445** "I galloped to . . ." W. P. Johnston 614; **445** prospect of concealing wound, Munford 22, Preston 4-18-62; **445** autopsy, Yandell 11-11-1877; **445** injection of whiskey, Munford 22; **445** escort to Corinth, Preston (*Memor.*) 5, 8; **445** Mrs. Inge cares for remains, Eisenschiml (*Shiloh*) 59, 60; **445** disposition of body, W. P. Johnston 688, 700; **445** "Bent on obtaining . . ." W. P. Johnston 690.

Index

509